THE COMPLETE WORKS

OF

ROBERT BURNS

POEMS SONGS AND LETTERS

BEING

THE COMPLETE WORKS

OF

ROBERT BURNS

EDITED FROM THE BEST PRINTED AND MANUSCRIPT AUTHORITIES
WITH GLOSSARIAL INDEX AND A BIOGRAPHICAL MEMOIR

BY

ALEXANDER SMITH

𝕷𝖔𝖓𝖉𝖔𝖓

MACMILLAN AND CO.

AND NEW YORK

1893

RICHARD CLAY AND SONS, LIMITED,
LONDON AND BUNGAY.

aster some thrashings, "I made an excellent English scholar ; and by the time I was ten or eleven years of age, I was a critic in substantives, verbs, and particles." Also we are told that in the family resided a certain old woman—Betty Davidson by name, as research has discovered—who had the largest collection in the country of tales and songs concerning devils, ghosts, fairies, &c.; and that to the recital of these Robert gave attentive ear, unconsciously laying up material for future *ums-O-Shanter*, and *Addresses to the Deil*. As for books, he had procured the *Life of Hannibal*, and the *History of Sir William Wallace ;* the first of a classical turn, lent by Mr. Murdoch, the second, purely traditionary, the property of a neighbouring blacksmith, constituting probably his entire secular library ; and in a letter to Mrs. Dunlop, he describes how the perusal of the latter moved him,—

"In those boyish days, I remember in particular being struck with that part of Wallace's story where these lines occur :

> Syne to the Leglen wood when it was late,
> To make a silent and a safe retreat.

chose a fine summer Sunday, the only day my line of life allowed, and walked alf a dozen miles to pay my respects to the Leglen wood, with as much devout nthusiasm as ever pilgrim did to Loretto, and explored every den and dell where could suppose my heroic countryman to have lodged."

When Mr. Murdoch left Mount Oliphant, the education of the family fell on the ther, who, when the boys came in from labour on the edge of the wintry twilight, t his candle and taught them arithmetic. He also when engaged in work with his sons, directed the conversation to improving subjects. He got books for them from a book society in Ayr ; among which are named Derham's *Physico and Astro-Theology*, and Ray's *Wisdom of God*. Stackhouse's *History of the Bible* was in the house, and from it Robert contrived to extract a considerable knowledge of ancient history. Mr. Murdoch sometimes visited the family and brought books ith him. On one occasion he read *Titus Andronicus* aloud at Mount Oliphant, and Robert's pure taste rose in a passionate revolt against its coarse cruelties and unspiritual horrors. When about fourteen years of age, he and his brother Gilbert were sent "week about during a summer quarter " to a parish school two or three miles distant from the farm to improve themselves in penmanship. Next year, about midsummer, Robert spent three weeks with his tutor, Murdoch, who had established himself in Ayr. The first week was given to a careful revision of the English Grammar, the remaining fortnight was devoted to French, and on his return he brought with him the *Adventures of Telemachus* and a *French Dictionary*, and with these he used to work alone during his evenings. He also turned his attention to Latin, but does not seem to have made much progress therein, although in after-life he could introduce a sentence or so of the ancient tongue to adorn his correspondence. By the time the family had left Mount Oliphant, he had torn the heart out of a good many books, among which were several theological works,

some of a philosophical nature, a few novels, the *Spectator, Shakespere, Pope's Hom*
and, above all, the *Works of Allan Ramsay*. These, with the Bible, a collection
English songs, and a collection of letters, were almost the only books he was
acquainted with when he broke out in literature. No great library certainly, but he
had a quick eye and ear, and all Ayrshire was an open page to him, filled with
strange matter, which he only needed to read off into passionate love-song
or blistering satire.

In his sixteenth year the family removed from Mount Oliphant to Lochlea. Here
Robert and Gilbert were employed regularly on the farm, and received from their
father 7*l.* per annum of wages. Up till now, Burns had led a solitary self-contained
life, with no companionship save his own thoughts and what books he could procure,
with no acquaintances save his father, his brother, and Mr. Murdoch. This seclusion
was now about to cease. In his seventeenth year, "to give his manners a finish"
he went to a country dancing school,—an important step in life for any young fellow,
a specially important step for a youth of his years, heart, brain, and passion. I
the Tarbolton dancing school the outer world with its fascinations burst upon him
It was like attaining majority and freedom. It was like coming up to London from
the provinces. Here he first felt the sweets of society, and could assure himself of
the truthfulness of his innate sense of superiority. At the dancing school, he encountered other young rustics laudably ambitious of "brushing up their manners,"
and, what was of more consequence, he encountered their partners also. This wa
his first season, and he was as gay as a young man of fortune who had entered on
his first London one. His days were spent in hard work, but the evenings were his
own, and these he seems to have spent almost entirely in sweethearting on his own
account, or on that of others. His brother tells us that he was almost constantly
in love. His inamoratas were the freckled beauties who milked cows and hoed
potatoes; but his passionate imagination attired them with the most wonderful
graces. He was Antony, and he found a Cleopatra—for whom the world were
well lost—in every harvest field. For some years onward he did not read
much; indeed, his fruitful reading, with the exception of *Fergusson's Poems*, of
which hereafter, was accomplished by the time he was seventeen; his leisure
being occupied in making love to rustic maids, where his big black eyes could
come into play. Perhaps on the whole, looking to poetic outcome, he could not
have employed himself to better purpose.

He was now rapidly getting perilous cargo on board. The Tarbolton dancing
school introduced him to unlimited sweethearting, and his nineteenth summer,
which he spent in the study of mensuration, at the school at Kirkoswald, made
him acquainted with the interior of taverns, and with "scenes of swaggering riot."
He also made the acquaintance of certain smugglers who frequented that bare and
deeply-coved coast, and seems to have been attracted by their lawless ways and
speeches. It is characteristic, that in the midst of his studies, he was upset by the

ms of a country girl who lived next door to the school. While taking the sun's
ude, he observed her walking in the adjoining garden, and Love put Trigo-
ometry to flight. During his stay at Kirkoswald, he had read *Shenstone* and
Thomson, and on his return home he maintained a literary correspondence with his
schoolfellows, and pleased his vanity with the thought that he could turn a sentence
with greater skill and neatness than any one of them.

For some time it had been Burns's habit to take a small portion of land from his
father for the purpose of raising flax ; and, as he had now some idea of settling in
life, it struck him that if he could add to his farmer-craft the accomplishment of flax-
dressing, it might not be unprofitable. He accordingly went to live with a relation of
his mother's in Irvine—Peacock by name—who followed that business, and with him
for some time he worked with diligence and success. But while welcoming the New
Year morning after a bacchanalian fashion, the premises took fire, and his schemes
were laid waste. Just at this time, too—to complete his discomfiture—he had been
jilted by a sweetheart, "who had pledged her soul to meet him in the field of
matrimony." In almost all the foul weather which Burns encountered, a woman
may be discovered flitting through it like a stormy petrel. His residence at Irvine
was a loss, in a worldly point of view, but there he ripened rapidly, both spiritually
and poetically. At Irvine, as at Kirkoswald, he made the acquaintance of persons
engaged in contraband traffic, and he tells us that a chief friend of his "spoke of
illicit love with the levity of a sailor—which, hitherto, I had regarded with horror.
There his friendship did me a mischief." About this time, too, John Rankine—to
whom he afterwards addressed several of his epistles—introduced him to St. Mary's
Lodge, in Tarbolton, and he became an enthusiastic Freemason. Of his mental
states and intellectual progress, we are furnished with numerous hints. He was
member of a debating club at Tarbolton, and the question for Hallowe'en still
exists in his handwriting. It is as follows :—" Suppose a young man, bred a farmer,
but without any fortune, has it in his power to marry either of two women, the one
a girl of large fortune, but neither handsome in person nor agreeable in conversation,
but who can manage the household affairs of a farm well enough ; the other of them
a girl every way agreeable in person, conversation, and behaviour, but without any
fortune ; which of them shall he choose ?" Not a bad subject for a collection of
clever rustics to sharpen their wits upon ! We may surmise that Burns found himself
as much superior in debate to his companions at the Bachelors' Club as he had
previously found himself superior to his Kirkoswald correspondents in letter-writting.
The question for the Hallowe'en discussion is interesting mainly in so far as it
indicates what kind of discussions were being at that time conducted in his own
brain ; and also how habitually, then and afterwards, his thinking grew out of his
personal condition and surroundings. A question of this kind interested him more
than whether, for instance, Cromwell deserved well of his country. Neither now
nor afterwards did he trouble himself much about far-removed things. He cared

for no other land than Caledonia.   He did not sing of Helen's beauty, but of the
beauty of the country girl he loved.   His poems were as much the product of his
own farm and its immediate neighbourhood, as were the clothes and shoes he wore,
the oats and turnips he grew.   Another aspect of him may be found in the letter
addressed to his father three days before the Irvine flax-shop went on fire.   It is
infected with a magnificent hypochondriasis.   It is written as by a Bolingbroke—
by a man who had played for a mighty stake, and who, when defeated, could smile
gloomily and turn fortune's slipperiness into parables.   And all the while the dark
philosophy and the rolling periods flowed from the pen of a country lad, whose
lodgings are understood to have cost a shilling per week, and "whose meal was
nearly out, but who was going to borrow till he got more."   One other circumstance
attending his Irvine life deserves notice—his falling in with a copy of *Fergusson's
Poems*.   For some time previously he had not written much, but *Fergusson* stirred
him with emulation ; and on his removal to Mossgiel, shortly afterwards, he in a
single winter poured forth more immortal verse—measured by mere quantity—than
almost any poet in the same space of time, either before his day or after.

Three months before the death of the elder Burnes, Robert and Gilbert
rented the farm of Mossgiel in the parish of Mauchline.   The farm consisted
of 119 acres, and its rent was 90*l*.   After the father's death the whole family
removed thither.   Burns was now twenty-four years of age, and come to his full
strength of limb, brain, and passion.   As a young farmer on his own account,
he mixed more freely than hitherto in the society of the country-side, and in a
more independent fashion.   He had the black eyes which Sir Walter saw afterwards in Edinburgh and remembered to have "glowed."   He had wit, which
convulsed the Masonic Meetings, and a rough-and-ready sarcasm with which he
flayed his foes.   Besides all this, his companionship at Irvine had borne its fruits.
He had become the father of an illegitimate child, had been rebuked for his
transgression before the congregation, and had, in revenge, written witty and
wicked verses on the reprimand and its occasion, to his correspondent Rankine.
And when we note here that he came into fierce collision with at least one section
of the clergy of his country, all the conditions have been indicated which went to
make up Burns the man, and Burns the poet.

Ayrshire was at this period a sort of theological bear-garden.   The more important clergymen of the district were divided into New Lights and Auld Lights ;
they wrangled in Church Courts, they wrote and harangued against each other ;
and, as the adherents of the one party or the other made up almost the entire
population, and as in such disputes Scotchmen take an extraordinary interest,
the county was set very prettily by the ears.   The Auld Light divines were strict
Calvinists, laying great stress on the doctrine of Justification by Faith, and inclined
generally to exercise spiritual authority after a somewhat despotic fashion.   The
New Light divines were less dogmatic, less inclined to religious gloom and acerbity,

and they possessed, on the whole, more literature and knowledge of the world. Burns became deeply interested in the theological warfare, and at once ranged himself on the liberal side. From his being a poet this was to have been expected, but various circumstances concurred in making his partisanship more than usually decided. The elder Burnes was, in his ways of thinking, a New Light, and his religious notions he impressed carefully on his children—his son consequently, in taking up the ground he did, was acting in accordance with received ideas and with early training. Besides, Burns's most important friends at this period— Mr. Gavin Hamilton, from whom he held his farm on a sub-lease, and Mr. Aitken, to whom the *Cotter's Saturday Night* was dedicated—were in the thick of the contest on the New Light side. Mr. Hamilton was engaged in personal dispute with the Rev. Mr. Auld—the clergyman who rebuked Burns—and Mr. Aitken had the management of the case of Dr. MacGill, who was cited before the local Church Courts on a charge of heterodoxy. Hamilton and Aitken held a certain position in the county—they were full of talent, they were hospitable, they were witty in themselves, and could appreciate wit in others. They were of higher social rank than Burns's associates had hitherto been, they had formed a warm friendship for him, and it was not unnatural that he should become their ally, and serve their cause with what weapons he had. Besides, wit has ever been a foe to the Puritan. Cavaliers fight with song and jest, as well as with sword and spear, and sometimes more effectively. Hudibras and Worcester are flung into opposite scales, and make the balance even. From training and temperament, Burns was an enemy of the Auld Light section ; conscious of his powers, and burning to distinguish himself, he searched for an opportunity as anxiously as ever did Irishman for a head at Donnybrook, and when he found it, he struck, without too curiously inquiring into the rights and wrongs of the matter. At Masonic Meetings, at the tables of his friends, at fairs, at gatherings round church-doors on Sundays, he argued, talked, joked, flung out sarcasms—to be gathered up, repeated and re-repeated—and maddened in every way the wild-boar of orthodoxy by the javelins of epigram. The satirical opportunity at length came, and Burns was not slow to take advantage of it. Two Auld Light divines, the Rev. John Russel and the Rev. Alex. Moodie, quarrelled about their respective parochial boundaries, and the question came before the Presbytery for settlement. In the court—when Burns was present—the reverend gentlemen indulged in coarse personal altercation, and the *Twa Herds* was the result. Copies of this satire were handed about, and for the first time Burns tasted how sweet a thing was applause. The circle of his acquaintances extended itself, and he could now call several clergymen of the moderate party his friends. The *Twa Herds* was followed by the tremendous satire of *Holy Willie's Prayer*, and by the *Holy Fair*—the last equally witty, equally familiar in its allusions to sacred things, but distinguished by short poetic touches, by descriptions of character and manners, unknown in Scottish poetry since the days of Dunbar.

These pieces caused great stir; friends admired and applauded; foes hated and reviled. His brother Gilbert spoke words of caution which, had Burns heeded, it would have been better for his fame. But to check such thunder in mid-volley was, perhaps, more than could have been expected of poetic flesh and blood.

Burns interested himself deeply in the theological disputes of his district, but he did not employ himself entirely in writing squibs against that section of the clergy which he disliked. He had already composed *Mailie's Elegy* and the *Epistle to Davie* —the first working in an element of humour ennobled by moral reflection, a peculiar manner in which he lived to produce finer specimens; the second almost purely didactic, and which he hardly ever surpassed—and as he was now in the full flush of inspiration, every other day produced its poem. He did not go far a-field for his subjects; he found sufficient inspiration in his daily life and the most familiar objects. The schoolmaster of Tarbolton had established a shop for groceries, and having a liking for the study of medicine, he took upon himself the airs of a physician, and advertised that "advice would be given in common disorders, at the shop, gratis." On one occasion, at the Tarbolton Mason-lodge, when Burns was present, the schoolmaster made a somewhat ostentatious display of his medical acquirements. To a man so easily moved as Burns, this hint was sufficient. On his way home from the Lodge the terrible grotesquerie of *Death and Dr. Hornbook* floated through his mind, and on the following afternoon the verses were repeated to Gilbert. Not long after, in a Sunday afternoon walk, he recited to Gilbert the *Cotter's Saturday Night* who described himself as electrified by the recital—as indeed he might well be. To Gilbert also the *Address to the Deil* was repeated while the two brothers were engaged with their carts in bringing home coals for family use. At this time, too, his poetic *Epistles to Lapraik* and others were composed—pieces which for *verve* and hurry and gush of versification seem to have been written at a sitting, yet for curious felicities of expression might have been under the file for years. It was Burns's habit, Mr. Chambers tells us, to keep his MSS. in the drawer of a little deal table in the garret at Mossgiel; and his youngest sister was wont, when he went out to afternoon labour, to slip up quietly and hunt for the freshly-written verses. Indeed, during the winter of 1785–86 Burns wrote almost all the poems which were afterwards published in the Kilmarnock edition.

But at this time he had other matters on hand than the writing of verses. The farm at Mossgiel was turning out badly; the soil was sour and wet, and, from mistakes in the matter of seed, the crops were failures. His prospects were made still darker by his relation with Jean Armour. He had made the acquaintance of this young woman at a penny wedding in Mauchline, shortly after he went to reside at Mossgiel, and the acquaintanceship, on his part at least, soon ripened into passion. In the spring of 1786, when baited with farming difficulties, he learned that Jean was about to become a mother, and the intelligence came on

m like a thunder-clap. Urged by a very proper *feeling, he resolved to make the* happy young woman all the reparation in his power, and accordingly he placed her hands a written acknowledgment of marriage—a document sufficient by the law of Scotland to legalize their connexion, though after a somewhat irregular fashion. When Mr. Armour heard of Jean's intimacy with Burns and its miserable result, he was moved with indignation, and he finally persuaded her to deliver into his hands Burns's written paper, and this document he destroyed, although, for anything he knew, he destroyed along with it his daughter's good fame. Burns's feelings at this crisis may be imagined. Pride, love, anger, despair, strove for mastery in his breast. Weary of his country, almost of his existence, and seeing ruin staring him in the face at Mossgiel, he resolved to seek better fortune and solace for a lacerated heart, in exile. He accordingly arranged with Dr. Dougla to act as book-keeper on his estate in Jamaica. In order to earn the passage money, he was advised to publish the wonderful verses then lying in the drawer of the deal table at Mossgiel. This advice jumped pleasantly enough with his own wishes, and without loss of time he issued his subscription papers and began to prepare for the press. He knew that his poems possessed merit; he felt that applause would sweeten his "good night." It is curious to think of Burns's wretched state—in a spiritual as well as a pecuniary sense—at this time, and of the centenary the other year which girdled the planet as with a blaze of festal fire and a roll of triumphal drums! Curious to think that the volume which Scotland regards as the most precious in her possession should have been published to raise nine pounds to carry its author into exile!

All the world has heard of Highland Mary—in life a maid-servant in the family of Mr. Hamilton, after death to be remembered with Dante's Beatrice and Petrarch's Laura. How Burns and Mary became acquainted we have little means of knowing—indeed the whole relationship is somewhat obscure—but Burns loved her as he loved no other woman, and her memory is preserved in the finest expression of his love and grief. Strangely enough, it seems to have been in the fierce rupture between himself and Jean that this white flower of love sprang up, sudden in its growth, brief in its passion and beauty. It was arranged that the lovers should become man and wife, and that Mary should return to her friends to prepare for her wedding. Before her departure there was a farewell scene. "On the second Sunday of May," Burns writes to Mr. Thomson, after an historical fashion which has something touching in it, "in a sequestered spot on the banks of the Ayr the interview took place." The lovers met and plighted solemn troth. According to popular statement, they stood on either side of a brook, they dipped their hands in the water, exchanged Bibles—and parted. Mary died at Greenock, and was buried in a dingy churchyard hemmed by narrow streets—beclanged now by innumerable hammers, and within a stone's throw of passing steamers. Information of her death was brought to Burns at Mossgiel; he went to the window to

read the letter, and the family noticed that on a sudden his face changed. He went out without speaking; they respected his grief and were silent. On the whole matter Burns remained singularly reticent; but years after, from a sudden geysir of impassioned song, we learn that through all that time she had never been forgotten.

Jean was approaching her confinement, and having heard that Mr. Armour was about to resort to legal measures to force him to maintain his expected progeny— an impossibility in his present circumstances—Burns left Mauchline and went to reside in the neighbourhood of Kilmarnock, where, in gloomy mood enough, he corrected his proof sheets. The volume appeared about the end of July, and, thanks to the exertions of his friends, the impression was almost immediately exhausted. Its success was decided. All Ayrshire rang with its praise. His friends were of course anxious that he should remain in Scotland; and as they possessed some influence, he lingered in Ayrshire, loth to depart, hoping that something would turn up, but quite undecided as to the complexion and nature of the desired something. Wronged as he considered himself to have been by the Armour family, he was still conscious of a lingering affection for Jean. The poems having made a conquest of Ayrshire, began to radiate out on every side. Professor Dugald Stewart, then resident at Catrine, had a copy of the poems, and Dr. Blair, who was on a visit to the professor, had his attention drawn to them, and expressed the warmest admiration. Mrs. Dunlop of Dunlop on opening the book had been electrified by the *Cotter's Saturday Night*, as Gilbert had been before her, and immediately sent an express to Burns at Mossgiel with a letter of praise and thanks. All this was pleasant enough, but it did not materially mend the situation. Burns could not live on praise alone, and accordingly, so soon as he could muster nine guineas from the sale of his book, he took a steerage passage in a vessel which was expected to sail from Greenock at the end of September. During the month of August he seems to have employed himself in collecting subscriptions, and taking farewell of his friends. Burns was an enthusiastic mason, and we can imagine that his last meeting with the Tarbolton Lodge would be a thing to remember. It *was* remembered, we learn from Mr. Chambers, by a surviving brother, John Lees. John said, "that Burns came in a pair of buckskins, out of which he would always pull the other shilling for the other bowl, till it was five in the morning. An awfu' night *that*." Care left outside the door, we can fancy how the wit would flash, and the big black eyes glow, on such an occasion!

The first edition of his poems being nearly exhausted, his friends encouraged him to produce a second forthwith; but on application, it was found that the Kilmarnock printer declined to undertake the risk, unless the price of the paper was advanced beforehand. This outlay Burns was at this time unable to afford. On hearing of the circumstance, his friend Mr. Ballantyne offered to advance the money, but urged him to proceed to Edinburgh and publish the second edition there. This advice commended itself to Burns's ambition, but for a while he

remained irresolute. Jean, meanwhile, had been confined of twins, and from one of his letters we learn that the "feelings of a father" kept him lingering in Ayrshire. News of the success of his poems came in upon him on every side. Dr. Lawrie, minister of Loudon, to whose family he had recently paid a visit, had forwarded a copy of the poems, with a sketch of the author's life, to Dr. Thomas Blacklock, and had received a letter from that gentleman, expressing the warmest admiration of the writer's genius, and urging that a second and larger edition should at once be proceeded with; adding, that "its intrinsic merits, and the exertions of the author's friends, might give the volume a more universal circulation than anything of the kind which has been published in my time." This letter, so full of encouragement, Dr. Lawrie carried at once to Mr. Gavin Hamilton, and Mr. Hamilton lost no time in placing it in Burns's hands. The poems had been favourably reviewed in the *Edinburgh Magazine* for October, and this number of the periodical, so interesting to all its inmates, would, no doubt, find its way to Mossgiel. Burns seems to have made up his mind to proceed to Edinburgh about the 18th November, a step which was warmly approved by his brother Gilbert; and when his resolution was taken, he acted upon it with promptitude.

He reached Edinburgh on the 28th November, 1786, and took up his residence with John Richmond, a Mauchline acquaintance, who occupied a room in Baxter's Close, Lawnmarket, for which he paid three shillings a week. Burns for some time after his arrival seems to have had no special object; he wandered about the city, looking down from the Castle on Princes Street; haunting Holyrood Palace and Chapel; standing with cloudy eyelid and hands meditatively knit beside the grave of Fergusson; and from the Canongate glancing up with interest on the quaint tenement in which Allan Ramsay kept his shop, wrote his poems, and curled the wigs of a departed generation of Scotsmen. At the time of Burns's arrival, the Old Town towered up from Holyrood to the Castle, picturesque, smoke-wreathed; and when the darkness came, its climbing tiers of lights and cressets were reflected in the yet existing Nor' Loch; and the grey uniform streets and squares of the New Town— from which the visitor to-day can look down on low wooded lands, the Forth, and Fife beyond—were only in course of erection. The literary society of the time was brilliant but exotic, like the French lily or the English rose. For a generation and more the Scottish philosophers, historians, and poets had brought their epigram from France as they brought their claret, and their humour from England as they brought their parliamentary intelligence. Blair of the *Grave* was a Scottish Dr. Young; Home of *Douglas* a Scottish Otway; Mackenzie a Scottish Addison; and Dr. Blair—so far as his criticism was concerned—a sort of Scottish Dr. Johnson. The Scotch brain was genuine enough; the faculty was native, but it poured itself into foreign moulds. The literary grandees wore decorations—honestly earned— but no one could discover amongst them the Order of the Thistle. These men, too, had done their work, and the burly black-eyed, humorous, passionate

ploughman came up amongst them, the herald of a new day and a new order of things ; the first king of a new literary empire, in which he was to be succeeded by Walter Scott,—then a lad of sixteen, engrossing deeds in his father's office, with the Tweed murmuring in his ears, and Melrose standing in the light of his opening imagination —with Hogg, Galt, Wilson, Lockhart and the rest, for his satraps and lieutenants.

Burns's arrival in Edinburgh was an historical event, far more important in itself, and in its issues, than either he or than any other person suspected.

He soon got to work, however. In Ayrshire he had made the acquaintance of Mr. Dalrymple, of Orangefield ; that gentleman introduced him to his brother-in-law, the Earl of Glencairn, then resident in Edinburgh ; and his lordship introduced him to William Creech, the leading publisher in the city, at whose shop the wits were wont to congregate. Creech undertook the publication of the new edition ; and, through the influence of Glencairn, it was arranged that the Caledonian Hunt should subscribe for a hundred copies, and that a guinea should be paid for each. Meantime, Mr. Mackenzie, in the *Lounger*, of date 9th December, wrote a glowing criticism on the poems, which smoothed a way for them into the politer circles. The new edition, dedicated to the Caledonian Hunt, appeared on the 21st April, 1787, containing a list of subscribers' names extending to more than thirty-eight pages. The Hunt, as we have seen, took one hundred copies, and several gentlemen and noblemen subscribed liberally—one taking twenty copies, a second forty copies, a third forty-two copies. The Scots Colleges in France and Spain are also set down as subscribers among individual names. This was splendid success, and Burns felt it. He was regarded as a phenomenon ; was asked hither and thither, frequently from kindness and pure admiration—often, however, to be merely talked with and stared at :—this he felt, too, and his vengeful spleen, well kept under on the whole, corroded his heart like a fierce acid. During the winter preceding the publication of the second edition, he was fêted and caressed. He was patronised by the Duchess of Gordon. Lord Glencairn was his friend, so also was Henry Erskine. He was frequently at Lord Monboddo's, where he admired the daughter's beauty more than the father's philosophy ; he breakfasted with Dr. Blair ; he walked in the mornings to the Braid Hills with Professor Dugald Stewart ; and he frequently escaped from these lofty circles to the Masonic Lodge, or to the supper-tables of convivial lawyers, where he felt no restraint, where he could be wounded by no patronage, and where he flashed and coruscated, and became the soul of the revel. Fashionable and lettered saloons were astonished by Burns's talk ; but the interior of taverns—and in Edinburgh tavern life was all but universal at the time—saw the brighter and more constant blaze. This sudden change of fortune—so different from his old life in the Irvine flax heckling-shop, or working the sour Mossgiel lands, or the post of a book-keeper in Jamaica, which he looked forward to, and so narrowly escaped—was not without its giddy and exciting

pleasures, and for pleasure of every kind Burns had the keenest relish. Now and again, too, in the earlier days of his Edinburgh life, when success wore its newest gloss, and applause had a novel sweetness, a spirt of exhilaration escaped him, not the less real that it was veiled in a little scornful exaggeration. In writing to Mr. Hamilton, he says : "For my own affairs, I am in a fair way of becoming as eminent as Thomas à Kempis, or John Bunyan ; and you may expect henceforth to see my birthday inserted among the wonderful events in the Poor Robin and Aberdeen Almanacks, along with Black Monday and the battle of Bothwell Bridge." In any case, if he did feel flattered by the attention paid him by society, he had time to cool and strike a balance in his friend Richmond's garret in the Lawnmarket—where he slept, Mr. Lockhart informs us, during the whole of that glittering and exciting winter.

Hitherto, the world had seen but little of Burns personally. It had heard his voice as of one singing behind the scenes, and been moved to admiration ; and when he presented himself in the full blaze of the footlights, he became the cynosure of every eye, and the point on which converged every critical opera-glass. Edinburgh and Burns confronted each other. Edinburgh "took stock" of Burns, Burns "took stock" of Edinburgh, and it is interesting to note the mutual impressions. From all that can be gathered from Dr. Blair, Professors Dugald Stewart, Walker, and others, Burns acquitted himself in his new circumstances admirably. He never lost head, he never let a word of exultation escape him, his deportment was everywhere respectful yet self-possessed ; he talked well and freely —for he knew he was expected to talk—but he did not engross conversation. His "deferential" address won his way to female favour : and the only two breaches of decorum which are recorded of him in society, may be palliated by his probable ignorance of his host's feelings and vanities on the first occasion, and on the second, by the peculiar provocation he received. Asked in Dr. Blair's house, and in Dr. Blair's presence, from which of the city preachers he had derived the greatest gratification, it would have been fulsome had Burns said, turning to the Doctor, "I consider you, Sir, the greatest pulpit orator I have ever heard." The question was a most improper one in the circumstances ; and if the company were thrown into a state of foolish embarrassment, and the host's feelings wounded by Burns giving the palm to his colleague—then the company were simply toadies of the sincerer sort, and the host less skilled in the world's ways than Burns, and possessed of less natural good-breeding. In the second instance when, in a sentence more remarkable for force than grace, he extinguished a clergyman who abused Gray's *Elegy,* but who could not quote a line of it correctly, he merely gave way to a swift and not ungenerous instinct—for which he was, no doubt, sorry the next moment. He cannot be defended altogether, although even here one can hardly help rendering him a sneaking approval. Bad language at a breakfast-table, and addressed to a clergyman, is improper—but, on the other hand, no clergyman has a right to be a

B   *b*

bore at a breakfast-table. Indeed, your critical and blundering bore, whether clergyman or no—all the more sedulously, perhaps, if he *be* a clergyman—should keep out of the way of a Burns. Evil is certain to befall him if he do not. It is pretty evident, however, from the records left, that Dr. Blair, Dugald Stewart, and others, did not really know Burns—did not, in fact, take much pains to know him. They never met him on frank, cordial, and brotherly terms. They looked on him curiously, as one looks on a strange insect, through a microscope. From their learned heights they regarded him as on the plain beneath. They were ever ready with advice, and counselled him to stand armed at points where no danger could possibly appear. Of all the good things in the world, advice is practically the least useful. If a man is fool enough to need advice, the chances are that he will be fool enough to resent it when given, or neglect it when the critical moment arrives. The Edinburgh literati did not quite well know what to make of Burns. He was a new thing under the sun, and they could not fall back on precedent. They patronised him kindly, heartily, for the most part—but still it was patronage. And it has come about that, in the lapse of seventy years, the relations of the parties have been quite reversed—as in dissolving views, the image of Burns has come out in bolder relief and brighter colours, while his patrons have lost outline, have dwindled, and become shadowy. Dr. Blair and Lord Monboddo will be remembered mainly by the circumstance that the one invited Burns to his evening entertainments, and the other to his breakfasts. Burns has kept that whole literary generation from oblivion, and from oblivion he will keep it yet awhile.

On the other hand, it is quite evident, that although Burns, during that brilliant winter, masked himself skilfully, he bore an inward smart. He felt that he was regarded as meteoric, a wonder ; that he did not fit into existing orders of things, and that in Edinburgh he had no familiar and received status. Consequently, he was never sure of his ground ; and while, for the most part, careful to offend no one, he was passionately jealous of condescension and suspicious of personal affront. The men amongst whom he mingled had their positions in the world, and in these positions they had the ease of use and wont. Their couches were made soft by the down of customariness. They had all the social proprieties and traditions at their backs. From the past, they flowered out socially and professionally. With Burns everything was different. He had in Edinburgh, so to speak, neither father nor mother. He had neither predecessor nor antecedent. He could roll in no groove made smooth by custom ; and hence it is, when in bitter mood, we find him making such extravagant claims for genius against dull rich men, or dull well-born men, or semi-dull men, who had been successful in the professions. He knew that genius was his sole claim to the notice of the brilliant personages he met night after night ; that but for it he was a small Ayrshire farmer, whom not one of those people would invite to their tables, or bid "Good day" to, if they met him

on a country road. It was admirable in Scott to waive, as he continually did, all claim to special regard on account of his genius, but it was easy for Scott to do this. Scott would have dined well every day of his life, he would have lived with cultivated and refined people, and would have enjoyed a fair share of social distinction, although he had never written *Marmion* or *Ivanhoe*. But Burns's sole title to notice *was* genius—take that from him, he was instantly denuded of his singing robes, and left in the hodden grey of the farmer, with a splash of mud on his top-boots. In his commonplace book—a very pool of Marah—which he kept at Edinburgh, there is an entry which brings all this out in a clear light.

"There are few of the sore evils under the sun give me more uneasiness and chagrin than the comparison how a man of genius, nay, of avowed worth, is received everywhere, with the reception which a mere ordinary character, decorated with the trappings and futile distinctions of fortune, meets. Imagine a man of abilities, his heart glowing with honest pride, conscious that men are born equal, still giving *honour to whom honour is due ;* he meets at a great man's table a Squire Something, or a Sir Somebody ; he knows the *noble* landlord, at heart, gives the bard, or whatever he is, a share of his good wishes, beyond, perhaps, any one at table ; yet how will it mortify him to see a fellow, whose abilities would scarcely have made an *eightpenny tailor*, and whose heart is not worth three farthings, meet with attention and notice, that are withheld from the son of genius and poverty !

"The noble Glencairn has wounded me to the soul here, because I dearly esteem, respect, and love him. He showed so much attention, engrossing attention, one day, to the only blockhead at table (the whole company consisted of his lordship, dunder-pate, and myself), that I was within half a point of throwing down my gage of contemptuous defiance ; but he shook my hand, and looked so benevolently good at parting. God bless him ! though I should never see him more, I shall love him until my dying day ! I am pleased to think I am so capable of the throes of gratitude, as I am miserably deficient in some other virtues.

"With Dr. Blair I am more at my ease. I never respect him with humble veneration ; but when he kindly interests himself in my welfare, or, still more, when he descends from his pinnacle, and meets me on equal ground in conversation, my heart overflows with what is called *liking*. When he neglects me for the mere carcase of greatness, or when his eye measures the difference of our points of elevation, I say to myself, with scarcely any emotion, what do I care for him, or his pomp either ? "

A man like Burns, living at a period when literature had not to any extent become a profession, could not find his place amongst the recognised forces of the world—was doomed for ever to be an outsider—and therein lay the tragedy of his life. He was continually making comparisons between his own evil fortune and the good fortune of others. Proud, suspicious, swift to take offence, when his

amour-propre was wounded, he was apt to salve it in the company of revellers whom he could meet on equal terms, and in whose society he could take out his revenge in sarcasm. As regards mere brain, he does not seem to have entertained any remarkable respect for the Edinburgh men of letters. He considered he had met as much intellectual capacity—unpolished and in the rough—in Torbolton debating societies, Mauchline masonic meetings, and at the tables of the writers of Kilmarnock and Ayr. He admitted, however, that his residence in Edinburgh had brought him in contact with something new—a refined and accomplished woman. The admission is important, and meeting it one fancies for a moment that one has caught some sort of explanation of his future life. What might have been the result had Burns secured a career in which his fancy and intellect could have exercised themselves, and a wife, who to affection added refinement and accomplishment, we may surmise, but cannot tell. A career he never secured ; and on his return to Ayrshire, in passionate blindness, he forged chains for himself which he could not break—which it would have been criminal in him to have attempted to break.

From Burns's correspondence while in Edinburgh we can see in what way he regarded his own position and prospects. He admitted that applause was pleasant ; he knew that, as a poet, he possessed some merit, but he constantly expressed his conviction that much of his success arose from the novelty of a poet appearing in his rank of life ; and he congratulates himself on the circumstance that—let literary reputation wax or wane—he had "an independence at the plough-tail" to fall back upon. He foresaw from the beginning that Edinburgh could be nothing more than a striking episode in his life, and that he was fated to return to the rural shades. Early in the year, he had some conversation with Mr. Patrick Miller, relative to his becoming a tenant on that gentleman's estate at Dalswinton, and had promised to run down to Dumfriesshire and look at the lands some time in the following May. That Mr. Miller was anxious to serve Burns, seems to have been generally known in Edinburgh ; for in Dr. Blair's letter, dated on 4th May, 1787, in answer to a note written by Burns on the previous day, intimating that he was about to leave town, the Doctor supposes that he is "going down to Dalswinton to look at some of Mr. Miller's farms." Before his return, Burns *did* intend to look at these farms, but at the moment farming was not the principal business in hand. He, in company with his young friend Ainslie, was on the wing for the south of Scotland—a district which was calling him with a hundred voices of tradition and ballad. On the day before starting, he sent Mr. Johnson, editor of the *Scot's Musical Museum*, a cordial letter, for he had entered with enthusiasm into that gentleman's work, and already written for it one or two songs—preliminary drops of the plenteous summer-shower which has kept so many secret places of the heart fresh and green.

The companions left Edinburgh on horseback on the 5th May. They visited

Dunse, Coldstream, Kelso, Jedburgh, Melrose, Dryburgh, and Yarrow—Burns scattering jokes and epigrams all the way. About the middle of the month Ainslie returned to Edinburgh, and Burns then crossed into England, saw Hexham and Newcastle, and returned home by Carlisle and Dumfries. From Dumfries he went to Dalswinton, looked over the estate, but did not seem much enamoured of its condition. He, however, arranged to meet Mr. Miller in August. He then came by Sanquhar to Mauchline, and dropped in upon his family unannounced. His meeting with these reticent hearts must be left to imagination. He went out from them obscure ; he returned to them illustrious, with a *nimbus* around his head. At home he renewed acquaintanceship with old friends, and found that Mr. Armour, who had treated him coldly in the day of his poverty and obscurity, was now inclined to regard him with a favourable eye—a circumstance which seems to have kindled Burns into unreasonable rage. "If anything," he writes to his correspondent Smith, "had been wanting to disgust me completely with the Armour family, their mean, servile compliance would have done it." The proud spirit which rankled in Edinburgh seems to have rankled no less bitterly in Ayrshire. A few days after he wrote to Mr. William Nicol, master of the High School, Edinburgh—then and afterwards one of his chiefest friends :—" I never, my friends, thought mankind very capable of anything generous ; but the stateliness of the patricians in Edinburgh, and the civility of my plebeian brethren (who perhaps formerly eyed me askance) since I returned home, have nearly put me out of conceit altogether with my species. I have bought a pocket Milton, which I carry perpetually about with me, in order to study the sentiments, the dauntless magnanimity, the intrepid, unyielding independence, the desperate daring, and noble defiance of hardship, in that great personage, Satan." At this precise period, it is somewhat hard to understand whence came the bitterness which wells up in almost every letter which Burns wrote. He was famous, he was even comparatively rich, but he had an eye which, constitutionally, regarded the seamy side of things. Probably, in no possible combination of fortunate circumstances could Burns have been a contented and happy man. He had Ulysses' "hungry heart," which could be satisfied with no shore, however green and pleasant, which must needs sail beyond the sunset. While residing at Mauchline, he accidentally met Jean, and affectionate intimacy was renewed, as if no anger or bitterness had ever estranged them.

Towards the end of June he went alone to the West Highlands, without any apparent motive, if not drawn by the memory of Mary Campbell. Of his movements in this trip we have no very precise information. At Inverary, where he could find accommodation neither in Castle nor Inn, he left an epigram which has become famous. In a letter to Mr. J. Smith—a fair specimen of his more familiar epistolary style—dated 30th June, we have some slight information respecting his doings, and a description of certain "high jinks" in the north, in which he was

an actor. Although the letter is dated as above, it does not state at what place it was written—Burns, perhaps, wishing to keep his secret.

" On our return, at a highland gentleman's hospitable mansion, we fell in with a merry party, and danced till the ladies left us, at three in the morning. Our dancing was none of the French or English insipid formal movements; the ladies sung Scotch songs like angels, at intervals; then we flew at ' Bab at the Bowster,' ' Tullochgorum,' ' Loch Erroch Side,' &c. like midges sporting in the mottie sun, or crows prognosticating a storm on a hairst day. When the dear lassies left us, we ranged round the bowl, to the good-fellow hour of six; except a few minutes that we went out to pay our devotions to the glorious lamp of day peering over the towering top of Ben Lomond. We all kneeled; our worthy landlor   son held the bowl, each man a full glass in his hand; and I, as priest, repeate   yming nonsense, like Thomas-a-Rhymer's prophecies, I suppose. After a small refreshment of the gifts of Somnus, we proceeded to spend the day on Loch Lomond, and reached Dumbarton in the evening. We dined at another good fellow's house, and consequently pushed the bottle; when we went out to mount our horses, we found ourselves ' No vera fou, but gaylie yet.' My two friends, and I, rode soberly down the Loch side, till by came a Highlandman at the gallop, on a tolerably good horse, but which had never known the ornaments of iron or leather. We scorned to be out-galloped by a Highlandman, so off we started, whip and spur. My companions, though seemingly gaily mounted, fell sadly astern; but my old mare, Jenny Geddes, one of the Rosinante family, strained past the Highlandman, in spite of all his efforts with the hair-halter. Just as I was passing him, Donald wheeled his horse, as if to cross before me, to mar my progress, when down came his horse, and threw his breekless rider in a clipt hedge; and down came Jenny Geddes over all, and my bardship between her and the Highlandman's horse. Jenny Geddes trode over me with such cautious reverence, that matters were not so bad as might have been expected; so I came off with a few cuts and bruises and a thorough resolution to be a pattern of sobriety for the future.

"I have yet fixed on nothing with respect to the serious business of life. I am, just as usual, a rhyming, mason-making, raking, aimless, idle fellow. However, I shall somewhere have a farm soon."

Whatever motive may have induced Burns to visit the West Highlands, he returned to Mossgiel somewhat shaken by the escapade related above. During the ensuing month he wrote his autobiographical sketch to Dr. Moore, and on the 7th August he returned to Edinburgh to settle business matters with his publisher, and to arrange other excursions through districts of the country in which he had a poetic interest.

Near the close of August, Burns and Nicol started on a northern tour. They went by Falkirk and Stirling, visited the field of Bannockburn, and on their return to Stirling, Burns, with a diamond which he had recently purchased—the most

unfortunate of all his investments, as it turned out—scribbled certain perilous verses on a window-pane of the inn. They then struck into Perthshire, admired the Falls of Moness, where Burns wrote *The Birks of Aberfeldy ;* visited Blair, the seat of the Duke of Athole, where they were hospitably entertained, and where Burns met his future patron, Mr. Graham, of Fintry, and narrowly missed meeting Mr. Dundas — a piece of ill-fortune which his biographers agree in lamenting. The travellers then proceeded to Inverness, went to Culloden, spent some time at the ruined cathedral at Elgin ; crossed the Spey, and visited the Duke of Gordon—which visit was cut short by an ebullition of wounded pride on the part of Nicol. From Castle Gordon they came by Banff to Aberdeen ; Burns then crossed into Kincardineshire — of which county his father was a native—and spent some time in hunting up his relations there. He then went to Montrose, where he met his cousin, Mr. James Burness, and returned to Edinburgh by Perth and Dundee.

In the beginning of October, according to Mr. Chambers,—for there seems to be a little obscurity as to date,—Burns, accompanied by Dr. Adair, set out on a visit to Sir William Murray, of Ochtertyre, and passing through Stirling, he broke the pane in the inn on which he had inscribed the treasonable lines. Unhappily, however, he could not by this means put them out of existence, as they had been widely copied and circulated, and were alive in many memories. At Ochtertyre he spent one or two pleasant days ; and while in the neighbourhood he took the opportunity of visiting Mrs. Bruce of Clackmannan, who was in possession of the helmet and sword of the Bruce, and with the latter she conferred on the poet and his guide the honour of knighthood, remarking as she did so, that she had a better right to give the title than some people. He returned to Edinburgh by Kinross and Queensferry, and while at Dunfermline some circumstances took place, trivial in themselves, but important as exhibiting what rapid changes took place in the weather of the poet's mind.

"At Dunfermline," says Dr. Adair, "we visited the ruined abbey and the abbey church, now consecrated to Presbyterian worship. Here I mounted the *cutty stool*, or stool of repentance, assuming the character of a penitent for fornication, while Burns from the pulpit addressed to me a ridiculous reproof and exhortation, parodied from that which had been delivered to himself in Ayrshire, where he had, as he assured me, once been one of seven who mounted the seat of shame together.

"In the churchyard two broad flagstones marked the grave of Robert Bruce, for whose memory Burns had more than common veneration. He knelt and kissed the stone with sacred fervour, and heartily execrated the worse than Gothic neglect of the first of Scottish heroes."

Burns was now resident in St. James's Square, in the house of William Cruick-shank, who was, like Nicol, connected with the Edinburgh High School. His

chief business was the arrangement of publishing matters with Creech, and he was anxious to come to some definite conclusion with Mr. Miller regarding a farm at Dalswinton. On his return from Ochtertyre he wrote that gentleman in practical terms enough : "I want to be a farmer in a small farm, about a plough-gang, in a pleasant country, under the auspices of a good landlord. I have no foolish notion of being a tenant on easier terms than another. To find a farm where one can live at all is not easy. I only mean living soberly, like an old style farmer, and joining personal industry. The banks of the Nith are as sweet poetic ground as any I ever saw ; and besides, sir, 'tis but justice to the feelings of my own heart, and the opinion of my best friends, to say that I would wish to call you landlord sooner than any landed gentleman I know. These are my views and wishes ; and in whatever way you think best to lay out your farms, I shall be happy to rent one of them. I shall certainly be able to ride to Dalswinton about the middle of next week." Burns, however, did not go to Dumfriesshire so early as he expected. There was dilatoriness on Creech's part regarding settlements as to the poems ; there was perhaps dilatoriness on Burns's part regarding the farm ; at all events, autumn had glided into winter, and he remained at Edinburgh without having come to a conclusion with either. The winter, however, was destined to open one of the strangest chapters in his strange story. At this time he made the acquaintance of Mrs. M'Lehose, the Clarinda of so many impassioned letters. This lady, who was possessed of no common beauty and intelligence, had been deserted by her husband, and was bringing up her children in somewhat narrow circumstances. They met at tea in the house of a common friend, and were pleased with each other's conversation. The second night after, Burns was to have drunk tea by invitation at the house of Mrs. M'Lehose, but having been upset the previous evening by a drunken coachman, and brought home with a knee severely bruised, he was obliged to forego that pleasure. He wrote the lady, giving the details of the accident, and expressing regret that he was unable to leave his room. The lady, who was of a temperament generous and impulsive, replied at once, giving utterance to *her* regret, and making Burns a formal proffer of her sympathy and friendship. Burns was enraptured, and returned an answer after the following fashion :—

"I stretch a point, indeed, my dearest madam, when I answer your card on the rack of my present agony. Your friendship, madam ! By heavens ! I was never proud before. * * * I swear solemnly (in all the terror of my former oath) to remember you in all the pride and warmth of friendship until—I cease to be !

"To-morrow, and every day till I see you, you shall hear from me.

"Farewell ! May you enjoy a better night's repose than I am likely to have."

The correspondence, so rapturously opened, proceeded quite as rapturously. It was arranged that in future Burns should sign himself *Sylvander*, and the lady *Clarinda*. Each day gave birth to its epistle. Poems were interchanged. Sighs

were wafted from St. James's Square to the Potterow. Clarinda was a "gloriously amiable fine woman," and Sylvander was her "devoted slave." Clarinda chid Sylvander tenderly for the warmth of his expressions. Sylvander was thrown into despair by the rebuke, but protested that he was not to blame. Who could behold her superior charms, her fine intelligence, and not love? who could love and be silent? Clarinda had strong Calvinistic leanings, and Sylvander, who could not pardon these things in Ayrshire clergymen, and was accustomed to call them by quite other names, was "delighted by her honest enthusiasm for religion." Clarinda was to be passing on a certain day through the square in which Sylvander lived, and promised to favour him with a nod, should she be so fortunate as to see him at his window; and wrote sorrowing, the day after, that she had been unable to discover his window. Sylvander was inconsolable. Not able to discover his window! He could almost throw himself over it for very vexation. His peace is spoiled for the day. He is sure the soul is capable of disease, for his has convulsed itself into an inflammatory fever, and so on. During this period of letter-writing, Burns and Mrs. M'Lehose had met several times in her own house, and on these occasions he had opportunities of making her aware of his dismal prospects. The results of his renewed intercourse with Jean on his return to Ayrshire were now becoming apparent; this was communicated to her along with other matters, and Mrs. M'Lehose was all forgiveness—tempered with rebuke, and a desire for a more Calvinistic way of thinking on his part on religious subjects. That the affection of Burns for the lady was rooted in anything deeper than fancy, and a natural delight in intelligence and a pleasing manner, may be doubted. His *Clarinda* letters are artificial, and one suspects the rhetorician in the swelling sentences and the exaggerated sentiment. With regard to Mrs. M'Lehose there can be no mistake. Her letters are far superior to Burns's, being simple, natural, and with a pathetic cadence in some portions which has not yet lost the power to affect. She loved Burns, and hoped, if he would but wait till existing ties were broken, to be united to him. But Burns could not wait, the correspondence drooped, and a year saw all his passion

> "Die away,
> And fade into the light of common day;"

the common day of Jean Armour, Ellisland, and the Excise.

When Burns at this period, confined to his room by an angry limb, in the middle of his Clarinda correspondence, and tortured with suspicions of Creech's insolvency —of which some ugly rumours had reached him—was made aware that Jean was about to become again a mother, and that her father had thrust her from his house in anger, he was perhaps more purely wretched than at any other period of his life. In his own breast there was passionate tumult and remorse. Look where he would, no blue spot was to be discovered in the entire sky of his prospects. He

had felt the sweetness of applause : he was now to experience the bitterness of the after-taste. He was a "lion" whose season had passed. His great friends seemed unwilling or unable to procure him a post. He had been torn from his old modes of life, and in the new order of things which surrounded him he could find nothing permanent, nothing that would cohere. Time was passing ; his life was purposeless ; he was doing nothing, effecting nothing ; he was flapping in the wind like an unbraced sail. At this juncture he resolved to bring matters to a conclusion, after one fashion or another. In his letters, the old scheme of emigration to the West Indies turns up bitterly for a moment. Then he bethought himself of a post in the Excise, which had always been a dream of his, and the possibility of his obtaining which had been discussed by his Ayrshire friends before he became famous. If such a position could be secured it would be at least something, something in itself, something to fall back upon should his farming schemes prove abortive. He accordingly wrote the Earl of Glencairn, soliciting his patronage, but the application appears to have been followed by no result. Mr. Graham, of Fintry, whose acquaintance Burns had made at Blair, the seat of the Duke of Athole, having heard of his wish, through the kind offices of Mr. Alexander Wood, the surgeon who attended him, immediately placed his name on the list of expectant officers. Having arranged his Excise business so far, he left Edinburgh to have another look at Mr. Miller's farms, and to come to an agreement, if possible. He took a friend with him on whose sagacity and business skill he could confide ; and after a deliberate inspection of the lands, he was better satisfied than he had been on a former occasion, and at once made an offer to Mr. Miller for the farm at Ellisland, which was accepted. On his return to Edinburgh he announced his resolution to his friend Miss Chalmers :

"Yesternight I completed a bargain with Mr. Miller, of Dalswinton, for the farm of Ellisland, on the banks of the Nith, between five and six miles above Dumfries. I begin at Whitsunday to build a house, drive lime, &c., and Heaven be my help ! for it will take a strong effort to bring my mind into the routine of business. I have discharged all the army of my former pursuits, fancies, and pleasures—a motley host ! and have literally and strictly retained only the ideas of a few friends, which I have incorporated into a life-guard."

Burns's business at this time in Edinburgh related to his settlement with Creech, which, after many delays, was about to take place. In all, he appears to have received between 400*l.* and 500*l.*, and out of this sum he advanced 180*l.* to his brother Gilbert, who was struggling manfully at Mossgiel. On the 24th March, with much business on hand, he left Edinburgh for Ayrshire, where he married Jean Armour—snapping thereby the chief link which bound him to the metropolis. This union, putting moral considerations out of the question altogether, was the most prudent course open to him, and it repaired the fabric of self-respect which had been, to some extent at least, broken down. For a time we hear nothing of

the "wandering stabs of remorse," and his letters breathe a quite unusual content-edness. He had made some little self-sacrifice, and he tasted the happiness which always arises from the consciousness of self-sacrifice. Besides, he had loved the girl, perhaps loved her all through, although the constant light of affection had, to himself as well as to others, been obscured by the glare of fiercer and more transitory fires ; and if so—the sacrifice not so great as he supposed it to be—he was plainly a gainer both ways. Burns was placed at this time in difficult circumstances, and he simply made the best of them. He could build only with the materials within reach. There was nothing left but to begin life again as a farmer, and it behoved him to wear russet on heart as well as on limb. In the heyday of his Edinburgh success he foresaw the probability of his return to the rural shades, and to these shades he had now returned—but he returned with reputation, experience, an unreproving conscience, some little money in hand, and with solider prospects of happiness than had ever yet fallen to his lot. Happiness he did taste for a few months—and then out of the future came the long shadows of disaster, fated not to pass away, but to gather deeper and darker over a grave which was dug too early —and yet too late.

When Burns entered into possession of Ellisland, at Whitsunday, 1788, he left his wife at Mauchline till the new dwelling-house should be erected. In the meantime he was sufficiently busy ; he had to superintend masons and carpenters, as well as look after more immediate farm matters. Besides, in order to qualify himself for holding his Excise Commission, he had to give attendance at Ayr for six weeks on the duties of his new profession. These occupations, together with occasional visits to his wife and family, kept him fully occupied. Hope had sprung up in his bosom like a Jonah's gourd, and while the greenness lasted he was happy enough. During his solitary life at Ellisland, he wrote two or three of his finest songs, each of them in praise of Jean, and each giving evidence that his heart was at rest. During this time, too, a somewhat extensive correspondence was kept up, and activity and hopefulness—only occasionally dashed by accesses of his constitutional melancholy—radiate through it all. As was natural, his letters relate, for the most part, to his marriage and his new prospects. As respects his marriage, he takes abundant care to make known that, acting as he had done, he had acted prudently ; that he had secured an admirable wife, and that in his new relationship he was entirely satisfied. If any doubt should exist as to Burns's satisfaction, it can arise only from his somewhat too frequent protestation of it. He takes care to inform his correspondents that he has actually married Jean, that he would have been a scoundrel had he declined to marry her, and that she possessed the sweetest temper and the handsomest figure in the country. The truth is, that, in the matter of matrimony, he could not very well help himself. He was aware that the match was far from a brilliant one, and as he really loved his wife, he had to argue down that feeling in his own heart ; he was aware that his correspondents did not con-

sider it brilliant, and he had also to argue down that feeling in theirs. Meanwhile, the house at Ellisland was getting finished. In the first week of December he brought home his wife, and in the pride of his heart he threw off a saucy little song,

"I hae a wife o' my ain,'

which quivers through every syllable of it with a homely and assured delight that laughs at all mischance. Mrs. Burns brought her children and a whole establishment of servants. The house was small, its accommodation was limited, and Burns sat at meals with his domestics, and on Sunday evenings, after the good old Scottish fashion, he duly catechised them. He has himself left on record that this was the happiest portion of his life. He had friends, with whom he maintained an intimate correspondence; he had a wife who loved him; his passionate and wayward heart was at rest in its own happiness; he could see the grain yellowing in his own fields; he had the Excise Commission in his pocket on which he could fall back if anything went wrong; and on the red scaur above the river, he could stride about, giving audience to incommunicable thought, while the Nith was hoarse with flood, and the moon was wading through clouds overhead. When should he have been happy, if not now?

Burns's farming operations during the second year of his occupancy of Ellisland were not successful, and in the more unrestrained letters of the period we find him complaining of his hard fate in being obliged to make one guinea do the work of five. As the expense of his family was now rapidly increasing, he requested to be allowed to enter at once on his duties as officer of Excise. That in his new mode of life he would encounter unpleasantnesses he knew, and was prepared for them; but he expected that Mrs. Burns would be able to manage the farm for the most part—in any case his salary as Exciseman would be a welcome addition to his means. He was appointed on application, he entered zealously on his duties, and as his district extended over ten parishes, he was forced to ride about two hundred miles per week. This work, taken in conjunction with labour at Ellisland, which, constantly getting into arrear, demanded fierce exertion at intervals, was too much for even his iron frame. He had attacks of illness, and his constitutional hypochondria ruled him with a darker sceptre than ever. It appears evident from his letters that he meant to make his fight at Ellisland, and that he considered the Excise as a second line of defence on which he could fall back in the event of defeat. At Ellisland he *was* defeated, and on his second line of defence he fell back grimly enough. An Excise officer is not a popular character in country districts where smugglers abound; and whatever degree of odium might attach to his new profession Burns was certain to feel more keenly than most. One can see that in his new relation his haughty spirit was ill at ease; that he suspected a sort of meanness in himself; and that the thought that he had in any way stooped or condescended was gall and wormwood. His bitterness on this matter escapes in

various and characteristic ways. At one time he treats the matter with imperial disdain, declaring that he does not intend " to seek honour from his profession ; " at another time in a set of impromptu verses he mocks at his occupation and him-self, illuminating the whole business with a flame of spleenful mirth. But the step he had taken was unquestionably a prudent one, and if it miscarried, it miscarried from foreign causes. From every account which survives, he was an excellent and zealous officer, and into his work he carried eyes which were at once sharp and kindly. It was not in his nature to be harsh or tyrannical. A word revealed secrets to him, a glance let him into the bearings of a case ; and while he saw that the interests of Government did not materially suffer, his good nature and kind-heartedness were always at hand to make matters as pleasant as possible. One or two of these Excise anecdotes are amongst the pleasantest remembrances we have of Burns. His professional prospects were on the whole far from despicable. On his farm he was losing money, health, and hope ; but in the Excise he looked forward to advancement—an Inspectorship or Supervisorship being regarded as within his reach.

If Ellisland had only been profitable, Burns might have been considered a fortu-nate man. For his own wants and for those of his family the cottage which he had built sufficed. The scenery around him was beautiful. He was on good terms with the neighbouring proprietors, and his reputation attracted visitors from many quarters. He procured books from Edinburgh and from the circulating library which—with that regard for mental means and appliances which seems to have been a characteristic of his race—he had established in the vicinity. Every other day letters and newspapers were arriving at Ellisland, connecting him with distant places and events ; and the stranger who dropped in upon him from London or Edinburgh, or even from places more remote, brought talk, ideas, observations on this thing and the other more or less valuable, stimulus, excitement—all tending to enrich intellectual life. And during this time he was no mental sluggard. He worked his brain as he worked his servants on the acres at Ellisland, or his horse as he rode on the scent of a smuggler through the Nithsdale moors. He carried on a multifarious correspondence, he wrote his letters carefully—only a little *too* carefully sometimes, for he is occasionally modish and over-dressed. Every other week he sent a packet of songs to Johnson for his *Museum*, which had now reached the third volume. He interested himself in local politics and scribbled election-eering ballads. One evening, when the past—heavy with unshed tears—lay near his heart, he composed the strain, *To Mary in Heaven ;* and in the course of one summer day, in a perfect riot and whirlwind of ecstasy, every faculty and power in full blossom, he dashed off *Tam O' Shanter*—immortal, unapproachable ! If Ellis-land had but paid, Burns might have been happy as farmer and poet,—or as Exciseman, farmer and poet,—for the characters were by no means incompatible.

But for his Excise salary Burns must have succumbed under farming difficul-

ties, he was now anxious to be quit of Ellisland, and to confine himself entirely to his official duties ; and it so happened that Mr. Miller was willing to release him of the portion of the lease which was yet to run, preparatory to a final sale of that part of the lands. The Ellisland crops were sold, and the sale was made the occasion of a drunken orgie. On the 1st September, Burns writes to Mr. Thomas Sloan :

"I sold my crop on this day se'en-night, and sold it very well. A guinea an acre on an average above value. But such a scene of drunkenness was hardly ever seen in this country. After the roup was over about thirty people engaged in a battle, every man for his own hand; and fought it out for three hours. Nor was the scene much better in the house. No fighting indeed, but folks lying drunk on the floor, and decanting, until both my dogs got so drunk by attending on them that they could not stand. You will easily guess how I enjoyed the scene, as I was no farther over than you used to see me."

In November Ellisland became the property of Mr. Morine, and Burns immediately sold his farm stock and implements—relinquishing for ever the plough-tail, at which he so often boasted that he had an independence—and removed with his wife and children to a small house in the Wee Vennel of Dumfries. On his removal he was appointed to an Excise division, which improved his salary. His income was now 70*l.* per annum.

It is at Dumfries that Burns's story first becomes really tragical. He had divorced himself from country scenery and the on-goings of rural life, which, up till now, formed an appropriate background for our ideas of him. Instead of the knowes and meadows of Mossgiel and Ellisland, with their lovely sunrises and twilights, we have to connect him with the streets, the gossip, and the dissipation of a third-rate Scottish town. He was no longer a farmer—he was a simple gauger, hoping to obtain a supervisorship. Proud as was his spirit, he was dependent on great friends ; and he condescended, on various occasions, to write epistles in prose and verse which fawned on a patron's hand. Natural inspiration and picturesqueness were taken out of his life. He turned down no more daisies, the horned moon hung no longer in the window-pane of the ale-house in which he drank ; the composition of theatrical prologues engaged his attention rather than the composition of poems of rustic life. He was never rich, but in Dumfries his poverty for the first time wears an aspect of painfulness. For the first time we hear of monetary difficulties, of obligations which he cannot conveniently meet, of debt. It was here, too, that certain weaknesses, which had lately grown upon him, attracted public notice. In Dumfries, as in Edinburgh at that time, there was a good deal of tavern-life, and much hard drinking at dinner and supper parties, and the like. Burns was famous— he had lived in dukes' houses, he corresponded with celebrated men, he could talk brilliantly, he had wit for every call as other men had spare silver, he could repeat his last poem or epigram—and as a consequence his society was in great request. It was something to have dined or supped in the company of Burns—if one ꞏꞏꞏ ꞏt

the rose, it was at least something to have been near the rose—and his host was proud of him, as he was proud of his haunch of venison, his claret, his silver *epergne.* Burns's good things circulated with the wine ; his wit gave a new relish to the fruit, and kindled an unwonted splendour in the brains of his listeners. Then strangers, passing through Dumfries, were naturally anxious to see the poet whose reputation had travelled so far. They invited him to the inns in which they were living, Burns consented, frequently the revel was loud and late, and when he rose—after the sun sometimes—he paid his share of the lawing with "a slice of his constitution." In his younger days he had been subjected to public rebuke by the Rev. Mr. Auld ; but since his marriage he seems to have been irreproachable in the matter of con-jugal fidelity. During, however, an unfortunate absence of his wife in Ayrshire he contracted a discreditable *liaison*, which resulted in the birth of a daughter. Mrs. Burns seems neither to have reproached nor complained ; she adopted the child, and brought it up in the same cradle with her own infant. If for his fault he had been subjected to domestic annoyance, he might have taken refuge in pride, and haughtily repelled reproaches ; but his wife's forgiveness allowed him to brood—and with what bitterness we can guess—over his misconduct. Doubtless the evil in his career at Dumfries has been exaggerated. Burns's position was full of peril —he was subjected to temptations which did not come in the way of ordinary men ; and if he drank hard, it was in an age when hard drinking was fashionable. If he sinned in this respect, he sinned in company with English prime ministers, Scotch Lords of Session, grave dignitaries of the Church in both countries, and with thousands of ordinary blockheads who went to their graves in the odour of sanctity, and whose epitaphs are a catalogue of all the virtues. Burns was a man set apart ; he was observed, he was talked about; and if he erred, it was like erring in the market-place. In any other inhabitant of Dumfries, misdemeanours such as Burns's would hardly have provoked remark ; what would have been unnoticed on the hodden grey of the farmer became a stain on the singing robe of the poet. That Burns should have led an unworthy life is to be deplored, but the truth is—and herein lies explanation, palliation perhaps—that in Dumfries he was somewhat a-weary of the sun. Not seldom he was desperate and at bay. He was neither in harmony with himself nor with the world. He had enjoyed one burst of brilliant success, and in the light of that success his life before and after looked darker than it actually was. The hope deferred of a supervisorship made his heart sick. He had succeeded as a poet, but in everything else failure had dogged his steps ; and out of that poetical success no permanent benefit had resulted, or seemed now in his need likely to result. In the east were the colours of the dawn, but the sun would not arise. His letters at this time breathe an almost uniform mood of exasperation and misery, and it is hard for a miserable man to be a good one. He is tempted to make strange alliances, and to pay a high price for forgetfulness. And over Burns's head at this time was suspended one other black

cloud, which, although it only burst in part, made the remainder of his life darker with its shadow.

Chief amongst Burns's friends during the early portion of his residence Dumfries were Mr. and Mrs. Riddel. They were in good circumstances, possessing a small estate in the neighbourhood of the town, and Burns was frequently their guest. Mrs. Riddel was young and pretty, and distinguished by literary taste and accomplishment. She wrote verses which Burns praised, and he introduced her to his friend Smellie, the naturalist, who was enchanted with her vivacity and talent. But this pleasant relationship was destined to be interrupted. On the occasion of a dinner-party at Woodley Park, the residence of Mr. Riddel, when wine flowed much too freely, Burns—in some not quite explained manner—grievously offended his hostess. On the following morning he apologised in prose and verse, threw the *onus* of his rudeness on Mr. Riddel's wine—which was the next thing to blaming Mr. Riddel himself—and in every way expressed regret for his conduct, and abhorrence of himself. These apologies do not seem to have been accepted, and for a time the friends ceased to meet. Burns was hurt and angry, and he made the lady he was accustomed to address in adoring verses and high-flown epistles the subject of cruel and unmanly lampoons. The estrangement was, of course, noised abroad, and people were inclined to side with the fashionable lady rather than with the Jacobinical exciseman. For a time at least, Dumfries regarded Burns with a lowering and suspicious eye, one reason of which may be found in his quarrel with the Riddels and its cause, and another in the political principles which he professed to hold, and to which he gave imprudent expression.

His immediate ancestors had perilled something in the cause of the Stuarts, and Burns, in his early days, was wont to wear a sentimental Jacobitism—for ornament's sake, like a ring on the finger, or a sprig of heather in the bonnet. This Jacobitism was fed by his sentiment and his poetry. It grew out of the House of Stuart as flowers grow out of the walls of ruins. But while he held the past in reverence, and respected aristocracy as an outcome of that past, a something around which tradition and ballad could gather, there was always a fierce democratic impulse in his mind, which raged at times like the ocean tide against the Bullers of Buchan. This democratic feeling, like his other feeling of Jacobitism, rested on no solid foundation. He had a strong feeling that genius and worth are always poor, that baseness and chicanery are always prosperous. He considered that the good things of this life were secured by the rascals more or less. The truth is, his Jacobitism sprang from his imagination, his Radicalism from his discontent; the one the offspring of the best portion of his nature, the other the offspring of the worst. Radicalism was originally born of hunger; and Burns, while denouncing the rulers of his country, was simply crying out under his own proper sore. He passionately carried particulars into generals. He was sick, and so was the whole body politic. He needed reform, so, of course, did the whole world, and it was more agreeable

begin with the world in the first instance. He was imprudent in the expression
his political opinions, and was continually doing himself injury thereby. He had
itten, as we have seen, treasonable verses on the inn window at Stirling; and
though on a subsequent visit he dashed out the pane, he could not by that
means destroy the copies which were in circulation. The writing of the verses
referred to was imprudent enough, but the expression of his Radicalism at Dumfries
—which was a transient mood, not a fixed principle with him—was more imprudent
ll. In the one case he was a private individual, anxious to enter the Excise;
the other, he had entered the Excise, was actually a Government officer, and in
eceipt of a Government salary. Besides, too, the times were troublous: there was
editious feeling in the country, France had become a volcano in active eruption,
nd European business was carried on in its portentous light. It became known
hat Burns looked with favour on the revolutionary party across the Channel, that
e read newspapers which were opposed to the Government, and, as a consequence,
the well-to-do inhabitants of Dumfries he was regarded with suspicion. This
spicion was, of course, wretched enough, but Burns need not have gone out of his
ay to incur it. He knew perfectly well that his Radicalism was based on no serious
nviction, that it grew out of personal discontent, and that the discontent was the
sult of wounded pride, and the consciousness that he had not shaped his life aright.
esides all this, he seems to have lost self-command; he was constantly getting into
crapes from which there could be no honourable extrication. He burned his fingers,
nd he did not dread the fire. To the Subscription Library in Dumfries he pre-
ented, amongst other volumes, a copy of *De Lolme on the British Constitution*, and
nscribed on the back of the portrait of the author, "Mr. Burns presents this book
o the Library, and begs they will take it as a creed of British liberty—until they
nd a better. R. B." And next morning he came to the bedside of the gentleman
who had the volume in custody, imploring to see *De Lolme*, as he feared he had
written something in it that might bring him into trouble. We hear of him at a
rivate dinner-party, when the health of Pitt was proposed, giving "The health of
George Washington—a better man," and of his being sulky that his toast was not
eceived. He had already sent a present of guns to the French Convention, with
hich our prospect of war was at this time becoming imminent; and at a later period
e find him quarrelling with an officer on the subject of another toast, and writing
pologies to the effect, firstly, that when the offence was committed he was drunk;
nd secondly, that he could not fight a duel, because he had the welfare of
thers to care for. When the Board of Excise ordered some inquiries to be made
egarding his political conduct, he wrote Mr. Graham of Fintry, declaring that "To
he British Constitution, on revolution principles, next after my God, I am most
evoutly attached." He was in a state of chronic exasperation at himself, at the
ch people of his acquaintance and of his immediate neighbourhood, and at the
orld generally; and his exasperation was continually blazing out in sarcasm and

invective. Curiously enough, too, when one thinks of it, during all this bitter time he was writing songs for Mr. Thomson, who had opened a correspondence with hi He was busy with *Chloris* and *Phillis*, while thrones were shaking, and the son Saint Louis knelt on the scaffold, and Marie Antoinette during her trial v beating out with weary fingers a piano tune on the bench before her. Every oth week up from Dumfries to Edinburgh came by the fly a packet of songs for the new publication. On one occasion came the stern war-ode, *Scots wha hae wi' Wal'* bled, which Mr. Thomson thought susceptible of improvement. But Burns inexorable; he liked his ode, and as it was it should remain. It has been . that by the more respectable circles in Dumfries Burns was regarded with suspic. if not with positive dislike. Some evidence of this will be found in the anecdote related by Mr. Lockhart. "Mr. M'Culloch," we are informed by that biographe "was seldom more grieved than when, riding into Dumfries one fine summ evening to attend a county ball, he saw Burns walking alone on the shady side the principal street of the town, while the opposite side was gay with successiv groups of ladies and gentlemen, all drawn together for the festivities of the night not one of whom appeared willing to recognise him. The horseman dismounted and joined Burns, who, on his proposing to him to cross the street, said, 'Nay nay, my young friend, that's all over now;' and quoted, after a pause, some verse of Lady Grizel Baillie's pathetic ballad :

> ' His bonnet stood ance fu' fair on his brow,
> His auld ane looked better than mony ane's new ;
> But now he let's wear ony gate it will hing,
> And casts himsel' dowie upon the corn-bing.

> ' Oh, were we young as we ance hae been,
> We sud hae been galloping down on yon green,
> And linking it ower the lily-white lea—
> And werena my heart light I wad die.'

Burns then turned the conversation, and took his young friend home with him till the time for the ball arrived."

This—with the exception of the actual close—was the darkest period in Burns's life. In a short time the horizon cleared a little. The quarrel with Mrs. Riddel was healed, and in a short time books and poems were exchanged between them as of yore. He appears also to have had again some hope of obtaining a supervisor-ship—the mirage that haunted his closing years. Meanwhile, political feeling had become less bitter ; and, in 1795, he exhibited his friendliness to the institutions of the country by entering himself one of a corps of volunteers which was raised in Dumfries, and by composing the spirited patriotic song, *Does haughty Gaul inva-sion threat ?* This song became at once popular ; and it showed the nation that the heart of the writer was sound at the core, that he hated anarchy and tyranny alike, and wished to steer a prudent middle course. Better days were dawning ; but by this time the hardships of his youth, his constant anxieties, his hoping

Of Burns, the man and poet, what is there left to be said? During his lifetime
was regarded as a phenomenon; and now, when he has been seventy years in
s grave, he is a phenomenon still. He came up from Ayrshire with all the sense
d shrewdness of its peasantry, the passion of its lovers, the piety of its circles of
mily worship, the wild mirth of its kirns and halloweens. Of all the great men
the North Country, his was incomparably the fullest soul. What fun he had,
hat melancholy, what pity, what anger, what passion, what homely sagacity,
hat sensitiveness! Of everything he was brimful and overflowing. It is difficult
carry a full cup and not to spill it. He had his errors, but they arose out of his
plendid and perilous richness. As a man he was full of natural goodness, but he
as unreticent even amongst poets. We know the best and the worst of him;
nd he has himself frankly told us that best and that worst. He had to fight with
dverse circumstances, he died before he had run his race, and his fame—greater
nan that of any other poet of his country—rests upon poems written swiftly, as
men write their letters, and on songs which came to him naturally as its carol comes
the blackbird.

Of all poets Burns was, perhaps, the most directly inspired. His poems did not
row—like stalactites—by the slow process of accretion; like Adam, they had no
nildhood—they awoke complete. Burns produced all his great effects by single
rokes. In his best things there is an impetus, a hurry, which gives one the idea
f boundless resource. To him a song was the occupation of a morning; his
oetic epistles drive along in a fiery sleet of words and images: his *Tam O' Shanter*
as written in a day—since Bruce fought Bannockburn, the best single day's work
one in Scotland Burns was never taken by surprise; he was ready for all calls
nd emergencies. He had not only—like Addison—a thousand-pound note at
ome, but he had—to carry out the image—plenty of loose intellectual coin in his
ocket. A richer man—with plenty of money in his purse, and able to get the
oney *out* of his purse when swift occasion required—Nature has seldom sent into
he world.

Born and bred as he was in the country, we find in Burns the finest pictures of
ural life. We smell continually the newly-turned earth, the hawthorn blossom,
he breath of kine. His shepherds and shepherdesses are not those who pipe and
nake love in Arcady and on Sèvres china—they actually work, receive wages,
ttend markets, hear sermons, go sweethearting, and, at times, before the con-
regation endure rebuke. The world he depicts is a real world, and the men and
vomen are also real. Burns had to sweat in the eye of Phœbus, and about all he
vrites there is an out-of-doors feeling. Although conversant with sunrises and
unsets, the processes of vegetation, and all the shows and forms of nature, he
eldom or never describes these things for their own sake; they are always kept
n subordination to the central human interest. Burns cared little for the natural
picturesque in itself; the moral picturesque touched him more nearly. An

old soldier in tattered scarlet interested him   he pr
ferred a gnarled character to a gnarled tree.   Arran hau
Ayrshire—Burns must daily have seen them f.   Mossgiel—ar
yet, to this most striking object in his range of v.   ere is not a sing
allusion in his letters and poems. If Wordsworth had been placed in the sam
environment, how he would have made his suns rise or set on Arran! Aft
all, it is usually the town-poets—men like Hunt and Keats—who go philanderir
after nature, who are enraptured by the graceful curvature of ferns and the colou
of mosses and lichens. Burns had an exquisite delight in Nature, especially in h
more sombre and gloomy aspects; but he took a deeper interest in man, and, as
consequence, the chief interest of his poems is of a moral kind. We value the
not so much for their colour, their harmony, their curious felicities of expression
as for the gleams of sagacity, the insight into character, the strong homely sens
and those wonderful short sentences scattered everywhere. Of those short lines an
sentences, now sly, now caustic, now broadly humorous, now purely didactic, n
writings, if Shakespeare's be excepted, have a greater abundance. They circulat
everywhere like current coin; they have passed like iron into the blood of our com
mon speech. Of Burns's conversation in Edinburgh we have little recorded that i
specially characteristic—and for this we blame not Burns, but his reporters. The
best thing—indeed, the only true and deep thing—is the simple statement which
struck Dugald Stewart so much when the pair were standing on the Braid hills
looking out on the fair morning world. Beneath were cottages, early sparrow
doubtless noisy in the thatch, pillars of blue smoke, telling of preparation o
breakfast for labourers afield, curling in the calm air. Burns took in the whole
landscape, and declared that, in his view, the worthiest object it contained was the
cluster of smoking cots, knowing as he did, what worth, what affection, what pious
contentment and happiness, nestled within them. This really is a gleam into the
man's inmost soul. Poetry, to him, lay in the cottage rather than in the tree that
overshadowed it, or the stream that sparkled past it. In one of his poems he lays
down the doctrine in express terms—

> "To mak a happy fireside clime
> To weans and wife,
> That's the true pathos and sublime
> Of human life."

The poetry of a man so intensely humane is certain to come home to the bosoms
and businesses of all other men—powerfully to the happy, more powerfully to the
miserable, who are ever in the majority. To the wretched, out of the Bible, there
is no such solace as the poetry of Burns. His genius comes to their hovels, their
poor bread wetted with tears, as Howard came to the strong places of pestilence—
irradiating, consoling; like the hearing of soft tones, like the touches of tender
hands. And then his large friendliness flows out in every direction. The "mouse"

Of Burns, the man and poet, what is there left to be said? During his lifetime he was regarded as a phenomenon; and now, when he has been seventy years in his grave, he is a phenomenon still. He came up from Ayrshire with all the sense and shrewdness of its peasantry, the passion of its lovers, the piety of its circles of family worship, the wild mirth of its kirns and halloweens. Of all the great men of the North Country, his was incomparably the fullest soul. What fun he had, what melancholy, what pity, what anger, what passion, what homely sagacity, what sensitiveness! Of everything he was brimful and overflowing. It is difficult to carry a full cup and not to spill it. He had his errors, but they arose out of his splendid and perilous richness. As a man he was full of natural goodness, but he was unreticent even amongst poets. We know the best and the worst of him; and he has himself frankly told us that best and that worst. He had to fight with adverse circumstances, he died before he had run his race, and his fame—greater than that of any other poet of his country—rests upon poems written swiftly, as men write their letters, and in songs which came to him naturally as its carol comes to the blackbird.

Of all poets Burns was, perhaps, the most directly inspired. His poems did not grow—like stalactites—by the slow process of accretion; like Adam, they had no childhood—they awoke complete. Burns produced all his great effects by single strokes. In his best things there is an impetus, a hurry, which gives one the idea of boundless resource. To him a song was the occupation of a morning; his poetic epistles drive along in a fiery sleet of words and images: his *Tam O' Shanter* was written in a day—since Bruce fought Bannockburn, the best single day's work done in Scotland Burns was never taken by surprise; he was ready for all calls and emergencies. He had not only—like Addison—a thousand-pound note at home, but he had—to carry out the image—plenty of loose intellectual coin in his pocket. A richer man—with plenty of money in his purse, and able to get the money *out* of his purse when swift occasion required—Nature has seldom sent into the world.

Born and bred as he was in the country, we find in Burns the finest pictures of rural life. We smell continually the newly-turned earth, the hawthorn blossom, the breath of kine. His shepherds and shepherdesses are not those who pipe and make love in Arcady and on Sèvres china—they actually work, receive wages, attend markets, hear sermons, go sweethearting, and, at times, before the congregation endure rebuke. The world he depicts is a real world, and the men and women are also real. Burns had to sweat in the eye of Phœbus, and about all he writes there is an out-of-doors feeling. Although conversant with sunrises and sunsets, the processes of vegetation, and all the shows and forms of nature, he seldom or never describes these things for their own sake; they are always kept in subordination to the central human interest. Burns cared little for the natural picturesque in itself; the moral picturesque touched him more nearly. An

old soldier in tattered scarlet interested him　　　　　ruin; he preferred a gnarled character to a gnarled tree.　The ridges of Arran haunt Ayrshire—Burns must daily have seen them from his door at Mossgiel—and yet, to this most striking object in his range of vision, there is not a single allusion in his letters and poems.　If Wordsworth had been placed in the same environment, how he would have made his suns rise or set on Arran!　After all, it is usually the town-poets—men like Hunt and Keats—who go philandering after nature, who are enraptured by the graceful curvature of ferns and the colours of mosses and lichens.　Burns had an exquisite delight in Nature, especially in her more sombre and gloomy aspects; but he took a deeper interest in man, and, as a consequence, the chief interest of his poems is of a moral kind.　We value them not so much for their colour, their harmony, their curious felicities of expression, as for the gleams of sagacity, the insight into character, the strong homely sense, and those wonderful short sentences scattered everywhere.　Of those short lines and sentences, now sly, now caustic, now broadly humorous, now purely didactic, no writings, if Shakespeare's be excepted, have a greater abundance.　They circulate everywhere like current coin; they have passed like iron into the blood of our common speech.　Of Burns's conversation in Edinburgh we have little recorded that is specially characteristic—and for this we blame not Burns, but his reporters.　The best thing—indeed, the only true and deep thing—is the simple statement which struck Dugald Stewart so much when the pair were standing on the Braid hills, looking out on the fair morning world.　Beneath were cottages, early sparrows doubtless noisy in the thatch, pillars of blue smoke, telling of preparation of breakfast for labourers afield, curling in the calm air.　Burns took in the whole landscape, and declared that, in his view, the worthiest object it contained was the cluster of smoking cots, knowing as he did, what worth, what affection, what pious contentment and happiness, nestled within them.　This really is a gleam into the man's inmost soul.　Poetry, to him, lay in the cottage rather than in the tree that overshadowed it, or the stream that sparkled past it.　In one of his poems he lays down the doctrine in express terms—

> "To mak a happy fireside clime
> 　　　To weans and wife,
> That's the true pathos and sublime
> 　　　Of human life."

The po　　a man so intensely humane is certain to come home to the bosoms and businesses of all other men—powerfully to the happy, more powerfully to the miserable, who are ever in the majority.　To the wretched, out of the Bible, there is no such solace as the poetry of Burns.　His genius comes to their hovels, their poor bread wetted with tears, as Howard came to the strong places of pestilence—irradiating, consoling; like the hearing of soft tones, like the touches of tender hands.　And then his large friendliness flows out in every direction.　The "mouse"

BIOGRAPHICAL PREFACE.

ROBERT BURNS was born about two miles to the south of Ayr, in the neighbourhood of Alloway Kirk and the Bridge of Doon, on the 25th January, 1759. The
cottage, a clay one, had been constructed by his father, and a week after the poet's
birth it gave way in a violent wind, and mother and child were carried at midnight to the shelter of a neighbour's dwelling.

When Burns became famous he wore, more however for ornament than use—
like the second jacket of a hussar—a certain vague Jacobitism. Both in his verses
and his letters he makes allusion to the constancy with which his ancestors followed
the banner of the Stuarts, and to the misfortunes which their loyalty brought upon
them. The family was a Kincardineshire one—in which county, indeed, it can be
traced pretty far back by inscriptions in churchyards, documents appertaining to
leases and the like—and the poet's grandfather and uncles were out, it is said, in
the Rebellion of 1715. When the title and estates of the Earl Marischal were
forfeited on account of the uprising, Burns's grandfather seems to have been brought
into trouble. He lost his farm, and his son came southward in search of
employment. The poet's father, who spelt his name Burnes, and who was
suspected of having a share in the Rebellion of 1745, came into the neighbourhood
of Edinburgh, where he obtained employment as a gardener. Afterwards he went
into Ayrshire, where, becoming overseer to Mr. Ferguson of Doonholm and
leasing a few acres of land, he erected a house and brought home his wife, Agnes
Brown, in December 1757. Robert was the firstborn. Brain, hypochondria, and
general superiority he inherited from his father; from his mother he drew his lyrical
gift, his wit, his mirth. She had a fine complexion, bright dark eyes, cheerful
spirits, and a memory stored with song and ballad—a love for which Robert drew
in with her milk.

In 1766, William Burnes removed to the farm of Mount Oliphant in the parish
of Ayr; but the soil was sour and bitter, and on the death of Mr. Ferguson, to
whom Mount Oliphant belonged, the management of the estate fell into the hands
of a factor, of whom all the world has heard. Disputes arose between the official
and the tenant. Harsh letters were read by the fireside at Mount Oliphant, and
were remembered years afterwards, bitterly enough, by at least one of the listeners.
Burness left his farm after an occupancy of six years, and removed to Lochlea, a
larger and better one in the parish of Tarbolton. Here, however, an unfortunate
difference arose between tenant and landlord as to the conditions of lease. Arbi-
ters were chosen, and a decision was given in favour of the proprietor. This

misfortune seems to have broken the spirit of Burnes.   He died of consumpt
on the 13th February, 1784, aged 63, weary enough of his long strife with pov
and ungenial soils, but not before he had learned to take pride in the abilities
his eldest son, and to tremble for his passions.

Burnes was an admirable specimen of the Scottish yeoman, or small farmer
the last century; for peasant he never was, nor did he come of a race of peasar
In his whole mental build and training he was superior to the people by wh
he was surrounded.   He had forefathers he could look back to; he had fam
traditions which he kept sacred.   Hard-headed, industrious, religious, somewl
austere, he ruled his household with a despotism, which affection and respect
the part of the ruled made light and easy.   To the blood of the Burneses a l
of knowledge was native as valour, in the old times, was native to the blood of t
Douglasses.   The poet's grandfather built a school at Clockenhill in Kincardir
the first known in that part of the country.   Burnes was of the same strai
and he resolved that his sons should have every educational advantage his mea
could allow.   To secure this he was willing to rise early and drudge late.   Acco
ingly, Robert, when six years old, was sent to a school at Alloway Mill; and
the removal of the teacher a few months afterwards to another post, Burnes,
conjunction with a few of his neighbours, engaged Mr. John Murdoch, boardir
him in their houses by turns, and paying him a small sum of money quarterl
Mr. Murdoch entered upon his duties, and had Robert and Gilbert for pupil
Under him they acquired reading, spelling, and writing; they were drilled
English grammar, taught to turn verse into prose, to substitute synonymous e
pressions for poetical words, and to supply ellipses.   He also attempted to tea
them a little Church music, but with no great success.   He seems to have take
to the boys, and to have been pleased with their industry and intelligenc
Gilbert was his favourite on account of his gay spirits and frolicksome lool
Robert was by comparison taciturn—distinctly stupid in the matter of psalmod
—and his countenance was swarthy, serious, and grave.

Our information respecting the family circle at Mount Oliphant, more interestin
now than that of any other contemporary Scottish family circle, is derived entirel
from the reminiscences of the tutor, and of Gilbert and Robert themselves.   An
however we may value every trivial fact and hint, and attempt to make it
window of insight, these days, as they passed on, seemed dull and matter-of-fa
enough to all concerned.   Mr. Murdoch considered his pupils creditably diligent
but nowise remarkable.   To Gilbert, these early years were made interesting whe
looked back upon in the light of his brother's glory.   Of that period, Robert wrot
a good deal at various times to various correspondents, when the world had becom
curious; but as in the case of all such writings, he unconsciously mixes the pa
with the present—looks back on his ninth year with the eyes of his th⟨irt⟩enth.   H
tells us that he was by no means a favourite with anybody; that thou⟨gh⟩   He cost th
                                                                      ⟨ev⟩er ou

is his "poor earth-born companion and fellow-mortal." He pities the "silly sheep," and the "chittering wing" of the bird perched on the frozen spray. The farmer speaks to his old mare "Maggie" as he would to a comrade, who had shared with him his struggles, toils, and triumphs. The poetry of Burns flows into a wintry world, like a tepid gulf-stream—mitigating harsh climates, breathing genial days, carrying with it spring-time and the cuckoo's note.

Of his humour again—which is merely his love laughing and playing antics in very extravagance of its joy—what can be said, except that it is the freshest, most original, most delightful in the world? What a riot of fun in *Tam O' Shanter;* what strange co-mixture of mirth and awfulness in *Death and Dr. Hornbook;* what extravaganza in the *Address to a Haggis!* To Burns's eye the world was dark enough, usually ; but on the gala days and carnivals of his spirit Mirth rules the hour, ragged Poverty dances all the lighter for his empty pockets, Death himself grins as he is poked in the lean ribs. And if, as is said, from the sweetest wine you can extract the sourest vinegar, one can fancy into what deadly satire this love will congeal itself, when it becomes hate. Burns hates his foe—be it man or doctrine—as intensely as he loves his mistress. *Holy Willie's Prayer* is a satirical crucifixion—slow, lingering, inexorable. He hated Hypocrisy, he tore its holy robe, and for the outrage Hypocrisy did not forgive him while he lived, nor has it yet learned to forgive him.

If we applaud the Roman Emperor who found Rome brick and left it marble, what shall we say of the man who found the songs of his country indelicate and left them pure—who made wholesome the air which the spirit and the affections breathe ? And Burns did this. He drove immodesty from love, and coarseness from humour. And not only did he purify existing Scottish Song ; he added to it all that it has of best and rarest. Since his day, no countryman of his, whatever may be his mood, need be visited by a sense of solitariness, or ache with a pent-up feeling. If he is glad, he will find a song as merry as himself ; if sad, he will find one that will sigh with his own woe. In Burns's Songs, love finds an exquisite companionship ; independence a backer and second ; conviviality a roaring table, and the best fellows round it ; patriotism a deeper love of country, and a gayer scorn of death than even its own. And in so adding to, and purifying Scottish song, Burns has conferred the greatest benefit on his countrymen that it is in the power of a poet to confer.

CHRONOLOGICAL TABLE

OF

BURNS'S LIFE AND WORKS.

ALLOWAY.

1759.

January 25.—Robert Burns born at Alloway, parish of Ayr, in a clay-built cottage, the work of his father's own hands. His father, William Burnes (so the family name was always written until changed by the poet), was a native of Kincardineshire, born November 11, 1721. His mother, Agnes Brown, born March 17, 1732, was daughter of a farmer in Carrick, Ayrshire. The poet's parents were married December 15, 1757. William Burnes was then a gardener and farm-overseer.

1765—(ÆTAT. SIX).

Sent to a school at Alloway Mill, kept by one Campbell, who was succeeded in May by John Murdoch, a young teacher of uncommon merit, engaged by William Burnes and four of his neighbours, who boarded him alternately at their houses, and guaranteed him a small salary. Two advantages were thus possessed by the poet—an excellent father and an excellent teacher.

MOUNT OLIPHANT.

1766—(SEVEN).

William Burnes removed to the farm of Mount Oliphant, two miles distant. His sons still attended Alloway school. The books used were a *Spelling Book*, the *New Testament*, the *Bible*, *Mason's Collection of Prose and Verse*, and *Fisher's English Grammar*.

1768—(NINE).

Murdoch gave up Alloway school. Visiting the Burnes family before his departure, he took with him, as a present, the play of *Titus Andronicus*; he read part of the play aloud, but the horrors of the scene shocked and distressed the children,

and Robert threatened to burn the book if it was left ! Instead of it Murdoch gave them a comedy, the *School for Love* (translated from the French) and an *English Grammar*. He had previously lent Robert a *Life of Hannibal*. "The earliest composition that I recollect taking any pleasure in," says the poet, "was the *Vision of Mirza* and a hymn of Addison's beginning *How are Thy servants blest, O Lord!* I particularly remember one half-stanza, which was music to my boyish ear—

> 'For though in dreadful whirls we hung
> High on the broken wave ! '"

He had found these in Mason's Collection. The latent seeds of poetry were further cultivated in his mind by an old woman living in the family, Betty David-son, who had a great store of tales, songs, ghost-stories, and legendary lore.

1770 — (ELEVEN).

By the time he was ten or eleven years of age he was an excellent English scholar, "a critic in substantives, verbs, and particles." After the departure of Murdoch, William Burnes was the only instructor of his sons and other children. He taught them arithmetic, and procured for their use *Salmon's Geographical Grammar*, *Derham's Physics and Astro-Theology*, and *Ray's Wisdom of God in the Creation*. These gave the boys some idea of Geography, Astronomy, and Natural History. He had also *Stackhouse's History of the Bible*, *Taylor's Scripture Doctrine of Original Sin*, a volume of *English History* (reigns of James I. and Charles I.). The blacksmith lent the common metrical *Life of Sir William Wallace* (which was read with Scottish fervour and enthusiasm), and a maternal uncle supplied a *Collection of Letters* by the wits of Queen Anne's reign, which inspired Robert with a strong desire to excel in letter-writing.

1772 — (THIRTEEN).

To improve their penmanship, William Burnes sent his sons, week about, during the summer quarter, to the parish school of Dalrymple, two or three miles distant. This year Murdoch was appointed teacher of English in Ayr school, and he re-newed his acquaintance with the Burnes family, sending them *Pope's Works* and "some other poetry."

1773 — (FOURTEEN).

Robert boarded three weeks with Murdoch at Ayr in order to revise his English Grammar. He acquired also a smattering of French, and on returning home he took with him a *French Dictionary* and *French Grammar*, and a copy of *Télémaque*. He attempted Latin, but soon abandoned it.

1774—(Fifteen).

His knowledge of French introduced him to some respectable families in Ayr (Dr. Malcolm's and others). A lady lent him the *Spectator*, Pope's *Homer*, and several other books. In this year began with him love and poetry. His partner in the harvest-field was a "bewitching creature" a year younger than himself, Nelly Kilpatrick, daughter of the blacksmith, who sang sweetly, and on her he afterwards wrote his first song and first effort at rhyme, *O, once I loved a bonie lass.*

1775—(Sixteen).

About this time Robert was the principal labourer on the farm. From the unproductiveness of the soil, the loss of cattle, and other causes, William Burnes had got into pecuniary difficulties, and the threatening letters of the factor (the landlord being dead) used to set the distressed family all in tears. The character of the factor is drawn in the *Tale of Two ~~Dogs~~*. The hard labour, poor living, and ~~led to t~~he poet's subsequent fits of melancholy ~~at the hea~~rt.

Dr. Currie

LOCHLEA.

1777—(Eighteen).

William Burnes and family remove to a larger farm at Lochlea, parish of Tarbolton. Take possession at Whitsunday. Affairs for a time look brighter, and all work diligently. Robert and Gilbert have £7 per annum each, as wages, from their father, and they also take land from him for the purpose of raising flax on their own account. "Though, when young, the poet was bashful and awkward in his intercourse with women, as he approached manhood his attachment to their society became very strong, and he was constantly the victim of some fair enslaver." (*Gilbert Burns.*) He was in the secret, he says, of all the loves of the parish of Tarbolton !

About this time Robert was the principal labourer on the farm. The inadequateness of the soil, the loss of cattle, and other causes, William Burnes fell into pecuniary difficulties, and the peace of the farm was destroyed.

1778—(Nineteen).

"I was," he says, "about eighteen or nineteen when I sketched the outlines of a tragedy." The whole had escaped his memory except a fragment of twenty lines : *All devil as I am, &c.*

The "Bachelors' Club
and five other
debate

choly, frequent headaches, and palpitation of the hea

1776—(Seventeen).

Spent his seventeenth summer (so in poet's MS. British Museum ; [?] altered the date to *nineteenth*) on a smuggling coast in Ayrshire, at Kirkoswald, purpose to learn mensuration, surveying, &c. He made good progress, though mixing somewhat in the dissipation of the place, which had then a flourishing contraband trade. Met the second of his poetical heroines, Peggy Thomson, on whom he afterwards wrote his fine song *Now westlin winds and slaught'ring guns.* The charms of this maiden "overset his trigonometry and set him off at a tangent from the sphere of his studies." On his return from Kirkoswald ("in my seventeenth year" he writes) he attended a dancing school to "give his manners a brush." His father had an antipathy to these meetings, and his going " in absolute defiance of his father's commands" (*sic* in orig.) was an "instance of rebellion" which he conceived brought on him the paternal resentment and even dislike. Gilbert Burns dissents altogether from this conclusion : the poet's extreme sensibility and regret for his one act of disobedience led him unconsciously to exaggerate the circumstances of the case. At Kirkoswald he had enlarged his reading by the addition of *Thomson's* and *Shenstone's Works*, and among the other books to which he had access at this period, besides those mentioned above, were some plays of Shakespeare, *Allan Ramsay's Works, Hervey's Meditations*, and a *Select Collection of English Songs* ("The Lark," 2 vols.). This last work was, he says, his *vade mecum ;* he pored over it driving his cart or walking to labour, and carefully noted the true tender or sublime from affectation and fustian. He composed this year two stanzas, *I dream'd I lay where flowers were springing.*

1780—(Twenty-one).

...ors' Club" established at Tarbolton by Robert and Gilbert Burns, ...her young men. Meetings were held once a month and questions ...ed. The sum expended by each member was not to exceed threepence.

1781—(Twenty-two).

David Sillar admitted a member of the Bachelors' Club. He describes Burns: "I recollect hearing his neighbours observe he had a great deal to say for himself, and that they suspected his principles (his religious principles). He wore the only tied hair in the parish, and in the church his plaid, which was of a particular colour, I think fillemot, he wrapped in a particular manner round his shoulders. Between sermons we often took a walk in the fields; in these walks I have frequently been struck by his facility in addressing the fair sex, and it was generally a death-blow to our conversation, however agreeable, to meet a female acquaintance. Some book he always carried and read when not otherwise employed. It was likewise his custom to read at table. In one of my visits to Lochlea, in time of a sowen supper, he was so intent on reading, I think *Tristram Shandy*, that his spoon falling out of his hand made him exclaim in a tone scarcely imitable, 'Alas, poor Yorick!'" The poet had now added to his collection of books Mackenzie's *Man of Feeling* (which he said he prized next to the Bible) and *Man of the World*, *Sterne's Works*, and Macpherson's *Ossian*. He would appear also to have had the poetical works of Young. Among the fair ones whose society he courted was a superior young woman, bearing the unpoetical name of Ellison Begbie. She

banks of the Nith. On the 19th settled with Creech, the profits from the Edinburgh edition and copyright being about 500*l*., of which the poet gave 180*l*. to his brother Gilbert, as a loan, to enable him to continue (with the family) at Mossgiel. In the latter end of April Burns was privately married to Jean Armour, and shortly afterwards wrote on her his two charming songs *Of a' the airts the wind can blaw* and *O, were I on Parnassus hill !*

ELLISLAND.

In June the poet went to reside on his farm, his wife remaining at Mauchline until a new house should be built at Ellisland. Formed the acquaintance of Captain Riddel of Glenriddel, a gentleman of literary and antiquarian tastes, who resided at Friars Carse, within a mile of Ellisland. On 28th June wrote *Verses in Friars Carse Hermitage.* August 5th, the poet at Mauchline made public acknowledgment of his marriage before the Kirk Session, at the same time giving "a guinea note for behoof of the poor." In December conducted Mrs. Burns to the banks of the Nith. *I hae a wife o' my ain !*

1789—(THIRTY).

Visited Edinburgh in February, and received about 50*l*. more of copyright money from Creech. August 18, son born to the poet, named Francis Wallace. About the same time received appointment to the Excise. October 16, the great bacchanalian contest for the Whistle took place at Friars Carse in presence of the poet. On the 20th of October (as calculated, and indeed proved by Mr. Chambers) the sublime and affecting lyric, *To Mary in Heaven*, was composed. Met Grose the antiquary at Friars Carse, and afterwards wrote the hum⸺ ⸺m *On Captain Grose's Peregrinations*. In December was⸺ ⸺d *The Five Carlines*.

1790—(THIRTY-ONE).

January 11.—Writes to Gilbert that his farm is a ruinous affair. On the 14th, addressing his friend Mr. Dunbar, W.S. relative to his Excise appointment, he says: "I found it a very convenient business to have 50*l*. per annum ; nor have I yet felt any of those mortifying circumstances in it I was led to fear." The duties were hard ; he had to ride at least 200 miles every week, but he still contributed largely to the *Scots Musical Museum*, wrote the elegy *On Captain Matthew Henderson* (one of the most exquisite of the poet's productions), and in autumn produced *Tam O' Shanter*, by universal assent the crowning glory and masterpiece of its author.

1791—(THIRTY-TWO).

In February wrote *Lament of Mary Queen of Scots*, and *Lament for James Earl of Glencairn*. In March had his right arm broken by the fall of his horse, and

d

was for some weeks disabled [fro]m writing. In this month also occurred an event which probably caused deepe[r pa]in than the broken arm. First, as Mr. Chambers says, " we have a poor girl lo[sing] the reputable world ;" (this was " Anna with the gowden locks," niece to the hostess of the Globe Tavern ;) " next we have Burns seeking an asylum for a helpless infant at his brother's ; then a magnanimous wife interposing with the almost romantically generous offer to become herself its nurse and guardian."* April 9, a third son born to the poet, and named William Nicol. At the close of the month the poet sold his crop at Ellisland, " and sold it well." Declined to attend the crowning of Thomson's bust at Ednam, but wrote verses for the occasion. In November made a short visit—his last—to Edinburgh, and shortly afterwards wrote his inimitable farewell to Clarinda, *Ae fond kiss and then we sever*. The fourth stanza of this song Sir Walter Scott said contained " the essence of a thousand love tales."

DUMFRIES.

At Martinmas (Nov. 11) the poet having disposed of his stock and other effects at Ellisland, and surrendered the lease of the farm to Mr. Miller the proprietor, removed with his family to the town of Dumfries. He occupied for a year and a half three rooms of a second floor on the north side of Bank Street (then called the Wee Vennel). On taking up his residence in the town, Burns was well received by the higher class of inhabitants and the neighbouring gentry. One of the most accomplished of the latter was Mrs. Walter Riddel (*née* Maria Woodley), then aged only about eighteen. This lady, with her husband, a brother of Captain Riddel of Glenriddel, lived on a small estate about four miles from Dumfries, which in compliment to the lady they called Woodley Park (now Goldielea).

1792—(Thirty-three).

February 27.—Burns behaved gallantly in seizing and boarding a smuggling brig in the Solway. The vessel, with her arms and stores, was sold by auction in Dumfries, and Burns purchased four carronades or small guns, for which he paid 3*l.* These he sent, with a letter, to the French Convention, but they were retained at Dover by the Custom-house authorities. This circumstance is supposed to have drawn on the poet the notice of his jealous superiors. He warmly sympathised with the French people in their struggle against despotism, and the Board of Excise ordered an inquiry into the poet's political conduct, though it is doubtful whether any reprimand was ever given him. In September Mr. George Thomson, Edinburgh, commenced his publication of national songs and melodies, and Burns

---

* Mrs. Burns was much attached to the child, who remained with her till she was seventeen years of age, when she married a soldier, John Thomson of the Stirling Militia. She is still living, and strongly resembles her father. Poor Anna the mother felt deeply the disgrace ; she, however, made a decent marriage in Leith, but died comparatively young, without any family by her husband.

cordially lent assistance to the unde
of pecuniary remuneration. On the 14th of Nov
the song of *Highland Mary*, and next month o
of all his ditties, *Duncan Gray cam here to woo*,

1793—(THIRTY-FOUR)

The poet continues his invaluable and disinterested
publication. In July he makes an excursion into Gall
Syme, stamp distributor, and according to that gen
statement on the subject is different) he compose
in the midst of a thunder-storm on the wilds of
Thomson in September, along with one no l
Whitsuntide the poet removed from the " Wee
per annum) in the Mill-hole Brae (now Burns
his death. His widow continued to occu

At a dinner-part
guests, having
accomplish
took pl

...ks of Johnson and Thomson, and he in favour of the Whig candidate, Mr. Heron. of Volunteers, enrolled in the month of March, song, *Does haughty Gaul invasion threat?* also ...es of *sweet myrtle let foreign lands reckon*, and ...s, *Last May a braw wooer*. The poet's health, ...nature age has set in.

...—(THIRTY-SEVEN).

796...elerated by an accidental circumstance. One ...Globe Tavern. There was deep snow on the ...down overpowered, by drowsiness and the ...ome hours in the open air. From the cold ...recovered. He still, however, continued ...ful and most touching of his lyrics was ...ing *Here's a health to ane I lo'e* ...ter to a brother exciseman, ...lness. In May, another ...And about the ...friend Johnson, ...ung lady, ...d with

1794—(THIRTY-F...

...exceeded in wine, was guilty of som...
...hostess, which she and her friends resente...
...parties, and for nearly a twelvemonth there was...
...place. During this interval Burns wrote several la...
wholly. Glenriddel died unreconciled to Burns, yet the latter honou...
unworthy of him as a man or as a poet. Apr...
sonnet. August 12, another son born to the poet, and n...
During this autumn and winter Burns wrote some of his fin...
the charms of Jane Lorimer, the "Chloris" of many a...
composed his lively song, the *Contented wi' little and cantie...*
intended as a picture of his own mind, but it is only, as Mr...
picture of one aspect of his own mind. Mr. Perry of the *Morni...*
engage Burns as a contributor to his paper; but the "...
declined, lest connexion with the Whig journal should i...
Excise. For a short time he acted as supervisor, and t...
were forgiven.

In January the poet composed his man...
a' that. His intercourse with Maria F...
occasionally a book, or a copy of...

1795—(THIR...

...song beg... ...his old ...
...aiden of eightee... ...present to a yo...
...to the poet in ... June 26th, inscrib...
...ad, *Wha will bu*... ...fort for health, Burns wen...
...oet writing despondi... Solway. There he was
Scots Musical Museu... ...imprinted on his
presented to Jessy Le... ...death was imprinted on his
...mes, *Jessy fair.* As a la... ...fatal, and some
...w, a sea-bathing hamlet on the... ...would prove fatal, and some
who thought "the stamp of death was imprinted on his...
vinced himself that his illness would prove fatal, and some
said to his wife, "Don't be afraid: I'll be more respected a...
...at present." Mrs. Riddel saw the poet
n dead, than when they parted to meet no more. On the 7th he wrote
...er Cunningham to move the Commissioners of Excise to
...of 50l. instead of reducing it, as was the rule in the case of
...35l. Mr. Findlater, his superior officer, says he had no
...done had the poet lived. On the 10th Burns wrote to
...ss condition, his debts, and his despair; and on the
...st to his father-in-law, stern old James Armour, that
...then in Fife, to come to the assistance of her
...the time of her confinement. His thoughts
ho had unaccountably been silent for some
...ndence: "With what pleasure did I use
...e adds, yet one pulse more to my poor
...n this dark hour of anguish came a

ess pop

Vennel

Street of ru.eness to the

ry warm. A rupture

it till intercourse tween the

mpoons on M. Riddel

4, Captain Riddel or

.ed his memory with a

.amed James Glencairn.

.hest songs, inspired by

.ic. In November he

wi' mair, which he

Chambers says, the

.ng *Chronicle* wishes to

.uly generous offer" is

.are his prospects in the

.ht that his political sins

.pendent song *For a' that and*

Riddel is renewed, and she sends him

verses, or a ticket for the theatre. He never

d 2

dear, w...
who proved ... the
election call... he ...
middle of Ju... and sler...
and requesting ...
This was ...
the verses... his ...
on the 4th of July ... Bro...
visited by Maria Riddel...
features." He was con...
time before this he had ...
hundred years after I a...
again on the 5th of July...
to his friend Alexand...
continue his full salary...
excisemen off duty, to ...
doubt this would have bee...
his brother as to his hopele...
same day he addressed a reque...
he would write to Mrs. Armo...
daughter, the poet's wife, d...
turned also to his friend Mrs. Du...
time. He recalled her interesting corr...
to break up the seal! The remembranc...
palpitating heart, Farewell!" Close o...

lawyer's letter urging payment—-and no doubt hinting at the serious consequences of non-payment—of a haberdasher's account. This legal missive served to conjure up before the distracted poet the image of a jail with all its horrors, and on the 12th he wrote two letters—one to his cousin in Montrose begging an advance of 10*l.*, and one to Mr. George Thomson imploring 5*l.* "Forgive, forgive me!" He left the sea-side on the 18th, weak and feverish, but was able the same day, on arriving at his house in Dumfries, to address a second note to James Armour, reiterating the wish expressed six days before, but without eliciting any reply— "Do, for Heaven's sake, send Mrs. Armour here immediately." From this period he was closely confined to bed (according to the statement of his widow), and was scarcely "*himself*" for half an hour together. He was aware of this infirmity, and told his wife that she was to touch him and remind him when he was going wrong. One day he got out of his bed, and his wife found him sitting in a corner of the room with the bed-clothes about him; she got assistance, and he suffered himself to be gently led back to bed. The day before he died he called very quickly and with a hale voice, "Gilbert! Gilbert!" On the morning of the 21st, at daybreak, death was obviously near at hand, and the children were sent for. They had been removed to the house of Jessy Lewars and her brother, in order that the poet's dwelling might be kept quiet, and they were now summoned back that they might have a last look of their illustrious father in life. He was insensible, his mind lost in delirium, and, according to his eldest son, his last words were, "That d——d rascal, Matthew Penn!"—an execration against the legal agent who had written the dunning letter. And so ended this sad and stormy life-drama, and the poet passed, as Mr. Carlyle has said, "not softly but speedily into that still country where the hail-storms and fire-showers do not reach, and the heaviest-laden wayfarer at length lays down his load." On the evening of Sunday, the 24th of July, the poet's remains were removed from his house to the Town Hall, and next day were interred with military honours.

CONTENTS.

CONTENTS TO THE LETTERS.

THE POEMS

OF

ROBERT BURNS.

POEMS.

THE TWA DOGS.

A TALE.

'TWAS in that place o' Scotland's isle,
That bears the name o' Auld King Coil,
Upon a bonie day in June,
When wearing thro' the afternoon,
Twa dogs, that were na thrang at hame,
Forgather'd ance upon a time.

The first I'll name, they ca'd him Cæsar,
Was keepit for his Honour's pleasure :
His hair, his size, his mouth, his lugs,
Shew'd he was nane o' Scotland's dogs ;
But whalpit some place far abroad,
Whare sailors gang to fish for Cod.

His locked, letter'd, braw brass collar,
Shew'd him the gentleman and scholar ;
But tho' he was o' high degree,
The fient a pride—nae pride had he ;
But wad hae spent an hour caressin,
Ev'n wi' a tinkler-gipsey's messin.
At kirk or market, mill or smiddie,
Nae tawted tyke, tho' e'er sae duddie,
But he wad stan't, as glad to see him,
An' stroan't on stanes and hillocks wi' him.

The tither was a ploughman's collie,
A rhyming, ranting, raving billie,
Wha for his friend and comrade had him,
An' in his freaks had Luath ca'd him,
After some dog in Highland sang,
Was made lang syne,—Lord knows how lang.

He was a gash an' faithfu' tyke,
As ever lap a sheugh or dike.
His honest, sonsie, baws'nt face,
Ay gat him friends in ilka place ;
His breast was white, his touzie back
Weel clad wi' coat o' glossy black ;
His gawcie tail, wi' upward curl,
Hung owre his hurdies wi' a swirl.

Nae doubt but they were fain o' ither,
An' unco pack an' thick thegither ;
Wi' social nose whyles snuff'd and snowkit ;
Whyles mice and moudieworts they howkit :
Whyles scour'd awa in lang excursion,
An' worry'd ither in diversion ;
Until wi' daffin weary grown,
Upon a knowe they sat them down,
An' there began a lang digression
About the lords o' the creation.

CÆSAR.

I've aften wonder'd, honest Luath,
What sort o' life poor dogs like you have ;
An' when the gentry's life I saw,
What way poor bodies liv'd ava.
Our Laird gets in his racked rents,
His coals, his kain, an' a' his stents :
He rises when he likes himsel ;
His flunkies answer at the bell ;
He ca's his coach ; he ca's his horse ;
He draws a bonie, silken purse
As lang's my tail, whare thro' the steeks,
The yellow letter'd Geordie keeks.
Frae morn to e'en, it's nought but toiling,
At baking, roasting, frying, boiling ;
An' tho' the gentry first are stechin,
Yet ev'n the ha' folk fill their pechan,
Wi' sauce, ragouts, and such like trashtrie,
That's little short o' downright wastrie.
Our Whipper-in, wee blastit wonner,
Poor worthless elf, it eats a dinner,
Better than ony tenant man
His Honour has in a' the lan :
An' what poor cot-folk pit their painch in,
I own it's past my comprehension.

LUATH.

Trowth, Cæsar, whyles they're fash't eneugh :
A cotter howkin in a sheugh,
Wi' dirty stanes biggin a dyke,
Baring a quarry, and siclike,
Himsel, a wife, he thus sustains,
A smytrie o' wee duddie weans,
An' nought but his han' darg, to keep
Them right an' tight in thack an' rape.
An' when they meet wi' sair disasters,
Like loss o' health, or want o' masters,
Ye maist wad think, a wee touch langer,
An' they maun starve o' cauld and hunger ;

But, how it comes, I never kend yet,
They're maistly wonderfu' contented ;
An' buirdly chiels, an' clever hizzies,
Are bred in sic a way as this is.

CÆSAR.

But then to see how ye're negleckit,
How huff'd, an' cuff'd, an' disrespeckit !
Lord, man, our gentry care as little
For delvers, ditchers, an' sic cattle,
They gang as saucy by poor folk,
As I wad by a stinking brock.
I've notic'd, on our Laird's court-day,
An' mony a time my heart's been wae,
Poor tenant bodies, scant o' cash,
How they maun thole a factor's snash :
He'll stamp an' threaten, curse an' swear,
He'll apprehend them, poind their gear ;
While they maun stan', wi' aspect humble,
An' hear it a', an' fear an' tremble !
I see how folk live that hae riches ;
But surely poor folk maun be wretches.

LUATH.

They're no sae wretched's ane wad think :
Tho' constantly on poortith's brink :
They're sae accustom'd wi' the sight,
The view o't gies them little fright.
Then chance an' fortune are sae guided,
They're ay in less or mair provided ;
An' tho' fatigu'd wi' close employment,
A blink o' rest's a sweet enjoyment.
The dearest comfort o' their lives,
Their grushie weans an' faithfu' wives :
The prattling things are just their pride,
That sweetens a' their fire-side.
An' whyles twalpennie worth o' nappy
Can mak the bodies unco happy ;
They lay aside their private cares,
To mind the Kirk and State affairs ;
They'll talk o' patronage an' priests,
Wi' kindling fury i' their breasts,
Or tell what new taxation's comin,
An' ferlie at the folk in Lon'on.
As bleak-fac'd Hallowmass returns,
They get the jovial, ranting kirns,
When rural life, o' ev'ry station,
Unite in common recreation ;
Love blinks, Wit slaps, an' social Mirth
Forgets there's Care upo' the earth.

That merry day the year begins,
'They bar the door on frosty winds;
The nappy reeks wi' mantling ream,
An' sheds a heart-inspiring steam;
The luntin pipe, an' sneeshin mill,
Are handed round wi' right guid will;
The cantie auld folks crackin crouse,
The young anes ranting thro' the house,—
My heart has been sae fain to see them,
That I for joy hae barket wi' them.

Still its owre true that ye hae said,
Sic game is now owre aften play'd.
There's monie a creditable stock
O' decent, honest, fawsont folk,
Are riven out baith root an' branch,
Some rascal's pridefu' greed to quench,
Wha thinks to knit himsel the faster
In favour wi' some gentle Master,
Wha, aiblins, thrang a parliamentin,
For Britain's guid his saul indentin—

CÆSAR.

Haith, lad, ye little ken about it;
For Britain's guid! guid faith! I doubt it.
Say rather, gaun as Premiers lead him,
An' saying *aye* or *no's* they bid him:
At operas an' plays parading,
Mortgaging, gambling, masquerading:
Or maybe, in a frolic daft,
To Hague or Calais taks a waft,
To make a tour, an' tak a whirl,
To learn *bon ton* an' see the worl'.
There, at Vienna or Versailles,
He rives his father's auld entails;
Or by Madrid he taks the rout,
To thrum guitars, an' fecht wi' nowt;
Or down Italian vista startles,
Whore-hunting amang groves o' myrtles:
Then bouses drumly German water,
To mak himsel look fair and fatter,
An' clear the consequential sorrows,
Love-gifts of Carnival Signoras.
For Britain's guid! for her destruction!
Wi' dissipation, feud, an' faction!

LUATH.

Hech, man! dear sirs! is that the gate
They waste sae mony a braw estate?
Are we sae foughten an' harass'd
For gear to gang that gate at last?

O would they stay aback frae courts,
An' please themsels wi' countra sports,
It wad for ev'ry ane be better,
The Laird, the Tenant, an' the Cotter!
For thae frank, rantin, ramblin billies,
Fient haet o' them's ill-hearted fellows :
Except for breaking o' their timmer,
Or speaking lightly o' their limmer,
Or shootin o' a hare or moor-cock,
The ne'er-a-bit they're ill to poor folk.
    But will ye tell me, Master Cæsar,
Sure great folk's life's a life o' pleasure?
Nae cauld nor hunger e'er can steer them,
The vera thought o't need na fear them.

CÆSAR.

    Lord, man, were ye but whyles whare I am,
The gentles ye wad ne'er envy 'em.
    It's true, they need na starve or sweat,
Thro' winter's cauld, or simmer's heat ;
They've nae sair wark to craze their banes,
An' fill auld age wi' grips an' granes :
But human bodies are sic fools,
For a' their colleges and schools,
That when nae real ills perplex them,
They mak enow themsels to vex them ;
An' ay the less they hae to sturt them,
In like proportion, less will hurt them.

    A country fellow at the pleugh,
His acre's till'd, he's right eneugh ;
A country girl at her wheel,
Her dizzen's done, she's unco weel :
But Gentlemen, an' Ladies warst,
Wi' ev'n down want o' wark are curst.
They loiter, lounging, lank, an' lazy ;
Tho' deil haet ails them, yet uneasy :
Their days insipid, dull, an' tasteless ;
Their nights unquiet, lang, an' restless ;
    An' ev'n their sports, their balls an' races,
Their galloping thro' public places,
There's sic parade, sic pomp, an' art,
The joy can scarcely reach the heart.
    The men cast out in party-matches,
Then sowther a' in deep debauches.
Ae night, they're mad wi' drink an' whoring,
Niest day their life is past enduring.
The Ladies arm-in-arm in clusters,
As great an' gracious a' as sisters ;
But hear their absent thoughts o' ither,
They're a' run deils an' jads thegither.

Whyles, owre the wee bit cup an' platie,
They sip the scandal potion pretty ;
Or lee-lang nights, wi' crabbit leuks,
Pore ower the devil's pictur'd beuks ;
Stake on a chance a farmer's stackyard,
An' cheat like ony unhang'd blackguard.
　　There's some exceptions, man an' woman ;
But this is Gentry's life in common.

By this, the sun was out o' sight,
An' darker gloamin brought the night :
The bum-clock humm'd wi' lazy drone,
The kye stood rowtin i' the loan ;
When up they gat, an' shook their lugs,
Rejoic'd they were na *men* but *dogs* ;
An' each took aff his several way,
Resolv'd to meet some ither day.

SCOTCH DRINK.

Gie him strong drink, until he wink,
　That's sinking in despair ;
An' liquor guid to fire his bluid,
　That's prest wi' grief an' care ;
There let him bouse, an' deep carouse,
　Wi' bumpers flowing o'er,
Till he forgets his loves or debts,
　An' minds his griefs no more.
　　　　Solomon's Proverbs, xxxi. 6, 7.

Let other Poets raise a fracas
'Bout vines, an' wines, an' drunken Bacchus,
An' crabbit names an' stories wrack us,
　　　　An' grate our lug,
I sing the juice Scotch bear can mak us,
　　　　In glass or jug.

O thou, my Muse ! guid auld Scotch Drink,
Whether thro' wimplin worms thou jink,
Or, richly brown, ream owre the brink,
　　　　In glorious faem,
Inspire me, till I lisp an' wink,
　　　　To sing thy name !

Let husky Wheat the haughs adorn,
An' Aits set up their awnie horn,
An' Pease an' Beans at een or morn,
　　　　Perfume the plain,
Leeze me on thee, John Barleycorn,
　　　　Thou King o' grain !

On thee aft Scotland chows her cood,
In souple scones, the wale o' food !
Or tumblin in the boiling flood
         Wi' kail an' beef ;
But when thou pours thy strong heart's blood,
           There thou shines chief.

Food fills the wame, an' keeps us livin ;
Tho' life's a gift no worth receivin,
When heavy-dragg'd wi' pine an' grievin ;
         But oil'd by thee,
The wheels o' life gae down-hill, scrievin,
         Wi' rattlin glee.

Thou clears the head o' doited Lear :
Thou cheers the heart o' drooping Care ;
Thou strings the nerves o' Labour sair,
         At 's weary toil :
Thou even brightens dark Despair
         Wi' gloomy smile.

Aft, clad in massy, siller weed,
Wi' Gentles thou erects thy head ;
Yet humbly kind, in time o' need,
         The poor man's wine,
His wee drap parritch, or his bread,
         Thou kitchens fine.

Thou art the life o' public haunts ;
But thee, what were our fairs and rants ?
Ev'n godly meetings o' the saunts,
         By thee inspir'd,
When gaping they besiege the tents,
         Are doubly fir'd.

That merry night we get the corn in !
O sweetly, then, thou reams the horn in !
Or reekin on a New-Year mornin
         In cog or bicker,
An' just a wee drap sp'ritual burn in,
         An' gusty sucker !

When Vulcan gies his bellows breath,
An' ploughmen gather wi' their graith,
O rare ! to see thee fizz an' freath
         I' th' lugget caup !
Then Burnewin comes on like Death
         At ev'ry chaup.

Nae mercy, then, for airn or steel ;
The brawnie, banic, ploughman chiel,
Brings hard owrehip, wi' sturdy wheel,
      The strong forehammer,
Till block an' studdie ring an' reel
      Wi' dinsome clamour.

When skirlin weanies see the light,
Thou maks the gossips clatter bright,
How fumblin' cuifs their dearies slight,
      Wae worth the name !
Nae Howdie gets a social night,
      Or plack frae them.

When neebors anger at a plea,
An' just as wud as wud can be,
How easy can the barley-bree
      Cement the quarrel !
It's aye the cheapest Lawyer's fee,
      To taste the barrel.

Alake ! that e'er my Muse has reason
To wyte her countrymen wi' treason !
But monie daily weet their weason
      Wi' liquors nice,
An' hardly, in a winter's season,
      E'er spier her price.

Wae worth that brandy, burning trash !
Fell source o' monie a pain an' brash !
Twins monie a poor, doylt, druken hash,
      O' half his days ;
An' sends, beside, auld Scotland's cash
      To her warst faes.

Ye Scots, wha wish auld Scotland well,
Ye chief, to you my tale I tell,
Poor plackless devils like mysel'
      It sets you ill,
Wi' bitter, dearthfu' wines to mell,
      Or foreign gill.

May gravels round his blather wrench,
An' gouts torment him, inch by inch,
Wha twists his gruntle wi' a glunch
      O' sour disdain,
Out owre a glass o' Whisky punch
      Wi' honest men !

O Whisky! soul o' plays an' pranks!
Accept a Bardie's gratefu' thanks!
When wanting thee, what tuneless cranks
      Are my poor verses!
Thou comes——they rattle i' their ranks
      At ither's a—s!

Thee, Ferintosh! O sadly lost!
Scotland, lament frae coast to coast!
Now colic-grips, an' barkin hoast,
      May kill us a';
For loyal Forbes' charter'd boast
      Is ta'en awa!

Thae curst horse-leeches o' th' Excise,
Wha mak the Whisky Stells their prize!
Haud up thy han,' Deil! ance, twice, thrice!
      There, seize the blinkers!
An' bake them up in brunstane pies
      For poor damn'd drinkers.

Fortune! if thou'll but gie me still
Hale breeks, a scone, an' Whisky gill,
An' rowth o' rhyme to rave at will,
      Tak' a' the rest,
An' deal't about as thy blind skill
      Directs thee best.

THE AUTHOR'S EARNEST CRY AND PRAYER.

TO THE RIGHT HONOURABLE AND HONOURABLE THE SCOTCH REPRESENTATIVES IN THE
HOUSE OF COMMONS.

Dearest of Distillation! last and best—
——How art thou lost!——
        PARODY ON MILTON.

YE Irish Lords, ye Knights an' Squires,
Wha represent our brughs an' shires,
An' doucely manage our affairs
      In Parliament,
To you a simple Bardie's prayers
      Are humbly sent.

Alas! my roupet Muse is hearse;
Your Honours' heart wi' grief 'twad pierce,
To see her sitten on her a—
      Low i' the dust,
An' scriechin out prosaic verse,
      An' like to brust!

Tell them wha hae the chief direction,
Scotland an' me's in great affliction,
E'er sin' they laid that curst restriction
                    On Aquavitæ;
An' rouse them up to strong conviction,
                    An' move their pity.

Stand forth, an' tell yon Premier Youth,
The honest, open, naked truth :
Tell him o' mine an' Scotland's drouth,
                    His servants humble :
The muckle devil blaw ye south,
                    If ye dissemble !

Does ony great man glunch an' gloom?
Speak out, an' never <u>fash your thumb</u> !
Let posts an' pensions sink or soom
                    Wi' them wha grant 'em :
If honestly they canna come,
                    Far better want 'em.

In gath'rin votes you were na slack ;
Now stand as tightly by your tack ;
Ne'er claw your lug, an' fidge your back,
                    An' hum an' haw ;
But raise your arm, an' tell your crack
                    Before them a'.

Paint Scotland greetin owre her thrissle ;
Her mutchkin stoup as toom's a whissle :
An' damn'd Excisemen in a bussle,
                    Seizin a Stell,
Triumphant crushin't like a mussel
                    Or lampit shell.

Then on the tither hand present her,
A blackguard Smuggler, right behint her,
An' cheek-for-chow, a chuffie Vintner,
                    Colleaguing join,
Picking her pouch as bare as Winter
                    Of a' kind coin.

Is there, that bears the name o' Scot,
But feels his heart's bluid rising hot,
To see his poor auld Mither's pot
                    Thus dung in staves,
An' plunder'd o' her hindmost groat
                    By gallows knaves?

Alas ! I'm but a nameless wight,
Trode i' the mire out o' sight !

But could I like Montgomeries fight,
        Or gab like Boswell,
There's some sark-necks I wad draw tight,
        An' tie some hose well.

God bless your Honours, can ye see't,
The kind, auld, cantie Carlin greet, *an old woman in high spirits*
An' no get warmly to your feet,
        An' gar them hear it?
An' tell them, wi' a patriot-heat,
        Ye winna bear it!

Some o' you nicely ken the laws, *know*
To round the period an' pause,
An' with rhetoric clause on clause
        To mak harangues;
Then echo thro' Saint Stephen's wa's *walls*
        Auld Scotland's wrangs. *wrongs*
                                I will warrant

Dempster, a true blue Scot I'se warran;
Thee, aith-detesting, chaste Kilkerran;
An' that glib-gabbet Highland Baron,
        The Laird o' Graham;
An' ane, a chap that's damn'd auldfarran,
        Dundas his name.

Erskine, a spunkie Norland billie;
True Campbells, Frederick an' Ilay;
An' Livingstone, the bauld Sir Willie;
        An' monie ithers,
Whom auld Demosthenes or Tully
        Might own for brithers.

Arouse, my boys! exert your mettle, *courage*
To get auld Scotland back her kettle;
Or faith! I'll wad my new pleugh-pettle, *plough*
        Ye'll see't or lang, *long*
She'll teach you, wi' a reekin whittle,
        Anither sang.

This while she's been in crankous mood, *irritated*
Her lost Militia fir'd her bluid;
(Deil na they never mair do guid,
        Play'd her that pliskie!)
An' now she's like to rin red-wud
        About her Whisky.

An' Lord, if ance they pit her till't,
Her tartan petticoat she'll kilt,
An' durk an' pistol at her belt,
        She'll tak the streets,
An' rin her whittle to the hilt,
        I' th' first she meets!

For God sake, Sirs ! then speak her fair,
An' straik her cannie wi' the hair,
An' to the *muckle house* repair,
             Wi' instant speed,
An' strive, wi' a' your wit and lear,
             To get remead.

Yon ill tongu'd tinkler, Charlie Fox,
May taunt you wi' his jeers an' mocks ;
But gie him't het, my hearty cocks !
             E'en cowe the cadie !
An' send him to his dicing-box
             An' sportin lady.

Tell yon guid bluid o' auld Boconnock's
I'll be his debt twa mashlum bonnocks,
An' drink his health in auld Nanse Tinnock's
             Nine times a-week,
If he some scheme, like tea an' winnocks,
             Wad kindly seek.

Could he some commutation broach,
I'll pledge my aith in guid braid Scotch,
He need na fear their foul reproach
             Nor erudition,
Yon mixtie-maxtie queer hotch-potch,
             The Coalition.

Auld Scotland has a raucle tongue ;
She's just a devil wi' a rung ;
An' if she promise auld or young
             To tak their part,
Tho' by the neck she should be strung,
             She'll no desert.

An' now, ye chosen Five-and-Forty,
May still your Mither's heart support ye ;
Then, though a Minister grow dorty,
             An' kick your place,
Ye'll snap your fingers, poor an' hearty,
             Before his face.

God bless your Honours a' your days,
Wi' sowps o' kail an' brats o' claise,
In spite o' a' the thievish kaes
             That haunt St. Jamie's !
Your humble Bardie sings an' prays
             While Rab his name is.

POSTSCRIPT.

Let half-starv'd slaves, in warmer skies,
See future wines, rich-clust'ring, rise;
Their lot auld Scotland ne'er envies,
　　　　　But blythe an' frisky,
She eyes her free-born, martial boys,
　　　　　Tak aff their Whisky.

What tho' their Phœbus kinder warms,
While fragrance blooms an' beauty charms!
When wretches range, in famish'd swarms,
　　　　　The scented groves,
Or hounded forth, dishonour arms
　　　　　In hungry droves.

Their gun's a burden on their shouther;
They downa bide the stink o' powther;
Their bauldest thought's a hank'ring swither
　　　　　To stan' or rin,
Till skelp—a shot—they're aff, a' throwther.
　　　　　To save their skin.

But bring a Scotsman frae his hill,
Clap in his cheek a Highland gill,
Say, such is royal George's will,
　　　　　An' there's the foe,
He has nae thought but how to kill
　　　　　Twa at a blow.

Nae cauld, faint-hearted doubtings tease him;
Death comes, wi' fearless eye he sees him;
Wi' bluidy han' a welcome gies him;
　　　　　An' when he fa's,
His latest draught o' breathin lea'es him
　　　　　In faint huzzas.

Sages their solemn een may steek,
An' raise a philosophic reek,
An' physically causes seek,
　　　　　In clime an' season;
But tell me Whisky's name in Greek,
　　　　　I'll tell the reason.

Scotland, my auld, respected Mither!
Tho' whyles ye moistify your leather,
Till whare ye sit, on craps o' heather,
　　　　　Ye tine your dam;
Freedom and Whisky gang thegither!
　　　　　Tak aff your dram!

THE HOLY FAIR.

A robe of seeming truth and trust
Hid crafty Observation;
And secret hung, with poison'd crust,
The dirk of Defamation:
A mask that like the gorget show'd,
Dye-varying on the pigeon;
And for a mantle large and broad,
He wrapt him in Religion.

HYPOCRISY À-LA-MODE.

UPON a simmer Sunday morn,
  When Nature's face is fair,
I walked forth to view the corn,
  An' snuff the caller air.
The risin' sun, owre Galston muirs,
  Wi' glorious light was glintin;
The hares were hirplin down the furrs,
  The lav'rocks they were chantin
            Fu' sweet that day.

As lightsomely I glowr'd abroad,
  To see a scene sae gay,
Three Hizzies, early at the road,
  Cam skelpin up the way.
Twa had manteeles o' dolefu' black,
  But ane wi' lyart lining;
The third, that gaed a wee a-back,
  Was in the fashion shining
            Fu' gay that day.

The twa appear'd like sisters twin,
  In feature, form, an' claes;
Their visage wither'd, lang an' thin,
  An' sour as ony slaes:
The third cam up, hap-step-an'-lowp,
  As light as ony lambie,
An' wi' a curchie low did stoop,
  As soon as e'er she saw me,
            Fu' kind that day.

Wi' bonnet aff, quoth I, 'Sweet lass,
  I think ye seem to ken me;
I'm sure I've seen that bonie face,
  But yet I canna name ye.'
Quo' she, an' laughin' as she spak,
  An' taks me by the han's,
'Ye, for my sake, hae gi'en the feck
  Of a' the ten comman's
            A screed some day.

'My name is Fun—your cronie dear,
　The nearest friend ye hae ;
An' this is Superstition here,
　An' that's Hypocrisy.
I'm gaun to Mauchline Holy Fair,
　To spend an hour in daffin :
Gin ye'll go there, yon runkl'd pair,
　We will get famous laughin
　　　　　　　　At them this day.'

Quoth I, ' With a' my heart, I'll do't ;
　I'll get my Sunday's sark on,
An' meet you on the holy spot ;
　Faith, we'se hae fine remarkin !'
Then I gaed hame at crowdie-time,
　An' soon I made me ready ;
For roads were clad, frae side to side,
　Wi' monie a wearie bodie,
　　　　　　　　In droves that day.

Here, farmers gash, in ridin graith
　Gaed hoddin by their cotters ;
There, swankies young, in braw braid-claith,
　Are springin owre the gutters.
The lasses, skelpin barefit, thrang,
　In silks an' scarlets glitter ;
Wi' sweet-milk cheese, in monie a whang,
　An' farls, bak'd wi' butter,
　　　　　　　　Fu' crump that day.

When by the plate we set our nose,
　Weel heaped up wi' ha'pence,
A greedy glowr Black Bonnet throws,
　An' we maun draw our tippence.
Then in we go to see the show, ✗
　On ev'ry side they're gath'rin,
Some carryin dails, some chairs an' stools,
　An' some are busy bleth'rin
　　　　　　　　Right loud that day.

Here stands a shed to fend the show'rs,
　An' screen our countra gentry ;
There, racer Jess, an' twa-three whores, ✗
　Are blinkin at the entry.
Here sits a raw o' tittlin jades,
　Wi' heaving breast an' bare neck,
An' there, a batch o' wabster lads,
　Blackguarding frae Kilmarnock
　　　　　　　　For fun this day.

Here, some are thinkin on their sins,
  An' some upo' their claes ;
Ane curses feet that fyl'd his shins,
  Anither sighs an' prays :
On this hand sits a chosen swatch,
  Wi' screw'd up, grace-proud faces ;
On that, a set o' chaps, at watch,
  Thrang winkin on the lasses
                    To chairs that day.

O happy is that man an' blest !
  Nae wonder that it pride him !
Wha's ain dear lass, that he likes best,
  Comes clinkin down beside him !
Wi' arm repos'd on the chair-back,
  He sweetly does compose him ;
Which, by degrees, slips round her neck,
  An's loof upon her bosom
                    Unkend that day.

Now a' the congregation o'er
  Is silent expectation ;
For Moodie speels the holy door,
  Wi' tidings o' damnation.
Should Hornie, as in ancient days,
  'Mang sons o' God present him,
The vera sight o' Moodie's face,
  To's ain het hame had sent him
                    Wi' fright that day.

Hear how he clears the points o' faith
  Wi' rattlin an' wi' thumpin !
Now meekly calm, now wild in wrath,
  He's stampin an' he's jumpin !
His lengthen'd chin, his turned-up snout,
  His eldritch squeel an' gestures,
O how they fire the heart devout,
  Like cantharidian plasters,
                    On sic a day !

But, hark ! the tent has chang'd its voice ;
  There's peace an' rest nae langer :
For a' the real judges rise,
  They canna sit for anger.
Smith opens out his cauld harangues,
  On practice and on morals ;
An' aff the godly pour in thrangs,
  To gie the jars an' barrels
                    A lift that day.

What signifies his barren shine
  Of moral pow'rs an' reason?
His English style, an' gesture fine,
  Are a' clean out o' season.
Like Socrates or Antonine,
  Or some auld pagan Heathen,
The moral man he does define,
  But ne'er a word o' faith in
      That's right that day.

In guid time comes an antidote
  Against sic poison'd nostrum;
For Peebles, frae the water-fit,
  Ascends the holy rostrum:
See, up he's got the word o' God
  An' meek an' mim has view'd it,
While Common Sense has ta'en the road,
  An' aff, an' up the Cowgate
      Fast, fast, that day.

Wee Miller, neist, the Guard relieves,
  An' Orthodoxy raibles,
Tho' in his heart he weel believes,
  An' thinks it auld wives' fables:
But, faith! the birkie wants a Manse,
  So, cannilie he hums them;
Altho' his carnal wit an' sense
  Like hafflins-wise o'ercomes him
      At times that day.

Now, butt an' ben, the Change-house fills,
  Wi' yill-caup Commentators:
Here's crying out for bakes an' gills,
  An' there the pint-stowp clatters;
While thick an' thrang, an' loud an' lang,
  Wi' logic, an' wi' Scripture,
They raise a din, that in the end
  Is like to breed a rupture
      O' wrath that day.

Leeze me on Drink! it gi'es us mair
  Than either School or College:
It kindles Wit, it waukens Lair,
  It pangs us fou o' Knowledge.
Be't whisky gill, or penny wheep,
  Or ony stronger potion,
It never fails, on drinkin' deep,
  To kittle up our notion
      By night or day.

c

The lads an' lasses, blythely bent
  To mind baith saul an' body,
Sit round the table, weel content,
  An' steer about the toddy.
On this ane's dress, an' that ane's leuk,
  They're makin observations ;
While some are cozie i' the neuk,
  An' formin assignations
                  To meet some day.

But now the Lord's ain trumpet touts,
  Till a' the hills are rairin,
An' echoes back return the shouts ;
  Black Russel is na spairin :
His piercing words, like Highlan swords,
  Divide the joints an' marrow ;
His talk o' Hell, whare devils dwell,
  Our vera 'sauls does harrow'
                  Wi' fright that day !

A vast, unbottom'd, boundless pit,
  Fill'd fou o' lowin brunstane,
Wha's ragin flame, an' scorchin heat,
  Wad melt the hardest whun-stane !
The half asleep start up wi' fear,
  An' think they hear it roarin,
When presently it does appear,
  'Twas but some neebor snorin
                  Asleep that day.

'Twad be owre lang a tale to tell
  How monie stories past,
An' how they crowded to the yill,
  When they were a' dismist :
How drink gaed round, in cogs an' caups,
  Amang the furms and benches ;
An' cheese an' bread, frae women's laps,
  Was dealt about in lunches,
                  An' dawds that day.

In comes a gaucie, gash Guidwife,
  An' sits down by the fire,
Syne draws her kebbuck an' her knife ;
  The lasses they are shyer.
The auld Guidmen, about the grace,
  Frae side to side they bother,
Till some ane by his bonnet lays,
  An' gi'es them't like a tether,
                  Fu' lang that day.

Waesucks ! for him that gets nae lass,
  Or lasses that hae naething !
Sma' need has he to say a grace,
  Or melvie his braw claithing !
O Wives, be mindfu', ance yoursel
  How bonie lads ye wanted,
An' dinna, for a kebbuck-heel,
    Let lasses be affronted
        On sic a day !

Now Clinkumbell, wi' rattling tow,
  Begins to jow an' croon ;
Some swagger hame, the best they dow,
  Some wait the afternoon.
At slaps the billies halt a blink,
  Till lasses strip their shoon :
Wi' faith an' hope, an' love an' drink,
  They're a' in famous tune
        For crack that day.

How monie hearts this day converts
  O' sinners and o' lasses !
Their hearts o' stane, gin night, are gane
  As saft as ony flesh is.
There's some are fou o' love divine,
  There's some are fou o' brandy ;
An' monie jobs that day begin,
  May end in Houghmagandie
        Some ither day.

DEATH AND DOCTOR HORNBOOK.

A TRUE STORY.

Some books are lies frae end to end,
And some great lies were never penn'd :
Ev'n Ministers, they hae been kenn'd,
        In holy rapture,
A rousing whid, at times, to vend,
        And nail't wi' Scripture.

But this that I am gaun to tell,
Which lately on a night befell,
Is just as true 's the Deil 's in hell
        Or Dublin city :
That e'er he nearer comes oursel
        's a muckle pity.

The Clachan yill had made me canty,
I wasna fou, but just had plenty ;
I stacher'd whyles, but yet took tent ay
    To free the ditches ;
An' hillocks, stanes, an' bushes, kenn'd ay
    Frae ghaists an' witches.

The rising moon began to glowr
The distant Cumnock hills out-owre :
To count her horns, wi' a' my pow'r,
    I set mysel ;
But whether she had three or four,
    I cou'd na tell.

I was come round about the hill,
And todlin down on Willie's mill,
Setting my staff, wi' a' my skill,
    To keep me sicker ;
Tho' leeward whyles, against my will,
    I took a bicker.

I there wi' Something did forgather,
That pat me in an eerie swither ;
An awfu' scythe, out-owre ae shouther,
    Clear-dangling, hang :
A three-taed leister on the ither
    Lay, large an' lang.

Its stature seem'd lang Scotch ells twa,
The queerest shape that e'er I saw,
For fient a wame it had ava,
    And then its shanks,
They were as thin, as sharp an' sma'
    As cheeks o' branks.

'Guid-een,' quo' I ; 'Friend ! hae ye been mawin,
When ither folk are busy sawin ?'
It seem'd to mak a kind o' stan',
    But naething spak ;
At length, says I, 'Friend, whare ye gaun,
    Will ye go back ?'

It spak right howe—'My name is Death,
But be na fley'd.'—Quoth I, 'Guid faith,
Ye're maybe come to stap my breath ;
    But tent me, billie :
I red ye weel, tak care o' skaith,
    See, there's a gully !'

'Gudeman,' quo' he, 'put up your whittle,
I'm no design'd to try its mettle ;

But if I did, I wad be kittle
                    To be mislear'd,
I wad na mind it, no that spittle
                    Out-owre my beard.'

'Weel, weel !' says I, 'a bargain be't ;
Come, gies your hand, an' sae we're gree't ;
We'll ease our shanks an' tak a seat,
                    Come gies your news ;
This while ye hae been mony a gate,
                    At mony a house.'

'Ay, ay !' quo' he, an' shook his head.
'It's e'en a lang, lang time indeed
Sin' I began to nick the thread,
                    An' choke the breath :
Folk maun do something for their bread,
                    An' sae maun Death.

' Sax thousand years are near-hand fled,
Sin' I was to the butching bred,
An' mony a scheme in vain's been laid,
                    To stap or scaur me ;
Till ane Hornbook's ta'en up the trade,
                    An' faith, he'll waur me.

' Ye ken Jock Hornbook i' the Clachan,
Deil mak his king's-hood in a spleuchan !
He's grown sae well acquaint wi' Buchan
                    An' ither chaps,
The weans haud out their fingers laughin
                    And pouk my hips.

' See, here's a scythe, and there's a dart,
They hae pierc'd mony a gallant heart ;
But Doctor Hornbook, wi' his art
                    And cursed skill,
Has made them baith no worth a f—t,
                    Damn'd haet they'll kill.

' 'Twas but yestreen, nae farther gaen,
I threw a noble throw at ane ;
Wi' less, I'm sure, I've hundreds slain :
                    But deil-ma-care,
It just play'd dirl on the bane,
                    But did nae mair.

' Hornbook was by, wi' ready art,
And had sae fortify'd the part,
That when I looked to my dart,
                    It was sae blunt,
Fient haet o't wad hae pierc'd the heart
                    O' a kail-runt.

' I drew my scythe in sic a fury,
I near-hand cowpit wi' my hurry,
But yet the bauld Apothecary
          Withstood the shock ;
I might as weel hae try'd a quarry
          O' hard whin rock.

' E'en them he canna get attended,
Altho' their face he ne'er had kend it,
Just sh — in a kail-blade, and send it,
          As soon's he smells't,
Baith their disease, and what will mend it,
          At once he tells't.

' And then, a' doctor's saws and whittles,
Of a' dimensions, shapes, an' mettles,
A' kinds o' boxes, mugs, an' bottles,
          He's sure to hae ;
Their Latin names as fast he rattles
          As A B C.

' Calces o' fossils, earths, and trees ;
True Sal-marinum o' the seas ;
The Farina of beans and pease,
          He has't in plenty ;
Aqua-fontis, what you please,
          He can content ye.

' Forbye some new, uncommon weapons,
Urinus Spiritus of capons ;
Or Mite-horn shavings, filings, scrapings,
          Distill'd *per se ;*
Sal-alkali o' Midge-tail clippings,
          And mony mae.'

' Waes me for Johnny Ged's Hole now,'
Quoth I, ' if that thae news be true !
His braw calf-ward whare gowans grew,
          Sae white and bonie,
Nae doubt they'll rive it wi' the plew ;
          They'll ruin Johnie !'

The creature grain'd an eldritch laugh,
And says, ' Ye needna yoke the pleugh,
Kirk-yards will soon be till'd eneugh,
          Tak ye nae fear :
They'll a' be trench'd wi' mony a sheugh
          In twa-three year.

'Whare I kill'd ane a fair strae-death,
By loss o' blood or want of breath,
This night I'm free to tak my aith,
   That Hornbook's skill
Has clad a score i' their last claith,
   By drap and pill.

'An honest Wabster to his trade,
Whase wife's twa nieves were scarce well-bred,
Gat tippence-worth to mend her head,
   When it was sair ;
The wife slade cannie to her bed,
   But ne'er spak mair.

'A countra Laird had ta'en the batts,
Or some curmurring in his guts,
His only son for Hornbook sets,
   An' pays him well.
The lad, for twa guid gimmer-pets,
   Was Laird himsel.

'A bonie lass, ye kend her name,
Some ill-brewn drink had hov'd her wame :
She trusts hersel, to hide the shame,
   In Hornbook's care ;
Horn sent her aff to her lang hame,
   To hide it there.

'That's just a swatch o' Hornbook's way ;
Thus goes he on from day to day,
Thus does he poison, kill, an' slay,
   An's weel pay'd for't ;
Yet stops me o' my lawfu' prey,
   Wi' his damn'd dirt.

'But, hark ! I'll tell you of a plot,
Tho' dinna ye be speaking o't ;
I'll nail the self-conceited Sot
   As dead's a herrin :
Niest time we meet, I'll wad a groat,
   He gets his fairin !'

But just as he began to tell,
The auld kirk-hammer strak the bell
Some wee, short hour ayont the twal,
   Which rais'd us baith :
I took the way that pleas'd mysel,
   And sae did Death.

THE BRIGS OF AYR.

A POEM.

INSCRIBED TO JOHN BALLANTINE, ESQ. AYR.

THE simple Bard, rough at the rustic plough,
Learning his tuneful trade from ev'ry bough ;
The chanting linnet, or the mellow thrush ;
Hailing the setting sun, sweet, in the green thorn bush ;
The soaring lark, the perching red-breast shrill,
Or deep-ton'd plovers, grey, wild-whistling o'er the hill
Shall he, nurst in the Peasant's lowly shed,
To hardy independence bravely bred,
By early poverty to hardship steel'd,
And train'd to arms in stern Misfortune's field ;
Shall he be guilty of their hireling crimes,
The servile, mercenary Swiss of rhymes ?
Or labour hard the panegyric close,
With all the venal soul of dedicating Prose ?
No ! though his artless strains he rudely sings,
And throws his hand uncouthly o'er the strings,
He glows with all the spirit of the Bard,
Fame, honest fame, his great, his dear reward.
Still, if some Patron's gen'rous care he trace,
Skill'd in the secret, to bestow with grace ;
When Ballantyne befriends his humble name
And hands the rustic Stranger up to fame,
With heartfelt throes his grateful bosom swells,
The godlike bliss, to give, alone excels.

'Twas when the stacks get on their winter-hap,
And thack and rape secure the toil-won crap ;
Potatoe-bings are snugged up frae skaith
O' coming Winter's biting, frosty breath ;
The bees, rejoicing o'er their summer toils,
Unnumber'd buds an' flow'rs, delicious spoils,
Seal'd up with frugal care in massive waxen piles,
Are doom'd by Man, that tyrant o'er the weak,
The death o' devils, smoor'd wi' brimstone reek :
The thund'ring guns are heard on ev'ry side,
The wounded coveys, reeling, scatter wide ;
The feather'd field-mates, bound by Nature's tie,
Sires, mothers, children, in one carnage lie :

(What warm, poetic heart, but inly bleeds,
And execrates man's savage, ruthless deeds!)
Nae mair the flow'r in field or meadow springs;
Nae mair the grove with airy concert rings,
Except perhaps the Robin's whistling glee,
Proud o' the height o' some bit half-lang tree :
The hoary morns precede the sunny days,
Mild, calm, serene, wide spreads the noontide blaze,
While thick the gossamour waves wanton in the rays.

'Twas in that season; when a simple Bard,
Unknown and poor, simplicity's reward,
Ae night, within the ancient brugh of Ayr,
By whim inspir'd, or haply prest wi' care,
He left his bed and took his wayward rout,
And down by Simpson's wheel'd the left about :
(Whether impell'd by all-directing Fate,
To witness what I after shall narrate ;
Or whether, rapt in meditation high,
He wander'd out he knew not where nor why:)
The drowsy Dungeon clock had number'd two,
And Wallace Tow'r had sworn the fact was true :
The tide-swoln Firth, wi' sullen-sounding roar,
Through the still night dash'd hoarse along the shore :
All else was hush'd as Nature's closèd e'e ;
The silent moon shone high o'er tow'r and tree :
The chilly frost, beneath the silver beam,
Crept, gently-crusting, owre the glittering stream.—
   When, lo ! on either hand the list'ning Bard,
The clanging sugh of whistling wings is heard ;
Two dusky forms dart thro' the midnight air,
Swift as the Gos drives on the wheeling hare ;
Ane on th' Auld Brig his airy shape uprears,
The ither flutters o'er the rising piers :
Our warlock Rhymer instantly descry'd
The Sprites that owre the Brigs of Ayr preside.
(That Bards are second-sighted is nae joke,
And ken the lingo of the sp'ritual folk ;
Fays, Spunkies, Kelpies, a', they can explain them,
And ev'n the vera deils they brawly ken them.)
Auld Brig appear'd o' ancient Pictish race,
The vera wrinkles Gothic in his face :
He seem'd as he wi' Time had warstl'd lang,
Yet, teughly doure, he bade an unco bang.
New Brig was buskit, in a braw new coat,
That he, at Lon'on, frae ane Adams got ;
In's hand five taper staves as smooth's a bead,
Wi' virls an' whirlygigums at the head.
The Goth was stalking round with anxious search,
Spying the time-worn flaws in ev'ry arch ;
It chanc'd his new-come neebor took his e'e,
And e'en a vex'd and angry heart had he !

Wi' thieveless sneer to see his modish mien,
He, down the water, gies him this guid-een :—

AULD BRIG.

I doubt na, Frien', ye'll think ye're nae sheep-shank,
Ance ye were streekit owre frae bank to bank !
But gin ye be a brig as auld as me,
Tho', faith ! that date, I doubt, ye'll never see ;
There'll be, if that day come, I'll wad a boddle,
Some fewer whigmeleeries in your noddle.

NEW BRIG.

Auld Vandal, ye but show your little mense,
Just much about it wi' your scanty sense ;
Will your poor, narrow foot-path of a street,
Where twa wheel-barrows tremble when they meet,
Your ruin'd, formless bulk o' stane and lime,
Compare wi' bonie Brigs o' modern time ?
There's men of taste wou'd tak the Ducat-stream,
Tho' they should cast the vera sark and swim,
Ere they would grate their feelings wi' the view
O' sic an ugly, Gothic hulk as you.

AULD BRIG.

Conceited gowk ! puff'd up wi' windy pride !
This mony a year I've stood the flood an' tide ;
And tho' wi' crazy eild I'm sair forfairn,
I'll be a Brig, when ye're a shapeless cairn !
As yet ye little ken about the matter,
But twa-three winters will inform ye better.
When heavy, dark, continued, a'-day rains,
Wi' deepening deluges o'erflow the plains ;
When from the hills where springs the brawling Coil,
Or stately Lugar's mossy fountains boil,
Or where the Greenock winds his moorland course
Or haunted Garpal draws his feeble source,
Arous'd by blust'ring winds an' spotting thowes ;
In mony a torrent down his snaw-broo rowes ;
While crashing ice, borne on the roaring spate,
Sweeps dams, an' mills, an' brigs, a' to the gate ;
And from Glenbuck, down to the Ratton-key,
Auld Ayr is just one lengthen'd, tumbling sea ;
Then down ye'll hurl, deil nor ye never rise !
And dash the gumlie jaups up to the pouring skies.
A lesson sadly teaching, to your cost,
That Architecture's noble art is lost !

NEW BRIG.

Fine Architecture, trowth, I needs must say't o't ;
The Lord be thankit that we've tint the gate o't !
Gaunt, ghastly, ghaist-alluring edifices,
Hanging with threat'ning jut, like precipices :

O'er arching, mouldy, gloom-inspiring coves,
Supporting roofs, fantastic, stony groves :
Windows and doors in nameless sculptures drest,
With order, symmetry, or taste unblest ;
Forms like some bedlam Statuary's dream,
The craz'd creations of misguided whim ;
Forms might be worshipp'd on the bended knee,
And still the second dread command be free,
Their likeness is not found on earth, in air, or sea.
Mansions that would disgrace the building taste
Of any mason reptile, bird, or beast ;
Fit only for a doited monkish race,
Or frosty maids forsworn the dear embrace,
Or cuifs of later times, wha held the notion,
That sullen gloom was sterling, true devotion ;
Fancies that our guid Brugh denies protection,
And soon may they expire, unblest with resurrection !

AULD BRIG.

O ye, my dear-remember'd, ancient yealins,
Were ye but here to share my wounded feelings !
Ye worthy Proveses, an' mony a Bailie,
Wha in the paths o' righteousness did toil ay ;
Ye dainty Deacons, an' ye douce Conveeners,
To whom our moderns are but causey-cleaners !
Ye godly Councils wha hae blest this town ;
Ye godly Brethren o' the sacred gown,
Wha meekly gie your hurdies to the smiters ;
And (what would now be strange) ye godly Writers ;
A' ye douce folk I've borne aboon the broo,
Were ye but here, what would ye say or do !
How would your spirits groan in deep vexation,
To see each melancholy alteration ;
And agonizing, curse the time and place
When ye begat the base, degen'rate race !
Nae langer Rev'rend Men, their country's glory,
In plain braid Scots hold forth a plain braid story
Nae langer thrifty Citizens, an' douce,
Meet owre a pint, or in the Council-house ;
But staumrel, corky-headed, graceless Gentry,
The herryment and ruin of the country ;
Men, three-parts made by Tailors and by Barbers,
Wha waste your weel-hain'd gear on damn'd new Brigs
        and Harbours !

NEW BRIG.

Now haud you there ! faith ye've said enough,
And muckle mair than ye can mak to through :
As for your Priesthood, I shall say but little,
Corbies and Clergy are a shot right kittle :

But, under favour o' your langer beard,
Abuse o' Magistrates might weel be spar'd :
To liken them to your auld-warld squad,
I must needs say, comparisons are odd.
In Ayr, Wag-wits nae mair can have a handle
To mouth 'a Citizen,' a term o' scandal :
Nae mair the Council waddles down the street,
In all the pomp of ignorant conceit;
Men wha grew wise priggin owre hops an' raisins,
Or gather'd lib'ral views in bonds and seisins.
If haply Knowledge, on a random tramp,
Had shor'd them wi' a glimmer of his lamp,
And would to Common-sense for once betray'd them,
Plain, dull Stupidity stept kindly in to aid them.

What farther clishmaclaver might been said,
What bloody wars, if Sprites had blood to shed,
No man can tell ; but all before their sight
A fairy train appear'd in order bright :
Adown the glittering stream they featly danc'd ;
Bright to the moon their various dresses glanc'd :
They footed o'er the wat'ry glass so neat,
The infant ice scarce bent beneath their feet :
While arts of Minstrelsy among them rung,
And soul-ennobling Bards heroic ditties sung.
O had M'Lauchlan, thairm-inspiring sage,
Been there to hear this heavenly band engage,
When thro' his dear strathspeys they bore with Highland rage,
Or when they struck old Scotia's melting airs,
The lover's raptur'd joys or bleeding cares;
How would his Highland lug been nobler fir'd,
And ev'n his matchless hand with finer touch inspir'd !
No guess could tell what instrument appear'd,
But all the soul of Music's self was heard ;
Harmonious concert rung in every part,
While simple melody pour'd moving on the heart.
The Genius of the Stream in front appears,
A venerable Chief, advanc'd in years;
His hoary head with water-lilies crown'd,
His manly leg with garter tangle bound.
Next came the loveliest pair in all the ring,
Sweet Female Beauty hand in hand with Spring ;
Then, crown'd with flow'ry hay, came Rural Joy,
And Summer, with his fervid-beaming eye :
All-cheering Plenty, with her flowing horn,
Led yellow Autumn wreath'd with nodding corn ;
Then Winter's time-bleach'd locks did hoary show,
By Hospitality with cloudless brow ;
Next follow'd Courage with his martial stride,
From where the Feal wild-woody coverts hide ;
Benevolence, with mild, benignant air,
A female form, came from the tow'rs of Stair :

Learning and Worth in equal measures trode
From simple Catrine, thy long-lov'd abode :
Last, white-rob'd Peace, crown'd with a hazel wreath,
To rustic Agriculture did bequeath
The broken, iron instruments of death :
At sight of whom our Sprites forgat their kindling wrath.

THE ORDINATION.

For sense, they little owe to frugal Heav'n—
To please the mob, they hide the little giv'n.

KILMARNOCK Wabsters, fidge and claw,
　An' pour your creeshie nations ;
An' ye wha leather rax an' draw,
　Of a' denominations ;
Swith to the Laigh Kirk, ane an' a',
　An' there tak up your stations ;
Then aff to Begbie's in a raw,
　An' pour divine libations
　　　　For joy this day.

Curst Common-sense, that imp o' hell,
　Cam in wi' Maggie Lauder ;
But Oliphant aft made her yell,
　An' Russel sair misca'd her ;
This day M'Kinlay takes the flail,
　An' he's the boy will blaud her !
He'll clap a shangan on her tail,
　An' set the bairns to daud her
　　　　Wi' dirt this day.

Mak haste an' turn king David owre,
　An' lilt wi' holy clangor ;
O' double verse come gie us four,
　An' skirl up the Bangor :
This day the Kirk kicks up a stoure,
　Nae mair the knaves shall wrang her,
For Heresy is in her pow'r,
　And gloriously she'll whang her
　　　　Wi' pith this day.

Come, let a proper text be read,
　An' touch it off wi' vigour,
How graceless Ham leugh at his Dad,
　Which made Canaan a niger :
Or Phineas drove the murdering blade,
　Wi' whore-abhorring rigour ;
Or Zipporah, the scauldin jad,
　Was like a bluidy tiger
　　　　I' th' Inn that day.

There, try his mettle on the creed,
　And bind him down wi' caution,
That Stipend is a carnal weed
　He takes but for the fashion ;
An' gie him o'er the flock, to feed,
　And punish each transgression ;
Especial, rams that cross the breed,
　Gie them sufficient threshin,
　　　　Spare them nae day.

Now auld Kilmarnock, cock thy tail,
　An' toss thy horns fu' canty ;
Nae mair thou'lt rowte out-owre the dale,
　Because thy pasture's scanty ;
For lapfu's large o' gospel kail
　Shall fill thy crib in plenty,
An runts o' grace the pick an' wale,
　No gi'en by way o' dainty,
　　　　But ilka day.

Nae mair by Babel streams we'll weep,
　To think upon our Zion ;
And hing our fiddles up to sleep,
　Like baby-clouts a-dryin :
Come, screw the pegs wi' tunefu' cheep,
　And o'er the thairms be tryin ;
Oh rare ! to see our elbucks wheep,
　And a' like lamb-tails flyin
　　　　Fu' fast this day !

Lang, Patronage, wi' rod o' airn,
　Has shor'd the Kirk's undoin,
As lately Fenwick, sair forfairn,
　Has proven to his ruin :
Our Patron, honest man ! Glencairn,
　He saw mischief was brewin ;
And like a godly, elect bairn,
　He's wal'd us out a true ane,
　　　　And sound this day.

Now Robinson harangue nae mair,
　But steek your gab for ever :
Or try the wicked town of Ayr,
　For there they'll think you clever ;
Or, nae reflection on your lear,
　Ye may commence a Shaver ;
Or to the Netherton repair,
　And turn a Carpet-weaver
　　　　　Aff-hand this day.

Mutrie and you were just a match,
　We never had sic twa drones :
Auld Hornie did the Laigh Kirk watch,
　Just like a winkin baudrons :
And ay he catch'd the tither wretch,
　To fry them in his caudrons ;
But now his Honour maun detach,
　Wi' a' his brimstone squadrons,
　　　　　Fast, fast this day.

See, see auld Orthodoxy's faes
　She's swingein thro' the city ;
Hark, how the nine-tail'd cat she plays !
　I vow it's unco pretty !
There, Learning, with his Greekish face,
　Grunts out some Latin ditty ;
And Common-sense is gaun, she says,
　To mak to Jamie Beattie
　　　　　Her plaint this day.

But there's Morality himsel,
　Embracing all opinions ;
Hear, how he gies the tither yell,
　Between his twa companions ;
See, how she peels the skin an' fell,
　As ane were peelin onions !
Now there, they're packed aff to hell,
　And banish'd our dominions,
　　　　　Henceforth this day.

O happy day ! rejoice, rejoice !
　Come bouse about the porter !
Morality's demure decoys
　Shall here nae mair find quarter :
M'Kinlay, Russel are the boys
　That heresy can torture ;
They'll gie her on a rape a hoyse,
　And cowe her measure shorter
　　　　　By th' head some day.

Come, bring the tither mutchkin in,
　And here's, for a conclusion,
To every New Light mother's son,
　From this time forth, Confusion :
If mair they deave us wi' their din,
　Or Patronage intrusion,
We'll light a spunk, and, ev'ry skin,
　We'll rin them aff in fusion
　　　　　Like oil, some day.

THE CALF.

TO THE REV. MR. JAMES STEVEN, ON HIS TEXT, MALACHI, CH. IV. VER. 2.

" And ye shall go forth, and grow up as calves of the stall."

RIGHT, Sir ! your text I'll prove it true,
　Tho' Heretics may laugh ;
For instance, there's yoursel just now,
　God knows, an unco Calf !

And should some Patron be so kind,
　As bless you wi' a kirk,
I doubt na, Sir, but then we'll find,
　Ye're still as great a Stirk.

But, if the Lover's raptur'd hour
　Shall ever be your lot,
Forbid it, ev'ry heavenly Power,
　You e'er should be a Stot !

Tho', when some kind, connubial Dear,
　Your but-and-ben adorns,
The like has been that you may wear
　A noble head of horns.

And, in your lug, most reverend James,
　To hear you roar and rowte,
Few men o' sense will doubt your claims
　To rank amang the Nowte.

And when ye're number'd wi' the dead,
　Below a grassy hillock,
Wi' justice they may mark your head—
　' Here lies a famous Bullock !'

ADDRESS TO THE DEIL.

O Prince! O Chief of many throned Pow'rs,
That led th' embattled Seraphim to war—

MILTON.

O THOU ! whatever title suit thee,
Auld Hornie, Satan, Nick, or Clootie,
Wha in yon cavern grim an' sootie,
          Clos'd under hatches,
Spairges about the brunstane cootie,
          To scaud poor wretches !

Hear me, auld Hangie, for a wee,
An' let poor damned bodies be ;
I'm sure sma' pleasure it can gie,
          Ev'n to a deil,
To skelp an' scaud poor dogs like me,
          An' hear us squeel !

Great is thy pow'r, an' great thy fame ;
Far kend an' noted is thy name ;
An' tho' yon lowin heugh's thy hame,
          Thou travels far ;
An' faith ! thou's neither lag nor lame,
          Nor blate nor scaur.

Whyles, ranging like a roarin lion
For prey, a' holes an' corners tryin ;
Whyles on the strong-wing'd Tempest flyin,
          Tirlin the kirks ;
Whyles, in the human bosom pryin,
          Unseen thou lurks.

I've heard my reverend Graunie say,
In lanely glens ye like to stray ;
Or where auld, ruin'd castles, gray,
          Nod to the moon,
Ye fright the nightly wand'rer's way,
          Wi' eldritch croon.

When twilight did my Graunie summon,
To say her pray'rs, douce, honest woman !
Aft yont the dyke she's heard you bummin,
          Wi' eerie drone ;
Or, rustlin, thro' the boortrees comin,
          Wi' heavy groan.

Ae dreary, windy, winter night,
The stars shot down wi' sklentin light,
Wi' you, mysel, I gat a fright,
          Ayont the lough ;
Ye, like a rash-buss, stood in sight,
          Wi' waving sugh.

The cudgel in my nieve did shake,
Each bristl'd hair stood like a stake,
When wi' an eldritch, stoor quaick, quaick,
          Amang the springs,
Awa ye squatter'd like a drake,
          On whistling wings.

Let warlocks grim, an' wither'd hags,
Tell how wi' you on ragweed nags,
They skim the muirs, an' dizzy crags,
          Wi' wicked speed ;
And in kirk-yards renew their leagues,
          Owre howkit dead.

Thence, countra wives, wi' toil an' pain,
May plunge an' plunge the kirn in vain ;
For, oh ! the yellow treasure's taen
          By witching skill ;
An' dawtit, twal-pint Hawkie's gaen
          As yell's the Bill.

Thence, mystic knots mak great abuse,
On young Guidmen, fond, keen, an' crouse ;
When the best wark-lume i' the house,
          By cantrip wit,
Is instant made no worth a louse,
          Just at the bit.

When thowes dissolve the snawy hoord,
An' float the jinglin icy-boord,
Then, Water-kelpies haunt the foord,
          By your direction,
An' nighted Trav'llers are allur'd
          To their destruction.

An' aft your moss-traversing Spunkies
Decoy the wight that late an' drunk is:
The bleezin, curst, mischievous monkies
       Delude his eyes,
Till in some miry slough he sunk is,
       Ne'er mair to rise.

When Masons' mystic word an' grip,
In storms an' tempests raise you up,
Some cock or cat your rage maun stop,
       Or, strange to tell !
The youngest Brother ye wad whip
       Aff straught to hell.

Lang syne, in Eden's bonie yard,
When youthfu' lovers first were pair'd,
An' all the soul of love they shar'd,
       The raptur'd hour,
Sweet on the fragrant, flow'ry swaird,
       In shady bow'r :

Then you, ye auld, snick-drawing dog !
Ye came to Paradise incog.
An' play'd on man a cursed brogue,
       (Black be you fa !)
An' gied the infant warld a shog,
       'Maist ruin'd a'.

D'ye mind that day, when in a bizz,
Wi' reekit duds, an' reestit gizz,
Ye did present your smoutie phiz,
       'Mang better folk,

An' sklented on the man of Uzz
       Your spitefu' joke ?

An' how ye gat him i' your thrall,
An' brak him out o' house an' hal',
While scabs an' blotches did him gall,
       Wi' bitter claw,
An' lows'd his ill-tongu'd, wicked Scawl,
       Was warst ava ?

But a' your doings to rehearse,
Your wily snares an' fechtin fierce,
Sin' that day Michael did you pierce,
       Down to this time,
Wad ding a' Lallan tongue, or Erse,
       In prose or rhyme.

An' now, auld Cloots, I ken ye're thinkin,
A certain Bardie's rantin, drinkin,
Some luckless hour will send him linkin,
       To your black pit ;
But, faith ! he'll turn a corner jinkin,
       An' cheat you yet.

But, fare you weel, auld Nickie-ben !
O wad ye tak a thought an' men' !
Ye aiblins might—I dinna ken—
       Still hae a stake—
I'm wae to think upo' yon den,
       Ev'n for your sake !

THE DEATH AND DYING WORDS OF POOR MAILIE, THE AUTHOR'S ONLY PET YOWE. ewe

AN UNCO MOURNFU' TALE.

As Mailie, an' her lambs thegither,
Was ae day nibbling on the tether,
Upon her cloot she coost a hitch,
An' owre she warsl'd in the ditch ;
There, groaning, dying, she did lie,
When Hughoc he cam doytin by.
   Wi' glowrin een, an' lifted han's,
Poor Hughoc like a statue stan's ;
He saw her days were near hand ended,
But, waes my heart ! he could na mend it !
He gapèd wide, but naething spak.
At length poor Mailie silence brak.

   'O thou, whase lamentable face
Appears to mourn my woefu' case !
My dying words attentive hear,
An' bear them to my Master dear.
   'Tell him, if e'er again he keep
As muckle gear as buy a sheep,
O, bid him never tie them mair
Wi' wicked strings o' hemp or hair !
But ca' them out to park or hill,
An' let them wander at their will ;
So may his flock increase, an' grow
To scores o' lambs, an' packs o' woo' !

'Tell him, he was a Master kin',
An' ay was guid to me an' mine ;
An' now my dying charge I gie him,
My helpless lambs, I trust them wi' him.
'O, bid him save their harmless lives,
Frae dogs, an' tods, an' butchers' knives!
But gie them guid cow-milk their fill,
Till they be fit to fend themsel :
An' tent them duly, e'en an' morn,
Wi' teats o' hay an' ripps o' corn.
'An' may they never learn the gaets
Of ither vile wanrestfu' pets !
To slink thro' slaps, an' reave an' steal,
At stacks o' pease, or stocks o' kail.
So may they, like their great Forbears,
For monie a year come thro' the sheers ;
So wives will gie them bits o' bread,
An' bairns greet for them when they're
    dead.
'My poor toop-lamb, my son an' heir,
O, bid him breed him up wi' care !
An', if he live to be a beast,
To pit some havins in his breast !

An' warn him, what I winna name,
To stay content wi' yowes at hame ;
An' no to rin an' wear his cloots,
Like ither menseless, graceless brutes.
'An' niest my yowie, silly thing,
Gude keep thee frae a tether string !
O, may thou ne'er forgather up
Wi' ony blastit, moorland toop ;
But ay keep mind to moop an' mell,
Wi' sheep o' credit like thysel !
'And now, my bairns, wi' my last
    breath
I lea'e my blessin wi' you baith :
An' when you think upo' your Mither,
Mind to be kind to ane anither.
'Now, honest Hughoc, dinna fail,
To tell my Master a' my tale ;
An' bid him burn this cursed tether,
An', for thy pains, thou'se get my blether.'

This said, poor Mailie turn'd her head,
An' clos'd her een amang the dead !

POOR MAILIE'S ELEGY.

LAMENT in rhyme, lament in prose,
Wi' saut tears trickling down your nose ;
Our Bardie's fate is at a close,
    Past a' remead ;
The last, sad cape-stane of his woes ;
    Poor Mailie's dead !

It's no the loss o' warl's gear,
That could sae bitter draw the tear,
Or mak our Bardie, dowie, wear
    The mourning weed :
He's lost a friend and neebor dear,
    In Mailie dead.

Thro' a' the toun she trotted by him ;
A lang half-mile she could descry him ;
Wi' kindly bleat, when she did spy him,
    She ran wi' speed :
A friend mair faithfu' ne'er cam nigh him,
    Than Mailie dead.

I wat she was a sheep o' sense,
An' could behave hersel wi' mense ;
I'll say't, she never brak a fence,
    Thro' thievish greed.
Our Bardie, lanely, keeps the spence
    Sin' Mailie's dead.

Or, if he wanders up the howe,
Her living image in her yowe
Comes bleating to him, owre the knowe,
    For bits o' bread ;
An' down the briny pearls rowe
    For Mailie dead.

She was nae get o' moorland tips,
Wi' tawted ket, an' hairy hips ;
For her forbears were brought in ships,
    Frae yont the Tweed :
A bonier fleesh ne'er cross'd the clips
    Than Mailie's dead.

Wae worth the man wha first did shape
That vile, wanchancie thing—a rape !
It maks guid fellows girn an' gape,
    Wi' chokin dread ;
An' Robin's bonnet wave wi' crape,
    For Mailie dead.

O, a' ye Bards on bonie Doon !
An' wha on Ayr your chanters tune !
Come, join the melancholious croon
    O' Robin's reed !
His heart will never get aboon !
    His Mailie's dead !

B

D

TO JAMES SMITH.

Friendship! mysterious cement of the soul!
Sweet'ner of Life, and solder of Society!
I owe thee much.————   BLAIR.

DEAR Smith, the sleeest, paukie thief,
That e'er attempted stealth or rief,
Ye surely hae some warlock-breef
      Owre human hearts ;
For ne'er a bosom yet was prief
      Against your arts.

For me, I swear by sun an' moon,
And ev'ry star that blinks aboon,
Ye've cost me twenty pair o' shoon
      Just gaun to see you ;
And ev'ry ither pair that's done,
      Mair taen I'm wi' you.

That auld, capricious carlin, Nature,
To mak amends for scrimpit stature,
She's turn'd you aff, a human creature
      On her first plan,
And in her freaks, on ev'ry feature,
      She's wrote, 'The Man.'

Just now I've taen the fit o' rhyme,
My barmie noddle's working prime,
My fancie yerkit up sublime
      Wi' hasty summon :
Hae ye a leisure-moment's time
      To hear what's comin ?

Some rhyme, a neebor's name to lash ;
Some rhyme (vain thought!) for needfu'
      cash ;
Some rhyme to court the countra clash,
      An' raise a din ;
For me, an *aim* I never fash ;
      I rhyme for fun.

The star that rules my luckless lot,
Has fated me the russet coat,
An' damn'd my fortune to the groat ;
      But, in requit,
Has blest me with a random shot
      O' countra wit.

This while my notion's taen a sklent,
To try my fate in guid, black prent ;
But still the mair I'm that way bent,
      Something cries, 'Hoolie !
I red you, honest man, tak tent !
      Ye'll shaw your folly.

'There's ither poets, much your betters,
Far seen in Greek, deep men o' letters,
Hae thought they had ensured their
      debtors,
      A' future ages ;
Now moths deform in shapeless tatters,
      Their unknown pages.'

Then farewel hopes o' laurel-boughs,
To garland my poetic brows !
Henceforth I'll rove where busy ploughs
      Are whistling thrang,
An' teach the lanely heights an' howes
      My rustic sang.

I'll wander on, wi' tentless heed
How never-halting moments speed,
Till fate shall snap the brittle thread ;
      Then, all unknown,
I'll lay me with th' inglorious dead,
      Forgot and gone !

But why o' Death begin a tale ?
Just now we're living sound an' hale ;
Then top and maintop crowd the sail,
      Heave Care o'er side !
And large, before Enjoyment's gale,
      Let's tak the tide.

This life, sae far's I understand,
Is a' enchanted fairy-land,
Where pleasure is the magic wand,
      That, wielded right,
Maks hours like minutes, hand in hand,
      Dance by fu' light.

The magic wand then let us wield :
For, ance that five-an'-forty's speel'd,
See, crazy, weary, joyless Eild,
　　Wi' wrinkl'd face,
Comes hostin, hirplin owre the field,
　　Wi' creepin pace.

When ance life's day draws near the
　　gloamin,
Then fareweel vacant careless roamin ;
An' fareweel cheerfu' tankards foamin,
　　An' social noise ;
An' fareweel dear deluding woman,
　　The joy of joys !

O life ! how pleasant in thy morning,
Young Fancy's rays the hills adorning !
Cold-pausing Caution's lesson scorning,
　　We frisk away,
Like schoolboys, at th' expected warning,
　　To joy and play.

We wander there, we wander here,
We eye the rose upon the brier,
Unmindful that the thorn is near,
　　Among the leaves :
And tho' the puny wound appear,
　　Short while it grieves.

Some, lucky, find a flow'ry spot,
For which they never toil'd nor swat ;
They drink the sweet and eat the fat,
　　But care or pain ;
And, haply, eye the barren hut
　　With high disdain.

With steady aim, some Fortune chase ;
Keen hope does ev'ry sinew brace ;
Thro' fair, thro' foul, they urge the race,
　　And seize the prey ;
Then canie, in some cozie place,
　　They close the day.

And others, like your humble servan',
Poor wights! nae rules nor roads observin,
To right or left, eternal swervin,
　　They zig-zag on ;
Till curst with age, obscure an' starvin,
　　They aften groan.

Alas ! what bitter toil an' straining—
But truce wi' peevish, poor complaining !
Is Fortune's fickle Luna waning ?
　　E'en let her gang !
Beneath what light she has remaining,
　　Let's sing our sang.

My pen I here fling to the door,
And kneel, ' Ye Pow'rs !' and warm
　　implore,
' Tho' I should wander Terra o'er,
　　In all her climes,
Grant me but this, I ask no more,
　　Ay rowth o' rhymes.

' Gie dreeping roasts to countra Lairds,
Till icicles hing frae their beards ;
Gie fine braw claes to fine Life-guards,
　　And Maids of Honour ;
And yill an' whisky gie to Cairds,
　　Until they sconner.

' A Title, Dempster merits it ;
A Garter gie to Willie Pitt ;
Gie Wealth to same be-ledger'd Cit,
　　In cent per cent ;
But gie me real, sterling Wit,
　　And I'm content.

' While Ye are pleased to keep me hale,
I'll sit down o'er my scanty meal,
Be't water-brose, or muslin-kail,
　　Wi' cheerfu' face,
As lang's the Muses dinna fail
　　To say the grace.'

An anxious e'e I never throws
Behint my lug, or by my nose ;
I jouk beneath Misfortune's blows
　　As weel's I may ;
Sworn foe to Sorrow, Care, and Prose,
　　I rhyme away.

O ye douce folk, that live by rule,
Grave, tideless-blooded, calm, and cool,
Compar'd wi' you—O fool ! fool ! fool !
　　How much unlike !
Your hearts are just a standing pool,
　　Your lives, a dyke !

Nae hair-brain'd sentimental traces,
In your unletter'd, nameless faces !
In arioso trills and graces
    Ye never stray,
But gravissimo, solemn basses
    Ye hum away.

Ye are sae grave, nae doubt ye're wise ;
Nae ferly tho' ye do despise
The hairum-scairum, ram-stam boys,

    The rattlin squad :
I see you upward cast your eyes—
    Ye ken the road.—

Whilst I —but I shall haud me there—
Wi' you I'll scarce gang ony where—
Then, Jamie, I shall say nae mair,
    But quat my sang,
Content with You to mak a pair,
    Whare'er I gang.

A DREAM.

Thoughts, words, and deeds, the Statute blames with reason ;
But surely DREAMS *were ne'er indicted Treason.*

[On reading, in the public papers, the Laureate's Ode, with the other parade of June 4, 1786, the author was no sooner dropt asleep, than he imagined himself transported to the Birth-day Levee ; and, in his dreaming fancy, made the following ADDRESS.]

GUID-MORNIN to your Majesty !
    May heaven augment your blisses,
On ev'ry new birth-day ye see ;
    A humble Bardie wishes !
My Bardship here, at your Levee,
    On sic a day as this is,
Is sure an uncouth sight to see,
    Amang thae Birth-day dresses
        Sae fine this day.

I see ye're complimented thrang,
    By mony a lord an' lady ;
' God save the King !' 's a cuckoo sang
    That's unco easy said ay ;
The Poets, too, a venal gang,
    Wi' rhymes weel-turn'd and ready,
Wad gar you trow ye ne'er do wrang,
    But ay unerring steady,
        On sic a day.

For me : before a Monarch's face,
    Ev'n *there* I winna flatter ;
For neither pension, post, nor place,
    Am I your humble debtor :
So, nae reflection on Your Grace,
    Your Kingship to bespatter ;
There's monie waur been o' the Race,
    And aiblins ane been better
        Than You this day.

'Tis very true, my sovereign King,
    My skill may weel be doubted :
But Facts are cheels that winna ding,
    An' downa be disputed :
Your Royal nest, beneath your wing,
    Is e'en right reft an' clouted,
And now the third part of the string,
    An' less, will gang about it
        Than did ae day.

Far be't frae me that I aspire
    To blame your legislation,
Or say, ye wisdom want, or fire,
    To rule this mighty nation ;
But, faith ! I muckle doubt, my Sire,
    Ye've trusted Ministration
To chaps, wha, in a barn or byre,
    Wad better fill'd their station
        Than courts yon day.

And now ye've gien auld Britain peace,
    Her broken shins to plaister ;
Your sair taxation does her fleece
    Till she has scarce a tester ;
For me, thank God, my life's a lease
    Nae bargain wearing faster,
Or, faith ! I fear that with the geese,
    I shortly boost to pasture
        I' the craft some day.

I'm no mistrusting Willie Pitt,
  When taxes he enlarges,
(An' Will's a true guid fallow's get,
  A name not envy spairges,)
That he intends to pay your debt,
  An' lessen a' your charges ;
But, God's sake ! let nae saving-fit
  Abridge your bonie barges
        An' boats this day.

Adieu, my Liege ! may freedom geck
  Beneath your high protection ;
An' may Ye rax Corruption's neck,
  And gie her for dissection !
But since I'm here, I'll no neglect,
  In loyal, true affection,
To pay your Queen, with due respect,
  My fealty an' subjection
        This great Birth-day.

Hail, Majesty most Excellent !
  While nobles strive to please Ye,
Will Ye accept a compliment
  A simple Poet gies Ye ?
Thae bonny bairntime Heav'n has lent,
  Still higher may they heeze Ye
In bliss, till Fate some day is sent,
  For ever to release Ye
        Frae care that day.

For you, young Potentate o' Wales,
  I tell your Highness fairly,
Down Pleasure's stream, wi' swelling sails
  I'm tauld ye're driving rarely ;
But some day ye may gnaw your nails,
  An' curse your folly sairly,
That ere ye brak Diana's pales,
  Or rattl'd dice wi' Charlie,
        By night or day.

Yet aft a ragged cowte's been known
  To mak a noble aiver ;
Sae, ye may doucely fill a Throne,
  For a' their clish-ma-claver :

There, Him at Agincourt wha shone,
  Few better were or braver ;
And yet, wi' funny, queer Sir John,
  He was an unco shaver
        For monie a day.

For you, right rev'rend Osnaburg,
  Nane sets the lawn-sleeve sweeter,
Altho' a ribban at your lug
  Wad been a dress completer :
As ye disown yon paughty dog
  That bears the Keys of Peter,
Then, swith ! an' get a wife to hug,
  Or, trouth ! ye'll stain the Mitre
        Some luckless day.

Young, royal Tarry Breeks, I learn,
  Ye've lately come athwart her ;
A glorious galley, stem and stern,
  Weel rigg'd for Venus' barter ;
But first hang out, that she'll discern
  Your hymeneal charter,
Then heave aboard your grapple airn,
  An', large upon her quarter,
        Come full that day.

Ye, lastly, bonie blossoms a',
  Ye royal Lasses dainty,
Heav'n mak you guid as weel as braw,
  An' gie you lads a-plenty :
But sneer na British boys awa',
  For Kings are unco scant ay ;
An' German Gentles are but sma',
  They're better just than want ay
        On onie day.

God bless you a' ! consider now
  Ye're unco muckle dautet ;
But, e'er the course o' life be through,
  It may be bitter sautet :
An' I hae seen their coggie fou,
  That yet hae tarrow't at it ;
But or the day was done, I trow,
  The laggen they hae clautet
        Fu' clean that day.

THE VISION.

DUAN FIRST.

THE sun had clos'd the winter day,
The Curlers quat their roarin play,
An' hunger'd Maukin taen her way
    To kail-yards green,
While faithless snaws ilk step betray
    Whare she has been.

The thresher's weary flingin-tree
The lee-lang day had tired me ;
And whan the day had clos'd his e'e,
    Far i' the west,
Ben i' the Spence, right pensivelie,
    I gaed to rest.

There, lanely, by the ingle-cheek,
I sat and ey'd the spewing reek,
That fill'd, wi' hoast-provoking smeek,
    The auld, clay biggin ;
An' heard the restless rattons squeak
    About the riggin.

All in this mottie, misty clime,
I backward mus'd on wasted time,
How I had spent my youthfu' prime,
    An' done nae-thing,
But stringin blethers up in rhyme,
    For fools to sing.

Had I to guid advice but harkit,
I might, by this, hae led a market,
Or strutted in a bank, and clarkit
    My cash-account :
While here, half-mad, half fed, half-sarkit,
    Is a' th' amount.

I started, mutt'ring, blockhead ! coof !
And heav'd on high my waukit loof,
To swear by a' yon starry roof,
    Or some rash aith,
That I, henceforth, would be rhyme-proof
    Till my last breath—

When click ! the string the snick did
    draw ;
And jee ! the door gaed to the wa' ;
And by my ingle-lowe I saw,
    Now bleezin bright,
A tight, outlandish Hizzie, braw,
    Come full in sight.

Ye need na doubt, I held my whisht ;
The infant aith, half-form'd, was crusht ;
I glowr'd as eerie's I'd been dusht
    In some wild glen ;
When sweet, like modest worth, she
    blusht,
    And stepped ben.

Green, slender, leaf-clad holly-boughs
Were twisted, gracefu', round her brows,
I took her for some Scottish Muse,
    By that same token ;
And come to stop these reckless vows,
    Would soon been broken.

A 'hair-brain'd, sentimental trace,'
Was strongly marked in her face ;
A wildly-witty, rustic grace
    Shone full upon her ;
Her eye, ev'n turn'd on empty space,
    Beam'd keen with Honour.

Down flow'd her robe, a tartan sheen,
Till half a leg was scrimply seen ;
And such a leg ! my bonie Jean
    Could only peer it ;
Sae straught, sae taper, tight, and clean,
    Nane else came near it.

Her mantle large, of greenish hue,
My gazing wonder chiefly drew ;
Deep lights and shades, bold-mingling,
    threw
    A lustre grand ;
And seem'd, to my astonish'd view
    A well-known Land.

Here, rivers in the sea were lost ;
There, mountains to the skies were tost :
Here, tumbling billows mark'd the coast
 With surging foam ;
There, distant shone Art's lofty boast,
 The lordly dome.

Here, Doon pour'd down his far-fetch'd
 floods ;
There, well-fed Irwine stately thuds,
Auld hermit Ayr staw thro' his woods,
 On to the shore ;
And many a lesser torrent scuds,
 With seeming roar.

Low, in a sandy valley spread,
An ancient Borough rear'd her head ;
Still, as in Scottish story read,
 She boasts a Race,
To ev'ry nobler virtue bred,
 And polish'd grace.

By stately tow'r or palace fair,
Or ruins pendent in the air,
Bold stems of Heroes, here and there,
 I could discern ;
Some seem'd to muse, some seem'd to
 dare,
 With feature stern.

My heart did glowing transport feel,
To see a Race heroic wheel,
And brandish round the deep-dy'd steel
 In sturdy blows ;
While back-recoiling seem'd to reel
 Their Suthron foes.

His COUNTRY'S SAVIOUR, mark him
 well !
Bold Richardton's heroic swell ;
The Chief on Sark who glorious fell,
 In high command ;
And He whom ruthless fates expel
 His native land.

There, where a sceptr'd Pictish shade
Stalk'd round his ashes lowly laid,
I mark'd a martial Race, pourtray'd
 In colours strong ;
Bold, soldier-featur'd, undismay'd
 They strode along.

Thro' many a wild, romantic grove,
Near many a hermit-fancy'd cove,
(Fit haunts for Friendship or for Love
 In musing mood,)
An aged Judge, I saw him rove,
 Dispensing good.

With deep-struck reverential awe
The learned Sire and Son I saw,
To Nature's God and Nature's law
 They gave their lore :
This, all its source and end to draw ;
 That, to adore.

Brydon's brave Ward I well could spy,
Beneath old Scotia's smiling eye ;
Who call'd on Fame, low standing by,
 To hand him on,
Where many a Patriot name on high,
 And Hero shone.

DUAN SECOND.

WITH musing-deep, astonish'd stare,
I view'd the heavenly-seeming Fair ;
A whisp'ring throb did witness bear,
 Of kindred sweet,
When with an elder Sister's air
 She did me greet.

' All hail ! my own inspired Bard !
In me thy native Muse regard !
Nor longer mourn thy fate is hard,
 Thus poorly low !
I come to give thee such reward
 As we bestow.

' Know, the great Genius of this land
Has many a light, aërial band,
Who, all beneath his high command,
 Harmoniously,
As Arts or Arms they understand,
 Their labours ply.

' They Scotia's Race among them share ;
Some fire the Soldier on to dare ;
Some rouse the Patriot up to bare
 Corruption's heart :
Some teach the Bard, a darling care,
 The tuneful art.

' 'Mong swelling floods of reeking gore,
They, ardent, kindling spirits pour ;
Or, 'mid the venal Senate's roar,
        They, sightless, stand,
To mend the honest Patriot lore,
        And grace the hand.

' And when the Bard, or hoary Sage,
Charm or instruct the future age,
They bind the wild, Poetic rage
        In energy,
Or point the inconclusive page
        Full on the eye.

' Hence, Fullarton, the brave and young ;
Hence, Dempster's zeal-inspired tongue ;
Hence, sweet harmonious Beattie sung
        His " Minstrel lays ; "
Or tore, with noble ardour stung,
        The Sceptic's bays.

' To lower orders are assign'd
The humbler ranks of human-kind,
The rustic Bard, the lab'ring Hind,
        The Artisan ;
All choose, as various they're inclin'd,
        The various man.

' When yellow waves the heavy grain,
The threat'ning storm some strongly rein ;
Some teach to meliorate the plain
        With tillage-skill ;
And some instruct the Shepherd-train,
        Blythe o'er the hill.

' Some hint the Lover's harmless wile ;
Some grace the Maiden's artless smile ;
Some soothe the Lab'rer's weary toil,
        For humble gains,
And make his cottage-scenes beguile
        His cares and pains.

' Some, bounded to a district-space,
Explore at large Man's infant race,
To mark the embryotic trace
        Of rustic Bard ;
And careful note each op'ning grace,
        A guide and guard.

' Of these am I—Coila my name ;
And this district as mine I claim,
Where once the Campbells, chiefs of
        fame,
        Held ruling pow'r :
I mark'd thy embryo-tuneful flame,
        Thy natal hour.

' With future hope, I oft would gaze,
Fond, on thy little early ways,
Thy rudely-caroll'd, chiming phrase,
        In uncouth rhymes,
Fir'd at the simple, artless lays
        Of other times.

' I saw thee seek the sounding shore,
Delighted with the dashing roar ;
Or when the North his fleecy store
        Drove thro' the sky,
I saw grim Nature's visage hoar
        Struck thy young eye.

' Or when the deep green-mantl'd Earth
Warm-cherish'd ev'ry flow'ret's birth,
And joy and music pouring forth
        In ev'ry grove,
I saw thee eye the gen'ral mirth
        With boundless love.

' When ripen'd fields, and azure skies,
Call'd forth the Reaper's rustling noise,
I saw thee leave their ev'ning joys,
        And lonely stalk,
To vent thy bosom's swelling rise
        In pensive walk.

' When youthful Love, warm-blushing
        strong,
Keen-shivering shot thy nerves along,
Those accents, grateful to thy tongue,
        Th' adored Name,
I taught thee how to pour in song,
        To soothe thy flame.

' I saw thy pulse's maddening play,
Wild send thee Pleasure's devious way,
Misled by Fancy's meteor ray,
        By Passion driven ;
But yet the light that led astray
        Was light from Heaven.

'I taught thy manners-painting strains,
The loves, the ways of simple swains,
Till now, o'er all my wide domains
    Thy fame extends ;
And some, the pride of Coila's plains,
    Become thy friends.

' Thou canst not learn, nor can I show,
To paint with Thomson's landscape-
    glow ;
Or wake the bosom-melting throe,
    With Shenstone's art ;
Or pour, with Gray, the moving flow
    Warm on the heart.

' Yet, all beneath th' unrivall'd rose,
The lowly daisy sweetly blows ;
Tho' large the forest's monarch throws
    His army shade,
Yet green the juicy hawthorn grows,
    Adown the glade.

' Then never murmur nor repine ;
Strive in thy humble sphere to shine ;
And trust me, not Potosi's mine,
    Nor King's regard,
Can give a bliss o'ermatching thine,
    A rustic Bard.

' To give my counsels all in one,
Thy tuneful flame still careful fan ;
Preserve the dignity of Man,
    With Soul erect ;
And trust, the Universal Plan
    Will all protect.

' And wear thou this '—she solemn said,
And bound the Holly round my head :
The polish'd leaves, and berries red,
    Did rustling play ;
And, like a passing thought, she fled
    In light away.

ADDRESS TO THE UNCO GUID, OR THE RIGIDLY RIGHTEOUS.

My son, these maxims make a rule,
    And lump them aye thegither;
The RIGID RIGHTEOUS *is a fool,*
    The RIGID WISE *anither:*
The cleanest corn that e'er was dight,
    May hae some pyles o' caff in;
So ne'er a fellow-creature slight
    For random fits o' daffin.
        SOLOMON.—Eccles. vii. 16.

O YE wha are sae guid yoursel,
    Sae pious and sae holy,
Ye've nought to do but mark and tell
    Your Neebour's fauts and folly !
Whase life is like a weel-gaun mill,
    Supply'd wi' store o' water,
The heapet happer's ebbing still,
    And still the clap plays clatter.

Hear me, ye venerable Core,
    As counsel for poor mortals,
That frequent pass douce Wisdom's door,
    For glaikit Folly's portals;
I, for their thoughtless, careless sakes,
    Would here propone defences,
Their donsie tricks, their black mistakes,
    Their failings and mischances.

Ye see your state wi' their's compar'd,
    And shudder at the niffer,
But cast a moment's fair regard,
    What maks the mighty differ ;
Discount what scant occasion gave
    That purity ye pride in,
And (what's aft mair than a' the lave)
    Your better art o' hiding.

Think, when your castigated pulse
    Gies now and then a wallop,
What raging must his veins convulse,
    That still eternal gallop ;
Wi' wind and tide fair i' your tail,
    Right on ye scud your sea-way ;
But in the teeth o' baith to sail,
    It maks an unco leeway.

See Social life and Glee sit down,
  All joyous and unthinking,
Till, quite transmugrify'd, they're grown
  Debauchery and Drinking :
O would they stay to calculate
  Th' eternal consequences ;
Or your more dreaded hell to state,
  Damnation of expenses !

Ye high, exalted, virtuous Dames,
  Ty'd up in godly laces,
Before ye gie poor Frailty names,
  Suppose a change o' cases ;
A dear lov'd lad, convenience snug,
  A treacherous inclination—
But, let me whisper i' your lug,
  Ye're aiblins nae temptation.
    perhaps

Then gently scan your brother Man,
  Still gentler sister Woman ;
Tho' they may gang a kennin wrang,
  To step aside is human :
One point must still be greatly dark,
  The moving *Why* they do it ;
And just as lamely can ye mark,
  How far perhaps they rue it.

Who made the heart, 'tis He alone
  Decidedly can try us,
He knows each chord its various tone,
  Each spring its various bias :
Then at the balance let's be mute,
  We never can adjust it ;
What's *done* we partly may compute,
  But know not what's *resisted*.

TAM SAMSON'S ELEGY.

An honest man's the noblest work of God.—POPE.

HAS auld Kilmarnock seen the Deil ?
Or great M'Kinlay thrawn his heel ?
Or Robinson again grown weel,
          To preach an' read ?
' Na, waur than a' ! ' cries ilka chiel,
          ' Tam Samson's dead ! '

Kilmarnock lang may grunt an' grane,
An' sigh, an' sab, an' greet her lane,
An' cleed her bairns, man, wife, an' wean,
          In mourning weed ;
To Death, she's dearly paid the kane,
          Tam Samson's dead !

The Brethren o' the mystic level
May hing their head in woefu' bevel,
While by their nose the tears will revel,
          Like ony bead ;
Death's gien the Lodge an unco devel,
          Tam Samson's dead !

When Winter muffles up his cloak,
And binds the mire like a rock ;
When to the loughs the Curlers flock
          Wi' gleesome speed,
Wha will they station at the *cock*,
          Tam Samson's dead ?

He was the king o' a' the Core,
To guard, or draw, or wick a bore,
Or up the rink like Jehu roar
          In time o' need ;
But now he lags on Death's *hog-score*,
          Tam Samson's dead !

Now safe the stately Sawmont sail,
And Trouts bedropp'd wi' crimson hail,
And Eels weel kend for souple tail,
          And Geds for greed,
Since dark in Death's *fish-creel* we wail
          Tam Samson dead !

Rejoice, ye birring Paitricks a' ;
Ye cootie Moorcocks, crousely craw ;
Ye Maukins, cock your fud fu' braw,
          Withouten dread ;
Your mortal Fae is now awa',
          Tam Samson's dead !

That woefu' morn be ever mourn'd
Saw him in shootin graith adorn'd,
While pointers round impatient burn'd,
          Frae couples freed ;
But, Och ! he gaed and ne'er return'd !
          Tam Samson's dead !

In vain auld age his body batters ;
In vain the gout his ancles fetters ;
In vain the burns came down like waters,
    An acre braid !
Now ev'ry auld wife, greetin, clatters,
    ' Tam Samson 's dead !'

Owre mony a weary hag he limpit,
An' ay the tither shot he thumpit,
Till coward Death behind him jumpit
    Wi' deadly feide ;
Now he proclaims, wi' tout o' trumpet,
    Tam Samson 's dead !

When at his heart he felt the dagger,
He reel'd his wonted bottle-swagger,
But yet he drew the mortal trigger
    Wi' weel-aim'd heed ;
' Lord, five !' he cry'd, an' owre did
    stagger ;
    Tam Samson 's dead !

Ilk hoary hunter mourn'd a brither ;
Ilk sportsman youth bemoan'd a father ;
Yon auld gray stane, amang the heather,
    Marks out his head,
Whare Burns has wrote, in rhyming
    blether,
    ' Tam Samson 's dead !'

There, low he lies, in lasting rest ;
Perhaps upon his mould'ring breast

Some spitefu' muirfowl bigs her nest,
    To hatch and breed ;
Alas ! nae mair he'll them molest !
    Tam Samson 's dead !

When August winds the heather wave,
And sportsmen wander by yon grave,
Three vollies let his mem'ry crave
    O' pouther an' lead,
Till Echo answer frae her cave,
    Tam Samson 's dead !

Heav'n rest his saul, whare'er he be !
Is th' wish o' mony mae than me :
He had twa faults, or maybe three,
    Yet what remead ?
Ae social, honest man want we :
    Tam Samson 's dead !

THE EPITAPH.

Tam Samson's weel-worn clay here lies,
    Ye canting zealots, spare him !
If honest worth in heaven rise,
    Ye'll mend or ye win near him.

PER CONTRA.

Go, Fame, an' canter like a filly
Thro' a' the streets an' neuks o' Killie,
Tell ev'ry social, honest billie
    To cease his grievin,
For yet, unskaith'd by Death's gleg gullie,
    Tam Samson 's livin !

HALLOWEEN.*

[The following Poem will, by many readers, be well enough understood ; but for the sake of those who are unacquainted with the manners and traditions of the country where the scene is cast, notes are added, to give some account of the principal charms and spells of that night, so big with prophecy to the peasantry in the west of Scotland. The passion of prying into futurity makes a striking part of the history of human nature, in its rude state, in all ages and nations ; and it may be some entertainment to a philosophic mind, if any such should honour the Author with a perusal, to see the remains of it, among the more unenlightened in our own.   R. B.]

> *Yes ! let the rich deride, the proud disdain,*
> *The simple pleasures of the lowly train ;*
> *To me more dear, congenial to my heart,*
> *One native charm, than all the gloss of art.*
> GOLDSMITH.

UPON that night, when Fairies light
  On Cassilis Downans† dance,
Or owre the lays, in splendid blaze,
  On sprightly coursers prance ;
Or for Colean the rout is ta'en,
  Beneath the moon's pale beams ;
There, up the Cove,‡ to stray an' rove
  Amang the rocks and streams
            To sport that night ;

Amang the bonie, winding banks,
  Where Doon rins, wimplin, clear,
Where Bruce§ ance rul'd the martial
    ranks,
  An' shook his Carrick spear,
Some merry, friendly, countra folks,
  Together did convene,
To burn their nits, an' pou their stocks,
  An' haud their Halloween
            Fu' blythe that night. .

The lasses feat, an' cleanly neat,
  Mair braw than when they're fine ;
Their faces blythe, fu' sweetly kythe,
  Hearts leal, an' warm, an' kin :
The lads sae trig, wi' wooer-babs,
  Weel knotted on their garten,
Some unco blate, an' some wi' gabs,
  Gar lasses' hearts gang startin
            Whyles fast at night.

Then, first an' foremost, thro' the kail,
  Their stocks‖ maun a' be sought ance :
They steek their een, an' grape an' wale,
  For muckle anes, an' straught anes.
Poor hav'rel Will fell aff the drift,
  An' wander'd thro' the Bow-kail,
An' pou't, for want o' better shift,
  A runt was like a sow-tail,
            Sae bow't that night.

* Is thought to be a night when witches, devils, and other mischief-making beings are all abroad on their baneful, midnight errands ; particularly those aërial pecple, the fairies, are said, on that night, to hold a grand anniversary.   R. B.
† Certain little, romantic, rocky, green hills, in the neighbourhood of the ancient seat of the Earls of Cassilis.   R. B.
‡ A noted cavern near Colean-house, called the Cove of Colean ; which, as well as Cassilis Downans, is famed in country story for being a favourite haunt of fairies.   R. B.
§ The famous family of that name, the ancestors of Robert, the great deliverer of his country, were Earls of Carrick.   R. B.
‖ The first ceremony of Halloween is, pulling each a *stock*, or plant of kail.   They must go out, hand in hand, with eyes shut, and pull the first they meet with.   Its being big or little, straight or crooked, is prophetic of the size and shape of the grand object of all their spells—the husband or wife.   If any *yird*, or earth, stick to the root, that is tocher, or fortune ; and the taste of the *custock*, that is, the heart of the stem, is indicative of the natural temper and disposition.   Lastly, the stems, or, to give them their ordinary appellation, the *runts*, are placed somewhere above the head of the door ; and the Christian names of the people whom chance brings into the house, are, according to the priority of placing the *runts*, the names in question.   R. B.

Then, straught or crooked, yird or nane,
  They roar an' cry a' throu'ther ;
The vera wee things, toddlin, rin,
  Wi' stocks out-owre their shouther ;
An' gif the custocks sweet or sour,
  Wi' joctelegs they taste them ;
Syne coziely, aboon the door,
  Wi' cannie care, they've plac'd them
        To lie that night.

The lasses staw frae 'mang them a'
  To pou their stalks o' corn ; *
But Rab slips out, an' jinks about,
  Behint the muckle thorn :
He grippet Nelly hard an' fast ;
  Loud skirl'd a' the lasses ;
But her tap-pickle maist was lost,
  When kiutlin i' the fause-house †
        Wi' him that night.

The auld guidwife's weel-hoordet nits ‡
  Are round an' round divided,
An' monie lads' and lasses' fates
  Are there that night decided :
Some kindle, couthie, side by side,
  An' burn thegither trimly ;
Some start awa, wi' saucy pride,
  An' jump out-owre the chimlie
        Fu' high that night.

Jean slips in twa, wi' tentie e'e ;
  Wha 'twas, she wadna tell ;
But this is Jock, and this is me,
  She says in to hersel :
He bleez'd owre her, an' she owre him,
  As they wad never mair part ;
Till fuff ! he started up the lum,
  An' Jean had e'en a sair heart
        To see't that night.

Poor Willie, wi' his bow-kail runt,
  Was brunt wi' primsie Mallie,
An' Mary, nae doubt, took the drunt,
  To be compar'd to Willie :
Mall's nit lap out, wi' pridefu' fling,
  An' her ain fit it brunt it ;
While Willie lap, an' swoor by jing,
  'Twas just the way he wanted
        To be that night.

Nell had the fause-house in her min',
  She pits hersel an' Rob in ;
In loving bleeze they sweetly join,
  Till white in ase they're sobbin :
Nell's heart was dancin at the view ;
  She whisper'd Rob to leuk for't :
Rob, stownlins, prie'd her bonnie mou,
  Fu' cozie in the neuk for't,
        Unseen that night.

But Merran sat behint their backs,
  Her thoughts on Andrew Bell ;
She lea'es them gashin at their cracks,
  An' slips out by hersel :
She thro' the yard the nearest taks,
  An' to the kiln she goes then,
An' darklins grapit for the bauks,
  And in the blue-clue § throws then,
        Right fear't that night.

An' aye she win't, an' ay she swat,
  I wat she made nae jaukin ;
Till something held within the pat,
  Guid Lord ! but she was quaukin !
But whether 'twas the Deil himsel,
  Or whether 'twas a bauk-en',
Or whether it was Andrew Bell,
  She did na wait on talkin
        To spier that night.

---

* They go to the barn-yard, and pull each, at three several times, a stalk of oats. If the third stalk wants the *tap-pickle*, that is, the grain at the top of the stalk, the party in question will come to the marriage-bed anything but a maid. R. B.

† When the corn is in a doubtful state, by being too green, or wet, the stack-builder, by means of old timber, &c. makes a large apartment in his stack, with an opening in the side which is fairest exposed to the wind : this he calls a *Fause-house.* R. B.

‡ Burning the nuts is a famous charm. They name the lad and the lass to each particular nut, as they lay them in the fire ; and accordingly as they burn quietly together, or start from beside one another, the course and issue of the courtship will be. R. B.

§ Whoever would, with success, try this spell, must strictly observe these directions : Steal out, all alone, to the *kiln*, and, darkling, throw into the *pot* a clue of blue yarn ; wind it in a new clue off the old one ; and, towards the latter end, something will hold the thread ; demand, *Wha hauds?* i. e. who holds? an answer will be returned from the kiln-pot, by naming the Christian and surname of your future spouse. R. B.

Wee Jenny to her Graunie says,
   ' Will ye go wi' me, Graunie ?
' I'll eat the apple * at the glass,
   ' I gat frae uncle Johnie :'
She fuff't her pipe wi' sic a lunt,
   In wrath she was sae vap'rin,
She notic't na, an aizle brunt
   Her braw new worset apron
           Out thro' that night.

' Ye little Skelpie-limmer's face !
   ' I daur you try sic sportin,
' As seek the foul Thief ony place,
   ' For him to spae your fortune ?
' Nae doubt but ye may get a sight !
   ' Great cause ye hae to fear it ;
' For monie a ane has gotten a fright,
   ' An' liv'd an' di'd deleeret,
           ' On sic a night.

' Ae Hairst afore the Sherra-moor,
   ' I mind't as weel's yestreen,
' I was a gilpey then, I'm sure
   ' I was na past fyfteen :
' The simmer had been cauld an' wat,
   ' An' stuff was unco' green ;
' An' ay a rantin kirn we gat,
   ' An' just on Halloween
           ' It fell that night.

' Our stibble-rig was Rab M'Graen,
   ' A clever, sturdy fallow ;
' His sin gat Eppie Sim wi' wean,
   ' That liv'd in Achmacalla ;
' He gat hemp-seed,† I mind it weel,
   ' An' he made unco light o't ;
' But monie a day was *by himsel*,
   ' He was sae sairly frighted
           ' That vera night.'

Then up gat fechtin Jamie Fleck,
   An' he swoor by his conscience,
That he could saw hemp-seed a peck ;
   For it was a' but nonsense :

The auld guidman raught down the pock,
   An' out a handfu' gied him ;
Syne bad him slip frae 'mang the folk,
   Sometime when nae ane see'd him,
           An' try't that night.

He marches thro' amang the stacks,
   Tho' he was something sturtin ;
The graip he for a harrow taks,
   An' haurls at his curpin :
An' ev'ry now an' then, he says,
   ' Hemp-seed, I saw thee,
' An' her that is to be my lass,
   ' Come after me an' draw thee
           ' As fast this night.'

He whistl'd up Lord Lenox' march,
   To keep his courage cheary ;
Altho' his hair began to arch,
   He was sae fley'd an' eerie :
Till presently he hears a squeak,
   An' then a grane an' gruntle ;
He by his shouther gae a keek,
   An' tumbl'd wi' a wintle
           Out-owre that night.

He roar'd a horrid murder-shout,
   In dreadfu' desperation !
An' young an' auld come rinnin out,
   An' hear the sad narration :
He swoor 'twas hilchin Jean M'Craw,
   Or crouchie Merran Humphie,
Till stop ! she trotted thro' them a' ;
   An' wha was it but *Grumphie*
           Asteer that night !

Meg fain wad to the barn gaen
   To winn three wechts o' naething ;‡
But for to meet the Deil her lane,
   She pat but little faith in :
She gies the Herd a pickle nits,
   And twa red-cheekit apples,
To watch, while for the barn she sets,
   In hopes to see Tam Kipples
           That vera night.

* Take a candle, and go alone to a looking-glass : eat an apple before it, and some traditions say, you should comb your hair all the time ; the face of your conjugal companion, *to be*, will be seen in the glass, as if peeping over your shoulder. R. B.

† Steal out unperceived, and sow a handful of hemp-seed ; harrowing it with anything you can conveniently draw after you. Repeat now and then, ' Hemp-seed, I saw thee, hemp-seed, I saw thee ; and him (or her) that is to be my true-love, come after me and pou thee.' Look over your left shoulder, and you will see the appearance of the person invoked, in the attitude of pulling hemp. Some traditions say, ' come after me, and shaw thee,' that is, show thyself : in which case it simply appears. Others omit the harrowing, and say, ' come after me, and harrow thee.' R. B.

‡ This charm must likewise be performed unperceived, and alone. You go to the *barn*, and

She turns the key, wi' cannie thraw,
  An' owre the threshold ventures ;
But first on Sawnie gies a ca',
  Syne bauldly in she enters ;
A ratton rattl'd up the wa',
  An' she cry'd, Lord preserve her !
An' ran thro' midden-hole an' a',
  An' pray'd wi' zeal an' fervour,
      Fu' fast that night.

They hoy't out Will, wi' sair advice ;
  They hecht him some fine braw ane ;
It chanc'd the stack he faddom't thrice *
  Was timmer-propt for thrawin :
He taks a swirlie, auld moss-oak,
  For some black, grousome Carlin ;
An' loot a winze, an' drew a stroke,
  Till skin in blypes cam haurlin
      Aff 's nieves that night.

A wanton widow Leezie was,
  As cantie as a kittlin ;
But Och ! that night, amang the shaws,
  She gat a fearfu' settlin !
She thro' the whins, an' by the cairn,
  An' owre the hill gaed scrievin,
Whare three lairds' lands met at a burn, †
  To dip her left sark-sleeve in,
      Was bent that night.

Whyles owre a linn the burnie plays,
  As thro' the glen it wimpl't ;
Whyles round a rocky scar it strays ;
  Whyles in a wiel it dimpl't ;

Whyles glitter'd to the nightly rays,
  Wi' bickering, dancing dazzle ;
Whyles cookit underneath the braes,
  Below the spreading hazel,
      Unseen that night.

Amang the brachens on the brae,
  Between her an' the moon,
The Deil, or else an outler Quey,
  Gat up an' gae a croon :
Poor Leezie's heart maist lap the hool ;
  Near lav'rock height she jumpit,
But mist a fit, an' in the pool
  Out-owre the lugs she plumpit,
      Wi' a plunge that night.

In order, on the clean hearth-stane,
  The luggies three ‡ are ranged ;
And ev'ry time great care is taen,
  To see them duly changed :
Auld uncle John, wha wedlock's joys
  Sin' Mar's-year did desire,
Because he gat the toom dish thrice,
  He heav'd them on the fire
      In wrath that night.

Wi' merry sangs, and friendly cracks,
  I wat they did na weary ;
And unco tales, an' funnie jokes,
  Their sports were cheap and cheary ;
Till butter'd So'ns, § wi' fragrant lunt,
  Set a' their gabs a-steerin ;
Syne, wi' a social glass o' strunt,
  They parted aff careerin
      Fu' blythe that night.

---

open both doors, taking them off the hinges, if possible ; for there is danger, that the *being*, about to appear, may shut the doors, and do you some mischief. Then take that instrument used in winnowing the corn, which, in our country dialect, we call a *wecht* ; and go through all the attitudes of letting down corn against the wind. Repeat it three times ; and the third time an apparition will pass through the barn, in at the windy door, and out at the other, having both the figure in question, and the appearance or retinue, marking the employment or station in life. R. B.

* Take an opportunity of going, unnoticed, to a *Bear-stack*, and fathom it three times round. The last fathom of the last time, you will catch in your arms the appearance of your future conjugal yoke-fellow. R. B.

† You go out, one or more (for this is a social spell), to a south running spring or rivulet, where ' three lairds' lands meet,' and dip your left shirt sleeve. Go to bed in sight of a fire, and hang your wet sleeve before it to dry. Lie awake ; and some time near midnight, an apparition, having the exact figure of the grand object in question, will come and turn the sleeve, as if to dry the other side of it. R. B.

‡ Take three dishes ; put clean water in one, foul water in another, leave the third empty : blindfold a person, and lead him to the hearth where the dishes are ranged ; he (or she) dips the left hand : if by chance in the clean water, the future husband or wife will come to the bar of matrimony, a maid : if in the foul, a widow : if in the empty dish, it foretells, with equal certainty, no marriage at all. It is repeated three times ; and every time the arrangement of the dishes is altered. R. B.

§ Sowens, with butter instead of milk to them, is always the *Halloween Supper*. R. B.

THE JOLLY BEGGARS

A CANTATA.

RECITATIVO.

WHEN lyart leaves bestrow the yird,
Or, wavering like the bauckie bird,
  Bedim cauld Boreas' blast :
When hailstanes drive wi' bitter skyte,
And infant frosts begin to bite,
  In hoary cranreuch drest ;
Ae night, at e'en, a merry core
  O' randie, gangrel bodies,
In Poosie-Nansie's held the splore,
  To drink their orra duddies :
    Wi' quaffing and laughing,
      They ranted and they sang ;
    Wi' jumping and thumping,
      The verra girdle rang.

First, niest the fire, in auld red rags,
Ane sat, weel brac'd wi' mealy bags,
  And knapsack a' in order ;
His doxy lay within his arm,
Wi' usquebae and blankets warm,
  She blinket on her sodger ;
An' aye he gies the towsie drab
  The tither skelpin' kiss,
While she held up her greedy gab,
  Just like an aumous dish ;
    Ilk smack still, did crack still,
      Just like a cadger's whip,
    Then staggering, and swaggering,
      He roar'd this ditty up—

AIR.

TUNE—' *Soldier's Joy.*'

I AM a son of Mars, who have been in many wars,
And show my cuts and scars wherever I come ;
This here was for a wench, and that other in a trench,
When welcoming the French at the sound of the drum.
               Lal de daudle, &c.

My 'prentiship I pass'd where my leader breath'd his last,
When the bloody die was cast on the heights of Abram ;
I serv'd out my trade when the gallant game was play'd,
And the Morro low was laid at the sound of the drum.
               Lal de daudle, &c.

I lastly was with Curtis, among the floating batt'ries,
And there I left for witness an arm and a limb :
Yet let my country need me, with Elliot to head me,
I'd clatter on my stumps at the sound of a drum.
               Lal de daudle, &c.

And now, tho' I must beg, with a wooden arm and leg,
And many a tatter'd rag hanging over my bum,
I'm as happy with my wallet, my bottle, and my callet,
As when I us'd in scarlet to follow a drum.
               Lal de daudle, &c.

What tho' with hoary locks, I must stand the winter shocks,
Beneath the woods and rocks, oftentimes for a home ;
When the t'other bag I sell, and the t'other bottle tell,
I could meet a troop of hell at the sound of the drum.

RECITATIVO.

He ended; and the kebars sheuk
  Aboon the chorus roar;
While frighted rattons backward leuk,
  And seek the benmost bore:

A fairy fiddler frae the neuk,
  He skirl'd out encore!
But up arose the martial chuck,
  And laid the loud uproar.

AIR.

TUNE—'*Soldier Laddie.*'

I ONCE was a maid, tho' I cannot tell when,
And still my delight is in proper young men;
Some one of a troop of dragoons was my daddie,
No wonder I'm fond of a sodger laddie.
        Sing, Lal de lal, &c.

The first of my loves was a swaggering blade,
To rattle the thundering drum was his trade;
His leg was so tight, and his cheek was so ruddy,
Transported I was with my sodger laddie.
        Sing, Lal de lal, &c

But the godly old chaplain left him in the lurch,
So the sword I forsook for the sake of the church;
He ventur'd the soul, I risked the body,
'Twas then I prov'd false to my sodger laddie.
        Sing, Lal de lal, &c.

Full soon I grew sick of my sanctified sot,
The regiment at large for a husband I got;
From the gilded spontoon to the fife I was ready,
I asked no more but a sodger laddie.
        Sing, Lal de lal, &c.

But the peace it reduc'd me to beg in despair,
Till I met my old boy at a Cunningham fair;
His rags regimental they flutter'd so gaudy,
My heart it rejoic'd at my sodger laddie.
        Sing, Lal de lal, &c.

And now I have liv'd—I know not how long,
And still I can join in a cup or a song;
But whilst with both hands I can hold the glass steady,
Here's to thee, my hero, my sodger laddie.
        Sing, Lal de lal, &c.

RECITATIVO.

Poor Merry Andrew, in the neuk
  Sat guzzling wi' a tinkler hizzie;
They mind't na wha the chorus teuk,
  Between themselves they were sae bizzy;

At length, wi' drink and courting dizzy,
  He stoitered up an' made a face;
Then turn'd, an' laid a smack on Grizzy,
  Syne tun'd his pipes wi' grave grimace.
        E

AIR.

TUNE—'*Auld Syr Symon.*'

SIR WISDOM's a fool when he's fou,
　Sir Knave is a fool in a session ;
He's there but a 'prentice I trow,
　But I am a fool by profession.

My grannie she bought me a beuk,
　And I held awa to the school ;
I fear I my talent misteuk,
　But what will ye hae of a fool ?

For drink I would venture my neck ;
　A hizzie's the half o' my craft ;
But what could ye other expect,
　Of ane that's avowedly daft ?

I ance was ty'd up like a stirk,
　For civilly swearing and quaffing ;
I ance was abus'd i' the kirk,
　For towzling a lass i' my daffin.

Poor Andrew that tumbles for sport,
　Let naebody name wi' a jeer ;
There's ev'n, I'm tauld, i' the court,
　A tumbler ca'd the Premier.

Observ'd ye, yon reverend lad
　Maks faces to tickle the mob ;
He rails at our mountebank squad—
　It's rivalship just i' the job.

And now my conclusion I'll tell,
　For faith I'm confoundedly dry ;
The chiel that's a fool for himsel',
　Gude Lord, is far dafter than I.

RECITATIVO.

Then niest outspak a raucle carlin,
Wha kent fu' weel to cleek the sterling,
For monie a pursie she had hooked,
And had in monie a well been dooked ;
Her dove had been a Highland laddie,
But weary fa' the waefu' woodie !
Wi' sighs and sabs, she thus began
To wail her braw John Highlandman :

AIR.

TUNE—'*O, an' ye were dead, Guidman.*'

A HIGHLAND lad my love was born,
The Lawlan' laws he held in scorn :
But he still was faithfu' to his clan,
My gallant braw John Highlandman.

CHORUS.

Sing, hey, my braw John Highland
　man !
Sing, ho, my braw John Highlandman!
There's no a lad in a' the lan'
Was match for my John Highlandman.

With his philibeg an' tartan plaid,
And gude claymore down by his side,
The ladies' hearts he did trepan,
My gallant braw John Highlandman.
　　　　　　Sing, hey, &c.

We rangèd a' from Tweed to Spey,
And liv'd like lords and ladies gay ;
For a Lawlan' face he feared nane,
My gallant braw John Highlandman.
　　　　　　Sing, hey, &c.

They banish'd him beyond the sea,
But ere the bud was on the tree,
Adown my cheeks the pearls ran,
Embracing my John Highlandman.
　　　　　　Sing, hey, &c.

But, oh ! they catch'd him at the last,
And bound him in a dungeon fast ;
My curse upon them every ane,
They've hang'd my braw John High-
　landman.
　　　　　　Sing, hey, &c.

And now a widow, I must mourn
The pleasures that will ne'er return ;
No comfort but a hearty can,
When I think on John Highlandman.
　　　　　　Sing, hey, &c.

RECITATIVO

A pigmy Scraper wi' his fiddle,
Wha us'd at trysts and fairs to driddle,
Her strappin limb and gaucy middle
　　(He reach'd nae higher),
Had hol't his heartie like a riddle,
　　And blawn't on fire.

Wi' hand on haunch, and upward ee,
He croon'd his gamut, one, two, three,
Then, in an Arioso key,
　　The wee Apollo
Set aff, wi' Allegretto glee,
　　His giga solo.

AIR.

LET me ryke up to dight that tear,
And go wi' me and be my dear,
And then your every care and fear
  May whistle owre the lave o't.

CHORUS.

I am a fiddler to my trade,
And a' the tunes that e'er I play'd,
The sweetest still to wife or maid,
  Was whistle owre the lave o't.

At kirns and weddings we'se be there,
And oh! sae nicely 's we will fare ;
We'll bouse about, till Daddie Care
  Sings whistle owre the lave o't.
                    I am, &c.

Sae merrily 's the banes we'll pyke,
And sun oursels about the dyke,
And at our leisure, when ye like,
  We'll whistle owre the lave o't.
                    I am, &c.

But bless me wi' your heav'n o' charms,
And while I kittle hair on thairms,
Hunger, cauld, and a' sic harms,
  May whistle owre the lave o't.
                    I am, &c.

RECITATIVO.

Her charms had struck a sturdy Caird,
  As well as poor Gut-scraper ;
He taks the fiddler by the beard,
  And draws a roosty rapier—

He swoor, by a' was swearing worth,
  To spit him like a pliver,
Unless he wad from that time forth
  Relinquish her for ever.

Wi' ghastly ee, poor tweedle-dee
  Upon his hunkers bended,
And pray'd for grace, wi' ruefu' face,
  And sae the quarrel ended.

But tho' his little heart did grieve
  When round the tinkler prest her,
He feign'd to snirtle in his sleeve,
  When thus the Caird address'd her :

AIR.

MY bonnie lass, I work in brass,
  A tinkler is my station ;
I've travell'd round all Christian ground
  In this my occupation ;
I've ta'en the gold, I've been enroll'd
  In many a noble squadron ;
But vain they search'd, when off I march'd
  To go and clout the cauldron.
                    I've ta'en the gold, &c.

Despise that shrimp, that wither'd imp,
  Wi' a' his noise and cap'rin',
And tak a share wi' those that bear
  The budget and the apron ;
And by that stoup, my faith and houp,
  And by that dear Kilbagie,
If e'er ye want, or meet wi' scant,
  May I ne'er weet my craigie.
                    And by that stoup, &c.

RECITATIVO.

The Caird prevail'd—th' unblushing fair
  In his embraces sunk,
Partly wi' love o'ercome sae sair,
  And partly she was drunk.
Sir Violino, with an air
  That show'd a man o' spunk,
Wish'd unison between the pair,
  And made the bottle clunk
            To their health that night.

But hurchin Cupid shot a shaft
  That play'd a dame a shavie,
The fiddler rak'd her fore and aft,
  Behint the chicken cavie.
Her lord, a wight o' Homer's craft,
  Tho' limpin' wi' the spavie,
He hirpl'd up, and lap like daft,
  And shor'd them Dainty Davie.
            O boot that night.

He was a care-defying blade
  As ever Bacchus listed,
Tho' Fortune sair upon him laid,
  His heart she ever miss'd it.
He had nae wish, but— to be glad,
  Nor want but—when he thirsted ;
He hated nought but—to be sad,
  And thus the Muse suggested
            His sang that night.
                    E 2

AIR.

Tune—'*For a' that, and a' that.*'

I AM a bard of no regard
 Wi' gentlefolks, an' a' that ;
But Homer-like, the glowran byke,
 Frae town to town I draw that.

CHORUS.

For a' that, and a' that,
 And twice as meikle 's a' that ;
I've lost but ane, I've twa behin',
 I've wife eneugh for a' that.

I never drank the Muses' stank,
 Castalia's burn, an' a' that ;
But there it streams, and richly reams,
 My Helicon I ca' that.
     For a' that, &c.

Great love I bear to a' the fair,
 Their humble slave, an' a' that ;
But lordly will, I hold it still
 A mortal sin to thraw that.
     For a' that, &c.

In raptures sweet, this hour we meet,
 Wi' mutual love, an' a' that ;
But for how lang the flie may stang,
 Let inclination law that.
     For a' that, &c.

Their tricks and craft hae put me daft,
 They've ta'en me in, and a' that ;
But clear your decks, and here's the sex !
 I like the jads for a' that.

 For a' that, and a' that,
  And twice as muckle 's a' that,
 My dearest bluid, to do them guid,
  They're welcome till't, for a' that.

RECITATIVO.

So sung the bard—and Nansie's wa's
Shook with a thunder of applause,
 Re-echo'd from each mouth ;
They toom'd their pocks, an' pawn'd their duds,
They scarcely left to co'er their fuds,
 To quench their lowan drouth.

Then owre again, the jovial thrang
 The poet did request,

To lowse his pack, an' wale a sang,
 A ballad o' the best ;
He, rising, rejoicing,
 Between his twa Deborahs,
Looks round him, an' found them
 Impatient for the chorus.

AIR.

Tune—'*Jolly Mortals, fill your Glasses.*'

SEE ! the smoking bowl before us,
 Mark our jovial ragged ring ;
Round and round take up the chorus,
 And in raptures let us sing :

CHORUS.

A fig for those by law protected !
 Liberty's a glorious feast !
Courts for cowards were erected,
 Churches built to please the priest.

What is title ? what is treasure ?
 What is reputation's care ?
If we lead a life of pleasure,
 'Tis no matter, how or where !
     A fig, &c.

With the ready trick and fable,
 Round we wander all the day ;
And at night, in barn or stable,
 Hug our doxies on the hay.
     A fig, &c.

Does the train-attended carriage
 Thro' the country lighter rove ?
Does the sober bed of marriage
 Witness brighter scenes of love ?
     A fig, &c.

Life is all a variorum,
 We regard not how it goes ;
Let them cant about decorum
 Who have characters to lose.
     A fig, &c.

Here's to budgets, bags, and wallets !
Here's to all the wandering train !
Here's our ragged brats and callets !
 One and all cry out, Amen !
     A fig, &c.

THE AULD FARMER'S NEW-YEAR MORNING SALUTATION
TO HIS AULD MARE, MAGGIE,

ON GIVING HER THE ACCUSTOMED RIPP OF CORN TO HANSEL IN THE NEW YEAR.

A GUID New-Year I wish thee, Maggie !
Hae, there's a ripp to thy auld baggie :
Tho' thou's howe-backit, now, an'
    knaggie,
        I've seen the day,
Thou could hae gane like ony staggie
        Out-owre the lay.

Tho' now thou's dowie, stiff, an' crazy,
An' thy auld hide's as white's a daisie,
I've seen thee dappl't, sleek an' glaizie,
        A bonie gray :
He should been tight that daur't to raize
    thee,
        Ance in a day.

Thou ance was i' the foremost rank,
A filly buirdly, steeve, an' swank,
An' set weel down a shapely shank,
        As e'er tread yird ;
An' could hae flown out-owre a stank,
        Like onie bird.

It's now some nine-an'-twenty year,
Sin' thou was my guid-father's meere ;
He gied me thee, o' tocher clear,
        An' fifty mark ;
Tho' it was sma', 'twas weel-won gear,
        An' thou was stark.

When first I gaed to woo my Jenny,
Ye then was trottin wi' your minnie :
Tho' ye was trickie, slee, an' funnie,
        Ye ne'er was donsie ;
But hamely, tawie, quiet, an' cannie,
        An' unco sonsie.

That day, ye pranc'd wi' muckle pride,
When ye bure hame my bonie bride ;
An' sweet an' gracefu' she did ride,
        Wi' maiden air !
Kyle-Stewart I could bragged wide,
        For sic a pair.

Tho' now ye dow but hoyte and hoble,
An' wintle like a saumont-coble,
That day ye was a jinker noble
        For heels an' win' !
An' ran them till they a' did wauble,
        Far, far behin'.

When thou an' I were young and skeigh,
An' stable-meals at fairs were driegh,
How thou wad prance, an' snore, an'
    skriegh
        An' tak the road !
Town's-bodies ran, and stood abeigh,
        An' ca't thee mad.

When thou was corn't, an' I was mellow,
We took the road ay like a swallow :
At Brooses thou had ne'er a fellow,
        For pith an' speed ;
But ev'ry tail thou pay't them hollow,
        Whare'er thou gaed.

The sma', droop-rumpl't, hunter cattle,
Might aiblins waur't thee for a brattle ;
But sax Scotch miles thou try't their
    mettle,
        An' gart them whaizle :
Nae whip nor spur, but just a wattle
        O' saugh or hazel.

Thou was a noble fittie-lan',
As e'er in tug or tow was drawn !
Aft thee an' I, in aught hours gaun,
        On guid March-weather,
Hae turn'd sax rood beside our han',
        For days thegither.

Thou never braindg't, an' fetch't, an'
    fliskit,
But thy auld tail thou wad hae whiskit,
An' spread abreed thy weel-fill'd brisket,
        Wi' pith an' pow'r,
Till spritty knowes wad rair't and riskit,
        An' slypet owre.

When frosts lay lang, an' snaws were
      deep,
An' threaten'd labour back to keep,
I gied thy cog a wee-bit heap
      Aboon the timmer ;
I ken'd my Maggie wad na sleep
      For that, or simmer.

In cart or car thou never reestit ;
The steyest brae thou wad hae face't it ;
Thou never lap, an' sten't, and breastit,
      Then stood to blaw ;
But just thy step a wee thing hastit,
      Thou snoov't awa.

My pleugh is now thy bairn-time a' :
Four gallant brutes as e'er did draw ;
Forbye sax mae, I've sell't awa,
      That thou hast nurst :
They drew me thretteen pund an' twa,
      The vera warst.

Monie a sair daurk we twa hae wrought,
An' wi' the weary warl' fought !
An' monie an anxious day, I thought
      We wad be beat !
Yet here to crazy age we're brought,
      Wi' something yet.

And think na, my auld, trusty servan',
That now perhaps thou's less deservin,
An' thy auld days may end in starvin,
      For my last fou,
A heapit stimpart, I'll reserve ane
      Laid by for you.

We've worn to crazy years thegither ;
We'll toyte about wi' ane anither ;
Wi' tentie care I'll flit thy tether
      To some hain'd rig,
Whare ye may nobly rax your leather,
      Wi' sma' fatigue.

TO A MOUSE, ON TURNING HER UP IN HER NEST WITH THE PLOUGH, NOVEMBER, 1785.

WEE, sleekit, cow'rin, tim'rous beastie,
O, what a panic's in thy breastie !
Thou need na start awa sae hasty,
      Wi' bickering brattle !
I wad be laith to rin an' chase thee,
      Wi' murd'ring pattle !

I'm truly sorry man's dominion
Has broken Nature's social union,
An' justifies that ill opinion,
      Which makes thee startle,
At me, thy poor, earth-born companion,
      An' fellow-mortal !

I doubt na, whiles, but thou may thieve ;
What then ? poor beastie, thou maun live !
A daimen-icker in a thrave
      'S a sma' request :
I'll get a blessin wi' the lave,
      And never miss't !

Thy wee bit housie, too, in ruin !
Its silly wa's the win's are strewin !
An' naething, now, to big a new ane,
      O' foggage green !
An' bleak December's winds ensuin,
      Baith snell an' keen !

Thou saw the fields laid bare and waste,
An' weary winter comin fast,
An' cozie here, beneath the blast,
      Thou thought to dwell,
Till crash ! the cruel coulter past,
      Out thro' thy cell.

That wee bit heap o' leaves an' stibble,
Has cost thee mony a weary nibble !
Now thou's turn'd out, for a' thy trouble,
      But house or hald,
To thole the winter's sleety dribble,
      An' cranreuch cauld !

But, Mousie, thou art no thy lane,
In proving foresight may be vain :
The best laid schemes o' mice an' men
      Gang aft a-gley,
An' lea'e us nought but grief an' pain,
      For promis'd joy.

Still thou art blest, compar'd wi' me !
The present only toucheth thee :
But, Och ! I backward cast my e'e
      On prospects drear !
An' forward, tho' I canna see,
      I guess an' fear !

A WINTER NIGHT.

Poor naked wretches, wheresoe'er you are,
That bide the pelting of this pitiless storm!
How shall your houseless heads, and unfed sides,
Your loop'd and window'd raggedness, defend you,
From seasons such as these?——
                                    SHAKESPEARE.

WHEN biting Boreas, fell and doure,
Sharp shivers thro' the leafless bow'r;
When Phœbus gies a short-liv'd glow'r,
            Far south the lift,
Dim-dark'ning thro' the flaky show'r,
            Or whirling drift:

Ae night the storm the steeples rocked,
Poor Labour sweet in sleep was locked,
While burns, wi' snawy wreeths up-choked,
            Wild-eddying swirl,
Or thro' the mining outlet bocked,
            Down headlong hurl.

List'ning, the doors an' winnocks rattle,
I thought me on the ourie cattle,
Or silly sheep, wha bide this brattle
            O' winter war,
And thro' the drift, deep-lairing, sprattle,
            Beneath a scar.

Ilk happing bird, wee, helpless thing!
That, in the merry months o' spring,
Delighted me to hear thee sing,
            What comes o' the
Whare wilt thou cow'r thy chittering win
            An' close thy e'e?

Ev'n you on murd'ring errands toil'd,
Lone from your savage homes exil'd,
The blood-stain'd roost, and sheep-cote spoil'd
            My heart forgets,
While pityless the tempest wild
            Sore on you beats.

Now Phœbe, in her midnight reign,
Dark muffl'd, view'd the dreary plain;
Still crowding thoughts, a pensive train,
            Rose in my soul,
When on my ear this plaintive strain,
            Slow, solemn, stole—

' Blow, blow, ye winds, with heavier gust !
' And freeze, thou bitter-biting frost !
' Descend, ye chilly, smothering snows !
' Not all your rage, as now, united shows
   ' More hard unkindness, unrelenting,
   ' Vengeful malice unrepenting,
' Than heav'n-illumin'd man on brother man bestows !
' See stern Oppression's iron grip,
   ' Or mad Ambition's gory hand,
' Sending, like blood-hounds from the slip,
   ' Woe, want, and murder o'er a land !
' Ev'n in the peaceful rural vale,
' Truth, weeping, tells the mournful tale,
' How pamper'd Luxury, Flatt'ry by her side,
   ' The parasite empoisoning her ear,
   ' With all the servile wretches in the rear,
' Looks o'er proud property, extended wide ;
   ' And eyes the simple rustic hind,
    ' Whose toil upholds the glitt'ring show,
   ' A creature of another kind,
   ' Some coarser substance, unrefin'd,
' Plac'd for her lordly use thus far, thus vile, below

' Where, where is Love's fond, tender throe,
' With lordly Honour's lofty brow,
   ' The pow'rs you proudly own ?
' Is there, beneath Love's noble name,
' Can harbour, dark, the selfish aim,
   ' To bless himself alone !
' Mark maiden-innocence a prey
   ' To love-pretending snares,
' This boasted honour turns away,
   ' Shunning soft pity's rising sway,
' Regardless of the tears, and unavailing pray'rs !
' Perhaps this hour, in mis'ry's squalid nest,
' She strains your infant to her joyless breast,
' And with a mother's fears shrinks at the rocking blast !

   ' Oh ye ! who, sunk in beds of down,
' Feel not a want but what yourselves create,
' Think, for a moment, on his wretched fate,
   ' Whom friends and fortune quite disown !
' Ill-satisfied keen nature's clam'rous call,
   ' Stretch'd on his straw he lays himself to sleep,
' While thro' the ragged roof and chinky wall,
' Chill o'er his slumbers, piles the drifty heap !
' Think on the dungeon's grim confine,
' Where guilt and poor misfortune pine !
' Guilt, erring man, relenting view ?
' But shall thy legal rage pursue

' The wretch, already crushèd low,
' By cruel fortune's undeservèd blow ?
' Affliction's sons are brothers in distress ;
' A brother to relieve, how exquisite the bliss ! '

I heard nae mair, for Chanticleer
   Shook off the pouthery snaw,
And hail'd the morning with a cheer,
   A cottage-rousing craw.

But deep this truth impress'd my mind—
   Thro' all His works abroad,
The heart benevolent and kind
   The most resembles God.

EPISTLE TO DAVIE, A BROTHER POET.

January—[1784].

WHILE winds frae aff Ben-Lomond blaw,
And bar the doors wi' driving snaw,
   And hing us owre the ingle,
I set me down, to pass the time,
And spin a verse or twa o' rhyme,
   In hamely, westlin jingle.
While frosty winds blaw in the drift,
   Ben to the chimla lug,
I grudge a wee the Great-folk's gift,
   That live sae bien an' snug :
     I tent less, and want less
      Their roomy fire-side ;
     But hanker and canker,
      To see their cursèd pride.

It's hardly in a body's pow'r,
To keep, at times, frae being sour,
   To see how things are shar'd ;
How best o' chiels are whyles in want,
While coofs on countless thousands rant,
   And ken na how to wair't :
But, Davie, lad, ne'er fash your head,
   Tho' we hae little gear,
We're fit to win our daily bread,
   As lang's we're hale and fier :
     ' Mair spier na, nor fear na,'
      Auld age ne'er mind a feg ;
     The last o't, the warst o't,
      Is only but to beg.

To lie in kilns and barns at e'en,
When banes are craz'd, and bluid is thin,
   Is, doubtless, great distress !

Yet then content could mak us blest ;
Ev'n then, sometimes, we'd snatch a taste
   Of truest happiness.
The honest heart that's free frae a'
   Intended fraud or guile,
However fortune kick the ba',
   Has ay some cause to smile :
     And mind still, you'll find still,
      A comfort this nae sma' ;
     Nae mair then, we'll care then,
      Nae farther can we fa'.

What tho', like commoners of air,
We wander out, we know not where,
   But either house or hal' ?
Yet nature's charms, the hills and woods,
The sweeping vales, and foaming floods,
   Are free alike to all.
In days when daisies deck the ground,
   And blackbirds whistle clear,
With honest joy our hearts will bound,
   To see the coming year :
     On braes when we please, then,
      We'll sit and sowth a tune ;
     Syne rhyme till't, we'll time till't,
      And sing't when we hae done.

It's no in titles nor in rank ;
It's no in wealth like Lon'on bank,
   To purchase peace and rest ;
It's no in making muckle, *mair :*
It's no in books, it's no in lear,
   To make us truly blest :

If happiness hae not her seat
  And centre in the breast,
We may be wise, or rich, or great,
  But never can be blest :
    Nae treasures, nor pleasures,
      Could make us happy lang ;
    The heart ay's the part ay,
      That makes us right or wrang.

Think ye, that sic as you and I,
Wha drudge and drive thro' wet an' dry,
  Wi' never-ceasing toil ;
Think ye, are we less blest than they,
Wha scarcely tent us in their way,
  As hardly worth their while ?
Alas ! how aft in haughty mood,
  God's creatures they oppress !
Or else, neglecting a' that's guid,
  They riot in excess !
    Baith careless, and fearless,
      Of either heav'n or hell !
    Esteeming, and deeming
      It's a' an idle tale !

Then let us cheerfu' acquiesce ;
Nor make our scanty pleasures less,
  By pining at our state ;
And, even should misfortunes come,
I, here wha sit, hae met wi' some,
  An's thankfu' for them yet.
They gie the wit of age to youth ;
  They let us ken oursel ;
They mak us see the naked truth,
  The real guid and ill.
    Tho' losses, and crosses,
      Be lessons right severe,
    There's wit there, ye'll get there,
      Ye'll find nae other where.

But tent me, Davie, ace o' hearts !
(To say aught less wad wrang the cartes,
  And flatt'ry I detest)
This life has joys for you and I ;
And joys that riches ne'er could buy ;
  And joys the very best.
There's a' the pleasures o' the heart,
  The lover an' the frien' ;
Ye hae your Meg, your dearest part,
  And I my darling Jean !

It warms me, it charms me,
  To mention but her name :
It heats me, it beets me,
  And sets me a' on flame !

O all ye pow'rs who rule above !
O Thou, whose very self art love !
  Thou know'st my words sincere !
The life-blood streaming thro' my heart,
Or my more dear immortal part,
  Is not more fondly dear !
When heart-corroding care and grief
  Deprive my soul of rest,
Her dear idea brings relief
  And solace to my breast.
    Thou Being, All-seeing,
      O hear my fervent pray'r ;
    Still take her, and make her
      Thy most peculiar care !

All hail, ye tender feelings dear !
The smile of love, the friendly tear,
  The sympathetic glow !
Long since, this world's thorny ways
Had number'd out my weary days,
  Had it not been for you !
Fate still has blest me with a friend,
  In every care and ill ;
And oft a more endearing band,
  A tie more tender still.
    It lightens, it brightens
      The tenebrific scene,
    To meet with, and greet with
      My Davie or my Jean.

O, how that name inspires my style !
The words come skelpin, rank and file,
  Amaist before I ken !
The ready measure rins as fine,
As Phœbus and the famous Nine
  Were glowrin owre my pen.
My spaviet Pegasus will limp,
  Till ance he's fairly het ;
And then he'll hilch, and stilt, and jimp,
  An' rin an unco fit :
    But lest then, the beast then,
      Should rue this hasty ride,
    I'll light now, and dight now
      His sweaty, wizen'd hide.

THE LAMENT,

OCCASIONED BY THE UNFORTUNATE ISSUE OF A FRIEND'S AMOUR.

Alas ! how oft does Goodness wound itself,
And sweet AFFECTION *prove the spring of woe !*

HOME.

O THOU pale Orb, that silent shines,
  While care-untroubled mortals sleep !
Thou seest a wretch that inly pines,
  And wanders here to wail and weep !
With woe I nightly vigils keep,
  Beneath thy wan, unwarming beam ;
And mourn, in lamentation deep,
  How life and love are all a dream.

I joyless view thy rays adorn
  The faintly-markèd, distant hill :
I joyless view thy trembling horn,
  Reflected in the gurgling rill :
My fondly-fluttering heart, be still !
  Thou busy pow'r, Remembrance, cease!
Ah ! must the agonizing thrill
  For ever bar returning peace !

No idly-feign'd poetic pains,
  My sad, love-lorn lamentings claim ;
No shepherd's pipe—Arcadian strains ;
  No fabled tortures, quaint and tame :
The plighted faith ; the mutual flame ;
  The oft attested Pow'rs above ;
The promis'd father's tender name :
  These were the pledges of my love !

Encircled in her clasping arms,
  How have the raptur'd moments flown!
How have I wish'd for fortune's charms,
  For her dear sake, and her's alone !
And must I think it ! is she gone,
  My secret heart's exulting boast ?
And does she heedless hear my groan ?
  And is she ever, ever lost ?

Oh ! can she bear so base a heart,
  So lost to honour, lost to truth,

As from the fondest lover part,
  The plighted husband of her youth !
Alas ! life's path may be unsmooth !
  Her way may lie thro' rough distress !
Then, who her pangs and pains will
    soothe,
  Her sorrows share, and make them
    less ?

Ye wingèd hours that o'er us past,
  Enraptur'd more, the more enjoy'd,
Your dear remembrance in my breast,
  My fondly-treasur'd thoughts em-
    ploy'd.
That breast, how dreary now, and void,
  For her too scanty once of room !
Ev'n ev'ry ray of hope destroy'd,
  And not a wish to gild the gloom !

The morn that warns th' approaching
    day,
  Awakes me up to toil and woe :
I see the hours in long array,
  That I must suffer, lingering, slow.
Full many a pang, and many a throe,
  Keen recollection's direful train,
Must wring my soul, ere Phœbus, low,
  Shall kiss the distant, western main.

And when my nightly couch I try,
  Sore-harass'd out with care and grief,
My toil-beat nerves, and tear-worn eye,
  Keep watchings with the nightly thief :
Or if I slumber, Fancy, chief,
  Reigns, haggard-wild, in sore affright :
Ev'n day, all-bitter, brings relief,
  From such a horror-breathing night.

O! thou bright Queen, who o'er th' expanse   [sway!
  Now highest reign'st, with boundless
Oft has thy silent-marking glance
  Observ'd us, fondly-wand'ring, stray!
The time, unheeded, sped away,
  While love's luxurious pulse beat high,
Beneath thy silver-gleaming ray,
    To mark the mutual-kindling eye.

Oh! scenes in strong remembrance set!
  Scenes, never, never to return!
Scenes, if in stupor I forget,
  Again I feel, again I burn!
From ev'ry joy and pleasure torn,
  Life's weary vale I'll wander thro';
And hopeless, comfortless, I'll mourn
  A faithless woman's broken vow.

DESPONDENCY.

AN ODE.

OPPRESS'D with grief, oppress'd with care,
A burden more than I can bear,
  I set me down and sigh:
O life! thou art a galling load,
Along a rough, a weary road,
  To wretches such as I!
Dim-backward as I cast my view,
  What sick'ning scenes appear!
What sorrows yet may pierce me thro',
  Too justly I may fear!
    Still caring, despairing,
      Must be my bitter doom;
    My woes here shall close ne'er,
      But with the closing tomb!

Happy, ye sons of busy life,
Who, equal to the bustling strife,
  No other view regard!
Ev'n when the wishèd end's deny'd,
Yet while the busy means are ply'd,
  They bring their own reward:
Whilst I, a hope-abandon'd wight,
  Unfitted with an aim,
Meet ev'ry sad returning night,
  And joyless morn the same;
    You, bustling, and justling,
      Forget each grief and pain;
    I, listless, yet restless,
      Find every prospect vain.

How blest the Solitary's lot,
Who, all-forgetting, all-forgot,
  Within his humble cell,
The cavern wild with tangling roots,
Sits o'er his newly-gather'd fruits,
  Beside his crystal well?

Or, haply, to his ev'ning thought,
  By unfrequented stream,
The ways of men are distant brought,
  A faint-collected dream:
    While praising, and raising
      His thoughts to Heav'n on high,
    As wand'ring, meand'ring,
      He views the solemn sky.

Than I, no lonely hermit plac'd,
Where never human footstep trac'd,
  Less fit to play the part;
The lucky moment to improve,
And just to stop, and just to move,
  With self-respecting art:
But ah! those pleasures, loves, and joys,
  Which I too keenly taste,
The Solitary can despise,
  Can want, and yet be blest!
    He needs not, he heeds not,
      Or human love or hate,
    Whilst I here, must cry here,
      At perfidy ingrate!

Oh! enviable, early days,   [maze,
When dancing thoughtless pleasure's
  To care, to guilt unknown!
How ill exchang'd for riper times,
To fee the follies, or the crimes,
  Of others, or my own!
Ye tiny elves that guiltless sport,
  Like linnets in the bush,
Ye little know the ills ye court,
  When manhood is your wish!
    The losses, the crosses,
      That active man engage!
    The fears all, the tears all,
      Of dim-declining age

WINTER.

A DIRGE.

THE wintry west extends his blast,
　And hail and rain does blaw ;
Or, the stormy north sends driving forth,
　The blinding sleet and snaw :
While, tumbling brown, the burn comes
　　down,
　And roars frae bank to brae :
And bird and beast in covert rest,
　And pass the heartless day.

" The sweeping blast, the sky o'ercast,"
　The joyless winter-day,
Let others fear, to me more dear
　Than all the pride of May :

The tempest's howl, it soothes my soul,
　My griefs it seems to join ;
The leafless trees my fancy please,
　Their fate resembles mine !

Thou Pow'r Supreme, whose mighty
　scheme
These woes of mine fulfil,
Here, firm, I rest, they must be best,
　Because they are Thy will !
Then all I want, (Oh ! do thou grant
　This one request of mine !)
Since to enjoy thou dost deny,
　Assist me to resign.

THE COTTER'S SATURDAY NIGHT.

INSCRIBED TO ROBERT AIKEN, ESQ. OF AYR.

Let not Ambition mock their useful toil,
　Their homely joys, and destiny obscure ;
Nor Grandeur hear, with a disdainful smile,
　The short and simple annals of the Poor.
　　　　　　　　　　　　　　GRAY.

MY lov'd, my honour'd, much respected friend !
　No mercenary bard his homage pays :
With honest pride, I scorn each selfish end ;
　My dearest meed, a friend's esteem and praise :
To you I sing, in simple Scottish lays,
　The lowly train in life's sequester'd scene ;
The native feelings strong, the guileless ways ;
　What Aiken in a cottage would have been ;
Ah ! tho' his worth unknown, far happier there, I ween.

November chill blaws loud wi' angry sugh ;
　The short'ning winter-day is near a close ;
The miry beasts retreating frae the pleugh ;
　The black'ning trains o' craws to their repose :
The toil-worn Cotter frae his labour goes,
　This night his weekly moil is at an end,
Collects his spades, his mattocks, and his hoes,
　Hoping the morn in ease and rest to spend,
And weary, o'er the moor, his course does hameward bend

At length his lonely cot appears in view,
　Beneath the shelter of an agèd tree;
Th' expectant wee-things, toddlin, stacher through
　To meet their Dad, wi' flichterin noise an' glee.
His wee bit ingle, blinkin bonilie,
　His clean hearth-stane, his thrifty wifie's smile,
The lisping infant prattling on his knee,
　Does a' his weary carking cares beguile,
An' makes him quite forget his labour an' his toil.

Belyve, the elder bairns come drapping in,
　At service out, amang the farmers roun';
Some ca' the pleugh, some herd, some tentie rin
　A cannie errand to a neebor town:
Their eldest hope, their Jenny, woman-grown,
　In youthfu' bloom, love sparkling in her e'e,
Comes hame, perhaps, to shew a braw new gown,
　Or deposite her sair-won penny-fee,
To help her parents dear, if they in hardship be.

With joy unfeign'd brothers and sisters meet,
　An' each for other's weelfare kindly spiers:
The social hours, swift-wing'd, unnotic'd fleet;
　Each tells the uncos that he sees or hears;
The parents, partial, eye their hopeful years;
　Anticipation forward points the view.
The mother, wi' her needle an' her sheers,
　Gars auld claes look amaist as weel's the new;
The father mixes a' wi' admonition due

Their master's an' their mistress's command,
　The younkers a' are warnèd to obey;
An' mind their labours wi' an eydent hand,
　An' ne'er, tho' out o' sight, to jauk or play:
An' O! be sure to fear the Lord alway,
　'An' mind your duty, duly, morn an' night!
Lest in temptation's path ye gang astray,
　Implore His counsel and assisting might:
They never sought in vain that sought the Lord aright!'

But hark! a rap comes gently to the door,
　Jenny, wha kens the meaning o' the same,
Tells how a neebor lad cam o'er the moor,
　To do some errands, and convoy her hame.
The wily mother sees the conscious flame
　Sparkle in Jenny's e'e, and flush her cheek;
Wi' heart-struck, anxious care, inquires his name,
　While Jenny hafflins is afraid to speak;
Weel pleas'd the mother hears, it's nae wild, worthless rake.

Wi' kindly welcome, Jenny brings him ben;
　A strappan youth; he takes the mother's eye;

Blythe Jenny sees the visit's no ill ta'en ;
  The father cracks of horses, pleughs, and kye.
The youngster's artless heart o'erflows wi' joy,
  But blate and laithfu', scarce can weel behave ;
The mother, wi' a woman's wiles, can spy
  What makes the youth sae bashfu' an' sae grave ;
Weel-pleas'd to think her bairn's respected like the lave.

O happy love ! where love like this is found !
  O heart-felt raptures ! bliss beyond compare !
I've pacèd much this weary, mortal round,
  And sage experience bids me this declare—
' If Heaven a draught of heavenly pleasure spare,
  One cordial in this melancholy vale,
'Tis when a youthful, loving, modest pair,
  In other's arms breathe out the tender tale,
Beneath the milk-white thorn that scents the ev'ning gale.

Is there, in human form, that bears a heart—
  A wretch ! a villain ! lost to love and truth !
That can, with studied, sly, ensnaring art,
  Betray sweet Jenny's unsuspecting youth ?
Curse on his perjur'd arts ! dissembling smooth !
  Are honour, virtue, conscience, all exil'd ?
Is there no pity, no relenting ruth,
  Points to the parents fondling o'er their child ?
Then paints the ruin'd maid, and their distraction wild !

But now the supper crowns their simple board,
  The healsome parritch, chief o' Scotia's food :
The soupe their only Hawkie does afford,
  That 'yont the hallan snugly chows her cood ;
The dame brings forth in complimental mood,
  To grace the lad, her weel-hain'd kebbuck, fell.
An' aft he's prest, an' aft he ca's it guid ;
  The frugal wifie, garrulous, will tell,
How 'twas a towmond auld, sin' lint was i' the bell.

The cheerfu' supper done, wi' serious face,
  They, round the ingle, form a circle wide ;
The sire turns o'er, wi' patriarchal grace,
  The big ha'-Bible, ance his father's pride :
His bonnet rev'rently is laid aside,
  His lyart haffets wearing thin an' bare ;
Those strains that once did sweet in Zion glide,
  He wales a portion with judicious care,
And ' Let us worship God !' he says, with solemn air.

They chant their artless notes in simple guise ;
  They tune their hearts, by far the noblest aim :
Perhaps Dundee's wild warbling measures rise,
  Or plaintive Martyrs, worthy of the name ;

Or noble Elgin beets the heav'nward flame,
    The sweetest far of Scotia's holy lays :
Compar'd with these, Italian trills are tame ;
    The tickl'd ears no heartfelt raptures raise ;
Nae unison hae they with our Creator's praise.

The priest-like father reads the sacred page,
    How Abram was the friend of God on high ;
Or Moses bade eternal warfare wage
    With Amalek's ungracious progeny ;
Or how the royal Bard did groaning lie
    Beneath the stroke of Heaven's avenging ire ;
Or Job's pathetic plaint, and wailing cry ;
    Or rapt Isaiah's wild, seraphic fire ;
Or other holy Seers that tune the sacred lyre.

Perhaps the Christian volume is the theme,
    How guiltless blood for guilty man was shed ;
How He, who bore in Heaven the second name,
    Had not on earth whereon to lay His head ;
How His first followers and servants sped ;
    The precepts sage they wrote to many a land :
How he, who lone in Patmos banishèd,
    Saw in the sun a mighty angel stand ;
And heard great Bab'lon's doom pronounc'd by Heaven's command.

Then kneeling down, to Heaven's Eternal King,
    The saint, the father, and the husband prays :
Hope ' springs exulting on triumphant wing,'
    That thus they all shall meet in future days :
There ever bask in uncreated rays,
    No more to sigh, or shed the bitter tear,
Together hymning their Creator's praise,
    In such society, yet still more dear ;
While circling Time moves round in an eternal sphere.

Compar'd with this, how poor Religion's pride,
    In all the pomp of method, and of art,
When men display to congregations wide
    Devotion's ev'ry grace, except the heart !
The Power, incens'd, the pageant will desert,
    The pompous strain, the sacerdotal stole ;
But haply, in some cottage far apart,
    May hear, well pleas'd, the language of the soul ;
And in his Book of Life the inmates poor enrol.

Then homeward all take off their sev'ral way ;
    The youngling cottagers retire to rest :
The parent-pair their secret homage pay,
    And proffer up to Heav'n the warm request,
That He who stills the raven's clam'rous nest,
    And decks the lily fair in flow'ry pride,

Would, in the way His wisdom sees the best,
   For them and for their little ones provide ;
But chiefly, in their hearts with grace divine preside.

From scenes like these old Scotia's grandeur springs,
   That makes her lov'd at home, rever'd abroad :
Princes and lords are but the breath of kings,
   ' An honest man's the noblest work of God : '
And certes, in fair virtue's heavenly road,
   The cottage leaves the palace far behind ;
What is a lordling's pomp ? a cumbrous load,
   Disguising oft the wretch of human kind,
Studied in arts of hell, in wickedness refin'd !

O Scotia ! my dear, my native soil !
   For whom my warmest wish to Heaven is sent !
Long may thy hardy sons of rustic toil
   Be blest with health, and peace, and sweet content !
And, Oh, may Heaven their simple lives prevent
   From luxury's contagion, weak and vile ;
Then, howe'er crowns and coronets be rent,
   A virtuous populace may rise the while,
And stand a wall of fire around their much-lov'd Isle.

O Thou ! who pour'd the patriotic tide
   That stream'd thro' Wallace's undaunted heart ;
Who dar'd to, nobly, stem tyrannic pride,
   Or nobly die, the second glorious part,
(The patriot's God, peculiarly thou art,
   His friend, inspirer, guardian, and reward !)
O never, never, Scotia's realm desert,
   But still the patriot, and the patriot-bard,
In bright succession raise, her ornament and guard !

MAN WAS MADE TO MOURN.

A DIRGE.

When chill November's surly blast
   Made fields and forests bare,
One ev'ning as I wander'd forth
   Along the banks of Ayr,
I spy'd a man, whose agèd step
   Seem'd weary, worn with care ;
His face was furrow'd o'er with years,
   And hoary was his hair.

Young stranger, whither wand'rest thou ?
   Began the rev'rend Sage ;
Does thirst of wealth thy step constrain,
   Or youthful pleasure's rage ?
B

Or, haply, prest with cares and woes,
   Too soon thou hast began
To wander forth, with me, to mourn
   The miseries of Man.

The sun that overhangs yon moors,
   Out-spreading far and wide,
Where hundreds labour to support
   A haughty lordling's pride ;
I've seen yon weary winter-sun
   Twice forty times return ;
And ev'ry time has added proofs,
   That Man was made to mourn.
F

O man! while in thy early years,
　How prodigal of time!
Mis-spending all thy precious hours,
　Thy glorious youthful prime!
Alternate follies take the sway;
　Licentious passions burn;
Which tenfold force give nature's law,
　That Man was made to mourn.

Look not alone on youthful prime,
　Or manhood's active might;
Man then is useful to his kind,
　Supported is his right,
But see him on the edge of life,
　With cares and sorrows worn,
Then age and want, Oh! ill-match'd
　　pair!
　Show Man was made to mourn.

A few seem favourites of fate,
　In pleasure's lap carest;
Yet, think not all the rich and great
　Are likewise truly blest.
But, Oh! what crowds in ev'ry land
　Are wretched and forlorn;
Thro' weary life this lesson learn,
　That Man was made to mourn.

Many and sharp the num'rous ills
　Inwoven with our frame!
More pointed still we make ourselves,
　Regret, remorse, and shame!
And man, whose heaven-erected face
　The smiles of love adorn,
Man's inhumanity to man
　Makes countless thousands mourn!

See yonder poor, o'erlabour'd wight,
　So abject, mean, and vile,
Who begs a brother of the earth
　To give him leave to toil;
And see his lordly fellow-worm
　The poor petition spurn,
Unmindful, tho' a weeping wife
　And helpless offspring mourn.

If I'm design'd yon lordling's slave,
　By nature's law design'd,
Why was an independent wish
　E'er planted in my mind?
If not, why am I subject to
　His cruelty, or scorn?
Or why has man the will and pow'r
　To make his fellow mourn?

Yet, let not this too much, my son,
　Disturb thy youthful breast;
This partial view of human-kind
　Is surely not the last!
The poor, oppressèd, honest man,
　Had never, sure, been born,
Had there not been some recompense
　To comfort those that mourn!

O Death! the poor man's dearest friend,
　The kindest and the best!
Welcome the hour my agèd limbs
　Are laid with thee at rest!
The great, the wealthy, fear thy blow,
　From pomp and pleasure torn;
But, Oh! a blest relief to those
　That weary-laden mourn!

╫ A PRAYER, IN THE PROSPECT OF DEATH.

O Thou unknown, Almighty Cause
　Of all my hope and fear!
In whose dread presence, ere an hour,
　Perhaps I must appear!

If I have wander'd in those paths
　Of life I ought to shun;
As something, loudly in my breast,
　Remonstrates I have done;

Thou know'st that Thou hast form'd me
　With passions wild and strong;

And list'ning to their witching voice
　Has often led me wrong.

Where human weakness has come short,
　Or frailty stept aside,
Do thou, All-Good! for such Thou art,
　In shades of darkness hide.

Where with intention I have err'd,
　No other plea I have,
But, Thou art good; and Goodness still
　Delighteth to forgive.

╫ *This is a sickly prayer, and not worthy of a Christian, much less in "the prospect of death". It is Christian neither in sentiment nor Theology. (? Dec. 1898)*

STANZAS ON THE SAME OCCASION.

WHY am I loth to leave this earthly scene?
  Have I so found it full of pleasing charms?
Some drops of joy with draughts of ill between:
  Some gleams of sunshine 'mid renewing storms;
Is it departing pangs my soul alarms?
  Or Death's unlovely, dreary, dark abode?
For guilt, for guilt, my terrors are in arms;
  I tremble to approach an angry God,
And justly smart beneath his sin-avenging rod.

Fain would I say, ' Forgive my foul offence!'
  Fain promise never more to disobey;
But, should my Author health again dispense,
  Again I might desert fair virtue's way;
Again in folly's path might go astray;
  Again exalt the brute, and sink the man;
Then how should I for Heavenly mercy pray,
  Who act so counter Heavenly mercy's plan?
Who sin so oft have mourn'd, yet to temptation ran?

O Thou, great Governor of all below!
  If I may dare a lifted eye to Thee,
Thy nod can make the tempest cease to blow,
  And still the tumult of the raging sea:
With that controlling pow'r assist ev'n me,
  Those headlong furious passions to confine,
For all unfit I feel my powers to be,
  To rule their torrent in th' allowed line;
O, aid me with Thy help, Omnipotence Divine!

LYING AT A REVEREND FRIEND'S HOUSE ONE NIGHT

THE AUTHOR LEFT THE FOLLOWING VERSES IN THE ROOM
WHERE HE SLEPT.

O THOU dread Pow'r, who reign'st above,
  I know Thou wilt me hear;
When for this scene of peace and love,
  I make my pray'r sincere.

The hoary sire—the mortal stroke,
  Long, long, be pleas'd to spare;
To bless his little filial flock,
  And show what good men are.

She, who her lovely offspring eyes
  With tender hopes and fears,
O, bless her with a mother's joys,
  But spare a mother's tears!

Their hope, their stay, their darling youth,
  In manhood's dawning blush;
Bless him, thou God of love and truth,
  Up to a parent's wish.

The beauteous, seraph sister-band,
  With earnest tears I pray,
Thou know'st the snares on ev'ry hand,
  Guide Thou their steps alway.

When soon or late they reach that coast,
  O'er life's rough ocean driven,
May they rejoice, no wand'rer lost,
  A family in Heaven!

THE FIRST PSALM.

THE man, in life wherever plac'd,
  Hath happiness in store,
Who walks not in the wicked's way,
  Nor learns their guilty lore :

Nor from the seat of scornful pride
  Casts forth his eyes abroad,
But with humility and awe
  Still walks before his God.

That man shall flourish like the trees
  Which by the streamlets grow ;

The fruitful top is spread on high,
  And firm the root below.

But he whose blossom buds in guilt
  Shall to the ground be cast,
And like the rootless stubble tost,
  Before the sweeping blast.

For why ? that God the good adore
  Hath giv'n them peace and rest,
But hath decreed that wicked men
  Shall ne'er be truly blest.

A PRAYER, UNDER THE PRESSURE OF VIOLENT
ANGUISH.

O THOU great Being ! what Thou art
  Surpasses me to know :
Yet sure I am, that known to Thee
  Are all Thy works below.

Thy creature here before Thee stands,
  All wretched and distrest ;
Yet sure those ills that wring my soul
  Obey Thy high behest.

Sure, Thou, Almighty, canst not act
  From cruelty or wrath !
O, free my weary eyes from tears,
  Or close them fast in death !

But if I must afflicted be,
  To suit some wise design ;
Then, man my soul with firm resolves
  To bear and not repine !

THE FIRST SIX VERSES OF THE NINETIETH PSALM.

O THOU, the first, the greatest friend
  Of all the human race !
Whose strong right hand has ever been
  Their stay and dwelling-place !

Before the mountains heav'd their heads
  Beneath Thy forming hand,
Before this ponderous globe itself
  Arose at Thy command ;

That pow'r which rais'd and still upholds
  This universal frame,
From countless, unbeginning time
  Was ever still the same.

Those mighty periods of years
  Which seem to us so vast,

Appear no more before Thy sight
  Than yesterday that's past.

Thou giv'st the word ; Thy creature, man,
  Is to existence brought ;
Again Thou say'st, ' Ye sons of men,
  Return ye into nought !'

Thou layest them, with all their cares,
  In everlasting sleep ;
As with a flood thou tak'st them off
  With overwhelming sweep.

They flourish like the morning flow'r,
  In beauty's pride array'd ;
But long ere night cut down it lies
  All wither'd and decay'd.

TO A MOUNTAIN DAISY,

ON TURNING ONE DOWN WITH THE PLOUGH, IN APRIL, 1786.

WEE, modest, crimson-tippèd flow'r,
Thou's met me in an evil hour ;
For I maun crush amang the stoure
  Thy slender stem.
To spare thee now is past my pow'r,
  Thou bonie gem.

Alas ! it's no thy neebor sweet,
The bonie Lark, companion meet !
Bending thee 'mang the dewy weet !
  Wi' spreckl'd breast,
When upward-springing, blythe, to greet
  The purpling east.

Cauld blew the bitter-biting north
Upon thy early, humble birth ;
Yet cheerfully thou glinted forth
  Amid the storm,
Scarce rear'd above the parent-earth
  Thy tender form.

The flaunting flow'rs our gardens yield,
High shelt'ring woods and wa's maun shield,
But thou, beneath the random bield
  O' clod or stane,
Adorns the histie stibble-field,
  Unseen, alane.

There, in thy scanty mantle clad,
Thy snawie bosom sun-ward spread,

Thou lifts thy unassuming head
  In humble guise ;
But now the share uptears thy bed,
  And low thou lies !

Such is the fate of artless Maid,
Sweet flow'ret of the rural shade !
By love's simplicity betray'd,
  And guileless trust,
Till she, like thee, all soil'd, is laid
  Low i' the dust.

Such is the fate of simple Bard,
On life's rough ocean luckless starr'd !
Unskilful he to note the card
  Of prudent lore,
Till billows rage, and gales blow hard,
  And whelm him o'er !

Such fate to suffering worth is giv'n,
Who long with wants and woes has striv'n,
By human pride or cunning driv'n
  To mis'ry's brink,
Till wrench'd of ev'ry stay but Heav'n,
  He, ruin'd, sink !

Ev'n thou who mourn'st the Daisy's fate,
That fate is thine—no distant date ;
Stern Ruin's ploughshare drives, elate,
  Full on thy bloom,
Till crush'd beneath the furrow's weight,
  Shall be thy doom !

TO RUIN.

ALL hail ! inexorable lord !
At whose destruction-breathing word
 The mightiest empires fall !
Thy cruel, woe-delighted train,
The ministers of grief and pain,
 A sullen welcome, all !
With stern-resolv'd, despairing eye,
 I see each aimèd dart ;
For one has cut my dearest tie,
 And quivers in my heart.
  Then low'ring, and pouring,
   The storm no more I dread ;
  Tho' thick'ning and black'ning
   Round my devoted head

And, thou grim pow'r, by life abhorr'd,
While life a pleasure can afford,
 Oh ! hear a wretch's pray'r !
No more I shrink appall'd, afraid ;
I court, I beg thy friendly aid,
 To close this scene of care !
When shall my soul, in silent peace,
 Resign life's joyless day ;
My weary heart its throbbings cease,
 Cold-mould'ring in the clay ?
  No fear more, no tear more,
   To stain my lifeless face,
  Enclasped, and grasped
   Within thy cold embrace !

TO MISS LOGAN, WITH BEATTIE'S POEMS,

FOR A NEW YEAR'S GIFT, JANUARY 1, 1787.

AGAIN the silent wheels of time
  Their annual round have driv'n,
And you, tho' scarce in maiden prime,
  Are so much nearer Heav'n.

No gifts have I from Indian coasts
  The infant year to hail ;

I send you more than India boasts,
  In Edwin's simple tale.

Our sex with guile and faithless love
  Is charg'd, perhaps too true ;
But may, dear Maid, each lover prove
  An Edwin still to you !

EPISTLE TO A YOUNG FRIEND.

MAY, 1786.

I LANG hae thought, my youthfu' friend,
  A something to have sent you,
Tho' it should serve nae ither end
  Than just a kind memento ;
But how the subject theme may gang,
  Let time and chance determine ;
Perhaps, it may turn out a sang,
  Perhaps, turn out a sermon.

Ye'll try the world soon, my lad,
  And, Andrew dear, believe me,
Ye'll find mankind an unco squad,
  And muckle they may grieve ye :
For care and trouble set your thought,
  Ev'n when your end 's attained ;
And a' your views may come to nought,
  Where ev'ry nerve is strained.

I'll no say, men are villains a' ;
  The real, harden'd wicked,
Wha hae nae check but human law,
  Are to a few restricked :
But Och ! mankind are unco weak,
  An' little to be trusted ;
If self the wavering balance shake,
  It's rarely right adjusted !

Yet they wha fa' in fortune's strife,
  Their fate we should na censure,
For still th' important end of life
  They equally may answer ;
A man may hae an honest heart,
  Tho' poortith hourly stare him ;
A man may tak a neebor's part,
  Yet hae nae cash to spare him.

Aye free, aff han' your story tell,
  When wi' a bosom crony ;
But still keep something to yoursel
  Ye scarcely tell to ony.
Conceal yoursel as weel 's ye can
  Frae critical dissection ;
But keek thro' ev'ry other man,
  Wi' sharpen'd, sly inspection.

The sacred lowe o' weel-plac'd love,
  Luxuriantly indulge it ;
But never tempt th' illicit rove,
  Tho' naething should divulge it ;
I wave the quantum o' the sin,
  The hazard o' concealing ;
But Och ! it hardens a' within,
  And petrifies the feeling !

To catch dame Fortune's golden smile,
  Assiduous wait upon her ;
And gather gear by ev'ry wile
  That 's justify'd by honour ;
Not for to hide it in a hedge,
  Nor for a train attendant ;
But for the glorious privilege
  Of being independent.

The fear o' hell 's a hangman's whip,
  To haud the wretch in order ;
But where ye feel your honour grip,
  Let that aye be your border :
Its slightest touches, instant pause—
  Debar a' side pretences ;
And resolutely keep its laws,
  Uncaring consequences.

The great Creator to revere,
　Must sure become the creature ;
But still the preaching cant forbear,
　And ev'n the rigid feature :
Yet ne'er with wits profane to range,
　Be complaisance extended ;
An Atheist-laugh's a poor exchange
　For Deity offended !

When ranting round in pleasure's ring,
　Religion may be blinded ;
Or if she gie a random sting,
　It may be little minded ;

But when on life we're tempest-driv'n,
　A conscience but a canker—
A correspondence fix'd wi' Heav'n
　Is sure a noble anchor !

Adieu, dear, amiable Youth !
　Your heart can ne'er be wanting !
May prudence, fortitude, and truth,
　Erect your brow undaunting !
In ploughman phrase, ' God send you
　Still daily to grow wiser ;　[speed,'
And may ye better reck the rede,
　Than ever did th' Adviser !

ON A SCOTCH BARD, GONE TO THE WEST INDIES.

A' YE wha live by sowps o' drink,
A' ye wha live by crambo-clink,
A' ye wha live an' never think,
　　　Come mourn wi' me !
Our billie's gi'en us a' a jink,
　　　An' owre the sea.

Lament him a' ye rantin core,
Wha dearly like a random-splore,
Nae mair he'll join the merry roar,
　　　In social key ;
For now he's taen anither shore,
　　　An' owre the sea !

The bonie lasses weel may wiss him,
And in their dear petitions place him :
The widows, wives, an' a' may bless him,
　　　Wi' tearfu' e'e ;
For weel I wat they'll sairly miss him
　　　That's owre the sea !

O Fortune, they hae room to grumble !
Hadst thou taen aff some drowsy bummle,
Wha can do nought but fyke an' fumble,
　　　'Twad been nae plea ;
But he was gleg as onie wumble,
　　　That's owre the sea !

Auld, cantie Kyle may weepers wear,
An' stain them wi' the saut, saut tear :
'Twill mak her poor, auld heart, I fear,
　　　In flinders flee ;
He was her Laureat monie a year
　　　That's owre the sea !

He saw misfortune's cauld nor-west
Lang mustering up a bitter blast ;
A jillet brak his heart at last,
　　　Ill may she be !
So, took a berth afore the mast,
　　　An' owre the sea.

To tremble under Fortune's cummock,
On scarce a bellyfu' o' drummock,
Wi' his proud, independent stomach,
　　　Could ill agree ;
So, row't his hurdies in a hammock,
　　　An' owre the sea.

He ne'er was gi'en to great misguidin',
Yet coin his pouches wad na bide in ;
Wi' him it ne'er was under hidin',
　　　He dealt it free :
The Muse was a' that he took pride in,
　　　That's owre the sea.

Jamaica bodies, use him weel,
An' hap him in a cozie biel ;
Ye'll find him ay' a dainty chiel,
　　　And fu' o' glee ;
He wad na wrang'd the vera deil,
　　　That's owre the sea.

Fareweel, my rhyme-composing billie !
Your native soil was right ill-willie ;
But may ye flourish like a lily,
　　　Now bonilie !
I'll toast ye in my hindmost gillie,
　　　Tho' owre the sea !

TO A HAGGIS.

FAIR fa' your honest, sonsie face,
Great chieftain o' the puddin-race !
Aboon them a' ye tak your place,
    Painch, tripe, or thairm :
Weel are ye wordy o' a grace
    As lang's my arm.

The groaning trencher there ye fill,
Your hurdies like a distant hill,
Your pin wad help to mend a mill
    In time o' need,
While thro' your pores the dews distil
    Like amber bead.

His knife see rustic labour dight,
An' cut you up wi' ready slight,
Trenching your gushing entrails bright
    Like onie ditch ;
And then, O what a glorious sight,
    Warm-reekin, rich !

Then, horn for horn they stretch an'
    strive,
Deil tak the hindmost, on they drive,
Till a' their weel-swall'd kytes belyve
    Are bent like drums ;
Then auld guidman, maist like to rive,
    Bethankit hums.

Is there that o'er his French ragout,
Or olio that wad staw a sow,
Or fricassee wad mak her spew
    Wi' perfect sconner,
Looks down wi' sneering, scornfu' view
    On sic a dinner !

Poor devil ! see him owre his trash,
As feckless as a wither'd rash,
His spindle shank a guid whip-lash,
    His nieve a nit :
Thro' bloody flood or field to dash,
    O how unfit !

But mark the rustic, haggis-fed,
The trembling earth resounds his tread,
Clap in his walie nieve a blade,
    He'll mak it whissle ;
An' legs, an' arms, an' heads will sned,
    Like taps o' thrissle.

Ye Pow'rs, wha mak mankind your care,
And dish them out their bill o' fare,
Auld Scotland wants nae stinking ware
    That jaups in luggies ;
But, if ye wish her gratefu' prayer,
    Gie her a Haggis !

A DEDICATION TO GAVIN HAMILTON, ESQ.

EXPECT na, Sir, in this narration,
A fleechin, fleth'rin Dedication,
To roose you up, an' ca' you guid,
An' sprung o' great an' noble bluid,
Because ye're sirnam'd like his Grace,
Perhaps related to the race ;
Then when I'm tir'd—and sae are ye,
Wi' mony a fulsome, sinfu' lie,
Set up a face, how I stop short,
For fear your modesty be hurt.

    This may do—maun do, Sir, wi' them
      wha   [fou ;
Maun please the great folk for a wame-
For me ! sae laigh I needna bow,

For, Lord be thankit, I can plough ;
And when I downa yoke a naig,
Then, Lord be thankit, I can beg ;
Sae I shall say, an' that's nae flatt'rin,
It's just sic Poet an' sic Patron.

    The Poet, some guid angel help him,
Or else, I fear, some ill ane skelp him !
He may do weel for a' he's done yet,
But only—he's no just begun yet.

    The Patron (Sir, ye maun forgie me,
I winna lie, come what will o' me),
On ev'ry hand it will allow'd be,
He's just—nae better than he should be.

I readily and freely grant,
He downa see a poor man want ;
What's no his ain he winna tak it,
What ance he says he winna break it ;
Ought he can lend he'll not refus't,
Till aft his guidness is abus'd ;
And rascals whyles that do him wrang,
Ev'n that, he does na mind it lang :
As master, landlord, husband, father,
He does na fail his part in either.

But then, nae thanks to him for a'
    that ;
Nae godly symptom ye can ca' that ;
It's naething but a milder feature
Of our poor, sinfu', corrupt nature :
Ye'll get the best o' moral works,
'Mang black Gentoos and pagan Turks,
Or hunters wild on Ponotaxi,
Wha never heard of orthodoxy.
That he's the poor man's friend in need,
The gentleman in word and deed,
It's no thro' terror of damnation ;
It's just a carnal inclination.

Morality, thou deadly bane,
Thy tens o' thousands thou hast slain !
Vain is his hope, whase stay and trust is
In moral mercy, truth, and justice !

No—stretch a point to catch a plack ;
Abuse a brother to his back ;
Steal thro' the winnock frae a whore,
But point the rake that taks the door :
Be to the poor like onie whunstane,
And haud their noses to the grunstane,
Ply ev'ry art o' legal thieving ;
No matter—stick to sound believing.

Learn three-mile pray'rs, an' half-
    mile graces,
Wi' weel-spread looves, an' lang, wry
    faces ;
Grunt up a solemn, lengthen'd groan,
And damn a' parties but your own ;
I'll warrant then, ye're nae deceiver,
A steady, sturdy, staunch believer.

O ye wha leave the springs of Calvin,
For gumlie dubs of your ain delvin !
Ye sons of heresy and error,
Ye'll some day squeel in quaking terror !

When vengeance draws the sword in
    wrath,
And in the fire throws the sheath ;
When Ruin, with his sweeping besom,
Just frets till Heav'n commission gies
    him :
While o'er the harp pale mis'ry moans, ⎞
And strikes the ever-deep'ning tones, ⎬
Still louder shrieks, and heavier groans ! ⎠

Your pardon, Sir, for this digression,
I maist forgat my Dedication ;
But when divinity comes 'cross me,
My readers still are sure to lose me.

So, Sir, ye see 'twas nae daft vapour,
But I maturely thought it proper,
When a' my works I did review,
To dedicate them, Sir, to You :
Because (ye need na tak it ill)
I thought them something like yoursel.

Then patronize them wi' your favour,
And your petitioner shall ever—
I had amaist said, ever pray :
But that's a word I need na say :
For prayin I hae little skill o't ;
I'm baith dead-sweer, an' wretched
    ill o't ;
But I'se repeat each poor man's pray'r,
That kens or hears about you, Sir.—

' May ne'er misfortune's gowling bark
Howl thro' the dwelling o' the Clerk !
May ne'er his gen'rous, honest heart,
For that same gen'rous spirit smart !
May Kennedy's far-honour'd name
Lang beet his hymeneal flame,
Till Hamiltons, at least a dizen,
Are frae their nuptial labours risen :
Five bonie lasses round their table,
And seven braw fellows, stout an' able,
To serve their King and Country weel,
By word, or pen, or pointed steel !
May health and peace, with mutual rays,
Shine on the evening o' his days ;
Till his wee, curlie John's ier-oe, ⎞
When ebbing life nae mair shall flow, ⎬
The last, sad, mournful rites bestow !' ⎠

I will not wind a lang conclusion,
Wi' complimentary effusion :

But whilst your wishes and endeavours
Are blest with Fortune's smiles and
    favours,
I am, dear Sir, with zeal most fervent,
Your much indebted, humble servant.

But if (which Pow'rs above prevent)
That iron-hearted carl, Want,
Attended in his grim advances,
By sad mistakes, and black mischances,
While hopes, and joys, and pleasures
    fly him,

Make you as poor a dog as I am,
Your humble servant then no more;
For who would humbly serve the poor?
But, by a poor man's hopes in Heav'n!
While recollection's pow'r is given,
If, in the vale of humble life,
The victim sad of fortune's strife,
I, thro' the tender gushing tear,
Should recognise my Master dear,
If friendless, low, we meet together,
Then, Sir, your hand—my Friend and
    Brother!

TO A LOUSE, ON SEEING ONE ON A LADY'S BONNET, AT CHURCH.

HA! whare ye gaun, ye crowlin ferlie!
Your impudence protects you sairly:
I canna say but ye strunt rarely,
    Owre gauze and lace;
Tho' faith, I fear ye dine but sparely
    On sic a place.

Ye ugly, creepin, blastit wonner,
Detested, shunn'd by saunt an' sinner,
How dare ye set your fit upon her,
    Sae fine a lady!
Gae somewhere else, and seek your
    dinner
    On some poor body.

Swith, in some beggar's haffet squattle;
There ye may creep, and sprawl, and
    sprattle
Wi' ither kindred, jumping cattle,
    In shoals and nations;
Whare horn nor bane ne'er dare unsettle
    Your thick plantations.

Now haud ye there, ye're out o' sight,
Below the fatt'rels, snug an' tight;
Na, faith ye yet! ye'll no be right
    Till ye've got on it,
The vera tapmost, tow'ring height
    O' Miss's bonnet.

My sooth! right bauld ye set your nose
    out,
As plump and gray as onie grozet;
O for some rank, mercurial rozet,
    Or fell, red smeddum,
I'd gie you sic a hearty doze o't,
    Wad dress your droddum!

I wad na been surpris'd to spy
You on an auld wife's flainen toy;
Or aiblins some bit duddie boy,
    On's wyliecoat;
But Miss's fine Lunardi! fie,
    How daur ye do't?

O, Jenny, dinna toss your head,
An' set your beauties a' abread!
Ye little ken what cursed speed
    The blastie's makin!
Thae winks and finger-ends, I dread,
    Are notice takin!

O wad some Pow'r the giftie gie us
To see oursels as others see us!
It wad frae monie a blunder free us
    And foolish notion:
What airs in dress an' gait wad lea'e us,
    And ev'n Devotion!

ADDRESS TO EDINBURGH.

EDINA ! Scotia's darling seat !
  All hail thy palaces and tow'rs,
Where once beneath a monarch's feet
  Sat Legislation's sov'reign pow'rs !
From marking wildly-scatter'd flow'rs,
  As on the banks of Ayr I stray'd,
And singing, lone, the ling'ring hours,
  I shelter in thy honour'd shade.

Here Wealth still swells the golden tide,
  As busy Trade his labours plies ;
There Architecture's noble pride
  Bids elegance and splendour rise ;
Here Justice, from her native skies,
  High wields her balance and her rod ;
There Learning, with his eagle eyes,
  Seeks Science in her coy abode.

Thy sons, Edina, social, kind,
  With open arms the stranger hail ;
Their views enlarg'd, their lib'ral mind,
  Above the narrow, rural vale ;
Attentive still to sorrow's wail,
  Or modest merit's silent claim :
And never may their sources fail !
  And never envy blot their name !

Thy daughters bright thy walks adorn,
  Gay as the gilded summer sky,
Sweet as the dewy milk-white thorn,
  Dear as the raptur'd thrill of joy !
Fair Burnet strikes th' adoring eye,
  Heaven's beauties on my fancy shine ;
I see the Sire of Love on high,
  And own his work indeed divine !

There watching high the least alarms,
  Thy rough, rude fortress gleams afar ;
Like some bold vet'ran, gray in arms,
  And mark'd with many a seamy scar :
The pond'rous wall and massy bar,
  Grim-rising o'er the rugged rock,
Have oft withstood assailing war,
  And oft repell'd th' invader's shock.

With awe-struck thought, and pitying
  tears,
  I view that noble, stately dome,
Where Scotia's kings of other years,
  Fam'd heroes, had their royal home :
Alas, how chang'd the times to come !
  Their royal name low in the dust !
Their hapless race wild-wand'ring roam !
  Tho' rigid law cries out, 'twas just !

Wild beats my heart, to trace your steps,
  Whose ancestors, in days of yore,
Thro' hostile ranks and ruin'd gaps
  Old Scotia's bloody lion bore :
Ev'n I who sing in rustic lore,
  Haply my sires have left their shed,
And fac'd grim danger's loudest roar,
  Bold-following where your fathers led !

Edina ! Scotia's darling seat !
  All hail thy palaces and tow'rs,
Where once beneath a monarch's feet
  Sat Legislation's sov'reign pow'rs !
From marking wildly-scatter'd flow'rs,
  As on the banks of Ayr I stray'd,
And singing, lone, the ling'ring hours,
  I shelter in thy honour'd shade.

EPISTLE TO JOHN LAPRAIK, AN OLD SCOTTISH BARD.

APRIL. 1, 1785.

WHILE briers an' woodbines budding
    green,
An' paitricks scraichin loud at e'en,
An' morning poussie whiddin seen,
      Inspire my Muse,
This freedom, in an unknown frien'
      I pray excuse.

On Fasten-een we had a rockin,
To ca' the crack and weave our stock-
    in ;
And there was muckle fun and jokin,
      Ye need na doubt ;
At length we had a hearty yokin
      At sang about.

There was ae sang, amang the rest,
Aboon them a' it pleas'd me best,
That some kind husband had addrest
  To some sweet wife :
It thirl'd the heart-strings thro' the breast,
  A' to the life.

I've scarce heard ought describ'd sae weel,
What gen'rous, manly bosoms feel ;
Thought I, 'Can this be Pope, or Steele,
  Or Beattie's wark !'
They tald me 'twas an odd kind chiel
  About Muirkirk.

It pat me fidgin-fain to hear't.
And sae about him there I spier't ;
Then a' that ken'd him round declar'd
  He had ingine,
That nane excell'd it, few cam near't,
  It was sae fine.

That, set him to a pint of ale,
An' either douce or merry tale,
Or rhymes an' sangs he'd made himsel,
  Or witty catches,
'Tween Inverness and Tiviotdale,
  He had few matches.

Then up I gat, an' swoor an aith,
Tho' I should pawn my pleugh and graith,
Or die a cadger pownie's death,
  At some dyke-back,
A pint an' gill I'd gie them baith
  To hear your crack.

But, first an' foremost, I should tell,
Amaist as soon as I could spell,
I to the crambo-jingle fell,
  Tho' rude an' rough,
Yet crooning to a body's sel,
  Does weel eneugh.

I am nae Poet, in a sense,
But just a Rhymer, like, by chance,
An' hae to learning nae pretence,
  Yet, what the matter ?
Whene'er my Muse does on me glance,
  I jingle at her.

Your critic-folk may cock their nose,
And say, ' How can you e'er propose,
You wha ken hardly verse frae prose,
  To mak a sang ?'
But, by your leaves, my learned foes,
  Ye're maybe wrang.

What's a' your jargon o' your schools,
Your Latin names for horns an' stools ;
If honest nature made you fools,
  What sairs your grammars ?
Ye'd better ta'en up spades and shools,
  Or knappin-hammers.

A set o' dull, conceited hashes,
Confuse their brains in college classes !
They gang in stirks, and come out asses,
  Plain truth to speak ;
An' syne they think to climb Parnassus
  By dint o' Greek!

Gie me ae spark o' Nature's fire,
That's a' the learning I desire ;
Then tho' I drudge thro' dub an' mire
  At pleugh or cart,
My Muse, though hamely in attire,
  May touch the heart.

O for a spunk o' Allan's glee,
Or Ferguson's, the bauld an' slee,
Or bright Lapraik's, my friend to be,
  If I can hit it !
That would be lear eneugh for me,
  If I could get it.

Now, Sir, if ye hae friends enow,
Tho' real friends, I b'lieve, are few,
Yet, if your catalogue be fou,
  I'se no insist,
But gif ye want ae friend that's true,
  I'm on your list.

I winna blaw about mysel,
As ill I like my fauts to tell ;
But friends, an' folks that wish me well,
  They sometimes roose me ;
Tho' I maun own, as monie still
  As far abuse me.

There's ae wee faut they whiles lay to me,
I like the lasses—Gude forgie me !
For monie a plack they wheedle frae me,

At dance or fair ;
Maybe some ither thing they gie me
They weel can spare.

But Mauchline race, or Mauchline fair,
I should be proud to meet you there ;
We'se gie ae night's discharge to care,
 If we forgather,
An' hae a swap o' rhymin-ware
 Wi' ane anither.

The four-gill chap, we'se gar him clatter,
An' kirsen him wi' reekin water ;
Syne we'll sit down an' tak our whitter,
 To cheer our heart ;
An' faith, we'se be acquainted better
 Before we part.

Awa, ye selfish, warly race,
Wha think that havins, sense, an' grace,

Ev'n love an' friendship, should give
 place
 To catch-the-plack !
I dinna like to see your face,
 Nor hear your crack.

But ye whom social pleasure charms,
Whose hearts the tide of kindness warms,
Who hold your being on the terms,
 ' Each aid the others,'
Come to my bowl, come to my arms,
 My friends, my brothers !

But to conclude my lang epistle,
As my auld pen's worn to the grissle ;
Twa lines frae you wad gar me fissle,
 Who am, most fervent,
While I can either sing, or whissle,
 Your friend and servant.

TO THE SAME.

April 21, 1785.

While new-ca'd kye rowte at the stake,
An' pownies reek in pleugh or braik,
This hour on e'enin's edge I take,
 To own I'm debtor,
To honest-hearted, auld Lapraik,
 For his kind letter.

Forjesket sair, with weary legs,
Rattlin the corn out-owre the rigs,
Or dealing thro' amang the naigs
 Their ten-hours' bite,
My awkart Muse sair pleads and begs,
 I would na write.

The tapetless, ramfeezl'd hizzie,
She's saft at best, and something lazy,
Quo' she, ' Ye ken, we've been sae busy,
 This month an' mair,
That trouth my head is grown quite
 dizzie,
 An' something sair.'

Her dowff excuses pat me mad ;
' Conscience,' says I, ' ye thowless jad !
I'll write, an' that a hearty blaud,
 This vera night ;
So dinna ye affront your trade,
 But rhyme it right.

' Shall bauld Lapraik, the king o' hearts,
Tho' mankind were a pack o' cartes,
Roose you sae weel for your deserts,
 In terms sae friendly,
Yet ye'll neglect to shaw your parts,
 An' thank him kindly ! '

Sae I gat paper in a blink,
An' down gaed stumpie in the ink :
Quoth I, ' Before I sleep a wink,
 I vow I'll close it ;
An' if ye winna mak it clink,
 By Jove I'll prose it ! '

Sae I've begun to scrawl, but whether
In rhyme, or prose, or baith thegither,
Or some hotch-potch that's rightly
 neither,
 Let time mak proof ;
But I shall scribble down some blether
 Just clean aff-loof.

My worthy friend, ne'er grudge an' carp,
Tho' fortune use you hard an' sharp ;
Come, kittle up your moorland harp
 Wi' gleesome touch !
Ne'er mind how fortune waft an' warp ;
 She's but a bitch.

She's gien me monie a jirt an' fleg,
Sin' I could striddle owre a rig ;
But, by the Lord, tho' I should beg
    Wi' lyart pow,
I'll laugh, an' sing, an' shake my leg,
    As lang's I dow !

Now comes the sax an' twentieth simmer,
I've seen the bud upo' the timmer,
Still persecuted by the limmer
    Frae year to year :
But yet, despite the kittle kimmer,
    I, Rob, am here.

Do ye envy the city Gent,
Behind a kist to lie an' sklent,
Or purse-proud, big wi' cent per cent ;
    An' muckle wame,
In some bit Brugh to represent
    A Bailie's name ?

Or is't the paughty, feudal Thane,
Wi' ruffl'd sark an' glancing cane,
Wha thinks himsel nae sheep-shank bane,
    But lordly stalks,
While caps and bonnets aff are taen,
    As by he walks ?

' O Thou wha gies us each guid gift !
Gie me o' wit an' sense a lift,
Then turn me, if Thou please, adrift,
    Thro' Scotland wide ;
Wi' cits nor lairds I wadna shift,
    In a' their pride ! '

Were this the charter of our state,
' On pain o' hell be rich an' great,'
Damnation then would be our fate,
    Beyond remead ;
But, thanks to Heaven ! that's no the gate
    We learn our creed.

For thus the royal mandate ran,
When first the human race began,
' The social, friendly, honest man,
    Whate'er he be,
'Tis he fulfils great Nature's plan,
    And none but he ! '

O mandate glorious and divine !
The followers of the ragged Nine,
Poor, thoughtless devils ! yet may shine,
    In glorious light,
While sordid sons of Mammon's line
    Are dark as night.

Tho' here they scrape, an' squeeze, an'
    growl,
Their worthless nievefu' of a soul
May in some future carcase howl,
    The forest's fright ;
Or in some day-detesting owl
    May shun the light.

Then may Lapraik and Burns arise,
To reach their native, kindred skies,
And sing their pleasures, hopes, an' joys,
    In some mild sphere,
Still closer knit in friendship's ties
    Each passing year !

TO WILLIAM SIMPSON.

OCHILTREE.

May, 1785.

I GAT your letter, winsome Willie ;
Wi' gratefu' heart I thank you brawlie;
Tho' I maun say't, I wad be silly,
    An' unco vain,
Should I believe, my coaxin billie,
    Your flatterin strain.

But I'se believe ye kindly meant it,
I sud be laith to think ye hinted
Ironic satire, sidelins sklented
    On my poor Musie ;
Tho' in sic phraisin terms ye've penn'd it,
    I scarce excuse ye.

My senses wad be in a creel,
Should I but dare a hope to speel,
Wi' Allan, or wi' Gilbertfield,
    The braes o' fame ;
Or Ferguson, the writer-chiel,
    A deathless name.

(O Ferguson ! thy glorious parts
Ill suited law's dry, musty arts !
My curse upon your whunstane hearts,
    Ye Enbrugh Gentry !
The tythe o' what ye waste at cartes
    Wad stow'd his pantry !)

Yet when a tale comes i' my head,
Or lasses gie my heart a screed,
As whiles they're like to be my dead,
    (O sad disease!)
I kittle up my rustic reed;
    It gies me ease.

Auld Coila, now, may fidge fu' fain,
She's gotten Poets o' her ain,
Chiels wha their chanters winna hain,
    But tune their lays,
Till echoes a' resound again
    Her weel-sung praise.

Nae Poet thought her worth his while,
To set her name in measur'd style;
She lay like some unkend-of isle,
    Beside New Holland,
Or whare wild-meeting oceans boil
    Besouth Magellan.

Ramsay an' famous Ferguson
Gied Forth an' Tay a lift aboon;
Yarrow an' Tweed, to monie a tune,
    Owre Scotland rings,
While Irwin, Lugar, Ayr, an' Doon,
    Naebody sings.

Th' Ilissus, Tiber, Thames, an' Seine,
Glide sweet in monie a tunefu' line!
But, Willie, set your fit to mine,
    An' cock your crest,
We'll gar our streams an' burnies shine
    Up wi' the best.

We'll sing auld Coila's plains an' fells,
Her moors red-brown wi' heather bells,
Her banks an' braes, her dens an' dells,
    Where glorious Wallace
Aft bure the gree, as story tells,
    Frae Southron billies.

At Wallace' name, what Scottish blood
But boils up in a spring-tide flood!
Oft have our fearless fathers strode
    By Wallace' side,
Still pressing onward, red-wat-shod,
    Or glorious dy'd.

O, sweet are Coila's haughs an' woods,
When lintwhites chant amang the buds,
And jinkin hares, in amorous whids,
    Their loves enjoy,
While thro' the braes the cushat croods
    Wi' wailfu' cry!

Ev'n winter bleak has charms to me
When winds rave thro' the naked tree;
Or frosts on hills of Ochiltree
    Are hoary gray;
Or blinding drifts wild-furious flee,
    Dark'ning the day!

O Nature! a' thy shews an' forms
To feeling, pensive hearts hae charms!
Whether the summer kindly warms,
    Wi' life an' light,
Or winter howls, in gusty storms,
    The lang, dark night!

The Muse, na Poet ever fand her,
Till by himsel he learn'd to wander,
Adown some trottin burn's meander,
    An' no think lang;
O sweet, to stray an' pensive ponder
    A heart-felt sang!

The warly race may drudge an' drive,
Hog-shouther, jundie, stretch, an' strive,
Let me fair Nature's face descrive,
    And I, wi' pleasure,
Shall let the busy, grumbling hive
    Bum owre their treasure.

Fareweel, 'my rhyme-composing brither!'
We've been owre lang unkenn'd to ither:
Now let us lay our heads thegither,
    In love fraternal:
May Envy wallop in a tether,
    Black fiend, infernal!

While Highlandmen hate tolls an' taxes;
While moorlan' herds like guid, fat
    braxies;
While Terra Firma, on her axis,
    Diurnal turns,
Count on a friend, in faith an' practice,
    In Robert Burns.

POSTSCRIPT

My memory's no worth a preen;
I had amaist forgotten clean,
Ye bade me write you what they mean
            By this New-Light,
'Bout which our herds sae aft have been
            Maist like to fight.

In days when mankind were but callans
At grammar, logic, an' sic talents,
They took nae pains their speech to
            balance,
            Or rules to gie,
But spak their thoughts in plain, braid
            Lallans,
            Like you or me.

In thae auld times, they thought the
            moon,
Just like a sark, or pair o' shoon,
Wore by degrees, till her last roon,
            Gaed past their viewin,
An' shortly after she was done,
            They gat a new one.

This past for certain, undisputed;
It ne'er cam i' their heads to doubt it,
Till chiels gat up an' wad confute it,
            An' ca'd it wrang;
An' muckle din there was about it,
            Baith loud an' lang.

Some herds, weel learn'd upo' the beuk,
Wad threap auld folk the thing misteuk;
For 'twas the auld moon turn'd a neuk,
            An' out o' sight,
An' backlins-comin, to the leuk,
            She grew mair bright.

This was deny'd, it was affirm'd;
The herds an' hissels were alarm'd:
The rev'rend gray-beards rav'd an'
            storm'd,
            That beardless laddies
Should think they better were inform'd
            Than their auld daddies.

Frae less to mair it gaed to sticks;
Frae words an' aiths to clours an' nicks;
An' monie a fallow gat his licks,
            Wi' hearty crunt;
An' some, to learn them for their tricks,
            Were hang'd an' brunt.

This game was play'd in monie lands,
An' auld-light caddies bure sic hands,
That, faith, the youngsters took the sands
            Wi' nimble shanks,
The lairds forbad, by strict commands,
            Sic bluidy pranks.

But new-light herds gat sic a cowe,
Folk thought them ruin'd stick-an-stowe,
Till now amaist on ev'ry knowe
            Ye'll find ane plac'd;
An' some, their new-light fair avow,
            Just quite barefac'd.

Nae doubt the auld-light flocks are
            bleatin;
Their zealous herds are vex'd an' sweatin;
Mysel, I've even seen them greetin
            Wi' girnin spite,
To hear the moon sae sadly lie'd on
            By word an' write.

But shortly they will cowe the louns!
Some auld-light herds in neebor towns
Are mind't, in things they ca' balloons,
            To tak a flight,
An' stay ae month amang the moons,
            An' see them right.

Guid observation they will gie them;
An' when the auld moon's gaun to lea'e
            them,
The hindmost shaird, they'll fetch it wi'
            them,
            Just i' their pouch,
An' when the new-light billies see them,
            I think they'll crouch!

Sae, ye observe that a' this clatter
Is naething but a ' moonshine matter;'
But tho' dull-prose folk Latin splatter
            In logic tulzie,
I hope, we Bardies ken some better
            Than mind sic brulzie.

EPISTLE TO JOHN RANKINE,

ENCLOSING SOME POEMS.

O ROUGH, rude, ready-witted Rankine,
The wale o' cocks for fun an' drinkin !
There's monie godly folks are thinkin,
   Your dreams an' tricks
Will send you, Korah-like, a-sinkin,
   Straught to auld Nick's.

Ye hae sae monie cracks an' cants,
And in your wicked, druken rants,
Ye mak a devil o' the saunts,
   An' fill them fou ;
And then their failings, flaws, an' wants,
   Are a' seen thro'.

Hypocrisy, in mercy spare it !
That holy robe, O dinna tear it !
Spare't for their sakes wha aften wear it,
   The lads in black ;
But your curst wit, when it comes near it,
   Rives't aff their back.

Think, wicked sinner, wha ye're skaithing,
It's just the blue-gown badge an' claithing
O' saunts ; tak that, ye lea'e them naithing
   To ken them by,
Frae ony unregenerate heathen
   Like you or I.

I've sent you here some rhyming ware,
A' that I bargain'd for, an' mair ;
Sae, when ye hae an hour to spare,
   I will expect,
Yon sang, ye'll sen't, wi' cannie care,
   And no neglect.

Tho', faith, sma' heart hae I to sing !
My Muse dow scarcely spread her wing !
I've play'd mysel a bonie spring,
   An' danc'd my fill !
I'd better gaen an' sair't the king
   At Bunker's Hill.

'Twas ae night lately, in my fun,
I gaed a roving wi' the gun,
An' brought a paitrick to the grun,
   A bonie hen,
And, as the twilight was begun,
   Thought nane wad ken.

The poor, wee thing was little hurt ;
I straikit it a wee for sport,
Ne'er thinkin they wad fash me for't ;
   But, Deil-ma-care !
Somebody tells the poacher-court
   The hale affair.

Some auld, us'd hands had ta'en a note,
That sic a hen had got a shot ;
I was suspected for the plot ;
   I scorn'd to lie ;
So gat the whissle o' my groat,
   An' pay't the fee.

But, by my gun, o' guns the wale,
An' by my pouther an' my hail,
An' by my hen, an' by her tail,
   I vow an' swear !
The game shall pay, o'er moor an' dale,
   For this, niest year.

As soon's the clockin-time is by,
An' the wee pouts begun to cry,
Lord, I'se hae sportin by an' by,
   For my gowd guinea ;
Tho' I should herd the buckskin kye
   For't, in Virginia.

Trowth, they had muckle for to blame !
'Twas neither broken wing nor limb,
But twa-three draps about the wame
   Scarce thro' the feathers ;
An' baith a yellow George to claim,
   An' thole their blethers !

It pits me aye as mad's a hare ;
So I can rhyme nor write nae mair ;
But pennyworths again is fair,
   When time's expedient :
Meanwhile I am, respected Sir,
   Your most obedient.

B

G

WRITTEN IN FRIARS-CARSE HERMITAGE,

ON NITH-SIDE.

THOU whom chance may hither lead,
Be thou clad in russet weed,
Be thou deckt in silken stole,
Grave these counsels on thy soul.
 ' Life is but a day at most,
Sprung from night, in darkness lost ;
Hope not sunshine ev'ry hour,
Fear not clouds will always lour.
    As Youth and Love, with sprightly
        dance,
Beneath thy morning star advance,
Pleasure with her syren air
May delude the thoughtless pair ;
Let Prudence bless Enjoyment's cup,
Then raptur'd sip, and sip it up.
    As thy day grows warm and high,
Life's meridian flaming nigh,
Dost thou spurn the humble vale ?
Life's proud summits wouldst thou scale?
Check thy climbing step, elate,
Evils lurk in felon wait :
Dangers, eagle-pinioned, bold,
Soar around each cliffy hold,
While cheerful Peace, with linnet song,
Chants the lowly dells among.
    As the shades of ev'ning close,
Beck'ning thee to long repose ;
As life itself becomes disease,
Seek the chimney-nook of ease.
There ruminate with sober thought,
On all thou'st seen, and heard, and
        wrought ;
And teach the sportive younkers round,
Saws of experience, sage and sound.
Say, man's true, genuine estimate,
The grand criterion of his fate,
Is not—art thou high or low ?
Did thy fortune ebb or flow ?
Did many talents gild thy span ?
Or frugal Nature grudge thee one ?
Tell them, and press it on their mind,
As thou thyself must shortly find,
The smile or frown of awful Heav'n
To Virtue or to Vice is giv'n.
Say, to be just, and kind, and wise,
There solid self-enjoyment lies ;
That foolish, selfish, faithless ways,

Lead to be wretched, vile, and base.
    Thus resign'd and quiet, creep
To the bed of lasting sleep ;
Sleep, whence thou shalt ne'er awake,
Night, where dawn shall never break,
Till future life, future no more,
To light and joy the good restore,
To light and joy unknown before.
    Stranger, go ! Heaven be thy guide !
Quod the Beadsman of Nith-side.

GLENRIDDEL HERMITAGE, *June 28th*, 1788.

FROM THE MS.

THOU whom chance may hither lead,
Be thou clad in russet weed,
Be thou deckt in silken stole,
Grave these maxims on thy soul.
    Life is but a day at most,
Sprung from night, in darkness lost ;
Hope not sunshine every hour,
Fear not clouds will always lour,
Happiness is but a name,
Make content and ease thy aim.
Ambition is a meteor gleam,
Fame, an idle restless dream :
Peace, the tenderest flower of spring ;
Pleasures, insects on the wing ;
Those that sip the dew alone,
Make the butterflies thy own ;
Those that would the bloom devour,
Crush the locusts, save the flower.
For the future be prepar'd,
Guard, wherever thou canst guard ;
But thy utmost duly done,
Welcome what thou canst not shun.
Follies past give thou to air,
Make their consequence thy care :
Keep the name of Man in mind,
And dishonour not thy kind.
Reverence, with lowly heart,
HIM whose wondrous work thou art :
Keep His goodness still in view,
Thy Trust, and Thy Example too.
Stranger, go ! Heaven be thy guide !
Quod the Beadsman of Nithe-side.

ODE, SACRED TO THE MEMORY OF MRS. OSWALD.

DWELLER in yon dungeon dark,
Hangman of creation, mark !
Who in widow-weeds appears,
Laden with unhonour'd years,
Noosing with care a bursting purse,
Baited with many a deadly curse !

STROPHE.

View the wither'd beldam s face —
Can thy keen inspection trace
Aught of humanity's sweet melting
    grace ?
Note that eye, 'tis rheum o'erflows,
Pity's flood there never rose.
See those hands, ne'er stretch'd to save,
Hands that took—but never gave.
Keeper of Mammon's iron chest,
Lo, there she goes, unpitied and unblest
She goes, but not to realms of ever-
    lasting rest !

ANTISTROPHE.

Plunderer of armies, lift thine eyes,
(A while forbear, ye tort'ring fiends,)
Seest thou whose step unwilling hither
    bends ?
No fallen angel, hurl'd from upper skies ;
'Tis thy trusty quondam mate,
Doom'd to share thy fiery fate,
She, tardy, hell-ward plies.

EPODE.

And are they of no more avail,
Ten thousand glitt'ring pounds a year ?
In other worlds can Mammon fail,
Omnipotent as he is here ?
O, bitter mock'ry of the pompous bier,
While down the wretched vital part is
    driv'n !
The cave-lodg'd beggar, with a
    conscience clear,
Expires in rags, unknown, and goes to
    Heav'n.

ELEGY ON CAPT. MATTHEW HENDERSON,

A GENTLEMAN WHO HELD THE PATENT FOR HIS HONOURS IMMEDIATELY FROM ALMIGHTY GOD.

But now his radiant course is run,
For Matthew's course was bright ;
His soul was like the glorious sun,
A matchless, Heav'nly Light.

O DEATH ! thou tyrant fell and bloody !
The meikle devil wi' a woodie
Haurl thee hame to his black smiddie,
    O'er hurcheon hides,
And like stock-fish come o'er his studdie
    Wi' thy auld sides !

He's gane, he's gane ! he's frae us torn,
The ae best fellow e'er was born !
Thee, Matthew, Nature's sel' shall
    mourn
      By wood and wild,
Where, haply, Pity strays forlorn,
    Frae man exil'd.

Ye hills, near neebors o' the starns,
That proudly cock your cresting cairns !
Ye cliffs, the haunts of sailing earns,
    Where echo slumbers !
Come join, ye Nature's sturdiest bairns,
    My wailing numbers !

Mourn, ilka grove the cushat kens !
Ye haz'lly shaws and briery dens !
Ye burnies, wimplin down your glens,
    Wi' toddlin din,
Or foaming strang, wi' hasty stens,
    Frae lin to lin.

Mourn, little harebells o'er the lee ;
Ye stately foxgloves fair to see ;
Ye woodbines hanging bonilie,
 In scented bow'rs ;
Ye roses on your thorny tree,
  The first o' flow'rs.

At dawn, when ev'ry grassy blade
Droops with a diamond at his head,
At ev'n, when beans their fragrance shed,
 I' th' rustling gale,
Ye maukins whiddin thro' the glade,
  Come join my wail.

Mourn, ye wee songsters o' the wood ;
Ye grouse that crap the heather bud ;
Ye curlews calling thro' a clud ;
 Ye whistling plover ;
And mourn, ye whirring paitrick brood ;
  He's gane for ever !

Mourn, sooty coots, and speckled teals,
Ye fisher herons, watching eels ;
Ye duck and drake, wi' airy wheels
 Circling the lake ;
Ye bitterns, till the quagmire reels,
  Rair for his sake.

Mourn, clam'ring craiks at close o' day,
'Mang fields o' flow'ring clover gay ;
And when ye wing your annual way
 Frae our cauld shore,
Tell thae far warlds, wha lies in clay,
  Wham we deplore.

Ye houlets, frae your ivy bow'r,
In some auld tree, or eldritch tow'r,
What time the moon, wi' silent glowr,
 Sets up her horn,
Wail thro' the dreary midnight hour
  Till waukrife morn !

O rivers, forests, hills, and plains !
Oft have ye heard my canty strains :
But now, what else for me remains
 But tales of woe ;
And frae my een the drapping rains
  Maun ever flow.

Mourn, spring, thou darling of the year !
Ilk cowslip cup shall kep a tear :
Thou, simmer, while each corny spear
 Shoots up its head,
Thy gay, green, flow'ry tresses shear,
  For him that's dead !

Thou, autumn, wi' thy yellow hair,
In grief thy sallow mantle tear !
Thou, winter, hurling thro' the air
 The roaring blast,
Wide o'er the naked world declare
  The worth we've lost !

Mourn him, thou sun, great source of
 light !
Mourn, empress of the silent night !
And you, ye twinkling starnies bright,
 My Matthew mourn !
For through your orbs he's ta'en his
 flight,
  Ne'er to return.

O Henderson ! the man ! the brother !
And art thou gone, and gone for ever ?
And hast thou crost that unknown river,
 Life's dreary bound ?
Like thee, where shall I find another,
  The world around ?

Go to your sculptur'd tombs, ye Great,
In a' the tinsel trash o' state !
But by thy honest turf I'll wait,
 Thou man of worth !
And weep thee ae best fellow's fate
  E'er lay in earth.

THE EPITAPH.

Stop, passenger ! my story's brief,
 And truth I shall relate, man ;
I tell nae common tale o' grief,
 For Matthew was a great man.

If thou uncommon merit hast,
 Yet spurn'd at fortune's door, man ;
A look of pity hither cast,
 For Matthew was a poor man.

If thou a noble sodger art,
 That passest by this grave, man,
There moulders here a gallant heart ;
 For Matthew was a brave man.

If thou on men, their works and ways,
  Canst throw uncommon light, man ;
Here lies wha weel had won thy praise,
  For Matthew was a bright man.

If thou at friendship's sacred ca'
  Wad life itself resign, man ;
The sympathetic tear maun fa',
  For Matthew was a kind man.

If thou art staunch without a stain,
  Like the unchanging blue, man ;

This was a kinsman o' thy ain,
  For Matthew was a true man.

If thou hast wit, and fun, and fire,
  And ne'er gude wine did fear, man ;
This was thy billie, dam, and sire,
  For Matthew was a queer man.

If ony whiggish whingin sot,
  To blame poor Matthew dare, man ;
May dool and sorrow be his lot,
  For Matthew was a rare man.

LAMENT OF MARY QUEEN OF SCOTS, ON THE APPROACH OF SPRING.

Now Nature hangs her mantle green
  On every blooming tree,
And spreads her sheets o' daisies white
  Out-owre the grassy lea :
Now Phœbus cheers the crystal streams,
  And glads the azure skies ;
But nought can glad the weary wight
  That fast in durance lies.

Now laverocks wake the merry morn,
  Aloft on dewy wing ;
The merle, in his noontide bow'r,
  Makes woodland echoes ring ;
The mavis mild wi' many a note,
  Sings drowsy day to rest :
In love and freedom they rejoice,
  Wi' care nor thrall opprest.

Now blooms the lily by the bank,
  The primrose down the brae ;
The hawthorn's budding in the glen,
  And milk-white is the slae :
The meanest hind in fair Scotland
  May rove their sweets amang ;
But I, the Queen of a' Scotland,
  Maun lie in prison strang.

I was the Queen o' bonie France,
  Where happy I hae been,
Fu' lightly rase I in the morn,
  As blythe lay down at e'en :

And I'm the sov'reign of Scotland,
  And mony a traitor there ;
Yet here I lie in foreign bands,
  And never-ending care.

But as for thee, thou false woman,
  My sister and my fae,
Grim vengeance, yet, shall whet a sword
  That thro' thy soul shall gae :
The weeping blood in woman's breast
  Was never known to thee ;
Nor th' balm that draps on wounds of woe
  Frae woman's pitying ee.

My son ! my son ! may kinder stars
  Upon thy fortune shine ;
And may those pleasures gild thy reign,
  That ne'er wad blink on mine !
God keep thee frae thy mother's faes,
  Or turn their hearts to thee :
And where thou meet'st thy mother's friend,
  Remember him for me !

Oh ! soon, to me, may summer-suns
  Nae mair light up the morn !
Nae mair, to me, the autumn winds
  Wave o'er the yellow corn !
And in the narrow house o' death
  Let winter round me rave ;
And the next flow'rs that deck the spring,
  Bloom on my peaceful grave !

EPISTLE TO R. GRAHAM, ESQ.

WHEN Nature her great master-piece design'd,
And fram'd her last, best work, the human mind,
Her eye intent on all the mazy plan,
She form'd of various parts the various man.
　　Then first she calls the useful many forth ;
Plain plodding industry, and sober worth :
Thence peasants, farmers, native sons of earth,
And merchandise' whole genus take their birth :
Each prudent cit a warm existence finds,
And all mechanics' many-apron'd kinds.
Some other rarer sorts are wanted yet,
The lead and buoy are needful to the net :
The caput mortuum of gross desires
Makes a material for mere knights and squires ;
The martial phosphorus is taught to flow,
She kneads the lumpish philosophic dough,
Then marks the unyielding mass with grave designs,
Law, physic, politics, and deep divines :
Last, she sublimes th' Aurora of the poles,
The flashing elements of female souls.
　　The order'd system fair before her stood,
Nature, well-pleas'd, pronounc'd it very good ;
But ere she gave creating labour o'er,
Half-jest, she try'd one curious labour more ;
Some spumy, fiery, ignis fatuus matter,
Such as the slightest breath of air might scatter ;
With arch alacrity and conscious glee
(Nature may have her whim as well as we,
Her Hogarth-art perhaps she meant to show it)
She forms the thing, and christens it—a Poet.
Creature, tho' oft the prey of care and sorrow,
When blest to-day, unmindful of to-morrow.
A being form'd t' amuse his graver friends,
Admir'd and prais'd—and there the homage ends :
A mortal quite unfit for Fortune's strife,
Yet oft the sport of all the ills of life ;
Prone to enjoy each pleasure riches give,
Yet haply wanting wherewithal to live :
Longing to wipe each tear, to heal each groan,
Yet frequent all unheeded in his own.
　　But honest Nature is not quite a Turk,
She laugh'd at first, then felt for her poor work.
Pitying the propless climber of mankind,
She cast about a standard tree to find ;
And, to support his helpless woodbine state,
Attach'd him to the generous truly great,

A title, and the only one I claim,
To lay strong hold for help on bounteous Graham.
  Pity the tuneful muses' hapless train,
Weak, timid landsmen on life's stormy main !
Their hearts no selfish stern absorbent stuff,
That never gives —tho' humbly takes enough ;
The little fate allows, they share as soon,
Unlike sage, proverb'd, wisdom's hard wrung boon.
The world were blest did bliss on them depend,
Ah, that " the friendly e'er should want a friend !"
Let prudence number o'er each sturdy son,
Who life and wisdom at one race begun,
Who feel by reason, and who give by rule,
(Instinct's a brute, and sentiment a fool !)
Who make poor ' will do ' wait upon ' I should '—
We own they're prudent, but who feels they're good ?
Ye wise ones, hence ! ye hurt the social eye !
God's image rudely etch'd on base alloy !
But come ye, who the godlike pleasure know,
Heaven's attribute distinguish'd—to bestow !
Whose arms of love would grasp the human race :
Come thou who giv'st with all a courtier's grace ;
Friend of my life, true patron of my rhymes !
Prop of my dearest hopes for future times.
Why shrinks my soul, half-blushing, half-afraid,
Backward, abash'd to ask thy friendly aid ?
I know my need, I know thy giving hand,
I crave thy friendship at thy kind command ;
But there are such who court the tuneful nine—
Heavens ! should the branded character be mine !
Whose verse in manhood's pride sublimely flows,
Yet vilest reptiles in their begging prose.
Mark, how their lofty independent spirit
Soars on the spurning wing of injur'd merit !
Seek not the proofs in private life to find ;
Pity the best of words should be but wind !
So, to heaven's gates the lark's shrill song ascends,
But grovelling on the earth the carol ends.
In all the clam'rous cry of starving want,
They dun benevolence with shameless front ;
Oblige them, patronize their tinsel lays,
They persecute you all your future days !
Ere my poor soul such deep damnation stain,
My horny fist assume the plough again ;
The piebald jacket let me patch once more ;
On eighteen-pence a week I've liv'd before.
Tho', thanks to Heaven, I dare even that last shift,
I trust, meantime, my boon is in thy gift ;
That, plac'd by thee upon the wish'd-for height,
Where, man and nature fairer in her sight,
My muse may imp her wing for some sublimer flight.

TO ROBERT GRAHAM, OF FINTRA, ESQ.

LATE crippl'd of an arm, and now a leg,
About to beg a pass for leave to beg ;
Dull, listless, teas'd, dejected, and deprest
(Nature is adverse to a cripple's rest) :
Will generous Graham list to his Poet's wail ?
(It soothes poor Misery, heark'ning to her tale,)
And hear him curse the light he first survey'd,
And doubly curse the luckless rhyming trade ?
   Thou, Nature, partial Nature, I arraign ;
Of thy caprice maternal I complain.
The lion and the bull thy care have found,
One shakes the forests, and one spurns the ground :
Thou giv'st the ass his hide, the snail his shell,
Th' envenom'd wasp, victorious, guards his cell. —
Thy minions, kings defend, control, devour,
In all th' omnipotence of rule and power. —
Foxes and statesmen, subtile wiles ensure ;
The cit and polecat stink, and are secure.
Toads with their poison, doctors with their drug,
The priest and hedgehog in their robes, are snug.
Ev'n silly woman has her warlike arts,
Her tongue and eyes, her dreaded spear and darts.
   But Oh ! thou bitter step-mother and hard,
To thy poor, fenceless, naked child—the Bard !
A thing unteachable in world's skill,
And half an idiot too, more helpless still.
No heels to bear him from the op'ning dun ;
No claws to dig, his hated sight to shun ;
No horns, but those by luckless Hymen worn,
And those, alas ! not Amalthea's horn :
No nerves olfact'ry, Mammon's trusty cur,
Clad in rich Dulness' comfortable fur,
In naked feeling, and in aching pride,
He bears th' unbroken blast from ev'ry side :
Vampyre booksellers drain him to the heart,
And scorpion critics cureless venom dart.
   Critics—appall'd I venture on the name,
Those cut-throat bandits in the paths of fame :
Bloody dissectors, worse than ten Monroes ;
He hacks to teach, they mangle to expose.
   His heart by causeless, wanton malice wrung,
By blockheads' daring into madness stung ;
His well-won bays, than life itself more dear,
By miscreants torn, who ne'er one sprig must wear :
Foil'd, bleeding, tortur'd in th' unequal strife,
The hapless Poet flounders on thro' life.
Till fled each hope that once his bosom fir'd,
And fled each Muse that glorious once inspir'd,

Low sunk in squalid, unprotected age,
Dead, even resentment, for his injur'd page,
He heeds or feels no more the ruthless critic's rage !
    So, by some hedge, the generous steed deceas'd,
For half-starv'd snarling curs a dainty feast ;
By toil and famine wore to skin and bone,
Lies, senseless of each tugging bitch's son.
    O Dulness ! portion of the truly blest !
Calm shelter'd haven of eternal rest !
Thy sons ne'er madden in the fierce extremes
Of Fortune's polar frost, or torrid beams.
If mantling high she fills the golden cup,
With sober selfish ease they sip it up ;
Conscious the bounteous meed they well deserve,
They only wonder " some folks " do not starve.
The grave sage hern thus easy picks his frog,
And thinks the mallard a sad worthless dog.
When disappointment snaps the clue of hope,
And thro' disastrous night they darkling grope,
With deaf endurance sluggishly they bear,
And just conclude that " fools are fortune's care."
So heavy, passive to the tempest's shocks,
Strong on the sign-post stands the stupid ox.
    Not so the idle Muses' mad-cap train,
Not such the workings of their moon-struck brain ;
In equanimity they never dwell,
By turns in soaring heav'n, or vaulted hell.
    I dread thee, Fate, relentless and severe,
With all a poet's, husband's, father's fear !
Already one strong-hold of hope is lost,
Glencairn, the truly noble, lies in dust ;
(Fled, like the sun eclips'd as noon appears,
And left us darkling in a world of tears :)
Oh ! hear my ardent, grateful, selfish pray'r !
Fintra, my other stay, long bless and spare !
Thro' a long life his hopes and wishes crown,
And bright in cloudless skies his sun go down !
May bliss domestic smooth his private path ;
Give energy to life ; and soothe his latest breath,
With many a filial tear circling the bed of death !

LAMENT FOR JAMES, EARL OF GLENCAIRN.

THE wind blew hollow frae the hills,
    By fits the sun's departing beam
Look'd on the fading yellow woods
    That wav'd o'er Lugar's winding
        stream :
Beneath a craigy steep, a Bard,
    Laden with years and meikle pain,
In loud lament bewail'd his lord,
    Whom death had all untimely taen.

He lean'd him to an ancient aik,
    Whose trunk was mould'ring down
        with years ;
His locks were bleachèd white wi' time,
    His hoary cheek was wet wi' tears ;
And as he touch'd his trembling harp,
    And as he tun'd his doleful sang,
The winds, lamenting thro' their caves,
    To echo bore the notes alang.

" Ye scatter'd birds that faintly sing,
  The reliques of the vernal quire !
Ye woods that shed on a' the winds
  The honours of the agèd year !
A few short months, and glad and gay,
  Again ye'll charm the ear and e'e ;
But nocht in all revolving time
  Can gladness bring again to me.

" I am a bending agèd tree,
  That long has stood the wind and rain;
But now has come a cruel blast,
  And my last hold of earth is gane :
Nae leaf o' mine shall greet the spring,
  Nae simmer sun exalt my bloom ;
But I maun lie before the storm,
  And ithers plant them in my room.

" I've seen so many changefu' years,
  On earth I am a stranger grown ;
I wander in the ways of men,
  Alike unknowing and unknown :
Unheard, unpitied, unreliev'd,
  I bear alane my lade o' care,
For silent, low, on beds of dust,
  Lie a' that would my sorrows share.

" And last (the sum of a' my griefs !)
  My noble master lies in clay ;
The flow'r amang our barons bold,
  His country's pride, his country's stay :
In weary being now I pine,
  For a' the life of life is dead,
And hope has left my agèd ken,
  On forward wing for ever fled.

" Awake thy last sad voice, my harp !
  The voice of woe and wild despair !
Awake, resound thy latest lay,
  Then sleep in silence evermair !
And thou, my last, best, only friend,
  That fillest an untimely tomb,
Accept this tribute from the Bard
  Thou brought from fortune's mirkest
    gloom.

" In Poverty's low barren vale, [round ;
  Thick mists, obscure, involv'd me
Though oft I turn'd the wistful eye,
  No ray of fame was to be found :
Thou found'st me, like the morning sun
  That melts the fogs in limpid air,
The friendless Bard, and rustic song,
  Became alike thy fostering care.

" O ! why has worth so short a date ?
  While villains ripen grey with time !
Must thou, the noble, gen'rous, great,
  Fall in bold manhood's hardy prime?
Why did I live to see that day ?
  A day to me so full of woe ?
O ! had I met the mortal shaft
  Which laid my benefactor low !

" The bridegroom may forget the bride
  Was made his wedded wife yestreen ;
The monarch may forget the crown
  That on his head an hour has been ;
The mother may forget the child
  That smiles sae sweetly on her knee;
But I'll remember thee, Glencairn,
  And a' that thou hast done for me ! "

LINES SENT TO SIR JOHN WHITEFORD,
OF WHITEFORD, BART. WITH THE FOREGOING POEM.

THOU, who thy honour as thy God rever'st,
Who, save thy mind's reproach, nought earthly fear'st,
To thee this votive offering I impart,
The tearful tribute of a broken heart.
The friend thou valued'st, I, the Patron, lov'd ;
His worth, his honour, all the world approv'd.
We'll mourn till we too go as he has gone,
And tread the dreary path to that dark world unknown.

TAM O' SHANTER.

A TALE.

Of Brownyis and of Bogilis full in this Buke.
GAWIN DOUGLAS.

WHEN chapman billies leave the street,
And drouthy neebors, neebors meet,
As market-days are wearing late,
An' folk begin to tak the gate;
While we sit bousing at the nappy,
An' getting fou and unco happy,
We think na on the lang Scots miles,
The mosses, waters, slaps, and styles,
That lie between us and our hame,
Whare sits our sulky sullen dame,
Gathering her brows like gathering storm,
Nursing her wrath to keep it warm.

This truth fand honest Tam o' Shanter,
As he frae Ayr ae night did canter,
(Auld Ayr, wham ne'er a town surpasses,
For honest men and bonie lasses.)

O Tam! hadst thou but been sae wise,
As ta'en thy ain wife Kate's advice!
She tauld thee weel thou wast a skellum,
A blethering, blustering, drunken blellum;
That frae November till October,
Ae market-day thou was na sober;
That ilka melder, wi' the miller,
Thou sat as lang as thou had siller;
That ev'ry naig was ca'd a shoe on,
The smith and thee gat roaring fou on;
That at the Lord's house, ev'n on Sunday,
Thou drank wi' Kirton Jean till Monday.
She prophesy'd that, late or soon,
Thou would be found deep drown'd in Doon;
Or catch'd wi' warlocks in the mirk,
By Alloway's auld haunted kirk.

Ah, gentle dames! it gars me greet,
To think how monie counsels sweet,
How mony lengthen'd, sage advices,
The husband frae the wife despises!

But to our tale: Ae market night,
Tam had got planted unco right;
Fast by an ingle, bleezing finely,
Wi' reaming swats, that drank divinely;
And at his elbow, Souter Johnny,
His ancient, trusty, drouthy crony;

Tam lo'ed him like a vera brither ;
They had been fou for weeks thegither.
The night drave on wi' sangs and clatter ;
And ay the ale was growing better :
The landlady and Tam grew gracious,
Wi' favours, secret, sweet, and precious :
The souter tauld his queerest stories ;
The landlord's laugh was ready chorus :
The storm without might rair and rustle,
Tam did na mind the storm a whistle.
      Care, mad to see a man sae happy,
E'en drown'd himsel amang the nappy :
As bees flee hame wi' lades o' treasure,
The minutes wing'd their way wi' pleasure ;
Kings may be blest, but Tam was glorious,
O'er a' the ills o' life victorious !
      But pleasures are like poppies spread,
You seize the flow'r, its bloom is shed
Or like the snow-falls in the river,
A moment white—then melts for ever ;
Or like the borealis race,
That flit ere you can point their place ;
Or like the rainbow's lovely form
Evanishing amid the storm.—
Nae man can tether time or tide ;—
The hour approaches Tam maun ride ;
That hour, o' night's black arch the key-stane,
That dreary hour he mounts his beast in ;
And sic a night he taks the road in,
As ne'er poor sinner was abroad in.
      The wind blew as 'twad blawn its last ;
The rattling show'rs rose on the blast ;
The speedy gleams the darkness swallow'd ;
Loud, deep, and lang, the thunder bellow'd :
That night, a child might understand,
The Deil had business on his hand.
      Weel mounted on his grey mare, Meg,
A better never lifted leg,
Tam skelpit on thro' dub and mire,
Despising wind, and rain, and fire ;
Whiles holding fast his gude blue bonnet ;
Whiles crooning o'er some auld Scots sonnet ;
Whiles glow'ring round wi' prudent cares,
Lest bogles catch him unawares ;
Kirk-Alloway was drawing nigh,
Whare ghaists and houlets nightly cry.—
      By this time he was cross the ford,
Whare in the snaw, the chapman smoor'd ;
And past the birks and meikle stane,
Whare drunken Charlie brak's neck-bane ;
And thro' the whins, and by the cairn,
Whare hunters fand the murder'd bairn ;

And near the thorn, aboon the well,
Whare Mungo's mither hang'd hersel.—
Before him Doon pours all his floods ;
The doubling storm roars thro' the woods ;
The lightnings flash from pole to pole ;
Near and more near the thunders roll :
When, glimmering thro' the groaning trees,
Kirk-Alloway seem'd in a bleeze ;
Thro' ilka bore the beams were glancing ;
And loud resounded mirth and dancing.—
 Inspiring bold John Barleycorn !
What dangers thou canst make us scorn !
Wi' tippenny, we fear nae evil ;
Wi' usquebae, we'll face the devil !—
The swats sae ream'd in Tammie's noddle,
Fair play, he car'd na deils a boddle.
But Maggie stood right sair astonish'd,
Till, by the heel and hand admonish'd,
She ventur'd forward on the light ;
And, vow ! Tam saw an unco sight !
Warlocks and witches in a dance ;
Nae cotillion brent new frae France,
But hornpipes, jigs, strathspeys, and reels,
Put life and mettle in their heels.
A winnock-bunker in the east,
There sat auld Nick, in shape o' beast ;
A towzie tyke, black, grim, and large,
To gie them music was his charge :
He screw'd the pipes and gart them skirl,
Till roof and rafters a' did dirl.—
Coffins stood round like open presses,
That shaw'd the dead in their last dresses ;
And by some devilish cantraip slight
Each in its cauld hand held a light,—
By which heroic Tam was able
To note upon the haly table,
A murderer's banes in gibbet airns ;
Twa span-lang, wee, unchristen'd bairns ;
A thief, new-cutted frae the rape,
Wi' his last gasp his gab did gape ;
Five tomahawks, wi' blude red rusted ;
Five scymitars, wi' murder crusted ;
A garter, which a babe had strangled ;
A knife, a father's throat had mangled,
Whom his ain son o' life bereft,
The grey hairs yet stack to the heft ;
Wi' mair o' horrible and awfu',
Which ev'n to name wad be unlawfu'.
 As Tammie glowr'd, amaz'd, and curious,
The mirth and fun grew fast and furious :
The piper loud and louder blew ;
The dancers quick and quicker flew ;

They reel'd, they set, they cross'd, they cleekit,
Till ilka carlin swat and reekit,
And coost her duddies to the wark,
And linket at it in her sark !
    Now Tam, O Tam ! had thae been queans,
A' plump and strapping in their teens ;
Their sarks, instead o' creeshie flannen,
Been snaw-white seventeen hunder linnen !
Thir breeks o' mine, my only pair,
That ance were plush, o' gude blue hair,
I wad hae gi'en them off my hurdies,
For ae blink o' the bonie burdies !
    But wither'd beldams, auld and droll,
Rigwooddie hags wad spean a foal,
Lowping and flinging on a crummock,
I wonder didna turn thy stomach.
    But Tam kend what was what fu' brawlie,
There was ae winsome wench and walie,
That night enlisted in the core,
(Lang after kend on Carrick shore ;
For mony a beast to dead she shot,
And perish'd mony a bonie boat,
And shook baith meikle corn and bear,
And kept the country-side.in fear,)
Her cutty sark, o' Paisley harn,
That while a lassie she had worn,
In longitude tho' sorely scanty,
It was her best, and she was vauntie. —
Ah ! little kend thy reverend grannie,
That sark she coft for her wee Nannie,
Wi' twa pund Scots ('twas a' her riches),
Wad ever grac'd a dance of witches !
    But here my muse her wing maun cour ;
Sic flights are far beyond her pow'r ;
To sing how Nannie lap and flang,
(A souple jade she was, and strang,)
And how Tam stood, like ane bewitch'd,
And thought his very een enrich'd ;
Even Satan glowr'd, and fidg'd fu' fain,
And hotch'd and blew wi' might and main :
Till first ae caper, syne anither,
Tam tint his reason a' thegither,
And roars out, " Weel done, Cutty-sark ! "
And in an instant all was dark :
And scarcely had he Maggie rallied,
When out the hellish legion sallied.
    As bees bizz out wi' angry fyke,
When plundering herds assail their byke ;
As open pussie's mortal foes,
When, pop ! she starts before their nose ;
As eager runs the market-crowd,
When, " Catch the thief ! " resounds aloud ;

So Maggie runs, the witches follow,
Wi' monie an eldritch skreech and hollow.
    Ah, Tam ! ah, Tam ! thou'll get thy fairin !
In hell they'll roast thee like a herrin !
In vain thy Kate awaits thy comin !
Kate soon will be a woefu' woman !
Now, do thy speedy utmost, Meg,
And win the key-stane of the brig :
There at them thou thy tail may toss,
A running stream they darena cross.
But ere the key-stane she could make,
The fient a tail she had to shake !
For Nannie, far before the rest,
Hard upon noble Maggie prest,
And flew at Tam wi' furious ettle ;
But little wist she Maggie's mettle—
Ae spring brought off her master hale,
But left behind her ain gray tail :
The carlin claught her by the rump,
And left poor Maggie scarce a stump.
    Now, wha this tale o' truth shall read,
Ilk man and mother's son, take heed ;
Whene'er to drink you are inclin'd,
Or cutty-sarks run in your mind,
Think, ye may buy the joys o'er dear,
Remember Tam o' Shanter's mare.

ON THE LATE CAPTAIN GROSE'S PEREGRINATIONS
THRO' SCOTLAND,

COLLECTING THE ANTIQUITIES OF THAT KINGDOM.

HEAR, Land o' Cakes, and brither
        Scots,
Frae Maidenkirk to Johnny Groats ;—
If there's a hole in a' your coats,
        I rede you tent it :
A chield's amang you taking notes,
        And, faith, he'll prent it.

If in your bounds ye chance to light
Upon a fine, fat, fodgel wight,
O' stature short, but genius bright,
        That's he, mark weel—
And wow ! he has an unco slight
        O' cauk and keel.

By some auld, houlet-haunted biggin,
Or kirk deserted by its riggin,
It's ten to ane ye'll find him snug in
        Some eldritch part,
Wi' deils, they say, Lord save's !
        colleaguin
        At some black art.—

Ilk ghaist that haunts auld ha' or chamer,
Ye gipsy-gang that deal in glamor,
And you deep read in hell's black
        grammar,
        Warlocks and witches,
Ye'll quake at his conjuring hammer,
        Ye midnight bitches.

It's tauld he was a sodger bred,
And ane wad rather fa'n than fled ;
But now he's quat the spurtle-blade,
    And dog-skin wallet,
And taen the—Antiquarian trade,
    I think they call it.

He has a fouth o' auld nick-nackets :
Rusty airn caps and jinglin jackets,
Wad haud the Lothians three in tackets,
    A towmont gude ;
And parritch-pats, and auld saut-backets,
    Before the Flood.

Of Eve's first fire he has a cinder ;
Auld Tubalcain's fire-shool and fender ;
That which distinguishèd the gender
    O' Balaam's ass ;
A broom-stick o' the witch of Endor,
    Weel shod wi' brass.

Forbye, he'll shape you aff, fu' gleg
The cut of Adam's philibeg ;
The knife that nicket Abel's craig
    He'll prove you fully,
It was a faulding jocteleg,
    Or lang-kail gullie.—

But wad ye see him in his glee,
For meikle glee and fun has he,
Then set him down, and twa or three
    Gude fellows wi' him ;
And port, O port ! shine thou a wee,
    And then ye'll see him !

Now, by the Pow'rs o' verse and prose !
Thou art a dainty chield, O Grose !—
Whae'er o' thee shall ill suppose,
    They sair misca' thee ;
I'd take the rascal by the nose,
    Wad say, Shame fa' thee !

ON SEEING A WOUNDED HARE LIMP BY ME,

WHICH A FELLOW HAD JUST SHOT AT.

[*April,* 1789.]

INHUMAN man ! curse on thy barb'rous art,
    And blasted be thy murder-aiming eye ;
    May never pity soothe thee with a sigh,
Nor ever pleasure glad thy cruel heart !

Go, live, poor wanderer of the wood and field,
    The bitter little that of life remains ;
    No more the thickening brakes and verdant plains
To thee shall home, or food, or pastime yield.

Seek, mangled wretch, some place of wonted rest,
    No more of rest, but now thy dying bed !
    The sheltering rushes whistling o'er thy head,
The cold earth with thy bloody bosom prest.

Oft as by winding Nith, I, musing, wait
    The sober eve, or hail the cheerful dawn,
    I'll miss thee sporting o'er the dewy lawn,
And curse the ruffian's aim, and mourn thy hapless fate.

ADDRESS TO THE SHADE OF THOMSON,

ON CROWNING HIS BUST AT EDNAM, ROXBURGH-SHIRE, WITH BAYS.

WHILE virgin Spring, by Eden's flood,
　Unfolds her tender mantle green,
Or pranks the sod in frolic mood,
　Or tunes Eolian strains between ;

While Summer with a matron grace
　Retreats to Dryburgh's cooling shade,
Yet oft, delighted, stops to trace
　The progress of the spiky blade ;

While Autumn, benefactor kind,
　By Tweed erects his agèd head,

And sees, with self-approving mind,
　Each creature on his bounty fed ;

While maniac Winter rages o'er
　The hills whence classic Yarrow flows,
Rousing the turbid torrent's roar,
　Or sweeping, wild, a waste of snows ;

So long, sweet Poet of the year,
　Shall bloom that wreath thou well
　　hast won ;
While Scotia, with exulting tear,
　Proclaims that Thomson was her son.

TO MISS CRUIKSHANK,

A VERY YOUNG LADY,

WRITTEN ON THE BLANK LEAF OF A BOOK, PRESENTED TO HER BY THE AUTHOR.

BEAUTEOUS rose-bud, young and gay,
Blooming in thy early May,
Never may'st thou, lovely Flow'r,
Chilly shrink in sleety show'r !
Never Boreas' hoary path,
Never Eurus' pois'nous breath,
Never baleful stellar lights,
Taint thee with untimely blights !
Never, never reptile thief
Riot on thy virgin leaf !
Nor even Sol too fiercely view
Thy bosom blushing still with dew !

May'st thou long, sweet crimson
　gem,
Richly deck thy native stem ;
Till some evening, sober, calm,
Dropping dews, and breathing balm,
While all around the woodland rings,
And every bird thy requiem sings ;
Thou, amid the dirgeful sound,
Shed thy dying honours round,
And resign to parent earth
The loveliest form she e'er gave birth.

ON READING, IN A NEWSPAPER,

THE DEATH OF JOHN M'LEOD, ESQ.

BROTHER TO A YOUNG LADY, A PARTICULAR FRIEND OF THE AUTHOR'S.

SAD thy tale, thou idle page,
　And rueful thy alarms :
Death tears the brother of her love
From Isabella's arms.
　B

Sweetly deckt with pearly dew
　The morning rose may blow ;
But cold successive noontide blasts
　May lay its beauties low.
　H

Fair on Isabella's morn
  The sun propitious smil'd ;
But, long ere noon, succeeding clouds
  Succeeding hopes beguil'd.

Fate oft tears the bosom chords
  That Nature finest strung :
So Isabella's heart was form'd,
  And so that heart was wrung.

Dread Omnipotence, alone,
  Can heal the wound He gave ;
Can point the brimful grief-worn eyes
  To scenes beyond the grave.

Virtue's blossoms there shall blow,
  And fear no withering blast ;
There Isabella's spotless worth
  Shall happy be at last.

THE HUMBLE PETITION OF BRUAR WATER
TO THE NOBLE DUKE OF ATHOLE.

My Lord, I know your noble ear
  Woe ne'er assails in vain ;
Embolden'd thus, I beg you 'll hear
  Your humble Slave complain,
How saucy Phœbus' scorching beams,
  In flaming summer-pride,
Dry-withering, waste my foamy streams,
  And drink my crystal tide.

The lightly-jumping glowrin trouts,
  That thro' my waters play,
If, in their random, wanton spouts,
  They near the margin stray ;
If, hapless chance ! they linger lang,
  I'm scorching up so shallow,
They're left the whitening stanes amang,
  In gasping death to wallow.

Last day I grat wi' spite and teen,
  As Poet Burns came by,
That to a Bard I should be seen
  Wi' half my channel dry :
A panegyric rhyme, I ween,
  Even as I was he shor'd me ;
But had I in my glory been,
  He, kneeling, wad ador'd me.

Here, foaming down the shelvy rocks,
  In twisting strength I rin ;
There, high my boiling torrent smokes,
  Wild-roaring o'er a linn :
Enjoying large each spring and well
  As Nature gave them me;
I am, altho' I say't mysel,
  Worth gaun a mile to see.

Would then my noble master please
  To grant my highest wishes,
He'll shade my banks wi' tow'ring trees,
  And bonie spreading bushes.
Delighted doubly then, my Lord,
  You'll wander on my banks,
And listen monie a grateful bird
  Return you tuneful thanks.

The sober laverock, warbling wild,
  Shall to the skies aspire ;
The gowdspink, Music's gayest child,
  Shall sweetly join the choir :
The blackbird strong, the lintwhite clear,
  The mavis mild and mellow ;
The robin pensive Autumn cheer,
  In all her locks of yellow :

This, too, a covert shall ensure,
  To shield them from the storm ;
And coward maukin sleep secure,
  Low in her grassy form :
Here shall the shepherd make his seat,
  To weave his crown of flow'rs ;
Or find a sheltering safe retreat,
  From prone-descending show'rs.

And here, by sweet endearing stealth,
  Shall meet the loving pair,
Despising worlds with all their wealth
  As empty, idle care :
The flow'rs shall vie in all their charms
  The hour of heav'n to grace,
And birks extend their fragrant arms,
  To screen the dear embrace.

Here haply too, at vernal dawn,
　Some musing bard may stray,
And eye the smoking, dewy lawn,
　And misty mountain, grey ;
Or, by the reaper's nightly beam,
　Mild-chequering thro' the trees,
Rove to my darkly dashing stream,
　Hoarse-swelling on the breeze.

Let lofty firs, and ashes cool,
　My lowly banks o'erspread,
And view, deep-bending in the pool,
　Their shadows' wat'ry bed !

Let fragrant birks in woodbines drest
　My craggy cliffs adorn ;
And, for the little songster's nest,
　The close embow'ring thorn.

So may Old Scotia's darling hope,
　Your little angel band,
Spring, like their fathers, up to prop
　Their honour'd native land !
So may thro' Albion's farthest ken,
　To social-flowing glasses
The grace be--" Athole's honest men,
　And Athole's bonie lasses !"

THE KIRK'S ALARM.

A SATIRE.

A Ballad Tune—*"Push about the Brisk Bowl."*

Orthodox, Orthodox, wha believe in John Knox,
　Let me sound an alarm to your conscience :
There's a heretic blast has been blawn i' the wast,
　" That what is not sense must be nonsense."

Dr. Mac, Dr. Mac, you should stretch on a rack,　*Dr. McGill—*
　To strike evil-doers wi' terror ;
To join faith and sense upon onie pretence,
　Is heretic, damnable error.

Town of Ayr, town of Ayr, it was mad, I declare,
　To meddle wi' mischief a-brewing ;
Provost John is still deaf to the church's relief,
　And orator Bob is its ruin.

D'rymple mild, D'rymple mild, tho' your heart's like a child,
　And your life like the new driven snaw,
Yet that winna save ye, auld Satan must have ye,
　For preaching that three's ane and twa.

Rumble John, Rumble John, mount the steps wi' a groan,
　Cry the book is wi' heresy cramm'd ;
Then lug out your ladle, deal brimstane like adle,
　And roar ev'ry note of the damn'd.

Simper James, Simper James, leave the fair Killie dames,
　There's a holier chase in your view ;
I'll lay on your head, that the pack ye'll soon lead,
　For puppies like you there's but few.

Singet Sawney, Singet Sawney, are ye herding the penny,
  Unconscious what evils await?
Wi' a jump, yell, and howl, alarm every soul,
  For the foul thief is just at your gate.

Daddy Auld, Daddy Auld, there's a tod in the fauld,
  A tod meikle waur than the Clerk;
Tho' ye can do little skaith, ye'll be in at the death,
  And gif ye canna bite, ye may bark.

Davie Bluster, Davie Bluster, if for a saint ye do muster,
  The corps is no nice of recruits:
Yet to worth let's be just, royal blood ye might boast,
  If the ass was the king of the brutes.

Jamy Goose, Jamy Goose, ye hae made but toom roose,
  In hunting the wicked Lieutenant;
But the Doctor's your mark, for the L——d's haly ark,
  He has cooper'd and caw'd a wrang pin in't.

Poet Willie, Poet Willie, gie the Doctor a volley,
  Wi' your "liberty's chain" and your wit;
O'er Pegasus' side ye ne'er laid a stride,
  Ye but smelt, man, the place where he sh-t.

Andro Gouk, Andro Gouk, ye may slander the book,
  And the book no the waur, let me tell ye!
Ye are rich, and look big, but lay by hat and wig,
  And ye'll hae a calf's head o' sma' value.

Barr Steenie, Barr Steenie, what mean ye? what mean ye?
  If ye'll meddle nae mair wi' the matter,
Ye may hae some pretence to havins and sense,
  Wi' people wha ken ye nae better.

Irvine Side, Irvine Side, wi' your turkeycock pride,
  Of manhood but sma' is your share;
Ye've the figure, 'tis true, even your faes will allow,
  And your friends they dare grant you nae mair.

Muirland Jock, Muirland Jock, when the Lord makes a rock
  To crush common sense for her sins,
If ill manners were wit, there's no mortal so fit
  To confound the poor Doctor at ance.

Holy Will, Holy Will, there was wit i' your skull,
  When ye pilfer'd the alms o' the poor;
The timmer is scant when ye're ta'en for a saint,
  Wha should swing in a rape for an hour.

Calvin's sons, Calvin's sons, seize your sp'ritual guns,
　　Ammunition you never can need ;
Your hearts are the stuff will be powther enough,
　　And your skulls are storehouses o' lead.

Poet Burns, Poet Burns, wi' your priest-skelping turns,
　　Why desert ye your auld native shire ?
You muse is a gipsie, e'en tho' she were tipsie,
　　She cou'd ca' us nae waur than we are.

ADDRESS TO THE TOOTHACHE,

WRITTEN WHEN THE AUTHOR WAS GRIEVOUSLY TORMENTED BY THAT DISORDER.

My curse upon your venom'd stang,
That shoots my tortur'd gums alang ;
And thro' my lugs gies monie a twang,
　　　　Wi' gnawing vengeance ;
Tearing my nerves wi' bitter pang,
　　　　Like racking engines !

When fevers burn, or ague freezes,
Rheumatics gnaw, or cholic squeezes ;
Our neighbour's sympathy may ease us,
　　　　Wi' pitying moan ;
But thee—thou hell o' a' diseases,
　　　　Ay mocks our groan !

Adown my beard the slavers trickle !
I throw the wee stools o'er the mickle,
As round the fire the giglets keckle
　　　　To see me loup ;
While, raving mad, I wish a heckle
　　　　Were in their doup.

O' a' the numerous human dools,
Ill har'sts, daft bargains, cutty-stools,
Or worthy friends rak'd i' the mools,
　　　　Sad sight to see !
The tricks o' knaves, or fash o' fools,
　　　　Thou bear'st the gree.

Where'er that place be priests ca' hell,
Whence a' the tones o' mis'ry yell,
And ranked plagues their numbers tell,
　　　　In dreadfu' raw,
Thou, Toothache, surely bear'st the bell
　　　　Amang them a' !

O thou grim mischief-making chiel,
That gars the notes of discord squeel,
Till daft mankind aft dance a reel
　　　　In gore a shoe-thick ;—
Gie a' the faes o' Scotland's weal
　　　　A towmont's Toothache !

WRITTEN WITH A PENCIL

OVER THE CHIMNEY-PIECE IN THE PARLOUR OF THE INN AT KENMORE, TAYMOUTH.

ADMIRING Nature in her wildest grace,
These northern scenes with weary feet I trace ;
O'er many a winding dale and painful steep,
Th' abodes of covey'd grouse and timid sheep,
My savage journey, curious, I pursue,
Till fam'd Breadalbane opens to my view.—
The meeting cliffs each deep-sunk glen divides,
The woods, wild scatter'd, clothe their ample sides ;

Th' outstretching lake, embosom'd 'mong the hills,
The eye with wonder and amazement fills ;
The Tay meand'ring sweet in infant pride,
The palace rising on his verdant side ;
The lawns wood-fringed in Nature's native taste
The hillocks dropt in Nature's careless haste ;
The arches striding o'er the new-born stream ;
The village, glittering in the noontide beam—

  *   *   *   *

Poetic ardours in my bosom swell,
Lone wand'ring by the hermit's mossy cell :
The sweeping theatre of hanging woods ;
Th' incessant roar of headlong tumbling floods–

  *   *   *   *   *

Here Poesy might wake her heav'n-taught lyre,
And look through Nature with creative fire ;
Here, to the wrongs of Fate half reconcil'd,
Misfortune's lighten'd steps might wander wild ;
And Disappointment, in these lonely bounds,
Find balm to soothe her bitter, rankling wounds :
Here heart-struck Grief might heav'nward stretch her scan,
And injur'd Worth forget and pardon man.

  *   *   *   *

ON THE BIRTH OF A POSTHUMOUS CHILD,

BORN IN PECULIAR CIRCUMSTANCES OF FAMILY DISTRESS.

SWEET flow'ret, pledge o' meikle love,
 And ward o' mony a prayer,
What heart o' stane wad thou na move,
 Sae helpless, sweet, and fair.

November hirples o'er the lea,
 Chill, on thy lovely form ;
And gane, alas ! the shelt'ring tree,
 Should shield thee frae the storm.

May He who gives the rain to pour,
 And wings the blast to blaw,
Protect thee frae the driving show'r,
 The bitter frost and snaw.

May He, the friend of woe and want,
 Who heals life's various stounds,
Protect and guard the mother plant,
 And heal her cruel wounds.

But late she flourish'd, rooted fast,
 Fair in the summer morn :
Now, feebly bends she in the blast,
 Unshelter'd and forlorn.

Blest be thy bloom, thou lovely gem,
 Unscath'd by ruffian hand !
And from thee many a parent stem
 Arise to deck our land.

WRITTEN WITH A PENCIL.

STANDING BY THE FALL OF FYERS, NEAR LOCH-NESS.

AMONG the heathy hills and ragged woods
The roaring Fyers pours his mossy floods ;
Till full he dashes on the rocky mounds,
Where, thro' a shapeless breach, his stream resounds.
As high in air the bursting torrents flow,
As deep recoiling surges foam below,
Prone down the rock the whitening sheet descends,
And viewless Echo's ear, astonished, rends.
Dim-seen, thro' rising mists and ceaseless show'rs,
The hoary cavern, wide-surrounding, low'rs.
Still, thro' the gap the struggling river toils,
And still, below, the horrid cauldron boils —
    *   *   *   *

SECOND EPISTLE TO DAVIE, A BROTHER POET.

AULD NEEBOR,

I'M three times doubly o'er your debtor,
For your auld-farrant, frien'ly letter ;
Tho' I maun say't, I doubt ye flatter,
        Ye speak sae fair,
For my puir, silly, rhymin clatter
        Some less maun sair.

Hale be your heart, hale be your fiddle ;
Lang may your elbuck jink and diddle,
To cheer you through the weary widdle
        O' war'ly cares,
Till bairns' bairns kindly cuddle
        Your auld gray hairs.

But Davie, lad, I'm red ye're glaikit ;
I'm tauld the Muse ye hae negleckit ;
An' gif it's sae, ye sud be licket
        Until ye fyke ;
Sic hauns as you sud ne'er be faikit,
        Be hain't wha like.

For me, I'm on Parnassus' brink,
Rivin' the words to gar them clink ;
Whyles daez't wi' love, whyles daez't
    wi' drink,
        Wi' jads or masons ;
An' whyles, but aye owre late, I think
        Braw sober lessons.

Of a' the thoughtless sons o' man,
Commend me to the Bardie clan ;
Except it be some idle plan
        O' rhymin clink,
The devil-haet, that I sud ban,
        They ever think.

Nae thought, nae view, nae scheme o'
        livin',
Nae cares to gie us joy or grievin' ;
But just the pouchie put the nieve in,
        An' while ought's there,
Then hiltie skiltie, we gae scrievin',
        An' fash nae mair.

Leeze me on rhyme ! it's aye a treasure,
My chief, amaist my only pleasure,
At hame, a-fiel', at wark, or leisure,
        The Muse, poor hizzie !
Tho' rough an' raploch be her measure,
        She's seldom lazy.

Haud to the Muse, my dainty Davie :
The warl' may play you monie a shavie ;
But for the Muse, she'll never leave ye,
        Tho' e'er sae puir,
Na, even tho' limpin' wi' the spavie
        Frae door tae door.

THE INVENTORY,

IN ANSWER TO THE USUAL MANDATE SENT BY A SURVEYOR OF THE TAXES, REQUIRING
A RETURN OF THE NUMBER OF HORSES, SERVANTS, CARRIAGES, ETC. KEPT.

SIR, as your mandate did request,
I send you here a faithfu' list,
O' gudes an' gear, an' a' my graith,
To which I'm clear to gi'e my aith.
  Imprimis then, for carriage cattle,
I have four brutes o' gallant mettle,
As ever drew afore a pettle ;
My han' afore's a gude auld has-been,
An' wight an' wilfu' a' his days been ;
My han' ahin's a weel gaun fillie,
That aft has borne me hame frae Killie,
An' your auld burrough monie a time,
In days when riding was nae crime—
But ance whan in my wooing pride
I like a blockhead boost to ride,
The wilfu' creature sae I pat to,
(Lord, pardon a' my sins an' that too !)
I play'd my fillie sic a shavie,
She's a' bedevil'd wi' the spavie.
My furr-ahin's a wordy beast,
As e'er in tug or tow was trac'd.—
The fourth's, a Highland Donald hastie,
A damn'd red-wud Kilburnie blastie.
Foreby a Cowte, o' Cowte's the wale,
As ever ran afore a tail ;
If he be spar'd to be a beast,
He'll draw me fifteen pun at least.—
  Wheel carriages I ha'e but few,
Three carts, an' twa are feckly new ;
Ae auld wheelbarrow, mair for token,
Ae leg, an' baith the trams, are broken ;
I made a poker o' the spin'le,
An' my auld mother brunt the trin'le.
  For men, I've three mischievous boys,
Run de'ils for rantin' an' for noise ;
A gaudsman ane, a thrasher t'other,
Wee Davock hauds the nowte in fother.
I rule them as I ought discreetly,
An' often labour them completely.

An' ay on Sundays duly nightly,
I on the questions tairge them tightly ;
Till faith, wee Davock's grown sae gleg,
Tho' scarcely langer than my leg,
He'll screed you aff Effectual Calling,
As fast as onie in the dwalling.—
  I've nane in female servan' station,
(Lord keep me ay frae a' temptation !)
I ha'e nae wife, and that my bliss is,
An' ye have laid nae tax on misses ;
An' then if kirk folks dinna clutch me,
I ken the devils dare na touch me.
Wi' weans I'm mair than weel contented,
Heav'n sent me ane mae than I wanted.
My sonsie smirking dear-bought Bess,
She stares the daddy in her face,
Enough of ought ye like but grace.
But her, my bonie sweet wee lady,
I've paid enough for her already,
An' gin ye tax her or her mither,
B' the Lord, ye'se get them a' thegither.
  And now, remember, Mr. Aiken,
Nae kind of license out I'm takin' ;
Frae this time forth, I do declare,
I'se ne'er ride horse nor hizzie mair ;
Thro' dirt and dub for life I'll paidle,
Ere I sae dear pay for a saddle ;
My travel a' on foot I'll shank it,
I've sturdy bearers, Gude be thankit !—
The Kirk an' you may tak' you that,
It puts but little in your pat ;
Sae dinna put me in your buke,
Nor for my ten white shillings luke.
  This list wi' my ain han' I wrote it,
Day an' date as under notit :
Then know all ye whom it concerns,
Subscripsi huic,

               ROBERT BURNS.

Mossgiel,
February 22nd, 1786.

THE WHISTLE.

A BALLAD.

I SING of a Whistle, a Whistle of worth,
I sing of a Whistle, the pride of the North,
Was brought to the court of our good Scottish king,
And long with this Whistle all Scotland shall ring.

Old Loda, still rueing the arm of Fingal,
The god of the bottle sends down from his hall—
'This Whistle's your challenge, in Scotland get o'er,
And drink them to hell, Sir, or ne'er see me more!'

Old poets have sung, and old chronicles tell,
What champions ventur'd, what champions fell;
The son of great Loda was conqueror still,
And blew on the Whistle their requiem shrill.

Till Robert, the lord of the Cairn and the Scaur,
Unmatch'd at the bottle, unconquer'd in war,
He drank his poor god-ship as deep as the sea,
No tide of the Baltic e'er drunker than he.

Thus Robert, victorious, the trophy has gain'd,
Which now in his house has for ages remain'd;
Till three noble chieftains, and all of his blood,
The jovial contest again have renew'd.

Three joyous good fellows, with hearts clear of flaw;
Craigdarroch, so famous for wit, worth, and law;
And trusty Glenriddel, so skill'd in old coins;
And gallant Sir Robert, deep-read in old wines.

Craigdarroch began, with a tongue smooth as oil,
Desiring Glenriddel to yield up the spoil;
Or else he would muster the heads of the clan,
And once more, in claret, try which was the man.

' By the gods of the ancients!' Glenriddel replies,
' Before I surrender so glorious a prize,
I'll conjure the ghost of the great Rorie More,
And bumper his horn with him twenty times o'er.'

Sir Robert, a soldier, no speech would pretend,
But he ne'er turn'd his back on his foe—or his friend,
Said, toss down the Whistle, the prize of the field,
And knee-deep in claret, he'd die ere he'd yield.

To the board of Glenriddel our heroes repair,
So noted for drowning of sorrow and care ;
But for wine and for welcome not more known to fame,
Than the sense, wit, and taste of a sweet lovely dame.

A bard was selected to witness the fray,
And tell future ages the feats of the day ;
A bard who detested all sadness and spleen,
And wish'd that Parnassus a vineyard had been.

The dinner being over, the claret they ply,
And ev'ry new cork is a new spring of joy ;
In the bands of old friendship and kindred so set,
And the bands grew the tighter the more they were wet.

Gay Pleasure ran riot as bumpers ran o'er ;
Bright Phœbus ne'er witness'd so joyous a core,
And vow'd that to leave them he was quite forlorn,
Till Cynthia hinted he'd see them next morn.

Six bottles a-piece had well wore out the night,
When gallant Sir Robert, to finish the fight,
Turn'd o'er in one bumper a bottle of red,
And swore 'twas the way that their ancestors did.

Then worthy Glenriddel, so cautious and sage,
No longer the warfare ungodly would wage ;
A high-ruling elder to wallow in wine !
He left the foul business to folks less divine.

The gallant Sir Robert fought hard to the end ;
But who can with Fate and quart bumpers contend ?
Though Fate said, a hero should perish in light ;
So up rose bright Phœbus—and down fell the knight.

Next up rose our bard, like a prophet in drink : —
' Craigdarroch, thou'lt soar when creation shall sink !
But if thou would flourish immortal in rhyme,
Come—one bottle more—and have at the sublime !

' Thy line, that have struggled for freedom with Bruce,
Shall heroes and patriots ever produce :
So thine be the laurel, and mine be the bay ;
The field thou hast won, by yon bright god of day !'

SKETCH

INSCRIBED TO THE RIGHT HON. C. J. FOX.

How Wisdom and Folly meet, mix, and unite ;
How Virtue and Vice blend their black and their white ;
How Genius, th' illustrious father of fiction,
Confounds rule and law, reconciles contradiction—
I sing ; If these mortals, the Critics, should bustle,
I care not, not I—let the Critics go whistle !

But now for a Patron, whose name and whose glory
At once may illustrate and honour my story.

Thou, first of our orators, first of our wits ;
Yet whose parts and acquirements seem just lucky hits ;
With knowledge so vast, and with judgment so strong,
No man, with the half of 'em, e'er could go wrong ;
With passions so potent, and fancies so bright,
No man with the half of 'em e'er could go right ;
A sorry, poor, misbegot son of the Muses,
For using thy name offers fifty excuses.
Good Lord, what is man ! for as simple he looks,
Do but try to develop his hooks and his crooks,
With his depths and his shallows, his good and his evil,
All in all, he's a problem must puzzle the devil.
On his one ruling Passion Sir Pope hugely labours,
That, like th' old Hebrew walking-switch, eats up its neighbours :
Mankind are his show-box—a friend, would you know him ?
Pull the string, Ruling Passion, the picture will show him.
What pity, in rearing so beauteous a system,
One trifling particular, Truth, should have miss'd him !
For, spite of his fine theoretic positions,
Mankind is a science defies definitions.

Some sort all our qualities each to its tribe,
And think Human-nature they truly describe ;
Have you found this, or t'other? there's more in the wind,
As by one drunken fellow his comrades you'll find.
But such is the flaw, or the depth of the plan
In the make of the wonderful creature call'd Man,
No two virtues, whatever relation they claim,
Nor even two different shades of the same,
Though like as was ever twin-brother to brother
Possessing the one shall imply you've the other.

But truce with abstraction, and truce with a muse,
Whose rhymes you'll perhaps, Sir, ne'er deign to peruse :
Will you leave your justings, your jars, and your quarrels,
Contending with Billy for proud-nodding laurels !

My much-honour'd Patron, believe your poor Poet,
Your courage much more than your prudence you show it,
In vain with Squire Billy for laurels you struggle,
He'll have them by fair trade, if not, he will smuggle;
Not cabinets even of kings would conceal 'em,
He'd up the back-stairs, and by G— he would steal 'em.
Then feats like Squire Billy's you ne'er can atchieve 'em,
It is not, outdo him—the task is, out-thieve him.

TO DR. BLACKLOCK.

ELLISLAND, 21ST OCT. 1789.

Wow, but your letter made me vauntie !
And are ye hale, and weel, and cantie ?
I kenn'd it still your wee bit jauntie
    Wad bring ye to :
Lord send you ay as weel's I want ye,
    And then ye'll do.

The ill-thief blaw the Heron south !
And never drink be near his drouth !
He tald mysel by word o' mouth,
    He'd tak my letter ;
I lippen'd to the chiel in trouth,
    And bade nae better.

But aiblins honest Master Heron
Had at the time some dainty fair one,
To ware his theologic care on,
    And holy study ;
And tir'd o' sauls to waste his lear on,
    E'en tried the body.

But what d'ye think, my trusty fier,
I'm turn'd a gauger—Peace be here !
Parnassian queens, I fear, I fear
    Ye'll now disdain me !
And then my fifty pounds a year
    Will little gain me.

Ye glaiket, gleesome, dainty damies,
Wha by Castalia's wimplin' streamies,
Lowp, sing, and lave your pretty limbies,
    Ye ken, ye ken,
That strang necessity supreme is
    'Mang sons o' men.

I hae a wife and twa wee laddies,
They maun hae brose and brats o'
    duddies ;
Ye ken yoursels my heart right proud is—
    I need na vaunt,
But I'll sned besoms—thraw saugh
    woodies,
        Before they want.

Lord help me thro' this warld o' care !
I'm weary sick o't late and air !
Not but I hae a richer share
    Than monie ithers ;
But why should ae man better fare,
    And a' men brithers ?

Come, Firm Resolve, take thou the van,
Thou stalk o' carl-hemp in man !
And let us mind, faint heart ne'er wan
    A lady fair ;
Wha does the utmost that he can,
    Will whyles do mair.

But to conclude my silly rhyme,
(I'm scant o' verse, and scant o' time,)
To make a happy fire-side clime
    To weans and wife,
That's the true pathos and sublime
    Of human life.

My compliments to sister Beckie ;
And eke the same to honest Lucky,
I wat she is a daintie chuckie,
    As e'er tread clay !
And gratefully, my guid auld cockie,
    I'm yours for ay.

                    ROBERT BURNS.

PROLOGUE,

SPOKEN AT THE THEATRE, DUMFRIES, ON NEW YEAR'S DAY EVENING. [1790.]

No song nor dance I bring from yon great city
That queens it o'er our taste—the more's the pity;
Tho , by-the-by, abroad why will you roam ?
Good sense and taste are natives here at home :
But not for panegyric I appear,
I come to wish you all a good new-year !
Old Father Time deputes me here before ye,
Not for to preach, but tell his simple story :
The sage grave ancient cough'd, and bade me say,
" You're one year older this important day."
If wiser too—he hinted some suggestion,
But 'twould be rude, you know, to ask the question ;
And with a would-be roguish leer and wink,
He bade me on you press this one word—" Think ! "
    Ye sprightly youths, quite flush with hope and spirit,
Who think to storm the world by dint of merit,
To you the dotard has a deal to say,
In his sly, dry, sententious, proverb way !
He bids you mind, amid your thoughtless rattle,
That the first blow is ever half the battle ;
That tho' some by the skirt may try to snatch him,
Yet by the forelock is the hold to catch him ;
That whether doing, suffering, or forbearing,
You may do miracles by persevering.
    Last, tho' not least in love, ye youthful fair,
Angelic forms, high Heaven's peculiar care !
To you old Bald-pate smooths his wrinkled brow,
And humbly begs you'll mind the important—*Now !*
To crown your happiness he asks your leave,
And offers bliss to give and to receive.
    For our sincere, tho' haply weak endeavours,
With grateful pride we own your many favours ;
And howsoe'er our tongues may ill reveal it,
Believe our glowing bosoms truly feel it.

ELEGY ON THE LATE MISS BURNET,

OF MONBODDO.

LIFE ne'er exulted in so rich a prize
As Burnet, lovely from her native skies ;
Nor envious death so triumph'd in a blow,
As that which laid th' accomplish'd Burnet low.

Thy form and mind, sweet maid, can I forget?
In richest ore the brightest jewel set!
In thee, high Heaven above was truest shown,
And by his noblest work the Godhead best is known.

In vain ye flaunt in summer's pride, ye groves;
　　Thou crystal streamlet with thy flowery shore,
Ye woodland choir that chant your idle loves,
　　Ye cease to charm—Eliza is no more!

Ye heathy wastes, immix'd with reedy fens;
　　Ye mossy streams, with sedge and rushes stor'd;
Ye rugged cliffs o'erhanging dreary glens,
　　To you I fly, ye with my soul accord.

Princes, whose cumbrous pride was all their worth,
　　Shall venal lays their pompous exit hail?
And thou, sweet excellence! forsake our earth,
　　And not a Muse in honest grief bewail?

We saw thee shine in youth and beauty's pride,
　　And virtue's light, that beams beyond the spheres:
But like the sun eclips'd at morning tide,
　　Thou left'st us darkling in a world of tears.

The parent's heart that nestled fond in thee,
　　That heart how sunk, a prey to grief and care;
So deckt the woodbine sweet yon aged tree,
　　So from it ravish'd, leaves it bleak and bare.

THE FOLLOWING POEM WAS WRITTEN

TO A GENTLEMAN WHO HAD SENT HIM A NEWSPAPER, AND OFFERED TO CONTINUE IT FREE OF EXPENSE.

KIND Sir, I've read your paper through,
And, faith, to me, 'twas really new!
How guess'd ye, Sir, what maist I
　　wanted?
This monie a day I've grain'd and
　　gaunted,
To ken what French mischief was
　　brewin';
Or what the drumlie Dutch were doin';
That vile doup-skelper, Emperor Joseph,
If Venus yet had got his nose off;
Or how the collieshangie works
Atween the Russians and the Turks;

Or if the Swede, before he halt,
Would play anither Charles the Twalt:
If Denmark, any body spak o't;
Or Poland, wha had now the tack o't;
How cut-throat Prussian blades were
　　hingin;
How libbet Italy was singin;
If Spaniard, Portuguese, or Swiss,
Were sayin or takin aught amiss:
Or how our merry lads at hame,
In Britain's court, kept up the game:
How royal George, the Lord leuk o'er
　　him!

Was managing St. Stephen's quorum ;
If sleekit Chatham Will was livin,
Or glaikit Charlie got his nieve in ;
How daddie Burke the plea was cookin,
If Warren Hastings' neck was yeukin ;
How cesses, stents, and fees were rax'd,
Or if bare a—s yet were tax'd ;
The news o' princes, dukes, and earls,
Pimps, sharpers, bawds, and opera-girls ;
If that daft buckie, Geordie Wales,
Was threshin still at hizzies' tails ;
Or if he was grown oughtlins douser,
And no a perfect kintra cooser.—
A' this and mair I never heard of ;

And, but for you, I might despair'd of.
So gratefu', back your news I send you,
And pray a' guid things may attend you !

Ellisland, Monday Morning, 1790.

*Remonstrance to the Gentleman to whom
the foregoing Poem was addressed.*

Dear Peter, dear Peter,
  We poor sons of metre
Are often negleckit, ye ken ;
  For instance, your sheet, man,
  (Though glad I'm to see't, man,)
I get it no ae day in ten. —R.B.

LINES ON AN INTERVIEW WITH LORD DAER.

THIS wot ye all whom it concerns,
I Rhymer Robin, alias Burns,
    October twenty-third,
A ne'er to be forgotten day,
Sae far I sprachled up the brae,
    I dinner'd wi' a Lord.

I've been at druken writers' feasts,
Nay, been bitch-fou 'mang godly priests,
    Wi' rev'rence be it spoken ;
I've even join'd the honour'd jorum,
When mighty Squireships of the quorum
    Their hydra drouth did sloken.

But wi' a Lord—stand out my shin ;
A Lord—a Peer—an Earl's son,
    Up higher yet, my bonnet !
And sic a Lord—lang Scotch ells twa,
Our Peerage he o'erlooks them a',
    As I look o'er my sonnet.

But, O for Hogarth's magic pow'r !
To show Sir Bardie's willyart glow'r,
    And how he star'd and stammer'd,

When goavan, as if led wi' branks,
An' stumpin on his ploughman shanks,
    He in the parlour hammer'd.

I sidling shelter'd in a nook,
An' at his Lordship steal't a look,
    Like some portentous omen ;
Except good sense and social glee,
An' (what surprised me) modesty,
    I marked nought uncommon.

I watch'd the symptoms o' the Great,
The gentle pride, the lordly state,
    The arrogant assuming ;
The fient a pride, nae pride had he,
Nor sauce, nor state that I could see,
    Mair than an honest ploughman.

Then from his lordship I shall learn,
Henceforth to meet with unconcern
    One rank as weel's another ;
Nae honest worthy man need care
To meet with noble youthful Daer,
    For he but meets a brother.

THE RIGHTS OF WOMAN.

PROLOGUE SPOKEN BY MISS FONTENELLE ON HER BENEFIT-NIGHT. [NOV. 26, 1792.]

WHILE Europe's eye is fix'd on mighty things,
The fate of Empires and the fall of Kings ;
While quacks of State must each produce his plan,
And even children lisp The Rights of Man ;

Amid the mighty fuss just let me mention,
The Rights of Woman merit some attention.
 First, in the Sexes' intermix'd connexion,
One sacred Right of Woman is, Protection.—
The tender flower that lifts its head, elate,
Helpless, must fall before the blasts of Fate,
Sunk on the earth, defac'd its lovely form,
Unless your shelter ward th' impending storm.
 Our second Right—but needless here is caution,
To keep that Right inviolate's the fashion,
Each man of sense has it so full before him,
He'd die before he'd wrong it—'tis Decorum.
There was, indeed, in far less polish'd days,
A time, when rough rude man had naughty ways ;
Would swagger, swear, get drunk, kick up a riot,
Nay, even thus invade a Lady's quiet !—
Now, thank our stars ! those Gothic times are fled ;
Now, well-bred men—and you are all well-bred !
Most justly think (and we are much the gainers)
Such conduct neither spirit, wit, nor manners.
 For Right the third, our last, our best, our dearest,
That Right to fluttering female hearts the nearest,
Which even the Rights of Kings in low prostration
Most humbly own—'tis dear, dear admiration !
In that blest sphere alone we live and move ;
There taste that life of life—immortal love.—
Sighs, tears, smiles, glances, fits, flirtations, airs,
'Gainst such an host what flinty savage dares—
When awful Beauty joins with all her charms,
Who is so rash as rise in rebel arms ?
 Then truce with kings, and truce with constitutions,
With bloody armaments and revolutions !
Let Majesty your first attention summon,
Ah ! ça ira ! THE MAJESTY OF WOMAN !

ADDRESS, SPOKEN BY MISS FONTENELLE,

ON HER BENEFIT-NIGHT, DECEMBER 4, 1795, AT THE THEATRE, DUMFRIES.

STILL anxious to secure your partial favour,
And not less anxious, sure, this night, than ever,
A Prologue, Epilogue, or some such matter,
'Twould vamp my bill, said I, if nothing better :
So sought a Poet, roosted near the skies,
Told him I came to feast my curious eyes ;
Said, nothing like his works was ever printed ;
And last, my Prologue-business slily hinted.
'Ma'am, let me tell you,' quoth my man of rhymes,
'I know your bent —these are no laughing times :

Can you—but, Miss, I own I have my fears—
Dissolve in pause—and sentimental tears?
With laden sighs, and solemn-rounded sentence,
Rouse from his sluggish slumbers fell Repentance ;
Paint Vengeance as he takes his horrid stand,
Waving on high the desolating brand,
Calling the storms to bear him o'er a guilty land ?'
    I could no more—askance the creature eyeing,
D'ye think, said I, this face was made for crying ?
I'll laugh, that's poz—nay, more, the world shall know it ;
And so, your servant ! gloomy Master Poet !
    Firm as my creed, Sirs, 'tis my fix'd belief,
That Misery's another word for Grief ;
I also think—so may I be a bride !
That so much laughter, so much life enjoy'd.
    Thou man of crazy care and ceaseless sigh,
Still under bleak Misfortune's blasting eye ;
Doom'd to that sorest task of man alive—
To make three guineas do the work of five :
Laugh in Misfortune's face—the beldam witch !
Say, you'll be merry, tho' you can't be rich.
    Thou other man of care, the wretch in love,
Who long with jiltish arts and airs hast strove ;
Who, as the boughs all temptingly project,
Measur'st in desperate thought—a rope—thy neck—
Or, where the beetling cliff o'erhangs the deep,
Peerest to meditate the healing leap :
Wouldst thou be cur'd, thou silly, moping elf ?
Laugh at her follies—laugh e'en at thyself :
Learn to despise those frowns now so terrific,
And love a kinder—that's your grand specific.
    To sum up all, be merry, I advise ;
And as we're merry, may we still be wise.

VERSES TO A YOUNG LADY.

WITH A PRESENT OF SONGS.

HERE, where the Scottish Muse immortal lives,
    In sacred strains and tuneful numbers join'd,
Accept the gift ; tho' humble he who gives,
    Rich is the tribute of the grateful mind.

So may no ruffian-feeling in thy breast
    Discordant jar thy bosom-chords among !
But Peace attune thy gentle soul to rest,
    Or Love, ecstatic, wake his seraph song !

Or Pity's notes, in luxury of tears,
    As modest Want the tale of woe reveals ;
While conscious Virtue all the strain endears,
    And heaven-born Piety her sanction seals !

POEM ON PASTORAL POETRY.

HAIL, Poesie ! thou Nymph reserv'd !
In chase o' thee, what crowds hae swerv'd
Frae common sense, or sunk enerv'd
      'Mang heaps o' clavers ;
And och ! o'er aft thy joes hae starv'd,
      'Mid a' thy favours !

Say, Lassie, why thy train amang,
While loud the trump's heroic clang,
And sock or buskin skelp alang
      To death or marriage ;
Scarce ane has tried the shepherd-sang
      But wi' miscarriage ?

In Homer's craft Jock Milton thrives ;
Eschylus' pen Will Shakespeare drives ;
Wee Pope, the knurlin, 'till him rives
      Horatian fame ;
In thy sweet sang, Barbauld, survives
      Even Sappho's flame.

But thee, Theocritus, wha matches ?
They're no herd's ballats, Maro's catches;
Squire Pope but busks his skinklin
    patches
      O' heathen tatters :
I pass by hunders, nameless wretches,
      That ape their betters.

In this braw age o' wit and lear,
Will nane the Shepherd's whistle mair
Blaw sweetly in its native air

And rural grace ;
And wi' the far-fam'd Grecian share
      A rival place ?

Yes ! there is ane ; a Scottish callan—
There's ane ; come forrit, honest Allan !
Thou need na jouk behint the hallan,
      A chiel sae clever ;
The teeth o' Time may gnaw Tamtallan,
      But thou's for ever !

Thou paints auld Nature to the nines,
In thy sweet Caledonian lines ;
Nae gowden stream thro' myrtles twines,
      Where Philomel,
While nightly breezes sweep the vines,
      Her griefs will tell !

In gowany glens thy burnie strays,
Where bonie lasses bleach their claes ;
Or trots by hazelly shaws and braes,
      Wi' hawthorns gray,
Where blackbirds join the shepherd's
    lays
      At close o' day.

Thy rural loves are nature's sel' ;
Nae bombast spates o' nonsense swell ;
Nae snap conceits ; but that sweet spell
      O' witchin' love ;
That charm that can the strongest quell,
      The sternest move.

WRITTEN ON THE BLANK LEAF OF THE LAST EDITION OF HIS POEMS,

PRESENTED TO THE LADY WHOM HE HAD OFTEN CELEBRATED
UNDER THE NAME OF CHLORIS.

'TIS Friendship's pledge, my young, fair
    friend,
  Nor thou the gift refuse,
Nor with unwilling ear attend
  The moralizing Muse.

Since thou, in all thy youth and charms,
  Must bid the world adieu,

(A world 'gainst peace in constant arms)
  To join the friendly few.

Since, thy gay morn of life o'ercast,
  Chill came the tempest's lower,
(And ne'er misfortune's eastern blast
  Did nip a fairer flower.)

Since life's gay scenes must charm no
  more,
  Still much is left behind ;
Still nobler wealth hast thou in store—
  The comforts of the mind !

Thine is the self-approving glow,
  On conscious honour's part ;

And, dearest gift of heaven below,
  Thine friendship's truest heart.

The joys refin'd of sense and taste,
  With every muse to rove :
And doubly were the poet blest,
  These joys could he improve.

POETICAL ADDRESS TO MR. WILLIAM TYTLER,

WITH THE PRESENT OF THE BARD'S PICTURE.

REVERED defender of beauteous Stuart,
  Of Stuart, a name once respected,
A name, which to love, was the mark of a true heart,
  But now 'tis despis'd and neglected.

Tho' something like moisture conglobes in my eye,
  Let no one misdeem me disloyal ;
A poor friendless wand'rer may well claim a sigh,
  Still more, if that wand'rer were royal.

My fathers that name have rever'd on a throne ;
  My fathers have fallen to right it ;
Those fathers would spurn their degenerate son,
  That name should he scoffingly slight it.

Still in prayers for King George I most heartily join,
  The Queen, and the rest of the gentry,
Be they wise, be they foolish, is nothing of mine ;
  Their title's avow'd by my country.

But why of this epocha make such a fuss,
  That gave us the Hanover stem ?
If bringing them over was lucky for us,
  I'm sure 'twas as lucky for them.

But, loyalty, truce ! we're on dangerous ground,
  Who knows how the fashions may alter ?
The doctrine, to-day, that is loyalty sound,
  To-morrow may bring us a halter.

I send you a trifle, a head of a bard,
  A trifle scarce worthy your care ;
But accept it, good Sir, as a mark of regard,
  Sincere as a saint's dying prayer.

Now life's chilly evening dim shades in your eye,
  And ushers the long dreary night ;
But you, like the star that athwart gilds the sky,
  Your course to the latest is bright.

SKETCH.—NEW-YEAR DAY. [1790.]

TO MRS. DUNLOP.

THIS day Time winds th' exhausted
          chain,
To run the twelvemonth's length again :
I see the old, bald-pated fellow,
With ardent eyes, complexion sallow,
Adjust the unimpair'd machine
To wheel the equal, dull routine.
    The absent lover, minor heir,
In vain assail him with their prayer,
Deaf, as my friend, he sees them press,
Nor makes the hour one moment less.
Will you (the Major's with the hounds,
The happy tenants share his rounds ;
Coila's fair Rachel's care to-day,
And blooming Keith's engaged with
          Gray)
From housewife cares a minute borrow—
—That grandchild's cap will do to-
          morrow—
And join with me a moralizing,
This day's propitious to be wise in.
    First, what did yesternight deliver ?
' Another year has gone for ever.'
And what is this day's strong suggestion?
' The passing moment's all we rest on !'
Rest on—for what ? what do we here ?
Or why regard the passing year ?

Will Time, amus'd with proverb'd lore,
Add to our date one minute more ?
A few days may, a few years must,
Repose us in the silent dust ;
Then is it wise to damp our bliss ?
Yes—all such reasonings are amiss !
The voice of Nature loudly cries,
And many a message from the skies,
That something in us never dies ;
That on this frail, uncertain state
Hang matters of eternal weight ;
That future-life in worlds unknown
Must take its hue from this alone ;
Whether as heavenly glory bright,
Or dark as misery's woful night.—
    Since then, my honor'd, first of friends,
On this poor being all depends ;
Let us th' important Now employ,
And live as those that never die.
    Tho' you, with days and honors
          crown'd,
Witness that filial circle round,
(A sight—life's sorrows to repulse ;
A sight—pale Envy to convulse ;)
Others may claim your chief regard ;
Yourself, you wait your bright reward.

EXTEMPORE, ON MR. WILLIAM SMELLIE,

AUTHOR OF THE PHILOSOPHY OF NATURAL HISTORY,
AND MEMBER OF THE ANTIQUARIAN AND ROYAL SOCIETIES OF EDINBURGH.

                To Crochallan came,
The old cock'd hat, the grey surtout, the same ;
His bristling beard just rising in its might,
'Twas four long nights and days to shaving night ;
His uncomb'd grizzly locks wild staring, thatch'd
A head for thought profound and clear, unmatch'd
Yet tho' his caustic wit was biting, rude,
His heart was warm, benevolent, and good.

INSCRIPTION FOR AN ALTAR

TO INDEPENDENCE, AT KERROUGHTRY, SEAT OF MR. HERON, WRITTEN IN SUMMER, 1795.

THOU of an independent mind,
With soul resolv'd, with soul resign'd;
Prepar'd Power's proudest frown to brave,
Who wilt not be, nor have a slave;
Virtue alone who dost revere,
Thy own reproach alone dost fear,
Approach this shrine, and worship here.

MONODY ON A LADY FAMED FOR HER CAPRICE.

How cold is that bosom which folly once fired,
  How pale is that cheek where the rouge lately glisten'd!
How silent that tongue which the echoes oft tir'd,
  How dull is that ear which to flattery so listen'd!

If sorrow and anguish their exit await,
  From friendship and dearest affection remov'd;
How doubly severer, Maria, thy fate,
  Thou diedst unwept, as thou livedst unlov'd.

Loves, Graces, and Virtues, I call not on you;
  So shy, grave, and distant, ye shed not a tear:
But come, all ye offspring of Folly so true,
  And flowers let us cull for Maria's cold bier.

We'll search thro' the garden for each silly flower,
  We'll roam through the forest for each idle weed;
But chiefly the nettle, so typical, shower,
  For none e'er approach'd her but rued the rash deed.

We'll sculpture the marble, we'll measure the lay;
  Here Vanity strums on her idiot lyre;
There keen Indignation shall dart on her prey,
  Which spurning Contempt shall redeem from his ire.

THE EPITAPH.

HERE lies, now a prey to insulting neglect,
  What once was a butterfly, gay in life's beam:
Want only of wisdom denied her respect,
  Want only of goodness denied her esteem.

SONNET, ON THE DEATH OF ROBERT RIDDEL, ESQ. OF GLENRIDDEL.

[*April,* 1794.]

No more ye warblers of the wood—no more !
 Nor pour your descant, grating on my soul ;
 Thou young-eyed Spring, gay in thy verdant stole,
More welcome were to me grim Winter's wildest roar.

How can ye charm, ye flow'rs, with all your dyes ?
 Ye blow upon the sod that wraps my friend :
 How can I to the tuneful strain attend ?
That strain flows round th' untimely tomb where Riddel lies.

Yes, pour, ye warblers, pour the notes of woe !
 And soothe the Virtues weeping o'er his bier :
 The Man of Worth, and has not left his peer,
Is in his "narrow house" for ever darkly low.

Thee, Spring, again with joys shall others greet ;
Me, mem'ry of my loss will only meet.

IMPROMPTU, ON MRS. RIDDEL'S BIRTHDAY, NOVEMBER 4, 1793.

OLD Winter with his frosty beard,
Thus once to Jove his prayer preferr'd, —
' What have I done of all the year,
To bear this hated doom severe ?
My cheerless suns no pleasure know ;
Night's horrid car drags, dreary slow ;
My dismal months no joys are crowning,
But spleeny English, hanging, drowning.
Now, Jove, for once be mighty civil,
To counterbalance all this evil ;
Give me, and I've no more to say,
Give me Maria's natal day !
That brilliant gift will so enrich me,
Spring, Summer, Autumn, cannot match me ;
''Tis done !' says Jove ; so ends my story,
And Winter once rejoic'd in glory.

TO A YOUNG LADY, MISS JESSY LEWARS, DUMFRIES,

WITH BOOKS WHICH THE BARD PRESENTED HER. [JUNE 26TH, 1796.]

THINE be the volumes, Jessy fair,
And with them take the Poet's prayer—
That fate may in her fairest page,
With every kindliest, best presage
Of future bliss, enrol thy name ;
With native worth, and spotless fame,
And wakeful caution still aware
Of ill—but chief, man's felon snare :
All blameless joys on earth we find,
And all the treasures of the mind—
These be thy guardian and reward ;
So prays thy faithful friend, the Bard.

VERSES

WRITTEN UNDER VIOLENT GRIEF.

Accept the gift a friend sincere
  Wad on thy worth be pressin' ;
Remembrance oft may start a tear,
But oh ! that tenderness forbear,
  Though 'twad my sorrows lessen.

My morning raise sae clear and fair,
  I thought sair storms wad never
Bedew the scene ; but grief and care
In wildest fury hae made bare
  My peace, my hope, for ever !

You think I'm glad ; oh, I pay weel
  For a' the joy I borrow,
In solitude—then, then I feel
I canna to mysel' conceal
  My deeply-ranklin' sorrow.

Farewell ! within thy bosom free
  A sigh may whiles awaken ;
A tear may wet thy laughin' ee,
For Scotia's son—ance gay like thee —
  Now hopeless, comfortless, forsaken !

EXTEMPORE TO MR. SYME,

ON REFUSING TO DINE WITH HIM,
AFTER HAVING BEEN PROMISED THE FIRST OF COMPANY, AND THE FIRST OF COOKERY.

17th December, 1795.

No more of your guests, be they titled or not,
  And cook'ry the first in the nation ;
Who is proof to thy personal converse and wit,
  Is proof to all other temptation.

TO MR. SYME,

WITH A PRESENT OF A DOZEN OF PORTER.

O, had the malt thy strength of mind,
  Or hops the flavour of thy wit,
'Twere drink for first of human kind,
  A gift that e'en for Syme were fit.

Jerusalem Tavern, Dumfries.

SONNET,

ON HEARING A THRUSH SING IN A MORNING WALK IN JANUARY, WRITTEN 25TH JANUARY, 1793,
THE BIRTH-DAY OF THE AUTHOR.

Sing on, sweet Thrush, upon the leafless bough ;
  Sing on, sweet bird, I listen to thy strain :
  See agèd Winter, 'mid his surly reign,
At thy blythe carol clears his furrow'd brow.

So in lone Poverty's dominion drear
  Sits meek Content with light unanxious heart,
  Welcomes the rapid moments, bids them part,
Nor asks if they bring aught to hope or fear.

I thank thee, Author of this opening day!
  Thou whose bright sun now gilds the orient skies!
  Riches denied, thy boon was purer joys,
What wealth could never give nor take away!

Yet come, thou child of poverty and care;
The mite high Heaven bestow'd, that mite with thee I'll share.

POEM, ADDRESSED TO MR. MITCHELL,

COLLECTOR OF EXCISE, DUMFRIES. [DECEMBER, 1795.]

FRIEND of the Poet, tried and leal,
Wha, wanting thee, might beg or steal;
Alake, alake, the meikle Deil
      Wi' a' his witches
Are at it, skelpin! jig and reel,
      In my poor pouches.

I modestly fu' fain wad hint it,
That one pound one, I sairly want it:
If wi' the hizzie down ye sent it,
      It would be kind;
And while my heart wi' life-blood dunted,
      I'd bear't in mind.

So may the auld year gang out moaning
To·see the new come laden, groaning,
Wi' double plenty o'er the loanin
      To thee and thine;
Domestic peace and comforts crowning
      The hale design.

POSTSCRIPT.

Ye've heard this while how I've been
      licket,
And by fell death was nearly nicket:
Grim loon! he gat me by the fecket,
      And sair me sheuk;
But by guid luck I lap a wicket,
      And turn'd a neuk.

But by that health, I've got a share o't,
And by that life, I'm promis'd mair o't,
My heal and weal I'll take a care o't
      A tentier way:
Then fareweel folly, hide and hair o't,
      For ance and aye.

SENT TO A GENTLEMAN WHOM HE HAD OFFENDED.

THE friend whom wild from wisdom's
      way
  The fumes of wine infuriate send;
(Not moony madness more astray;)
  Who but deplores that hapless friend?

Mine was th' insensate frenzied part,
  Ah why should I such scenes out-
      live?
Scenes so abhorrent to my heart!
  'Tis thine to pity and forgive.

POEM ON LIFE,

ADDRESSED TO COLONEL DE PEYSTER, DUMFRIES, 1796.

My honour'd Colonel, deep I feel
Your interest in the Poet's weal;
Ah! now sma' heart hae I to speel
   The steep Parnassus,
Surrounded thus by bolus pill,
   And potion glasses.

O what a canty warld were it,
Would pain, and care, and sickness
   spare it;
And fortune favour worth and merit,
   As they deserve:
(And aye a rowth, roast beef and claret;
   Syne wha wad starve?)

Dame Life, tho' fiction out may trick her,
And in paste gems and fripp'ry deck her;
Oh! flick'ring, feeble, and unsicker
   I've found her still,
Aye wav'ring like the willow wicker,
   'Tween good and ill.

Then that curst carmagnole, auld Satan,
Watches, like baudrons by a rattan,
Our sinfu' saul to get a claut on
   Wi' felon ire;
Syne, whip! his tail ye'll ne'er cast
   saut on,
   He's off like fire.

Ah Nick! ah Nick! it isna fair,
First shewing us the tempting ware,
Bright wines and bonie lasses rare,
   To put us daft;
Syne weave, unseen, thy spider snare
   O' hell's damn'd waft.

Poor man, the flie, aft bizzies by,
And aft as chance he comes thee nigh,
Thy auld damn'd elbow yeuks wi' joy,
   And hellish pleasure;
Already in thy fancy's eye,
   Thy sicker treasure.

Soon heels-o'er-gowdie! in he gangs,
And like a sheep-head on a tangs,
Thy girning laugh enjoys his pangs
   And murd'ring wrestle,
As, dangling in the wind, he hangs
   A gibbet's tassel.

But lest you think I am uncivil,
To plague you with this draunting drivel,
Abjuring a' intentions evil,
   I quat my pen:
The Lord preserve us frae the Devil!
   Amen! amen!

TO ROBERT GRAHAM, ESQ. OF FINTRY,

ON RECEIVING A FAVOUR.

I CALL no Goddess to inspire my strains,
A fabled Muse may suit a Bard that
   feigns;
Friend of my life! my ardent spirit burns,
And all the tribute of my heart returns,
For boons recorded, goodness ever new,
The gift still dearer, as the giver you.

Thou orb of day! thou other paler light!
And all ye many sparkling stars of night;
If aught that giver from my mind efface;
If I that giver's bounty e'er disgrace;
Then roll to me, along your wand'ring
   spheres,
Only to number out a villain's years!

EPITAPH ON A FRIEND.

An honest man here lies at rest,
As e'er God with his image blest;
The friend of man, the friend of truth;
The friend of age, and guide of youth:

Few hearts like his, with virtue warm'd,
Few heads with knowledge so inform'd:
If there's another world, he lives in bliss;
If there is none, he made the best of this.

VERSES WRITTEN AT SELKIRK,

ADDRESSED TO MR. CREECH, 13TH MAY, 1787.

AULD chuckie Reekie's sair distrest,
Down droops her ance weel burnish't
          crest,
Nae joy her bonie buskit nest
          Can yield ava,
Her darling bird that she lo'es best,
          Willie's awa!

O Willie was a witty wight,
And had o' things an unco slight;
Auld Reekie ay he keepit tight,
          An' trig an' braw:
But now they'll busk her like a fright,
          Willie's awa!

The stiffest o' them a' he bow'd;
The bauldest o' them a' he cow'd;
They durst nae mair than he allow'd,
          That was a law:
We've lost a birkie weel worth gowd,
          Willie's awa!

Now gawkies, tawpies, gowks, and
          fools,
Frae colleges and boarding-schools,
May sprout like simmer puddock-stools
          In glen or shaw,
He wha could brush them down to mools,
          Willie's awa!

The brethren o' the Commerce-Chaumer
May mourn their loss wi' doolfu' clamour;
He was a dictionar and grammar
          Amang them a';
I fear they'll now mak mony a stammer,
          Willie's awa!

Nae mair we see his levee door
Philosophers and Poets pour,
And toothy critics by the score,
          In bloody raw,
The adjutant o' a' the core,
          Willie's awa!

Now worthy Gregory's Latin face,
Tytler's and Greenfield's modest grace;
Mackenzie, Stewart, sic a brace
          As Rome ne'er saw;
They a' maun meet some ither place,
          Willie's awa!

Poor Burns e'en Scotch drink canna
          quicken,
He cheeps like some bewilder'd chicken
Scar'd frae its minnie and the cleckin
          By hoodie-craw;
Grief's gien his heart an unco kickin',
          Willie's awa!

Now ev'ry sour-mou'd grinnin' blellum,
And Calvin's folk, are fit to fell him;
And self-conceited critic skellum
          His quill may draw;
He wha could brawlie ward their bellum,
          Willie's awa!

Up wimpling stately Tweed I've sped,
And Eden scenes on crystal Jed,
And Ettrick banks now roaring red,
          While tempests blaw;
But every joy and pleasure's fled,
          Willie's awa!

May I be Slander's common speech;
A text for infamy to preach;
And lastly, streekit out to bleach
          In winter snaw;
When I forget thee, WILLIE CREECH,
          Tho' far awa!

May never wicked Fortune touzle him!
May never wicked men bamboozle him!
Until a pow as auld's Methusalem
          He canty claw!
Then to the blessed, New Jerusalem
          Fleet wing awa!

INSCRIPTION ON THE TOMBSTONE

ERECTED BY BURNS TO THE MEMORY OF FERGUSSON.

"Here lies Robert Fergusson, Poet,
Born September 5th, 1751—
Died 16th October, 1774."

No sculptur'd marble here, nor pompous lay,
    ' No storied urn nor animated bust ; '
This simple stone directs pale Scotia's way
    To pour her sorrows o'er her Poet's dust.

She mourns, sweet tuneful youth, thy hapless fate,
    Tho' all the powers of song thy fancy fir'd,
Yet Luxury and Wealth lay by in State,
    And thankless starv'd what they so much admir'd.

This humble tribute with a tear he gives,
    A brother Bard, he can no more bestow :
But dear to fame thy Song immortal lives,
    A nobler monument than Art can show.

A GRACE BEFORE DINNER.

O THOU, who kindly dost provide
    For every creature's want !
We bless thee, God of Nature wide,
    For all thy goodness lent :

And, if it please thee, Heavenly Guide,
    May never worse be sent ;
But whether granted, or denied,
    Lord, bless us with content !
                    Amen !

A VERSE

COMPOSED AND REPEATED BY BURNS, TO THE MASTER OF THE HOUSE, ON TAKING LEAVE
AT A PLACE IN THE HIGHLANDS, WHERE HE HAD BEEN HOSPITABLY ENTERTAINED.

WHEN death's dark stream I ferry o'er,
    A time that surely shall come ;
In Heaven itself I'll ask no more,
    Than just a Highland welcome.

LIBERTY.

A FRAGMENT.

THEE, Caledonia, thy wild heaths among,
Thee, famed for martial deed and sacred song,
    To thee I turn with swimming eyes ;
Where is that soul of Freedom fled ?
Immingled with the mighty dead !
    Beneath the hallow'd turf where Wallace lies !
Hear it not, Wallace, in thy bed of death !
    Ye babbling winds, in silence sweep ;
    Disturb not ye the hero's sleep,
Nor give the coward secret breath.

Is this the power in Freedom's war,
  That wont to bid the battle rage?
Behold that eye which shot immortal hate,
  Crushing the despot's proudest bearing,
That arm which, nerved with thundering fate,
  Brav'd usurpation's boldest daring!
One quench'd in darkness like the sinking star,
And one the palsied arm of tottering, powerless age.

FRAGMENT OF AN ODE

TO THE MEMORY OF PRINCE CHARLES EDWARD STUART.

FALSE flatterer, Hope, away!
Nor think to lure us as in days of yore;
  We solemnize this sorrowing natal-day
To prove our loyal truth; we can no more;
  And owning Heaven's mysterious sway,
    Submissive low adore.

Ye honour'd mighty dead!
Who nobly perish'd in the glorious cause,
Your king, your country, and her laws!
  From great Dundee who smiling victory led,
And fell a martyr in her arms
(What breast of northern ice but warms?)
  To bold Balmerino's undying name,
Whose soul of fire, lighted at heaven's high flame,
Deserves the proudest wreath departed heroes claim.

Nor unavenged your fate shall be,
  It only lags the fatal hour;
Your blood shall with incessant cry
  Awake at last th' unsparing power;
As from the cliff, with thundering course,
  The snowy ruin smokes along,
With doubling speed and gathering force,
Till deep it crashing whelms the cottage in the vale!
So vengeance   *   *   *   *

ELEGY ON THE DEATH OF ROBERT RUISSEAUX.

Now Robin lies in his last lair,
He'll gabble rhyme, nor sing nae mair,
Cauld poverty, wi' hungry stare,
  Nae mair shall fear him:
Nor anxious fear, nor cankert care,
  E'er mair come near him.

To tell the truth, they seldom fash't him,
Except the moment that they crush't
  him;
For sune as chance or fate had husht 'em,

    Tho' e'er sae short,
Then wi' a rhyme or sang he lasht 'em,
    And thought it sport.

Tho' he was bred to kintra wark,
And counted was baith wight and stark,
Yet that was never Robin's mark
    To mak a man;
But tell him, he was learn'd and clark,
    Ye roos'd him than!

ANSWER TO VERSES ADDRESSED TO THE POET

BY THE GUIDWIFE OF WAUCHOPE-HOUSE. [1787.]

GUIDWIFE,
I MIND it weel, in early date,
When I was beardless, young and blate,
　An' first could thresh the barn,
Or haud a yokin at the pleugh,
An' tho' forfoughten sair eneugh,
　Yet unco proud to learn :
When first amang the yellow corn
　A man I reckon'd was,
And wi' the lave ilk merry morn
　Could rank my rig and lass,
　　Still shearing, and clearing
　　The tither stooked raw,
　　Wi' claivers, an' haivers,
　　Wearing the day awa :

Ev'n then a wish, (I mind its power,)
A wish that to my latest hour
　Shall strongly heave my breast ;
That I for poor auld Scotland's sake,
Some usefu' plan, or beuk could make,
　Or sing a sang at least.
The rough bur-thistle, spreading wide
　Amang the bearded bear,
I turn'd the weeder-clips aside,
　An' spar'd the symbol dear :
　　No nation, no station,
　　My envy e'er could raise ;
　　A Scot still, but blot still,
　　I knew nae higher praise.

But still the elements o' sang
In formless jumble, right an' wrang,
　Wild floated in my brain ;
Till on that har'st I said before,
My partner in the merry core,
　She rous'd the forming strain :
I see her yet, the sonsie quean,
　That lighted up my jingle,

Her witching smile, her pauky een,
　That gart my heart-strings tingle ;
　　I fired, inspired,
　　　At ev'ry kindling keek,
　　But bashing, and dashing,
　　　I feared aye to speak.

Health to the sex, ilk guid chiel says,
Wi' merry dance in winter days,
　An' we to share in common :
The gust o' joy, the balm of woe,
The saul o' life, the heav'n below,
　Is rapture-giving woman.
Ye surly sumphs, who hate the name,
　Be mindfu' o' your mither :
She, honest woman, may think shame
　That ye're connected with her,
　　Ye're wae men, ye're nae men,
　　That slight the lovely dears ;
　　To shame ye, disclaim ye,
　　Ilk honest birkie swears.

For you, no bred to barn or byre,
Wha sweetly tune the Scottish lyre,
　Thanks to you for your line :
The marled plaid ye kindly spare,
By me should gratefully be ware ;
　'Twad please me to the nine.
I'd be more vauntie o' my hap,
　Douce hingin' owre my curple,
Than ony ermine ever lap,
　Or proud imperial purple.
　　Farewell then, lang heal then,
　　　An' plenty be your fa' :
　　May losses and crosses
　　　Ne'er at your hallan ca'.

March, 1787.

TO J. LAPRAIK.

SEPT. 13TH, 1785.

GUID speed an' furder to you, Johny,
Guid health, hale han's, and weather
　bonie
Now when ye're nickan down fu' cany

The staff o' bread,
May ye ne'er want a stoup o' bran'y
　To clear your head.

May Boreas never thresh your rigs,
Nor kick your rickles aff their legs,
Sendin' the stuff o'er muirs an' hags
  Like drivin' wrack ;
But may the tapmast grain that wags
  Come to the sack.

I'm bizzie too, an' skelpin' at it,
But bitter, daudin showers hae wat it,
Sae my auld stumpie pen I gat it
  Wi' muckle wark,
An' took my jocteleg an' whatt it,
  Like onie clerk.

It's now twa month that I'm your debtor,
For your braw, nameless, dateless letter,
Abusin' me for harsh ill-nature
  On holy men,
While Deil a hair yoursel' ye're better,
  But mair profane.

But let the kirk-folk ring their bells,
Let's sing about our noble sels ;
We'll cry nae jads frae heathen hills
  To help, or roose us,
But browster wives an' whisky stills,
  They are the Muses.

Your friendship, Sir, I winna quat it,
An' if ye make objections at it,
Then han' in nieve some day we'll knot it,
  An' witness take,
An' when wi' Usquebae we've wat it
  It winna break.

But if the beast and branks be spar'd
Till kye be gaun without the herd,
An' a' the vittel in the yard,
  An' theekit right,
I mean your ingle-side to guard
  Ae winter night.

Then muse-inspirin' aqua-vitæ
Shall make us baith sae blithe an' witty
Till ye forget ye're auld an' gatty,
  An' be as canty
As ye were nine years less than thretty,
  Sweet ane an' twenty !

But stooks are cowpet wi' the blast,
An' now the sinn keeks in the west,
Then I maun rin amang the rest
  An' quit my chanter ;
Sae I subscribe mysel in haste,
  Yours, Rab the Ranter.

THE TWA HERDS. [APRIL 1785.]

Blockheads with reason wicked wits abhor,
But Fool with Fool is barbarous civil war.

        POPE.

O a' ye pious godly flocks,
Weel fed on pastures orthodox,
Wha now will keep you frae the fox,
  Or worrying tykes ?
Or wha will tent the waifs and crocks,
  About the dykes ?

The twa best herds in a' the wast,
That e'er gae gospel horn a blast,
These five and twenty summers past,
  O dool to tell !
Hae had a bitter black out-cast,
  Atween themsel.

O, Moodie, man, and wordy Russel,
How could you raise so vile a bustle,
Ye'll see how new-light herds will whistle,
  And think it fine !
The Lord's cause ne'er gat sic a twistle,
  Sin' I hae min'.

O, Sirs, whae'er wad hae expeckit,
Your duty ye wad sae negleckit,
Ye wha were ne'er by lairds respeckit,
  To wear the plaid,
But by the brutes themselves eleckit
  To be their guide.

What flock wi' Moodie's flock could rank,
Sae hale and hearty every shank,
Nae poison'd soor Arminians tank
    He let them taste,
Frae Calvin's well, aye clear, they drank:
    O' sic a feast !

The thummart wil'-cat, brock and tod,
Weel kend his voice thro' a' the wood,
He smell'd their ilka hole and road,
    Baith out and in,
And weel he lik'd to shed their bluid,
    And sell their skin.

What herd like Russel tell'd his tale,
His voice was heard thro' muir and dale,
He kend the Lord's sheep, ilka tail,
    O'er a' the height,
And saw gin they were sick or hale,
    At the first sight.

He fine a mangy sheep could scrub,
Or nobly fling the gospel club,
And new-light herds could nicely drub,
    Or pay their skin,
Could shake them owre the burning dub,
    Or heave them in.

Sic twa—O ! do I live to see't,
Sic famous twa should disagreet,
An' names, like 'villain,' 'hypocrite,'
    Ilk ither gi'en,
While new-light herds wi' laughin' spite,
    Say, 'neither's liein' !

A' ye wha tent the gospel fauld,
There's Duncan deep, and Peebles shaul,
But chiefly thou, apostle Auld,
    We trust in thee,
That thou wilt work them, hot and cauld,
    Till they agree.

Consider, Sirs, how we're beset,
There's scarce a new herd that we get,

But comes frae 'mang that cursed set
    I winna name,
I hope frae heaven to see them yet
    In fiery flame.

Dalrymple has been lang our fae,
M'Gill has wrought us meikle wae,
And that curs'd rascal ca'd M'Quhae,
    And baith the Shaws,
That aft hae made us black and blae,
    Wi' vengefu' paws.

Auld Wodrow lang has hatch'd mischief,
We thought aye death wad bring relief,
But he has gotten, to our grief,
    Ane to succeed him,
A chiel wha'll soundly buff our beef ;
    I meikle dread him.

And monie a ane that I could tell,
Wha fain would openly rebel,
Forby turn-coats amang oursel,
    There's Smith for ane,
I doubt he's but a grey nick quill,
    And that ye'll fin'.

O ! a' ye flocks, owre a' the hills,
By mosses, meadows, moors, and fells,
Come join your counsels and your skills,
    To cowe the lairds,
And get the brutes the power themsels
    To choose their herds.

Then Orthodoxy yet may prance,
And Learning in a woody dance,
And that fell cur ca'd Common Sense,
    That bites sae sair,
Be banish'd owre the seas to France ;
    Let him bark there.

Then Shaw's and D'rymple's eloquence,
M'Gill's close nervous excellence,
M'Quhae's pathetic manly sense,
    And guid M'Math,
Wi' Smith, wha thro' the heart can glance,
    May a' pack aff.

TO THE REV. JOHN M'MATH,

ENCLOSING A COPY OF HOLY WILLIE'S PRAYER, WHICH HE HAD REQUESTED.

Sept. 17th, 1785.

WHILE at the stook the shearers cowr
To shun the bitter blaudin' show'r,
Or in gulravage rinnin scour
        To pass the time,
To you I dedicate the hour
        In idle rhyme.

My Musie, tir'd wi' monie a sonnet
On gown, an' ban', an' douse black bonnet,
Is grown right eerie now she's done it,
        Lest they shou'd blame her,
An' rouse their holy thunder on it,
        And anathem her.

I own 'twas rash, and rather hardy,
That I, a simple countra bardie,
Shou'd meddle wi' a pack so sturdy,
        Wha, if they ken me,
Can easy, wi' a single wordie,
        Lowse hell upon me.

But I gae mad at their grimaces,
Their sighin', cantin', grace-proud faces,
Their three-mile prayers, and hauf-mile graces,
        Their raxin' conscience,
Whase greed, revenge, an' pride disgraces
        Waur nor their nonsense.

There's Gaun, misca't waur than a beast,
Wha has mair honour in his breast
Than monie scores as guid's the priest
        Wha sae abus'd him ;
An' may a bard no crack his jest
        What way they've us'd him ?

See him, the poor man's friend in need,
The gentleman in word an' deed,
An' shall his fame an' honour bleed
        By worthless skellums,
An' no a Muse erect her head
        To cowe the blellums ?

O Pope, had I thy satire's darts
To gie the rascals their deserts,
I'd rip their rotten, hollow hearts,
   An' tell aloud
Their jugglin' hocus-pocus arts
    To cheat the crowd.

God knows, I'm no the thing I shou'd be,
Nor am I even the thing I could be,
But, twenty times, I rather would be
   An atheist clean,
Than under gospel colours hid be,
    Just for a screen.

An honest man may like a glass,
An honest man may like a lass,
But mean revenge, an' malice fause,
   He'll still disdain,
An' then cry zeal for gospel laws,
    Like some we ken.

They tak religion in their mouth ;
They talk o' mercy, grace, an' truth,
For what ? to gie their malice skouth
   On some puir wight,
An' hunt him down, o'er right an' ruth,
    To ruin straight.

All hail, Religion ! maid divine !
Pardon a muse sae mean as mine,
Who in her rough imperfect line
   Thus daurs to name thee ;
To stigmatize false friends of thine
    Can ne'er defame thee.

Tho' blotcht an' foul wi' monie a stain,
An' far unworthy of thy train,
Wi' trembling voice I tune my strain
   To join wi' those,
Who boldly daur thy cause maintain
    In spite o' foes :

In spite o' crowds, in spite o' mobs,
In spite of undermining jobs,
In spite o' dark banditti stabs
   At worth an' merit,
By scoundrels, even wi' holy robes,
    But hellish spirit.

O Ayr! my dear, my native ground !
Within thy presbyterial bound,
A candid lib'ral band is found
   Of public teachers,
As men, as Christians too, renown'd,
   An' manly preachers.

Sir, in that circle you are nam'd ;
Sir, in that circle you are fam'd ;
An' some, by whom your doctrine's blam'd,
   (Which gies you honour,)
Even, Sir, by them your heart's esteem'd,
   An' winning manner.

Pardon this freedom I have ta'en,
An' if impertinent I've been,
Impute it not, good Sir, in ane
   Whase heart ne'er wrang'd ye,
But to his utmost would befriend
   Ought that belang'd ye.

HOLY WILLIE'S PRAYER.

O Thou, wha in the Heavens dost
   dwell,
Wha, as it pleases best thysel',
Sends ane to heaven and ten to hell,
   A' for thy glory,
And no for onie guid or ill
   They've done afore thee !

I bless and praise thy matchless might,
Whan thousands thou hast left in night,
That I am here afore thy sight,
   For gifts an' grace,
A burnin an' a shinin light,
   To a' this place.

What was I, or my generation,
That I should get sic exaltation ?
I, wha deserve sic just damnation,
   For broken laws,
Five thousand years 'fore my creation,
   Thro' Adam's cause.

When frae my mither's womb I fell,
Thou might hae plunged me in hell,
To gnash my gums, to weep and wail,
   In burnin' lake,
Where damnèd devils roar and yell,
   Chain'd to a stake.

Yet I am here a chosen sample,
To show thy grace is great and ample ;
I'm here a pillar in thy temple,
   Strong as a rock,
A guide, a buckler, an example
   To a' thy flock.

O Lord, thou kens what zeal I bear,
When drinkers drink, and swearers
   swear,
And singin there and dancin here,
   Wi' great an' sma':
For I am keepit by thy fear,
   Free frae them a'.

But yet, O Lord ! confess I must,
At times I'm fash'd wi' fleshly lust,
An' sometimes too, wi' warldly trust,
   Vile self gets in ;
But thou remembers we are dust,
   Defil'd in sin.

O Lord ! yestreen, thou kens, wi' Meg—
Thy pardon I sincerely beg,
O ! may it ne'er be a livin plague
   To my dishonour,
An' I'll ne'er lift a lawless leg
   Again upon her.

Besides I farther maun allow,
Wi' Lizzie's lass, three times I trow ;
But Lord, that Friday I was fou,
　　　When I came near her,
Or else thou kens thy servant true
　　　Wad ne'er hae steer'd her.

May be thou lets this fleshly thorn
Beset thy servant e'en and morn,
Lest he owre high and proud should turn,
　　　'Cause he's sae gifted ;
If sae, thy hand maun e'en be borne,
　　　Until thou lift it.

Lord, bless thy chosen in this place,
For here thou hast a chosen race ;
But God confound their stubborn face,
　　　And blast their name,
Wha bring thy elders to disgrace,
　　　An' public shame.

Lord, mind Gawn Hamilton's deserts,
He drinks, an' swears, an' plays at cartes,
Yet has sae monie takin arts,
　　　Wi' grit an' sma',
Frae God's ain priest the people's hearts
　　　He steals awa'.

An' whan we chasten'd him therefore,
Thou kens how he bred sic a splore,
As set the warld in a roar

O' laughin at us ;
Curse thou his basket and his store,
　　　Kail and potatoes.

Lord, hear my earnest cry an' pray'r,
Against that presbyt'ry o' Ayr,
Thy strong right hand, Lord, make it
　　bare,
　　　Upo' their heads ;
Lord, weigh it down, and dinna spare,
　　　For their misdeeds.

O Lord my God, that glib-tongu'd Aiken,
My very heart and soul are quakin,
To think how we stood sweatin, shakin,
　　　An' p—d wi' dread,
While he, wi' hingin lips an' snakin,
　　　Held up his head.

Lord, in the day of vengeance try him ;
Lord, visit them wha did employ him,
And pass not in thy mercy by 'em,
　　　Nor hear their pray'r :
But, for thy people's sake, destroy 'em,
　　　And dinna spare

But, Lord, remember me and mine
Wi' mercies temp'ral and divine,
That I for gear and grace may shine,
　　　Excell'd by nane,
An' a' the glory shall be thine,
　　　Amen, Amen.

EPITAPH ON HOLY WILLIE.

HERE Holy Willie's sair worn clay
　　Taks up its last abode ;
His saul has taen some other way,
　　I fear the left-hand road.

Stop ! there he is, as sure's a gun,
　　Poor silly body, see him ;
Nae wonder he's as black's the grun,
　　Observe wha's standing wi' him.

Your brunstane devilship, I see,
　　Has got him there before ye ;

But haud your nine-tail cat a-wee,
　　Till ance you've heard my story.

Your pity I will not implore,
　　For pity ye have nane ;
Justice, alas ! has gien him o'er,
　　And mercy's day is gane.

But hear me, Sir, deil as ye are,
　　Look something to your credit ;
A coof like him wad stain your name,
　　If it were kent ye did it.

K 2

ON SCARING SOME WATER FOWL

IN LOCH-TURIT, A WILD SCENE AMONG THE HILLS OF OCHTERTYRE.

WHY, ye tenants of the lake,
For me your wat'ry haunt forsake?
Tell me, fellow-creatures, why
At my presence thus you fly?
Why disturb your social joys,
Parent, filial, kindred ties?—
Common friend to you and me,
Nature's gifts to all are free:
Peaceful keep your dimpling wave,
Busy feed, or wanton lave;
Or, beneath the sheltering rock,
Bide the surging billow's shock.
   Conscious, blushing for our race,
Soon, too soon, your fears I trace.
Man, your proud, usurping foe,
Would be lord of all below;
Plumes himself in Freedom's pride,
Tyrant stern to all beside.
   The eagle, from the cliffy brow,
Marking you his prey below,

In his breast no pity dwells,
Strong Necessity compels.
But Man, to whom alone is giv'n
A ray direct from pitying Heav'n,
Glories in his heart humane—
And creatures for his pleasure slain.
   In these savage, liquid plains,
Only known to wand'ring swains,
Where the mossy riv'let strays,
Far from human haunts and ways;
All on Nature you depend,
And life's poor season peaceful spend.
   Or, if man's superior might
Dare invade your native right,
On the lofty ether borne,
Man with all his pow'rs you scorn;
Swiftly seek, on clanging wings,
Other lakes and other springs;
And the foe you cannot brave,
Scorn at least to be his slave.

TO GAVIN HAMILTON, ESQ. MAUCHLINE,

RECOMMENDING A BOY.

Mosgaville, May 3, 1786.

I HOLD it, Sir, my bounden duty,
To warn you how that Master Tootie,
   Alias Laird M'Gaun,
Was here to lure the lad away
'Bout whom ye spak the tither day,
   An' wad hae don't aff han':
But lest he learn the callan tricks,
As faith I muckle doubt him,
Like scrapin' out auld Crummie's nicks,
   An' tellin' lies about them;
As lieve then I'd have then,
   Your clerkship he should sair,
If sae be, ye may be
   Not fitted otherwhere.

Altho' I say't, he's gleg enough,
An' 'bout a house that's rude an' rough,
   The boy might learn to swear;
But then wi' you, he'll be sae taught,
An' get sic fair example straught,
   I hae na onie fear.
Ye'll catechize him every quirk,

An' shore him weel wi' hell;
An' gar him follow to the kirk——
   —Ay when ye gang yoursel.
If ye then, maun be then
   Frae hame this comin' Friday,
Then please, Sir, to lea'e, Sir,
   The orders wi' your lady.

My word of honour I ha'e gi'en,
In Paisley John's, that night at e'en,
   To meet the Warld's worm:
To try to get the twa to gree,
An' name the airles an' the fee,
   In legal mode an' form:
I ken he weel a snick can draw,
   When simple bodies let him;
An' if a Devil be at a',
   In faith he's sure to get him.
To phrase you an' praise you,
   Ye ken your Laureat scorns:
The pray'r still, you share still,
   Of grateful Minstrel   BURNS.

EPISTLE TO MR. M'ADAM,

OF CRAIGEN-GILLAN, IN ANSWER TO AN OBLIGING LETTER HE SENT IN THE
COMMENCEMENT OF MY POETIC CAREER.

SIR, o'er a gill I gat your card,
    I trow it made me proud ;
' See wha taks notice o' the Bard ! '
    I lap and cry'd fu' loud.

' Now deil-ma-care about their jaw,
    The senseless, gawky million ;
I'll cock my nose aboon them a',
    I'm roos'd by Craigen-Gillan ! '

'Twas noble, Sir ; 'twas like yoursel,
    To grant your high protection :
A great man's smile, ye ken fu' weel,
    Is aye a blest infection.

Tho', by his banes wha in a tub
    Match'd Macedonian Sandy !

On my ain legs, thro' dirt and dub,
    I independent stand ay. —

And when those legs to gude, warm kail,
    Wi' welcome canna bear me ;
A lee dyke-side, a sybow-tail,
    And barley-scone shall cheer me.

Heaven spare you lang to kiss the breath
    O' monie flow'ry simmers !
And bless your bonie lasses baith,
    I'm tald they're loosome kimmers !

And God bless young Dunaskin's laird,
    The blossom of our gentry !
And may he wear an auld man's beard,
    A credit to his country.

TO CAPTAIN RIDDEL, GLENRIDDEL.

EXTEMPORE LINES ON RETURNING A NEWSPAPER.

Ellisland, Monday Evening.

YOUR News and Review, Sir, I've read through and through, Sir,
    With little admiring or blaming ;
The papers are barren of home-news or foreign,
    No murders or rapes worth the naming.

Our friends the Reviewers, those chippers and hewers
    Are judges of mortar and stone, Sir ;
But of meet, or unmeet, in a fabrick complete,
    I'll boldly pronounce they are none, Sir.

My goose-quill too rude is to tell all your goodness
    Bestow'd on your servant, the Poet ;
Would to God I had one like a beam of the sun,
    And then all the world, Sir, should know it !

VERSES

WHOSE is that noble, dauntless brow?
  And whose that eye of fire?
And whose that generous princely mien
  Even rooted foes admire?

Stranger, to justly shew that brow,
  And mark that eye of fire,
Would take His hand, whose vernal
    tints
  His other works admire.

Bright as a cloudless summer sun,
  With stately port he moves;
His guardian seraph eyes with awe
  The noble ward he loves.

Among the illustrious Scottish sons
  That chief thou may'st discern;
Mark Scotia's fond returning eye,
  It dwells upon Glencairn.

TO TERRAUGHTY, ON HIS BIRTHDAY.

HEALTH to the Maxwells' vet'ran Chief!
Health, aye unsour'd by care or grief:
Inspir'd, I turn'd Fate's sibyl leaf
      This natal morn,
I see thy life is stuff o' prief,
      Scarce quite half worn.

This day thou metes threescore eleven,
And I can tell that bounteous Heaven
(The second-sight, ye ken, is given
      To ilka Poet)
On thee a tack o' seven times seven
      Will yet bestow it.

If envious buckies view wi' sorrow
Thy lengthen'd days on this blest morrow,
May desolation's lang-teeth'd harrow,

      Nine miles an hour,
Rake them, like Sodom and Gomorrah,
      In brunstane stoure—

But for thy friends, and they are monie,
Baith honest men and lassies bonie,
May couthie fortune, kind and cannie,
      In social glee,
Wi' mornings blithe and e'enings funny
      Bless them and thee!

Fareweel, auld birkie! Lord be near ye,
And then the Deil he daurna steer ye:
Your friends aye love, your faes aye
    fear ye;
      For me, shame fa' me,
If neist my heart I dinna wear ye
      While BURNS they ca' me.

TO A LADY,

FAIR Empress of the Poet's soul,
  And Queen of Poetesses;
Clarinda, take this little boon,
  This humble pair of glasses.

And fill them high with generous juice,
  As generous as your mind;

And pledge me in the generous toast—
  'The whole of human kind!'

'To those who love us!'—second fill;
  But not to those whom we love;
Lest we love those who love not us!
  A third—'to thee and me, Love!'

THE VOWELS.

A TALE.

'Twas where the birch and sounding thong are ply'd,
The noisy domicile of pedant pride ;
Where ignorance her darkening vapour throws,
And cruelty directs the thickening blows ;
Upon a time, Sir Abece the great,
In all his pedagogic powers elate,
His awful chair of state resolves to mount,
And call the trembling Vowels to account.
　First enter'd A, a grave, broad, solemn wight,
But ah ! deform'd, dishonest to the sight !
His twisted head look'd backward on his way,
And flagrant from the scourge, he grunted, *ai!*
　Reluctant, E stalk'd in ; with piteous race
The jostling tears ran down his honest face !
That name, that well-worn name, and all his own,
Pale he surrenders at the tyrant's throne !
The pedant stifles keen the Roman sound
Not all his mongrel diphthongs can compound ;
And next, the title following close behind,
He to the nameless, ghastly wretch assign'd.
　The cobweb'd gothic dome resounded, Y !
In sullen vengeance, I, disdain'd reply :
The pedant swung his felon cudgel round,
And knock'd the groaning vowel to the ground !
　In rueful apprehension enter'd O,
The wailing minstrel of despairing woe ;
Th' Inquisitor of Spain the most expert,
Might there have learnt new mysteries of his art :
So grim, deform'd, with horrors entering U,
His dearest friend and brother scarcely knew !
　As trembling U stood staring all aghast,
The pedant in his left hand clutch'd him fast,
In helpless infants' tears he dipp'd his right,
Baptiz'd him *eu,* and kick'd him from his sight.

SKETCH.

A little, upright, pert, tart, tripping wight,
And still his precious self his dear delight ;
Who loves his own smart shadow in the streets
Better than e'er the fairest she he meets :
A man of fashion too, he made his tour,
Learn'd vive la bagatelle, et vive l'amour ;
So travell'd monkeys their grimace improve,
Polish their grin, nay, sigh for ladies' love.

Much specious lore, but little understood ;
Veneering oft outshines the solid wood :
His solid sense—by inches you must tell,
But mete his cunning by the old Scots ell ;
His meddling vanity, a busy fiend,
Still making work his selfish craft must mend.

PROLOGUE

FOR MR. SUTHERLAND'S BENEFIT-NIGHT, DUMFRIES. [1790.]

WHAT needs this din about the town o' Lon'on,
How this new play an' that new sang is comin' ?
Why is outlandish stuff sae meikle courted ?
Does nonsense mend like whisky, when imported ?
Is there nae poet, burning keen for fame,
Will try to gie us sangs and plays at hame ?
For comedy abroad he need na toil,
A fool and knave are plants of every soil ;
Nor need he hunt as far as Rome and Greece
To gather matter for a serious piece ;
There's themes enow in Caledonian story,
Would show the tragic muse in a' her glory.
   Is there no daring Bard will rise, and tell
How glorious Wallace stood, how hapless fell ?
Where are the Muses fled that could produce
A drama worthy o' the name o' Bruce ;
How here, even here, he first unsheath'd the sword
'Gainst mighty England and her guilty lord ;
And after monie a bloody, deathless doing,
Wrench'd his dear country from the jaws of ruin ?
O for a Shakespeare or an Otway scene,
To draw the lovely, hapless Scottish Queen !
Vain all th' omnipotence of female charms
'Gainst headlong, ruthless, mad Rebellion's arms.
She fell, but fell with spirit truly Roman,
To glut the vengeance of a rival woman ;
A woman, tho' the phrase may seem uncivil,
As able and as cruel as the devil !
One Douglas lives in Home's immortal page,
But Douglases were heroes every age :
And tho' your fathers, prodigal of life,
A Douglas follow'd to the martial strife,
Perhaps, if bowls row right, and Right succeeds,
Ye yet may follow where a Douglas leads !
   As ye hae generous done, if a' the land
Would tak the Muses' servants by the hand ;
Not only hear, but patronize, befriend them,
And where ye justly can commend, commend them ;
And aiblins when they winna stand the test,
Wink hard and say, the folks hae done their best !

Would a' the land do this, then I'll be caution
Ye'll soon hae poets o' the Scottish nation,
Will gar Fame blaw until her trumpet crack,
And warsle time an' lay him on his back !
  For us and for our stage should onie spier,
' Whase aught thae chiels maks a' this bustle here ? '
My best leg foremost, I'll set up my brow,
We hae the honour to belong to you !
We're your ain bairns, e'en guide us as ye like,
But like good mithers, shore before ye strike—
And gratefu' still I hope ye'll ever find us,
For a' the patronage and meikle kindness
We've got frae a' professions, sets and ranks :
God help us ! we're but poor—ye'se get but thanks.

ELEGY ON THE YEAR 1788,

SKETCH.

For Lords or Kings I dinna mourn,
E'en let them die—for that they're born :
But oh ! prodigious to reflec' !
A Towmont, Sirs, is gane to wreck !
O Eighty-eight, in thy sma' space
What dire events hae taken place !
Of what enjoyments thou hast reft us !
In what a pickle thou hast left us !
  The Spanish empire's tint a head,
And my auld teethless Bawtie's dead !
The tulzie's sair 'tween Pitt an' Fox,
An' our gudewife's wee birdy cocks ;
The tane is game, a bludie devil,
But to the hen-birds unco civil ;
The tither's something dour o' treadin,
But better stuff ne'er claw'd a midden.
  Ye ministers, come mount the poupit,
An' cry till ye be haerse an' roupet,
For Eighty-eight he wish'd you weel,
And gied you a' baith gear an' meal ;

E'en monie a plack, and monie a peck.
Ye ken yoursels, for little feck.
  Ye bonie lasses, dight your een,
For some o' you hae tint a frien' ;
In Eighty-eight, ye ken, was ta'en
What ye'll ne'er hae to gie again.
  Observe the very nowt an' sheep,
How dowf and daviely they creep ;
Nay, even the yirth itsel does cry,
For E'mbrugh wells are grutten dry.
  O Eighty-nine, thou's but a bairn,
An' no owre auld, I hope, to learn !
Thou beardless boy, I pray tak care,
Thou now has got thy daddie's chair,
Nae hand-cuff'd, mizzl'd, hap-shackl'd
         Regent,
But, like himsel, a full free agent.
Be sure ye follow out the plan
Nae waur than he did, honest man :
As muckle better as you can.

January 1, 1789.

VERSES WRITTEN UNDER THE PORTRAIT OF FERGUSSON THE POET,

IN A COPY OF THAT AUTHOR'S WORKS
PRESENTED TO A YOUNG LADY IN EDINBURGH, MARCH 19TH, 1787.

Curse on ungrateful man, that can be pleas'd,
And yet can starve the author of the pleasure !
O thou, my elder brother in misfortune,
By far my elder brother in the Muses,
With tears I pity thy unhappy fate !
Why is the Bard unpitied by the world,
Yet has so keen a relish of its pleasures ?

LAMENT (*see* NOTE),

WRITTEN AT A TIME WHEN THE POET WAS ABOUT TO LEAVE SCOTLAND.

O'ER the mist-shrouded cliffs of the lone mountain straying,
　　Where the wild winds of winter incessantly rave,
What woes wring my heart while intently surveying
　　The storm's gloomy path on the breast of the wave.

Ye foam-crested billows, allow me to wail,
　　Ere ye toss me afar from my lov'd native shore ;
Where the flower which bloom'd sweetest in Coila's green vale,
　　The pride of my bosom, my Mary's no more.

No more by the banks of the streamlet we'll wander,
　　And smile at the moon's rimpled face in the wave ;
No more shall my arms cling with fondness around her,
　　For the dew-drops of morning fall cold on her grave.

No more shall the soft thrill of love warm my breast,
　　I haste with the storm to a far distant shore ;
Where unknown, unlamented, my ashes shall rest,
　　And joy shall revisit my bosom no more.

D E L I A.

AN ODE.

FAIR the face of orient day,
Fair the tints of op'ning rose ;
But fairer still my Delia dawns,
More lovely far her beauty blows.

Sweet the lark's wild-warbled lay,
Sweet the tinkling rill to hear ;
But, Delia, more delightful still
Steal thine accents on mine ear.

The flower-enamour'd busy bee
The rosy banquet loves to sip ;
Sweet the streamlet's limpid lapse
To the sun-brown'd Arab's lip ;

But, Delia, on thy balmy lips
Let me, no vagrant insect, rove !
O let me steal one liquid kiss !
For oh ! my soul is parch'd with love !

ON THE DEATH OF SIR JAMES HUNTER BLAIR.

THE lamp of day, with ill-presaging glare,
　　Dim, cloudy, sunk beneath the western wave ;
Th' inconstant blast howl'd thro' the dark'ning air,
　　And hollow whistl'd in the rocky cave.

Lone as I wander'd by each cliff and dell,
　　Once the lov'd haunts of Scotia's royal train ;
Or 'mus'd where limpid streams, once hallow'd well,
　　Or mould'ring ruins mark the sacred fane.

Th' increasing blast roar'd round the beetling rocks,
   The clouds swift-wing'd flew o'er the starry sky,
The groaning trees untimely shed their locks,
   And shooting meteors caught the startled eye.

The paly moon rose in the livid east,
   And 'mong the cliffs disclos'd a stately Form,
In weeds of woe that frantic beat her breast,
   And mix'd her wailings with the raving storm.

Wild to my heart the filial pulses glow,
   'Twas Caledonia's trophied shield I view'd :
Her form majestic droop'd in pensive woe,
   The lightning of her eye in tears imbued.

Revers'd that spear, redoubtable in war,
   Reclin'd that banner, erst in fields unfurl'd,
That like a deathful meteor gleam'd afar,
   And brav'd the mighty monarchs of the world.—

' My patriot son fills an untimely grave !'
   With accents wild and lifted arms she cried ;
' Low lies the hand that oft was stretch'd to save,
   Low lies the heart that swell'd with honest pride !

' A weeping country joins a widow's tear,
   The helpless poor mix with the orphan's cry ;
The drooping arts surround their patron's bier,
   And grateful science heaves the heartfelt sigh.—

' I saw my sons resume their ancient fire ;
   I saw fair Freedom's blossoms richly blow ;
But, ah ! how hope is born but to expire !
   Relentless fate has laid their guardian low.—

' My patriot falls, but shall he lie unsung,
   While empty greatness saves a worthless name ?
No ; every Muse shall join her tuneful tongue,
   And future ages hear his growing fame.

' And I will join a mother's tender cares,
   Thro' future times to make his virtues last,
That distant years may boast of other Blairs,'—
   She said, and vanish'd with the sweeping blast.

TO MISS FERRIER,

ENCLOSING THE ELEGY ON SIR J. H. BLAIR.

NAE heathen name shall I prefix
  Frae Pindus or Parnassus ;
Auld Reekie dings them a' to sticks,
  For rhyme-inspiring lasses.

Jove's tunefu' dochters three times three
  Made Homer deep their debtor ;
But, gi'en the body half an ee,
  Nine Ferriers wad done better !

Last day my mind was in a bog,
  Down George's Street I stoited ;

A creeping cauld prosaic fog
  My very senses doited.

Do what I dought to set her free,
  My saul lay in the mire ;
Ye turned a neuk—I saw your ee—
  She took the wing like fire !

The mournfu' sang I here enclose,
  In gratitude I send you ;
And wish and pray in rhyme sincere,
  A' gude things may attend you !

WRITTEN ON THE BLANK LEAF

OF A COPY OF THE FIRST EDITION [OF HIS POEMS], WHICH I PRESENTED TO AN OLD SWEETHEART, THEN MARRIED.

ONCE fondly lov'd, and still remember'd dear,
  Sweet early object of my youthful vows,
Accept this mark of friendship, warm, sincere ;
  Friendship ! 'tis all cold duty now allows.

And when you read the simple artless rhymes,
  One friendly sigh for him, he asks no more,
Who distant burns in flaming torrid climes,
  Or haply lies beneath th' Atlantic roar.

THE POET'S WELCOME TO HIS ILLEGITIMATE CHILD.

THOU'S welcome, wean ! mishanter fa'
    me,
If ought of thee, or of thy mammy,
Shall ever danton me, or awe me,
      My sweet wee lady,
Or if I blush when thou shalt ca' me
      Tit-ta or daddy.

Wee image of my bonie Betty,
I fatherly will kiss and daut thee,
As dear an' near my heart I set thee
      Wi' as gude will,
As a' the priests had seen me get thee
      That's out o' hell.

What tho' they ca' me fornicator,
An' tease my name in kintra clatter :
The mair they talk I'm kent the better,
      E'en let them clash ;
An auld wife's tongue's a feckless matter
      To gie ane fash.

Sweet fruit o' monie a merry dint,
My funny toil is now a' tint,
Sin' thou came to the warl asklent,
      Which fools may scoff at ;
In my last plack thy part's be in't—
      The better haff o't.

An' if thou be what I wad hae thee,
An' tak the counsel I shall gie thee,
A lovin' father I'll be to thee,
  If thou be spar'd ;
Thro' a' thy childish years I'll ee thee,
  An' think't weel war'd.

Gude grant that thou may aye inherit
Thy mither's person, grace, an' merit,
An' thy poor worthless daddy's spirit,
  Without his failins,
'Twill please me mair to hear an' see't,
  Than stockit mailins.

LETTER TO JOHN GOUDIE, KILMARNOCK,

ON THE PUBLICATION OF HIS ESSAYS.

O Goudie ! terror of the Whigs,
Dread o' black coats and rev'rend wigs,
Sour Bigotry, on her last legs,
  Girnin' looks back,
Wishin' the ten Egyptian plagues
  Wad seize you quick.

Poor gapin' glowrin' Superstition,
Waes me ! she's in a sad condition ;
Fy, bring Black-Jock, her state physician,
  To see her water ;
Alas ! there's ground o' great suspicion
  She'll ne'er get better.

Auld Orthodoxy lang did grapple,
But now she's got an unco' ripple ;
Haste, gie her name up i' the chapel,

  Nigh unto death ;
See how she fetches at the thrapple,
  An' gasps for breath.

Enthusiasm's past redemption,
Gaen in a galloping consumption,
Not a' the quacks, with a' their gumption,
  Will ever mend her,
Her feeble pulse gies strong presumption,
  Death soon will end her.

'Tis you and Taylor are the chief,
Wha are to blame for this mischief ;
But gin the Lord's ain folks gat leave,
  A toom tar-barrel
An' twa red peats wad send relief,
  An' end the quarrel.

LETTER TO JAMES TENNANT, GLENCONNER.

Auld comrade dear and brither sinner,
How's a' the folk about Glenconner ;
How do you this blae eastlin wind,
That's like to blaw a body blind ?
For me, my faculties are frozen,
My dearest member nearly dozen'd.
I've sent you here by Johnie Simson,
Twa sage philosophers to glimpse on ;
Smith, wi' his sympathetic feeling,
An' Reid, to common sense appealing.
Philosophers have fought an' wrangled,
An' meikle Greek an' Latin mangled,
Till wi' their logic-jargon tir'd,
An' in the depth of Science mir'd,
To common sense they now appeal,
What wives an' wabsters see an' feel.
But, hark ye, friend, I charge you strictly,
Peruse them, an' return them quickly,

For now I'm grown sae cursed douse,
I pray an' ponder butt the house,
My shins, my lane, I there sit roastin',
Perusing Bunyan, Brown, an' Boston ;
Till by an' by, if I haud on,
I'll grunt a real Gospel-groan:
Already I begin to try it,
To cast my een up like a pyet,
When by the gun she tumbles o'er,
Flutt'ring an' gaspin in her gore :
Sae shortly you shall see me bright,
A burning an' a shining light.
 My heart-warm love to guid auld Glen,
The ace an' wale of honest men :
When bending down wi' auld grey hairs,
Beneath the load of years and cares,
May He who made him still support him,
An' views beyond the grave comfort him.

His worthy fam'ly far and near,
God bless them a' wi' grace and gear !
  My auld school-fellow, Preacher
    Willie,
The manly tar, my mason Billie,
An' Auchenbay, I wish him joy ;
If he's a parent, lass or boy,
May he be dad, and Meg the mither
Just five-and-forty years thegither !
An' no forgetting wabster Charlie,
I'm tauld he offers very fairly.
An' Lord, remember singing Sannock,
Wi' hale-breeks, saxpence, an' a bannock.
An' next, my auld acquaintance, Nancy,
Since she is fitted to her fancy ;
An' her kind stars hae airted till her
A good chiel wi' a pickle siller.
My kindest, best respects I sen' it,
To cousin Kate an' sister Janet ;

Tell them frae me, wi' chiels be cautious,
For, faith, they'll aiblins fin' them
    fashious :
To grant a heart is fairly civil,
But to grant a maidenhead's the devil.—
An' lastly, Jamie, for yoursel,
May guardian angels tak a spell,
An' steer you seven miles south o' hell :
But first, before you see heav'n's glory,
May ye get monie a merry story,
Monie a laugh, and monie a drink,
An' aye enough o' needfu' clink.
    Now fare ye weel, an' joy be wi' you,
For my sake this I beg it o' you,
Assist poor Simson a' ye can,
Ye'll fin' him just an honest man ;
Sae I conclude and quat my chanter,
Your's, saint or sinner,
                    ROB THE RANTER.

EPISTLE FROM ESOPUS TO MARIA.

FROM those drear solitudes and frowzy cells,
Where infamy with sad repentance dwells ;
Where turnkeys make the jealous portal fast,
And deal from iron hands the spare repast ;
Where truant 'prentices, yet young in sin,
Blush at the curious stranger peeping in ;
Where strumpets, relics of the drunken roar,
Resolve to drink, nay, half to whore, no more ;
Where tiny thieves not destin'd yet to swing,
Beat hemp for others, riper for the string :
From these dire scenes my wretched lines I date,
To tell Maria her Esopus' fate.
' Alas ! I feel I am no actor here ! '
'Tis real hangmen, real scourges bear !
Prepare, Maria, for a horrid tale
Will turn thy very rouge to deadly pale ;
Will make thy hair, tho' erst from gipsy poll'd,
By barber woven, and by barber sold,
Though twisted smooth with Harry's nicest care,
Like hoary bristles to erect and stare.
The hero of the mimic scene, no more
I start in Hamlet, in Othello roar ;
Or haughty Chieftain, 'mid the din of arms,
In Highland bonnet woo Malvina's charms ;
While sans culottes stoop up the mountain high,
And steal from me Maria's prying eye.

Bless'd Highland bonnet !   Once my proudest dress,
Now prouder still, Maria's temples press.
I see her wave thy towering plumes afar,
And call each coxcomb to the wordy war.
I see her face the first of Ireland's sons,
And even out-Irish his Hibernian bronze ;
The crafty colonel leaves the tartan'd lines,
For other wars, where he a hero shines :
The hopeful youth, in Scottish senate bred,
Who owns a Bushby's heart without the head,
Comes 'mid a string of coxcombs to display,
That *veni, vidi, vici,* is his way ;
The shrinking bard adown an alley skulks,
And dreads a meeting worse than Woolwich hulks ;
Though there, his heresies in church and state
Might well award him Muir and Palmer's fate :
Still she undaunted reels and rattles on,
And dares the public like a noontide sun.
(What scandal call'd Maria's jaunty stagger,
The ricket reeling of a crooked swagger ?
Whose spleen e'en worse than Burns's venom when
He dips in gall unmix'd his eager pen, —
And pours his vengeance in the burning line,
Who christen'd thus Maria's lyre divine ;
The idiot strum of vanity bemused,
And even th' abuse of poesy abused ;
Who call'd her verse a parish workhouse, made
For motley, foundling fancies, stolen or stray'd ?)
A workhouse ! ah, that sound awakes my woes,
And pillows on the thorn my rack'd repose !
In durance vile here must I wake and weep,
And all my frowzy couch in sorrow steep ;
That straw where many a rogue has lain of yore,
And vermin'd gipsies litter'd heretofore.

Why, Lonsdale, thus thy wrath on vagrants pour,
Must earth no rascal, save thyself, endure ?
Must thou alone in guilt immortal swell,
And make a vast monopoly of hell ?
Thou know'st, the virtues cannot hate thee worse,
The vices also, must they club their curse ?
Or must no tiny sin to others fall,
Because thy guilt's supreme enough for all ?

Maria, send me too thy griefs and cares ;
In all of thee sure thy Esopus shares.
As thou at all mankind the flag unfurls,
Who on my fair-one satire's vengeance hurls ?
Who calls thee pert, affected, vain coquette,
A wit in folly, and a fool in wit ?
Who says that fool alone is not thy due,
And quotes thy treacheries to prove it true ?

Our force united on thy foes we'll turn,
And dare the war with all of woman born :
For who can write and speak as thou and I ?
My periods that decyphering defy,
And thy still matchless tongue that conquers all reply.

ON A SUICIDE.

EARTH'D up here lies an imp o' hell,
    Planted by Satan's dibble—
Poor silly wretch, he's damn'd himsel'
    To save the Lord the trouble.

A FAREWELL.

FAREWELL, dear Friend ! may guid luck hit you,
And, mang her favourites admit you !
If e'er Detraction shore to smit you,
    May nane believe him !
And ony De'il that thinks to get you,
    Good Lord deceive him.

THE FAREWELL.

FAREWELL, old Scotia's bleak domains,
Far dearer than the torrid plains
  Where rich ananas blow !
Farewell, a mother's blessing dear !
A brother's sigh ! a sister's tear !
  My Jean's heart-rending throe !
Farewell, my Bess ! tho' thou'rt bereft
  Of my parental care ;
A faithful brother I have left,
  My part in him thou'lt share !
    Adieu too, to you too,
      My Smith, my bosom frien' ;
    When kindly you mind me,
      O then befriend my Jean !

When bursting anguish tears my heart,
From thee, my Jeany, must I part ?
  Thou weeping answ'rest 'no !'
Alas ! misfortune stares my face,
And points to ruin and disgrace,
  I for thy sake must go !
Thee, Hamilton, and Aiken dear,
  A grateful, warm adieu !
I, with a much-indebted tear,
  Shall still remember you !
    All-hail then, the gale then,
      Wafts me from thee, dear shore !
    It rustles, and whistles,
      I'll never see thee more !

EPISTLE TO ROBERT GRAHAM, ESQ.
OF FINTRY:

ON THE CLOSE OF THE DISPUTED ELECTION BETWEEN SIR JAMES JOHNSTONE AND CAPTAIN MILLER, FOR THE DUMFRIES DISTRICT OF BOROUGHS.

FINTRY, my stay in worldly strife,
Friend o' my Muse, friend o' my life,
    Are ye as idle's I am ?
Come then, wi' uncouth, kintra fleg,
O'er Pegasus I'll fling my leg,
    And ye shall see me try him.

I'll sing the zeal Drumlanrig bears
Who left the all-important cares
     Of princes and their darlings ;
And, bent on winning borough towns,
Came shaking hands wi' wabster loons,
     And kissing barefit carlins.

Combustion thro' our boroughs rode
Whistling his roaring pack abroad
     Of mad unmuzzled lions ;
As Queensberry buff and blue unfurl'd,
And Westerha' and Hopeton hurl'd
     To every Whig defiance.

But cautious Queensberry left the war,
Th' unmanner'd dust might soil his star ;
     Besides, he hated bleeding ;
But left behind him heroes bright,
Heroes in Cæsarean fight,
     Or Ciceronian pleading.

O ! for a throat like huge Mons-Meg,
To muster o'er each ardent Whig
     Beneath Drumlanrig's banner !
Heroes and heroines commix,
All in the field of politics,
     To win immortal honour.

M'Murdo and his lovely spouse,
(Th' enamour'd laurels kiss her brows !)
     Led on the loves and graces :
She won each gaping burgess' heart,
While he, all-conquering, play'd his part
     Among their wives and lasses.

Craigdarroch led a light-arm'd corps,
Tropes, metaphors and figures pour,
     Like Hecla streaming thunder :
Glenriddel, skill'd in rusty coins,
Blew up each Tory's dark designs,
     And bared the treason under.

In either wing two champions fought,
Redoubted Staig, who set at nought
     The wildest savage Tory :
And Welsh, who ne'er yet flinch'd his ground,
High-waved his magnum-bonum round
     With Cyclopean fury.

Miller brought up th' artillery ranks,
The many-pounders of the Banks,
     Resistless desolation !

While Maxwelton, that baron bold,
'Mid Lawson's port entrench'd his hold,
          And threaten'd worse damnation.

To these what Tory hosts oppos'd,
With these what Tory warriors clos'd,
          Surpasses my descriving:
Squadrons extended long and large,
With furious speed rush to the charge,
          Like raging devils driving.

What verse can sing, what prose narrate,
The butcher deeds of bloody fate
          Amid this mighty tulzie!
Grim Horror girn'd—pale Terror roar'd,
As Murther at his thrapple shor'd,
          And Hell mix'd in the brulzie.

As Highland crags by thunder cleft,
When lightnings fire the stormy lift,
          Hurl down with crashing rattle;
As flames among a hundred woods;
As headlong foam a hundred floods;
          Such is the rage of battle!

The stubborn Tories dare to die;
As soon the rooted oaks would fly
          Before th' approaching fellers:
The Whigs come on like Ocean's roar,
When all his wintry billows pour
          Against the Buchan Bullers.

Lo, from the shades of Death's deep night,
Departed Whigs enjoy the fight,
          And think on former daring:
The muffled murtherer of Charles
The Magna Charta flag unfurls,
          All deadly gules its bearing.

Nor wanting ghosts of Tory fame,
Bold Scrimgeour follows gallant Graham,
          Auld Covenanters shiver.
(Forgive, forgive, much wrong'd Montrose!
Now death and hell engulf thy foes,
          Thou liv'st on high for ever!)

Still o'er the field the combat burns,
The Tories, Whigs, give way by turns;
          But Fate the word has spoken,
For woman's wit and strength o' man,
Alas! can do but what they can!
          The Tory ranks are broken.

O that my een were flowing burns !
My voice a lioness that mourns
  Her darling cubs' undoing !
That I might greet, that I might cry,
While Tories fall, while Tories fly,
  And furious Whigs pursuing !

What Whig but melts for good Sir James ?
Dear to his country by the names
  Friend, patron, benefactor !
Not Pulteney's wealth can Pulteney save !
And Hopeton falls, the generous brave !
  And Stewart, bold as Hector !

Thou, Pitt, shalt rue this overthrow ;
And Thurlow growl a curse of woe ;
  And Melville melt in wailing !
How Fox and Sheridan rejoice !
And Burke shall sing, 'O Prince, arise,
  Thy power is all-prevailing ! '

For your poor friend, the Bard, afar
He only hears and sees the war,
  A cool spectator purely !
So, when the storm the forest rends,
The robin in the hedge descends,
  And sober chirps securely.

STANZAS ON THE DUKE OF QUEENSBERRY.

How shall I sing Drumlanrig's Grace,
Discarded remnant of a race
  Once great in martial story ?
His forbears' virtues all contrasted—
The very name of Douglas blasted—
  His that inverted glory.

Hate, envy, oft the Douglas bore ;
But he has superadded more,
  And sunk them in contempt :
Follies and crimes have stain'd the name,
But, Queensberry, thine the virgin claim,
  From aught that's good exempt.

VERSES

ON THE DESTRUCTION OF THE WOODS NEAR DRUMLANRIG.

As on the banks o' wandering Nith,
 Ae smiling simmer-morn I stray'd,
And traced its bonie howes and haughs,
 Where linties sang and lambkins
  play'd.
I sat me down upon a craig,
 And drank my fill o' fancy's dream,
When, from the eddying deep below,
 Uprose the genius of the stream.

Dark, like the frowning rock, his
  brow,
 And troubled, like his wintry wave,
And deep, as sughs the boding wind
 Amang his eaves, the sigh he gave—
'And came ye here, my son,' he cried,
 'To wander in my birken shade ?
To muse some favourite Scottish theme,
 Or sing some favourite Scottish maid.

L 2

' There was a time, it's nae lang syne,
　Ye might hae seen me in my pride,
When a' my banks sae bravely saw
　Their woody pictures in my tide ;
When hanging beech and spreading elm
　Shaded my stream sae clear and cool,
And stately oaks their twisted arms
　Threw broad and dark across the pool ;

' When glinting, through the trees,
　　　appear'd
　The wee white cot aboon the mill,
And peacefu' rose its ingle reek,
　That slowly curlèd up the hill.
But now the cot is bare and cauld,
　Its branchy shelter's lost and gane,
And scarce a stinted birk is left
　To shiver in the blast its lane.'

' Alas !' said I, ' what ruefu' chance
　Has twined ye o' your stately trees ?
Has laid your rocky bosom bare ?
Has stripp'd the cleeding o' your bracs ?
Was it the bitter eastern blast,
　That scatters blight in early spring ?
Or was't the wil'fire scorch'd their
　　　boughs,
　Or canker-worm wi' secret sting ? '

' Nae eastlin blast,' the sprite replied ;
　' It blew na here sae fierce and fell,
And on my dry and halesome banks
　Nae canker-worms get leave to dwell :
Man ! cruel man !' the genius sigh'd—
　As through the cliffs he sank him
　　　down—
' The worm that gnaw'd my bonie trees,
　That reptile wears a ducal crown.'

EPISTLE TO MAJOR LOGAN.

HAIL, thairm-inspirin', rattlin' Willie !
Though fortune's road be rough an' hilly
To every fiddling, rhyming billie,
　　　We never heed,
But take it like the unback'd filly,
　　　Proud o' her speed.

When idly goavan whyles we saunter,
Yirr, fancy barks, awa' we canter
Uphill, down brae, till some mishanter,
　　　Some black bog-hole,
Arrests us, then the scathe an' banter
　　　We're forced to thole.

Hale be your heart ! Hale be your fiddle !
Lang may your elbuck jink and diddle,
To cheer you through the weary widdle
　　　O' this wild warl',
Until you on a crummock driddle
　　　A gray-hair'd carl.

Come wealth, come poortith, late or
　　　soon,
Heaven send your heart-strings ay in
　　　tune,
And screw your temper-pins aboon
　　　A fifth or mair,
The melancholious, lazie croon,
　　　O' cankrie care.

May still your life from day to day
Nae ' lente largo ' in the play,
But ' allegretto forte ' gay
　　　Harmonious flow
A sweeping, kindling, bauld strathspey—
　　　Encore ! Bravo !

A blessing on the cheery gang
Wha dearly like a jig or sang,
An' never think o' right an' wrang
　　　By square an' rule,
But as the clegs o' feeling stang
　　　Are wise or fool.

My hand-waled curse keep hard in chase
The harpy, hoodock, purse-proud race,
Wha count on poortith as disgrace—
　　　Their tuneless hearts !
May fire-side discords jar a base
　　　To a' their parts !

But come, your hand, my careless brither,
I' th' ither warl' if there's anither,
An' that there is I've little swither
　　　About the matter ;
We cheek for chow shall jog thegither,
　　　I'se ne'er bid better.

We've faults and failings — granted
    clearly,
We're frail backsliding mortals merely,
Eve's bonie squad priests wyte them
    sheerly
        For our grand fa' ;
But still, but still, I like them dearly—
        God bless them a' !

Ochon for poor Castalian drinkers,
When they fa' foul o' earthly jinkers,
The witching cursed delicious blinkers
        Hae put me hyte,
And gart me weet my waukrife winkers,
        Wi' girnin spite.

But by yon moon !—and that's high
    swearin'—
An' every star within my hearin' !
An' by her een wha was a dear ane !
        I'll ne'er forget ;
I hope to gie the jads a clearin'
        In fair play yet.

Mossgiel, 30th October, 1786.

My loss I mourn, but not repent it,
I'll seek my pursie whare I tint it,
Ance to the Indies I were wonted,
        Some cantraip hour,
By some sweet elf I'll yet be dinted,
        Then, *vive l'amour !*

Faites mes baissemains respectueuse,
To sentimental sister Susie,
An' honest Lucky ; no to roose you,
        Ye may be proud,
That sic a couple Fate allows ye
        To grace your blood.

Nae mair at present can I measure,
An' trowth my rhymin' ware's nae
    treasure ;
But when in Ayr, some half hour's
    leisure,
        Be't light, be't dark,
Sir Bard will do himself the pleasure
        To call at Park.

                    ROBERT BURNS.

EPITAPH ON THE POET'S DAUGHTER.

HERE lies a rose, a budding rose,
    Blasted before its bloom ;
Whose innocence did sweets disclose
    Beyond that flower's perfume.
To those who for her loss are grieved,
    This consolation's given—
She's from a world of woe relieved,
    And blooms a rose in heaven.

EPITAPH ON GABRIEL RICHARDSON

HERE Brewer Gabriel's fire's extinct,
    And empty all his barrels :
He's blest—if, as he brew'd, he drink,
    In upright honest morals.

ON STIRLING.

HERE Stuarts once in glory reign'd,
And laws for Scotland's weal ordain'd ;
But now unroof'd their palace stands,
Their sceptre's sway'd by other hands ;
The injured Stuart line is gone,
A race outlandish fills their throne.
An idiot race to honour lost,
Who know them best, despise them most.

LINES

ON BEING TOLD THAT THE ABOVE VERSES WOULD AFFECT HIS PROSPECTS.

RASH mortal, and slanderous poet, thy name
Shall no longer appear in the records of fame ;
Dost not know that old Mansfield, who writes like the Bible,
Says the more 'tis a truth, sir, the more 'tis a libel ?

REPLY TO THE MINISTER OF GLADSMUIR.

LIKE Esop's lion, Burns says, sore I feel
All others scorn—but damn that ass's heel.

EPISTLE TO HUGH PARKER.

IN this strange land, this uncouth clime,
A land unknown to prose or rhyme ;
Where words ne'er crost the Muse's
    heckles,
Nor limpit in poetic shackles ;
A land that prose did never view it,
Except when drunk he stacher't through
    it ;
Here, ambush'd by the chimla cheek,
Hid in an atmosphere of reek,
I hear a wheel thrum i' the neuk,
I hear it—for in vain I leuk.—
The red peat gleams, a fiery kernel,
Enhusked by a fog infernal :
Here, for my wonted rhyming raptures,
I sit and count my sins by chapters ;
For life and spunk like ither Christians,
I'm dwindled down to mere existence,
Wi' nae converse but Gallowa' bodies,
Wi' nae kend face but Jenny Geddes.
Jenny, my Pegasean pride !
Dowie she saunters down Nithside,
And ay a westlin leuk she throws,
While tears hap o'er her auld brown
    nose !

Was it for this, wi' canny care,
Thou bure the Bard through many a
    shire ?
At howes or hillocks never stumbled,
And late or early never grumbled ?—
O, had I power like inclination,
I'd heeze thee up a constellation,
To canter with the Sagitarre,
Or loup the ecliptic like a bar ;
Or turn the pole like any arrow ;
Or, when auld Phœbus bids good-
    morrow,
Down the zodiac urge the race,
And cast dirt on his godship's face ;
For I could lay my bread and kail
He'd ne'er cast saut upo' thy tail.—
Wi' a' this care and a' this grief,
And sma', sma' prospect of relief,
And nought but peat reek i' my head,
How can I write what ye can read ?—
Tarbolton, twenty-fourth o' June,
Ye'll find me in a better tune ;
But till we meet and weet our whistle,
Tak this excuse for nae epistle.

ROBERT BURNS.

ADDRESS OF BEELZEBUB

TO THE PRESIDENT OF THE HIGHLAND SOCIETY.

LONG life, my Lord, an' health be yours,
Unskaith'd by hunger'd Highland boors ;
Lord grant nae duddie desperate beggar,
Wi' dirk, claymore, or rusty trigger,
May twin auld Scotland o' a life

She likes—as lambkins like a knife.
Faith, you and Applecross were right
To keep the Highland hounds in sight,
I doubt na' ! they wad bid nae better
Than let them ance out owre the water

Than up amang thae lakes and seas
They'll mak' what rules and laws they
    please ;
Some daring Hancock, or a Franklin,
May set their Highland bluid a ranklin' ;
Some Washington again may head them,
Or some Montgomery fearless lead them,
Till God knows what may be effected
When by such heads and hearts
    directed ;
Poor dunghill sons of dirt and mire
May to Patrician rights aspire !
Nae sage North, now, nor sager Sack-
    ville,
To watch and premier o'er the pack vile,
An' whare will ye get Howes and
    Clintons
To bring them to a right repentance,
To cowe the rebel generation,
An' save the honour o' the nation ?
They an' be d——d ! what right hae
    they
To meat or sleep, or light o' day !
Far less to riches, pow'r, or freedom,
But what your lordship likes to gie them?

But hear, my lord ! Glengarry, hear !
Your hand 's owre light on them, I fear ;
Your factors, grieves, trustees, and
    bailies,
I canna' say but they do gaylies ;
They lay aside a' tender mercies,

June 1, Anno Mundi 5790.

An' tirl the hallions to the birses ;
Yet while they're only poind't and
    herriet,
They'll keep their stubborn Highland
    spirit ;
But smash them ! crash them a' to
    spails !
An' rot the dyvors i' the jails !
The young dogs, swinge them to the
    labour !
Let wark an' hunger mak' them sober !
The hizzies, if they're aughtlins fawsont,
Let them in Drury-lane be lesson'd !
An' if the wives an' dirty brats
E'en thigger at your doors an' yetts
Flaffan wi' duds an' grey wi' beas',
Frightin' awa your deucks an' geese,
Get out a horsewhip or a jowler,
The langest thong, the fiercest growler,
An gar the tatter'd gypsies pack
Wi' a' their bastarts on their back !
Go on, my lord ! I lang to meet you,
An' in my house at hame to greet you ;
Wi' common lords ye shanna mingle,
The benmost neuk beside the ingle,
At my right han' assign'd your seat
'Tween Herod's hip an' Polycrate,—
Or if you on your station tarrow
Between Almagro and Pizarro,
A seat, I'm sure, ye're weel deservin't ;
An' till ye come—Your humble servant,

BEELZEBUB.

TO MR. JOHN KENNEDY.

Now Kennedy, if foot or horse
E'er bring you in by Mauchline Corss,
Lord man, there's lasses there wad force
    A hermit's fancy,
And down the gate in faith they're worse
    And mair unchancy.

But as I'm sayin' please step to Dow's
And taste sic gear as Johnny brews,
Till some bit callan brings me news
    That you are there,
And if we dinna had a bouze
    I'se ne'er drink mair.

It's no I like to sit an' swallow,
Then like a swine to puke an' wallow,
But gie me just a true good fallow

    Wi' right ingine,
And spunkie ance to make us mellow,
    And then we'll shine.

Now if ye're ane o' warl's folk,
Wha rate the wearer by the cloak,
An' sklent on poverty their joke,
    Wi' bitter sneer,
Wi' you no friendship I will troke
    Nor cheap nor dear.

But if, as I'm informèd weel,
Ye hate as ill's the vera deil,
The flinty hearts that canna feel—
    Come, Sir, here's tae you ;
Hae there's my haun' I wiss you weel,
    And gude be wi' you.

ON THE DEATH OF ROBERT DUNDAS, ESQ.

OF ARNISTON, LATE LORD PRESIDENT OF THE COURT OF SESSION.

LONE on the bleaky hills the straying flocks
Shun the fierce storms among the sheltering rocks ;
Down from the rivulets, red with dashing rains,
The gathering floods burst o'er the distant plains ;
Beneath the blasts the leafless forests groan ;
The hollow caves return a sullen moan.

Ye hills, ye plains, ye forests, and ye caves,
Ye howling winds, and wintry swelling waves !
Unheard, unseen, by human ear or eye,
Sad to your sympathetic scenes I fly ;
Where to the whistling blast and water's roar,
Pale Scotia's recent wound I may deplore.

O heavy loss, thy country ill could bear !
A loss these evil days can ne'er repair !
Justice, the high vicegerent of her God,
Her doubtful balance eyed, and sway'd her rod ;
Hearing the tidings of the fatal blow,
She sunk, abandon'd to the wildest woe.

Wrongs, injuries, from many a darksome den,
Now gay in hope explore the paths of men :
See from his cavern grim Oppression rise,
And throw on Poverty his cruel eyes ;
Keen on the helpless victim see him fly,
And stifle, dark, the feebly-bursting cry :

Mark ruffian Violence, distain'd with crimes,
Rousing elate in these degenerate times ;
View unsuspecting Innocence a prey,
As guileful Fraud points out the erring way :
While subtile Litigation's pliant tongue
The life-blood equal sucks of Right and Wrong :
Hark, injured Want recounts th' unlisten'd tale,
And much-wrong'd Mis'ry pours th' unpitied wail !

Ye dark waste hills, and brown unsightly plains,
To you I sing my grief-inspired strains :
Ye tempests, rage ! ye turbid torrents, roll !
Ye suit the joyless tenor of my soul.
Life's social haunts and pleasures I resign,
Be nameless wilds and lonely wanderings mine,
To mourn the woes my country must endure,
That wound degenerate ages cannot cure.

TO JOHN M'MURDO, ESQ.

O, COULD I give thee India's wealth,
  As I this trifle send !
Because thy joy in both would be
  To share them with a friend.

But golden sands did never grace
  The Heliconian stream ;
Then take what gold could never buy —
  An honest Bard's esteem.

ON THE DEATH OF A LAP-DOG,

NAMED ECHO.

IN wood and wild, ye warbling throng,
  Your heavy loss deplore ;
Now half-extinct your powers of song,
  Sweet Echo is no more.

Ye jarring, screeching things around,
  Scream your discordant joys ;
Now half your din of tuneless sound
  With Echo silent lies.

LINES WRITTEN AT LOUDON MANSE.

THE night was still, and o'er the hill
  The moon shone on the castle wa' ;
The mavis sang, while dew-drops hang
  Around her, on the castle wa'.

Sae merrily they danced the ring,
  Frae eenin' till the cock did craw ;
And aye the o'erword o' the spring,
  Was Irvine's bairns are bonie a'.

ORTHODOX, ORTHODOX.

A SECOND VERSION OF THE KIRK'S ALARM.

ORTHODOX, orthodox,
  Who believe in John Knox,
Let me sound an alarm to your con-
    science—
    There's an heretic blast,
    Has been blawn i' the wast
That what is not sense must be nonsense,
    Orthodox,
That what is not sense must be nonsense.

Doctor Mac, Doctor Mac,
  Ye should stretch on a rack,
To strike evil-doers wi' terror ;
    To join faith and sense,
    Upon any pretence,
Was heretic damnable error,
    Doctor Mac,
Was heretic damnable error.

Town of Ayr, town of Ayr,
  It was rash, I declare,
To meddle wi' mischief a-brewing ;

Provost John is still deaf
  To the church's relief,
And orator Bob is its ruin,
    Town of Ayr,
And orator Bob is its ruin.

D'rymple mild, D'rymple mild,
  Tho' your heart's like a child,
And your life like the new-driven snaw,
    Yet that winna save ye,
    Old Satan must have ye
For preaching that three's ane an' twa,
    D'rymple mild,
For preaching that three's ane an' twa.

Calvin's sons, Calvin's sons,
  Seize your spiritual guns,
Ammunition ye never can need ;
    Your hearts are the stuff,
    Will be powder enough,
And your skulls are a storehouse of lead,
    Calvin's sons,
And your skulls are a storehouse of lead.

Rumble John, Rumble John,
Mount the steps with a groan,
Cry the book is with heresy cramm'd;
Then lug out your ladle,
Deal brimstone like aidle,
And roar every note o' the damn'd,
         Rumble John,
And roar every note o' the damn'd.

Simper James, Simper James,
Leave the fair Killie dames,
There's a holier chase in your view;
I'll lay on your head,
That the pack ye'll soon lead,
For puppies like you there's but few,
         Simper James,
For puppies like you there's but few.

Singet Sawnie, Singet Sawnie,
Are ye herding the penny,
Unconscious what danger awaits?
With a jump, yell, and howl,
Alarm every soul,
For Hannibal's just at your gates,
         Singet Sawnie,
For Hannibal's just at your gates.

Andrew Gowk, Andrew Gowk,
Ye may slander the book,
And the book nought the waur—let me
    tell you;
Tho' ye're rich and look big,
Yet lay by hat and wig,
And ye'll hae a calf's-head o' sma' value,
         Andrew Gowk,
And ye'll hae a calf's-head o' sma' value.

Poet Willie, Poet Willie,
Gie the doctor a volley,
Wi' your 'liberty's chain' and your wit:
O'er Pegasus' side,
Ye ne'er laid a stride,
Ye only stood by when he sh—'
         Poet Willie,
Ye only stood by when he sh—.

Bar Steenie, Bar Steenie,
What mean ye? what mean ye?
If ye'll meddle nae mair wi' the matter,
Ye may hae some pretence, man,
To havins and sense, man,
Wi' people that ken you nae better,
         Bar Steenie,
Wi' people that ken you nae better.

Jamie Goose, Jamie Goose,
Ye hae made but toom roose,
O' hunting the wicked lieutenant;
But the doctor's your mark,
For the Lord's holy ark,
He has cooper'd and ca'd a wrong pin
    in't,
         Jamie Goose,
He has cooper'd and ca'd a wrong pin
    in't.

Davie Bluster, Davie Bluster,
For a saunt if ye muster,
It's a sign they're no nice o' recruits,
Yet to worth let's be just,
Royal blood ye might boast,
If the ass were the King o' the brutes,
         Davie Bluster,
If the ass were the King o' the brutes.

Muirland George, Muirland George,
Whom the Lord made a scourge,
To claw common sense for her sins;
If ill manners were wit,
There's no mortal so fit
To confound the poor doctor at ance,
         Muirland George,
To confound the poor doctor at ance.

Cessnockside, Cessnockside,
Wi' your turkey-cock pride,
O' manhood but sma' is your share!
Ye've the figure, it's true,
Even our foes maun allow,
And your friends daurna say ye hae mair,
         Cessnockside,
And your friends daurna say ye hae mair.

Daddie Auld, Daddie Auld,
There's a tod i' the fauld,
A tod meikle waur than the clerk;
Tho' ye downa do skaith,
Ye'll be in at the death,
And if ye canna bite ye can bark,
         Daddie Auld,
And if ye canna bite ye can bark.

Poet Burns, Poet Burns,
Wi' your priest-skelping turns,
Why desert ye your auld native shire?
Tho' your Muse is a gipsy,
Yet were she even tipsy,
She could ca' us nae waur than we are,
Poet Burns,
She could ca' us nae waur than we are.

POSTSCRIPT.

Afton's Laird, Afton's Laird,
When your pen can be spared,
A copy o' this I bequeath,
On the same sicker score
I mentioned before,
To that trusty auld worthy Clackleith,
Afton's Laird,
To that trusty auld worthy Clackleith.

THE SELKIRK GRACE.

SOME hae meat, and canna eat,
And some wad eat that want it;
But we hae meat and we can eat,
And sae the Lord be thanket.

ELEGY ON THE DEATH OF PEG NICHOLSON.

PEG NICHOLSON was a gude bay mare,
As ever trode on airn;
But now she's floating down the Nith,
An' past the mouth o' Cairn.

Peg Nicholson was a gude bay mare,
An' rode thro' thick an' thin;
But now she's floating down the Nith,
An' wanting even the skin.

Peg Nicholson was a gude bay mare,
An' ance she bare a priest;
But now she's floating down the Nith,
For Solway fish a feast.

Peg Nicholson was a gude bay mare,
An' the priest he rode her sair;
An' meikle oppress'd an' bruised she was,
As priest-rid cattle are.

ON SEEING MISS FONTENELLE

IN A FAVOURITE CHARACTER.

SWEET naïveté of feature,
Simple, wild, enchanting elf,
Not to thee, but thanks to Nature,
Thou art acting but thyself.

Wert thou awkward, stiff, affected,
Spurning nature, torturing art;
Loves and graces all rejected,
Then indeed thou'dst act a part.

THE SOLEMN LEAGUE AND COVENANT.

THE Solemn League and Covenant
Now brings a smile, now brings a tear;
But sacred Freedom, too, was theirs:
If thou'rt a slave, indulge thy sneer.

ON MISS JESSY LEWARS.

TALK not to me of savages
    From Afric's burning sun,
No savage e'er could rend my heart,
    As, Jessy, thou hast done.

But Jessy's lovely hand in mine,
    A mutual faith to plight,
Not ev'n to view the heavenly choir,
    Would be so blest a sight.

EPITAPH ON MISS JESSY LEWARS.

SAY, Sages, what's the charm on earth
    Can turn Death's dart aside?
It is not purity and worth,
    Else Jessy had not died.

THE RECOVERY OF JESSY LEWARS.

BUT rarely seen since Nature's birth,
    The natives of the sky,
Yet still one Seraph's left on earth,
    For Jessy did not die.

THE TOAST.

FILL me with the rosy wine,
Call a toast, a toast divine;
Give the Poet's darling flame,
Lovely Jessy be the name;
Then thou mayest freely boast,
Thou hast given a peerless toast.

THE KIRK OF LAMINGTON.

As cauld a wind as ever blew,
A caulder kirk, and in't but few;
As cauld a minister's e'er spak,
Ye'se a' be het ere I come back.

WRITTEN ON A BLANK LEAF

OF ONE OF MISS HANNAH MORE'S WORKS, WHICH SHE HAD GIVEN HIM.

THOU flattering mark of friendship kind,
Still may thy pages call to mind
    The dear, the beauteous donor:
Though sweetly female every part,
Yet such a head, and more the heart,
    Does both the sexes honour.
She show'd her tastes refined and just
When she selected thee,
Yet deviating own I must,
    For so approving me.
        But kind still, I'll mind still
            The giver in the gift;
        I'll bless her and wiss her
            A Friend above the Lift.

INSCRIPTION ON A GOBLET.

WRITTEN IN THE HOUSE OF MR. SYME.

THERE's death in the cup—sae beware !
   Nay, more—there is danger in touching ;
But wha can avoid the fell snare ?
   The man and his wine's sae bewitching !

THE BOOK-WORMS.

THROUGH and through the inspired leaves,
   Ye maggots, make your windings ;
But, oh ! respect his lordship's taste,
   And spare his golden bindings.

ON ROBERT RIDDEL.

To Riddel, much-lamented man,
   This ivied cot was dear ;
Reader, dost value matchless worth ?
   This ivied cot revere.

WILLIE CHALMERS.

WI' braw new branks in mickle pride,
   And eke a braw new brechan,
My Pegasus I'm got astride,
   And up Parnassus pechin ;
Whiles owre a bush wi' downward crush,
   The doited beastie stammers ;
Then up he gets, and off he sets
   For sake o' Willie Chalmers.

I doubt na, lass, that weel kenn'd name
   May cost a pair o' blushes ;
I am nae stranger to your fame
   Nor his warm urged wishes.
Your bonie face sae mild and sweet,
   His honest heart enamours,
And faith ye'll no be lost a whit,
   Tho' waired on Willie Chalmers.

Auld Truth hersel' might swear ye're fair,
   And Honour safely back her,
And Modesty assume your air,
   And ne'er a ane mistak' her :
And sic twa love-inspiring een
   Might fire even holy Palmers ;
Nae wonder then they've fatal been
   To honest Willie Chalmers.

I doubt na fortune may you shore
   Some mim-mou'd pouther'd priestie,
Fu' lifted up wi' Hebrew lore,
   And band upon his breastie :
But oh ! what signifies to you,
   His lexicons and grammars ;
The feeling heart's the royal blue,
   And that's wi' Willie Chalmers.

Some gapin' glowrin' countra laird,
   May warsle for your favour ;
May claw his lug, and straik his beard,
   And host up some palaver.
My bonie maid, before ye wed
   Sic clumsy-witted hammers,
Seek Heaven for help, and barefit skelp
   Awa' wi' Willie Chalmers.

Forgive the Bard ! my fond regard
   For ane that shares my bosom,
Inspires my muse to gie 'm his dues,
   For de'il a hair I roose him.
May powers aboon unite you soon,
   And fructify your amours,—
And every year come in mair dear
   To you and Willie Chalmers.

TO JOHN TAYLOR.

WITH Pegasus upon a day,
　Apollo weary flying,
Through frosty hills the journey lay,
　On foot the way was plying.

Poor slip-shod giddy Pegasus
　Was but a sorry walker;
To Vulcan then Apollo goes,
　To get a frosty calker.

OBliging Vulcan fell to work,
　Threw by his coat and bonnet,
And did Sol's business in a crack;
　Sol paid him with a sonnet.

Ye Vulcan's sons of Wanlockhead,
　Pity my sad disaster;
My Pegasus is poorly shod—
　I'll pay you like my master.

LINES WRITTEN ON A BANK-NOTE.

WAE worth thy power, thou cursed leaf!
Fell source o' a' my woe and grief!
For lack o' thee I've lost my lass!
For lack o' thee I scrimp my glass!
I see the children of affliction
Unaided, thro' thy curs'd restriction.
I've seen the oppressor's cruel smile,
Amid his hapless victim's spoil.
For lack o' thee I leave this much-lov'd shore,
Never, perhaps, to greet old Scotland more.

　　　　　　　　　　R. B.　*Kyle.*

THE LOYAL NATIVES' VERSES.

YE sons of sedition, give ear to my song,
Let Syme, Burns, and Maxwell pervade every throng,
With Cracken the attorney, and Mundell the quack,
Send Willie the monger to hell with a smack.

These verses were handed over the table to Burns at a convivial meeting, and he endorsed the subjoined reply:

BURNS—EXTEMPORE.

YE true 'Loyal Natives,' attend to my song,
In uproar and riot rejoice the night long;
From envy and hatred your corps is exempt;
But where is your shield from the darts of contempt?

REMORSE.

OF all the numerous ills that hurt our peace,
That press the soul, or wring the mind with anguish,
Beyond comparison the worst are those
That to our folly or our guilt we owe.
In every other circumstance, the mind
Has this to say—'It was no deed of mine;'

But when to all the evil of misfortune
This sting is added—' Blame thy foolish self !'
Or worser far, the pangs of keen Remorse ;
The torturing, gnawing consciousness of guilt—
Of guilt, perhaps, where we've involvèd others ;
The young, the innocent, who fondly lov'd us,
Nay, more, that very love their cause of ruin !
O burning hell ! in all thy store of torments,
There's not a keener lash !
Lives there a man so firm, who, while his heart
Feels all the bitter horrors of his crime,
Can reason down its agonizing throbs ;
And, after proper purpose of amendment,
Can firmly force his jarring thoughts to peace ?
O, happy ! happy ! enviable man !
O glorious magnanimity of soul !

THE TOAD-EATER.

WHAT of earls with whom you have supt,
   And of dukes that you dined with yestreen ?
Lord ! a louse, Sir, is still but a louse,
   Though it crawl on the curls of a Queen.

TO ———.

Mossgiel, —— 1786.

SIR,
   YOURS this moment I unseal,
     And faith I am gay and hearty !
   To tell the truth an' shame the Deil
     I am as fu' as Bartie :

But foorsday, Sir, my promise leal
   Expect me o' your party,
If on a beastie I can speel,
   Or hurl in a cartie.   R. B.

'IN VAIN WOULD PRUDENCE.'

IN vain would Prudence, with decorous sneer,
Point out a cens'ring world, and bid me fear ;
Above that world on wings of love I rise,
I know its worst—and can that worst despise.
' Wrong'd, injur'd, shunn'd ; unpitied, unredrest,
The mock'd quotation of the scorner's jest.'
Let Prudence' direst bodements on me fall,
Clarinda, rich reward ! o'erpays them all !

THOUGH FICKLE FORTUNE.'

THOUGH fickle Fortune has deceiv'd me,
   She promis'd fair and perform'd but ill ;
Of mistress, friends, and wealth bereav'd me,
   Yet I bear a heart shall support me still. —

I'll act with prudence as far's I'm able,
    But if success I must never find,
Then come misfortune, I bid thee welcome,
    I'll meet thee with an undaunted mind.—

'I BURN, I BURN.'

'I BURN, I burn, as when thro' ripen'd corn
By driving winds the crackling flames are borne,'
Now maddening, wild, I curse that fatal night ;
Now bless the hour which charm'd my guilty sight.
In vain the laws their feeble force oppose :
Chain'd at his feet they groan, Love's vanquish'd foes
In vain religion meets my sinking eye ;
I dare not combat—but I turn and fly ;
Conscience in vain upbraids th' unhallow'd fire ;
Love grasps his scorpions—stifled they expire !
Reason drops headlong from his sacred throne,
Your dear idea reigns and reigns alone :
Each thought intoxicated homage yields,
And riots wanton in forbidden fields !

    By all on high adoring mortals know !
    By all the conscious villain fears below !
    By your dear self !—the last great oath I swear ;
    Nor life nor soul were ever half so dear !

EPIGRAM ON A NOTED COXCOMB.

LIGHT lay the earth on Billy's breast,
    His chicken heart so tender ;
But build a castle on his head,
    His skull will prop it under.

TAM THE CHAPMAN.

As Tam the Chapman on a day
Wi' Death forgather'd by the way,
Weel pleas'd, he greets a wight sae famous,
And Death was nae less pleased wi' Thomas,
Wha cheerfully lays down the pack,
And there blaws up a hearty crack ;
His social, friendly, honest heart,
Sae tickled Death they could na part :
Sae after viewing knives and garters,
Death takes him hame to gie him quarters.

TO DR. MAXWELL,

ON MISS JESSY STAIG'S RECOVERY.

MAXWELL, if merit here you crave,
　　That merit I deny :
You save fair Jessy from the grave !
　　An Angel could not die.

FRAGMENT.

Now health forsakes that angel face,
　　Nae mair my Dearie smiles ;
Pale sickness withers ilka grace,
　　And a' my hopes beguiles.

The cruel powers reject the prayer
　　I hourly mak' for thee ;
Ye heavens, how great is my despair,
　　How can I see him dee !

THERE'S NAETHIN LIKE THE HONEST NAPPY.

THERE'S naethin like the honest nappy !
Whaur'll ye e'er see men sae happy,
Or women sonsie, saft an' sappy,
　　　　'Tween morn an' morn,
As them wha like to taste the drappie
　　　　In glass or horn.

I've seen me daez't upon a time ;
I scarce could wink or see a styme ;
Just ae hauf mutchkin does me prime,
　　　　Ought less is little,
Then back I rattle on the rhyme
　　　　As gleg's a whittle !

PROLOGUE,

SPOKEN BY MR. WOODS, ON HIS BENEFIT-NIGHT, MONDAY, APRIL 16, 1787.

WHEN by a generous public's kind acclaim,
That dearest meed is granted—honest fame ;
When here your favour is the actor's lot,
Nor even the man in private life forgot ;
What breast so dead to heav'nly virtue's glow,
But heaves impassion'd with the grateful throe ?
　Poor is the task to please a barb'rous throng,
It needs no Siddons' power in Southern's song :
But here an ancient nation, fam'd afar
For genius, learning high, as great in war—
Hail, Caledonia ! name for ever dear !
Before whose sons I'm honour'd to appear !
Where every science, every nobler art—
That can inform the mind, or mend the heart,
Is known ; as grateful nations oft have found,
Far as the rude barbarian marks the bound.
Philosophy, no idle, pedant dream,
Here holds her search, by heaven-taught Reason's beam ;
Here History paints with elegance and force,
The tide of Empire's fluctuating course ;

B　　　　　　　　M

Here Douglas forms wild Shakespeare into plan,
And Harley rouses all the god in man.
When well-form'd taste and sparkling wit unite,
With manly love, or female beauty bright,
(Beauty, where faultless symmetry and grace
Can only charm us in the second place,)
Witness my heart, how oft with panting fear,
As on this night, I've met these judges here!
But still the hope Experience taught to live,
Equal to judge—you're candid to forgive.
No hundred-headed Riot here we meet,
With decency and law beneath his feet,
Nor Insolence assumes fair Freedom's name ;
Like Caledonians, you applaud or blame.
　　O Thou, dread Power ! whose empire-giving hand
Has oft been stretch'd to shield the honour'd land,
Strong may she glow with all her ancient fire ;
May every son be worthy of his sire ;
Firm may she rise with generous disdain
At Tyranny's, or direr Pleasure's chain ;
Still self-dependent in her native shore,
Bold may she brave grim Danger's loudest roar,
Till Fate the curtain drop on worlds to be no more.

NATURE'S LAW.

A POEM HUMBLY INSCRIBED TO G. H. ESQ.

Great nature spoke, observant man obeyed.
　　　　　　　　　　　　　　　　POPE.

LET other heroes boast their scars,
　The marks of sturt and strife :
And other Poets sing of wars,
　The plagues of human life ;
Shame fa' the fun ; wi' sword and gun
　To slap mankind like lumber !
I sing his name and nobler fame,
　Wha multiplies our number.

Great Nature spoke, with air benign,
' Go on, ye human race !
' This lower world I you resign ;
　' Be fruitful and increase.
' The liquid fire of strong desire
　' I've pour'd it in each bosom ;
' Here, in this hand, does mankind stand,
　' And there, is Beauty's blossom !'

The Hero of these artless strains,
　A lowly Bard was he,
Who sung his rhymes in Coila's plains
　With meikle mirth an' glee ;
Kind Nature's care had given his share,
　Large, of the flaming current ;
And, all devout, he never sought
　To stem the sacred torrent.

He felt the powerful, high behest,
　Thrill, vital, thro' and thro' ;
And sought a correspondent breast,
　To give obedience due ;
Propitious Powers screen'd the young
　flow'rs,
　From mildews of abortion ;
And lo ! the Bard, a great reward,
　Has got a double portion !

Auld, cantie Coil may count the day,
  As annual it returns,
The third of Libra's equal sway,
  That gave another Burns,
With future rhymes, an' other times,
  To emulate his sire ;
To sing auld Coil in nobler style
  With more poetic fire.

Ye Powers of peace, and peaceful song,
  Look down with gracious eyes ;
And bless auld Coila, large and long,
  With multiplying joys.
Long may she stand to prop the land,
  The flow'r of ancient nations ;
And Burnses spring, her fame to sing,
  To endless generations !

THE CATS LIKE KITCHEN.

THE cats like kitchen ;
  The dogs like broo ;
The lasses like the lads weel,
  And th' auld wives too.

CHORUS.
And we're a' noddin,
  Nid, nid, noddin,
We're a' noddin fou at e'en.

TRAGIC FRAGMENT.

ALL devil as I am, a damned wretch,
A harden'd, stubborn, unrepenting villain,
Still my heart melts at human wretchedness ;
And with sincere tho' unavailing sighs
I view the helpless children of distress.
With tears of indignation I behold th' oppressor
Rejoicing in the honest man's destruction,
Whose unsubmitting heart was all his crime.
Even you, ye helpless crew, I pity you ;
Ye, whom the seeming good think sin to pity ;
Ye poor, despis'd, abandon'd vagabonds,
Whom Vice, as usual, has turn'd o'er to Ruin.
O but for kind, tho' ill-requited friends,
I had been driven forth like you forlorn,
The most detested, worthless wretch among you !
O injur'd God ! Thy goodness has endow'd me
With talents passing most of my compeers,
Which I in just proportion have abus'd,
As far surpassing other common villains,
As Thou in natural parts hadst given me more.

EXTEMPORE.

ON PASSING A LADY'S CARRIAGE. [MRS. MARIA RIDDEL'S.]

IF you rattle along like your mistress's tongue,
  Your speed will out-rival the dart :
But, a fly for your load, you'll break down on the road,
  If your stuff be as rotten's her heart.

FRAGMENTS.

YE hae lien a' wrang, lassie,
　Ye've lien a' wrang;
Ye've lien in an unco bed,
　And wi' a fremit man.
O ance ye danced upon the knowes,
　And ance ye lightly sang—
But in herrying o' a bee byke,
　I'm rad ye've got a stang.

O GIE my love brose, brose,
　Gie my love brose and butter;
For nane in Carrick or Kyle
　Can please a lassie better.
The lav'rock lo'es the grass,
　The muirhen lo'es the heather;
But gie me a braw moonlight,
　And me and my love together.

LASS, when your mither is frae hame,
　Might I but be sae bauld
As come to your bower-window,
　And creep in frae the cauld,
As come to your bower-window,
　And when it's cauld and wat,
Warm me in thy sweet bosom;
　Fair lass, wilt thou do that?

Young man, gif ye should be sae kind,
　When our gudewife's frae hame,
As come to my bower-window,
　Whare I am laid my lane,
And warm thee in my bosom –
　But I will tell thee what,
The way to me lies through the kirk;
　Young man, do ye hear that?

I MET a lass, a bonie lass,
　Coming o'er the braes o' Couper,
Bare her leg and bright her een,
　And handsome ilka bit about her.
Weel I wat she was a quean
　Wad made a body's mouth to water;
Our Mess John, wi' his lyart pow,
　His haly lips wad lickit at her.

O WAT ye what my minnie did,
　My minnie did, my minnie did,
O wat ye what my minnie did,
　On Tysday 'teen to me, jo?
She laid me in a saft bed,
　A saft bed, a saft bed,
She laid me in a saft bed,
　And bade gudeen to me, jo.

An' wat ye what the parson did,
　The parson did, the parson did,
An' wat ye what the parson did,
　A' for a penny fee, jo?
He loosed on me a lang man,
　A mickle man, a strang man,
He loosed on me a lang man,
　That might hae worried me, jo.

An' I was but a young thing,
　A young thing, a young thing,
An' I was but a young thing,
　Wi' nane to pity me, jo.
I wat the kirk was in the wyte,
　In the wyte, in the wyte,
To pit a young thing in a fright,
　An' loose a man on me, jo.

O CAN ye labour lea, young man,
　An' can ye labour lea;
Gae back the gate ye cam' again,
　Ye'se never scorn me.

I feed a man at Martinmas,
　Wi' arle pennies three;
An' a' the faut I fan' wi' him,
　He couldna labour lea.

The stibble rig is easy plough'd,
　The fallow land is free;
But wha wad keep the handless coof,
　That couldna labour lea?

JENNY M'Craw, she has ta'en to the heather,
Say, was it the covenant carried her thither ;
Jenny M'Craw to the mountains is gane,
Their leagues and their covenants a' she has ta'en ;
My head and my heart, now quo' she, are at rest,
And as for the lave, let the Deil do his best.

THE last braw bridal that I was at,
   'Twas on a Hallowmass day,
And there was routh o' drink and fun,
   And mickle mirth and play.
The bells they rang, and the carlins sang,
   And the dames danced in the ha' ;
The bride went to bed wi' the silly
     bridegroom,
   In the midst o' her kimmers a'.

O THOU, in whom we live and move,
   Who mad'st the sea and shore,
Thy goodness constantly we prove,
   And grateful would adore.
And if it please thee, Pow'r above,
   Still grant us with such store ;
The friend we trust, the fair we love,
   And we desire no more.

LORD, we thank an' thee adore,
   For temp'ral gifts we little merit ;
At present we will ask no more,
   Let William Hyslop give the spirit.

THERE came a piper out o' Fife,
   I watna what they ca'd him ;
He play'd our cousin Kate a spring,
   When fient a body bade him.
And ay the mair he hotch'd an' blew,
   The mair that she forbade him.

THE black-headed eagle,
   As keen as a beagle,
He hunted o'er height and owre howe ;
   But fell in a trap
   On the braes o' Gemappe,
E'en let him come out as he dowe.

EPITAPH ON WILLIAM NICOL.

YE maggots feast on Nicol's brain,
   For few sic feasts ye've gotten ;
And fix your claws in Nicol's heart,
   For de'il a bit o'ts rotten.

ANSWER TO A POETICAL EPISTLE

SENT THE AUTHOR BY A TAILOR.

WHAT ails ye now, ye lousie bitch,
To thresh my back at sic a pitch ?
Losh, man ! hae mercy wi' your natch,
   Your bodkin's bauld,
I didna suffer ha'f sae much
   Frae Daddie Auld.

What tho' at times when I grow crouse,
I gi'e their wames a random pouse,
Is that enough for you to souse
   Your servant sae ?
Gae mind your seam, ye prick-the-louse,
   An' jag-the-flae.

King David o' poetic brief,
Wrought 'mang the lasses such mischief
As fill'd his after life wi' grief
 An' bloody rants,
An' yet he's rank'd amang the chief
 O' lang-syne saunts.

And maybe, Tam, for a' my cants,
My wicked rhymes, an' drucken rants,
I'll gie auld cloven Clooty's haunts
 An unco slip yet,
An' snugly sit amang the saunts,
 At Davie's hip yet.

But fegs, the Session says I maun
Gae fa' upo' anither plan,
Than garren lasses cowp the cran
 Clean heels owre body,
And sairly thole their mither's ban
 Afore the howdy.

This leads me on, to tell for sport,
How I did wi' the Session sort—
Auld Clinkum at the Inner port
 Cry'd three times, 'Robin!
Come hither, lad, an' answer for't,
 Ye're blam'd for jobbin'.'

Wi' pinch I put a Sunday's face on,
An' snoov'd awa' before the Session—
I made an open fair confession,
 I scorn'd to lie;
An' syne Mess John, beyond expression,
 Fell foul o' me.

A furnicator-loun he call'd me,
An' said my fau't frae bliss expell'd me;
I own'd the tale was true he tell'd me,
 'But what the matter?'
Quo' I, 'I fear unless ye geld me,
 I'll ne'er be better.'

'Geld you!' quo' he, 'and whatfore no?
If that your right hand, leg or toe,
Should ever prove your sp'ritual foe,
 You shou'd remember
To cut if aff, an' whatfore no
 Your dearest member?'

'Na, na,' quo' I, 'I'm no for that,
Gelding's nae better than 'tis ca't,
I'd rather suffer for my faut,
 A hearty flewit,
As sair owre hip as ye can draw't,
 Tho' I should rue it.

'Or gin ye like to end the bother,
To please us a', I've just ae ither,
When next wi' yon lass I forgather,
 Whate'er betide it,
I'll frankly gi'e her't a' thegither,
 An' let her guide it.'

But, Sir, this pleas'd them warst ava,
An' therefore, Tam, when that I saw,
I said, 'Gude night,' and cam awa,
 And left the Session;
I saw they were resolved a'
 On my oppression.

EXTEMPORE LINES,

IN ANSWER TO A CARD FROM AN INTIMATE FRIEND OF BURNS, WISHING HIM
TO SPEND AN HOUR AT A TAVERN.

THE King's most humble servant I,
 Can scarcely spare a minute;
But I'll be wi' ye by an' bye;
 Or else the Deil's be in it.

MY bottle is my holy pool,
That heals the wounds o' care an' dool,
And pleasure is a wanton trout,
An' ye drink it, ye'll find him out.

LINES

WRITTEN EXTEMPORE IN A LADY'S POCKET-BOOK. [MISS KENNEDY, SISTER-IN-LAW OF GAVIN HAMILTON.]

GRANT me, indulgent Heav'n, that I may live
To see the miscreants feel the pains they give;
Deal Freedom's sacred treasures free as air,
Till slave and despot be but things which were.

THE HENPECK'D HUSBAND.

CURS'D be the man, the poorest wretch in life,
The crouching vassal to the tyrant wife!
Who has no will but by her high permission;
Who has not sixpence but in her possession;
Who must to her his dear friend's secret tell;
Who dreads a curtain lecture worse than hell.
Were such the wife had fallen to my part,
I'd break her spirit, or I'd break her heart:
I'd charm her with the magic of a switch,
I'd kiss her maids, and kick the perverse bitch.

EPITAPH ON A HENPECK'D COUNTRY SQUIRE.

As father Adam first was fool'd,
A case that's still too common,
Here lies a man a woman rul'd,
The Devil rul'd the woman.

EPIGRAM ON SAID OCCASION.

O DEATH, hadst thou but spar'd his life
Whom we, this day, lament!
We freely wad exchang'd the wife,
And a' been weel content.

Ev'n as he is, cauld in his graff,
The swap we yet will do't;
Take thou the carlin's carcase aff,
Thou'se get the saul o' boot.

ANOTHER.

ONE Queen Artemisia, as old stories tell,
When depriv'd of her husband she loved so well,
In respect for the love and affection he'd show'd her,
She reduc'd him to dust and she drank up the powder.

But Queen Netherplace, of a diff'rent complexion,
When call'd on to order the fun'ral direction,
Would have eat her dead lord, on a slender pretence,
Not to shew her respect, but --to save the expense.

VERSES

WE came na here to view your warks
  In hopes to be mair wise,
But only, lest we gang to hell,
  It may be nae surprise.

But when we tirl'd at your door,
  Your porter dought na hear us;
Sae may, shou'd we to hell's yetts come,
  Your billy Satan sair us!

LINES

ON BEING ASKED WHY GOD HAD MADE MISS DAVIES SO LITTLE
AND MRS. * * * SO LARGE.

Written on a Pane of Glass in the Inn at Moffat.

ASK why God made the gem so small,
  An' why so huge the granite?
Because God meant mankind should set
  That higher value on it.

EPIGRAM.

WRITTEN AT INVERARY.

WHOE'ER he be that sojourns here,
  I pity much his case,
Unless he come to wait upon
  The Lord their God, his Grace.

There's naething here but Highland pride,
  And Highland scab and hunger;
If Providence has sent me here,
  'Twas surely in his anger.

A TOAST.

GIVEN AT A MEETING OF THE DUMFRIES-SHIRE VOLUNTEERS, HELD TO COMMEMORATE
THE ANNIVERSARY OF RODNEY'S VICTORY, APRIL 12TH, 1782.

INSTEAD of a Song, boys, I'll give you a Toast,—
Here's the memory of those on the twelfth that we lost:
That we lost, did I say? nay, by heav'n, that we found,
For their fame it shall last while the world goes round.
The next in succession, I'll give you the King,
Whoe'er would betray him, on high may he swing!
And here's the grand fabric, our free Constitution,
As built on the base of the great Revolution;
And longer with Politics, not to be cramm'd,
Be Anarchy curs'd, and be Tyranny damn'd;
And who would to Liberty e'er prove disloyal,
May his son be a hangman, and he his first trial!

LINES

SAID TO HAVE BEEN WRITTEN BY BURNS, WHILE ON HIS DEATH-BED, TO JOHN RANKINE,
AYRSHIRE, AND FORWARDED TO HIM IMMEDIATELY AFTER THE POET'S DECEASE.

HE who of Rankine sang, lies stiff and dead ;
And a green grassy hillock hides his head ;
Alas ! alas ! a devilish change indeed !

VERSES ADDRESSED TO J. RANKINE,

ON HIS WRITING TO THE POET, THAT A GIRL IN THAT PART OF THE COUNTRY
WAS WITH CHILD TO HIM.

I AM a keeper of the law
In some sma' points, altho' not a' ;
Some people tell me gin I fa',
    Ae way or ither,
The breaking of ae point, tho' sma',
    Breaks a' thegither.

I hae been in for't ance or twice,
And winna say owre far for thrice,
Yet never met with that surprise
    That broke my rest,
But now a rumour's like to rise,
    A whaup's i' the nest.

ON SEEING THE BEAUTIFUL SEAT OF LORD GALLOWAY.

WHAT dost thou in that mansion fair ?
    Flit, Galloway, and find
Some narrow, dirty, dungeon cave,
    The picture of thy mind !

ON THE SAME.

NO Stewart art thou, Galloway,
    The Stewarts all were brave ;
Besides, the Stewarts were but fools,
    Not one of them a knave.

ON THE SAME.

BRIGHT ran thy line, O Galloway,
    Thro' many a far-fam'd sire !
So ran the far-fam'd Roman way,
    So ended in a mire !

TO THE SAME,

ON THE AUTHOR BEING THREATENED WITH HIS RESENTMENT.

SPARE me thy vengeance, Galloway,
    In quiet let me live :
I ask no kindness at thy hand,
    For thou hast none to give.

VERSES TO J. RANKINE.

AE day, as Death, that grusome carl,
Was driving to the tither warl'
A mixtie-maxtie motley squad,
And monie a guilt-bespotted lad ;
Black gowns of each denomination,
And thieves of every rank and station,
From him that wears the star and garter,
To him that wintles in a halter ;
Asham'd himsel to see the wretches,
He mutters, glowrin at the bitches,

'By God I'll not be seen behint them,
Nor 'mang the sp'ritual core present
    them,
Without at least, ae honest man,
To grace this damn'd infernal clan.'
By Adamhill a glance he threw,
'Lord God!' quoth he, 'I have it now,
There's just the man I want, i' faith,'
And quickly stoppit Rankine's breath.

EXTEMPORANEOUS EFFUSION,

ON BEING APPOINTED TO THE EXCISE.

SEARCHING auld wives' barrels,
    Och, hon ! the day !
That clarty barm should stain my laurels ;
    But—what'll ye say ?
These movin' things, ca'd wives and weans,
Wad move the very hearts o' stanes !

ON HEARING THAT THERE WAS FALSEHOOD IN THE REV. DR. B——'S VERY LOOKS.

THAT there is falsehood in his looks
    I must and will deny ;
They say their master is a knave—
    And sure they do not lie.

POVERTY.

IN politics if thou wouldst mix,
    And mean thy fortunes be ;
Bear this in mind,—be deaf and blind,
    Let great folks hear and see.

ON A SCHOOLMASTER

IN CLEISH PARISH, FIFESHIRE.

HERE lie Willie Michie's banes ;
    O Satan. when ye tak him,
Gie him the schoolin' of your weans,
    For clever deils he'll mak them !

LINES

WRITTEN AND PRESENTED TO MRS. KEMBLE, ON SEEING HER IN THE CHARACTER
OF YARICO IN THE DUMFRIES THEATRE, 1794.

KEMBLE, thou cur'st my unbelief
    Of Moses and his rod ;
At Yarico's sweet notes of grief
    The rock with tears had flow'd.

LINES.

I MURDER hate by field or flood,
    Tho' glory's name may screen us ;
In wars at hame I'll spend my blood,
    Life-giving war of Venus.

The deities that I adore
    Are social Peace and Plenty,
I'm better pleased to make one more,
    Than be the death of twenty.

LINES

WRITTEN ON A WINDOW, AT THE KING'S ARMS TAVERN, DUMFRIES.

YE men of wit and wealth, why all this sneering
    'Gainst poor Excisemen ? give the cause a hearing ;
What are your landlords' rent-rolls ? taxing ledgers :
    What premiers, what ? even Monarchs' mighty gaugers :
Nay, what are priests, those seeming godly wise men ?
    What are they, pray, but spiritual Excisemen ?

LINES

WRITTEN ON THE WINDOW OF THE GLOBE TAVERN, DUMFRIES.

THE graybeard, Old Wisdom, may boast of his treasures,
    Give me with gay Folly to live :
I grant him his calm-blooded, time-settled pleasures,
    But Folly has raptures to give.

EXTEMPORE IN THE COURT OF SESSION.

TUNE—'*Killiecrankie.*'

LORD ADVOCATE.

HE clench'd his pamphlets in his fist,
    He quoted and he hinted,
Till in a declamation-mist,
    His argument he tint it :
He gaped for't, he graped for't,
    He fand it was awa, man ;
But what his common sense came short,
    He eked out wi' law, man.

MR. ERSKINE.

Collected Harry stood awee,
    Then open'd out his arm, man ;
His lordship sat wi' ruefu' e'e,
    And ey'd the gathering storm, man :
Like wind-driv'n hail it did assail,
    Or torrents owre a linn, man ;
The Bench sae wise, lift up their eyes,
    Half-wauken'd wi' the din, man.

LINES

WRITTEN UNDER THE PICTURE OF MISS BURNS. [SEE PAGE 473.]

CEASE, ye prudes, your envious railing,
  Lovely Burns has charms—confess :
True it is, she had one failing,
  Had a woman ever less ?

ON MISS J. SCOTT, OF AYR.

OH ! had each Scot of ancient times
  Been, Jeanie Scott, as thou art,
The bravest heart on English ground
  Had yielded like a coward.

EPIGRAM ON CAPTAIN FRANCIS GROSE,

THE CELEBRATED ANTIQUARY.

THE Devil got notice that Grose was a-dying,
So whip ! at the summons, old Satan came flying ;
But when he approach'd where poor Francis lay moaning,
And saw each bed-post with its burden a-groaning,
Astonish'd ! confounded ! cry'd Satan, ' By God,
I'll want 'im, ere I take such a damnable load.'

EPIGRAM ON ELPHINSTONE'S TRANSLATION OF MARTIAL'S EPIGRAMS.

O THOU whom Poetry abhors,
Whom Prose had turnèd out of doors,
Heard'st thou yon groan ?—proceed no further,
'Twas laurel'd Martial calling murther.

EPITAPH ON A COUNTRY LAIRD,

NOT QUITE SO WISE AS SOLOMON.

BLESS Jesus Christ, O Cardoness,
  With grateful lifted eyes,
Who said that not the soul alone,
  But body too, must rise :
For had he said, ' The soul alone
  From death I will deliver,'
Alas, alas ! O Cardoness,
  Then thou hadst slept for ever !

EPITAPH ON A NOISY POLEMIC.

BELOW thir stanes lie Jamie's banes :
O Death, it's my opinion,
Thou ne'er took such a bleth'rin' bitch
Into thy dark dominion !

EPITAPH ON WEE JOHNNY.

Hic jacet wee Johnny.

WHOE'ER thou art, O reader, know
That death has murder'd Johnie !
An' here his body lies fu' low——
For saul he ne'er had ony.

EPITAPH ON A CELEBRATED RULING ELDER.

HERE souter Hood in Death does sleep ;
To Hell, if he's gane thither,
Satan, gie him thy gear to keep,
He'll haud it weel thegither.

EPITAPH FOR ROBERT AIKEN, ESQ.

KNOW thou, O stranger to the fame
Of this much lov'd, much honour'd name,
(For none that knew him need be told)
A warmer heart death ne'er made cold.

EPITAPH FOR GAVIN HAMILTON, ESQ.

THE poor man weeps—here Gavin sleeps,
Whom canting wretches blam'd :
But with such as he, where'er he be,
May I be sav'd or damn'd !

A BARD'S EPITAPH.

Is there a whim-inspired fool,
Owre fast for thought, owre hot for rule,
Owre blate to seek, owre proud to snool,
    Let him draw near ;
And owre this grassy heap sing dool,
    And drap a tear.

Is there a Bard of rustic song,
Who, noteless, steals the crowds among,
That weekly this area throng,
    O, pass not by !
But, with a frater-feeling strong,
    Here, heave a sigh.

Is there a man whose judgment clear,
Can others teach the course to steer,
Yet runs, himself, life's mad career,
　　Wild as the wave ;
Here pause—and, thro' the starting tear,
　　Survey this grave.

The poor Inhabitant below
Was quick to learn and wise to know,
And keenly felt the friendly glow,
　　And *softer flame*,
But thoughtless follies laid him low,
　　And stain'd his name !

Reader, attend—whether thy soul
Soars fancy's flights beyond the pole,
Or darkling grubs this earthly hole,
　　In low pursuit ;
Know, prudent, cautious *self-control*
　　Is wisdom's root.

EPITAPH ON MY FATHER.

O YE, whose cheek the tear of pity stains,
　　Draw near with pious rev'rence and attend !
Here lie the loving husband's dear remains,
　　The tender father, and the gen'rous friend.

The pitying heart that felt for human woe ;
　　The dauntless heart that fear'd no human pride ;
The friend of man, to vice alone a foe ;
　　'For ev'n his failings lean'd to virtue's side.'

EPITAPH ON JOHN DOVE,

INNKEEPER, MAUCHLINE.

HERE lies Johnny Pidgeon ;
What was his religion ?
Wha e'er desires to ken,
To some other warl'
Maun follow the carl,
For here Johnny Pidgeon had nane !

Strong ale was ablution,—
Small beer persecution,
A dram was memento mori ;
But a full flowing bowl
Was the saving his soul,
And port was celestial glory.

EPITAPH ON JOHN BUSHBY,

WRITER, IN DUMFRIES.

HERE lies John Bushby, honest man !
Cheat him, Devil, if you can.

EPITAPH ON A WAG IN MAUCHLINE.

LAMENT him, Mauchline husbands a',
　　He aften did assist ye ;
For had ye staid whole weeks awa,
　　Your wives they ne'er had miss'd ye.

Ye Mauchline bairns, as on ye pass
　　To school in bands thegither,
O tread ye lightly on his grass,
　　Perhaps he was your father.

EPITAPH ON A PERSON NICKNAMED 'THE MARQUIS,'

WHO DESIRED BURNS TO WRITE ONE ON HIM.

HERE lies a mock Marquis whose titles were shamm'd,
If ever he rise, it will be to be damn'd.

EPITAPH ON WALTER R—— [RIDDEL].

SIC a reptile was Wat,
  Sic a miscreant slave,
That the worms ev'n damn'd him
  When laid in his grave.
'In his flesh there's a famine,'
  A starv'd reptile cries ;
'An' his heart is rank poison,'
  Another replies.

ON HIMSELF.

HERE comes Burns
  On Rosinante ;
She's d—— poor,
  But he's d—— canty !

GRACE BEFORE MEAT.

O LORD, when hunger pinches sore,
  Do thou stand us in need,
And send us from thy bounteous store,
  A tup or wether head ! Amen.

ON COMMISSARY GOLDIE'S BRAINS.

LORD, to account who dares thee call,
  Or e'er dispute thy pleasure ?
Else why within so thick a wall
  Enclose so poor a treasure ?

IMPROMPTU

ON AN INNKEEPER NAMED BACON, WHO INTRUDED HIMSELF INTO ALL COMPANIES.

AT Brownhill we always get dainty good cheer,
And plenty of bacon each day in the year ;
We've all things that's nice, and mostly in season,
But why always *Bacon*—come, give me a reason ?

ADDRESSED TO A LADY

WHOM THE AUTHOR FEARED HE HAD OFFENDED.

RUSTICITY'S ungainly form
  May cloud the highest mind ;
But when the heart is nobly warm,
  The good excuse will find.

Propriety's cold cautious rules
  Warm fervour may o'erlook ;
But spare poor sensibility
  The ungentle, harsh rebuke.

EPIGRAM.

WHEN ——, deceased, to the devil went down,
'Twas nothing would serve him but Satan's own crown ;
'Thy fool's head,' quoth Satan, 'that crown shall wear never,
I grant thou'rt as wicked, but not quite so clever.'

. LINES INSCRIBED ON A PLATTER.

MY blessings on ye, honest wife,
    I ne'er was here before :
Ye've wealth o' gear for spoon and
    knife—
Heart could not wish for more.

Heaven keep you clear of sturt and
    strife,
    Till far ayont four score,
And by the Lord o' death and life,
    I'll ne'er gae by your door !

TO ——.

YOUR billet, sir, I grant receipt ;
Wi' you I'll canter ony gate, ·——
Though 'twere a trip to yon blue warl',
Whare birkies march on burning marl :
Then, sir, God willing, I'll attend ye,
And to his goodness I commend ye.
                                    R. BURNS.

ON MR. M'MURDO.

BLEST be M'Murdo to his latest day,
No envious cloud o'ercast his evening ray ;
No wrinkle furrow'd by the hand of care,
Nor even sorrow add one silver hair !
Oh, may no son the father's honour stain,
Nor ever daughter give the mother pain.

TO A LADY

WHO WAS LOOKING UP THE TEXT DURING SERMON.

FAIR maid, you need not take the hint,
    Nor idle texts pursue :
'Twas *guilty sinners* that he meant—
    Not *angels* such as you !

IMPROMPTU.

How daur ye ca' me howlet-faced,
    Ye ugly, glowering spectre ?
My face was but the keekin' glass,
    An' there ye saw your picture.

TO MR. MACKENZIE, SURGEON, MAUCHLINE.

FRIDAY first's the day appointed
By the Right Worshipful anointed,
  To hold our grand procession ;
To get a blad o' Johnie's morals,
And taste a swatch o' Manson's barrels
  I' the way of our profession.

The Master and the Brotherhood
  Would a' be glad to see you ;

For me I would be mair than proud
  To share the mercies wi' you.
If Death, then, wi' skaith, then,
  Some mortal heart is hechtin',
Inform him, and storm him,
  That Saturday you'll fecht him.

ROBERT BURNS.

Mossgiel, An. M. 5790.

TO A PAINTER.

DEAR ——, I'll gie ye some advice
  You'll tak it no uncivil :
You shouldna paint at angels mair,
  But try and paint the devil.

To paint an angel's kittle wark,
  Wi' auld Nick there's less danger ;
You'll easy draw a weel-kent face,
  But no sae weel a stranger.

LINES WRITTEN ON A TUMBLER.

YOU'RE welcome, Willie Stewart ;
  You're welcome, Willie Stewart ;
There's ne'er a flower that blooms in
    May,
  That's half sae welcome's thou art.

Come, bumpers high, express your joy,
  The bowl we maun renew it ;

The tappit-hen, gae bring her ben,
  To welcome Willie Stewart.

May foes be strang, and friends be
    slack,
  Ilk action may he rue it ;
May woman on him turn her back,
  That wrangs thee, Willie Stewart !

ON MR. W. CRUIKSHANK
OF THE HIGH SCHOOL, EDINBURGH.

HONEST Will to heaven is gane,
  And mony shall lament him ;
His faults they a' in Latin lay,
  In English nane e'er kent them.

B

N

SONGS.

THE LASS O' BALLOCHMYLE.

TUNE—'*Miss Forbes's Farew.ll to Banff, or Ettrick Banks.*'

'TWAS even—the dewy fields were
    green,
  On every blade the pearls hang ;
The Zephyrs wanton'd round the bean,
  And bore its fragrant sweets alang :
In every glen the Mavis sang,
  All nature listening seem'd the while :
Except where green-wood echoes rang,
  Amang the braes o' Ballochmyle.

With careless step I onward stray'd,
  My heart rejoic'd in nature's joy,
When musing in a lonely glade,
  A maiden fair I chanc'd to spy ;
Her look was like the morning's eye,
  Her hair like nature's vernal smile,
Perfection whisper'd passing by,
  Behold the lass o' Ballochmyle !

Fair is the morn in flowery May,
  And sweet is night in Autumn mild,
When roving thro' the garden gay,
  Or wandering in a lonely wild :

But Woman, Nature's darling child !
  There all her charms she does compile;
Ev'n there her other works are foil'd
  By the bonie lass o' Ballochmyle.

O, had she been a country maid,
  And I the happy country swain,
Tho' shelter'd in the lowest shed
  That ever rose on Scotland's plain !
Thro' weary winter's wind and rain,
  With joy, with rapture, I would toil;
And nightly to my bosom strain
  The bonie lass o' Ballochmyle.

Then pride might climb the slipp'ry steep,
  Where fame and honours lofty shine ;
And thirst of gold might tempt the deep,
  Or downward seek the Indian mine :
Give me the cot below the pine,
  To tend the flocks or till the soil,
And every day have joys divine,
  With the bonie lass o' Ballochmyle.

SONG OF DEATH.

A GAELIC AIR.

SCENE.—*A field of battle. Time of the day—Evening. The wounded and dying of the
victorious army are supposed to join in the song.*

FAREWELL, thou fair day, thou green earth, and ye skies,
  Now gay with the broad setting sun !
Farewell, loves and friendships, ye dear, tender ties,
  Our race of existence is run !

Thou grim King of Terrors, thou life's gloomy foe,
  Go, frighten the coward and slave !
Go, teach them to tremble, fell Tyrant ! but know,
  No terrors hast thou for the brave !

Thou strik'st the dull peasant—he sinks in the dark,
  Nor saves e'en the wreck of a name :
Thou strik'st the young hero—a glorious mark !
  He falls in the blaze of his fame !

In the field of proud honour—our swords in our hands,
  Our King and our Country to save—
While victory shines on life's last ebbing sands,
  O ! who would not die with the brave !

MY AIN KIND DEARIE O.

WHEN o'er the hill the eastern star
  Tells bughtin-time is near, my jo ;
And owsen frae the furrow'd field
  Return sae dowf and wearie O ;
Down by the burn, where scented birks
  Wi' dew are hanging clear, my jo,
I'll meet thee on the lea-rig,
  My ain kind dearie O.

In mirkest glen, at midnight hour,
  I'd rove, and ne'er be eerie O,
If thro' that glen I gaed to thee,
  My ain kind dearie O.

Altho' the night were ne'er sae wild,
  And I were ne'er sae wearie O,
I'd meet thee on the lea-rig,
  My ain kind dearie O.

The hunter lo'es the morning sun,
  To rouse the mountain deer, my jo ;
At noon the fisher seeks the glen,
  Along the burn to steer, my jo ;
Gie me the hour o' gloamin grey,
  It maks my heart sae cheery O,
To meet thee on the lea-rig,
  My ain kind dearie O.

AULD ROB MORRIS.

THERE'S auld Rob Morris that wons in yon glen,
He's the king o' gude fellows and wale of auld men ;
He has gowd in his coffers, he has owsen and kine,
And ae bonie lassie, his darling and mine.

She's fresh as the morning, the fairest in May ;
She's sweet as the ev'ning amang the new hay ;
As blythe and as artless as the lamb on the lea,
And dear to my heart as the light to my ee.

But oh ! she's an heiress, auld Robin's a laird,
And my daddie has nought but a cot-house and yard ;
A wooer like me maunna hope to come speed,
The wounds I must hide that will soon be my dead.

The day comes to me, but delight brings me nane ;
The night comes to me, but my rest it is gane :
I wander my lane, like a night-troubled ghaist,
And I sigh as my heart it wad burst in my breast

O had she but been of a lower degree,
I then might hae hop'd she wad smil'd upon me ;
O how past descriving had then been my bliss,
As now my distraction no words can express !

N 2

NAEBODY.

I HAE a wife o' my ain,
    I'll partake wi' naebody;
I'll tak cuckold frae nane,
    I'll gie cuckold to naebody.

I hae a penny to spend,
    There—thanks to naebody;
I hae naething to lend,
    I'll borrow frae naebody.

I am naebody's lord,
    I'll be slave to naebody;
I hae a guid braid sword,
    I'll tak dunts frae naebody.

I'll be merry and free,
    I'll be sad for naebody;
If naebody care for me,
    I'll care for naebody.

MY WIFE'S A WINSOME
WEE THING.

SHE is a winsome wee thing,
She is a handsome wee thing,
She is a bonie wee thing,
This sweet wee wife o' mine.

I never saw a fairer,
I never lo'ed a dearer,
And neist my heart I'll wear her,
For fear my jewel tine.

She is a winsome wee thing,
She is a handsome wee thing,
She is a bonie wee thing,
This sweet wee wife o' mine.

The warld's wrack, we share o't,
The warstle and the care o't;
Wi' her I'll blythely bear it,
And think my lot divine.

DUNCAN GRAY.

DUNCAN GRAY came here to woo,
    Ha, ha, the wooing o't,
On blythe yule night when we were fou,
    Ha, ha, the wooing o't.

Maggie coost her head fu' high,
Look'd asklent and unco skeigh,
Gart poor Duncan stand abeigh;
    Ha, ha, the wooing o't.

Duncan fleech'd, and Duncan pray'd;
    Ha, ha, &c.
Meg was deaf as Ailsa Craig,
    Ha, ha, &c.
Duncan sigh'd baith out and in,
Grat his een baith bleer't and blin',
Spak o' lowpin o'er a linn;
    Ha, ha, &c.

Time and chance are but a tide,
    Ha, ha, &c.
Slighted love is sair to bide,
    Ha, ha, &c.
Shall I, like a fool, quoth he,
For a haughty hizzie die?
She may gae to—France for me!
    Ha, ha, &c.

How it comes let doctors tell,
    Ha, ha, &c.
Meg grew sick—as he grew well,
    Ha, ha, &c.
Something in her bosom wrings,
For relief a sigh she brings;
And O, her een, they spak sic things!
    Ha, ha, &c.

Duncan was a lad o' grace,
    Ha, ha, &c.
Maggie's was a piteous case,
    Ha, ha, &c.
Duncan couldna be her death,
Swelling pity smoor'd his wrath;
Now they're crouse and cantie baith!
    Ha, ha, the wooing o't.

O POORTITH.

TUNE—'*I had a Horse.*'

O POORTITH cauld, and restless love,
    Ye wreck my peace between ye;
Yet poortith a' I could forgive,
    An' 'twerena for my Jeanie.
    O why should fate sic pleasure have,
        Life's dearest bands untwining?
    Or why sae sweet a flower as love
        Depend on Fortune's shining?

This warld's wealth when I think on,
  Its pride, and a' the lave o't;
Fie, fie on silly coward man,
  That he should be the slave o't.
      O why, &c.

Her een sae bonie blue betray
  How she repays my passion;
But prudence is her o'erword aye,
  She talks of rank and fashion.
      O why, &c.

O wha can prudence think upon,
  And sic a lassie by him?
O wha can prudence think upon,
  And sae in love as I am?
      O why, &c.

How blest the humble cotter's fate!
  He woos his simple dearie;
The silly bogles, wealth and state,
  Can never make them eerie.
    O why should fate sic pleasure have,
      Life's dearest bands untwining?
    Or why sae sweet a flower as love
      Depend on Fortune's shining?

GALLA WATER.

THERE'S braw braw lads on Yarrow
      braes,
  That wander thro' the blooming
      heather;
But Yarrow braes nor Ettrick shaws
  Can match the lads o' Galla Water.

But there is ane, a secret ane,
  Aboon them a' I lo'e him better;
And I'll be his, and he'll be mine,
  The bonie lad o' Galla Water.

Altho' his daddie was nae laird,
  And tho' I hae nae meikle tocher;
Yet rich in kindest, truest love,
  We'll tent our flocks by Galla Water.

It ne'er was wealth, it ne'er was wealth,
  That coft contentment, peace or plea-
      sure;
The bands and bliss o' mutual love,
  O that's the chiefest warld's treasure!

LORD GREGORY.

O MIRK, mirk is this midnight hour,
  And loud the tempest's roar;
A waefu' wanderer seeks thy tow'r,
  Lord Gregory, ope thy door.

An exile frae her father's ha',
  And a' for loving thee;
At least some pity on me shaw,
  If love it mayna be.

Lord Gregory, mind'st thou not the grove,
  By bonie Irwine side,
Where first I own'd that virgin-love,
  I lang, lang had denied?

How aften didst thou pledge and vow,
  Thou wad for aye be mine!
And my fond heart, itsel sae true,
  It ne'er mistrusted thine.

Hard is thy heart, Lord Gregory,
  And flinty is thy breast:
Thou dart of heaven that flashest by,
  O wilt thou give me rest!

Ye mustering thunders from above,
  Your willing victim see!
But spare, and pardon my fause love,
  His wrangs to heaven and me!

OPEN THE DOOR TO ME, OH!

WITH ALTERATIONS.

OH, open the door, some pity to shew,
  Oh, open the door to me, Oh!
Tho' thou hast been false, I'll ever prove true,
  Oh, open the door to me, Oh!

Cauld is the blast upon my pale cheek,
　　But caulder thy love for me, Oh !
The frost that freezes the life at my heart,
　　Is nought to my pains frae thee, Oh !

The wan moon is setting behind the white wave,
　　And time is setting with me, Oh !
False friends, false love, farewell ! for mair
　　I'll ne'er trouble them, nor thee, Oh !

She has open'd the door, she has open'd it wide ;
　　She sees his pale corse on the plain, Oh !
My true love, she cried, and sank down by his side,
　　Never to rise again, Oh !

MEG O' THE MILL.

Air—'*O, bonie Lass, will you lie in a Barrack.*'

O KEN ye what Meg o' the Mill has gotten,
An' ken ye what Meg o' the Mill has gotten ?
She has gotten a coof wi' a claut o' siller,
And broken the heart o' the barley Miller.

The Miller was strappin, the Miller was ruddy ;
A heart like a lord, and a hue like a lady ;
The Laird was a widdiefu', bleerit knurl ;
She's left the guid fellow and ta'en the churl.

The Miller he hecht her a heart leal and loving ;
The Laird did address her wi' matter mair moving,
A fine pacing horse wi' a clear chained bridle,
A whip by her side, and a bonie side-saddle.

O wae on the siller, it is sae prevailing ;
And wae on the love that is fix'd on a mailen!
A tocher's nae word in a true lover's parle,
But, gie me my love, and a fig for the warl !

JESSIE.

Tune—'*Bonie Dundee.*'

TRUE hearted was he, the sad swain o' the Yarrow,
　　And fair are the maids on the banks o' the Ayr,
But by the sweet side o' the Nith's winding river,
　　Are lovers as faithful, and maidens as fair :
To equal young Jessie seek Scotland all over ;
　　To equal young Jessie you seek it in vain,
Grace, beauty, and elegance, fetter her lover,
　　And maidenly modesty fixes the chain.

O, fresh is the rose in the gay, dewy morning,
    And sweet is the lily at evening close ;
But in the fair presence o' lovely young Jessie,
    Unseen is the lily, unheeded the rose.
Love sits in her smile, a wizard ensnaring ;
    Enthron'd in her een he delivers his law :
And still to her charms she alone is a stranger !
    Her modest demeanour's the jewel of a'.

WANDERING WILLIE.

HERE awa, there awa, wandering Willie,
    Here awa, there awa, haud awa hame ;
Come to my bosom, my ain only dearie,
    Tell me thou bring'st me my Willie the same.

Winter winds blew loud and cauld at our parting,
    Fears for my Willie brought tears in my ee ;
Welcome now simmer, and welcome my Willie,
    The simmer to nature, my Willie to me !

Rest, ye wild storms, in the cave of your slumbers ;
    How your dread howling a lover alarms !
Wauken, ye breezes, row gently, ye billows,
    And waft my dear laddie ance mair to my arms.

But oh, if he's faithless, and minds na his Nannie,
    Flow still between us, thou wide-roaring main ;
May I never see it, may I never trow it,
    But, dying, believe that my Willie's my ain.

LOGAN BRAES.

TUNE—'*Logan Water.*'

O LOGAN, sweetly didst thou glide
That day I was my Willie's bride ;
And years sinsyne hae o'er us run,
Like Logan to the simmer sun.
But now thy flow'ry banks appear
Like drumlie winter, dark and drear,
While my dear lad maun face his faes,
Far, far frae me and Logan Braes.

Again the merry month o' May
Has made our hills and valleys gay ;
The birds rejoice in leafy bowers,
The bees hum round the breathing
    flowers ;
Blithe morning lifts his rosy eye,
And evening's tears are tears of joy :
My soul, delightless, a' surveys,
While Willie's far frae Logan Braes.

Within yon milk-white hawthorn bush,
Amang her nestlings, sits the thrush ;
Her faithfu' mate will share her toil,
Or wi' his song her cares beguile :
But I wi' my sweet nurslings here,
Nae mate to help, nae mate to cheer,
Pass widow'd nights and joyless days,
While Willie's far frae Logan Braes.

O wae upon you, men o' state,
That brethren rouse to deadly hate !
As ye mak monie a fond heart mourn,
Sae may it on your heads return !
How can your flinty hearts enjoy
The widow's tears, the orphan's cry ?
But soon may peace bring happy days,
And Willie hame to Logan Braes !

THERE WAS A LASS.

TUNE—'*Bonie Jean.*'

THERE was a lass, and she was fair,
  At kirk and market to be seen,
When a' the fairest maids were met,
  The fairest maid was bonie Jean.

And ay she wrought her mammie's wark,
  And ay she sang sae merrily :
The blythest bird upon the bush
  Had ne'er a lighter heart than she.

But hawks will rob the tender joys
  That bless the little lintwhite's nest ;
And frost will blight the fairest flowers,
  And love will break the soundest rest.

Young Robie was the brawest lad,
  The flower and pride of a' the glen ;
And lie had owsen, sheep and kye,
  And wanton naigies nine or ten.

He gaed wi' Jeanie to the tryste,
  He danc'd wi' Jeanie on the down ;
And lang ere witless Jeanie wist,
  Her heart was tint, her peace was
    stown.

As in the bosom o' the stream
  The moon-beam dwells at dewy e'en ;
So trembling, pure, was tender love,
  Within the breast o' bonie Jean.

And now she works her mammie's wark,
  And aye she sighs wi' care and pain ;
Yet wistna what her ail might be,
  Or what wad mak her weel again.

But didna Jeanie's heart loup light,
  And didna joy blink in her ee,
As Robie tauld a tale o' love,
  Ae e'enin on the lily lea ?

The sun was sinking in the west,
  The birds sang sweet in ilka grove ;
His cheek to hers he fondly prest,
  And whisper'd thus his tale o' love :

O Jeanie fair, I lo'e thee dear ;
  O canst thou think to fancy me ?
Or wilt thou leave thy mammie's cot,
  And learn to tent the farms wi' me?

At barn or byre thou shaltna drudge,
  Or naething else to trouble thee ;
But stray amang the heather-bells,
  And tent the waving corn wi' me.

Now what could artless Jeanie do ?
  She had nae will to say him na :
At length she blush'd a sweet consent,
  And love was ay between them twa.

PHILLIS THE FAIR.

TUNE—'*Robin Adair.*'

WHILE larks with little wing
  Fann'd the pure air,
Tasting the breathing spring,
  Forth I did fare :
Gay the sun's golden eye
Peep'd o'er the mountains high ;
Such thy morn ! did I cry,
  Phillis the fair.

In each bird's careless song
  Glad did I share ;
While yon wild flowers among,
  Chance led me there :
Sweet to the opening day,
Rosebuds bent the dewy spray ;
Such thy bloom ! did I say,
  Phillis the fair.

Down in a shady walk,
  Doves cooing were,
I mark'd the cruel hawk
  Caught in a snare :
So kind may Fortune be,
Such make his destiny,
He who would injure thee,
  Phillis the fair.

BY ALLAN STREAM.

TUNE—'*Allan Water.*'

BY Allan stream I chanc'd to rove,
  While Phœbus sank beyond Benleddi ;
The winds were whispering thro' the
    grove,
  The yellow corn was waving ready :
I listen'd to a lover's sang,
  And thought on youthfu' pleasures
    monie ;
And ay the wildwood echoes rang—
  O, dearly do I love thee, Annie !

O, happy be the woodbine bower,
  Nae nightly bogle mak it eerie ;
Nor ever sorrow stain the hour,
  The place and time I met my dearie !
Her head upon my throbbing breast,
  She, sinking, said 'I'm thine for ever !'
While monie a kiss the seal imprest,
  The sacred vow, we ne'er should sever.

The haunt o' spring's the primrose brae,
  The simmer joys the flocks to follow ;
How cheery thro' her shortening day
  Is autumn, in her weeds o' yellow !
But can they melt the glowing heart,
  Or chain the soul in speechless pleasure,
Or, thro' each nerve the rapture dart,
  Like meeting her, our bosom's treasure ?

HAD I A CAVE.

Tune—'*Robin Adair.*'

Had I a cave on some wild, distant shore,
Where the winds howl to the waves' dashing roar ;
    There would I weep my woes,
    There seek my lost repose,
    Till grief my eyes should close,
        Ne'er to wake more.

Falsest of womankind, canst thou declare
All thy fond plighted vows—fleeting as air ?
    To thy new lover hie,
    Laugh o'er thy perjury,
    Then in thy bosom try,
        What peace is there !

WHISTLE, AND I'LL COME TO YOU, MY LAD.

Tune—'*My Jo, Janet.*'

O whistle, and I'll come to you, my lad ;
O whistle, and I'll come to you, my lad :
Tho' father and mither and a' should gae mad,
O whistle, and I'll come to you, my lad.

But warily tent, when ye come to court me,
And come na unless the back-yett be a-jee ;
Syne up the back-stile, and let naebody see,
And come as ye were na comin to me.
And come, &c.
    O whistle, &c.

At kirk, or at market, whene'er ye meet me,
Gang by me as tho' that ye car'd na a flie :
But steal me a blink o' your bonie black ee,
Yet look as ye were na lookin at me.
Yet look, &c.
    O whistle, &c.

Ay vow and protest that ye care na for me,
And whiles ye may lightly my beauty a wee ;
But court na anither, tho' jokin ye be,
For fear that she wyle your fancy frae me.
For fear, &c.
    O whistle, &c.

HUSBAND, HUSBAND, CEASE YOUR STRIFE.

TUNE—'*My Jo, Janet.*'

HUSBAND, husband, cease your strife,
  Nor longer idly rave, sir;
Tho' I am your wedded wife,
  Yet I am not your slave, sir.

' One of two must still obey,
  Nancy, Nancy;
Is it man or woman, say,
  My spouse, Nancy?'

If 'tis still the lordly word,
  Service and obedience;
I'll desert my sov'reign lord,
  And so good-bye allegiance!

' Sad will I be, so bereft,
  Nancy, Nancy!
Yet I'll try to make a shift,
  My spouse, Nancy.'

My poor heart then break it must,
  My last hour I'm near it:
When you lay me in the dust,
  Think, think how you will bear it.

' I will hope and trust in Heaven,
  Nancy, Nancy;
Strength to bear it will be given,
  My spouse, Nancy.'

Well, sir, from the silent dead
  Still I'll try to daunt you;
Ever round your midnight bed
  Horrid sprites shall haunt you.

' I'll wed another, like my dear
  Nancy, Nancy;
Then all hell will fly for fear,
  My spouse, Nancy.'

DELUDED SWAIN.

TUNE—'*The Collier's Dochter.*'

DELUDED swain, the pleasure
  The fickle Fair can give thee,
Is but a fairy treasure,
  Thy hopes will soon deceive thee.

The billows on the ocean,
  The breezes idly roaming,
The clouds' uncertain motion,
  They are but types of woman.

O! art thou not ashamed
  To doat upon a feature?
If man thou wouldst be named,
  Despise the silly creature.

Go, find an honest fellow;
  Good claret set before thee:
Hold on till thou art mellow,
  And then to bed in glory.

SONG.

TUNE—'*The Quaker's Wife.*'

THINE am I, my faithful fair,
  Thine, my lovely Nancy;
Ev'ry pulse along my veins,
  Ev'ry roving fancy.

To thy bosom lay my heart,
  There to throb and languish:
Tho' despair had wrung its core,
  That would heal its anguish.

Take away these rosy lips,
  Rich with balmy treasure!
Turn away thine eyes of love,
  Lest I die with pleasure!

What is life when wanting love?
  Night without a morning!
Love's the cloudless summer sun,
  Nature gay adorning.

WILT THOU BE MY DEARIE?

A NEW SCOTS SONG.

TUNE—'*The Sutor's Dochter.*'

WILT thou be my dearie?
When sorrow wrings thy gentle heart,
Wilt thou let me cheer thee?
By the treasure of my soul,
That's the love I bear thee!
I swear and vow that only thou
Shalt ever be my dearie—
Only thou, I swear and vow,
Shalt ever be my dearie.

Lassie, say thou lo'es me ;
Or if thou wilt na be my ain,
Say na thou'lt refuse me :
If it winna, canna be,
Thou for thine may choose me,
Let me, lassie, quickly die,
Trusting that thou lo'es me—
Lassie, let me quickly die,
Trusting that thou lo'es me.

BANKS OF CREE.

TUNE—'*The Flowers of Edinburgh.*'

HERE is the glen, and here the bower,
All underneath the birchen shade ;
The village-bell has toll'd the hour,
O what can stay my lovely maid ?

'Tis not Maria's whispering call ;
'Tis but the balmy breathing gale,
Mixt with some warbler's dying fall,
The dewy star of eve to hail.

It is Maria's voice I hear !
So calls the woodlark in the grove
His little faithful mate to cheer,
At once 'tis music—and 'tis love.

And art thou come? and art thou true ?
O welcome, dear, to love and me !
And let us all our vows renew,
Along the flow'ry banks of Cree.

ON THE SEAS AND FAR AWAY.

TUNE—'*O'er the Hills and far away.*'

How can my poor heart be glad,
When absent from my Sailor lad ?
How can I the thought forego,
He's on the seas to meet the foe ?
Let me wander, let me rove,
Still my heart is with my love ;
Nightly dreams and thoughts by day
Are with him that's far away.

CHORUS.

On the seas and far away,
On stormy seas and far away ;
Nightly dreams and thoughts by day
Are aye with him that's far away.

When in summer's noon I faint,
As weary flocks around me pant,
Haply in this scorching sun
My Sailor's thund'ring at his gun :
Bullets, spare my only joy !
Bullets, spare my darling boy !
Fate, do with me what you may,
Spare but him that's far away !
　　On the seas, &c.

At the starless midnight hour,
When winter rules with boundless
　　power ;
As the storms the forest tear,
And thunders rend the howling air,
Listening to the doubling roar,
Surging on the rocky shore,
All I can—I weep and pray,
For his weal that's far away.
　　On the seas, &c.

Peace, thy olive wand extend,
And bid wild War his ravage end,
Man with brother man to meet,
And as a brother kindly greet :
Then may heaven with prosp'rous gales
Fill my Sailor's welcome sails,
To my arms their charge convey,
My dear lad that's far away.
　　On the seas, &c.

HARK ! THE MAVIS.

TUNE—'*Ca' the Yowes to the Knowes.*'

CHORUS.

Ca' the yowes to the knowes,
Ca' them where the heather grows,
Ca' them where the burnie rows,
　　My bonie dearie.

HARK ! the mavis' evening sang
Sounding Clouden's woods amang,
Then a faulding let us gang,
　　My bonie dearie.
　　Ca' the, &c.

We'll gae down by Clouden side,
Thro' the hazels spreading wide,
O'er the waves that sweetly glide
　　To the moon sae clearly.
　　Ca' the, &c.

Yonder Clouden's silent towers,
Where at moonshine midnight hours,
O'er the dewy-bending flowers,
    Fairies dance sae cheery.
      Ca' the, &c.

Ghaist nor bogle shalt thou fear ;
Thou'rt to love and Heaven sae dear,
Nocht of ill may come thee near,
    My bonie dearie.
      Ca' the, &c.

Fair and lovely as thou art,
Thou hast stown my very heart ;
I can die—but canna part,
    My bonie dearie.
      Ca' the, &c.

While waters wimple to the sea ;
While day blinks in the lift sae hie ;
Till clay-cauld death shall blin' my ee,
    Ye shall be my dearie.
      Ca' the, &c.

SHE SAYS SHE LO'ES ME BEST OF A'.

TUNE—'*Onagh's Water-fall.*'

SAE flaxen were her ringlets,
    Her eyebrows of a darker hue,
Bewitchingly o'erarching
    Twa laughing een o' bonie blue.
Her smiling, sae wyling,
    Wad make a wretch forget his woe ;
What pleasure, what treasure,
    Unto these rosy lips to grow !
Such was my Chloris' bonie face,
    When first her bonie face I saw,
And aye my Chloris' dearest charm,
    She says she lo'es me best of a'.

Like harmony her motion ;
    Her pretty ancle is a spy
Betraying fair proportion,
    Wad make a saint forget the sky ;
Sae warming, sae charming,
    Her faultless form and gracefu' air ;
Ilk feature—auld Nature
    Declar'd that she could do nae mair:
Hers are the willing chains o' love,
    By conquering beauty's sovereign law ;
And aye my Chloris' dearest charm,
    She says she lo'es me best of a'.

Let others love the city,
    And gaudy show at sunny noon ;
Gie me the lonely valley,
    The dewy eve, and rising moon
Fair beaming, and streaming
    Her silver light the boughs amang ;
While falling, recalling,
    The amorous thrush concludes his
      sang :
There, dearest Chloris, wilt thou rove
    By wimpling burn and leafy shaw,
And hear my vows o' truth and love,
    And say thou lo'es me best of a' ?

HOW LANG AND DREARY.

TUNE—'*Cauld Kail in Aberdeen.*'

How lang and dreary is the night,
    When I am frae my dearie ;
I restless lie frae e'en to morn,
    Tho' I were ne'er sae weary.

CHORUS.

For oh, her lanely nights are lang ;
    And oh, her dreams are eerie ;
And oh, her widow'd heart is sair,
    That's absent frae her dearie.

When I think on the lightsome days
    I spent wi' thee, my dearie,
And now that seas between us roar,
    How can I be but eerie !
      For oh, &c.

How slow ye move, ye heavy hours ;
    The joyless day how drearie !
It wasna sae ye glinted by,
    When I was wi' my dearie.
      For oh, &c.

THE LOVER'S MORNING SALUTE TO HIS MISTRESS.

TUNE—'*Deil tak the Wars.*'

SLEEP'ST thou, or wak'st thou, fairest
    creature ?
Rosy morn now lifts his eye,
Numbering ilka bud which Nature
    Waters wi' the tears o' joy :
Now thro' the leafy woods,
And by the reeking floods,

Wild Nature's tenants freely, gladly
    stray ;
  The lintwhite in his bower
Chants o'er the breathing flower ;
  The lav'rock to the sky
Ascends wi' sangs o' joy,
While the sun and thou arise to bless
    the day.

Phœbus, gilding the brow o' morning,
  Banishes ilk darksome shade,
Nature gladdening and adorning ;
  Such to me my lovely maid.
When absent frae my fair,
  The murky shades o' care
With starless gloom o'ercast my sullen
    sky :
  But when, in beauty's light,
  She meets my ravish'd sight,
  When thro' my very heart
  Her beaming glories dart—
'Tis then I wake to life, to light, and joy.

LASSIE WI' THE LINT-WHITE LOCKS.

Tune—'*Rothiemurchus's Rant.*'

CHORUS.

Lassie wi' the lint-white locks,
  Bonie lassie, artless lassie,
Wilt thou wi' me tent the flocks ?
  Wilt thou be my dearie O ?

Now nature cleeds the flowery lea,
And a' is young and sweet like thee ;
O wilt thou share its joys wi' me,
  And say thou'lt be my dearie O ?
    Lassie wi', &c.

And when the welcome simmer-shower
Has cheer'd ilk drooping little flower,
We'll to the breathing woodbine bower
  At sultry noon, my dearie O.
    Lassie wi', &c.

When Cynthia lights, wi' silver ray,
The weary shearer's hameward way,
Thro' yellow waving fields we'll stray,
  And talk o' love, my dearie O.
    Lassie wi', &c.

And when the howling wintry blast
Disturbs my lassie's midnight rest ;
Enclasped to my faithfu' breast,
  I'll comfort thee, my dearie O.
    Lassie wi' the lint-white locks,
    Bonie lassie, artless lassie,
    Wilt thou wi' me tent the flocks ?
    Wilt thou be my dearie O ?

THE AULD MAN.

Tune—'*The Death of the Linnet.*'

But lately seen in gladsome green
  The woods rejoic'd the day,
Thro' gentle showers the laughing
    flowers
  In double pride were gay :
But now our joys are fled,
  On winter blasts awa !
Yet maiden May, in rich array,
  Again shall bring them a'.

But my white pow, nae kindly thowe
  Shall melt the snaws of age ;
My trunk of eild, but buss or bield,
  Sinks in time's wintry rage.
Oh, age has weary days,
  And nights o' sleepless pain !
Thou golden time o' youthfu' prime,
  Why com'st thou not again ?

FAREWELL, THOU STREAM.

Tune—'*Nancy's to the Greenwood gane.*

Farewell, thou stream that winding
    flows
  Around Eliza's dwelling !
O Mem'ry ! spare the cruel throes
  Within my bosom swelling :
Condemn'd to drag a hopeless chain,
  And yet in secret languish,
To feel a fire in ev'ry vein,
  Nor dare disclose my anguish.

Love's veriest wretch, unseen, unknown,
  I fain my griefs would cover :
The bursting sigh, th' unweeting groan,
  Betray the hapless lover.

I know thou doom'st me to despair,
　Nor wilt nor canst relieve me ;
But oh, Eliza, hear one prayer,
　For pity's sake forgive me !

The music of thy voice I heard,
　Nor wist while it enslav'd me ;

I saw thine eyes, yet nothing fear'd,
　Till fears no more had sav'd me :
Th' unwary sailor thus aghast,
　The wheeling torrent viewing,
'Mid circling horrors sinks at last
　In overwhelming ruin.

CONTENTED WI' LITTLE.

TUNE—'*Lumps o' pudding.*'

CONTENTED wi' little, and cantie wi' mair,
Whene'er I forgather wi' sorrow and care,
I gie them a skelp as they're creepin' alang,
Wi' a cog o' gude swats, and an auld Scottish sang.

I whyles claw the elbow o' troublesome thought ;
But man is a soger, and life is a faught :
My mirth and gude humour are coin in my pouch,
And my freedom's my lairdship nae monarch dare touch.

A towmond o' trouble, should that be my fa',
A night o' gude fellowship sowthers it a' ;
When at the blythe end of our journey at last,
Wha the deil ever thinks o' the road he has past ?

Blind Chance, let her snapper and stoyte on her way,
Be't to me, be't frae me, e'en let the jad gae :
Come ease, or come travail ; come pleasure or pain,
My warst word is—' Welcome, and welcome again ! '

MY NANNIE'S AWA.

TUNE—'*There'll never be peace till Jamie comes hame.*'

Now in her green mantle blythe Nature arrays,
And listens the lambkins that bleat o'er the braes,
While birds warble welcomes in ilka green shaw ;
But to me it's delightless—my Nannie's awa.

The snaw-drap and primrose our woodlands adorn,
And violets bathe in the weet o' the morn :
They pain my sad bosom, sae sweetly they blaw,
They mind me o' Nannie—my Nannie's awa.

Thou laverock that springs frae the dews o' the lawn,
The shepherd to warn o' the grey-breaking dawn,
And thou, mellow mavis, that hails the night-fa',
Gie over for pity—my Nannie's awa.

Come autumn sae pensive, in yellow and grey,
And soothe me wi' tidings o' nature's decay ;
The dark, dreary winter, and wild-driving snaw,
Alane can delight me—now Nannie's awa.

SWEET FA'S THE EVE.

TUNE—'*Craigieburn-wood.*'

SWEET fa's the eve on Craigie-burn,
 And blythe awakes the morrow,
But a' the pride o' spring's return
 Can yield me nocht but sorrow.

I see the flowers and spreading trees,
 I hear the wild birds singing ;
But what a weary wight can please,
 And care his bosom wringing ?

Fain, fain would I my griefs impart,
 Yet dare na for your anger ;
But secret love will break my heart,
 If I conceal it langer.

If thou refuse to pity me,
 If thou shalt love anither,
When yon green leaves fa' frae the tree,
 Around my grave they'll wither.

O LASSIE, ART THOU SLEEPING YET ?

TUNE—'*Let me in this ae night.*'

O LASSIE, art thou sleeping yet ?
Or art thou wakin, I would wit ?
For love has bound me hand and foot,
 And I would fain be in, jo.

CHORUS.

O let me in this ae night,
 This ae, ae, ae night ;
For pity's sake this ae night,
 O rise and let me in, jo.

Thou hear'st the winter wind and weet,
Nae star blinks thro' the driving sleet ;
Tak pity on my weary feet,
 And shield me frae the rain, jo.
 O let me in, &c.

The bitter blast that round me blaws,
Unheeded howls, unheeded fa's ;
The cauldness o' thy heart's the cause
 Of a' my grief and pain, jo.
 O let me in, &c.

HER ANSWER.

O TELL na me o' wind and rain,
Upbraid na me wi' cauld disdain !
Gae back the gait ye cam again,
 I winna let you in, jo.

CHORUS.

I tell you now this ae night,
 This ae, ae, ae night ;
And ance for a' this ae night,
 I winna let you in, jo.

The snellest blast, at mirkest hours,
That round the pathless wand'rer pours,
Is nocht to what poor she endures,
 That's trusted faithless man, jo.
 I tell you now, &c.

The sweetest flower that deck'd the mead,
Now trodden like the vilest weed ;
Let simple maid the lesson read,
 The weird may be her ain, jo.
 I tell you now, &c.

The bird that charm'd his summer-day.
Is now the cruel fowler's prey ;
Let witless, trusting woman say
 How aft her fate's the same, jo.
 I tell you now, &c.

SONG.

TUNE—'*Humours of glen.*'

THEIR groves o' sweet myrtles let foreign lands reckon,
 Where bright-beaming summers exalt the perfume ;
Far dearer to me yon lone glen o' green breckan,
 Wi' the burn stealing under the lang yellow broom.

Far dearer to me are yon humble broom bowers,
 Where the blue-bell and gowan lurk lowly unseen :
For there, lightly tripping amang the wild flowers,
 A listening the linnet, aft wanders my Jean.

Tho' rich is the breeze in their gay sunny valleys,
    And cauld Caledonia's blast on the wave ;
Their sweet-scented woodlands that skirt the proud palace,
    What are they ?   The haunt of the tyrant and slave !

The slave's spicy forests, and gold-bubbling fountains,
    The brave Caledonian views wi' disdain ;
He wanders as free as the winds of his mountains,
    Save love's willing fetters, the chains o' his Jean.

'TWAS NA HER BONIE BLUE EE.

TUNE—*' Laddie, lie near me.'*

'TWAS na her bonie blue ee was my ruin ;
Fair tho' she be, that was ne'er my undoing ;
'Twas the dear smile when naebody did mind us,
'Twas the bewitching, sweet, stown glance o' kindness.

Sair do I fear that to hope is denied me,
Sair do I fear that despair maun abide me ;
But tho' fell fortune should fate us to sever,
Queen shall she be in my bosom for ever.

Chloris, I'm thine wi' a passion sincerest,
And thou hast plighted me love o' the dearest !
And thou'rt the angel that never can alter,
Sooner the sun in his motion would falter.

ADDRESS TO THE WOODLARK.

TUNE—*' Where'll bonie Ann lie.'*

O STAY, sweet warbling woodlark, stay,
Nor quit for me the trembling spray,
A hapless lover courts thy lay,
    Thy soothing fond complaining.

Again, again that tender part,
That I may catch thy melting art ;
For surely that wad touch her heart,
    Wha kills me wi' disdaining.

Say, was thy little mate unkind,
And heard thee as the careless wind ?
Oh, nocht but love and sorrow join'd
    Sic notes o' wae could wauken.

Thou tells o' never-ending care ;
O' speechless grief, and dark despair ;
For pity's sake, sweet bird, nae mair !
    Or my poor heart is broken !

HOW CRUEL ARE THE PARENTS.

TUNE—*' John Anderson my Jo.'*

How cruel are the parents
    Who riches only prize,
And to the wealthy booby
    Poor woman sacrifice.
Meanwhile the hapless daughter
    Has but a choice of strife ;
To shun a tyrant father's hate,
    Become a wretched wife.

The ravening hawk pursuing,
    The trembling dove thus flies,
To shun impelling ruin
    A while her pinions tries ;
Till of escape despairing,
    No shelter or retreat,
She trusts the ruthless falconer,
    And drops beneath his feet.

MARK YONDER POMP.

TUNE—' Deil tak the wars.'

MARK yonder pomp of costly fashion,
    Round the wealthy, titled bride :
But when compar'd with real passion,
    Poor is all that princely pride.
    What are their showy treasures ?
    What are their noisy pleasures ?
The gay, gaudy glare of vanity and art :
    The polish'd jewel's blaze
    May draw the wond'ring gaze,
    And courtly grandeur bright
    The fancy may delight,
But never, never can come near the
            heart.
    But did you see my dearest Chloris,
        In simplicity's array ;
Lovely as yonder sweet opening flower
        is,
    Shrinking from the gaze of day.
    O then, the heart alarming,
    And all resistless charming,
In Love's delightful fetters she chains
        the willing soul !
    Ambition would disown
    The world's imperial crown ;
    Even Avarice would deny
    His worshipp'd deity,
And feel thro' every vein Love's rap-
        tures roll.

I SEE A FORM, I SEE A FACE.

TUNE—' This is no my ain house.'

O THIS is no my ain lassie,
    Fair tho' the lassie be ;
O weel ken I my ain lassie,
    Kind love is in her ee.

I see a form, I see a face,
Ye weel may wi' the fairest place :
It wants, to me, the witching grace,
    The kind love that's in her ee.
        O this is no, &c.

She's bonie, blooming, straight, and tall,
And lang has had my heart in thrall ;
And aye it charms my very saul,
    The kind love that's in her ee.
        O this is no, &c.

B

A thief sae pawkie is my Jean,
To steal a blink, by a' unseen ;
But gleg as light are lovers' een,
    When kind love is in the ee.
        O this is no, &c.

It may escape the courtly sparks,
It may escape the learned clerks ;
But weel the watching lover marks
    The kind love that's in her ee.
        O this is no, &c.

O BONIE WAS YON ROSY BRIER.

TUNE—' I wish my love was in a mire.'

O BONIE was yon rosy brier,
    That blooms sae fair frae haunt o' man ;
And bonie she, and ah, how dear !
    It shaded frae the e'enin sun.

Yon rosebuds in the morning dew,
    How pure amang the leaves sae green ;
But purer was the lover's vow
    They witness'd in their shade yestreen.

All in its rude and prickly bower,
    That crimson rose, how sweet and fair !
But love is far a sweeter flower
    Amid life's thorny path o' care.

The pathless wild, and wimpling burn,
    Wi' Chloris in my arms, be mine ;
And I, the world, nor wish, nor scorn,
    Its joys and griefs alike resign.

FORLORN, MY LOVE.

TUNE—' Let me in this ae night.'

FORLORN, my love, no comfort near,
Far, far from thee, I wander here ;
Far, far from thee, the fate severe
    At which I most repine, love.

CHORUS.

O wert thou, love, but near me,
    But near, near, near me ;
How kindly thou wouldst cheer me,
    And mingle sighs with mine, love

O

Around me scowls a wintry sky,
That blasts each bud of hope and joy;
And shelter, shade, nor home have I,
   Save in those arms of thine, love.
     O wert, &c.

Cold, alter'd friendship's cruel part,
To poison fortune's ruthless dart—

Let me not break thy faithful heart,
   And say that fate is mine, love.
     O wert, &c.

But dreary tho' the moments fleet,
O let me think we yet shall meet!
That only ray of solace sweet
   Can on thy Chloris shine, love.
     O wert, &c.

LAST MAY A BRAW WOOER.

Tune—'Lothian Lassie.'

Last May a braw wooer cam down the lang glen,
   And sair wi' his love he did deave me:
I said there was naething I hated like men,
   The deuce gae wi'm to believe me, believe me,
   The deuce gae wi'm to believe me.

He spak o' the darts in my bonie black een,
   And vow'd for my love he was dying;
I said he might die when he liked for Jean:
   The Lord forgie me for lying, for lying,
   The Lord forgie me for lying!

A weel-stocked mailen, himsel for the laird,
   And marriage aff-hand, were his proffers:
I never loot on that I kend it, or car'd;
   But thought I might hae waur offers, waur offers,
   But thought I might hae waur offers.

But what wad ye think? in a fortnight or less,
   The deil tak his taste to gae near her!
He up the lang loan to my black cousin Bess,
   Guess ye how, the jad! I could bear her, could bear her,
   Guess ye how, the jad! I could bear her.

But a' the niest week as I fretted wi' care,
   I gaed to the tryste o' Dalgarnock,
And wha but my fine fickle lover was there.
   I glowr'd as I'd seen a warlock, a warlock,
   I glowr'd as I'd seen a warlock.

But owre my left shouther I gae him a blink,
   Lest neebors might say I was saucy;
My wooer he caper'd as he'd been in drink,
   And vow'd I was his dear lassie, dear lassie,
   And vow'd I was his dear lassie

I spier'd for my cousin fu' couthy and sweet,
  Gin she had recover'd her hearin,
And how her new shoon fit her auld shachl't feet—
  But, heavens ! how he fell a swearin, a swearin,
  But, heavens ! how he fell a swearin.

He begged, for Gudesake ! I wad be his wife,
  Or else I wad kill him wi' sorrow :
So e'en to preserve the poor body in life,
  I think I maun wed him to-morrow, to-morrow,
  I think I maun wed him to-morrow.

HEY FOR A LASS WI' A TOCHER.

TUNE—'*Balinamona ora.*'

AWA wi' your witchcraft o' beauty's alarms,
The slender bit beauty you grasp in your arms :
O, gie me the lass that has acres o' charms,
O, gie me the lass wi' the weel-stockit farms.

CHORUS.

  Then hey, for a lass wi' a tocher, then hey, for a lass
    wi' a tocher,
  Then hey, for a lass wi' a tocher ; the nice yellow
    guineas for me.

Your beauty's a flower in the morning that blows,
And withers the faster, the faster it grows ;
But the rapturous charm o' the bonie green knowes,
Ilk spring they're new deckit wi' bonie white yowes.
    Then hey, &c.

And e'en when this beauty your bosom has blest,
The brightest o' beauty may cloy, when possest ;
But the sweet yellow darlings wi' Geordie imprest,
The langer ye hae them—the mair they're carest.
    Then hey, &c.

ALTHO' THOU MAUN NEVER BE MINE.

TUNE—'*Here's a health to them that's awa, Hiney.*'

CHORUS.

Here's a health to ane I lo'e dear,
Here's a health to ane I lo'e dear ;
Thou art as sweet as the smile when fond lovers meet,
And soft as their parting tear—Jessy !
O 2

ALTHO' thou maun never be mine,
  Altho' even hope is denied ;
'Tis sweeter for thee despairing,
  Than aught in the world beside—Jessy !
    Here's a health, &c.

I mourn thro' the gay, gaudy day,
  As, hopeless, I muse on thy charms :
But welcome the dream o' sweet slumber,
  For then I am lockt in thy arms—Jessy !
    Here's a health, &c.

I guess by the dear angel smile,
  I guess by the love-rolling ee ;
But why urge the tender confession
  'Gainst fortune's fell cruel decree—Jessy !
    Here's a health, &c.

THE BIRKS OF ABERFELDY.

CHORUS.

Bonie lassie, will ye go, will ye go,
    will ye go,
Bonie lassie, will ye go to the Birks of
    Aberfeldy ?

Now simmer blinks on flowery braes,
And o'er the crystal streamlet plays,
Come let us spend the lightsome days
    In the Birks of Aberfeldy.
      Bonie lassie, &c.

While o'er their heads the hazels hing,
The little birdies blythly sing,
Or lightly flit on wanton wing
    In the Birks of Aberfeldy.
      Bonie lassie, &c.

The braes ascend like lofty wa's,
The foaming stream deep roaring fa's,
O'erhung wi' fragrant spreading shaws,
    The Birks of Aberfeldy.
      Bonie lassie, &c.

The hoary cliffs are crown'd wi' flowers,
White o'er the linns the burnie pours,
And rising, weets wi' misty showers
    The Birks of Aberfeldy.
      Bonie lassie, &c.

Let fortune's gifts at random flee,
They ne'er shall draw a wish frae me,
Supremely blest wi' love and thee,
    In the Birks of Aberfeldy.
      Bonie lassie, &c.

THE YOUNG HIGHLAND ROVER.

TUNE—'*Morag.*'

LOUD blaw the frosty breezes,
  The snaws the mountains cover ;
Like winter on me seizes,
  Since my young Highland Rover
  Far wanders nations over.
Where'er he go, where'er he stray,
  May Heaven be his warden :
Return him safe to fair Strathspey,
  And bonie Castle-Gordon !

The trees now naked groaning,
  Shall soon wi' leaves be hinging,
The birdies dowie moaning,
  Shall a' be blythely singing,
  And every flower be springing,
Sae I'll rejoice the lee-lang day,
  When by his mighty warden
My youth's return'd to fair Strathspey,
  And bonie Castle-Gordon.

STAY, MY CHARMER.

Tune—'*An gille dubh ciar dhubh.*'

Stay, my charmer, can you leave me?
Cruel, cruel to deceive me!
Well you know how much you grieve
  me ;
  Cruel charmer, can you go?
  Cruel charmer, can you go?

By my love so ill requited ;
By the faith you fondly plighted ;
By the pangs of lovers slighted ;
  Do not, do not leave me so !
  Do not, do not leave me so !

FULL WELL THOU KNOW'ST.

Tune—'*Rothiemurchus's rant.*'

CHORUS.

Fairest maid on Devon banks,
  Crystal Devon, winding Devon,
Wilt thou lay that frown aside,
  And smile as thou wert wont to do ?

Full well thou know'st I love thee dear,
Couldst thou to malice lend an ear ?
O, did not love exclaim, " Forbear,
  Nor use a faithful lover so ? "
    Fairest maid, &c.

Then come, thou fairest of the fair,
Those wonted smiles, O, let me share ;
And by thy beauteous self I swear,
  No love but thine my heart shall
  know.
    Fairest maid, &c.

STRATHALLAN'S LAMENT.

Thickest night, o'erhang my dwelling !
  Howling tempests, o'er me rave !
Turbid torrents, wintry swelling,
  Still surround my lonely cave !

Crystal streamlets gently flowing,
  Busy haunts of base mankind,
Western breezes softly blowing,
  Suit not my distracted mind.

In the cause of right engag'd,
  Wrongs injurious to redress,
Honour's war we strongly wag'd,
  But the heavens deny'd success.

Ruin's wheel has driven o'er us,
  Not a hope that dare attend ;
The wide world is all before us—
  But a world without a friend !

RAVING WINDS AROUND HER BLOWING.

Tune—'*M'Gregor of Ruara's lament.*

Raving winds around her blowing,
Yellow leaves the woodlands strowing,
By a river hoarsely roaring,
Isabella stray'd deploring :
" Farewell, hours that late did measure
Sunshine days of joy and pleasure ;
Hail, thou gloomy night of sorrow,
Cheerless night that knows no morrow !

" O'er the past too fondly wandering,
On the hopeless future pondering ;
Chilly grief my life-blood freezes,
Fell despair my fancy seizes.
Life, thou soul of every blessing,
Load to misery most distressing,
O, how gladly I'd resign thee,
And to dark oblivion join thee ! "

MUSING ON THE ROARING OCEAN.

Tune—'*Druimion dubh.*'

Musing on the roaring ocean
  Which divides my love and me ;
Wearying Heaven in warm devotion,
  For his weal where'er he be.

Hope and fear's alternate billow
  Yielding late to nature's law ;
Whisp'ring spirits round my pillow
  Talk of him that's far awa.

Ye whom sorrow never wounded,
  Ye who never shed a tear,
Care-untroubled, joy-surrounded,
  Gaudy day to you is dear.

Gentle night, do thou befriend me ;
  Downy sleep, the curtain draw ;
Spirits kind, again attend me,
  Talk of him that's far awa !

BLYTHE WAS SHE.

Tune—'*Andro and his cuttie gun.*'

CHORUS.

Blythe, blythe and merry was she,
  Blythe was she but and ben :
Blythe by the banks of Ern,
  And blythe in Glenturit glen.

By Ochtertyre grows the aik,
  On Yarrow banks, the birken shaw ;
But Phemie was a bonier lass
  Than braes o' Yarrow ever saw.
    Blythe, &c.

Her looks were like a flower in May,
  Her smile was like a simmer morn ;
She tripped by the banks of Ern
  As light's a bird upon a thorn.
    Blythe, &c.

Her bonie face it was as meek
  As onie lamb's upon a lee ;
The evening sun was ne'er sae sweet
  As was the blink o' Phemie's ee.
    Blythe, &c.

The Highland hills I've wander'd wide,
  And o'er the Lowlands I hae been ;
But Phemie was the blythest lass
  That ever trod the dewy green.
    Blythe, &c.

PEGGY'S CHARMS.

Tune—'*Neil Gow's lamentation for
Abercairny.*'

Where, braving angry winter's storms,
  The lofty Ochils rise,
Far in their shade my Peggy's charms
  First blest my wondering eyes.
As one who, by some savage stream,
  A lonely gem surveys,
Astonish'd doubly, marks it beam
  With art's most polish'd blaze.

Blest be the wild, sequester'd shade,
  And blest the day and hour,
Where Peggy's charms I first survey'd,
  When first I felt their pow'r !
The tyrant death with grim control
  May seize my fleeting breath ;
But tearing Peggy from my soul
  Must be a stronger death.

THE LAZY MIST.

Irish Air—'*Coolun.*'

The lazy mist hangs from the brow of the hill,
Concealing the course of the dark-winding rill ;
How languid the scenes, late so sprightly, appear,
As autumn to winter resigns the pale year !
The forests are leafless, the meadows are brown,
And all the gay foppery of summer is flown :
Apart let me wander, apart let me muse,
How quick time is flying, how keen fate pursues ;
How long I have lived, but how much lived in vain
How little of life's scanty span may remain :
What aspects, old Time, in his progress, has worn ;
What ties, cruel fate in my bosom has torn.
How foolish, or worse, till our summit is gain'd !
And downward, how weaken'd, how darken'd, how pain'd !
This life's not worth having with all it can give,
For something beyond it poor man sure must live.

A ROSE-BUD BY MY EARLY WALK.

TUNE—'*The Shepherd's Wife.*'

A ROSE-BUD by my early walk,
Adown a corn-enclosèd bawk,
Sae gently bent its thorny stalk,
  All on a dewy morning.

Ere twice the shades o' dawn are fled,
In a' its crimson glory spread,
And drooping rich the dewy head,
  It scents the early morning.

Within the bush, her covert nest
A little linnet fondly prest,
The dew sat chilly on her breast
  Sae early in the morning.

She soon shall see her tender brood,
The pride, the pleasure o' the wood,
Amang the fresh green leaves bedew'd,
  Awake the early morning.

So thou, dear bird, young Jeany fair,
On trembling string or vocal air,
Shalt sweetly pay the tender care
  That tents thy early morning.

So thou, sweet rose-bud, young and gay,
Shalt beauteous blaze upon the day,
And bless the parent's evening ray
  That watch'd thy early morning.

TIBBIE, I HAE SEEN THE DAY.

TUNE—'*Invercauld's reel.*'

CHORUS.

O Tibbie, I hae seen the day,
  Ye would na been sae shy;
For laik o' gear ye lightly me,
  But, trowth, I care na by.

YESTREEN I met you on the moor,
Ye spak na, but gaed by like stoure:
Ye geck at me because I'm poor,
  But fient a hair care I.
    O Tibbie, I hae, &c.

I doubt na, lass, but ye may think,
Because ye hae the name o' clink,
That ye can please me at a wink,
  Whene'er ye like to try.
    O Tibbie, I hae, &c.

But sorrow tak him that's sae mean,
Altho' his pouch o' coin were clean,
Wha follows ony saucy quean
  That looks sae proud and high.
    O Tibbie, I hae, &c.

Altho' a lad were e'er sae smart,
If that he want the yellow dirt,
Ye'll cast your head anither airt,
  And answer him fu' dry.
    O Tibbie, I hae, &c.

But if ye hae the name o' gear,
Ye'll fasten to him like a brier,
Tho' hardly he, for sense or lear,
  Be better than the kye.
    O Tibbie, I hae, &c.

But, Tibbie, lass, tak my advice,
Your daddy's gear maks you sae nice;
The deil a ane wad spier your price,
  Were ye as poor as I.
    O Tibbie, I hae, &c.

There lives a lass in yonder park,
I would na gie her in her sark,
For thee wi' a' thy thousand mark;
  Ye need na look sae high.
    O Tibbie, I hae, &c.

I LOVE MY JEAN.

TUNE—'*Miss Admiral Gordon's Strathspey.*'

OF a' the airts the wind can blaw,
  I dearly like the west,
For there the bonie lassie lives,
  The lassie I lo'e best:
There wild woods grow, and rivers row,
  And monie a hill between;
But day and night my fancy's flight
  Is ever wi' my Jean.

I see her in the dewy flowers,
  I see her sweet and fair:
I hear her in the tunefu' birds,
  I hear her charm the air:
There's not a bonie flower that springs
  By fountain, shaw, or green;
There's not a bonie bird that sings,
  But minds me o' my Jean.

O, WERE I ON PARNASSUS' HILL!

Tune—'My Love is lost to me.'

O, were I on Parnassus' hill !
Or had of Helicon my fill ;
That I might catch poetic skill,
     To sing how dear I love thee.
But Nith maun be my Muse's well,
My Muse maun be thy bonie sel ;
On Corsincon I'll glowr and spell,
     And write how dear I love thee.

Then come, sweet Muse, inspire my lay !
For a' the lee-lang simmer's day,
I could na sing, I could na say,
     How much, how dear, I love thee.
I see thee dancing o'er the green,
Thy waist sae jimp, thy limbs sae clean,
Thy tempting looks, thy roguish een—
     By Heaven and earth I love thee !

By night, by day, a-field, at hame,
The thoughts o' thee my breast inflame ;
And aye I muse and sing thy name—
     I only live to love thee.
Tho' I were doom'd to wander on,
Beyond the sea, beyond the sun,
Till my last weary sand was run ;
     Till then—and then I'd love thee.

THE BLISSFUL DAY.

Tune—'Seventh of November.'

The day returns, my bosom burns,
     The blissful day we twa did meet ;
Tho' winter wild in tempest toil'd,
     Ne'er summer-sun was half sae sweet.
Than a' the pride that loads the tide,
     And crosses o'er the sultry line ;
Than kingly robes, than crowns and
          globes,
     Heaven gave me more, it made thee
          mine.

While day and night can bring delight,
     Or nature aught of pleasure give ;
While joys above my mind can move,
     For thee, and thee alone, I live !
When that grim foe of life below
     Comes in between to make us part ;
The iron hand that breaks our band,
     It breaks my bliss—it breaks my heart.

THE BRAES O' BALLOCHMYLE.

Tune—'Miss Forbes's farewell to Banff.'

The Catrine woods were yellow seen,
     The flowers decay'd on Catrine lee,
Nae lav'rock sang on hillock green,
     But nature sicken'd on the ee.
Thro' faded groves Maria sang,
     Hersel in beauty's bloom the whyle,
And aye the wild-wood echoes rang,
     Fareweel the braes o' Ballochmyle.

Low in your wintry beds, ye flowers,
     Again ye'll flourish fresh and fair ;
Ye birdies dumb, in with'ring bowers,
     Again ye'll charm the vocal air.
But here, alas ! for me nae mair
     Shall birdie charm, or floweret smile ;
Fareweel the bonie banks of Ayr,
     Fareweel, fareweel, sweet Balloch-
          myle.

THE HAPPY TRIO.

Tune—'Willie brew'd a peck o' maut.'

O, Willie brew'd a peck o' maut,
     And Rob and Allan cam to see ;
Three blyther hearts, that lee-lang night,
     Ye wad na find in Christendie.

CHORUS.

We are na fou, we're no that fou,
     But just a drappie in our ee ;
The cock may craw, the day may daw,
     And ay we'll taste the barley bree.

Here are we met, three merry boys,
     Three merry boys, I trow, are we ;
And monie a night we've merry been,
     And monie mae we hope to be !
          We are na fou, &c.

It is the moon, I ken her horn,
     That's blinkin in the lift sae hie ;
She shines sae bright to wyle us hame,
     But by my sooth she'll wait a wee !
          We are na fou, &c.

Wha first shall rise to gang awa,
     A cuckold, coward loun is he !
Wha first beside his chair shall fa',
     He is the King among us three !
          We are na fou, &c.

THE BLUE-EYED LASSIE.

TUNE—'*The blathrie o't.*'

I GAED a waefu' gate yestreen,
  A gate, I fear, I'll dearly rue ;
I gat my death frae twa sweet een,
  Twa lovely een o' bonie blue.
'Twas not her golden ringlets bright,
  Her lips like roses wat wi' dew,
Her heaving bosom lily-white ;—
  It was her een sae bonie blue.

She talk'd, she smil'd, my heart she
    wyl'd,
  She charm'd my soul I wist na how ;
And ay the stound, the deadly wound,
  Cam frae her een sae bonie blue.
But spare to speak, and spare to speed ;
  She'll aiblins listen to my vow :
Should she refuse, I'll lay my dead
  To her twa een sae bonie blue.

JOHN ANDERSON MY JO.

JOHN ANDERSON my jo, John,
  When we were first acquent,
Your locks were like the raven,
  Your bonie brow was brent ;
But now your brow is beld, John,
  Your locks are like the snaw ;
But blessings on your frosty pow,
  John Anderson my jo.

John Anderson my jo, John,
  We clamb the hill thegither ;
And monie a canty day, John,
  We've had wi' ane anither :
Now we maun totter down, John,
  But hand in hand we'll go,
And sleep thegither at the foot,
  John Anderson my jo.

TAM GLEN.

TUNE—'*The mucking o' Geordie's byre.*'

MY heart is a breaking, dear Tittie,
  Some counsel unto me come len',
To anger them a' is a pity ;
  But what will I do wi' Tam Glen ?

I'm thinking, wi' sic a braw fellow,
  In poortith I might mak a fen' ;
What care I in riches to wallow,
  If I maunna marry Tam Glen ?

There's Lowrie the laird o' Dumeller,
  'Guid-day to you, brute !' he comes
    ben :
He brags and he blaws o' his siller,
  But when will he dance like Tam
    Glen ?

My minnie does constantly deave me,
  And bids me beware o' young men ;
They flatter, she says, to deceive me ;
  But wha can think sae o' Tam Glen?

My dad lie says, gin I'll forsake him,
  He'll gie me guid hunder marks ten :
But, if it's ordain'd I maun take him,
  O wha will I get but Tam Glen?

Yestreen at the Valentines' dealing,
  My heart to my mou gied a sten :
For thrice I drew ane without failing,
  And thrice it was written, Tam Glen.

The last Halloween I was waukin
  My droukit sark-sleeve, as ye ken ;
His likeness cam up the house staukin—
  And the very grey breeks o' Tam
    Glen !

Come counsel, dear Tittie, don't tarry ;
  I'll gie you my bonie black hen,
Gif ye will advise me to marry
  The lad I lo'e dearly, Tam Glen.

GANE IS THE DAY.

TUNE—'*Guidwife count the lawin.*'

GANE is the day, and mirk's the night,
But we'll ne'er stray for faute o' light,
For ale and brandy's stars and moon,
And bluid-red wine's the risin' sun.

CHORUS.

Then guidwife count the lawin, the
  lawin, the lawin,
Then guidwife count the lawin, and
  bring a coggie mair.

There's wealth and ease for gentlemen,
And semple-folk maun fecht and fen',
But here we're a' in ae accord,
For ilka man that's drunk 's a lord.
  Then guidwife count, &c.

My coggie is a haly pool,
That heals the wounds o' care and dool ;
And pleasure is a wanton trout,
An' ye drink it a' ye'll find him out.
  Then guidwife count, &c.

MY TOCHER'S THE JEWEL.

O MEIKLE thinks my luve o' my beauty,
  And meikle thinks my luve o' my kin ;
But little thinks my luve I ken brawlie
  My Tocher's the jewel has charms for him.
It's a' for the apple he'll nourish the tree ;
  It's a' for the hiney he'll cherish the bee ;
My laddie's sae meikle in luve wi' the siller,
  He canna hae luve to spare for me.

Your proffer o' luve's an airle-penny,
  My Tocher's the bargain ye wad buy;
But an ye be crafty, I am cunnin,
  Sae ye wi' anither your fortune maun try.
Ye're like to the timmer o' yon rotten wood ;
  Ye're like to the bark o' yon rotten tree ;
Ye'll slip frae me like a knotless thread,
  And ye'll crack your credit wi' mae nor me.

WHAT CAN A YOUNG LASSIE DO WI' AN OLD MAN?

TUNE—' *What can a Lassie do.*'

WHAT can a young lassie, what shall a young lassie,
  What can a young lassie do wi' an auld man?
Bad luck on the penny that tempted my minnie
  To sell her poor Jenny for siller an' lan' !
    Bad luck on the penny, &c.

He's always compleenin frae mornin to e'enin,
  He hosts and he hirples the weary day lang :
He's doylt and he's dozin, his bluid it is frozen,
  O, dreary's the night wi' a crazy auld man !

He hums and he hankers, he frets and he cankers,
  I never can please him do a' that I can ;
He's peevish, and jealous of a' the young fellows :
  O, dool on the day, I met wi' an auld man !

My auld auntie Katie upon me takes pity,
  I'll do my endeavour to follow her plan ;
I'll cross him, and rack him, until I heart-break him,
  And then his auld brass will buy me a new pan.

O, FOR ANE AND TWENTY, TAM!

TUNE—'*The Moudiewort.*'

CHORUS.

An O for ane and twenty, Tam!
An hey, sweet ane and twenty, Tam!
I'll learn my kin a rattlin sang,
An I saw ane and twenty, Tam.

THEY snool me sair, and haud me down,
And gar me look like bluntie, Tam!
But three short years will soon wheel
    roun',
And then comes ane and twenty, Tam.
    An O for ane, &c.

A gleib o' lan', a claut o' gear,
Was left me by my auntie, Tam;
At kith or kin I need na spier,
An I saw ane and twenty, Tam.
    An O for ane, &c.

They'll hae me wed a wealthy coof,
Tho' I mysel' hae plenty, Tam;
But hear'st thou, laddie, there's my loof,
I'm thine at ane and twenty, Tam!
    An O for ane, &c.

THE BONIE WEE THING.

TUNE—'*The Lads of Saltcoats.*'

BONIE wee thing, cannie wee thing,
Lovely wee thing, was thou mine,
I wad wear thee in my bosom,
Lest my jewel I should tine.

Wishfully I look and languish
In that bonie face o' thine;
And my heart it stounds wi' anguish,
Lest my wee thing be na mine.

Wit, and grace, and love, and beauty,
In ae constellation shine;
To adore thee is my duty,
Goddess o' this soul o' mine!
    Bonie wee, &c.

THE BANKS OF NITH.

TUNE—'*Robie Donna Gorach.*'

THE Thames flows proudly to the sea,
Where royal cities stately stand;
But sweeter flows the Nith to me,
Where Cummins ance had high com-
    mand:
When shall I see that honour'd land,
That winding stream I love so dear!
Must wayward fortune's adverse hand
For ever, ever keep me here?

How lovely, Nith, thy fruitful vales,
Where spreading hawthorns gaily
    bloom;
How sweetly wind thy sloping dales,
Where lambkins wanton thro' the
    broom!
Tho' wandering, now, must be my doom,
Far from thy bonie banks and braes,
May there my latest hours consume,
Amang the friends of early days!

BESSY AND HER SPINNIN WHEEL.

TUNE—'*Bottom of the Punch Bowl.*'

O LEEZE me on my spinnin wheel,
O leeze me on my rock and reel;
Frae tap to tae that cleeds me bien,
And haps me fiel and warm at e'en!
I'll set me down and sing and spin,
While laigh descends the simmer sun,
Blest wi' content, and milk and meal—
O leeze me on my spinnin wheel.

On ilka hand the burnies trot,
And meet below my theekit cot;
The scented birk and hawthorn white,
Across the pool their arms unite,
Alike to screen the birdie's nest,
And little fishes' caller rest:
The sun blinks kindly in the biel',
Where blythe I turn my spinnin wheel

On lofty aiks the cushats wail,
And echo cons the doolfu' tale;
The lintwhites in the hazel braes,
Delighted, rival ither's lays:

The craik amang the claver hay,
The paitrick whirrin o'er the ley,
The swallow jinkin round my shiel,
Amuse me at my spinnin wheel.

Wi' sma' to sell, and less to buy,
Aboon distress, below envy,
O wha wad leave this humble state,
For a' the pride of a' the great?
Amid their flarin, idle toys,
Amid their cumbrous, dinsome joys,
Can they the peace and pleasure feel
Of Bessy at her spinnin wheel?

COUNTRY LASSIE.

TUNE—'*John, come kiss me now.*'

IN simmer when the hay was mawn,
And corn wav'd green in ilka field,
While claver blooms white o'er the lea,
And roses blaw in ilka bield;
Blythe Bessie in the milking shiel,
Says, 'I'll be wed, come o't what
will;'
Out spak a dame in wrinkled eild,
'O' guid advisement comes nae ill.

'It's ye hae wooers monie ane,
And, lassie, ye're but young ye ken;
Then wait a wee, and cannie wale
A routhie butt, a routhie ben:
There's Johnie o' the Buskie-glen,
Fu' is his barn, fu' is his byre;
Tak this frae me, my bonie hen,
It's plenty beets the luver's fire.'

'For Johnie o' the Buskie-glen
I dinna care a single flie;
He lo'es sae weel his craps and kye,
He has nae luve to spare for me:
But blithe's the blink o' Robie's ee,
And weel I wat he lo'es me dear:
Ae blink o' him I wad nae gie
For Buskie-glen and a' his gear.'

'O thoughtless lassie, life's a faught!
The canniest gate, the strife is sair;
But aye fu' han't is fechtin best,
A hungry care's an unco care:
But some will spend, and some will
spare,
An' wilfu' folk maun hae their will;

Syne as ye brew, my maiden fair,
Keep mind that ye maun drink the
yill.'

'O, gear will buy me rigs o' land,
And gear will buy me sheep and kye;
But the tender heart o' leesome luve
The gowd and siller canna buy:
We may be poor—Robie and I,
Light is the burden luve lays on;
Content and luve brings peace and joy,
What mair hae queens upon a throne?'

FAIR ELIZA.

TUNE -' *The bonie brucket Lassie.*'

TURN again, thou fair Eliza,
Ae kind blink before we part,
Rue on thy despairing lover!
Canst thou break his faithfu' heart?
Turn again, thou fair Eliza;
If to love thy heart denies,
For pity hide the cruel sentence
Under friendship's kind disguise!

Thee, dear maid, hae I offended?
The offence is loving thee;
Canst thou wreck his peace for ever,
Wha for thine wad gladly die?
While the life beats in my bosom,
Thou shalt mix in ilka throe:
Turn again, thou lovely maiden,
Ae sweet smile on me bestow.

Not the bee upon the blossom,
In the pride o' sinny noon;
Not the little sporting fairy,
All beneath the simmer moon;
Not the poet in the moment
Fancy lightens in his ee,
Kens the pleasure, feels the rapture,
That thy presence gies to me.

SHE'S FAIR AND FAUSE.

SHE'S fair and fause that causes my
smart,
I lo'ed her meikle and lang:
She's broken her vow, she's broken my
heart,
And I may e'en gae hang.

A coof cam in wi' rowth o' gear,
And I hae tint my dearest dear,
But woman is but warld's gear,
　Sae let the bonie lass gang.

Whae'er ye be that woman love,
　To this be never blind,

Nae ferlie 'tis tho' fickle she prove,
　A woman has't by kind :
O Woman lovely, Woman fair !
An Angel form 's faun to thy share,
'Twad been o'er meikle to gien thee
　mair,
I mean an Angel mind.

THE POSIE.

O LUVE will venture in, where it daur na weel be seen,
O luve will venture in, where wisdom ance has been ;
But I will down yon river rove, amang the wood sae green,
　And a' to pu' a Posie to my ain dear May.

The primrose I will pu', the firstling o' the year,
And I will pu' the pink, the emblem o' my dear,
For she's the pink o' womankind, and blooms without a peer :
　And a' to be a Posie to my ain dear May.

I'll pu' the budding rose, when Phœbus peeps in view,
For it's like a baumy kiss o' her sweet bonie mou ;
The hyacinth's for constancy, wi' its unchanging blue,
　And a' to be a Posie to my ain dear May.

The lily it is pure, and the lily it is fair,
And in her lovely bosom I'll place the lily there ;
The daisy's for simplicity and unaffected air,
　And a' to be a Posie to my ain dear May.

The hawthorn I will pu', wi' its locks o' siller grey,
Where, like an aged man, it stands at break o' day,
But the songster's nest within the bush I winna tak away ;
　And a' to be a Posie to my ain dear May.

The woodbine I will pu' when the e'ening star is near,
And the diamond drops o' dew shall be her een sae clear :
The violet's for modesty which weel she fa's to wear,
　And a' to be a Posie to my ain dear May.

I'll tie the Posie round wi' the silken band o' luve,
And I'll place it in her breast, and I'll swear by a' above,
That to my latest draught o' life the band shall ne'er remuve,
　And this will be a Posie to my ain dear May.

THE BANKS O' DOON.

Tune—' The Caledonian Hunt s delight.'

YE banks and braes o' bonie Doon,
　　How can ye bloom sae fresh and fair !
How can ye chant, ye little birds,
　　,And I sae weary fu' o' care !
Thou'lt break my heart, thou warbling
　　bird,
　　　That wantons thro' the flowering
　　　　thorn :
Thou minds me o' departed joys,
　　Departed—never to return.

Thou'lt break my heart, thou bonie bird,
　　That sings beside thy mate,
For sae I sat, and sae I sang,
　　And wist na o' my fate.
Aft hae I rov'd by bonie Doon,
　　To see the rose and woodbine twine;
And ilka bird sang o' its luve,
　　And fondly sae did I o' mine.

Wi' lightsome heart I pu'd a rose,
　　Fu' sweet upon its thorny tree ;
And my fause luver stole my rose,
　　But ah ! he left the thorn wi' me.
Wi' lightsome heart I pu'd a rose
　　Upon a morn in June ;
And sae I flourish'd on the morn,
　　And sae was pu'd on noon.

VERSION PRINTED IN THE MUSICAL MUSEUM.

YE flowery banks o' bonie Doon,
　　How can ye blume sae fair !
How can ye chant, ye little birds,
　　And I sae fu' o' care.

Thou'll break my heart, thou bonie
　　bird,
　　That sings upon the bough ;
Thou minds me o' the happy days,
　　When my fause luve was true.

Thou'll break my heart, thou bonie
　　bird,
　　That sings beside thy mate ;
For sae I sat, and sae I sang,
　　And wist na o' my fate.

Aft hae I rov'd by bonie Doon,
　　To see the wood-bine twine,
And ilka bird sang o' its love,
　　And sae did I o' mine.

Wi' lightsome heart I pu'd a rose
　　Frae off its thorny tree ;
And my fause luver staw the rose,
　　But left the thorn wi' me.

GLOOMY DECEMBER.

ANCE mair I hail thee, thou gloomy December !
　　Ance mair I hail thee wi' sorrow and care ;
Sad was the parting thou makes me remember,
　　Parting wi' Nancy, oh ! ne'er to meet mair.
Fond lovers' parting is sweet painful pleasure,
　　Hope beaming mild on the soft parting hour ;
But the dire feeling, O farewell for ever,
　　Is anguish unmingl'd and agony pure.

Wild as the winter now tearing the forest,
　　Till the last leaf o' the summer is flown,
Such is the tempest has shaken my bosom,
　　Since my last hope and last comfort is gone ;
Still as I hail thee, thou gloomy December,
　　Still shall I hail thee wi' sorrow and care ;
For sad was the parting thou makes me remember,
　　Parting wi' Nancy, oh ! ne'er to meet mair.

BEHOLD THE HOUR.

Tune—'*Oran Gaoil.*'

Behold the hour, the boat arrive !
  Thou goest, thou darling of my heart :
Sever'd from thee can I survive ?
  But fate has will'd, and we must part !
I'll often greet this surging swell ;
  Yon distant isle will often hail :
'E'en here I took the last farewell ;
  There latest mark'd her vanish'd sail.'

Along the solitary shore,
  While flitting sea-fowls round me cry,
Across the rolling, dashing roar,
  I'll westward turn my wistful eye :
'Happy, thou Indian grove,' I'll say,
  'Where now my Nancy's path may be !
'While thro' thy sweets she loves to stray,
  O tell me, does she muse on me ?'

WILLIE'S WIFE.

Tune—'*Tibbie Fowler in the Glen.*'

Willie Wastle dwalt on Tweed,
  The spot they ca'd it Linkumdoddie,
Willie was a wabster guid,
  Cou'd stown a clue wi' onie bodie ;

He had a wife was dour and din,
  O Tinkler Madgie was her mither ;
  Sic a wife as Willie had,
  I wad na gie a button for her.

She has an ee, she has but ane,
  The cat has twa the very colour :
Five rusty teeth, forbye a stump,
  A clapper tongue wad deave a miller ;
A whiskin beard about her mou,
  Her nose and chin they threaten ither ;
    Sic a wife, &c.

She's bow-hough'd, she's hein shinn'd,
  Ae limpin leg a hand-breed shorter ;
She's twisted right, she's twisted left,
  To balance fair in ilka quarter :
She has a hump upon her breast,
  The twin o' that upon her shouther ;
    Sic a wife, &c.

Auld baudrons by the ingle sits,
  An' wi' her loof her face a-washin ;
But Willie's wife is nae sae trig,
  She dights her grunzie wi' a hushion ;
Her walie nieves like midden-creels,
  Her face wad fyle the Logan-water ;
    Sic a wife as Willie had,
    I wad na gie a button for her.

AFTON WATER.

Flow gently, sweet Afton, among thy green braes,
Flow gently, I'll sing thee a song in thy praise ;
My Mary's asleep by thy murmuring stream,
Flow gently, sweet Afton, disturb not her dream.

Thou stock-dove whose echo resounds thro' the glen,
Ye wild whistling blackbirds in yon thorny den,
Thou green-crested lapwing, thy screaming forbear,
I charge you disturb not my slumbering fair.

How lofty, sweet Afton, thy neighbouring hills,
Far mark'd with the courses of clear, winding rills ;
There daily I wander as noon rises high,
My flocks and my Mary's sweet cot in my eye.

How pleasant thy banks and green valleys below,
Where wild in the woodlands the primroses blow ;
There oft as mild ev'ning weeps over the lea,
The sweet-scented birk shades my Mary and me.

Thy crystal stream, Afton, how lovely it glides,
And winds by the cot where my Mary resides ;
How wanton thy waters her snowy feet lave,
As gathering sweet flow'rets she stems thy clear wave.

Flow gently, sweet Afton, among thy green braes,
Flow gently, sweet river, the theme of my lays ;
My Mary's asleep by thy murmuring stream,
Flow gently, sweet Afton, disturb not her dream.

LOUIS, WHAT RECK I BY THEE?

Tune—' *My Mother's aye glowring o'er me.*'

Louis, what reck I by thee,
   Or Geordie on his ocean ?
Dyvour, beggar loons to me,
   I reign in Jeanie's bosom.

Let her crown my love her law,
   And in her breast enthrone me :
Kings and nations, swith awa !
   Reif randies, I disown ye !

BONIE BELL.

The smiling spring comes in rejoicing,
   And surly winter grimly flies :
Now crystal clear are the falling waters,
   And bonie blue are the sunny skies ;
Fresh o'er the mountains breaks forth
     the morning,
   The ev'ning gilds the ocean's swell ;
All creatures joy in the sun's returning,
   And I rejoice in my bonie Bell.

The flowery spring leads sunny summer,
   And yellow autumn presses near,
Then in his turn comes gloomy winter,
   Till smiling spring again appear.
Thus seasons dancing, life advancing,
   Old Time and Nature their changes
     tell,
But never ranging, still unchanging
   I adore my bonie Bell.

FOR THE SAKE OF SOMEBODY.

Tune—' *The Highland Watch's farewell.*'

My heart is sair, I dare na tell,
   My heart is sair for somebody ;
I could wake a winter night,
   For the sake o' somebody !

Oh-hon ! for somebody !
   Oh-hey ! for somebody !
I could range the world around,
   For the sake o' somebody.

Ye powers that smile on virtuous love,
   O, sweetly smile on somebody !
Frae ilka danger keep him free,
   And send me safe my somebody.
     Oh-hon ! for somebody !
     Oh-hey ! for somebody !
I wad do—what wad I not ?
For the sake o' somebody !

O MAY, THY MORN.

O May, thy morn was ne'er sae sweet,
   As the mirk night o' December ;
For sparkling was the rosy wine,
   And private was the chamber :
And dear was she I dare na name,
   But I will aye remember.
     And dear, &c.

And here's to them, that, like oursel,
   Can push about the jorum,
And here's to them that wish us weel,
   May a' that's guid watch o'er them ;
And here's to them we dare na tell,
   The dearest o' the quorum.
     And here's to, &c.

THE LOVELY LASS OF INVERNESS.

The lovely lass o' Inverness,
   Nae joy nor pleasure can she see ;
For e'en and morn she cries, alas !
   And aye the saut tear blins her ee :
Drumossie moor, Drumossie day,
   A waefu' day it was to me ;
For there I lost my father dear,
   My father dear, and brethren three.

Their winding-sheet the bluidy clay,
  Their graves are growing green to see;
And by them lies the dearest lad
  That ever blest a woman's ee !
Now wae to thee, thou cruel lord,
  A bluidy man I trow thou be ;
For monie a heart thou hast made sair,
  That ne'er did wrang to thine or thee.

A RED, RED ROSE.

Tune—'*Wishaw's favourite.*'

O, MY luve's like a red, red rose,
  That's newly sprung in June :
O, my luve's like the melodie
  That's sweetly play'd in tune.

As fair art thou, my bonie lass,
  So deep in luve am I :
And I will luve thee still, my dear,
  Till a' the seas gang dry.

Till a' the seas gang dry, my dear,
  And the rocks melt wi' the sun :
I will luve thee still, my dear,
  While the sands o' life shall run.

And fare thee weel, my only luve,
  And fare thee weel awhile !
And I will come again, my luve,
  Tho' it were ten thousand mile.

O, WAT YE WHA'S IN YON TOWN ?

Tune—'*The bonie Lass in yon town.*'

O, WAT ye wha's in yon town,
  Ye see the e'enin sun upon ?
The fairest dame's in yon town,
  That e'enin sun is shining on.

Now haply down yon gay green shaw,
  She wanders by yon spreading tree :
How blest, ye flow'rs that round her blaw,
  Ye catch the glances o' her e'e !

How blest, ye birds that round her sing,
  And welcome in the blooming year,
And doubly welcome be the spring,
  The season to my Lucy dear !

B

The sun blinks blithe on yon town,
  And on yon bonie braes of Ayr ;
But my delight in yon town,
  And dearest bliss, is Lucy fair.

Without my love, not a' the charms
  O' Paradise could yield me joy ;
But gie me Lucy in my arms,
  And welcome Lapland's dreary sky.

My cave wad be a lover's bower,
  Tho' raging winter rent the air ;
And she a lovely little flower,
  That I wad tent and shelter there.

O sweet is she in yon town,
  Yon sinkin sun's gane down upon ;
A fairer than's in yon town,
  His setting beam ne'er shone upon.

If angry fate is sworn my foe,
  And suffering I am doom'd to bear ;
I careless quit all else below,
  But spare me, spare me Lucy dear.

For while life's dearest blood is warm,
  Ae thought frae her shall ne'er depart,
And she—as fairest is her form,
  She has the truest, kindest heart.

A VISION.

Tune—'*Cunnock Psalms.*'

As I stood by yon roofless tower,
  Where the wa' flower scents the dewy
    air,
Where the howlet mourns in her ivy
    bower,
  And tells the midnight moon her care ;

CHORUS.

A lassie, all alone was making her moan,
  Lamenting our lads beyond the sea :
In the bluidy wars they fa', and our
    honour's gane an' a',
  And broken-hearted we maun die.

The winds were laid, the air was still,
  The stars they shot alang the sky ;
The fox was howling on the hill,
  And the distant-echoing glens reply.

P

The stream, adown its hazelly path,
    Was rushing by the ruin'd wa's,
Hasting to join the sweeping Nith,
    Whase distant roarings swell and fa's.

The cauld blue north was streaming forth
    Her lights, wi' hissing, eerie din ;
Athort the lift they start and shift,
    Like fortune's favours, tint as win.

By heedless chance I turn'd mine eyes,
    And, by the moonbeam, shook to see
A stern and stalwart ghaist arise,
    Attir'd as minstrels wont to be.

Had I a statue been o' stane,
    His darin look had daunted me :
And on his bonnet grav'd was plain
    The sacred posy—Libertie !

And frae his harp sic strains did flow,
    Might rous'd the slumbering dead to
        hear ;
But oh, it was a tale of woe,
    As ever met a Briton's ear !

He sang wi' joy his former day,
    He weeping wail'd his latter times ;
But what he said it was nae play,
    I winna venture't in my rhymes.

O, WERT THOU IN THE CAULD BLAST.

TUNE—' *The Lass of Livingstone.*'

O, WERT thou in the cauld blast,
    On yonder lea, on yonder lea,
My plaidie to the angry airt,
    I'd shelter thee, I'd shelter thee.
Or did misfortune's bitter storms
    Around thee blaw, around thee blaw,
Thy bield should be my bosom,
    To share it a', to share it a'.

Or were I in the wildest waste,
    Of earth and air, of earth and air,
The desart were a paradise,
    If thou wert there, if thou wert there.
Or were I monarch o' the globe,
    Wi' thee to reign, wi' thee to reign,
The only jewel in my crown
    Wad be my queen, wad be my queen.

THE HIGHLAND LASSIE.

TUNE—' *The deuks dang o'er my daddy.*'

NAE gentle dames, tho' e'er sae fair,
Shall ever be my Muse's care ;
Their titles a' are empty show ;
Gie me my Highland lassie, O.

CHORUS.

Within the glen sae bushy, O,
    Aboon the plain sae rushy, O,
I set me down wi' right good will
    To sing my Highland lassie, O.

Oh, were yon hills and valleys mine,
Yon palace and yon gardens fine !
The world then the love should know
I bear my Highland lassie, O.
    Within the glen, &c.

But fickle fortune frowns on me,
And I maun cross the raging sea ;
But while my crimson currents flow
I'll love my Highland lassie, O.
    Within the glen, &c.

Altho' thro' foreign climes I range,
I know her heart will never change,
For her bosom burns with honour's glow,
My faithful Highland lassie, O.
    Within the glen, &c.

For her I'll dare the billow's roar,
For her I'll trace a distant shore,
That Indian wealth may lustre throw
Around my Highland lassie, O.
    Within the glen, &c.

She has my heart, she has my hand,
By sacred truth and honour's band !
Till the mortal stroke shall lay me low,
I'm thine, my Highland lassie, O.

    Fareweel the glen sae bushy, O !
    Fareweel the plain sae rushy, O !
    To other lands I now must go,
    To sing my Highland lassie, O !

JOCKEY'S TA'EN THE PART-ING KISS.

JOCKEY'S ta'en the parting kiss,
    O'er the mountains he is gane ;
And with him is a' my bliss,
    Nought but griefs with me remain.

Spare my luve, ye winds that blaw,
  Plashy sleets and beating rain !
Spare my luve, thou feathery snaw,
  Drifting o'er the frozen plain !

When the shades of evening creep
  O'er the day's fair, gladsome ee,
Sound and safely may he sleep,
  Sweetly blithe his waukening be !

He will think on her he loves,
  Fondly he'll repeat her name ;
For where'er he distant roves,
  Jockey's heart is still at hame.

PEGGY'S CHARMS.

My Peggy's face, my Peggy's form,
The frost of hermit age might warm ;
My Peggy's worth, my Peggy's mind,
Might charm the first of human kind.
I love my Peggy's angel air,
Her face so truly, heavenly fair,
Her native grace so void of art ;
But I adore my Peggy's heart.

The lily's hue, the rose's dye,
The kindling lustre of an eye ;
Who but owns their magic sway,
Who but knows they all decay !
The tender thrill, the pitying tear,
The generous purpose, nobly dear,
The gentle look that rage disarms,
These are all immortal charms.

UP IN THE MORNING EARLY.

CHORUS.

Up in the morning's no for me,
  Up in the morning early ;
When a' the hills are cover'd wi' snaw,
  I'm sure it's winter fairly.

Cauld blaws the wind frae east to west,
  The drift is driving sairly ;
Sae loud and shrill's I hear the blast,
  I'm sure it's winter fairly.

The birds sit chittering in the thorn,
  A' day they fare but sparely ;
And lang's the night frae e'en to morn,
  I'm sure it's winter fairly.
    Up in the morning, &c.

THO' CRUEL FATE.

Tho' cruel fate should bid us part,
  As far's the pole and line ;
Her dear idea round my heart
  Should tenderly entwine.

Tho' mountains frown and deserts howl,
  And oceans roar between ;
Yet, dearer than my deathless soul,
  I still would love my Jean.

* * * * *

I DREAM'D I LAY WHERE FLOWERS WERE SPRINGING.

I dream'd I lay where flowers were
    springing
  Gaily in the sunny beam ;
List'ning to the wild birds singing,
  By a falling, crystal stream :
Straight the sky grew black and daring ;
  Thro' the woods the whirlwinds rave ;
Trees with agèd arms were warring,
  O'er the swelling, drumlie wave.

Such was my life's deceitful morning,
  Such the pleasures I enjoy'd ;
But lang or noon, loud tempests storming
  A' my flowery bliss destroy'd.
Tho' fickle fortune has deceiv'd me,
  She promis'd fair, and perform'd but ill ;
Of monie a joy and hope bereav'd me,
  I bear a heart shall support me still.

BONIE ANN.

Ye gallants bright, I red you right,
  Beware o' bonie Ann :
Her comely face sae fu' o' grace,
  Your heart she will trepan.
Her een sae bright, like stars by night,
  Her skin is like the swan ;
Sae jimpy lac'd her genty waist,
  That sweetly ye might span.

Youth, grace, and love, attendant move,
  And pleasure leads the van ;
In a' their charms, and conquering arms,
  They wait on bonie Ann.
The captive bands may chain the hands,
  But love enslaves the man :
Ye gallants braw, I red you a',
  Beware o' bonie Ann.

P 2

MY BONIE MARY.

Go fetch to me a pint o' wine,
    An' fill it in a silver tassie ;
That I may drink before I go,
    A service to my bonie lassie.
The boat rocks at the pier o' Leith ;
    Fu' loud the wind blaws frae the ferry ;
The ship rides by the Berwick-law,
    And I maun leave my bonie Mary.

The trumpets sound, the banners fly,
    The glittering spears are rankèd ready ;
The shouts o' war are heard afar,
    The battle closes thick and bloody ;
But it's no the roar o' sea or shore
    Wad mak me langer wish to tarry ;
Nor shout o' war that's heard afar,
    It's leaving thee, my bonie Mary.

MY HEART'S IN THE HIGHLANDS.

My heart's in the Highlands, my heart is not here ;
My heart's in the Highlands a-chasing the deer ;
Chasing the wild deer, and following the roe,
My heart's in the Highlands wherever I go.
Farewell to the Highlands, farewell to the North,
The birth-place of valour, the country of worth ;
Wherever I wander, wherever I rove,
The hills of the Highlands for ever I love.

Farewell to the mountains high cover'd with snow ;
Farewell to the straths and green valleys below ;
Farewell to the forests and wild-hanging woods ;
Farewell to the torrents and loud-pouring floods.
My heart's in the Highlands,-my heart is not here ;
My heart's in the Highlands a-chasing the deer ;
Chasing the wild deer, and following the roe,
My heart's in the Highlands, wherever I go.

THERE'S A YOUTH IN THIS CITY.

Tune—'*Neil Gow's lament.*'

There's a youth in this city, it were a great pity,
    That he from our lasses should wander awa ;
For he's bonie and braw, weel favour'd witha',
    And his hair has a natural buckle and a'.
His coat is the hue of his bonnet sae blue ;
    His fecket is white as the new-driven snaw ;
His hose they are blae, and his shoon like the slae,
    And his clear siller buckles they dazzle us a'.
       His coat is the hue, &c.

For beauty and fortune the laddie 's been courtin ;
    Weel-featur'd, weel-tocher'd, weel-mounted and braw ;
But chiefly the siller, that gars him gang till her,
    The pennie's the jewel that beautifies a'.
There's Meg wi' the mailin, that fain wad a haen him,
    And Susy whase daddy was Laird o' the ha' ;
There's lang-tocher'd Nancy maist fetters his fancy,
    —But the laddie's dear sel he lo'es dearest of a'.

THE RANTIN DOG THE DADDIE O'T.

Tune—'*East nook o' Fife.*'

O WHA my babie-clouts will buy?
Wha will tent me when I cry?
Wha will kiss me whare I lie?
  The rantin dog the daddie o't.

Wha will own he did the faut?
Wha will buy my groanin maut?
Wha will tell me how to ca't?
  The rantin dog the daddie o't.

When I mount the creepie-chair,
Wha will sit beside me there?
Gie me Rob, I seek nae mair,
  The rantin dog the daddie o't.

Wha will crack to me my lane?
Wha will mak me fidgin fain?
Wha will kiss me o'er again?
  The rantin dog the daddie o't.

I DO CONFESS THOU ART SAE FAIR.

I DO confess thou art sae fair,
  I wad been o'er the lugs in luve;
Had I not found the slightest prayer
  That lips could speak, thy heart
    could muve.

I do confess thee sweet, but find
  Thou art sae thriftless o' thy sweets,
Thy favours are the silly wind
  That kisses ilka thing it meets.

See yonder rose-bud rich in dew,
  Amang its native briers sae coy,
How soon it tines its scent and hue
  When pu'd and worn a common toy!

Sic fate ere lang shall thee betide,
  Tho' thou may gaily bloom a while;
Yet soon thou shalt be thrown aside,
  Like onie common weed and vile.

YON WILD MOSSY MOUNTAINS.

YON wild mossy mountains sae lofty and wide,
That nurse in their bosom the youth o' the Clyde,
Where the grouse lead their coveys thro' the heather to feed,
And the shepherd tents his flock as he pipes on his reed:
    Where the grouse, &c.

Not Gowrie's rich valley, nor Forth's sunny shores,
To me hae the charms o' yon wild mossy moors;
For there, by a lanely, sequester'd clear stream,
Resides a sweet lassie, my thought and my dream.

Amang thae wild mountains shall still be my path,
Ilk stream foaming down its ain green narrow strath;
For there, wi' my lassie, the day lang I rove,
While o'er us unheeded fly the swift hours o' love.

She is not the fairest, altho' she is fair;
O' nice education but sma' is her share;
Her parentage humble as humble can be,
But I lo'e the dear lassie because she lo'es me.

To beauty what man but maun yield him a prize,
In her armour of glances, and blushes, and sighs?
And when wit and refinement hae polish'd her darts,
They dazzle our een, as they fly to our hearts.

But kindness, sweet kindness, in the fond sparkling ee,
Has lustre outshining the diamond to me;
And the heart-beating love, as I'm clasp'd in her arms,
O, these are my lassie's all-conquering charms!

WHA IS THAT AT MY BOWER DOOR?

WHA is that at my bower door?
    O wha is it but Findlay;
Then gae your gate, ye'se nae be here!
    Indeed maun I, quo' Findlay.
What mak ye sae like a thief?
    O come and see, quo' Findlay;
Before the morn ye'll work mischief;
    Indeed will I, quo' Findlay.

Gif I rise and let you in;
    Let me in, quo' Findlay;
Ye'll keep me waukin wi' your din;
    Indeed will I, quo' Findlay.
In my bower if ye should stay;
    Let me stay, quo' Findlay;
I fear ye'll bide till break o' day;
    Indeed will I, quo' Findlay.

Here this night if ye remain;
    I'll remain, quo' Findlay;
I dread ye'll learn the gate again;
    Indeed will I, quo' Findlay.
What may pass within this bower—
    Let it pass, quo' Findlay;
Ye maun conceal till your last hour;
    Indeed will I, quo' Findlay.

FAREWELL TO NANCY.

AE fond kiss, and then we sever!
Ae fareweel, alas, for ever!
Deep in heart-wrung tears I'll pledge thee,
Warring sighs and groans I'll wage thee.
Who shall say that fortune grieves him
While the star of hope she leaves him?
Me, nae cheerfu' twinkle lights me,
Dark despair around benights me.

I'll ne'er blame my partial fancy,
Naething could resist my Nancy;
But to see her, was to love her;
Love but her, and love for ever.
Had we never lov'd sae kindly,
Had we never lov'd sae blindly,
Never met—or never parted,
We had ne'er been broken hearted.

Fare thee weel, thou first and fairest!
Fare thee weel, thou best and dearest!
Thine be ilka joy and treasure,
Peace, enjoyment, love, and pleasure.

Ae fond kiss, and then we sever;
Ae fareweel, alas, for ever!
Deep in heart-wrung tears I pledge thee,
Warring sighs and groans I'll wage thee.

THE BONIE BLINK O' MARY'S EE.

Now bank an' brae are claith'd in green,
    An' scatter'd cowslips sweetly spring,
By Girvan's fairy haunted stream
    The birdies flit on wanton wing.
To Cassillis' banks when e'ening fa's,
    There wi' my Mary let me flee,
There catch her ilka glance o' love,
    The bonie blink o' Mary's ee!

The chield wha boasts o' warld's wealth,
    Is aften laird o' meikle care;
But Mary she is a' my ain,
    Ah, fortune canna gie me mair!
Then let me range by Cassillis' banks
    Wi' her the lassie dear to me,
And catch her ilka glance o' love,
    The bonie blink o' Mary's ee!

OUT OVER THE FORTH.

OUT over the Forth I look to the north,
    But what is the north and its High-
        lands to me?
The south nor the east gie ease to my
        breast,
    The far foreign land, or the wild
        rolling sea.

But I look to the west, when I gae to
        rest,
    That happy my dreams and my
        slumbers may be;
For far in the west lives he I lo'e best,
    The lad that is dear to my babie and
        me.

THE BONIE LAD THAT'S FAR AWAY.

TUNE—'*Owre the hills and far away.*'

O HOW can I be blithe and glad,
    Or how can I gang brisk and braw,
When the bonie lad that I lo'e best
    Is o'er the hills and far awa?

It's no the frosty winter wind,
 It's no the driving drift and snaw ;
But ay the tear comes in my ee,
 To think on him that's far awa.

My father pat me frae his door,
 My friends they hae disown'd me a' :
But I hae ane will tak my part,
 The bonie lad that's far awa.

A pair o' gloves he gae to me,
 And silken snoods he gae me twa ;
And I will wear them for his sake,
 The bonie lad that's far awa.

The weary winter soon will pass,
 And spring will cleed the birken-
 shaw :
And my sweet babie will be born,
 And he'll came hame that's far awa.

THE GOWDEN LOCKS
OF ANNA.

Tune—'*Banks of Banna.*'

Yestreen I had a pint o' wine,
 A place where body saw na' ;
Yestreen lay on this breast o' mine
 The gowden locks of Anna.

The hungry Jew in wilderness
 Rejoicing o'er his manna,
Was naething to my hinny bliss
 Upon the lips of Anna.

Ye monarchs, tak the east and west,
 Frae Indus to Savannah !
Gie me within my straining grasp
 The melting form of Anna.
There I'll despise imperial charms,
 An Empress or Sultana,
While dying raptures in her arms,
 I give and take with Anna !

Awa, thou flaunting god o' day !
 Awa, thou pale Diana !
Ilk star gae hide thy twinkling ray
 When I'm to meet my Anna.
Come, in thy raven plumage, night,
 Sun, moon, and stars withdrawn a' ;
And bring an angel pen to write
 My transports wi' my Anna !

POSTSCRIPT.

The kirk and state may join, and tell
 To do such things I mauna :
The kirk and state may gae to hell,
 And I'll gae to my Anna.
She is the sunshine o' my ee,
 To live but her I canna ;
Had I on earth but wishes three,
 The first should be my Anna.

BANKS OF DEVON.

How pleasant the banks of the clear-winding Devon,
 With green-spreading bushes, and flowers blooming fair !
But the boniest flower on the banks of the Devon
 Was once a sweet bud on the braes of the Ayr.

Mild be the sun on this sweet blushing flower,
 In the gay rosy morn as it bathes in the dew !
And gentle the fall of the soft vernal shower,
 That steals on the evening each leaf to renew.

O, spare the dear blossom, ye orient breezes,
 With chill hoary wing as ye usher the dawn !
And far be thou distant, thou reptile that seizes
 The verdure and pride of the garden and lawn !

Let Bourbon exult in his gay gilded lilies,
 And England triumphant display her proud rose ;
A fairer than either adorns the green valleys
 Where Devon, sweet Devon, meandering flows.

ADOWN WINDING NITH.

TUNE—'*The muckin o' Geordie's byre.*'

ADOWN winding Nith I did wander,
  To mark the sweet flowers as they
    spring ;
Adown winding Nith I did wander,
  Of Phillis to muse and to sing.

CHORUS.

Awa wi' your belles and your beauties,
  They never wi' her can compare ;
Whaever has met wi' my Phillis,
  Has met wi' the queen o' the fair.

The daisy amus'd my fond fancy,
  So artless, so simple, so wild ;
Thou emblem, said I, o' my Phillis,
  For she is Simplicity's child.
      Awa, &c.

The rose-bud's the blush o' my charmer,
  Her sweet balmy lip when 'tis prest :
How fair and how pure is the lily,
  But fairer and purer her breast.
      Awa, &c.

Yon knot of gay flowers in the arbour,
  They ne'er wi' my Phillis can vie :
Her breath is the breath o' the woodbine,
  Its dew-drop o' diamond, her eye.
      Awa, &c.

Her voice is the song of the morning
  That wakes through the green-spread-
    ing grove
When Phœbus peeps over the mountains,
  On music, and pleasure, and love.
      Awa, &c.

But beauty how frail and how fleeting,
  The bloom of a fine summer's day !
While worth in the mind o' my Phillis
  Will flourish without a decay.
      Awa, &c.

STREAMS THAT GLIDE.

TUNE—'*Morag.*'

STREAMS that glide in orient plains,
Never bound by winter's chains !
Glowing here on golden sands,
There commix'd with foulest stains
From tyranny's empurpled bands :

These, their richly-gleaming waves,
I leave to tyrants and their slaves ;
Give me the stream that sweetly laves
  The banks by Castle Gordon.

Spicy forests, ever gay,
Shading from the burning ray
Hapless wretches sold to toil,
Or the ruthless native's way,
Bent on slaughter, blood, and spoil :
Woods that ever verdant wave,
I leave the tyrant and the slave,
Give me the groves that lofty brave
  The storms, by Castle Gordon.

Wildly here without control,
Nature reigns and rules the whole ;
In that sober pensive mood,
Dearest to the feeling soul,
She plants the forest, pours the flood ;
Life's poor day I'll musing rave,
And find at night a sheltering cave,
Where waters flow and wild woods wave,
  By bonie Castle Gordon.

THE DE'IL'S AWA' WI' THE EXCISEMAN.

THE De'il cam fiddling thro' the town,
  And danc'd awa wi' the Exciseman ;
And ilka wife cry'd 'Auld Mahoun,
  We wish you luck o' your prize, man.

'We'll mak our maut, and brew our
    drink,
  We'll dance, and sing, and rejoice,
    man ;
And monie thanks to the muckle
    black De'il
  That danc'd awa wi' the Excise-
    man.

'There's threesome reels, and foursome
    reels,
  There's hornpipes and strathspeys,
    man ;
But the ae best dance e'er cam to our lan',
  Was—the De'il's awa wi' the Excise-
    man.
    We'll mak our maut,' &c.

BLITHE HAE I BEEN ON YON HILL.

Tune—'*Liggeram cosh.*'

Blithe hae I been on yon hill,
As the lambs before me ;
Careless ilka thought and free,
As the breeze flew o'er me :
Now nae langer sport and play,
Mirth or sang can please me ;
Lesley is sae fair and coy,
Care and anguish seize me.

Heavy, heavy is the task,
Hopeless love declaring :
Trembling, I dow nocht but glowr,
Sighing, dumb, despairing !
If she winna ease the thraws
In my bosom swelling,
Underneath the grass-green sod
Soon maun be my dwelling.

O WERE MY LOVE YON LILAC FAIR.

Tune—'*Hughie Graham.*'

O were my love yon lilac fair,
Wi' purple blossoms to the spring ;
And I, a bird to shelter there,
When wearied on my little wing ;

How I wad mourn, when it was torn
By autumn wild, and winter rude !

But I wad sing on wanton wing,
When youthfu' May its bloom renew'd.

O gin my love were yon red rose
That grows upon the castle wa',
And I mysel' a drap o' dew,
Into her bonie breast to fa' !

Oh, there beyond expression blest,
I'd feast on beauty a' the night ;
Seal'd on her silk-saft faulds to rest,
Till fley'd awa' by Phœbus' light.

COME, LET ME TAKE THEE.

Tune—'*Cauld kail.*'

Come, let me take thee to my breast,
And pledge we ne'er shall sunder ;
And I shall spurn as vilest dust
The warld's wealth and grandeur :
And do I hear my Jeanie own
That equal transports move her ?
I ask for dearest life alone
That I may live to love her.

Thus in my arms, wi' all thy charms,
I clasp my countless treasure ;
I'll seek nae mair o' heaven to share,
Than sic a moment's pleasure :
And by thy een, sae bonie blue,
I swear I'm thine for ever !
And on thy lips I seal my vow,
And break it shall I never.

WHERE ARE THE JOYS.

Tune—'*Saw ye my Father?*'

Where are the joys I have met in the morning,
That danc'd to the lark's early sang ?
Where is the peace that awaited my wand'ring,
At evening the wild woods amang ?

No more a-winding the course of yon river,
And marking sweet flow'rets so fair :
No more I trace the light footsteps of pleasure,
But sorrow and sad sighing care.

Is it that summer's forsaken our valleys,
  And grim, surly winter is near ?
No, no, the bees humming round the gay roses,
  Proclaim it the pride of the year.

Fain would I hide what I fear to discover,
  Yet long, long too well have I known :
All that has caus'd this wreck in my bosom,
  Is Jenny, fair Jenny alone.

Time cannot aid me, my griefs are immortal,
  Nor hope dare a comfort bestow :
Come, then, enamour'd and fond of my anguish,
  Enjoyment I'll seek in my woe.

O SAW YE MY DEAR.

Tune—'*When she cam ben she bobbit.*'

O SAW ye my dear, my Phely ?
O saw ye my dear, my Phely ?
She's down i' the grove, she's wi' a new
    love,
  She winna come hame to her Willy.

What says she, my dearest, my Phely ?
What says she, my dearest, my Phely ?
She lets thee to wit that she has thee
    forgot,
  And for ever disowns thee her Willy.

O had I ne'er seen thee, my Phely !
O had I ne'er seen thee, my Phely !
As light as the air, and fause as thou's
    fair,
  Thou'st broken the heart o' thy Willy.

THOU HAST LEFT ME EVER, JAMIE.

Tune—'*Fee him, father.*'

THOU hast left me ever, Jamie,
  Thou hast left me ever ;
Thou hast left me ever, Jamie,
  Thou hast left me ever.
Aften hast thou vow'd that death
  Only should us sever ;
Now thou'st left thy lass for aye—
  I maun see thee never, Jamie,
  I'll see thee never !

Thou hast me forsaken, Jamie,
  Thou hast me forsaken ;
Thou hast me forsaken, Jamie,
  Thou hast me forsaken.
Thou canst love anither jo,
  While my heart is breaking ;
Soon my weary een I'll close—
  Never mair to waken, Jamie,
  Ne'er mair to waken !

MY CHLORIS.

Tune—'*My lodging is on the cold ground.*'

My Chloris, mark how green the groves,
  The primrose banks how fair :
The balmy gales awake the flowers,
  And wave thy flaxen hair.

The lav'rock shuns the palace gay,
  And o'er the cottage sings :
For Nature smiles as sweet, I ween,
  To shepherds as to kings.

Let minstrels sweep the skilfu' string
  In lordly lighted ha' :
The shepherd stops his simple reed,
  Blythe, in the birken shaw.

The princely revel may survey
  Our rustic dance wi' scorn ;
But are their hearts as light as ours
  Beneath the milk-white thorn ?

The shepherd, in the flowery glen,
  In shepherd's phrase will woo :
The courtier tells a finer tale,
  But is his heart as true ?

These wild-wood flowers I've pu'd, to
    deck
  That spotless breast o' thine :
The courtier's gems may witness love—
  But 'tis na love like mine.

CHARMING MONTH OF MAY.

Tune—'*Dainty Davie.*'

It was the charming month of May,
When all the flowers were fresh and gay,
One morning, by the break of day,
  The youthful, charming Chloe ;

From peaceful slumber she arose,
Girt on her mantle and her hose,
And o'er the flowery mead she goes,
  The youthful, charming Chloe.

CHORUS.

Lovely was she by the dawn,
  Youthful Chloe, charming Chloe,
Tripping o'er the pearly lawn,
  The youthful, charming Chloe.

The feather'd people you might see
Perch'd all around on every tree,
In notes of sweetest melody
  They hail the charming Chloe ;

Till, painting gay the eastern skies,
The glorious sun began to rise,
Out-rival'd by the radiant eyes
  Of youthful, charming Chloe.
    Lovely was she, &c.

LET NOT WOMAN E'ER
COMPLAIN.

Tune—'*Duncan Gray.*'

Let not woman e'er complain
  Of inconstancy in love ;
Let not woman e'er complain,
  Fickle man is apt to rove :

Look abroad through Nature's range,
  Nature's mighty law is change ;
Ladies, would it not be strange,
  Man should then a monster prove ?

Mark the winds, and mark the skies ;
  Ocean's ebb, and ocean's flow :
Sun and moon but set to rise,
  Round and round the seasons go.

Why then ask of silly man,
  To oppose great Nature's plan ?
We'll be constant while we can—
  You can be no more, you know.

O PHILLY.

Tune—'*The sow's tail.*'

HE.

O Philly, happy be that day
When, roving thro' the gather'd hay,
My youthfu' heart was stown away,
  And by thy charms, my Philly.

SHE.

O Willy, aye I bless the grove
Where first I own'd my maiden love,
Whilst thou didst pledge the Powers
    above
  To be my ain dear Willy.

HE.

As songsters of the early year
Are ilka day mair sweet to hear,
So ilka day to me mair dear
  And charming is my Philly.

SHE.

As on the brier the budding rose
Still richer breathes and fairer blows,
So in my tender bosom grows
  The love I bear my Willy.

HE.

The milder sun and bluer sky,
That crown my harvest cares wi' joy,
Were ne'er sae welcome to my eye
  As is a sight o' Philly.

SHE.

The little swallow's wanton wing,
Tho' wafting o'er the flowery spring,
Did ne'er to me sic tidings bring
    As meeting o' my Willy.

HE.

The bee that thro' the sunny hour
Sips nectar in the opening flower,
Compar'd wi' my delight is poor,
    Upon the lips o' Philly.

SHE.

The woodbine in the dewy weet
When evening shades in silence meet
Is nocht sae fragrant or sae sweet
    As is a kiss o' Willy.

HE.

Let fortune's wheel at random rin,
And fools may tyne, and knaves may
    win;
My thoughts are a' bound up in ane,
    And that's my ain dear Philly.

SHE.

What's a' the joys than gowd can gie!
I care na wealth a single flie;
The lad I love's the lad for me,
    And that's my ain dear Willy.

JOHN BARLEYCORN.

A BALLAD.

THERE was three Kings into the east,
    Three Kings both great and high,
And they hae sworn a solemn oath
    John Barleycorn should die.

They took a plough and plough'd him
    down,
    Put clods upon his head,
And they hae sworn a solemn oath
    John Barleycorn was dead.

But the cheerfu' Spring came kindly on,
    And show'rs began to fall;
John Barleycorn got up again,
    And sore surpris'd them all.

The sultry suns of Summer came,
    And he grew thick and strong,
His head weel arm'd wi' pointed spears,
    That no one should him wrong.

The sober Autumn enter'd mild,
    When he grew wan and pale;
His bending joints and drooping head
    Show'd he began to fail.

His colour sicken'd more and more,
    He faded into age;
And then his enemies began
    To shew their deadly rage.

They've ta'en a weapon, long and sharp,
    And cut him by the knee;
Then tied him fast upon a cart,
    Like a rogue for forgerie.

They laid him down upon his back,
    And cudgell'd him full sore;
They hung him up before the storm,
    And turn'd him o'er and o'er.

They filled up a darksome pit
    With water to the brim,
They heaved in John Barleycorn,
    There let him sink or swim.

They laid him out upon the floor,
    To work him farther woe,
And still, as signs of life appear'd,
    They toss'd him to and fro.

They wasted, o'er a scorching flame,
    The marrow of his bones;
But a miller us'd him worst of all,
    For he crush'd him between two stones.

And they hae ta'en his very heart's blood,
    And drank it round and round;
And still the more and more they drank,
    Their joy did more abound.

John Barleycorn was a hero bold,
    Of noble enterprise,
For if you do but taste his blood,
    'Twill make your courage rise;

'Twill make a man forget his woe;
    'Twill heighten all his joy:
'Twill make the widow's heart to sing,
    Tho' the tear were in her eye.

Then let us toast John Barleycorn,
    Each man a glass in hand;
And may his great posterity
    Ne'er fail in old Scotland!

CANST THOU LEAVE ME THUS?

Tune—'*Roy's Wife.*

Canst thou leave me thus, my Katy ?
Canst thou leave me thus, my Katy ?
Well thou know'st my aching heart,
And canst thou leave me thus for pity?

Is this thy plighted, fond regard,
Thus cruelly to part, my Katy ?
Is this thy faithful swain's reward—
An aching, broken heart, my Katy ?
    Canst thou, &c.

Farewell ! and ne'er such sorrows tear
That fickle heart of thine, my Katy !
Thou may'st find those will love thee
    dear—
But not a love like mine, my Katy.
    Canst thou, &c.

ON CHLORIS BEING ILL.

Tune—'*Aye waukin o.*'

Long, long the night,
    Heavy comes the morrow,
While my soul's delight
    Is on her bed of sorrow.

Can I cease to care,
    Can I cease to languish,
While my darling fair
    Is on the couch of anguish ?
        Long, &c.

Every hope is fled,
    Every fear is terror ;
Slumber e'en I dread,
    Every dream is horror.
        Long, &c.

Hear me, Pow'rs divine !
    Oh, in pity hear me !
Take aught else of mine,
    But my Chloris spare me !
        Long, &c.

WHEN GUILFORD GOOD OUR PILOT STOOD.

A FRAGMENT.

Tune—'*Gillicrankie.*'

WHEN Guilford good our Pilot stood,
    An' did our hellim thraw, man,
Ae night, at tea, began a plea,
    Within America, man :
Then up they gat the maskin-pat,
    And in the sea did jaw, man ;
An' did nae less, in full Congress,
    Than quite refuse our law, man.

Then thro' the lakes Montgomery takes,
    I wat he was na slaw, man ;
Down Lowrie's burn he took a turn,
    And Carleton did ca', man :
But yet, what-reck, he, at Quebec,
    Montgomery-like did fa', man,
Wi' sword in hand, before his band,
    Amang his en'mies a', man.

Poor Tammy Gage, within a cage
    Was kept at Boston ha', man ;
Till Willie Howe took o'er the knowe
    For Philadelphia, man :
Wi' sword an' gun he thought a sin
    Guid Christian bluid to draw, man ;
But at New York, wi' knife an' fork,
    Sir Loin he hacked sma', man.

Burgoyne gaed up, like spur an' whip,
    Till Fraser brave did fa', man ;
Then lost his way, ae misty day,
    In Saratoga shaw, man.
Cornwallis fought as lang's he dought,
    An' did the Buckskins claw, man ;
But Clinton's glaive frae rust to save,
    He hung it to the wa', man.

Then Montague, an' Guilford too,
    Began to fear a fa', man ;
And Sackville doure, wha stood the
        stoure,
    The German Chief to thraw, man :
For Paddy Burke, like ony Turk,
    Nae mercy had at a', man ;
An' Charlie Fox threw by the box,
    An' lows'd his tinkler jaw, man.

Then Rockingham took up the game ;
    Till death did on him ca', man ;
When Shelburne meek held up his cheek,
    Conform to gospel law, man ;
Saint Stephen's boys, wi' jarring noise,
    They did his measures thraw, man,
For North an' Fox united stocks,
    An' bore him to the wa', man.

Then Clubs an' Hearts were Charlie's
        cartes,
    He swept the stakes awa', man,
Till the Diamond's Ace, of Indian race,
    Led him a sair *faux pas*, man :
The Saxon lads, wi' loud placads,
    On Chatham's boy did ca', man ;
An' Scotland drew her pipe, an' blew,
    ' Up, Willie, waur them a', man ! '

Behind the throne then Grenville 's gone,
    A secret word or twa, man ;
While slee Dundas arous'd the class
    Be-north the Roman wa', man ;
An' Chatham's wraith, in heavenly graith,
    (Inspired Bardies saw, man,)
Wi' kindling eyes cry'd, ' Willie, rise !
    Would I hae fear'd them a', man ? '

But, word an' blow, North, Fox, and Co.
    Gowff'd Willie like a ba', man,
Till Suthron raise, an' coost their claise
    Behind him in a raw, man ;
An' Caledon threw by the drone,
    An' did her whittle draw, man ;
An' swoor fu' rude, thro' dirt an' blood,
    To make it guid in law, man.

*   *   *   *   *

THE RIGS O' BARLEY.

Tune—' *Corn rigs are bonie.* '

It was upon a Lammas night,
    When corn rigs are bonie,
Beneath the moon's unclouded light,
    I held awa to Annie :
The time flew by, wi' tentless heed,
    Till 'tween the late and early,
Wi' sma' persuasion she agreed,
    To see me thro' the barley.

The sky was blue, the wind was still,
    The moon was shining clearly ;
I set her down, wi' right good will,
    Amang the rigs o' barley ;
I ken't her heart was a' my ain ;
    I lov'd her most sincerely ;
I kiss'd her owre and owre again
    Amang the rigs o' barley.

I lock'd her in my fond embrace ;
    Her heart was beating rarely ;
My blessings on that happy place,
    Amang the rigs o' barley !
But by the moon and stars so bright,
    That shone that hour so clearly !
She ay shall bless that happy night
    Amang the rigs o' barley.

I hae been blythe wi' comrades dear ;
    I hae been merry drinking ;
I hae been joyfu' gath'rin gear ;
    I hae been happy thinking :
But a' the pleasures e'er I saw,
    Tho' three times doubl'd fairly,
That happy night was worth them a',
    Amang the rigs o' barley.

CHORUS.

Corn rigs, an' barley rigs,
    An' corn rigs are bonie :
I 'll ne'er forget that happy night,
    Amang the rigs wi' Annie.

FAREWELL TO ELIZA.

Tune—' *Gilderoy.* '

From thee, Eliza, I must go,
    And from my native shore ;
The cruel fates between us throw
    A boundless ocean's roar :
But boundless oceans, roaring wide,
    Between my Love and me,
They never, never can divide
    My heart and soul from thee.

Farewell, farewell, Eliza dear,
    The maid that I adore !
A boding voice is in mine ear,
    We part to meet no more !
But the last throb that leaves my heart,
    While death stands victor by,
That throb, Eliza, is thy part,
    And thine that latest sigh !

MY NANIE, O.

BEHIND yon hills where Stinchar flows,
  'Mang moors an' mosses many, O,
The wintry sun the day has clos'd,
  And I'll awa' to Nanie, O.

The westlin wind blaws loud an' shill ;
  The night's baith mirk and rainy, O :
But I'll get my plaid, an' out I'll steal,
  An' owre the hill to Nanie, O.

My Nanie's charming, sweet, an' young :
  Nae artfu' wiles to win ye, O :
May ill befa' the flattering tongue
  That wad beguile my Nanie, O.

Her face is fair, her heart is true,
  As spotless as she's bonie, O :
The op'ning gowan, wat wi' dew,
  Nae purer is than Nanie, O.

A country lad is my degree,
  An' few there be that ken me, O ;
But what care I how few they be,
  I'm welcome aye to Nanie, O.

My riches a's my penny-fee,
  An' I maun guide it cannie, O ;
But warl's gear ne'er troubles me,
  My thoughts are a', my Nanie, O.

Our auld Guidman delights to view
  His sheep an' kye thrive bonie, O ;
But I'm as blythe that hauds his pleugh,
  An' has nae care but Nanie, O.

Come weel, come woe, I care na by,
  I'll tak what Heav'n will send me, O ;
Nae ither care in life have I,
  But live, an' love my Nanie, O.

GREEN GROW THE RASHES.

A FRAGMENT.

CHORUS.

Green grow the rashes, O ;
  Green grow the rashes, O ;
The sweetest hours that e'er I spend,
  Are spent amang the lasses, O !

THERE'S nought but care on ev'ry han',
  In ev'ry hour that passes, O ;
What signifies the life o' man,
  An' 'twere na for the lasses, O.
    Green grow, &c.

The warly race may riches chase,
  An' riches still may fly them, O ;
An' tho' at last they catch them fast,
  Their hearts can ne'er enjoy them, O.
    Green grow, &c.

But gie me a canny hour at e'en,
  My arms about my dearie, O ;
An' warly cares, an' warly men,
  May a' gae tapsalteerie, O !
    Green grow, &c.

For you sae douse, ye sneer at this,
  Ye're nought but senseless asses, O :
The wisest man the warl' saw,
  He dearly lov'd the lasses, O.
    Green grow, &c.

Auld Nature swears, the lovely dears
  Her noblest work she classes, O ;
Her prentice han' she tried on man,
  An' then she made the lasses, O.
    Green grow, &c.

*　　*　　*　　*　　*

NOW WESTLIN WINDS.

TUNE—'*I had a horse, I had nae mair.*'

Now westlin winds and slaught'ring
    guns
  Bring autumn's pleasant weather ;
The moorcock springs, on whirring
    wings,
  Amang the blooming heather :
Now waving grain, wide o'er the plain,
  Delights the weary farmer ;
And the moon shines bright, when I
    rove at night
  To muse upon my charmer.

The partridge loves the fruitful fells ;
  The plover loves the mountains ;
The woodcock haunts the lonely dells ;
  The soaring hern the fountains :

Thro' lofty groves the cushat roves,
  The path of man to shun it ;
The hazel bush o'erhangs the thrush,
  The spreading thorn the linnet.

Thus ev'ry kind their pleasure find,
  The savage and the tender ;
Some social join, and leagues combine ;
  Some solitary wander ;
Avaunt, away ! the cruel sway,
  Tyrannic man's dominion ;
The sportsman's joy, the murd'ring cry,
  The flutt'r.ng, gory pinion !

But, Peggy dear, the ev'ning's clear,
  Thick flies the skimming swallow ;

The sky is blue, the fields in view,
  All fading-green and yellow :
Come let us stray our gladsome way,
  And view the charms of nature ;
The rustling corn, the fruited thorn,
  And ev'ry happy creature.

We'll gently walk, and sweetly talk,
  Till the silent moon shine clearly ;
I'll grasp thy waist, and, fondly prest,
  Swear how I love thee dearly :
Not vernal show'rs to budding flow'rs,
  Not autumn to the farmer,
So dear can be, as thou to me,
  My fair, my lovely charmer !

THE BIG-BELLIED BOTTLE.

Tune—'*Prepare, my dear brethren, to the tavern let's fly.*'

No churchman am I for to rail and to write,
No statesman nor soldier to plot or to fight,
No sly man of business contriving a snare,
For a big-belly'd bottle 's the whole of my care.

The peer I don't envy, I give him his bow ;
I scorn not the peasant, tho' ever so low ;
But a club of good fellows, like those that are there,
And a bottle like this, are my glory and care.

Here passes the squire on his brother—his horse ;
There centum per centum, the cit with his purse ;
But see you the Crown how it waves in the air,
There a big-belly'd bottle still eases my care.

The wife of my bosom, alas ! she did die ;
For sweet consolation to church I did fly ;
I found that old Solomon proved it fair,
That the big-belly'd bottle 's a cure for all care.

I once was persuaded a venture to make ;
A letter inform'd me that all was to wreck ;
But the pursy old landlord just waddled up stairs,
With a glorious bottle that ended my cares.

' Life's cares they are comforts,' a maxim laid down
By the bard, what d'ye call him, that wore the black gown
And, faith, I agree with th' old prig to a hair,
For a big-belly'd bottle 's a heav'n of a care.

A STANZA ADDED IN A MASON LODGE.

Then fill up a bumper, and make it o'erflow,
And honours masonic prepare for to throw ;
May every true brother of the compass and square
Have a big-belly'd bottle when harass'd with care.

THE AUTHOR'S FAREWELL TO HIS NATIVE COUNTRY.

Tune—'*Roslin Castle.*'

THE gloomy night is gath'ring fast,
Loud roars the wild inconstant blast,
Yon murky cloud is foul with rain,
I see it driving o'er the plain ;
The hunter now has left the moor,
The scatter'd coveys meet secure,
While here I wander, prest with care,
Along the lonely banks of Ayr.

The Autumn mourns her rip'ning corn
By early Winter's ravage torn ;
Across her placid, azure sky,
She sees the scowling tempest fly :
Chill runs my blood to hear it rave,
I think upon the stormy wave,
Where many a danger I must dare,
Far from the bonie banks of Ayr.

'Tis not the surging billow's roar,
'Tis not that fatal, deadly shore ;
Tho' death in ev'ry shape appear,
The wretched have no more to fear :
But round my heart the ties are bound,
That heart transpierc'd with many a
     wound :
These bleed afresh, those ties I tear,
To leave the bonie banks of Ayr.

Farewell, old Coila's hills and dales,
Her heathy moors and winding vales ;
The scenes where wretched fancy roves,
Pursuing past, unhappy loves !
Farewell, my friends ! Farewell, my
     foes !
My peace with these, my love with
     those—
The bursting tears my heart declare,
Farewell, the bonie banks of Ayr !

THE FAREWELL.

TO THE BRETHREN OF ST. JAMES'S LODGE,
TARBOLTON.

Tune—'*Guid night, and joy be wi' you a' !*'

ADIEU ! a heart-warm, fond adieu !
Dear brothers of the mystic tie !
Ye favour'd, ye enlighten'd few,
Companions of my social joy !
B

Tho' I to foreign lands must hie,
Pursuing Fortune's slidd'ry ba',
With melting heart, and brimful eye,
I'll mind you still, tho' far awa'.

Oft have I met your social band,
And spent the cheerful, festive night;
Oft, honour'd with supreme command,
Presided o'er the sons of light :
And by that hieroglyphic bright,
Which none but craftsmen ever saw !
Strong mem'ry on my heart shall write
Those happy scenes when far awa' !

May freedom, harmony, and love,
Unite you in the grand design,
Beneath th' Omniscient eye above,
The glorious Architect Divine !
That you may keep th' unerring line,
Still rising by the plummet's law,
Till Order bright, completely shine,
Shall be my pray'r when far awa'.

And You, farewell ! whose merits claim,
Justly, that highest badge to wear !
Heav'n bless your honour'd, noble name,
To Masonry and Scotia dear !
A last request permit me here,
When yearly ye assemble a',
One round, I ask it with a tear,
To him, the Bard that's far awa'.

AND MAUN I STILL ON MENIE DOAT.

Tune—'*Jockey's grey breeks.*'

AGAIN rejoicing nature sees
Her robe assume its vernal hues,
Her leafy locks wave in the breeze,
All freshly steep'd in morning dews.

CHORUS.

And maun I still on Menie doat,
And bear the scorn that's in her e'e ?
For it's jet, jet black, an' it's like a hawk,
An' it winna let a body be !

In vain to me the cowslips blaw,
In vain to me the vi'lets spring;
In vain to me, in glen or shaw,
The mavis and the lintwhite sing.
And maun I still, &c.

Q

The merry ploughboy cheers his team,
　Wi' joy the tentie seedsman stalks,
But life to me's a weary dream,
　A dream of ane that never wauks.
　　And maun I still, &c.

The wanton coot the water skims,
　Amang the reeds the ducklings cry,
The stately swan majestic swims,
　And every thing is blest but I.
　　And maun I still, &c.

The sheep-herd steeks his faulding slap,
　And owre the moorlands whistles
　　shill,
Wi' wild, unequal, wand'ring step
　I meet him on the dewy hill.
　　And maun I still, &c.

And when the lark, 'tween light and
　　dark,
　Blythe waukens by the daisy's side,
And mounts and sings on flittering
　　wings,
　A woe-worn ghaist I hameward glide.
　　And maun I still, &c.

Come Winter, with thine angry howl,
　And raging bend the naked tree;
Thy gloom will soothe my cheerless soul,
　When Nature all is sad like me!
　　And maun I still on Menie doat,
　　　And bear the scorn that's in her
　　　　e'e?
　　For it's jet, jet black, an' it's like a
　　　hawk,
　　　An' it winna let a body be!

HIGHLAND MARY.

TUNE—'*Katharine Ogie.*'

YE banks, and braes, and streams around
　The castle o' Montgomery,
Green be your woods, and fair your
　　flowers,
　Your waters never drumlie!
There simmer first unfauld her robes,
　And there the langest tarry;
For there I took the last fareweel
　O' my sweet Highland Mary.

How sweetly bloom'd the gay green birk,
　How rich the hawthorn's blossom,
As underneath their fragrant shade
　I clasp'd her to my bosom!
The golden hours, on angel wings,
　Flew o'er me and my dearie;
For dear to me, as light and life,
　Was my sweet Highland Mary.

Wi' monie a vow, and lock'd embrace,
　Our parting was fu' tender;
And, pledging aft to meet again,
　We tore oursels asunder;
But oh! fell death's untimely frost,
　That nipt my flower sae early!
Now green's the sod, and cauld's the
　　clay,
　That wraps my Highland Mary!

O pale, pale now, those rosy lips,
　I aft hae kiss'd sae fondly!
And closed for ay the sparkling glance,
　That dwelt on me sae kindly!
And mould'ring now in silent dust,
　That heart that lo'ed me dearly!
But still within my bosom's core
　Shall live my Highland Mary.

AULD LANG SYNE.

SHOULD auld acquaintance be forgot,
　And never brought to min'?
Should auld acquaintance be forgot,
　And days o' lang syne?

CHORUS.

　For auld lang syne, my dear,
　　For auld lang syne,
　We'll tak a cup o' kindness yet,
　　For auld lang syne.

We twa hae run about the braes,
　And pu'd the gowans fine;
But we've wander'd mony a weary foot
　Sin auld lang syne.
　　For auld, &c.

We twa hae paidl't i' the burn,
　From mornin sun till dine;
But seas between us braid hae roar'd
　Sin auld lang syne.
　　For auld, &c.

And here's a hand, my trusty fiere,
  And gie's a hand o' thine ;
And we'll tak a right guid willie-waught,
  For auld lang syne.
    For auld, &c.

And surely ye'll be your pint-stowp,
  And surely I'll be mine ;
And we'll tak a cup o' kindness yet
  For auld lang syne.
    For auld, &c.

BANNOCKBURN.

ROBERT BRUCE'S ADDRESS TO HIS ARMY.

TUNE—'*Hey tuttie tattie.*'

SCOTS, wha hae wi' Wallace bled,
Scots, wham Bruce has aften led ;
Welcome to your gory bed,
  Or to glorious victorie.

Now's the day, and now's the hour ;
See the front o' battle lower ;
See approach proud Edward's power—
  Edward ! chains and slaverie !

Wha will be a traitor knave ?
Wha can fill a coward's grave ?
Wha sae base as be a slave ?
  Traitor ! coward ! turn and flee !

Wha for Scotland's King and law
Freedom's sword will strongly draw,
Free-man stand, or free-man fa' ?
  Caledonian ! on wi' me !

By oppression's woes and pains !
By your sons in servile chains !
We will drain our dearest veins,
  But they shall—they *shall* be free !

Lay the proud usurpers low !
Tyrants fall in every foe !
Liberty's in every blow !
  Forward ! let us do, or die !

THE GALLANT WEAVER.

TUNE—'*The auld wife ayont the fire.*'

WHERE Cart rins rowin to the sea,
By monie a flow'r and spreading tree,
There lives a lad, the lad for me,
  He is a gallant weaver.

Oh I had wooers aught or nine,
They gied me rings and ribbons fine ;
And I was fear'd my heart would tine,
  And I gied it to the weaver.

My daddie sign'd my tocher-band,
To gie the lad that has the land ;
But to my heart I'll add my hand,
  And gie it to the weaver.

While birds rejoice in leafy bowers ;
While bees rejoice in opening flowers ;
While corn grows green in simmer
    showers,
  I'll love my gallant weaver.

SONG.

ANNA, thy charms my bosom fire,
  And waste my soul with care ;
But ah ! how bootless to admire,
  When fated to despair !

Yet in thy presence, lovely fair,
  To hope may be forgiven ;
For sure, 'twere impious to despair
  So much in sight of heaven.

FOR A' THAT AND A' THAT.

Is there, for honest poverty,
  That hangs his head, and a' that ?
The coward-slave, we pass him by,
  We dare be poor for a' that !
    For a' that, and a' that,
    Our toils obscure, and a' that ;
    The rank is but the guinea stamp ;
    The man's the gowd for a' that.

What tho' on hamely fare we dine,
  Wear hodden-grey, and a' that ;
Gie fools their silks, and knaves their
    wine,
  A man's a man for a' that.
    For a' that, and a' that,
    Their tinsel show, and a' that ;
    The honest man, tho' e'er sae poor,
    Is King o' men for a' that.

Q 2

Ye see yon birkie, ca'd a lord,
  Wha struts, and stares, and a' that ;
Tho' hundreds worship at his word,
  He's but a coof for a' that :
    For a' that, and a' that,
      His riband, star, and a' that,
    The man of independent mind,
      He looks and laughs at a' that.

A prince can mak a belted knight,
  A marquis, duke, and a' that ;
But an honest man's aboon his might,
  Guid faith he mauna fa' that !
    For a' that, and a' that,
      Their dignities, and a' that,
    The pith o' sense, and pride o'
      worth,
      Are higher rank than a' that.

Then let us pray that come it may,
  As come it will for a' that ;
That sense and worth, o'er a' the earth,
  May bear the gree, and a' that.
    For a' that, and a' that,
      It's coming yet, for a' that,
    That man to man, the warld o'er,
      Shall brothers be for a' that.

DAINTY DAVIE.

Now rosy May comes in wi' flowers,
  To deck her gay, green spreading
    bowers ;
And now comes in my happy hours,
  To wander wi' my Davie.

CHORUS.

Meet me on the warlock knowe,
  Dainty Davie, dainty Davie,
There I'll spend the day wi' you,
  My ain dear dainty Davie.

The crystal waters round us fa',
The merry birds are lovers a',
The scented breezes round us blaw,
  A wandering wi' my Davie.
           Meet me, &c.

When purple morning starts the hare,
To steal upon her early fare,
Then through the dews I will repair,
  To meet my faithfu' Davie.
           Meet me, &c.

When day, expiring in the west,
The curtain draws o' Nature's rest,
I flee to his arms I lo'e best,
  And that's my ain dear Davie.
           Meet me, &c.

TO MR. CUNNINGHAM.

Tune—'*The hopeless lover.*'

Now spring has clad the groves in green,
  And strew'd the lea wi' flowers ;
The furrow'd waving corn is seen
  Rejoice in fostering showers ;
While ilka thing in nature join
  Their sorrows to forego,
O why thus all alone are mine
  The weary steps of woe !

The trout within yon wimpling burn
  Glides swift, a silver dart,
And safe beneath the shady thorn
  Defies the angler's art :
My life was once that careless stream,
  That wanton trout was I ;
But love, wi' unrelenting beam,
  Has scorch'd my fountain dry.

The little flow'ret's peaceful lot,
  In yonder cliff that grows,
Which, save the linnet's flight, I wot,
  Nae ruder visit knows,
Was mine ; till love has o'er me past,
  And blighted a' my bloom,
And now beneath the withering blast
  My youth and joy consume.

The waken'd lav'rock warbling springs,
  And climbs the early sky,
Winnowing blithe her dewy wings
  In morning's rosy eye ;
As little reckt I sorrow's power,
  Until the flowery snare
O' witching love, in luckless hour,
  Made me the thrall o' care.

O had my fate been Greenland's snows
  Or Afric's burning zone,
Wi' man and nature leagu'd my foes,
  So Peggy ne'er I'd known !
The wretch whase doom is, "Hope nae
    mair ! "
  What tongue his woes can tell !
Within whose bosom, save despair,
  Nae kinder spirits dwell.

CLARINDA.

CLARINDA, mistress of my soul,
　The measur'd time is run!
The wretch beneath the dreary pole
　So marks his latest sun.

To what dark cave of frozen night
　Shall poor Sylvander hie ;
Depriv'd of thee, his life and light,
　The sun of all his joy?

We part—but by these precious drops
　That fill thy lovely eyes !
No other light shall guide my steps
　Till thy bright beams arise.

She, the fair sun of all her sex,
　Has blest my glorious day :
And shall a glimmering planet fix
　My worship to its ray ?

WHY, WHY TELL THY LOVER.

TUNE—'*Caledonian Hunt's delight.*'

WHY, why tell thy lover,
　Bliss he never must enjoy ?
Why, why undeceive him,
　And give all his hopes the lie ?
O why, while fancy, raptur'd, slumbers,
　Chloris, Chloris all the theme !
Why, why wouldst thou, cruel,
　Wake thy lover from his dream ?

CALEDONIA.

TUNE—'*Caledonian Hunt's delight.*'

THERE was once a day, but old Time then was young,
　That brave Caledonia, the chief of her line,
From some of your northern deities sprung :
　(Who knows not that brave Caledonia's divine ?)
From Tweed to the Orcades was her domain,
　To hunt, or to pasture, or do what she would :
Her heavenly relations there fixed her reign,
　And pledg'd her their godheads to warrant it good.

A lambkin in peace, but a lion in war,
　The pride of her kindred the heroine grew ;
Her grandsire, old Odin triumphantly swore,
　' Whoe'er shall provoke thee, th' encounter shall rue ! '
With tillage or pasture at times she would sport
　To feed her fair flocks by her green rustling corn :
But chiefly the woods were her fav'rite resort,
　Her darling amusement, the hounds and the horn.

Long quiet she reign'd ; till thitherward steers
　A flight of bold eagles from Adria's strand ;
Repeated, successive, for many long years,
　They darken'd the air, and they plunder'd the land.
Their pounces were murder, and terror their cry,
　They conquer'd and ruin'd a world beside ;
She took to her hills, and her arrows let fly,
　The daring invaders they fled or they died.

The fell Harpy-raven took wing from the north,
　The scourge of the seas, and the dread of the shore ;
The wild Scandinavian boar issu'd forth
　To wanton in carnage and wallow in gore :

O'er countries and kingdoms their fury prevail'd,
    No arts could appease them, no arms could repel ·
But brave Caledonia in vain they assail'd,
    As Largs well can witness, and Loncartie tell.

The Cameleon-savage disturb'd her repose,
    With tumult, disquiet, rebellion, and strife ;
Provok'd beyond bearing, at last she arose,
    And robb'd him at once of his hopes and his life :
The Anglian lion, the terror of France,
    Oft prowling, ensanguin'd the Tweed's silver flood ;
But, taught by the bright Caledonian lance,
    He learned to fear in his own native wood.

Thus bold, independent, unconquer'd, and free,
    Her bright course of glory for ever shall run :
For brave Caledonia immortal must be ;
    I'll prove it from Euclid as clear as the sun :
Rectangle-triangle, the figure we'll choose,
    The upright is Chance, and old Time is the base ;
But brave Caledonia's the hypothenuse ;
    Then ergo, she'll match them, and match them always.

ON THE BATTLE OF SHERIFF-MUIR,

BETWEEN THE DUKE OF ARGYLE AND THE
EARL OF MAR.

TUNE—'*The Cameronian rant.*'

'O CAM ye here the fight to shun,
    Or herd the sheep wi' me, man ?
Or were you at the Sherra-muir,
    And did the battle see, man ?'
I saw the battle, sair and teugh,
And reeking-red ran monie a sheugh,
My heart, for fear, gae sough for sough,
To hear the thuds, and see the cluds
O' clans frae woods, in tartan duds,
    Wha glaum'd at Kingdoms three,
    man.

The red-coat lads, wi' black cockades,
    To meet them were na slaw, man ;
They rush'd and push'd, and blude out-
    gush'd,
    And monie a bouk did fa', man :
And great Argyle led on his files,
I wat they glanced twenty miles :

They hack'd and hash'd, while broad-
    swords clash'd,
And thro' they dash'd, and hew'd and
    smash'd,
    Till fey men died awa, man.

But had you seen the philibegs,
    And skyrin tartan trews, man,
When in the teeth they dar'd our whigs,
    And covenant true blues, man ;
In lines extended lang and large,
When bayonets oppos'd the targe,
And thousands hasten'd to the charge,
Wi' Highland wrath they frae the sheath
Drew blades o' death, till, out of breath,
    They fled like frighted doos, man.

'O how deil, Tam, can that be true?
    The chase gaed frae the north, man :
I saw mysel, they did pursue
    The horsemen back to Forth, man ;
And at Dumblane, in my ain sight,
They took the brig wi' a' their might,
And straught to Stirling wing'd their
    flight ;
But, cursed lot ! the gates were shut,
And monie a huntit, poor red-coat,
    For fear amaist did swarf, man.'

My sister Kate cam up the gate
  Wi' crowdie unto me, man ;
She swore she saw some rebels run
  Frae Perth unto Dundee, man :
Their left-hand general had nae skill,
The Angus lads had nae guid-will,
That day their neebors' blood to spill ;
For fear, by foes, that they should lose
Their cogs o' brose ; all crying woes,
  And so it goes, you see, man.

They've lost some gallant gentlemen
  Amang the Highland clans, man ;
I fear my lord Panmure is slain,
  Or fallen in whiggish hands, man :
Now wad ye sing this double fight,
Some fell for wrang, and some for right ;
But monie bade the world guid-night ;
Then ye may tell, how pell and mell,
By red claymores, and muskets' knell,
Wi' dying yell, the tories fell,
  And whigs to hell did flee, man.

THE DUMFRIES VOLUNTEERS.

TUNE—'*Push about the jorum.*'

April, 1759.

DOES haughty Gaul invasion threat ?
  Then let the loons beware, Sir,
There's wooden walls upon our seas,
  And volunteers on shore, Sir.
The Nith shall run to Corsincon,
  And Criffel sink to Solway,
Ere we permit a foreign foe
  On British ground to rally !
      Fal de ral, &c.

O let us not like snarling tykes
  In wrangling be divided ;
Till, slap, come in an unco loon
  And wi' a rung decide it.
Be Britain still to Britain true,
  Amang oursels united ;
For never but by British hands
  Maun British wrangs be righted !
      Fal de ral, &c.

The kettle o' the kirk and state,
  Perhaps a claut may fail in't ;
But deil a foreign tinkler loon
  Shall ever ca' a nail in't.

Our fathers' bluid the kettle bought,
  And wha wad dare to spoil it ;
By heaven, the sacrilegious dog
  Shall fuel be to boil it.
      Fal de ral, &c.

The wretch that wad a tyrant own,
  And the wretch his true-born brother,
Who would set the mob aboon the
    throne,
  May they be damned together !
Who will not sing, ' God save the King,'
  Shall hang as high's the steeple ;
But while we sing, ' God save the King,'
  We'll ne'er forget the People.

O WHA IS SHE THAT LO'ES ME ?

TUNE—'*Morag.*'

O WHA is she that lo'es me,
  And has my heart a-keeping ?
O sweet is she that lo'es me,
  As dews o' simmer weeping,
  In tears the rose-buds steeping.

CHORUS.

  O that's the lassie o' my heart,
    My lassie ever dearer ;
  O that's the queen o' womankind,
    And ne'er a ane to peer her.

If thou shalt meet a lassie,
  In grace and beauty charming,
That e'en thy chosen lassie,
  Erewhile thy breast sae warming,
  Had ne'er sic powers alarming ;
    O that's, &c.

If thou hadst heard her talking,
  And thy attentions plighted,
That ilka body talking,
  But her by thee is slighted,
  And thou art all delighted ;
    O that's, &c.

If thou hast met this fair one ;
  When frae her thou hast parted,
If every other fair one,
  But her, thou hast deserted,
  And thou art broken-hearted ;
    O that's, &c.

CAPTAIN GROSE.

TUNE—'*Sir John Malcolm.*'

KEN ye ought o' Captain Grose?
　Igo, and ago,
If he's amang his friends or foes?
　Iram, coram, dago.

Is he South, or is he North?
　Igo, and ago,
Or drowned in the river Forth?
　Iram, coram, dago.

Is he slain by Highland bodies?
　Igo, and ago,
And eaten like a wether-haggis?
　Iram, coram, dago.

Is he to Abram's bosom gane?
　Igo, and ago,
Or haudin Sarah by the wame?
　Iram, coram, dago.

Where'er he be, the Lord be near him!
　Igo, and ago,
As for the deil, he daur na steer him.
　Iram, coram, dago.

But please transmit th' enclosed letter,
　Igo, and ago,
Which will oblige your humble debtor.
　Iram, coram, dago.

So may ye hae auld stanes in store,
　Igo, and ago,
The very stanes that Adam bore.
　Iram, coram, dago.

So may ye get in glad possession,
　Igo, and ago,
The coins o' Satan's coronation!
　Iram, coram, dago.

WHISTLE OWRE THE LAVE O'T.

FIRST when Maggy was my care,
Heaven, I thought, was in her air;
Now we're married—spier nae mair—
　Whistle owre the lave o't.

Meg was meek, and Meg was mild,
Bonie Meg was nature's child—
Wiser men than me's beguil'd;—
　Whistle owre the lave o't.

How we live, my Meg and me,
How we love and how we 'gree,
I care na by how few may see—
　Whistle owre the lave o't.

Wha I wish were maggots' meat,
Dish'd up in her winding sheet,
I could write—but Meg maun see't—
　Whistle owre the lave o't.

O, ONCE I LOV'D A BONIE LASS.

TUNE—'*I am a Man unmarried.*'

O, ONCE I lov'd a bonie lass,
　Ay, and I love her still,
And whilst that virtue warms my breast
　I'll love my handsome Nell.
　　　　Fal lal de ral, &c.

As bonie lasses I hae seen,
　And monie full as braw,
But for a modest gracefu' mien
　The like I never saw.

A bonie lass, I will confess,
　Is pleasant to the ee,
But without some better qualities
　She's no a lass for me.

But Nelly's looks are blithe and sweet,
　And what is best of a',
Her reputation is complete,
　And fair without a flaw.

She dresses aye sae clean and neat,
　Both decent and genteel:
And then there's something in her gait
　Gars onie dress look weel.

A gaudy dress and gentle air
　May slightly touch the heart,
But it's innocence and modesty
　That polishes the dart.

'Tis this in Nelly pleases me,
　'Tis this enchants my soul!
For absolutely in my breast
　She reigns without control.
　　　　Fal lal de ral, &c.

YOUNG JOCKEY.

YOUNG Jockey was the blithest lad
  In a' our town or here awa ;
Fu' blithe he whistled at the gaud,
  Fu' lightly danc'd he in the ha' !
He roos'd my een sae bonie blue,
  He roos'd my waist sae genty sma' ;
An' aye my heart came to my mou,
  When ne'er a body heard or saw.

My Jockey toils upon the plain,
  Thro' wind and weed, thro' frost
    and snaw ;
And o'er the lea I look fu' fain
  When Jockey's owsen hameward ca'.
An' aye the night comes round again,
  When in his arms he takes me a' ;
An' aye he vows he'll be my ain
  As lang's he has a breath to draw.

M'PHERSON'S FAREWELL.

FAREWELL, ye dungeons dark and strong,
  The wretch's destinie :
M'Pherson's time will not be long
  On yonder gallows tree.

CHORUS.

Sae rantingly, sae wantonly,
  Sae dauntingly gaed he ;
He play'd a spring and danc'd it
    round,
  Below the gallows tree.

Oh, what is death but parting breath?—
  On monie a bloody plain
I've dar'd his face, and in this place
  I scorn him yet again !
    Sae rantingly, &c.

Untie these bands from off my hands,
  And bring to me my sword !
And there's no a man in all Scotland,
  But I'll brave him at a word.
    Sae rantingly, &c.

I've liv'd a life of sturt and strife ;
  I die by treacherie :
It burns my heart I must depart
  And not avengèd be.
    Sae rantingly, &c.

Now farewell light, thou sunshine bright,
  And all beneath the sky !
May coward shame distain his name,
  The wretch that dares not die !
    Sae rantingly, &c.

THE DEAN OF FACULTY.
A NEW BALLAD.

TUNE—' *The Dragon of Wantley.*'

DIRE was the hate at old Harlaw
  That Scot to Scot did carry ;
And dire the discord Langside saw,
  For beauteous, hapless Mary :
But Scot with Scot ne'er met so hot,
  Or were more in fury seen, Sir,
Than 'twixt Hal and Bob for the famous
    job—
  Who should be Faculty's Dean, Sir.

This Hal for genius, wit and lore,
  Among the first was number'd ;
But pious Bob, 'mid learning's store,
  Commandment the tenth remember'd.
Yet simple Bob the victory got,
  And won his heart's desire ;
Which shews that heaven can boil the pot,
  Though the devil piss in the fire.

Squire Hal besides had, in this case,
  Pretensions rather brassy,
For talents to deserve a place
  Are qualifications saucy ;
So their worships of the Faculty,
  Quite sick of merit's rudeness,
Chose one who should owe it all, d'ye see,
  To their gratis grace and goodness.

As once on Pisgah purg'd was the sight
  Of a son of Circumcision,
So may be, on this Pisgah height,
  Bob's purblind, mental vision ;
Nay, Bobby's mouth may be open'd yet,
  Till for eloquence you hail him,
And swear he has the Angel met
  That met the Ass of Balaam.

In your heretic sins may ye live and die,
  Ye heretic eight and thirty !
But accept, ye sublime Majority,
  My congratulations hearty.
With your Honors and a certain King,
  In your servants this is striking—
The more incapacity they bring,
  The more they're to your liking.

I'LL AY CA' IN BY YON TOWN.

I'LL ay ca' in by yon town,
   And by yon garden green again ;
I'll ay ca' in by yon town,
   And see my bonie Jean again.

There's nane sall ken, there's nane sall
      guess,
   What brings me back the gate again,
But she, my fairest faithfu' lass,
   And stownlins we sall meet again.

She'll wander by the aiken tree
   When trystin-time draws near again ;
And when her lovely form I see,
   O haith, she's doubly dear again !

A BOTTLE AND FRIEND.

HERE'S a bottle and an honest friend !
   What wad ye wish for mair, man ?
Wha kens, before his life may end,
   What his share may be o' care, man ?
Then catch the moments as they fly,
   And use them as ye ought, man :—
Believe me, happiness is shy,
   And comes not ay when sought, man.

I'LL KISS THEE YET.

TUNE—'*The Braes o' Balquhidder.*'

CHORUS.

I'll kiss thee yet, yet,
   And I'll kiss thee o'er again,
An' I'll kiss thee yet, yet,
   My bonie Peggy Alison !

ILK care and fear, when thou art near,
   I ever mair defy them, O ;
Young Kings upon their hansel throne
   Are no sae blest as I am, O !
      I'll kiss thee, &c.

When in my arms, wi' a' thy charms,
   I clasp my countless treasure, O ;
I seek nae mair o' Heaven to share,
   Than sic a moment's pleasure, O !
      I'll kiss thee, &c.

And by thy een sae bonie blue,
   I swear I'm thine for ever, O ;—
And on thy lips I seal my vow,
   And break it shall I never, O !
      I'll kiss thee, &c.

ON CESSNOCK BANKS.

TUNE—'*If he be a Butcher neat and trim.*'

ON Cessnock banks a lassie dwells ;
   Could I describe her shape and mien ;
Our lasses a' she far excels,
   An' she has twa sparkling rogueish
      een.

She's sweeter than the morning dawn
   When rising Phœbus first is seen,
And dew-drops twinkle o'er the lawn ;
   An' she has twa sparkling rogueish
      een.

She's stately like yon youthful ash
   That grows the cowslip braes between,
And drinks the stream with vigour fresh ;
   An' she has twa sparkling rogueish
      een.

She's spotless like the flow'ring thorn
   With flow'rs so white and leaves so
      green,
When purest in the dewy morn ;
   An' she has twa sparkling rogueish
      een.

Her looks are like the vernal May,
   When ev'ning Phœbus shines serene,
While birds rejoice on every spray ;
   An' she has twa sparkling rogueish
      een.

Her hair is like the curling mist
   That climbs the mountain-sides at
      e'en,
When flow'r-reviving rains are past ;
   An' she has twa sparkling rogueish
      een.

Her forehead's like the show'ry bow,
   When gleaming sunbeams intervene
And gild the distant mountain's brow ;
   An' she has twa sparkling rogueish
      een.

Her cheeks are like yon crimson gem,
   The pride of all the flowery scene,
Just opening on its thorny stem ;
   An' she has twa sparkling rogueish
      een.

Her teeth are like the nightly snow
  When pale the morning rises keen,
While hid the murmuring streamlets
    flow ;
    An' she has twa sparkling rogueish
      een.

Her lips are like yon cherries ripe,
  That sunny walls from Boreas screen ;
They tempt the taste and charm the
    sight ;
    An' she has twa sparkling rogueish
      een.

Her teeth are like a flock of sheep,
  With fleeces newly washen clean,
That slowly mount the rising steep :
    An' she has twa glancin' sparklin'
      een.

Her breath is like the fragrant breeze
  That gently stirs the blossom'd bean,
When Phœbus sinks behind the seas ;
    An' she has twa sparkling rogueish
      een.

Her voice is like the ev'ning thrush
  That sings on Cessnock banks unseen,
While his mate sits nestling in the bush;
    An' she has twa sparkling rogueish
      een.

But it's not her air, her form, her face,
  Tho' matching beauty's fabled queen,
'Tis the mind that shines in ev'ry
    grace,
    An' chiefly in her rogueish een.

PRAYER FOR MARY.

TUNE—' *Blue Bonnets.*'

POWERS celestial, whose protection
  Ever guards the virtuous fair,
While in distant climes I wander,
  Let my Mary be your care :
Let her form sae fair and faultless,
  Fair and faultless as your own ;
Let my Mary's kindred spirit
  Draw your choicest influence down.

Make the gales you waft around her
  Soft and peaceful as her breast ;
Breathing in the breeze that fans her,
  Soothe her bosom into rest :
Guardian angels, O protect her,
  When in distant lands I roam ;
To realms unknown while fate exiles me,
  Make her bosom still my home.

YOUNG PEGGY.

TUNE—' *Last time I cam o'er the Muir.*'

YOUNG Peggy blooms our bonniest
    lass,
  Her blush is like the morning,
The rosy dawn, the springing grass,
  With early gems adorning :
Her eyes outshine the radiant beams
  That gild the passing shower,
And glitter o'er the crystal streams,
  And cheer each fresh'ning flower.

Her lips more than the cherries bright,
  A richer dye has grac'd them ;
They charm th' admiring gazer's sight,
  And sweetly tempt to taste them :
Her smile is as the ev'ning mild,
  When feather'd pairs are courting,
And little lambkins wanton wild,
  In playful bands disporting.

Were Fortune lovely Peggy's foe,
  Such sweetness would relent her,
As blooming Spring unbends the
    brow
  Of surly, savage Winter.
Detraction's eye no aim can gain
  Her winning powers to lessen ;
And fretful envy grins in vain,
  The poison'd tooth to fasten.

Ye Pow'rs of Honour, Love, and
    Truth,
  From ev'ry ill defend hre ;
Inspire the highly favour'd youth
  The destinies intend her ;
Still fan the sweet connubial flame
  Responsive in each bosom ;
And bless the dear parental name
  With many a filial blossom.

THERE'LL NEVER BE PEACE TILL JAMIE COMES HAME.

A SONG.

By yon castle wa', at the close of the day,
I heard a man sing, tho' his head it was grey :
And as he was singing, the tears fast down came—
There'll never be peace till Jamie comes hame.

The church is in ruins, the state is in jars,
Delusions, oppressions, and murderous wars ;
We dare na weel say't, but we ken wha's to blame—
There'll never be peace till Jamie comes hame.

My seven braw sons for Jamie drew sword,
And now I greet round their green beds in the yerd ;
It brak the sweet heart o' my faithfu' auld dame—
There'll never be peace till Jamie comes hame.

Now life is a burden that bows me down,
Sin' I tint my bairns, and he tint his crown ;
But till my last moment my words are the same—
There'll never be peace till Jamie comes hame.

THERE WAS A LAD.

TUNE—'*Dainty Davie.*'

There was a lad was born in Kyle,
But what'n a day o' what'n a style
I doubt it's hardly worth the while
    To be sae nice wi' Robin.

    Robin was a rovin' Boy,
        Rantin' rovin', rantin' rovin' ;
    Robin was a rovin' Boy,
        Rantin' rovin' Robin.

Our monarch's hindmost year but ane
Was five-and-twenty days begun,
'Twas then a blast o' Janwar win'
    Blew hansel in on Robin.

The gossip keekit in his loof,
Quo' scho wha lives will see the proof,
This waly boy will be nae coof,
    I think we'll ca' him Robin.

He'll hae misfortunes great and sma',
But ay a heart aboon them a' ;
He'll be a credit till us a',
    We'll a' be proud o' Robin.

But sure as three times three mak nine,
I see by ilka score and line,
This chap will dearly like our kin',
    So leeze me on thee, Robin.

Guid faith, quo' scho, I doubt you, Sir,
Ye gar the lasses lie aspar,
But twenty fauts ye may hae waur,
    So blessings on thee, Robin !

    Robin was a rovin' Boy,
        Rantin' rovin', rantin' rovin' ;
    Robin was a rovin' Boy,
        Rantin' rovin' Robin.

TO MARY.

TUNE—'*Ewe-bughts, Marion.*'

Will ye go to the Indies, my Mary,
    And leave auld Scotia's shore ?
Will ye go to the Indies, my Mary,
    Across the Atlantic's roar ?

O sweet grows the lime and the orange,
    And the apple on the pine ;
But a' the charms o' the Indies
    Can never equal thine.

I hae sworn by the Heavens to my Mary,
　I hae sworn by the Heavens to be true;
And sae may the Heavens forget me,
　When I forget my vow !

O plight me your faith, my Mary,
　And plight me your lily-white hand ;
O plight me your faith, my Mary,
　Before I leave Scotia's strand.

We hae plighted our troth, my Mary,
　In mutual affection to join,
And curst be the cause that shall part us !
　The hour, and the moment o' time !

MARY MORISON.

TUNE—'*Bide ye yet.*'

O MARY, at thy window be,
　It is the wish'd, the trysted hour !
Those smiles and glances let me see,
　That make the miser's treasure poor ;
How blythely wad I bide the stoure,
　A weary slave frae sun to sun ;
Could I the rich reward secure,
　The lovely Mary Morison.

Yestreen, when to the trembling string
　The dance gaed thro' the lighted ha',
To thee my fancy took its wing,
　I sat, but neither heard or saw :
Tho' this was fair, and that was braw,
　And yon the toast of a' the town,
I sigh'd, and said amang them a',
　'Ye are na Mary Morison.'

O Mary, canst thou wreck his peace,
　Wha for thy sake wad gladly die?
Or canst thou break that heart of his,
　Whase only faut is loving thee ?
If love for love thou wilt na gie,
　At least be pity to me shown !
A thought ungentle canna be
　The thought o' Mary Morison.

THE SODGER'S RETURN.

TUNE—'*The Mill Mill O.*'

WHEN wild war's deadly blast was
　　blawn,
　And gentle peace returning,

Wi' mony a sweet babe fatherless,
　And mony a widow mourning :
I left the lines and tented field,
　Where lang I'd been a lodger,
My humble knapsack a' my wealth,
　A poor and honest sodger.

A leal, light heart was in my breast,
　My hand unstain'd wi' plunder ;
And for fair Scotia, hame again
　I cheery on did wander.
I thought upon the banks o' Coil,
　I thought upon my Nancy,
I thought upon the witching smile
　That caught my youthful fancy.

At length I reach'd the bonie glen,
　Where early life I sported ;
I pass'd the mill, and trysting thorn,
　Where Nancy aft I courted :
Wha spied I but my ain dear maid,
　Down by her mother's dwelling !
And turn'd me round to hide the flood
　That in my een was swelling.

Wi' alter'd voice, quoth I, Sweet lass,
　Sweet as yon hawthorn blossom,
O ! happy, happy may he be,
　That's dearest to thy bosom !
My purse is light, I've far to gang,
　And fain wad be thy lodger ;
I've serv'd my King and Country lang—
　Take pity on a sodger !

Sae wistfully she gaz'd on me,
　And lovelier was than ever :
Quo' she, a sodger ance I lo'ed,
　Forget him shall I never :
Our humble cot, and hamely fare,
　Ye freely shall partake it,
That gallant badge, the dear cockade,
　Ye're welcome for the sake o't.

She gaz'd—she redden'd like a rose—
　Syne pale like onie lily ;
She sank within my arms, and cried,
　Art thou my ain dear Willie ?
By Him who made yon sun and sky,
　By whom true love's regarded,
I am the man ; and thus may still
　True lovers be rewarded !

The wars are o'er, and I'm come hame,
  And find thee still true-hearted ;
Tho' poor in gear, we're rich in love,
  And mair we'se ne'er be parted.
Quo' she, My grandsire left me gowd,
  A mailen plenish'd fairly ;
And come, my faithful sodger lad,
  Thou'rt welcome to it dearly !

For gold the merchant ploughs the main.
  The farmer ploughs the manor ;
But glory is the sodger's prize ;
  The sodger's wealth is honour :
The brave poor sodger ne'er despise,
  Nor count him as a stranger,
Remember he's his Country's stay
  In day and hour o' danger.

MY FATHER WAS A FARMER.

TUNE—' *The Weaver and his Shuttle, O.*'

My Father was a Farmer upon the Carrick border, O
And carefully he bred me in decency and order, O
He bade me act a manly part, though I had ne'er a farthing, O
For without an honest manly heart, no man was worth regarding, O.

Then out into the world my course I did determine, O
Tho' to be rich was not my wish, yet to be great was charming, O
My talents they were not the worst ; nor yet my education, O
Resolv'd was I, at least to try, to mend my situation, O.

In many a way, and vain essay, I courted fortune's favour ; O
Some cause unseen still stept between, to frustrate each endeavour, O
Sometimes by foes I was o'erpower'd ; sometimes by friends forsaken ; O
And when my hope was at the top, I still was worst mistaken, O.

Then sore harass'd, and tir'd at last, with fortune's vain delusion ; O
I dropt my schemes, like idle dreams, and came to this conclusion ; O
The past was bad, and the future hid ; its good or ill untried ; O
But the present hour was in my pow'r, and so I would enjoy it, O.

No help, nor hope, nor view had I ; nor person to befriend me ; O
So I must toil, and sweat and broil, and labour to sustain me, O
To plough and sow, to reap and mow, my father bred me early ; O
For one, he said, to labour bred, was a match for fortune fairly, O.

Thus all obscure, unknown, and poor, thro' life I'm doom'd to wander, O
Till down my weary bones I lay in everlasting slumber ; O
No view nor care, but shun whate'er might breed me pain or sorrow ; O
I live to-day as well's I may, regardless of to-morrow, O.

But cheerful still, I am as well as a monarch in a palace, O
Tho' fortune's frown still hunts me down, with all her wonted malice ; O
I make indeed my daily bread, but ne'er can make it farther ; O
But as daily bread is all I need, I do not much regard her, O.

When sometimes by my labour I earn a little money, O
Some unforeseen misfortune comes generally upon me ; O
Mischance, mistake, or by neglect, or my good-natur'd folly ; O
But come what will, I've sworn it still, I'll ne'er be melancholy, O.

All you who follow wealth and power, with unremitting ardour, O
The more in this you look for bliss, you leave your view the farther ; O
Had you the wealth Potosi boasts, or nations to adore you, O
A cheerful honest-hearted clown I will prefer before you, O.

A MOTHER'S LAMENT FOR THE DEATH OF HER SON.

TUNE—'*Finlayston House.*'

FATE gave the word, the arrow sped,
　And pierc'd my darling's heart ;
And with him all the joys are fled
　Life can to me impart !
By cruel hands the sapling drops,
　In dust dishonour'd laid :
So fell the pride of all my hopes,
　My age's future shade.

The mother-linnet in the brake
　Bewails her ravish'd young ;
So I, for my lost darling's sake,
　Lament the live-day long.
Death, oft I've fear'd thy fatal blow,
　Now, fond, I bare my breast,
O, do thou kindly lay me low
　With him I love, at rest !

BONIE LESLEY.

TUNE—'*The Collier's bonie Dochter.*'

O SAW ye bonie Lesley
　As she gaed o'er the border ?
She's gane, like Alexander,
　To spread her conquests farther.

To see her is to love her,
　And love but her for ever ;
For Nature made her what she is,
　And ne'er made sic anither !

Thou art a queen, Fair Lesley,
　Thy subjects we, before thee :
Thou art divine, Fair Lesley,
　The hearts o' men adore thee.

The Deil he could na scaith thee,
　Or aught that wad belang thee ;
He'd look into thy bonie face,
　And say, 'I canna wrang thee.'

The Powers aboon will tent thee ;
　Misfortune sha'na steer thee ;
Thou'rt like themselves sae lovely,
　That ill they'll ne'er let near thee.

Return again, Fair Lesley,
　Return to Caledonie !
That we may brag, we hae a lass
　There's nane again sae bonie.

AMANG THE TREES.

TUNE—'*The King of France, he rade a race.*'

AMANG the trees where humming bees
　At buds and flowers were hinging, O
Auld Caledon drew out her drone,
　And to her pipe was singing ; O
'Twas Pibroch, Sang, Strathspey, or
　Reels,
She dirl'd them aff fu' clearly, O
When there cam a yell o' foreign squeels,
　That dang her tapsalteerie, O—

Their capon craws and queer ha ha's,
　They made our lugs grow eerie ; O
The hungry bike did scrape and pike
　Till we were wae and wearie : O—
But a royal ghaist wha ance was cas'd
　A prisoner aughteen year awa,
He fir'd a fiddler in the north
　That dang them tapsalteerie, O.

*　　*　　*　　*

WHEN FIRST I CAME TO STEWART KYLE.

TUNE—'*I had a horse and I had nae mair.*'

WHEN first I came to Stewart Kyle,
　My mind it was na steady,
Where'er I gaed, where'er I rade,
　A mistress still I had aye :
But when I came roun' by Mauchline
　town,
　Not dreadin' onie body,
My heart was caught before I thought,
　And by a Mauchline lady.

*　　*　　*　　*

ON SENSIBILITY.

TO MY DEAR AND MUCH HONOURED FRIEND,
MRS. DUNLOP, OF DUNLOP.

AIR—'*Sensibility.*'

SENSIBILITY, how charming,
　Thou, my friend, canst truly tell ;
But distress, with horrors arming,
　Thou hast also known too well !

Fairest flower, behold the lily,
　Blooming in the sunny ray :
Let the blast sweep o'er the valley,
　See it prostrate on the clay.

Hear the wood-lark charm the forest,
　Telling o'er his little joys ;
Hapless bird ! a prey the surest
　To each pirate of the skies.

Dearly bought the hidden treasure
　Finer feelings can bestow ;
Chords that vibrate sweetest pleasure
　Thrill the deepest notes of woe.

MONTGOMERIE'S PEGGY.

Tune—'Galla Water.'

Altho' my bed were in yon muir,
　Amang the heather, in my plaidie,
Yet happy, happy would I be,
　Had I my dear Montgomerie's Peggy.

When o'er the hill beat surly storms,
　And winter nights were dark and rainy,
I'd seek some dell, and in my arms
　I'd shelter dear Montgomerie's Peggy.

Were I a Baron proud and high,
　And horse and servants waiting ready,
Then a' 'twad gie o' joy to me,
　The sharin't wi' Montgomerie's Peggy.

　　*　　*　　*　　*

ON A BANK OF FLOWERS.

On a bank of flowers, in a summer day,
　For summer lightly drest,
The youthful blooming Nelly lay,
　With love and sleep opprest ;

When Willie, wand'ring thro' the wood,
Who for her favour oft had sued ;
He gaz'd, he wish'd, he fear'd, he blush'd,
　And trembled where he stood.

Her closed eyes, like weapons sheath'd,
　Were seal'd in soft repose ;
Her lips, still as she fragrant breath'd,
　It richer dy'd the rose.

The springing lilies sweetly prest,
Wild-wanton kiss'd her rival breast ;
He gaz'd, he wish'd, he fear'd, he blush'd,
　His bosom ill at rest.

Her robes, light waving in the breeze,
　Her tender limbs embrace !
Her lovely form, her native ease,
　All harmony and grace !

Tumultuous tides his pulses roll,
A faltering ardent kiss he stole ;
He gaz'd, he wish'd, he fear'd, he blush'd,
　And sigh'd his very soul.

As flies the partridge from the brake
　On fear-inspired wings ;
So Nelly, starting, half awake,
　Away affrighted springs :

But Willie follow'd—as he should,
He overtook her in the wood :
He vow'd, he pray'd, he found the maid
　Forgiving all, and good.

O RAGING FORTUNE'S
WITHERING BLAST.

O raging fortune's withering blast
　Has laid my leaf full low ! O
O raging fortune's withering blast
　Has laid my leaf full low ! O.

My stem was fair, my bud was green,
　My blossom sweet did blow ; O
The dew fell fresh, the sun rose mild,
　And made my branches grow ; O.

But luckless fortune's northern storms
　Laid a' my blossoms low, O
But luckless fortune's northern storms
　Laid a' my blossoms low, O.

EVAN BANKS. (See note.)

Tune—'Savourna Delish.'

Slow spreads the gloom my soul desires,
The sun from India's shore retires :
To Evan Banks with temp'rate ray,
Home of my youth, he leads the day.

Oh Banks to me for ever dear !
Oh stream, whose murmurs still I hear !
All, all my hopes of bliss reside
Where Evan mingles with the Clyde.

And she, in simple beauty drest,
Whose image lives within my breast ;
Who trembling heard my parting sigh,
And long pursued me with her eye :

Does she, with heart unchang'd as mine,
Oft in the vocal bowers recline ?
Or, where yon grot o'erhangs the tide,
Muse while the Evan seeks the Clyde ?

Ye lofty Banks that Evan bound,
Ye lavish woods that wave around,
And o'er the stream your shadows throw,
Which sweetly winds so far below ;

What secret charm to mem'ry brings,
All that on Evan's border springs !
Sweet Banks ! ye bloom by Mary's side :
Blest stream ! she views thee haste to
 Clyde.

Can all the wealth of India's coast
Atone for years in absence lost !
Return, ye moments of delight,
With richer treasures bless my sight !

Swift from this desert let me part,
And fly to meet a kindred heart !
No more may aught my steps divide
From that dear stream which flows to
 Clyde !

WOMEN'S MINDS.

TUNE—'*For a' that.*'

THO' women's minds like winter winds
 May shift and turn, and a' that,
The noblest breast adores them maist,
 A consequence I draw that.

  For a' that, and a' that,
   And twice as meikle's a' that,
  The bonie lass that I loe best
   She'll be my ain for a' that.

Great love I bear to all the fair,
 Their humble slave, and a' that ;
But lordly will, I hold it still
 A mortal sin to thraw that.
  For a' that, &c.

B

But there is ane aboon the lave,
 Has wit, and sense, and a' that ;
A bonie lass, I like her best,
 And wha a crime dare ca' that ?
  For a' that, &c.

In rapture sweet this hour we meet,
 Wi' mutual love and a' that ;
But for how lang the flie may stang,
 Let inclination law that.
  For a' that, &c.

Their tricks and craft hae put me daft,
 They've ta'en me in, and a' that ;
But clear your decks, and here's 'The
  Sex !'
 I like the jades for a' that.
  For a' that, &c.

TO MARY IN HEAVEN.

TUNE—'*Miss Forbes' farewell to Banff.*'

THOU lingering star, with less'ning ray,
 That lov'st to greet the early morn,
Again thou usher'st in the day
 My Mary from my soul was torn.
O Mary ! dear departed shade !
 Where is thy place of blissful rest ?
Seest thou thy lover lowly laid ?
 Hear'st thou the groans that rend his
  breast ?

That sacred hour can I forget ?
 Can I forget the hallow'd grove,
Where by the winding Ayr we met,
 To live one day of parting love ?
Eternity will not efface
 Those records dear of transports past ;
Thy image at our last embrace ;
 Ah ! little thought we 'twas our last !

Ayr gurgling kiss'd his pebbled shore,
 O'erhung with wild woods, thick'ning
  green ;
The fragrant birch, and hawthorn hoar,
 Twin'd am'rous round the raptur'd
  scene.
The flowers sprang wanton to be prest,
 The birds sang love on ev'ry spray,
Till too, too soon, the glowing west
 Proclaim'd the speed of winged day.

F

Still o'er these scenes my mem'ry wakes,
    And fondly broods with miser care !
Time but the impression deeper makes,
    As streams their channels deeper wear.
My Mary, dear departed shade !
    Where is thy blissful place of rest ?
Seest thou thy lover lowly laid ?
    Hear'st thou the groans that rend his
        breast ?

TO MARY.

COULD aught of song declare my pains,
    Could artful numbers move thee,
The Muse should tell, in labour'd strains,
    O Mary, how I love thee !

They who but feign a wounded heart
    May teach the lyre to languish ;
But what avails the pride of art,
    When wastes the soul with anguish ?

Then let the sudden bursting sigh
    The heart-felt pang discover ;
And in the keen, yet tender eye,
    O read th' imploring lover !

For well I know thy gentle mind
    Disdains art's gay disguising ;
Beyond what fancy e'er refin'd,
    The voice of nature prizing.

O LEAVE NOVELS.

O LEAVE novels, ye Mauchline belles,
    Ye're safer at your spinning wheel ;
Such witching books are baited hooks
    For rakish rooks, like Rob Mossgiel.

Your fine Tom Jones and Grandisons,
    They make your youthful fancies reel,
They heat your brains, and fire your veins,
    And then you're prey for Rob Moss-
        giel.

Beware a tongue that's smoothly hung ;
    A heart that warmly seems to feel ;
That feeling heart but acts a part,
    'Tis rakish art in Rob Mossgiel.

The frank address, the soft caress,
    Are worse than poison'd darts of steel,
The frank address, and politesse,
    Are all finesse in Rob Mossgiel.

ADDRESS TO GENERAL DUMOURIER.

A PARODY ON ROBIN ADAIR.

YOU'RE welcome to Despots, Dumou-
    rier ;
You're welcome to Despots, Dumourier ;
How does Dampière do ?
Aye, and Bournonville too ?
Why did they not come along with you,
    Dumourier ?

I will fight France with you, Dumourier ;
I will fight France with you, Dumourier ;
I will fight France with you,
I will take my chance with you ;
By my soul I'll dance a dance with you,
    Dumourier.

Then let us fight about, Dumourier ;
Then let us fight about, Dumourier ;
Then let us fight about,
Till freedom's spark is out,
Then we'll be damn'd no doubt—Du-
    mourier.

SWEETEST MAY.

SWEETEST May, let love inspire thee ;
Take a heart which he designs thee ;
As thy constant slave regard it ;
For its faith and truth reward it.

Proof o' shot to birth or money,
Not the wealthy, but the bonie ;
Not high-born, but noble-minded,
In love's silken band can bind it !

ONE NIGHT AS I DID WANDER.

TUNE—'*John Anderson my Jo.*'

ONE night as I did wander,
    When corn begins to shoot,
I sat me down to ponder,
    Upon an auld tree root :

Auld Ayr ran by before me,
    And bicker'd to the seas ;
A cushat crooded o'er me
    That echoed thro' the braes.
      *   *   *   *

THE WINTER IT IS PAST.

A FRAGMENT.

THE winter it is past, and the simmer comes at last,
　And the small birds sing on every tree ;
Now every thing is glad, while I am very sad,
　Since my true love is parted from me.

The rose upon the brier by the waters running clear,
　May have charms for the linnet or the bee ;
Their little loves are blest, and their little hearts at rest,
　But my true love is parted from me.

FRAGMENT.

HER flowing locks, the raven's wing,
　Adown her neck and bosom hing ;
How sweet unto that breast to cling,
　And round that neck entwine her !

Her lips are roses wet wi' dew !
　O, what a feast her bonie mou !
Her cheeks a mair celestial hue,
　A crimson still diviner !

THE CHEVALIER'S LAMENT.

TUNE—'*Captain O'Kean.*'

THE small birds rejoice in the green leaves returning,
　The murmuring streamlet winds clear thro' the vale ;
The hawthorn trees blow in the dews of the morning,
　And wild scatter'd cowslips bedeck the green dale :

But what can give pleasure, or what can seem fair,
　While the lingering moments are number'd by care ?
No flowers gaily springing, nor birds sweetly singing,
　Can soothe the sad bosom of joyless despair.

The deed that I dar'd could it merit their malice,
　A King or a Father to place on his throne ?
His right are these hills, and his right are these valleys,
　Where the wild beasts find shelter, but I can find none.

But 'tis not my sufferings thus wretched, forlorn,
　My brave gallant friends, 'tis your ruin I mourn :
Your deeds prov'd so loyal in hot bloody trial,
　Alas ! can I make you no sweeter return ?

THE BELLES OF MAUCHLINE.

TUNE—'*Bonnie Dundee.*'

IN Mauchline there dwells six proper young Belles,
　The pride of the place and it's neighbourhood a',
Their carriage and dress, a stranger would guess,
　In Lon'on or Paris they'd gotten it a' :

Miss Miller is fine, Miss Markland's divine,
　Miss Smith she has wit, and Miss Betty is braw :
There's beauty and fortune to get wi' Miss Morton,
　But Armour's the jewel for me o' them a'.

R 2

THE TARBOLTON LASSES.

If ye gae up to yon hill-tap,
  Ye'll there see bonie Peggy;
She kens her father is a laird,
  And she forsooth's a leddy.

There Sophy tight, a lassie bright,
  Besides a handsome fortune :
Wha canna win her in a night,
  Has little art in courting.

Gae down by Faile, and taste the ale,
  And tak a look o' Mysie ;
She's dour and din, a deil within,
  But aiblins she may please ye.

If she be shy, her sister try,
  Ye'll maybe fancy Jenny,
If ye'll dispense wi' want o' sense—
  She kens hersel she's bonie.

As ye gae up by yon hill-side,
  Speer in for bonie Bessy ;
She'll gi'e ye a beck, and bid ye light,
  And handsomely address ye.

There's few sae bony, nane sae gude,
  In a' King George' dominion ;
If ye should doubt the truth o' this—
  It's Bessy's ain opinion !

THE TARBOLTON LASSES.

In Tarbolton, ye ken, there are proper young men,
  And proper young lasses and a', man ;
But ken ye the Ronalds that live in the Bennals,
  They carry the gree frae them a', man.

Their father's a laird, and weel he can spare 't,
  Braid money to tocher them a', man,
To proper young men, he'll clink in the hand
  Gowd guineas a hunder or twa, man.

There's ane they ca' Jean, I'll warrant ye've seen
  As bonie a lass or as braw, man,
But for sense and guid taste she'll vie wi' the best,
  And a conduct that beautifies a', man.

The charms o' the min', the langer they shine,
  The mair admiration they draw, man ;
While peaches and cherries, and roses and lilies,
  They fade and they wither awa, man.

If ye be for Miss Jean, tak this frae a frien',
  A hint o' a rival or twa, man,
The Laird o' Blackbyre wad gang through the fire,
  If that wad entice her awa, man.

The Laird o' Braehead has been on his speed,
  For mair than a towmond or twa, man,
The Laird o' the Ford will straught on a board,
  If he canna get her at a', man.

Then Anna comes in, the pride o' her kin,
  The boast of our bachelors a', man :
Sae sonsy and sweet, sae fully complete,
  She steals our affections awa, man.

If I should detail the pick and the wale
    O' lasses that live here awa, man,
The fault wad be mine, if they didna shine,
    The sweetest and best o' them a', man.

I lo'e her mysel, but darena weel tell,
    My poverty keeps me in awe, man,
For making o' rhymes, and working at times,
    Does little or naething at a', man.

Yet I wadna choose to let her refuse,
    Nor ha'e 't in her power to say na, man,
For though I be poor, unnoticed, obscure,
    My stomach's as proud as them a', man.

Though I canna ride in weel-booted pride,
    And flee o'er the hills like a craw, man,
I can haud up my head wi' the best o' the breed,
    Though fluttering ever so braw, man.

My coat and my vest, they are Scotch o' the best,
    O' pairs o' guid breeks I ha'e twa, man,
And stockings and pumps to put on my stumps,
    And ne'er a wrang steek in them a', man.

My sarks they are few, but five o' them new,
    Twal' hundred, as white as the snaw, man,
A ten-shilling's hat, a Holland cravat ;
    There are no mony poets sae braw, man.

I never had frien's, weel stockit in means,
    To leave me a hundred or twa, man,
Nae weel tochered aunts, to wait on their drants,
    And wish them in hell for it a', man.

I never was canny for hoarding o' money,
    Or claughtin't together at a', man,
I've little to spend, and naething to lend,
    But deevil a shilling I awe, man.
    *   *   *   *   *

HERE'S A HEALTH TO THEM THAT'S AWA.

HERE'S a health to them that's awa,
Here's a health to them that's awa ;
And wha winna wish guid luck to our
    cause,
May never guid luck be their fa' !
It's guid to be merry and wise,
It's guid to be honest and true,
It's guid to support Caledonia's cause,
And bide by the buff and the blue.

Here's a health to them that's awa,
Here's a health to them that's awa,
Here's a health to Charlie the chief o'
    the clan,
Altho' that his band be but sma'.
May liberty meet wi' success !
May prudence protect her frae evil !
May tyrants and tyranny tine in the mist,
And wander their way to the devil !

Here's a health to them that's awa,
Here's a health to them that's awa ;
Here's a health to Tammie, the Norland
    laddie,
That lives at the lug o' the law !
Here's freedom to him that wad read,
Here's freedom to him that wad write !
There's nane ever fear'd that the truth
    should be heard,
But they wham the truth wad indite.
Here's a health to them that's awa,
Here's a health to them that's awa,
Here's Chieftain M'Leod, a Chieftain
    worth gowd,
Tho' bred among mountains o' snaw !

I'M OWRE YOUNG TO MARRY YET.

I AM my mammie's ae bairn,
    Wi' unco folk I weary, Sir ;
And lying in a man's bed,
    I'm fley'd wad mak me eerie, Sir.

CHORUS.

I'm owre young, I'm owre young,
    I'm owre young to marry yet ;
I'm owre young, 'twad be a sin
    To tak me frae my mammie yet.

My mammie coft me a new gown,
    The kirk maun hae the gracing o't ;
Were I to lie wi' you, kind Sir,
    I'm fear'd ye'd spoil the lacing o't.
        I'm owre young, &c.

Hallowmas is come and gane,
    The nights are lang in winter, Sir ;
And you an' I in ae bed,
    In troth I dare na venture, Sir.
        I'm owre young, &c.

Fu' loud and shrill the frosty wind
    Blaws thro' the leafless timmer, Sir ;
But if ye come this gate again,
    I'll aulder be gin simmer, Sir.
        I'm owre young, &c.

DAMON AND SYLVIA.

TUNE—'*The tither morn, as I forlorn.*'

YON wand'ring rill, that marks the hill,
    And glances o'er the brae, Sir :
Slides by a bower where monie a flower
    Sheds fragrance on the day, Sir.

There Damon lay, with Sylvia gay ;
    To love they thought nae crime, Sir ;
The wild-birds sang, the echoes rang,
    While Damon's heart beat time, Sir.

MY LADY'S GOWN THERE'S GAIRS UPON'T.

CHORUS.

My lady's gown there's gairs upon't,
    And gowden flowers sae rare
        upon't ;
But Jenny's jimps and jirkinet,
    My lord thinks muckle mair upon't.

MY lord a-hunting he is gane,
But hounds or hawks wi' him are nane,
By Colin's cottage lies his game,
If Colin's Jenny be at hame.
        My lady's gown, &c.

My lady's white, my lady's red,
And kith and kin o' Cassillis' blude,
But her ten-pund lands o' tocher guid
Were a' the charms his lordship lo'ed.
        My lady's gown, &c.

Out o'er yon muir, out o'er yon moss,
Whare gor-cocks thro' the heather pass,
There wons auld Colin's bonie lass,
A lily in a wilderness.
        My lady's gown, &c.

Sae sweetly move her genty limbs,
Like music notes o' lover's hymns :
The diamond dew in her een sae blue,
Where laughing love sae wanton swims.
        My lady's gown, &c.

My lady's dink, my lady's drest,
The flower and fancy o' the west ;
But the lassie that a man lo'es best,
O that's the lass to make him blest.
        My lady's gown, &c.

O AY MY WIFE SHE DANG ME.

CHORUS.

O ay my wife she dang me,
An' aft my wife did bang me ;
If ye gie a woman a' her will,
Guid faith she'll soon o'ergang ye.

ON peace and rest my mind was bent,
And fool I was I marry'd ;
But never honest man's intent
As cursedly miscarry'd.

Some sa'r o' comfort still at last,
When a' thir days are done, man,
My pains o' hell on earth are past,
I'm sure o' bliss aboon, man.
O ay my wife, &c.

THE BANKS OF NITH.

A BALLAD.

To thee, lov'd Nith, thy gladsome plains,
Where late wi' careless thought I
rang'd,
Though prest wi' care and sunk in woe,
To thee I bring a heart unchang'd.

I love thee, Nith, thy banks and braes,
Tho' mem'ry there my bosom tear ;
For there he rov'd that brake my heart,
Yet to that heart, ah, still how dear !

BONIE PEG.

As I came in by our gate end,
As day was waxin' weary,
O wha came tripping down the street,
But bonie Peg, my dearie !

Her air sae sweet, and shape complete,
Wi' nae proportion wanting,
The Queen of Love did never move
Wi' motion mair enchanting.

Wi' linked hands, we took the sands
Adown yon winding river ;
And, oh ! that hour and broomy bower,
Can I forget it ever ?

O LAY THY LOOF IN MINE, LASS.

CHORUS.

O lay thy loof in mine, lass,
In mine, lass, in mine, lass,
And swear in thy white hand, lass,
That thou wilt be my ain.

A SLAVE to love's unbounded sway,
He aft has wrought me meikle wae ;
But now he is my deadly fae,
Unless thou be my ain.
O lay thy loof, &c.

There's monie a lass has broke my rest,
That for a blink I hae lo'ed best ;
But thou art Queen within my breast,
For ever to remain.
O lay thy loof, &c.

O GUID ALE COMES.

CHORUS.

O guid ale comes, and guid ale goes,
Guid ale gars me sell my hose,
Sell my hose, and pawn my shoon,
Guid ale keeps my heart aboon.

I HAD sax owsen in a pleugh,
They drew a' weel eneugh,
I sell'd them a' just ane by ane ;
Guid ale keeps my heart aboon.

Guid ale hauds me bare and busy,
Gars me moop wi' the servant hizzie,
Stand i' the stool when I hae done,
Guid ale keeps my heart aboon.
O guid ale comes, &c.

O WHY THE DEUCE.

EXTEMPORE. APRIL, 1782.

O WHY the deuce should I repine,
And be an ill foreboder ?
I'm twenty-three, and five feet nine—
I'll go and be a sodger.

I gat some gear wi' meikle care,
I held it weel thegither ;
But now it's gane and something mair,
I'll go and be a sodger.

POLLY STEWART.

TUNE—*' Ye're welcome, Charley Stewart.'*

CHORUS.

O lovely Polly Stewart,
  O charming Polly Stewart,
There's ne'er a flower that blooms in
    May,
  That's half so fair as thou art.

THE flower it blaws, it fades, it fa's,
  And art can ne'er renew it ;
But worth and truth eternal youth
  Will gie to Polly Stewart.

May he, whase arms shall fauld thy
    charms,
  Possess a leal and true heart ;
To him be given to ken the heaven
  He grasps in Polly Stewart.
    O lovely, &c.

ROBIN SHURE IN HAIRST.

CHORUS.

Robin shure in hairst,
  I shure wi' him,
Fient a heuk had I,
  Yet I stack by him.

I GAED up to Dunse,
  To warp a wab o' plaiden,
At his daddie's yett,
  Wha met me but Robin.

Was na Robin bauld,
  Tho' I was a cotter,
Play'd me sick a trick
  And me the eller's dochter ?

Robin promis'd me
  A' my winter vittle ;
Fient haet he had but three
  Goose feathers and a whittle.
    Robin shure, &c.

THE FIVE CARLINS.

AN ELECTION BALLAD. 1789.

TUNE—*' Chevy Chase.'*

THERE were five Carlins in the south,
  They fell upon a scheme,
To send a lad to Lon'on town
  To bring us tidings hame.

Not only bring us tidings hame,
  But do our errands there,
And aiblins gowd and honour baith
  Might be that laddie's share.

There was Maggie by the banks o'
    Nith,
  A dame wi' pride eneugh ;
And Marjorie o' the monie Lochs,
  A Carlin auld an' teugh.

And blinkin Bess o' Annandale,
  That dwells near Solway side,
And whisky Jean that took her gill
  In Galloway so wide.

And auld black Joan frae Creighton
    peel,
  O' gipsy kith an' kin,
Five wighter Carlins were na foun'
  The south kintra within.

To send a lad to Lon'on town
  They met upon a day,
And monie a Knight and monie a
    Laird,
  That errand fain would gae.

O ! monie a Knight and monie a Laird,
  This errand fain would gae ;
But nae ane could their fancy please,
  O ! ne'er a ane but twae.

The first ane was a belted Knight,
  Bred o' a border clan,
An' he wad gae to Lon'on town,
  Might nae man him withstan' :

And he wad do their errands weel,
  And meikle he wad say,
And ilka ane at Lon'on court
  Wad bid to him guid day.

Then neist came in a sodger youth,
  And spak wi' modest grace,
An' he wad gae to Lon'on town,
  If sae their pleasure was.

He wad na hecht them courtly gift,
  Nor meikle speech pretend ;
But he wad hecht an honest heart
  Wad ne'er desert his friend.

Now wham to choose and wham refuse,
  To strife thae Carlins fell ;
For some had gentle folk to please,
  And some wad please themsel.

Then out spak mim-mou'd Meg o' Nith,
  An' she spak out wi' pride,
An' she wad send the sodger youth
  Whatever might betide.

For the auld guidman o' Lon'on court
  She didna care a pin,
But she wad send the sodger youth
  To greet his eldest son.

Then up sprang Bess o' Annandale :
  A deadly aith she's ta'en,
That she wad vote the border Knight,
  Tho' she should vote her lane.

For far aff fowls hae feathers fair,
  An' fools o' change are fain :
But I hae tried the border Knight,
  I'll try him yet again.

Says auld black Joan frae Creighton
    peel,
  A Carlin stoor and grim,
The auld guidman or young guidman,
  For me may sink or swim !

For fools may freit o' right and wrang,
  While knaves laugh them to scorn :
But the sodgers' friends hae blawn the
    best,
  Sae he shall bear the horn.

Then whisky Jean spak o'er her drink,
  Ye weel ken kimmers a'
The auld guidman o' Lon'on court,
  His back's been at the wa'.

And monie a friend that kiss'd his caup,
  Is now a frammit wight ;
But it's ne'er sae wi' whisky Jean,—
  We'll send the border Knight.

Then slow raise Marjorie o' the Lochs,
  And wrinkled was her brow ;
Her ancient weed was russet gray,
  Her auld Scots bluid was true.

There's some great folks set light by me,
  I set as light by them ;
But I will send to Lon'on town,
  Wha I lo'e best at hame.

So how this weighty plea will end,
  Nae mortal wight can tell ;
God grant the King and ilka man
  May look weel to himsel' !

THE DEUK'S DANG O'ER MY DADDIE.

THE bairns gat out wi' an unco shout,
  The deuk's dang o'er my daddie, O !
The fient ma care, quo' the feirie auld
    wife,
  He was but a paidlin body, O !
He paidles out, and he paidles in,
  An' he paidles late and early, O ;
This seven lang years I hae lien by his
    side,
  An' he is but a fusionless carlie, O.

O haud your tongue, my feirie auld
    wife,
  O haud your tongue now, Nansie, O :
I've seen the day, and sae hae ye,
  Ye wadna been sae donsie, O ;
I've seen the day ye butter'd my brose,
  And cuddl'd me late and earlie, O ;
But downa do's come o'er me now,
  And, oh, I find it sairly, O !

THE LASS THAT MADE THE BED TO ME.

WHEN Januar' wind was blawing cauld,
  As to the north I took my way,
The mirksome night did me enfauld,
  I knew na where to lodge till day.

By my good luck a maid I met,
  Just in the middle o' my care ;
And kindly she did me invite
  To walk into a chamber fair.

I bow'd fu' low unto this maid,
  And thank'd her for her courtesie ;
I bow'd fu' low unto this maid,
  And bade her mak a bed to me.

She made the bed baith large and wide,
  Wi' twa white hands she spread it
    down ;
She put the cup to her rosy lips,
  And drank, ' Young man, now sleep
    ye soun.'

She snatch'd the candle in her hand,
  And frae my chamber went wi' speed ;
But I call'd her quickly back again
  To lay some mair below my head.

A cod she laid below my head,
  And served me wi' due respect ;
And to salute her wi' a kiss,
  I put my arms about her neck.

' Haud aff your hands, young man,'
    she says,
  ' And dinna sae uncivil be :
If ye hae onie love for me,
  O wrang na my virginitie !'

Her hair was like the links o' gowd,
  Her teeth were like the ivorie ;
Her cheeks like lilies dipt in wine,
  The lass that made the bed to me.

Her bosom was the driven snaw,
  Twa drifted heaps sae fair to see ;
Her limbs the polish'd marble stane,
  The lass that made the bed to me.

I kiss'd her owre and owre again,
  And aye she wist na what to say ;
I laid her between me and the wa',—
  The lassie thought na lang till day.

Upon the morrow when we rose,
  I thank'd her for her courtesie ;
But aye she blush'd, and aye she sigh'd,
  And said, ' Alas ! ye've ruin'd me.'

I clasp'd her waist, and kiss'd her syne,
  While the tear stood twinkling in her
    ee ;
I said, ' My lassie, dinna cry,
  For ye ay shall make the bed to me.'

She took her mither's Holland sheets,
  And made them a' in sarks to me :
Blythe and merry may she be,
  The lass that made the bed to me.

The bonie lass made the bed to me,
  The braw lass made the bed to me :
I'll ne'er forget till the day I die,
  The lass that made the bed to me !

THE UNION.

Tune—'*Such a parcel of rogues in a nation.*'

FAREWEEL to a' our Scottish fame,
  Fareweel our ancient glory !
Fareweel even to the Scottish name,
  Sae fam'd in martial story !
Now Sark rins o'er the Solway sands,
  And Tweed rins to the ocean,
To mark where England's province
    stands ;
  Such a parcel of rogues in a nation.

What guile or force could not subdue,
  Through many warlike ages,
Is wrought now by a coward few,
  For hireling traitors' wages.
The English steel we could disdain,
  Secure in valour's station,
But English gold has been our bane ;
  Such a parcel of rogues in a nation !

O would, or had I seen the day
  That treason thus could sell us,
My auld grey head had lien in clay,
  Wi' Bruce and loyal Wallace !
But pith and power, till my last hour
  I'll mak this declaration,
We're bought and sold for English gold :
  Such a parcel of rogues in a nation !

THERE WAS A BONIE LASS.

THERE was a bonie lass, and a bonie,
    bonie lass,
  And she lo'ed her bonie laddie dear ;
Till war's loud alarms tore her laddie
    frae her arms,
  Wi' monie a sigh and tear.

Over sea, over shore, where the cannons
    loudly roar,
  He still was a stranger to fear :
And nocht could him quell, or his
    bosom assail,
  But the bonie lass he lo'ed sae dear.

MY HARRY WAS A GALLANT GAY.

TUNE—'*Highlander's lament.*'

My Harry was a gallant gay,
  Fu' stately strade he on the plain!
But now he's banish'd far away,
  I'll never see him back again.

CHORUS.

O for him back again,
  O for him back again,
I wad gie a' Knockhaspie's land,
  For Highland Harry back again.

When a' the lave gae to their
    bed,
  I wander dowie up the glen ;
I sit me down and greet my fill,
  And ay I wish him back again.
    O for him, &c.

O were some villains hangit high,
  And ilka body had their ain,
Then I might see the joyfu' sight,
  My Highland Harry back again ¦
    O for him, &c.

TIBBIE DUNBAR.

TUNE — '*Johnny M'Gill.*'

O WILT thou go wi' me, sweet Tibbie Dunbar ?
O wilt thou go' wi' me, sweet Tibbie Dunbar ?
Wilt thou ride on a horse, or be drawn in a car,
Or walk by my side, O sweet Tibbie Dunbar ?
I care na thy daddie, his lands and his money,
I care na thy kin, sae high and sae lordly :
But say thou wilt hae me for better for waur,
And come in thy coatie, sweet Tibbie Dunbar.

WEE WILLIE.

WEE Willie Gray, and his leather wallet ;
Peel a willow-wand, to be him boots and jacket :
The rose upon the briar will be him trouse and doublet,
The rose upon the briar will be him trouse and doublet !
Wee Willie Gray, and his leather wallet ;
Twice a lily flower will be him sark and cravat ;
Feathers of a flee wad feather up his bonnet,
Feathers of a flee wad feather up his bonnet.

CRAIGIE-BURN-WOOD.

CHORUS.

Beyond thee, dearie, beyond thee,
    dearie,
And O to be lying beyond thee,
O sweetly, soundly, weel may he sleep,
  That's laid in the bed beyond thee.

SWEET closes the evening on Craigie-
    burn-wood,
And blythely awakens the morrow ;
But the pride of the spring in the Craigie-
    burn-wood
Can yield to me nothing but sorrow.
  Beyond thee, &c.

I see the spreading leaves and flowers,
  I hear the wild birds singing ;
But pleasure they hae nane for me,
  While care my heart is wringing.
    Beyond thee, &c.

I canna tell, I maun na tell,
  I dare na for your anger;
But secret love will break my heart
  If I conceal it langer.
    Beyond thee, &c.

I see thee gracefu', straight and tall,
  I see thee sweet and bonie,
But oh, what will my torments be,
  If thou refuse thy Johnie !
    Beyond thee, &c.

To see thee in anither's arms,
    In love to lie and languish,
'Twad be my dead, that will be seen,
    My heart wad burst wi' anguish.
        Beyond thee, &c.

But, Jeanie, say thou wilt be mine,
    Say, thou lo'es nane before me ;
An' a' my days o' life to come,
    I'll gratefully adore thee.
        Beyond thee, &c.

HERE'S HIS HEALTH IN WATER!

Tune—' *The job of journey-work.*'

Altho' my back be at the wa',
    And tho' he be the fautor ;
Altho' my back be at the wa',
    Yet, here's his health in water !
O ! wae gae by his wanton sides,
    Sae brawlie he could flatter ;
Till for his sake I'm slighted sair,
    And dree the kintra clatter.
But tho' my back be at the wa',
    And tho' he be the fautor ;
But tho' my back be at the wa',
    Yet, here's his health in water !

AS DOWN THE BURN THEY TOOK THEIR WAY.

As down the burn they took their way,
    And thro' the flowery dale ;
His cheeks to hers he aft did lay,
    And love was ay the tale.

With ' Mary, when shall we return,
    Sic pleasure to renew ?'
Quoth Mary, ' Love, I like the burn,
    And ay shall follow you.'

LADY ONLIE.

Tune—' *Ruffian's rant.*'

A' the lads o' Thornie-bank,
    When they gae to the shore o' Bucky,
They'll step in an' tak' a pint
    Wi' Lady Onlie, honest Lucky !
    Ladie Onlie, honest Lucky,
        Brews good ale at shore o' Bucky;
    I wish her sale for her gude ale,
        The best on a' the shore o' Bucky.

Her house sae bien, her curch sae clean,
    I wat she is a dainty chucky ;
And cheerlie blinks the ingle-gleed
    Of Lady Onlie, honest Lucky !
    Lady Onlie, honest Lucky,
        Brews gude ale at shore o' Bucky ;
    I wish her sale for her gude ale,
        The best on a' the shore o' Bucky.

AS I WAS A WANDERING.

Tune—' *Rinn meudial mo mhealladh.*'

As I was a wand'ring ae midsummer e'enin',
    The pipers and youngsters were making their game ;
Amang them I spied my faithless fause lover,
    Which bled a' the wounds o' my dolour again.

Weel, since he has left me, may pleasure gae wi' him ;
    I may be distress'd, but I winna complain ;
I flatter my fancy I may get anither,
    My heart it shall never be broken for ane.

I could na get sleeping till dawin' for greetin',
    The tears trickled down like the hail and the rain ;
Had I na got greetin', my heart wad a broken,
    For, oh ! love forsaken's a tormenting pain.

Altho' he has left me for greed o' the siller,
    I dinna envy him the gains he can win ;
I rather wad bear a' the lade o' my sorrow
    Than ever hae acted sae faithless to him.

Weel, since he has left me, may pleasure gae wi' him,
    I may be distress'd, but I winna complain ;
I flatter my fancy I may get anither,
    My heart it shall never be broken for ane.

BANNOCKS O' BARLEY.

TUNE—'*The Killogie.*'

BANNOCKS o' bear meal,
    Bannocks o' barley ;
Here's to the Highlandman's
    Bannocks o' barley.
Wha in a brulzie
    Will first cry a parley ?
Never the lads wi'
    The bannocks o' barley.

Bannocks o' bear meal,
    Bannocks o' barley ;
Here's to the lads wi'
    The bannocks o' barley ;
Wha in his wae-days
    Were loyal to Charlie ?
Wha but the lads wi'
    The bannocks o' barley.

OUR THRISSLES FLOURISHED FRESH AND FAIR.

TUNE — '*Awa Whigs, awa.*'

CHORUS.

Awa Whigs, awa !
Awa Whigs, awa !
Ye're but a pack o' traitor louns,
Ye'll do nae good at a'.

OUR thrissles flourish'd fresh and fair,
    And bonie bloom'd our roses ;
But Whigs came like a frost in June,
    And wither'd a' our posies.

Our ancient crown's fa'n in the dust—
    Deil blin' them wi' the stoure o't ;
And write their names in his black
    beuk,
Wha gae the Whigs the power o't.

Our sad decay in Church and State
    Surpasses my descriving ;
The Whigs came o'er us for a curse,
    And we hae done with thriving.

Grim vengeance lang has ta'en a nap,
    But we may see him wauken ;
Gude help the day when royal heads
    Are hunted like a maukin.

Awa Whigs, awa !
    Awa Whigs, awa !
Ye're but a pack o' traitor louns,
    Ye'll do nae gude at a'.

PEG-A-RAMSEY.

TUNE—'*Cauld is the e'enin' blast.*'

CAULD is the e'enin' blast
    O' Boreas o'er the pool,
And dawin' it is dreary
    When birks are bare at Yule.

O bitter blaws the e'enin' blast
    When bitter bites the frost,
And in the mirk and dreary drift
    The hills and glens are lost.

Ne'er sae murky blew the night
    That drifted o'er the hill,
But bonie Peg-a-Ramsey
    Gat grist to her mill.

COME BOAT ME O'ER TO CHARLIE.

TUNE—'*O'er the water to Charlie.*'

COME boat me o'er, come row me o'er,
    Come boat me o'er to Charlie ;
I'll gie John Ross another bawbee,
    To boat me o'er to Charlie.

We'll o'er the water and o'er the
        sea,
    We'll o'er the water to Charlie ;
Come weal, come woe, we'll gather
        and go,
    And live or die wi' Charlie.

I lo'e weel my Charlie's name,
    Tho' some there be abhor him :
But O, to see auld Nick gaun hame,
    And Charlie's faes before him !

I swear and vow by moon and stars,
    And sun that shines so early,
If I had twenty thousand lives,
    I'd die as aft for Charlie.
    We'll o'er the water and o'er the
        sea,
    We'll o'er the water to Charlie ;
Come weal, come woe, we'll gather
        and go,
    And live or die with Charlie !

BRAW LADS OF GALLA WATER.

TUNE—' *Galla Water.*'

CHORUS.

Braw, braw lads of Galla Water ;
    O braw lads of Galla Water !
I'll kilt my coats aboon my knee,
    And follow my love through the
        water.

SAE fair her hair, sae brent her brow,
Sae bonie blue her een, my dearie ;
Sae white her teeth, sae sweet her mou',
The mair I kiss she's ay my dearie.

O'er yon bank and o'er yon brae,
O'er yon moss amang the heather ;
I'll kilt my coats aboon my knee,
And follow my love through the water.

Down amang the broom, the broom,
Down amang the broom, my dearie,
The lassie lost a silken snood,
    That cost her mony a blirt and bleary.
    Braw, braw lads of Galla Water ;
    O braw lads of Galla Water :
    I'll kilt my coats aboon my knee,
        And follow my love through the
        water.

COMING THROUGH THE RYE.

TUNE—'*Coming through the rye.*'

COMING through the rye, poor body,
    Coming through the rye,
She draiglet a' her petticoatie,
    Coming through the rye.
Jenny's a' wat, poor body,
    Jenny's seldom dry ;
She draiglet a' her petticoatie,
    Coming through the rye.

Gin a body meet a body—
    Coming through the rye ;
Gin a body kiss a body—
    Need a body cry ?

Gin a body meet a body
    Coming through the glen,
Gin a body kiss a body—
    Need the world ken ?
Jenny's a' wat, poor body ;
    Jenny's seldom dry ;
She draiglet a' her petticoatie,
    Coming through the rye.

THE LASS OF ECCLEFECHAN.

TUNE—' *Jacky Latin.*'

GAT ye me, O gat ye me,
    O gat ye me wi' naething ?
Rock and reel, and spinnin' wheel,
    A mickle quarter basin.
Bye attour, my gutcher has
    A hich house and a laigh ane,
A' forbye, my bonie sel',
    The toss of Ecclefechan.

O haud your tongue now, Luckie Laing,
    O haud your tongue and jauner ;
I held the gate till you I met,
    Syne I began to wander :
I tint my whistle and my sang,
    I tint my peace and pleasure ;
But your green graff, now, Luckie
        Laing,
    Wad airt me to my treasure.

THE SLAVE'S LAMENT.

IT was in sweet Senegal that my foes did me enthral,
　For the lands of Virginia, O ;
Torn from that lovely shore, and must never see it more,
　And alas I am weary, weary, O !

All on that charming coast is no bitter snow or frost,
　Like the lands of Virginia, O ;
There streams for ever flow, and there flowers for ever blow,
　And alas I am weary, weary, O !

The burden I must bear, while the cruel scourge I fear,
　In the lands of Virginia, O ;
And I think on friends most dear, with the bitter, bitter tear,
　And alas I am weary, weary, O !

HAD I THE WYTE.

TUNE—' Had I the wyte she bade me.'

HAD I the wyte, had I the wyte,
　Had I the wyte she bade me ;
She watch'd me by the hie-gate side,
　And up the loan she shaw'd me ;
And when I wadna venture in,
　A coward loon she ca'd me ;
Had kirk and state been in the gate,
　I lighted when she bade me.

Sae craftilie she took me ben,
　And bade me make nae clatter ;
'For our ramgunshoch glum gudeman
　Is out and owre the water : '
Whae'er shall say I wanted grace,
　When I did kiss and dawte her,
Let him be planted in my place,
　Syne say I was the fautor.

Could I for shame, could I for shame,
　Could I for shame refused her ?
And wadna manhood been to blame,
　Had I unkindly used her ?
He clawed her wi' the ripplin-kame,
　And blue and bluidy bruised her ;
When sic a husband was frae hame,
　What wife but had excused her ?

I dighted ay her een sae blue,
　And bann'd the cruel randy ;
And weel I wat her willing mou'
　Was e'en like sugar-candy.
A gloamin-shot it was I trow,
　I lighted on the Monday ;
But I cam through the Tysday's dew,
　To wanton Willie's brandy.

HEE BALOU.

TUNE—' The Highland balou.'

HEE balou ! my sweet wee Donald,
Picture o' the great Clanronald ;
Brawlie kens our wanton chief
Wha got my young Highland thief.

Leeze me on thy bonie craigie,
An' thou live, thou'll steal a naigie :
Travel the country thro' and thro',
And bring hame a Carlisle cow.

Thro' the Lawlands, o'er the border,
Weel, my babie, may thou furder :
Herry the louns o' the laigh countree,
Syne to the Highlands hame to me.

HER DADDIE FORBAD.

TUNE—' Jumpin' John.'

HER daddie forbad, her minnie forbad ;
　Forbidden she wadna be :
She wadna trow't, the browst she brew'd
　Wad taste sae bitterlie.
　　The lang lad they ca' Jumpin' John
　　　Beguiled the bonie lassie,
　　The lang lad they ca' Jumpin' John
　　　Beguiled the bonie lassie.

A cow and a cauf, a yowe and a hauf,
　And thretty gude shillin's and three ;
A vera gude tocher, a cotter-man's
　dochter,
　The lass with the bonie black ee.
　　The lang lad they ca' Jumpin' John
　　　Beguiled the bonie lassie,
　　The lang lad they ca' Jumpin John
　　　Beguiled the bonie lassie.

HERE'S TO THY HEALTH, MY BONIE LASS.

Tune—'Laggan Burn.'

HERE'S to thy health, my bonie lass,
  Gude night, and joy be wi' thee;
I'll come nae mair to thy bower door,
  To tell thee that I lo'e thee.
O dinna think, my pretty pink,
  But I can live without thee:
I vow and swear I dinna care
  How lang ye look about ye.

Thou'rt ay sae free informing me
  Thou hast nae mind to marry;
I'll be as free informing thee
  Nae time hae I to tarry.
I ken thy friends try ilka means,
  Frae wedlock to delay thee;
Depending on some higher chance—
  But fortune may betray thee.

I ken they scorn my low estate,
  But that does never grieve me;
But I'm as free as any he,
  Sma' siller will relieve me.
I count my health my greatest wealth,
  Sae lang as I'll enjoy it:
I'll fear nae scant, I'll bode nae want,
  As lang's I get employment.

But far aff fowls hae feathers fair,
  And ay until ye try them:
Tho' they seem fair, still have a care,
  They may prove waur than I am.
But at twal at night, when the moon
    shines bright,
  My dear, I'll come and see thee;
For the man that lo'es his mistress weel
  Nae travel makes him weary.

HEY, THE DUSTY MILLER.

Tune—'The Dusty Miller.'

HEY, the dusty miller,
  And his dusty coat;
He will win a shilling,
  Or he spend a groat.
    Dusty was the coat,
    Dusty was the colour,
    Dusty was the kiss
      That I got frae the miller.

Hey, the dusty miller,
  And his dusty sack;
Leeze me on the calling
  Fills the dusty peck.
    Fills the dusty peck,
      Brings the dusty siller;
    I wad gie my coatie
      For the dusty miller.

THE CARDIN' O'T.

Tune—'Salt Fish and Dumplings.'

I COFT a stane o' haslock woo',
  To make a coat to Johnny o't;
For Johnny is my only jo,
  I lo'e him best of ony yet.
    The cardin' o't, the spinnin' o't;
      The warpin' o't, the winnin' o't;
    When ilka ell cost me a groat,
      The tailor staw the lynin o't.

For though his locks be lyart gray,
  And though his brow be beld aboon;
Yet I hae seen him on a day,
  The pride of a' the parishen.
    The cardin' o't, the spinnin' o't,
      The warpin' o't, the winnin' o't;
    When ilka ell cost me a groat,
      The tailor staw the lynin o't.

THE JOYFUL WIDOWER.

Tune—'Maggy Lauder.'

I MARRIED with a scolding wife
  The fourteenth of November;
She made me weary of my life,
  By one unruly member.
Long did I bear the heavy yoke,
  And many griefs attended;
But, to my comfort be it spoke,
  Now, now her life is ended.

We lived full one-and-twenty years
  A man and wife together;
At length from me her course she steer'd,
  And gone I know not whither:
Would I could guess, I do profess,
  I speak, and do not flatter,
Of all the women in the world,
  I never could come at her.

Her body is bestowèd well,
  A handsome grave does hide her ;
But sure her soul is not in hell,
  The deil would ne'er abide her.
I rather think she is aloft,
  And imitating thunder ;
For why,—methinks I hear her voice
Tearing the clouds asunder.

THENIEL MENZIE'S BONIE MARY.

TUNE—'*The Ruffian's rant.*'

IN coming by the brig o' Dye,
  At Darlet we a blink did tarry ;
As day was dawin in the sky
  We drank a health to bonie Mary.
    Theniel Menzie's bonie Mary,
      Theniel Menzie's bonie Mary ;
    Charlie Gregor tint his plaidie,
      Kissin' Theniel's bonie Mary.

Her een sae bright, her brow sae white,
  Her haffet locks as brown's a berry,
An' ay they dimpled wi' a smile
  The rosy cheeks o' bonie Mary.
    Theniel Menzie's bonie Mary,
      Theniel Menzie's bonie Mary ;
    Charlie Gregor tint his plaidie,
      Kissin' Theniel's bonie Mary.

We lap an' danced the lee-lang day,
  Till piper lads were wae an' weary,
But Charlie gat the spring to pay
  For kissin' Theniel's bonie Mary.
    Theniel Menzie's bonie Mary,
      Theniel Menzie's bonie Mary ;
    Charlie Gregor tint his plaidie,
      Kissin' Theniel's bonie Mary.

THE FAREWELL.

TUNE—'*It was a' for our rightfu' King.*'

IT was a' for our rightfu' King,
  We left fair Scotland's strand ;
It was a' for our rightfu' King
  We e'er saw Irish land,
      My dear ;
  We e'er saw Irish land.
B

Now a' is done that men can do,
  And a' is done in vain ;
My love and native land farewell,
  For I maun cross the main,
      My dear ;
  For I maun cross the main.

He turn'd him right and round about
  Upon the Irish shore ;
And gae his bridle-reins a shake,
  With adieu for evermore,
      My dear ;
  With adieu for evermore.

The sodger from the wars returns,
  The sailor frae the main ;
But I hae parted frae my love,
  Never to meet again,
      My dear ;
  Never to meet again.

When day is gane, and night is come,
  And a' folk bound to sleep ;
I think on him that's far awa',
  The lee-lang night, and weep,
      My dear ;
  The lee-lang night, and weep.

IT IS NA, JEAN, THY BONIE FACE.

TUNE—'*The Maid's Complaint.*'

IT is na, Jean, thy bonie face,
  Nor shape that I admire,
Although thy beauty and thy grace
  Might weel awake desire.
Something, in ilka part o' thee,
  To praise, to love, I find ;
But dear as is thy form to me,
  Still dearer is thy mind.

Nae mair ungen'rous wish I hae,
  Nor stronger in my breast,
Than if I canna mak thee sae,
  At least to see thee blest.
Content am I, if Heaven shall give
  But happiness to thee :
And as wi' thee I'd wish to live,
  For thee I'd bear to die.

S

JAMIE, COME TRY ME.

Tune—'*Jamie, come try me.*'

CHORUS.

Jamie, come try me,
Jamie, come try me ;
If thou would win my love,
Jamie, come try me.

If thou should ask my love,
Could I deny thee ?
If thou would win my love,
Jamie, come try me.

If thou should kiss me, love,
Wha could espy thee ?
If thou wad be my love,
Jamie, come try me.
Jamie, come try me &c.

LANDLADY, COUNT THE LAWIN.

Tune—'*Hey tutti, taiti.*'

Landlady, count the lawin,
The day is near the dawin ;
Ye're a' blind drunk, boys,
And I'm but jolly fou.
Hey tutti, taiti,
How tutti, taiti—
Wha's fou now ?

Cog an' ye were ay fou,
Cog an' ye were ay fou,
I wad sit and sing to you
If ye were ay fou.

Weel may ye a' be !
Ill may we never see !
God bless the King, boys,
And the companie !
Hey tutti, taiti,
How tutti, taiti—
Wha's fou now ?

MY LOVE SHE'S BUT A LASSIE YET.

Tune—'*Lady Badinscoth's reel.*'

My love she's but a lassie yet ;
My love she's but a lassie yet ;
We'll let her stand a year or twa,
She'll no be half sae saucy yet.

I rue the day I sought her, O,
I rue the day I sought her, O ;
Wha gets her needs na say she's woo'd,
But he may say he's bought her, O !

Come, draw a drap o' the best o't yet ;
Come, draw a drap o' the best o't yet ;
Gae seek for pleasure where ye will,
But here I never miss'd it yet.
We're a' dry wi' drinking o't,
We're a' dry wi' drinking o't ;
The minister kiss'd the fiddler's wife,
An' could na preach for thinkin' o't.

MY HEART WAS ANCE.

Tune—'*To the weavers gin ye go.*'

My heart was ance as blythe and free
As simmer days were lang,
But a bonie, westlin weaver lad
Has gart me change my sang.
To the weavers gin ye go, fair
maids,
To the weavers gin ye go ;
I rede you right gang ne'er at
night,
To the weavers gin ye go.

My mither sent me to the town,
To warp a plaiden wab ;
But the weary, weary warpin o't
Has gart me sigh and sab.

A bonie westlin weaver lad
Sat working at his loom ;
He took my heart as wi' a net,
In every knot and thrum.

I sat beside my warpin-wheel,
And ay I ca'd it roun' ;
But every shot and every knock,
My heart it gae a stoun.

The moon was sinking in the west
Wi' visage pale and wan,
As my bonie westlin weaver lad
Convoy'd me through the glen.

But what was said, or what was done,
  Shame fa' me gin I tell ;
But oh ! I fear the kintra soon
  Will ken as weel's mysel.

To the weavers gin ye go, fair maids,
  To the weavers gin ye go ;
I rede you right gang ne'er at night,
  To the weavers gin ye go.

LOVELY DAVIES.

TUNE—*'Miss Muir.'*

O HOW shall I, unskilfu', try
  The poet's occupation,
The tunefu' powers, in happy hours,
  That whisper inspiration ?
Even they maun dare an effort mair,
  Than aught they ever gave us,
Or they rehearse, in equal verse,
  The charms o' lovely Davies.

Each eye it cheers, when she appears,
  Like Phœbus in the morning,
When past the shower, and ev'ry flower
  The garden is adorning.
As the wretch looks o'er Siberia's shore,
  When winter-bound the wave is ;
Sae droops our heart when we maun part
  Frae charming lovely Davies.

Her smile's a gift, frae 'boon the lift,
  That maks us mair than princes ;
A scepter'd hand, a King's command,
  Is in her darting glances :
The man in arms, 'gainst female charms,
  Even he her willing slave is ;
He hugs his chain, and owns the reign
  Of conquering, lovely Davies.

My Muse to dream of such a theme,
  Her feeble powers surrender ;
The eagle's gaze alone surveys
  The sun's meridian splendour :
I wad in vain essay the strain,
  The deed too daring brave is ;
I'll drap the lyre, and mute admire
  The charms o' lovely Davies.

KENMURE'S ON AND AWA.

TUNE — *'O Kenmure's on and awa, Willie.*

O KENMURE'S on and awa, Willie !
  O Kenmure's on and awa !
And Kenmure's lord 's the bravest lord
  That ever Galloway saw.

Success to Kenmure's band, Willie !
  Success to Kenmure's band ;
There's no a heart that fears a Whig
  That rides by Kenmure's hand.

Here's Kenmure's health in wine, Willie !
  Here's Kenmure's health in wine ;
There ne'er was a coward o' Kenmure's
  Nor yet o' Gordon's line.   [blude,

O Kenmure's lads are men, Willie !
  O Kenmure's lads are men ;
Their hearts and swords are metal true—
  And that their faes shall ken.

They'll live or die wi' fame, Willie !
  They'll live or die wi' fame ;
But soon, wi' sounding victorie,
  May Kenmure's lord come hame.

Here's him that's far awa, Willie !
  Here's him that's far awa ;
And here's the flower that I love best—
  The rose that's like the snaw !

THE CAPTAIN'S LADY.

TUNE—*'O mount and go.'*
CHORUS.

O mount and go,
  Mount and make you ready ;
O mount and go,
  And be the Captain's Lady.

WHEN the drums do beat,
  And the cannons rattle,
Thou shalt sit in state,
  And see thy love in battle.

When the vanquish'd foe
  Sues for peace and quiet,
To the shades we'll go,
  And in love enjoy it.

  O mount and go,
    Mount and make you ready ;
  O mount and go,
    And be the Captain's Lady.
              S 2

LADY MARY ANN.

Tune—'*Cragtown's growing.*'

O, Lady Mary Ann
  Looks o'er the castle wa',
She saw three bonie boys
  Playing at the ba';
The youngest he was
  The flower amang them a';
My bonie laddie's young,
  But he's growin' yet.

O father! O father!
  An' ye think it fit,
We'll send him a year
  To the college yet:
We'll sew a green ribbon
  Round about his hat,
And that will let them ken
  He's to marry yet.

Lady Mary Ann
  Was a flower i' the dew,
Sweet was its smell,
  And bonie was its hue!
And the langer it blossom'd
  The sweeter it grew;
For the lily in the bud
  Will be bonier yet.

Young Charlie Cochran
  Was the sprout of an aik;
Bonie and bloomin'
  And straught was its make:
The sun took delight
  To shine for its sake,
And it will be the brag
  O' the forest yet.

The simmer is gane
  When the leaves they were green,
And the days are awa
  That we hae seen:
But far better days
  I trust will come again,
For my bonie laddie's young,
  But he's growin' yet.

THE HIGHLAND WIDOW'S LAMENT.

Oh! I am come to the low countrie,
  Och-on, och-on, och-rie!
Without a penny in my purse,
  To buy a meal to me.

It was nae sae in the Highland hills,
  Och-on, och-on, och-rie!
Nae woman in the country wide
  Sae happy was as me.

For then I had a score o' kye,
  Och-on, och-on, och-rie!
Feeding on yon hills so high,
  And giving milk to me.

And there I had three score o' yowes,
  Och-on, och-on, och-rie!
Skipping on yon bonie knowes,
  And casting woo' to me.

I was the happiest of the clan,
  Sair, sair may I repine;
For Donald was the brawest lad,
  And Donald he was mine.

Till Charlie Stewart cam at last,
  Sae far to set us free;
My Donald's arm was wanted then,
  For Scotland and for me.

Their waefu' fate what need I tell,
  Right to the wrang did yield:
My Donald and his country fell
  Upon Culloden's field.

Oh! I am come to the low countrie,
  Och-on, och-on, och-rie!
Nae woman in the world wide
  Sae wretched now as me.

MERRY HAE I BEEN TEETHIN' A HECKLE.

Tune—'*Lord Breadalbane's March.*'

O MERRY hae I been teethin' a heckle,
  And merry hae I been shapin' a spoon;
O merry hae I been cloutin a kettle,
  And kissin' my Katie when a' was done.

O a' the lang day I ca' at my hammer,
    An' a' the lang day I whistle and sing,
A' the lang night I cuddle my kimmer,
    An' a' the lang night as happy's a King.

Bitter in dool I lickit my winnins,
    O' marrying Bess, to gie her a slave :
Bless'd be the hour she cool'd in her linnens,
    And blythe be the bird that sings on her grave.
Come to my arms, my Katie, my Katie,
    An' come to my arms, and kiss me again !
Drunken or sober, here's to thee, Katie !
    And bless'd be the day I did it again.

RATTLIN', ROARIN' WILLIE.

TUNE—' *Rattlin,' roarin' Willie.'*

O RATTLIN', roarin' Willie,
    O, he held to the fair,
An' for to sell his fiddle,
    An' buy some other ware ;
But parting wi' his fiddle,
    The saut tear blin't his ee ;
And rattlin', roarin' Willie,
    Ye're welcome hame to me !

O Willie, come sell your fiddle,
    O sell your fiddle sae fine ;

O Willie, come sell your fiddle,
    And buy a pint o' wine !
If I should sell my fiddle,
    The warl' would think I was mad ;
For mony a rantin' day
    My fiddle and I hae had.

As I cam by Crochallan,
    I cannily keekit ben—
Rattlin', roarin' Willie
    Was sitting at yon board en',
Sitting at yon board en',
    And amang guid companie ;
Rattlin', roarin' Willie,
    Ye're welcome hame to me !

O MALLY'S MEEK, MALLY'S SWEET.

O MALLY's meek, Mally's sweet,
    Mally's modest and discreet,
Mally's rare, Mally's fair,
    Mally's every way complete.
As I was walking up the street,
    A barefit maid I chanced to meet ;
But O the road was very hard
    For that fair maiden's tender feet.

It were mair meet that those fine feet
    Were weel laced up in silken shoon,
And 'twere more fit that she should sit
    Within yon chariot gilt aboon.

Her yellow hair, beyond compare,
    Comes trinkling down her swan-white neck,
And her two eyes, like stars in skies,
    Would keep a sinking ship frae wreck.
O Mally's meek, Mally's sweet,
    Mally's modest and discreet,
Mally's rare, Mally's fair,
    Mally's every way complete.

SAE FAR AWA.

Tune—'*Dalkeith Maiden Bridge.*'

O SAD and heavy should I part,
  But for her sake sae far awa ;
Unknowing what my way may thwart
  My native land sae far awa.
Thou that of a' things Maker art,
  That form'd this Fair sae far awa,
Gie body strength, then I'll ne'er start
  At this my way sae far awa.

How true is love to pure desert,
  So love to her, sae far awa :
And nocht can heal my bosom's smart,
  While, oh ! she is sae far awa.
Nane other love, nane other dart,
  I feel but her's, sae far awa ;
But fairer never touch'd a heart
  Than her's, the fair sae far awa.

O STEER HER UP.

Tune—'*O steer her up, and haud her gaun.*'

O STEER her up, and haud her gaun—
  Her mother's at the mill, jo ;
And gin she winna take a man,
  E'en let her take her will, jo :
First shore her wi' a kindly kiss,
  And ca' another gill, jo,
And gin she take the thing amiss,
  E'en let her flyte her fill, jo.

O steer her up, and be na blate,
  An' gin she tak it ill, jo,
Then lea'e the lassie till her fate,
  And time nae langer spill, jo :
Ne'er break your heart for ae rebute,
  But think upon it still, jo ;
Then gin the lassie winna do't,
  Ye'll fin' anither will, jo.

O, WHAR DID YE GET.

Tune—'*Bonie Dundee.*'

O, WHAR did ye get that hauver meal bannock ?
  O silly blind body, O dinna ye see ?
I gat it frae a brisk young sodger laddie,
  Between Saint Johnston and bonie Dundee.
O gin I saw the laddie that gae me't !
  Aft has he doudled me on his knee ;
May Heaven protect my bonie Scots laddie,
  And send him safe hame to his babie and me !

My blessin's upon thy sweet wee lippie,
  My blessin's upon thy bonie e'e brie !
Thy smiles are sae like my blythe sodger laddie,
  Thou's ay the dearer and dearer to me !
But I'll big a bower on yon bonie banks,
  Where Tay rins wimplin' by sae clear ;
And I'll cleed thee in the tartan sae fine,
  And mak thee a man like thy daddie dear.

THE FÊTE CHAMPÊTRE.

Tune—'*Killiecrankie.*'

O WHA will to Saint Stephen's house,
  To do our errands there, man ?
O wha will to Saint Stephen's house,
  O' th' merry lads of Ayr, man ?
Or will we send a man-o'-law ?
  Or will we send a sodger ?
Or him wha led o'er Scotland a'
  The meikle Ursa-Major ?

Come, will ye court a noble lord,
  Or buy a score o' lairds, man ?
For worth and honour pawn their word,
  Their vote shall be Glencaird's, man ?
Ane gies them coin, ane gies them wine,
  Anither gies them clatter ;
Anbank, wha guess'd the ladies' taste,
  He gies a Fête Champêtre.

When Love and Beauty heard the news,
  The gay green-woods amang, man ;
Where gathering flowers and busking
    bowers,
  They heard the blackbird's sang,
    man ;
A vow, they seal'd it with a kiss
  Sir Politics to fetter,
As their's alone, the patent-bliss,
  To hold a Fête Champêtre.

Then mounted Mirth, on gleesome wing,
  O'er hill and dale she flew, man ;
Ilk wimpling burn, ilk crystal spring,
  Ilk glen and shaw she knew, man :
She summon'd every social sprite,
  That sports by wood or water,
On th' bonie banks of Ayr to meet,
  And keep this Fête Champêtre.

Cauld Boreas, wi' his boisterous crew,
  Were bound to stakes like kye, man;
And Cynthia's car, o' silver fu',
  Clamb up the starry sky, man :
Reflected beams dwell in the streams,
  Or down the current shatter ;
The western breeze steals through the
    trees,
  To view this Fête Champêtre.

How many a robe sae gaily floats !
  What sparkling jewels glance, man !
To Harmony's enchanting notes,
  As moves the mazy dance, man !
The echoing wood, the winding flood,
  Like Paradise did glitter,
When angels met, at Adam's yett,
  To hold their Fête Champêtre.

When Politics came there, to mix
  And make his ether-stane, man !
He circled round the magic ground,
  But entrance found he nane, man :
He blush'd for shame, he quat his name,
  Forswore it, every letter,
Wi' humble prayer to join and share
  This festive Fête Champêtre.

SIMMER'S A PLEASANT TIME.

Tune—'Ay waukin, O.'

Simmer's a pleasant time,
  Flow'rs of ev'ry colour ;
The water rins o'er the heugh,
  And I long for my true lover.
    Ay waukin O,
      Waukin still and wearie :
    Sleep I can get nane
      For thinking on my dearie.

When I sleep I dream,
  When I wauk I'm eerie ;
Sleep I can get nane
  For thinking on my dearie.

Lanely night comes on,
  A' the lave are sleeping ;
I think on my bonie lad
  And I bleer my een with greetin'.
    Ay waukin O,
      Waukin still and wearie ;
    Sleep I can get nane
      For thinking on my dearie.

THE BLUDE RED ROSE AT YULE MAY BLAW.

Tune—' To daunton me.'

The blude red rose at Yule may blaw,
The simmer lilies bloom in snaw,
The frost may freeze the deepest sea ;
But an auld man shall never daunton me.

To daunton me, and me sae young,
Wi' his fause heart and flatt'ring tongue,
That is the thing you ne'er shall see ;
For an auld man shall never daunton me.

For a' his meal and a' his maut,
For a' his fresh beef and his saut,
For a' his gold and white monie,
An auld man shall never daunton me.

His gear may buy him kye and yowes,
His gear may buy him glens and knowes ;
But me he shall not buy nor fee,
For an auld man shall never daunton me.

He hirples twa fauld as he dow,
Wi' his teethless gab and his auld beld pow,
And the rain rains down frae his red bleer'd ee—
That auld man shall never daunton me.

To daunton me, and me sae young,
Wi' his fause heart and flatt'ring tongue,
That is the thing you ne'er shall see ;
For an auld man shall never daunton me.

THE HIGHLAND LADDIE.

Tune—'If thou'lt play me fair play.'

THE boniest lad that e'er I saw,
　Bonie laddie, Highland laddie,
Wore a plaid and was fu' braw,
　Bonie Highland laddie.
On his head a bonnet blue,
　Bonie laddie, Highland laddie,
His royal heart was firm and true,
　Bonie Highland laddie.

Trumpets sound and cannons roar,
　Bonie lassie, Lawland lassie,
And a' the hills wi' echoes roar,
　Bonie Lawland lassie.
Glory, Honour, now invite,
　Bonie lassie, Lawland lassie,
For Freedom and my King to fight,
　Bonie Lawland lassie.

The sun a backward course shall take,
　Bonie laddie, Highland laddie,
Ere aught thy manly courage shake ;
　Bonie Highland laddie.
Go, for yoursel procure renown,
　Bonie laddie, Highland laddie,
And for your lawful King his crown,
　Bonie Highland laddie !

THE COOPER O' CUDDIE.

Tune—'Bab at the bowster.'

THE cooper o' Cuddie cam here
　awa,
And ca'd the girrs out owre us a'—
And our gude-wife has gotten a ca'
　That anger'd the silly gude-man, O.
We'll hide the cooper behind the door,
Behind the door, behind the door ;
We'll hide the cooper behind the door,
　And cover him under a mawn, O.

He sought them out, he sought them in,
Wi', Deil hae her ! and, Deil hae
　him !
But the body was sae doited and blin',
　He wist na where he was gaun, O.

They cooper'd at e'en, they cooper'd at
　morn,
Till our gude-man has gotten the scorn ;
On ilka brow she's planted a horn,
　And swears that they shall stan', O.
We'll hide the cooper behind the door,
Behind the door, behind the door ;
We'll hide the cooper behind the door,
　And cover him under a mawn, O.

NITHSDALE'S WELCOME HAME.

THE noble Maxwells and their powers
　Are coming o'er the border,
And they'll gae bigg Terreagle's towers,
　An' set them a' in order,
And they declare Terreagle's fair,
　For their abode they choose it;
There's no a heart in a' the land,
　But's lighter at the news o't.

Tho' stars in skies may disappear,
　And angry tempests gather;
The happy hour may soon be near
　That brings us pleasant weather:
The weary night o' care and grief
　May hae a joyful morrow;
So dawning day has brought relief—
　Fareweel our night o' sorrow!

THE TAILOR.

TUNE—'*The Tailor fell thro' the bed, thimbles an' a'.*'

THE Tailor fell thro' the bed, thimbles an' a',
The Tailor fell thro' the bed, thimbles an' a';
The blankets were thin, and the sheets they were sma',
The Tailor fell thro' the bed, thimbles an' a'.

The sleepy bit lassie, she dreaded nae ill,
The sleepy bit lassie, she dreaded nae ill;
The weather was cauld, and the lassie lay still,
She thought that a tailor could do her nae ill.

Gie me the groat again, canny young man;
Gie me the groat again, canny young man;
The day it is short, and the night it is lang,
The dearest siller that ever I wan!

There's somebody weary wi' lying her lane;
There's somebody weary wi' lying her lane;
There's some that are dowie, I trow wad be fain
To see the bit tailor come skippin' again.

THE TITHER MORN.

THE tither morn,
　When I forlorn,
Aneath an aik sat moaning,
　I did na trow,
　I'd see my Jo,
Beside me, gain the gloaming.
　But he sae trig,
　Lap o'er the rig,
And dawtingly did cheer me,
　When I, what reck,
　Did least expec',
To see my lad so near me.

　His bonnet he,
　A thought ajee,
Cock'd sprush when first he clasp'd
　　me;
　And I, I wat,
　Wi' fainness grat,
While in his grips he press'd me,

Deil tak' the war!
　I late and air,
Hae wish'd since Jock departed;
　But now as glad
　I'm wi' my lad,
As short syne broken-hearted.

　Fu' aft at e'en
　Wi' dancing keen,
When a' were blythe and merry,
　I car'd na by,
　Sae sad was I
In absence o' my dearie.
　But, praise be blest,
　My mind's at rest,
I'm happy wi' my Johnny:
　At kirk and fair,
　I'se ay be there,
And be as canty's ony.

THE CARLE OF KELLYBURN BRAES.

TUNE—'*Kellyburn braes.*'

THERE lived a carle on Kellyburn braes
   (Hey, and the rue grows bonie wi' thyme),
And he had a wife was the plague o' his days ;
   And the thyme it is wither'd, and rue is in prime.

Ae day as the carle gaed up the lang glen
   (Hey, and the rue grows bonie wi' thyme),
He met wi' the Devil ; says, 'How do you fen ?'
   And the thyme it is wither'd, and rue is in prime.

'I've got a bad wife, sir ; that's a' my complaint'
   (Hey, and the rue grows bonie wi' thyme),
'For, saving your presence, to her ye're a saint ;'
   And the thyme it is wither'd, and rue is in prime.

'It's neither your stot nor your staig I shall crave
   (Hey, and the rue grows bonie wi' thyme),
'But gie me your wife, man, for her I must have ;'
   And the thyme it is wither'd, and rue is in prime.

'O welcome, most kindly,' the blythe carle said
   (Hey, and the rue grows bonie wi' thyme),
'But if ye can match her, ye're waur nor ye're ca'd ;'
   And the thyme it is wither'd, and rue is in prime.

The Devil has got the auld wife on his back
   (Hey, and the rue grows bonie wi' thyme),
And, like a poor pedlar, he's carried his pack ;
   And the thyme it is wither'd, and rue is in prime.

He's carried her hame to his ain hallan-door
   (Hey, and the rue grows bonie wi' thyme),
Syne bad her gae in, for a b—h and a w—e ;
   And the thyme it is wither'd, and rue is in prime.

Then straight he makes fifty, the pick o' his band
   (Hey, and the rue grows bonie wi' thyme),
Turn out on her guard in the clap of a hand ;
   And the thyme it is wither'd, and rue is in prime.

The carlin gaed thro' them like ony wud bear
   (Hey, and the rue grows bonie with thyme),
Whae'er she gat hands on came near her nae mair ;
   And the thyme it is wither'd, and rue is in prime.

A reekit wee Devil looks over the wa'
   (Hey, and the rue grows bonie wi' thyme),
'O, help, master, help, or she'll ruin us a' ;'
   And the thyme it is wither'd, and rue is in prime.

The Devil he swore by the edge o' his knife
  (Hey, and the rue grows bonie with thyme),
He pitied the man that was tied to a wife ;
  And the thyme it is wither'd, and rue is in prime.

The Devil he swore by the kirk and the bell
  (Hey, and the rue grows bonie wi' thyme),
He was not in wedlock, thank heav'n, but in hell ;
  And the thyme it is wither'd, and rue is in prime.

Then Satan has travell'd again wi' his pack
  (Hey, and the rue grows bonie wi' thyme),
And to her auld husband he's carried her back ;
  And the thyme it is wither'd, and rue is in prime.

'I hae been a Devil the feck o' my life '
  (Hey, and the rue grows bonie wi' thyme),
'But ne'er was in hell, till I met wi' a wife ; '
  And the thyme it is wither'd, and rue is in prime.

THERE WAS A LASS.

Tune—'*Duncan Davison.*'

There was a lass, they ca'd her Meg,
  And she held o'er the moors to spin ;
There was a lad that follow'd her,
  They ca'd him Duncan Davison.
The moor was driegh, and Meg was skiegh,
  Her favour Duncan could na win ;
For wi' the rock she wad him knock,
  And ay she shook the temper-pin.

As o'er the moor they lightly foor,
  A burn was clear, a glen was green,
Upon the banks they eased their shanks,
  And ay she set the wheel between :
But Duncan swore a haly aith,
  That Meg should be a bride the morn ;
Then Meg took up her spinnin' graith,
  And flung them a' out o'er the burn.

We'll big a house—a wee, wee house,
  And we will live like King and Queen,
Sae blythe and merry we will be
  When ye set by the wheel at e'en.
A man may drink and no be drunk ;
  A man may fight and no be slain ;
A man may kiss a bonie lass,
  And ay be welcome back again.

THE WEARY PUND O' TOW.

TUNE—' *The weary pund o' tow.*'

THE weary pund, the weary pund,
  The weary pund o' tow ;
I think my wife will end her life
  Before she spin her tow.
I bought my wife a stane o' lint
  As gude as e'er did grow ;
And a' that she has made o' that,
  Is ae poor pund o' tow.

There sat a bottle in a bole,
  Beyond the ingle low,
And ay she took the tither souk
  To drouk the stowrie tow.

Quoth I, For shame, ye dirty dame,
  Gae spin your tap o' tow !
She took the rock, and wi' a knock
  She brak it o'er my pow.

At last her feet—I sang to see't—
  Gaed foremost o'er the knowe ;
And or I wad anither jad,
  I'll wallop in a tow.
    The weary pund, the weary pund,
      The weary pund o' tow !
    I think my wife will end her life
      Before she spin her tow.

THE PLOUGHMAN.

TUNE—' *Up wi' the Ploughman.*'

THE ploughman he's a bonie lad,
  His mind is ever true, jo,
His garters knit below his knee,
  His bonnet it is blue, jo.

CHORUS.

Then up wi't a', my ploughman lad,
  And hey, my merry ploughman ;
Of a' the trades that I do ken,
  Commend me to the ploughman.

My ploughman he comes hame at e'en,
  He's aften wat and weary ;
Cast off the wat, put on the dry,
  And gae to bed, my Dearie !
    Up wi't a', &c.

I will wash my ploughman's hose,
  And I will dress his o'erlay ;
I will mak my ploughman's bed,
  And cheer him late and early.
    Up wi't a', &c.

I hae been east, I hae been west,
  I hae been at Saint Johnston,
The boniest sight that e'er I saw
  Was the ploughman laddie dancin'.
    Up wi't a', &c.

Snaw-white stockins on his legs,
  And siller buckles glancin' ;
A gude blue bannet on his head,
  And O, but he was handsome !
    Up wi't a', &c.

Commend me to the barn-yard,
  And the corn-mou', man ;
I never gat my coggie fou
  Till I met wi' the ploughman.
    Up wi't a', &c.

THE CARLES OF DYSART.

TUNE—' *Hey, ca' thro'.*'

UP wi' the carles of Dysart,
  And the lads o' Buckhaven,
And the kimmers o' Largo,
  And the lasses o' Leven.
    Hey, ca' thro', ca' thro',
      For we hae mickle ado ;
    Hey, ca' thro', ca' thro',
      For we hae mickle ado.

We hae tales to tell,
  And we hae sangs to sing ;
We hae pennies to spend,
  And we hae pints to bring.

We'll live a' our days,
  And them that come behin',
Let them do the like,
  And spend the gear they win.
    Hey, ca' thro', ca' thro',
      For we hae mickle ado ;
    Hey, ca' thro', ca' thro',
      For we hae mickle ado.

WEARY FA' YOU, DUNCAN GRAY.

TUNE—'*Duncan Gray.*'

WEARY fa' you, Duncan Gray—
Ha, ha, the girdin o't !
Wae gae by you, Duncan Gray—
Ha, ha, the girdin o't !
When a' the lave gae to their play,
Then I maun sit the lee-lang day,
And jog the cradle wi' my tae,
And a' for the girdin o't.

Bonie was the Lammas moon—
Ha, ha, the girdin o't !
Glowrin' a' the hills aboon—
Ha, ha, the girdin o't !
The girdin brak, the beast cam down,
I tint my curch, and baith my shoon ;
Ah ! Duncan, ye're an unco loon—
Wae on the bad girdin o't !

But, Duncan, gin ye'll keep your aith —
Ha, ha, the girdin o't !
Ise bless you wi' my hindmost breath —
Ha, ha, the girdin o't !
Duncan, gin ye'll keep your aith,
The beast again can bear us baith,
And auld Mess John will mend the skaith,
And clout the bad girdin o't.

MY HOGGIE.

TUNE—'*What will I do gin my Hoggie die?*'

WHAT will I do gin my Hoggie die ?
My joy, my pride, my Hoggie !
My only beast, I had na mae,
And vow but I was vogie !

The lee-lang night we watch'd the fauld,
Me and my faithfu' doggie ;
We heard nought but the roaring linn,
Amang the braes sae scroggie ;

But the howlet cry'd frae the castle wa',
The blitter frae the boggie,
The tod reply'd upon the hill,
I trembled for my Hoggie.

When day did daw, and cocks did craw,
The morning it was foggie ;
An' unco tyke lap o'er the dyke,
And maist has kill'd my Hoggie.

WHERE HAE YE BEEN.

TUNE—'*Killiecrankie.*'

WHARE hae ye been sae braw, lad ?
Where hae ye been sae brankie, O ?
O, whare hae ye been sae braw, lad ?
Cam ye by Killiecrankie, O ;
An' ye had been whare I hae been,
Ye wad na been so cantie, O ;
An' ye had seen what I had seen,
On the braes o' Killiecrankie, O.

I fought at land, I fought at sea ;
At hame I fought my auntie, O ;
But I met the Devil an' Dundee,
On the braes o' Killiecrankie, O.
The bauld Pitcur fell in a furr,
An' Clavers got a clankie, O ;
Or I had fed an Athole gled,
On the braes o' Killiecrankie, O.

COCK UP YOUR BEAVER.

TUNE—'*Cock up your beaver.*'

WHEN first my brave Johnnie lad
Came to this town,
He had a blue bonnet
That wanted the crown ;
But now he has gotten
A hat and a feather,—
Hey, brave Johnnie lad,
Cock up your beaver !

Cock up your beaver,
And cock it fu' sprush,
We'll over the border
And gie them a brush ;
There's somebody there
We'll teach better behaviour—
Hey, brave Johnnie lad,
Cock up your beaver !

THE HERON BALLADS.

FIRST BALLAD.

WHOM will you send to London town,
To Parliament and a' that ?
Or wha in a' the country round
The best deserves to fa' that ?

For a' that, an' a' that,
Thro' Galloway and a' that !
Where is the laird or belted
   knight
That best deserves to fa' that ?

Wha sees Kerroughtree's open yett,
   And wha is't never saw that ?
Wha ever wi' Kerroughtree meets
   And has a doubt of a' that ?
      For a' that, an' a' that,
      Here's Heron yet for a' that !
      The independent patriot,
      The honest man, an' a' that.

Tho' wit and worth in either sex,
   St. Mary's Isle can shaw that ;
Wi' dukes an' lords let Selkirk mix,
   And weel does Selkirk fa' that.
      For a' that, an' a' that,
      Here's Heron yet for a' that !
      The independent commoner
      Shall be the man for a' that.

But why should we to nobles jouk,
   And is't against the law then ?
For why, a lord may be a gouk,
   Wi' ribbon, star, an' a' that.
      For a' that, an' a' that,
      Here's Heron yet for a' that !
      A lord may be a lousy loun,
      Wi' ribbon, star, an' a' that.

A beardless boy comes o'er the hills,
   Wi' uncle's purse an' a' that ;
But we'll hae ane frae 'mang oursels,
   A man we ken, an' a' that.
      For a' that, an' a' that,
      Here's Heron yet for a' that !
      For we're not to be bought an'
         sold
      Like naigs, an' nowt, an' a' that.

Then let us drink the Stewartry,
   Kerroughtree's laird, an' a' that,
Our representative to be,
   For weel he's worthy a' that.
      For a' that, an' a' that,
      Here's Heron yet for a' that !
      A House of Commons such as
         he,
      They would be blest that saw
         that.

THE ELECTION.

· SECOND BALLAD.

Fy, let us a' to Kirkcudbright,
   For there will be bickerin' there ;
For Murray's light-horse are to muster,
   And O, how the heroes will swear !
An' there will be Murray commander,
   And Gordon the battle to win ;
Like brothers they'll stand by each
      other,
   Sae knit in alliance an' kin.

An' there will be black-lippit Johnnie,
   The tongue o' the trump to them a' ;
An' he get na hell for his haddin'
   The Deil gets na justice ava' ;
An' there will be Kempleton's birkie,
   A boy no sae black at the bane,
But, as for his fine nabob fortune,
   We'll e'en let the subject alane.

An' there will be Wigton's new sheriff,
   Dame Justice fu' brawlie has sped,
She's gotten the heart of a Bushby,
   But, Lord, what's become o' the head ?
An' there will be Cardoness, Esquire,
   Sae mighty in Cardoness' eyes ;
A wight that will weather damnation,
   For the Devil the prey will despise.

An' there will be Douglasses doughty,
   New christ'ning towns far and near !
Abjuring their democrat doings,
   By kissing the — o' a peer ;
An' there will be Kenmure sae gen'rous
   Whose honour is proof to the storm,
To save them from stark reprobation
   He lent them his name to the firm.

But we winna mention Redcastle,
   The body e'en let him escape !
He'd venture the gallows for siller,
   An' 'twere na the cost o' the rape.
An' where is our King's lord lieutenant,
   Sae fam'd for his gratefu' return ?
The billie is gettin' his questions,
   To say in St. Stephen's the morn.

An' there will be lads o' the gospel,
   Muirhead wha's as good as he's true ;
An' there will be Buittle's apostle,
   Wha's more o' the black than the blue ;

An' there will be folk from St. Mary's,
 A house o' great merit and note,
The deil ane but honours them highly,—
 The deil ane will gie them his vote !

An' there will be wealthy young Richard,
 Dame Fortune should hing by the
  neck ;
For prodigal, thriftless bestowing—
 His merit had won him respect :
An' there will be rich brother nabobs,
 Though nabobs, yet men of the first ;
An' there will be Collieston's whiskers,
 An' Quintin, o' lads not the worst.

An' there will be stamp-office Johnnie,
 Tak tent how ye purchase a dram ;
An' there will be gay Cassencarrie,
 An' there will be gleg Colonel Tam ;
An' there will be trusty Kerroughtree,
 Whose honour was ever his law,
If the virtues were pack'd in a parcel,
 His worth might be sample for a'.

An' can we forget the auld major,
 Wha'll ne'er be forgot in the Greys ;
Our flatt'ry we'll keep for some other,
 Him only 'tis justice to praise.
An' there will be maiden Kilkerran,
 And also Barskimming's gude knight ;
An' there will be roarin' Birtwhistle,
 Wha, luckily, roars in the right.

An' there, frae the Niddisdale's borders,
 Will mingle the Maxwells in droves ;
Teugh Johnnie, staunch Geordie, an'
  Walie,
 That griens for the fishes an' loaves ;
An' there will be Logan MacDowall,
 Sculdudd'ry an' he will be there,
An' also the wild Scot o' Galloway,
 Sodgerin', gunpowder Blair.

Then hey the chaste interest o'
  Broughton,
 An' hey for the blessings 'twill bring !
It may send Balmaghie to the Commons,
 In Sodom 'twould make him a King ;
An' hey for the sanctified Murray,
 Our land who wi' chapels has stor'd ;
He founder'd his horse among harlots,
 But gied the auld naig to the Lord.

AN EXCELLENT NEW SONG.

THIRD BALLAD. (MAY 1796.)

WHA will buy my troggin,
 Fine election ware ;
Broken trade o' Broughton,
 A' in high repair.
  Buy braw troggin,
   Frae the banks o' Dee ·
  Wha wants troggin
   Let him come to me.

There's a noble Earl's
 Fame and high renown,
For an auld sang—
 It's thought the gudes were stown.
  Buy braw troggin, &c.

Here's the worth o' Broughton
 In a needle's ee ;
Here's a reputation
 Tint by Balmaghie.
  Buy braw troggin, &c.

Here's an honest conscience
 Might a prince adorn ;
Frae the downs o' Tinwald—
 So was never worn.
  Buy braw troggin, &c.

Here's its stuff and lining,
 Cardoness' head ;
Fine for a sodger
 A' the wale o' lead.
  Buy braw troggin, &c.

Here's a little wadset
 Buittles scrap o' truth,
Pawn'd in a gin-shop
 Quenching holy drouth.
  Buy braw troggin, &c.

Here's armorial bearings
 Frae the manse o' Urr ;
The crest, an auld crab-apple
 Rotten at the core.
  Buy braw troggin, &c.

Here is Satan's picture,
 Like a bizzard gled,
Pouncing poor Redcastle
 Sprawlin' as a taed.
  Buy braw troggin, &c.

Here's the worth and wisdom
  Collieston can boast ;
By a thievish midge
  They had been nearly lost.
      Buy braw troggin, &c.

Here is Murray's fragments
  O' the ten commands ;
Gifted by black Jock
  To get them aff his hands.
      Buy braw troggin, &c.

Saw ye e'er sic troggin ?
  If to buy ye're slack,
Hornie's turnin' chapman, —
  He'll buy a' the pack.
      Buy braw troggin, &c.

JOHN BUSHBY'S LAMENTATION.

TUNE—'*The Babes in the Wood.*

'TWAS in the seventeen hunder year
  O' grace and ninety-five,
That year I was the wae'est man
  O' ony man alive.

In March the three-and-twentieth morn,
  The sun raise clear and bright ;
But oh I was a waefu' man
  Ere to-fa' o' the night.

Yerl Galloway lang did rule this land,
  Wi' equal right and fame,
And thereto was his kinsman join'd
  The Murray's noble name.

Yerl Galloway lang did rule the land,
  Made me the judge o' strife ;
But now Yerl Galloway's sceptre's broke,
  And eke my hangman's knife.

'Twas by the banks o' bonie Cree,
  Beside Kirkcudbright's towers,
The Stewart and the Murray there
  Did muster a' their powers.

The Murray, on the auld gray yaud,
  Wi' wingèd spurs did ride,
That auld gray yaud, yea, Nidsdale rade,
  He staw upon Nidside.

An' there had na been the yerl himsel',
  O there had been nae play ;
But Garlies was to London gane,
  And sae the kye might stray.

And there was Balmaghie, I ween,
  In front rank he wad shine ;
But Balmaghie had better been
  Drinking Madeira wine.

Frae the Glenkens came to our aid,
  A chief o' doughty deed ;
In case that worth should wanted be,
  O' Kenmure we had need.

And by our banners march'd Muirhead,
  And Buittle was na slack ;
Whase haly priesthood nane can stain,
  For wha can dye the black ?

And there sae grave Squire Cardoness,
  Look'd on till a' was done ;
Sae, in the tower o' Cardoness,
  A howlet sits at noon.

And there led I the Bushby clan,
  My gamesome billie Will ;
And my son Maitland, wise as brave,
  My footsteps follow'd still.

The Douglas and the Heron's name
  We set nought to their score ;
The Douglas and the Heron's name
  Had felt our weight before.

But Douglasses o' weight had we,
  The pair o' lusty lairds,
For building cot-houses sae famed,
  And christening kail-yards.

And there Redcastle drew his sword,
  That ne'er was stained wi' gore,
Save on a wanderer lame and blind,
  To drive him frae his door.

And last came creeping Collieston,
  Was mair in fear than wrath ;
Ae knave was constant in his mind,
  To keep that knave frae scaith.

YE SONS OF OLD KILLIE.

TUNE—'*Shawnboy.*'

YE sons of old Killie, assembled by Willie,
　To follow the noble vocation ;
Your thrifty old mother has scarce such another
　To sit in that honour'd station.
I've little to say, but only to pray,
　As praying's the ton of your fashion ;
A prayer from the Muse you well may excuse,
　'Tis seldom her favourite passion.

Ye powers who preside o'er the wind and the tide,
　Who marked each element's border ;
Who formed this frame with beneficent aim,
　Whose sovereign statute is order ;
Within this dear mansion may wayward contention
　Or withered envy ne'er enter ;
May secrecy round be the mystical bound,
　And brotherly love be the centre !

YE JACOBITES BY NAME.

TUNE—'*Ye Jacobites by name.*'

YE Jacobites by name, give an ear, give an ear ;
　Ye Jacobites by name, give an ear ;
　　Ye Jacobites by name,
　　Your fautes I will proclaim,
　　　Your doctrines I maun blame—
　　　　You shall hear.

What is right and what is wrang, by the law, by the law ?
What is right and what is wrang by the law ?
　What is right and what is wrang ?
　A short sword and a lang,
　　A weak arm, and a strang
　　　For to draw.

What makes heroic strife, fam'd afar, fam'd afar,
What makes heroic strife fam'd afar ?
　What makes heroic strife ?
　To whet th' assassin's knife,
　　Or hunt a parent's life
　　　Wi' bluidie war.

Then let your schemes alone, in the state, in the state ;
Then let your schemes alone in the state ;
　Then let your schemes alone,
　Adore the rising sun,
　　And leave a man undone
　　　To his fate.

T

SONG—AH, CHLORIS.

TUNE—'*Major Graham.*'

AH, Chloris, since it may na be,
  That thou of love wilt hear ;
If from the lover thou maun flee,
  Yet let the friend be dear.

Altho' I love my Chloris mair
  Than ever tongue could tell ;
My passion I will ne'er declare,
  I'll say, I wish thee well :

Tho' a' my daily care thou art,
  And a' my nightly dream,
I'll hide the struggle in my heart,
  And say it is esteem.

WHAN I SLEEP I DREAM.

WHAN I sleep I dream,
  Whan I wauk I'm eerie,
Sleep I canna get,
  For thinkin' o' my dearie.

Lanely night comes on,
  A' the house are sleeping,
I think on the bonie lad
  That has my heart a keeping.
      Ay waukin O, waukin ay and
          wearie,
      Sleep I canna get, for thinkin' o'
          my dearie.

Lanely night comes on,
  A' the house are sleeping,
I think on my bonie lad,
  An' I bleer my een wi' greetin' !
      Ay waukin, &c.

KATHARINE JAFFRAY.

THERE liv'd a lass in yonder dale,
  And down in yonder glen, O ;
And Katharine Jaffray was her name,
  Weel known to many men, O.

Out came the Lord of Lauderdale
  Out frae the south countrie, O,
All for to court this pretty maid,
  Her bridegroom for to be, O.

He's tell'd her father and mother baith,
  As I hear sindry say, O ;
But he has na tell'd the lass hersel'
  Till on her wedding day, O.

Then came the Laird o' Lochinton
  Out frae the English border,
All for to court this pretty maid,
  All mounted in good order.

THE COLLIER LADDIE.

O WHARE live ye my bonie lass,
  And tell me how they ca' ye ?
My name, she says, is Mistress Jean,
  And I follow my Collier laddie.

O see ye not yon hills and dales
  The sun shines on sae brawly :
They a' are mine, and they shall be thine,
  If ye'll leave your Collier laddie.

And ye shall gang in rich attire,
  Weel buskit up fu' gaudy ;
And ane to wait at every hand,
  If ye'll leave your Collier laddie.

Tho' ye had a' the sun shines on,
  And the earth conceals sae lowly ;
I would turn my back on you and it a ,
  And embrace my Collier laddie.

I can win my five pennies in a day,
  And spend it at night full brawlie ;
I can mak my bed in the Collier's neuk,
  And lie down wi' my Collier laddie.

Loove for loove is the bargain for me,
  Tho' the wee cot-house should haud
      me ;   [bread,
And the warld before me to win my
  And fare fa' my Collier laddie.

WHEN I THINK ON THE HAPPY DAYS.

WHEN I think on the happy days
  I spent wi' you, my dearie ;
And now what lands between us lie,
  How can I be but eerie !

How slow ye move, ye heavy hours,
  As ye were wae and weary !
It was na sae ye glinted by
  When I was wi' my dearie.

YOUNG JAMIE, PRIDE OF A' THE PLAIN.

TUNE—'*The Carlin o' the Glen.*'

Young Jamie, pride of a' the plain,
Sae gallant and sae gay a swain ;
Tho' a' our lasses he did rove,
And reign'd resistless King of Love :
But now wi' sighs and starting tears,
He strays amang the woods and briers;

Or in the glens and rocky caves
His sad complaining dowie raves :
I wha sae late did range and rove,
And changed with every moon my love,
I little thought the time was near,
Repentance I should buy sae dear ;
The slighted maids my torment see,
And laugh at a' the pangs I dree ;
While she, my cruel, scornfu' fair,
Forbids me e'er to see her mair !

THE HEATHER WAS BLOOMING.

The heather was blooming, the meadows were mawn,
Our lads gaed a hunting, ae day at the dawn,
O'er moors and o'er mosses and monie a glen,
At length they discover'd a bonie moor-hen.
    I red you beware at the hunting, young men ;
    I red you beware at the hunting, young men ;
    Tak some on the wing, and some as they spring,
    But cannily steal on a bonie moor-hen.

Sweet brushing the dew from the brown heather bells,
Her colours betray'd her on yon mossy fells ;
Her plumage outlustred the pride o' the spring,
And O ! as she wanton'd gay on the wing.
    I red, &c.

Auld Phœbus himsel, as he peep'd o'er the hill,
In spite at her plumage he tried his skill :
He levell'd his rays where she bask'd on the brae—
His rays were outshone, and but mark'd where she lay.
    I red, &c.

They hunted the valley, they hunted the hill,
The best of our lads wi' the best o' their skill ;
But still as the fairest she sat in their sight,
Then, whirr ! she was over, a mile at a flight.
    I red, &c.

*   *   *   *

WAE IS MY HEART.

Wae is my heart, and the tear's in my ee ;
Lang, lang, joy's been a stranger to me :
Forsaken and friendless my burden I bear,
And the sweet voice o' pity ne'er sounds in my ear.

Love, thou hast pleasures ; and deep hae I loved ;
Love, thou hast sorrows ; and sair hae I proved :
But this bruised heart that now bleeds in my breast,
I can feel its throbbings will soon be at rest.

O if I were where happy I hae been ;
Down by yon stream and yon bonie castle green :
For there he is wand'ring and musing on me,
Wha wad soon dry the tear frae Phillis's ee.

T 2

EPPIE M'NAB.

O saw ye my dearie, my Eppie M'Nab?
O saw ye my dearie, my Eppie M'Nab?
She's down in the yard, she's kissin' the laird,
She winna come hame to her ain Jock Rab.
O come thy ways to me, my Eppie M'Nab!
O come thy ways to me, my Eppie M'Nab!
Whate'er thou has done, be it late, be it soon,
Thou's welcome again to thy ain Jock Rab.

What says she, my dearie, my Eppie M'Nab?
What says she, my dearie, my Eppie M'Nab?
She lets thee to wit, that she has thee forgot,
And for ever disowns thee, her ain Jock Rab.
O had I ne'er seen thee, my Eppie M'Nab!
O had I ne'er seen thee, my Eppie M'Nab!
As light as the air, and fause as thou's fair,
Thou's broken the heart o' thy ain Jock Rab.

AN, O! MY EPPIE.

An' O! my Eppie,
My jewel, my Eppie!
Wha wadna be happy
   Wi' Eppie Adair?
By love, and by beauty,
By law, and by duty,
I swear to be true to
   My Eppie Adair!

An' O! my Eppie,
My jewel, my Eppie!
Wha wadna be happy
   Wi' Eppie Adair?
A' pleasure exile me,
Dishonour defile me,
If e'er I beguile thee,
   My Eppie Adair!

GUDEEN TO YOU, KIMMER.

Gudeen to you, Kimmer,
   And how do ye do?
Hiccup, quo' Kimmer,
   The better that I'm fou.
      We're a' noddin, nid nid noddin,
      We're a' noddin at our house at
         hame.

Kate sits i' the neuk,
   Suppin' hen broo;
Deil tak Kate
   An' she be a noddin too!
      We're a' noddin, &c.

How's a' wi' you, Kimmer,
   And how do ye fare?
A pint o' the best o't,
   And twa pints mair.
      We're a' noddin, &c.

How's a' wi' you, Kimmer,
   And how do ye thrive;
How mony bairns hae ye?
   Quo' Kimmer, I hae five.
      We're a' noddin, &c.

Are they a' Johny's?
   Eh! atweel no:
Twa o' them were gotten
   When Johny was awa.
      We're a' noddin, &c.

Cats like milk,
   And dogs like broo;
Lads like lasses weel,
   And lasses lads too.
      We're a' noddin, &c.

O THAT I HAD NE'ER BEEN MARRIED.

O THAT I had ne'er been married,
 I wad never had nae care ;
Now I've gotten wife and bairns,
 An' they cry crowdie ever mair.
 Ance crowdie, twice crowdie,
  Three times crowdie in a day ;
 Gin ye crowdie ony mair,
  Ye'll crowdie a' my meal away.

Waefu want and hunger fley me,
 Glowrin by the hallen en' ;
Sair I fecht them at the door,
 But ay I'm eerie they come ben.
 Ance crowdie, &c.

THERE'S NEWS, LASSES.

THERE'S news, lasses, news,
 Gude news I've to tell,
There's a boat fu' o' lads
 Come to our town to sell.
 The wean wants a cradle,
  An' the cradle wants a cod,
 An' I'll no gang to my bed
  Until I get a nod.

Father, quo' she, Mither, quo' she,
 Do what ye can,
I'll no gang to my bed
 Till I get a man.
 The wean, &c.

I hae as gude a craft rig
 As made o' yird and stane ;
And waly fu' the ley-crap
 For I maun till'd again.
 The wean, &c.

SCROGGAM.

THERE was a wife wonn'd in Cockpen,
 Scroggam ;
She brew'd gude ale for gentlemen,
Sing auld Cowl, lay you down by me,
Scroggam, my dearie, ruffum.

The gudewife's dochter fell in a fever,
 Scroggam ;
The priest o' the parish fell in anither,
Sing auld Cowl, lay you down by me,
Scroggam, my dearie, ruffum.

They laid the twa i' the bed thegither,
 Scroggam ;
That the heat o' the tane might cool
 the tither,
Sing auld Cowl, lay you down by me,
Scroggam, my dearie, ruffum.

FRAE THE FRIENDS AND LAND I LOVE.

FRAE the friends and land I love,
 Driven by Fortune's felly spite,
Frae my best belov'd I rove,
 Never mair to taste delight ;
Never mair maun hope to find
 Ease frae toil, relief frae care :
When remembrance wrecks the mind,
 Pleasures but unveil despair.

Brightest climes shall mirk appear,
 Desart ilka blooming shore,
Till the Fates, nae mair severe,
 Friendship, love, and peace restore ;
Till revenge, wi' laurell'd head,
 Bring our banish'd hame again ;
And ilka loyal, bonie lad
 Cross the seas and win his ain.

THE LADDIES BY THE BANKS O' NITH.

ELECTION BALLAD, 1789.

TUNE—' *Up and waur them a'.*'

THE laddies by the banks o' Nith
 Wad trust his Grace wi' a', Jamie,
But he'll sair them as he sair'd the king—
 Turn tail and rin awa, Jamie.
  Up and waur them a', Jamie,
   Up and waur them a' ;
  The Johnstons hae the guidin' o't,
   Ye turncoat Whigs, awa.

The day he stude his country's friend,
 Or gied her faes a claw, Jamie,
Or frae puir man a blessin' wan,
 That day the duke ne'er saw, Jamie.

But wha is he, his country's boast ?
 Like him there is na twa, Jamie ;
There's no a callant tents the kye,
 But kens o' Westerha', Jamie.

To end the wark, here's Whistlebirk,
 Lang may his whistle blaw, Jamie ;
And Maxwell true o' sterling blue,
 And we'll be Johnstons a', Jamie.

THE BONIE LASS OF ALBANY.

Tune—'Mary's dream.'

My heart is wae, and unco wae,
　To think upon the raging sea,
That roars between her gardens green
　And the bonie Lass of Albany.

This lovely maid's of royal blood
　That ruled Albion's kingdoms three,
But oh, alas, for her bonie face,
　They hae wrang'd the Lass of Albany.

In the rolling tide of spreading Clyde
　There sits an isle of high degree,
And a town of fame whose princely
　　　name
　Should grace the Lass of Albany.

But there's a youth, a witless youth,
　That fills the place where she should
　　　be ;
We'll send him o'er to his native shore,
　And bring our ain sweet Albany.

Alas the day, and wo the day,
　A false usurper wan the gree,
Who now commands the towers and
　　　lands—
　The royal right of Albany.

We'll daily pray, we'll nightly pray,
　On bended knees most ferventlie,
The time may come, with pipe and
　　　drum
　We'll welcome hame fair Albany.

SONG.

Tune—'Maggy Lauder.'

When first I saw fair Jeanie's face,
　I couldna tell what ailed me,
My heart went fluttering pit-a-pat,
　My een they almost failed me.
She's aye sae neat, sae trim, sae tight,
　All grace does round her hover,
Ae look deprived me o' my heart,
　And I became a lover.
She's aye, aye sae blythe, sae gay,
　She's aye so blythe and cheerie ;
She's aye sae bonie, blythe, and gay,
　O gin I were her dearie !

Had I Dundas's whole estate,
　Or Hopetoun's wealth to shine in ;
Did warlike laurels crown my brow,
　Or humbler bays entwining—
I'd lay them a' at Jeanie's feet,
　Could I but hope to move her,
And prouder than a belted knight,
　I'd be my Jeanie's lover.
　　She's aye, aye sae blythe, sae
　　　gay, &c.

But sair I fear some happier swain
　Has gained sweet Jeanie's favour :
If so, may every bliss be hers,
　Though I maun never have her :
But gang she east, or gang she west,
　'Twixt Forth and Tweed all over,
While men have eyes, or ears, or taste,
　She'll always find a lover.
　　She's aye, aye sae blythe, sae
　　　gay, &c.

APPENDIX.

THE following *Elegy, Extempore Verses to Gavin Hamilton,* and *Versicles on Sign-posts,* now for the first time published, are extracted, it is supposed, from the copy of his *Common-place Book* which Burns presented to Mrs. Dunlop of Dunlop. The copy, after having been in the hands of several persons, and at each remove denuded of certain pages, came into the possession of Mr. Stillie, bookseller, Princes Street, Edinburgh, some years since, and is now the property of Mr. Macmillan. Besides the following poems, it contains two stanzas never before published of the *Epitaph on Robert Fergusson,* versions of *There was a Lad was born in Kyle,* and *Gordon Castle,* differing in some respects from those commonly printed ; all of which have been embodied in the notes to the present edition. In the *Common-place book,* the *Elegy* is thus introduced :—"The following poem is the work of some hapless unknown son of the Muses, who deserved a better fate. There is a great deal of 'The Voice of Cona,' in his solitary mournful notes ; and had the sentiments been clothed in Shenstone's language, they would have been no discredit even to that elegant poet." Burns, it will be seen, does not claim the authorship, and, from internal evidence, the Editor is of opinion that it was not written by him. Still, the *Elegy,* so far at least as the Editor is aware, exists no-where else ; and if Burns did not actually compose it, he at least thought it worthy of being copied with his own hand into a book devoted almost exclusively to his own compositions. Even if it were certain that Burns was not the author, still, the knowledge that he admired it, and that through his agency it alone exists, is considered sufficient excuse for its admission here. The *Extempore Verses to Gavin Hamilton* are as certainly Burns's as is *Death and Dr. Hornbook,* or the *Address to the Deil.* The dialect, the turn of phrase, the glittering surface of sarcasm, with the strong under-current of sense, and the peculiar off-hand impetuosity of idea and illustration, unmistakeably indicate Burns's hand, and his only. In the *Common-place Book,* no date is given ; but from the terms of the two closing stanzas, it would appear that the voyage to Jamaica was in contemplation at the period of its composition. The last stanza is almost identical in thought and expression with the closing lines of the well-known *Dedication to Gavin Hamilton,* which was written at that time, and which appeared in the first edition of the Poems printed at Kilmarnock.

The *Versicles on Signposts* have the following introduction :—"The everlasting surliness of a Lion, Saracen's head, &c. or the unchanging blandness of the Land-lord welcoming a traveller, on some sign-posts, would be no bad similes of the constant affected fierceness of a Bully, or the eternal simper of a Frenchman or a Fiddler." The Versicles themselves are of little worth, and are indebted entirely to their paternity for their appearance here.

ELEGY.

STRAIT is the spot and green the sod,
    From whence my sorrows flow :
And soundly sleeps the ever dear
    Inhabitant below.

Pardon my transport, gentle shade,
    While o'er the turf I bow !
Thy earthly house is circumscrib'd,
    And solitary now.

Not one poor stone to tell thy name,
    Or make thy virtues known :
But what avails to me, to thee,
    The sculpture of a stone ?

I'll sit me down upon this turf,
    And wipe away this tear :
The chill blast passes swiftly by,
    And flits around thy bier.

Dark is the dwelling of the Dead,
    And sad their house of rest :
Low lies the head by Death's cold arm
    In aweful fold embrac'd.

I saw the grim Avenger stand
    Incessant by thy side ;
Unseen by thee, his deadly breath
    Thy lingering frame destroy'd.

Pale grew the roses on thy cheek,
    And wither'd was thy bloom,
Till the slow poison brought thy youth
    Untimely to the tomb.

Thus wasted are the ranks of men,
    Youth, Health, and Beauty fall :
The ruthless ruin spreads around,
    And overwhelms us ail.

Behold where round thy narrow house
    The graves unnumber'd lie !
The multitudes that sleep below
    Existed but to die.

Some, with the tottering steps of Age,
    Trod down the darksome way :
And some, in youth's lamented prime,
    Like thee, were torn away.

Yet these, however hard their fate,
    Their native earth receives :
Amid their weeping friends they died,
    And fill their fathers' graves.

From thy lov'd friends when first thy
    heart
    Was taught by Heaven to flow :
Far, far remov'd, the ruthless stroke
    Surpris'd and laid thee low.

At the last limits of our isle,
    Wash'd by the western wave,
Touch'd by thy fate, a thoughtful bard
    Sits lonely on thy grave.

Pensive he eyes, before him spread,
    The deep, outstretch'd and vast ;
His mourning notes are borne away
    Along the rapid blast.

And while, amid the silent Dead
    Thy hapless fate he mourns,
His own long sorrows freshly bleed,
    And all his grief returns.

Like thee, cut off in early youth
    And flower of beauty's pride,
His friend, his first and only joy,
    His much loved Stella, died.

Him, too, the stern impulse of Fate
    Resistless bears along ;
And the same rapid tide shall whelm
    The Poet and the Song.

The tear of pity which he shed,
    He asks not to receive ;
Let but his poor remains be laid
    Obscurely in the grave.

His grief-worn heart, with truest joy,
    Shall meet the welcome shock :
His airy harp shall lie unstrung
    And silent on the rock.

O, my dear maid, my Stella, when
    Shall this sick period close :
And lead the solitary bard
    To his beloved repose ?

EXTEMPORE

TO MR. GAVIN HAMILTON.

To you, Sir, this summons I've sent,
    Pray whip till the pownie is fraething ;
But if you demand what I want,
    I honestly answer you, naething.

Ne'er scorn a poor Poet like me,
  For idly just living and breathing,
While people of every degree
  Are busy employed about—naething.

Poor Centum-per-centum may fast,
  And grumble his hurdies their claith-
    ing;
He'll find, when the balance is cast,
  He's gane to the devil for—naething.

The courtier cringes and bows,
  Ambition has likewise its plaything;
A coronet beams on his brows :
  And what is a coronet ?—naething.

Some quarrel the Presbyter gown,
  Some quarrel Episcopal graithing,
But every good fellow will own
  Their quarrel is all about—naething.

The lover may sparkle and glow,
  Approaching his bonie bit gay thing :
But marriage will soon let him know
  He's gotten a buskit up naething.

The Poet may jingle and rhyme
  In hopes of a laureate wreathing,
And when he has wasted his time
  He's kindly rewarded with naething.

The thundering bully may rage,
  And swagger and swear like a
    heathen;
But collar him fast, I'll engage,
  You'll find that his courage is naething.

Last night with a feminine whig,
  A Poet she could na put faith in,
But soon we grew lovingly big,
  I taught her, her terrors were naething.

Her whigship was wonderful pleased,
  But charmingly tickled wi' ae thing ;

Her fingers I lovingly squeezed,
  And kissed her and promised her—
    naething.

The priest anathemas may threat,—
  Predicament, Sir, that we're baith in;
But when honour's reveillé is beat,
  The holy artillery's naething.

And now, I must mount on the wave,
  My voyage perhaps there is death in :
But what of a watery grave ?
  The drowning a Poet is naething.

And now, as grim death's in my thought,
  To you, Sir, I make this bequeathing :
My service as long as ye've aught,
  And my friendship, by G—, when
    ye've naething.

VERSICLES ON SIGN-POSTS.

He looked
Just as your Sign-post lions do,
As fierce, and quite as harmless too.

PATIENT STUPIDITY.

So heavy, passive to the tempests' shocks,
Strong on the Sign-post stands the stupid
  Ox.

His face with smile eternal drest,
Just like the Landlord to his guest,
High as they hang with creaking din,
To index out the Country Inn.

A head, pure, sinless quite of brain and
  soul,
The very image of a Barber's Poll ;
It shows a human face and wears a wig,
And looks, when well preserved, amazing
  big.

THE
LETTERS OF BURNS.

THE

LETTERS OF BURNS.

No. I.

TO MISS ELLISON BEGBIE.

[ALTHOUGH the exact date of the correspondence with Miss Ellison Begbie cannot be ascertained, there appears to be good reason for attributing it to some time about 1780-1, and for believing that they are the earliest letters of the poet which have been preserved. Ellison was the daughter of a small farmer, and was engaged, at the time of the correspondence, as domestic servant to a family on the banks of the Cessnock. She was an amiable, intelligent, but not particularly handsome girl, and Burns was evidently serious in his desire to marry her. It was on the eve of his removal to Irvine to try his hand at flax-dressing, with a view to getting the means of marriage, that he learned the hopelessness of his passion. Ellison had already given her heart to another. She was the heroine of the song, " On Cessnock Banks."]

LOCHLEA.

I VERILY believe, my dear E., that the pure genuine feelings of love are as rare in the world as the pure genuine principles of virtue and piety. This I hope will account for the uncommon style of all my letters to you. By uncommon, I mean their being written in such a serious manner, which, to tell you the truth, has made me often afraid lest you should take me for some zealous bigot, who conversed with his mistress as he would converse with his minister. I don't know how it is, my dear; for though, except your company, there is nothing on earth gives me so much pleasure as writing to you, yet it never gives me those giddy raptures so much talked of among lovers. I have often thought that if a well-grounded affection be not really a part of virtue, 'tis some thing extremely akin to it. Whenever the thought of my E. warms my heart, every feeling of humanity, every principle of generosity kindles in my breast. It extinguishes every dirty spark of malice and envy which are but too apt to infest me. I grasp every creature in the arms of universal benevolence, and equally participate in the pleasures of the happy, and sympathise with the miseries of the unfortunate. I assure you, my dear, I often look up to the Divine Disposer of events with an eye of gratitude for the blessing which I hope He intends to bestow on me in bestowing you. I sincerely wish that He may bless my endeavours to make your

life as comfortable and happy as possible, both in sweetening the rougher parts of my natural temper, and bettering the unkindly circumstances of my fortune. This, my dear, is a passion, at least in my view, worthy of a man, and I will add worthy of a Christian. The sordid earth-worm may profess love to a woman's person, whilst in reality his affection is centered in her pocket : and the slavish drudge may go a-wooing as he goes to the horse-market to choose one who is stout and firm, and as we may say of an old horse, one who will be a good drudge and draw kindly. I disdain their dirty, puny ideas. I would be heartily out of humour with myself, if I thought I were capable of having so poor a notion of the sex, which were designed to crown the pleasures of society. Poor devils ! I don't envy them their happiness who have such notions. For my part I propose quite other pleasures with my dear partner.—R. B.

No. II.

TO THE SAME.

My dear E.   LOCHLEA.

I do not remember, in the course of your acquaintance and mine, ever to have heard your opinion on the ordinary way of falling in love amongst people of our station in life : I do not mean the persons who proceed in the way of bargain, but those whose affection is really placed on the person.

Though I be, as you know very well, but a very awkward lover myself, yet as I have some opportunities of observing the conduct of others who are much better skilled in the affair of courtship than I am, I often think it is owing to lucky chance more than to good management, that there are not more unhappy marriages than usually are.

It is natural for a young fellow to like the acquaintance of the females, and customary for him to keep them company when occasion serves : some one of them is more agreeable to him than the rest ; there is something, he knows not what, pleases him, he knows not how, in her company. This I take to be what is called love with the greater part of us ; and I must own, my dear E., it is a hard game such a one as you have to play when you meet with such a lover. You cannot refuse but he is sincere, and yet though you use him ever so favourably, perhaps in a few months, or at farthest in a year or two, the same unaccountable fancy may make him as distractedly fond of another, whilst you are quite forgot. I am aware that perhaps the next time I have the pleasure of seeing you, you may bid me take my own lesson home, and tell me that the passion I have professed for you is perhaps one of those transient flashes I have been describing ; but I hope, my dear E., you will do me the justice to believe me, when I assure you that the love I have for you is founded on the sacred principles of virtue and honour, and by consequence so long as you continue possessed of those amiable qualities which first inspired my passion for you, so long must I continue to love you. Believe me, my dear, it is love like this alone which can render the marriage state

happy. People may talk of flames and raptures as long as they please, and a warm fancy, with a flow of youthful spirits, may make them feel something like what they describe ; but sure I am the nobler faculties of the mind, with kindred feelings of the heart, can only be the foundation of friendship, and it has always been my opinion that the married life was only friendship in a more exalted degree. If you will be so good as to grant my wishes and it shall please Providence to spare us to the latest period of life, I can look forward and see that even then, though bent down with wrinkled age ; even then, when all other worldly circumstances will be indifferent to me, I will regard my E. with the tenderest affection, and for this plain reason, because she is still possessed of these noble qualities, improved to a much higher degree, which first inspired my affection for her.

> "O happy state ! when souls each other draw,
> When love is liberty, and nature law."

I know were I to speak in such a style to many a girl, who thinks herself possessed of no small share of sense, she would think it ridiculous ; but the language of the heart is, my dear E., the only courtship I shall ever use to you.

When I look over what I have written, I am sensible that it is vastly different from the ordinary style of courtship, but I shall make no apology—I know your good nature will excuse what your good sense may see amiss.—R. B.

No. III.

TO THE SAME.

LOCHLEA.

I HAVE often thought it a peculiarly unlucky circumstance in love, that though in every other situation in life telling the truth is not only the safest, but actually by far the easiest way of proceeding, a lover is never under greater difficulty in acting, or more puzzled for expression, than when his passion is sincere, and his intentions are honourable. I do not think that it is very difficult for a person of ordinary capacity to talk of love and fondness which are not felt, and to make vows of constancy and fidelity which are never intended to be performed, if he be villain enough to practise such detestable conduct : but to a man whose heart glows with the principles of integrity and truth, and who sincerely loves a woman of amiable person, uncommon refinement of sentiment, and purity of manners —to such an one, in such circumstances, I can assure you, my dear, from my own feelings at this present moment, courtship is a task indeed. There is such a number of foreboding fears, and distrustful anxieties crowd into my mind when I am in your company, or when I sit down to write to you, that what to speak or what to write I am altogether at a loss.

There is one rule which I have hitherto practised, and which I shall invariably keep with you, and that is, honestly to tell you the plain truth.

There is something so mean and unmanly in the arts of dissimulation and falsehood, that I am surprised they can be acted by any one in so noble, so generous a passion, as virtuous love. No, my dear E., I shall never endeavour to gain your favour by such detestable practices. If you will be so good and so generous as to admit me for your partner, your companion, your bosom friend through life, there is nothing on this side of eternity shall give me greater transport; but I shall never think of purchasing your hand by any arts unworthy of a man, and I will add, of a Christian. There is one thing, my dear, which I earnestly request of you, and it is this: that you would soon either put an end to my hopes by a peremptory refusal, or cure me of my fears by a generous consent.

It would oblige me much if you would send me a line or two when convenient. I shall only add further that, if a behaviour regulated (though perhaps but very imperfectly) by the rules of honour and virtue, if a heart devoted to love and esteem you, and an earnest endeavour to promote your happiness; if these are qualities you would wish in a friend, in a husband, I hope you shall ever find them in your real friend and sincere lover,—R. B.

No. IV.
TO THE SAME.

LOCHLEA.

I OUGHT, in good manners, to have acknowledged the receipt of your letter before this time, but my heart was so shocked with the contents of it, that I can scarcely yet collect my thoughts so as to write you on the subject. I will not attempt to describe what I felt on receiving your letter. I read it over and over, again and again, and though it was in the politest language of refusal, still it was peremptory; "you were sorry you could not make me a return, but you wish me," what, without you, I never can obtain, "you wish me all kind of happiness." It would be weak and unmanly to say that without you I never can be happy; but sure I am, that sharing life with you would have given it a relish, that, wanting you, I can never taste.

Your uncommon personal advantages, and your superior good sense, do not so much strike me: these, possibly, may be met with in a few instances in others; but that amiable goodness, that tender feminine softness, that endearing sweetness of disposition, with all the charming offspring of a warm feeling heart—these I never again expect to meet with in such a degree in this world. All these charming qualities, heightened by an education much beyond anything I have ever met in any woman I ever dared to approach, have made an impression on my heart that I do not think the world can ever efface. My imagination has fondly flattered myself with a wish—I dare not say it ever reached a hope—that possibly I might one day call you mine. I had formed the most delightful images, and my fancy fondly brooded over them;

but now I am wretched for the loss of what I really had no right to expect. I must now think no more of you as a mistress: still I presume to ask to be admitted as a friend. As such I wish to be allowed to wait on you, and as I expect to remove in a few days a little further off, and you, I suppose, will soon leave this place, I wish to see or hear from you soon: and if an expression should perhaps escape me rather too warm for friendship, I hope you will pardon it in, my dear Miss —— (pardon me the dear expression for once), . . . R. B.

No. V.
TO WILLIAM BURNES.

[His disappointed love, his distaste for the dull, laborious employment of flax-heckling, and the unpromising nature of the speculation, combined, with a severe nervous malady, to throw Burns into a state of painful mental depression. It was a time, as he afterwards said, which he could not recall without a shudder.]

HONOURED SIR,   *Irvine, December 27th, 1781.*

I have purposely delayed writing, in the hope that I should have the pleasure of seeing you on New Year's Day; but work comes so hard upon us, that I do not choose to be absent on that account, as well as for some other little reasons which I shall tell you at meeting. My health is nearly the same as when you were here, only my sleep is a little sounder, and on the whole I am rather better than otherwise, though I mend by very slow degrees. The weakness of my nerves has so debilitated my mind that I dare neither review past events,* nor look forward into futurity; for the least anxiety or perturbation in my breast produces most unhappy effects on my whole frame. Sometimes, indeed, when for an hour or two my spirits are a little lightened, I *glimmer* a little into futurity; but my principal, and indeed my only pleasurable employment, is looking backwards and forwards in a moral and religious way. I am quite transported at the thought that ere long, perhaps very soon, I shall bid an eternal adieu to all the pains, and uneasinesses, and disquietudes of this weary life; for I assure you I am heartily tired of it, and if I do not very much deceive myself, I could contentedly and gladly resign it.

> " The soul uneasy, and confined at home,
> Rests and expatiates in a life to come."

It is for this reason I am more pleased with the 15th, 16th, and 17th verses of the 7th chapter of Revelations, than with any ten times as many verses in the whole Bible, and would not exchange the noble enthusiasm with which they inspire me for all that this world has to offer. As for this world, I despair of ever making a figure in it. I am not formed for the bustle of the busy, nor the flutter of the gay. I shall never again be capable of entering into such scenes. Indeed, I am altogether unconcerned at the thoughts of this life. I foresee that poverty and obscurity probably await me, and I am in some measure prepared, and daily preparing to meet them. I have but just time and paper to return you my grateful thanks

* In all Dr. Currie's four editions (1800—1803) the word " wants " is here given, an obvious misprint for " events."

R   U

for the lessons of virtue and piety you have given me, which were too much neglected at the time of giving them, but which I hope have been remembered ere it is yet too late. Present my dutiful respects to my mother, and my compliments to Mr. and Mrs. Muir ; and with wishing you a merry New Year's Day, I shall conclude. I am, honoured Sir,

Your dutiful Son,
ROBERT BURNESS.

P.S. My meal is nearly out, but I am going to borrow till I get more.

No. VI.

TO MR. JOHN MURDOCH,

SCHOOLMASTER, STAPLES INN BUILDINGS, LONDON.

[John Murdoch, before his removal to London, kept the school of Lochlea, where the sons of William Burnes were for a time his pupils.]

DEAR SIR,   LOCHLEA, 15*th January*, 1783.

As I have an opportunity of sending you a letter without putting you to that expense which any production of mine would but ill repay, I embrace it with pleasure, to tell you that I have not forgotten, nor ever will forget, the many obligations I lie under to your kindness and friendship.

I do not doubt, Sir, but you will wish to know what has been the result of all the pains of an indulgent father, and a masterly teacher ; and I wish I could gratify your curiosity with such a recital as you will be pleased with ; but that is what I am afraid will not be the case. I have, indeed, kept pretty clear of vicious habits ; and, in this respect, I hope, my conduct will not disgrace the education I have gotten ; but, as a man of the world, I am most miserably deficient. One would have thought that, bred as I have been, under a father who has figured pretty well as *un homme des affaires*, I might have been what the world calls a pushing, active fellow ; but to tell you the truth, Sir, there is hardly anything more my reverse. I seem to be one sent into the world, to see and observe ; and I very easily compound with the knave who tricks me of my money, if there be anything original about him, which shows me human nature in a different light from anything I have seen before. In short, the joy of my heart is to " study men, their manners, and their ways ;" and for this darling subject, I cheerfully sacrifice every other con- sideration. I am quite indolent about those great concerns that set the bustling, busy sons of care agog ; and if I have to answer for the present hour, I am very easy with regard to anything further. Even the last shift of the unfortunate and the wretched does not much terrify me : I know that even then my talent for what country folks call " a sensible crack," when once it is sanctified by a hoary head, would procure me so much esteem, that even then—I would learn to be happy.* However, I am

---

* He evidently means as a wandering beggar.

under no apprehensions about that ; for though indolent, yet so far as an extremely delicate constitution permits, I am not lazy ; and in many things, especially in tavern matters, I am a strict economist : not, indeed, for the sake of the money ; but one of the principal parts in my composition is a kind of pride of stomach ; and I scorn to fear the face of any man living : above everything, I abhor as hell, the idea of sneaking in a corner to avoid a dun—possibly some pitiful, sordid wretch, who in my heart I despise and detest. 'Tis this, and this alone, that endears economy to me. In the matter of books, indeed, I am very profuse. My favourite authors are of the sentimental kind, such as Shenstone, particularly his " Elegies ;" Thomson ; " Man of Feeling "—a book I prize next to the Bible ; " Man of the World ;" Sterne, especially his " Sentimental Journey ;" Macpherson's " Ossian," &c. : these are the glorious models after which I endeavour to form my conduct, and 'tis incongruous, 'tis absurd to suppose that the man whose mind glows with sentiments lighted up at the sacred flame—the man whose heart distends with benevolence to all the human race—he " who can soar above this little scene of things "—can he descend to mind the paltry concerns about which the terræfilial race fret, and fume, and vex themselves ! Oh how the glorious triumph swells my heart ! I forget that I am a poor, insignificant devil, unnoticed and unknown, stalking up and down fairs and markets, when I happen to be in them, reading a page or two of mankind, and " catching the manners living as they rise," whilst the men of business jostle me on every side, as an idle incumbrance in their way . . . .

Dear Sir, yours,
R. B.

No. VII.

COMMON-PLACE BOOK.

[The following " Observations " were written between 1783 and 1785, and were sent by Burns to Mr. Robert Riddel, with the following note :—" My dear Sir,—On rummaging over some old papers I lighted on a MS. of my early years, in which I had determined to write myself out ; as I was placed by fortune among a class of men to whom my ideas would have been nonsense. I had meant that the book should have lain by me, in the fond hope that some time or other, even after I was no more, my thoughts would fall into the hands of somebody capable of appreciating their value."]

Observations, Hints, Songs, Scraps of Poetry, &c., by Robert Burness ; a man who had little art in making money, and still less in keeping it ; but was, however, a man of some sense, a great deal of honesty, and unbounded good-will to every creature, rational and irrational. —As he was but little indebted to scholastic education, and bred at a plough-tail, his performances must be strongly tinctured with his unpolished, rustic way of life ; but as I believe they are really his own, it may be some entertainment to a curious observer of human nature to see how a ploughman thinks and feels under the pressure of love, ambition,

anxiety, grief, with the like cares and passions, which, however diversified by the modes and manners of life, operate pretty much alike, I believe, on all the species.

" There are numbers in the world who do not want sense to make a figure, so much as an opinion of their own abilities to put them upon recording their observations, and allowing them the same importance which they do to those that appear in print."—SHENSTONE.

" Pleasing, when youth is long expired, to trace
The forms our pencil or our pen designed !
Such was our youthful air, and shape, and face,
Such the soft image of our youthful mind."—*Ibid.*

April, 1783.

Notwithstanding all that has been said against love, respecting the folly and weakness it leads a young inexperienced mind into ; still I think it in a great measure deserves the highest encomiums that have been passed upon it. If anything on earth deserves the name of rapture or transport, it is the feelings of green eighteen in the company of the mistress of his heart, when she repays him with an equal return of affection.

August.

There is certainly some connexion between love and music and poetry ; and, therefore, I have always thought it a fine touch of nature, that passage in a modern love-composition :—

" As towards her cot he jogged along,
Her name was frequent in his song."

For my own part I never had the least thought or inclination of turn-ing poet till I got once heartily in love, and then rhyme and song were in a manner the spontaneous language of my heart. The following com-position was the first of my performances, and done at an early period of my life, when my heart glowed with honest warm simplicity ; un-acquainted and uncorrupted with the ways of a wicked world. The per-formance is, indeed, very puerile and silly ; but I am always pleased with it, as it recalls to my mind those happy days when my heart was yet honest, and my tongue was sincere. The subject of it was a young girl* who really deserved all the praises I have bestowed on her. I not only had this opinion of her then—but I actually think so still, now that the spell is long since broken, and the charm at an end :—

O once I lov'd a bonnie lass. (*Page* 232.)

Lest my works should be thought below criticism ; or meet with a critic who, perhaps, will not look on them with so candid and favourable an eye ; I am determined to criticise them myself.

The first distich of the first stanza is quite too much in the flimsy strain of our ordinary street ballads ; and, on the other hand, the second distich is too much in the other extreme. The expression is a little awkward, and the sentiment too serious. Stanza the second I am well pleased with ; and I think it conveys a fine idea of that amiable part of the

* "Handsome Nell,"—Nelly Kirkpatrick, his first sweetheart.

sex—the agreeables ; or what in our Scotch dialect we call a sweet sonsy lass. The third stanza has a little of the flimsy turn in it ; and the third line has rather too serious a cast. The fourth stanza is a very indifferent one ; the first line is, indeed, all in the strain of the second stanza, but the rest is mostly expletive. The thoughts in the fifth stanza come finely up to my favourite idea—a sweet sonsy lass : the last line, however, halts a little. The same sentiments are kept up with equal spirit and tenderness in the sixth stanza ; but the second and fourth lines ending with short syllables hurt the whole. The seventh stanza has several minute faults ; but I remember I composed it in a wild enthusiasm of passion, and to this hour I never recollect it but my heart melts, my blood sallies at the remembrance.

September.

I entirely agree with that judicious philosopher, Mr. Smith, in his excellent Theory of Moral Sentiments, that remorse is the most painful sentiment that can embitter the human bosom. Any ordinary pitch of fortitude may bear up tolerably well under those calamities in the procurement of which we ourselves have had no hand ; but when our own follies or crimes have made us miserable and wretched, to bear up with manly firmness, and at the same time have a proper penitential sense of our misconduct, is a glorious effort of self-command.

> Of all the numerous ills that hurt our peace,
> That press the soul, or wring the mind with anguish,
> Beyond comparison the worst are those
> That to our folly or our guilt we owe.
> In every other circumstance the mind
> Has this to say—' It was no deed of mine ;'
> But when to all the evil of misfortune
> This sting is added—' Blame thy foolish self ;'
> Or worser far, the pangs of keen remorse ;
> The torturing, gnawing, consciousness of guilt—
> Of guilt, perhaps, where we've involved others ;
> The young, the innocent, who fondly lov'd us,
> Nay, more, that very love their cause of ruin !
> O burning hell ! in all thy store of torments
> There's not a keener lash !
> Lives there a man so firm, who, while his heart
> Feels all the bitter horrors of his crime,
> Can reason down its agonizing throbs ;
> And, after proper purpose of amendment,
> Can firmly force his jarring thoughts to peace ?
> O happy ! happy ! enviable man !
> O glorious magnanimity of soul !

March, 1784.

I have often observed, in the course of my experience of human life, that every man, even the worst, has something good about him ; though very often nothing else than a happy temperament of constitution inclining him to this or that virtue. For this reason, no man can say in what degree any other person, besides himself, can be, with strict justice, called wicked. Let any of the strictest character for regularity of conduct among us, examine impartially how many vices he has never been guilty of, not from any care or vigilance, but for want of opportunity, or some

accidental circumstance intervening ; how many of the weaknesses of mankind he has escaped, because he was out of the line of such temptation ; and, what often, if not always, weighs more than all the rest, how much he is indebted to the world's good opinion, because the world does not know all : I say, any man who can thus think, will scan the failings, nay, the faults and crimes, of mankind around him, with a brother's eye.

I have often courted the acquaintance of that part of mankind commonly known by the ordinary phrase of blackguards, sometimes farther than was consistent with the safety of my character ; those who, by thoughtless prodigality or headstrong passions, have been driven to ruin Though disgraced by follies, nay, sometimes stained with guilt, I have yet found among them, in not a few instances, some of the noblest virtues, magnanimity, generosity, disinterested friendship, and even modesty.

April.

As I am what the men of the world, if they knew such a man, would call a whimsical mortal, I have various sources of pleasure and enjoyment, which are in a manner peculiar to myself, or some here and there such other out-of-the-way person. Such is the peculiar pleasure I take in the season of winter, more than the rest of the year. This, I believe, may be partly owing to my misfortunes giving my mind a melancholy cast : but there is something even in the

> " Mighty tempest, and the hoary waste,
> Abrupt and deep, stretch'd o'er the buried earth,'' —

which raises the mind to a serious sublimity, favourable to everything great and noble. There is scarcely any earthly object gives me more—I do not know if I should call it pleasure—but something which exalts me, something which enraptures me—than to walk in the sheltered side of a wood, or high plantation, in a cloudy winter day, and hear the stormy wind howling among the trees, and raving over the plain. It is my best season for devotion : my mind is wrapt up in a kind of enthusiasm to Him, who, in the pompous language of the Hebrew bard, " walks on the wings of the wind." In one of these seasons, just after a train of misfortunes, I composed the following :—

The wintry west extends his blast. (*Page* 61.)

Shenstone finely observes, that love verses, writ without any real passion, are the most nauseous of all conceits ; and I have often thought that no man can be a proper critic of love-composition, except he himself, in one or more instances, have been a warm votary of this passion. As I have been all along a miserable dupe to love, and have been led into a thousand weaknesses and follies by it, for that reason I put the more confidence in my critical skill, in distinguishing foppery and conceit from real passion and nature. Whether the following song will stand the test, I will not pretend to say, because it is my own ; only I can say it was, at the time, genuine from the heart :—

Behind yon hills, &c. (*Page* 223.)

March, 1784.

There was a certain period of my life that my spirit was broke by repeated losses and disasters, which threatened, and indeed effected, the utter ruin of my fortune. My body, too, was attacked by that most dreadful distemper, a hypochondria, or confirmed melancholy. In this wretched state, the recollection of which makes me yet shudder, I hung my harp on the willow-trees, except in some lucid intervals, in one of which I composed the following :—

O thou Great Being ! what thou art. (*Page* 68.)

April.

The following song is a wild rhapsody, miserably deficient in versification ; but as the sentiments are the genuine feelings of my heart, for that reason I have a particular pleasure in conning it over :—

My father was a farmer upon the Carrick border.

(*Page* 238.)

April.

I think the whole species of young men may be naturally enough divided into two grand classes, which I shall call the *grave* and the *merry ;* though, by the by, these terms do not with propriety enough express my ideas. The grave I shall cast into the usual division of those who are goaded on by the love of money, and those whose darling wish is to make a figure in the world. The merry are the men of pleasure of all denominations ; the jovial lads, who have too much fire and spirit to have any settled rule of action ; but, without much deliberation, follow the strong impulses of nature : the thoughtless, the careless, the indolent—in particular *he* who, with a happy sweetness of natural temper, and a cheerful vacancy of thought, steals through life—generally, indeed, in poverty and obscurity ; but poverty and obscurity are only evils to him who can sit gravely down and make a repining comparison between his own situation and that of others ; and lastly, to grace the quorum, such are, generally, those whose heads are capable of all the towerings of genius, and whose hearts are warmed with all the delicacy of feeling.

August.

The foregoing was to have been an elaborate dissertation on the various species of men ; but as I cannot please myself in the arrangement of my ideas, I must wait till farther experience and nicer observation throw more light on the subject.—In the meantime I shall set down the following fragment, which, as it is the genuine language of my heart, will enable anybody to determine which of the classes I belong to :—

There's nought but care on ev'ry han',
In ev'ry hour that passes, O. (*Page* 223.)

As the grand end of human life is to cultivate an intercourse with that BEING to whom we owe life, with every enjoyment that renders life delightful ; and to maintain an integritive conduct towards our fellow-creatures ; that so, by forming piety and virtue into habit, we may be fit

members for that society of the pious and the good which reason and revelation teach us to expect beyond the grave, I do not see that the turn of mind and pursuits of such an one as the above verses describe—one who spends the hours and thoughts which the vocations of the day can spare with Ossian, Shakspeare, Thomson, Shenstone, Sterne, &c.; or, as the maggot takes him, a gun, a fiddle, or a song to make or mend; and at all times some heart's-dear bonnie lass in view—I say I do not see that the turn of mind and pursuits of such an one are in the least more inimical to the sacred interests of piety and virtue, than the even lawful bustling and straining after the world's riches and honours: and I do not see but he may gain heaven as well—which, by the by, is no mean consideration —who steals through the vale of life, amusing himself with every little flower that fortune throws in his way, as he who, straining straight forward, and perhaps bespattering all about him, gains some of life's little eminences, where, after all, he can only see and be seen a little more conspicuously than what, in the pride of his heart, he is apt to term the poor, indolent devil he has left behind him.

August.

A Prayer, when fainting fits, and other alarming symptoms of a pleurisy or some other dangerous disorder, which indeed still threatens me, first put nature on the alarm :—

> O Thou unknown, Almighty Cause
> Of all my hope and fear! (*Page 66.*)

August.

Misgivings in the hour of despondency and prospect of death :—

> Why am I loth to leave this earthly scene? (*Page 67.*)

EGOTISMS FROM MY OWN SENSATIONS.

May [1784?].

I don't well know what is the reason of it, but somehow or other, though I am, when I have a mind, pretty generally beloved, yet I never could get the art of commanding respect: I imagine it is owing to my being deficient in what Sterne calls "that understrapping virtue of discretion." I am so apt to a *lapsus linguæ*, that I sometimes think the character of a certain great man I have read of somewhere is very much *à-propos* to myself—that he was a compound of great talents and great folly.—N.B. To try if I can discover the causes of this wretched infirmity, and, if possible, to mend it.

[Here follow the song *Tho' cruel Fate should bid us part*, page 211; the fragment *One night as I did wander*, page 242; *There was a lad was born in Kyle*, page 236; *Elegy on the death of Robert Ruisseaux*, page 124.]

August.

However I am pleased with the works of our Scotch poets, particularly the excellent Ramsay, and the still more excellent Fergusson, yet I am hurt to see other places of Scotland, their towns, rivers, woods, haughs, &c. immortalized in such celebrated performances, while my dear native country, the ancient baileries of Carrick, Kyle, and Cunningham, famous

both in ancient and modern times for a gallant and warlike race of inhabitants; a country where civil, and particularly religious liberty have ever found their first support, and their last asylum; a country, the birth-place of many famous philosophers, soldiers, and statesmen, and the scene of many important events recorded in Scottish history, particularly a great many of the actions of the glorious Wallace, the saviour of his country; yet, we never have had one Scotch poet of any eminence, to make the fertile banks of Irvine, the romantic woodlands and sequestered scenes on Ayr, and the heathy mountainous source and winding sweep of Doon, emulate Tay, Forth, Ettrick, Tweed, &c. This is a complaint I would gladly remedy, but, alas! I am far unequal to the task, both in native genius and education. Obscure I am, and obscure I must be, though no young poet, nor young soldier's heart, ever beat more fondly for fame than mine:—

> " And if there is no other scene of being
> Where my insatiate wish may have its fill,
> This something at my heart that heaves for room,
> My best, my dearest part, was made in vain."

August.

A Fragment—

When first I came to Stewart Kyle. (*Page* 239.)

September.

There is a great irregularity in the old Scotch songs, a redundancy of syllables with respect to that exactness of accent and measure that the English poetry requires, but which glides in, most melodiously, with the respective tunes to which they are set. For instance, the fine old song of " The Mill, Mill, O," to give it a plain, prosaic reading, it halts prodigiously out of measure; on the other hand, the song set to the same tune in Bremner's collection of Scotch songs, which begins, " To Fanny fair could I impart," &c. it is most exact measure: and yet, let them both be sung before a real critic, one above the biases of prejudices, but a thorough judge of nature,—how flat and spiritless will the last appear, how trite, and lamely methodical, compared with the wild-warbling cadence, the heart-moving melody of the first! This is particularly the case with all those airs which end with a hypermetrical syllable. There is a degree of wild irregularity in many of the compositions and fragments which are daily sung to them by my compeers, the common people—a certain happy arrangement of old Scotch syllables, and yet, very frequently, nothing, not even like rhyme, or sameness of jingle, at the ends of the lines. This has made me sometimes imagine that perhaps it might be possible for a Scotch poet, with a nice judicious ear, to set compositions to many of our most favourite airs, particularly that class of them mentioned above, independent of rhyme altogether.

There is a noble sublimity, a heart-melting tenderness, in some of our ancient ballads, which show them to be the work of a masterly hand: and it has often given me many a heart-ache to reflect that such glorious old

bards—bards who very probably owed all their talents to native genius, yet have described the exploits of heroes, the pangs of disappointment, and the meltings of love, with such fine strokes of nature—that their very names (oh how mortifying to a bard's vanity!) are now " buried among the wreck of things which were."

O ye illustrious names unknown! who could feel so strongly and describe so well: the last, the meanest of the Muses' train—one who, though far inferior to your flights, yet eyes your path, and with trembling wing would sometimes soar after you—a poor rustic bard unknown, pays this sympathetic pang to your memory! Some of you tell us, with all the charms of verse, that you have been unfortunate in the world—unfortunate in love: he, too, has felt the loss of his little fortune, the loss of friends, and, worse than all, the loss of the woman he adored. Like you, all his consolation was his Muse: she taught him in rustic measures to complain. Happy could he have done it with your strength of imagination and flow of verse! May the turf lie lightly on your bones! and may you now enjoy that solace and rest which this world rarely gives to the heart tuned to all the feelings of poesy and love!

September.

[Here follows the song on *Montgomerie's Peggy*, page 240.]

There is a fragment in imitation of an old Scotch song, well known among the country ingle sides. I cannot tell the name, neither of the song nor the tune, but they are in fine unison with one another. By the way, these old Scottish airs are so nobly sentimental, that when one would compose to them, to "south the tune," as our Scotch phrase is, over and over, is the readiest way to catch the inspiration, and raise the bard into that glorious enthusiasm so strongly characteristic of our old Scotch poetry. I shall here set down one verse of the piece mentioned above, both to mark the song and tune I mean, and likewise as a debt I owe to the author, as the repeating of that verse has lighted up my flame a thousand times :—

> When clouds in skies do come together—
> To hide the brightness of the weather,
> There will surely be some pleasant weather
> When a' their storms are past and gone.*
>
> Though fickle Fortune has deceived me,
> She promised fair and perform'd but ill ;
> Of mistress, friends, and wealth bereav'd me,—
> Yet I bear a heart shall support me still.
>
> I'll act with prudence as far as I'm able ;
> But if success I must never find,
> Then come misfortune, I bid thee welcome,
> I'll meet thee with an undaunted mind.

The above was an extempore, under the pressure of a heavy train of misfortunes, which, indeed, threatened to undo me altogether. It was just at the close of that dreadful period mentioned already ; and though

---

* Alluding to the misfortunes he feelingly laments before this verse. [This is the author's note.]

the weather has brightened up a little with me, yet there has always been since a tempest brewing round me in the grim sky of futurity, which I pretty plainly see will some time or other, perhaps ere long, overwhelm me, and drive me into some doleful dell, to pine in solitary, squalid wretchedness.—However, as I hope my poor country Muse, who, all rustic, awkward, and unpolished as she is, has more charms for me than any other of the pleasures of life beside—as I hope she will not then desert me, I may even then learn to be, if not happy, at least easy, and south a sang to soothe my misery.

'Twas at the same time I set about composing an air in the old Scotch style. I am not musical scholar enough to prick down my tune properly, so it can never see the light, and perhaps 'tis no great matter ; but the following were the verses I composed to suit it :—

> O raging fortune's withering blast
> Has laid my leaf full low, O ! (*Page* 240.)

The tune consisted of three parts, so that the above verses just went through the whole air.

October 1785.

If ever any young man, in the vestibule of the world, chance to throw his eye over these pages, let him pay a warm attention to the following observations, as I assure him they are the fruit of a poor devil's dear-bought experience. I have literally, like that great poet and great gallant, and by consequence that great fool, Solomon, "turned my eyes to behold madness and folly." Nay, I have, with all the ardour of a lively, fanciful, and whimsical imagination, accompanied with a warm, feeling, poetic heart, shaken hands with their intoxicating friendship.

In the first place, let my pupil, as he tenders his own peace, keep up a regular, warm intercourse with the Deity.

No. VIII.

TO MR. JAMES BURNES,

WRITER, MONTROSE.

[James Burnes was Robert's cousin, the son of his father's elder brother, and grandfather of Sir Alex. Burnes, of Afghan fame.]

DEAR SIR, LOCHLEA, 21*st June*, 1783.

My father received your favour of the 10th current; and as he has been for some months very poorly in health, and is in his own opinion (and, indeed, in almost everybody's else) in a dying condition, he has only, with great difficulty, written a few farewell lines to each of his brothers-in-law. For this melancholy reason, I now hold the pen for him to thank you for your kind letter, and to assure you, Sir, that it shall not be my fault if my father's correspondence in the north die with him. My brother writes to John Caird, and to him I must refer you for the news of our family.

I shall only trouble you with a few particulars relative to the wretched state of this country. Our markets are exceedingly high; oatmeal 17*d*. and 18*d*. per peck, and not to be got even at that price. We have indeed been pretty well supplied with quantities of white peas from England and elsewhere, but that resource is likely to fail us, and what will become of us then, particularly the very poorest sort, Heaven only knows. This country, till of late, was flourishing incredibly in the manufacture of silk, lawn, and carpet weaving; and we are still carrying on a good deal in that way, but much reduced from what it was. We had also a fine trade in the shoe way, but now entirely ruined, and hundreds driven to a starving condition on account of it. Farming is also at a very low ebb with us. Our lands, generally speaking, are mountainous and barren; and our landholders, full of ideas of farming gathered from the English and the Lothians, and other rich soils in Scotland, make no allowance for the odds of the quality of land, and consequently stretch us much beyond what in the event we will be found able to pay. We are also much at a loss for want of proper methods in our improvements of farming. Necessity compels us to leave our old schemes, and few of us have opportunities of being well informed in new ones. In short, my dear Sir, since the unfortunate beginning of this American war, and its as unfortunate conclusion, this country has been, and still is, decaying very fast. Even in higher life, a couple of our Ayrshire noblemen, and the major part of our knights and squires, are all insolvent. A miserable job of a Douglas, Heron, and Co.'s bank, which no doubt you heard of, has undone numbers of them; and imitating English and French, and other foreign luxuries and fopperies, has ruined as many more. There is a great trade of smuggling carried on along our coasts, which, however destructive to the interests of the kingdom at large, certainly enriches this corner of it, but too often at the expense of our morals. However, it enables individuals to make, at least for a time, a splendid appearance; but Fortune, as is usual with her when she is uncommonly lavish of her favours, is generally even with them at last: and happy were it for numbers of them if she would leave them no worse than when she found them.

My mother sends you a small present of a cheese; 'tis but a very little one, as our last year's stock is sold off; but if you could fix on any correspondent in Edinburgh or Glasgow, we would send you a proper one in the season. Mrs. Black promises to take the cheese under her care so far, and then to send it to you by the Stirling carrier.

I shall conclude this long letter with assuring you that I shall be very happy to hear from you, or any of our friends in your country, when opportunity serves.

My father sends you, probably for the last time in this world, his warmest wishes for your welfare and happiness; and my mother and the rest of the family desire to enclose their kind compliments to you, Mrs. Burness, and the rest of your family, along with those of,

Dear Sir,

Your affectionate Cousin,

R. B.

No. IX.

TO THE SAME.

[William Burnes died on the 13th February, 1784. On his deathbed he owned there was one of his family for whose future he feared, and Robert being then alone in the room with his father and sister (Mrs. Begg) asked, "Oh, father, is it me you mean?" The old man said it was; and Robert, turning to the window, burst into tears. William Burnes lies buried in Alloway Kirkyard. On the small headstone over his grave are some lines by his son, lamenting his loss, and commemorating his virtues.]

DEAR COUSIN, LOCHLEA, *17th February*, 1784.

I would have returned you my thanks for your kind favour of the 13th Dec. sooner, had it not been that I waited to give you an account of that melancholy event which, for some time past, we have from day to day expected.

On the 13th current I lost the best of fathers. Though, to be sure, we had long warning of the impending stroke, still the feelings of nature claim their part, and I cannot recollect the tender endearments and parental lessons of the best of friends and ablest of instructors, without feeling what perhaps the calmer dictates of reason would partly condemn.

I hope my father's friends in your country will not let their connexion in this place die with him. For my part I shall ever with pleasure, with pride, acknowledge my connexion with those who were allied by the ties of blood and friendship to a man whose memory I shall ever honour and revere. . . .

No. X.

TO THE SAME.

[This letter, it will be observed, is dated from Mossgiel, whither, on Mr. Burnes' death, the family removed from Lochlea. The old man's affairs were in a very embarrassed condition, and his two sons and two grown daughters had to rank as creditors of their father for arrears of wages in order to save part of the Lochlea stocking for their new venture. "Mossgiel," says Gilbert Burns, "was stocked by the property and individual savings of the whole family, and was a joint concern among us. Every member of the family was allowed ordinary wages for the labour he performed on the farm. My brother's allowance and mine were £7 per annum each. And during the whole time this family concern lasted, which was four years, as well as during the preceding period at Lochlea, his expenses never in any one year exceeded his slender income."]

MOSSGIEL, *August*, 1784.

WE have been surprised with one of the most extraordinary phenomena in the moral world which, I dare say, has happened in the course of this half century. We have had a party of Presbytery Relief, as they call themselves, for some time in this country. A pretty thriving society of

them has been in the burgh of Irvine for some years past, till about two years ago, a Mrs. Buchan,* from Glasgow, came among them and began to spread some fanatical notions of religion among them, and, in a short time, made many converts; and among others their preacher, Mr. White, who upon that account has been suspended and formally deposed by his brethren. He continued, however, to preach in private to his party, and was supported, both he and their spiritual mother, as they affect to call old Buchan, by the contributions of the rest, several of whom were in good circumstances; till, in spring last, the populace rose and mobbed Mrs. Buchan and put her out of the town; on which, all her followers voluntarily quitted the place likewise, and with such precipitation, that many of them never shut their doors behind them; one left a washing on the green, another a cow bellowing at the crib without food, or anybody to mind her; and after several stages, they are fixed at present in the neighbourhood of Dumfries. Their tenets are a strange jumble of enthusiastic jargon; among others, she pretends to give them the Holy Ghost by breathing on them, which she does with postures and practices that are scandalously indecent; they have likewise disposed of all their effects, and hold a community of goods, and live nearly an idle life, carrying on a great farce of pretended devotion in barns and woods, where they lodge and lie all together, and hold likewise a community of women, as it is another of their tenets that they can commit no moral sin. I am personally acquainted with most of them, and I can assure you the above mentioned are facts.

This, my dear Sir, is one of the many instances of the folly of leaving the guidance of sound reason and common-sense in matters of religion.

Whenever we neglect or despise these sacred monitors, the whimsical notions of a perturbated brain are taken for the immediate influences of the Deity, and the wildest fanaticism, and the most inconstant absurdities, will meet with abettors and converts. Nay, I have often thought, that the more out-of-the-way and ridiculous the fancies are, if once they are sanctified under the sacred name of religion, the unhappy mistaken votaries are the more firmly glued to them.—R. B.

---

* Allan Cunningham gives the following interesting note on Mrs. Buchan and her followers:—
"The Buchanites were a small community of enthusiasts, who believed the time to be at hand when there would neither be marriage nor giving in marriage—when the ground, instead of thistles and heather, would yield spontaneously the finest fruits—when all things under the sun would be in common—and 'Our Lady,' so they called Mrs. Buchan, reign spiritual queen of the earth. At first they held the doctrine of immediate translation, but a night spent in wild prayer, wild song, and wilder sermons on the top of a cold hill rebuked this part of their belief, but strengthened them in the opinion regarding their empire on earth; and confirmed 'Our Lady' in the resolution of making a tour through her imaginary dominions. She accordingly moved towards Nithsdale with all her people—some were in carts, some were on horseback, and not a few on foot. She rode in front upon a white pony; and often halted to lecture them upon the loveliness of the land, and to cheer them with food from what she called her 'Garner of mercy,' and with drink from a large cup called 'The comforter.' She addressed all people as she passed along with much mildness, and spoke to them in the language of their callings. 'James Macleish,' she said to a gardener, who went to see her, 'quit Mr. Copland's garden, and come and work in that of the Lord.'—'Thank ye,' answered James, 'but he was na owre kind to the last gardener he had.' 'Our Lady' died at Auchengibard-hill in Galloway, and her followers were dispersed. A few of the more resolute believers took a farm: the women spun and made large quantities of linen; the men ploughed and sowed, and made articles of turnery: their lives were inoffensive and their manners gentle: they are now all dead and gone." An interesting History of the Buchanites has been written by Mr. Joseph Train.

No. XI.

TO MISS ———.

[This and the following letter may be assigned to 1784-5.]

My dear Countrywoman,

I am so impatient to show you that I am once more at peace with you, that I send you the book I mentioned directly, rather than wait the uncertain time of my seeing you. I am afraid I have mislaid or lost Collins' Poems, which I promised to Miss Irvin. If I can find them, I will forward them by you ; if not, you must apologize for me.

I know you will laugh at it when I tell you that your piano and you together have played the deuce somehow about my heart. My breast has been widowed these many months, and I thought myself proof against the fascinating witchcraft ; but I am afraid you will "feelingly convince me what I am." I say, I am afraid, because I am not sure what is the matter with me. I have one miserable bad symptom ; when you whisper, or look kindly to another, it gives me a draught of damnation. I have a kind of wayward wish to be with you ten minutes by yourself, though what I would say, Heaven above knows, for I am sure I know not. I have no formed design in all this ; but just, in the nakedness of my heart, write you down a mere matter-of-fact story. You may perhaps give yourself airs of distance on this, and that will completely cure me ; but I wish you would not : just let us meet, if you please, in the old beaten way of friendship.

I will not subscribe myself your humble servant, for that is a phrase, I think, at least fifty miles off from my heart ; but I will conclude with sincerely wishing that the Great Protector of innocence may shield you from the barbed dart of calumny, and hand you by the covert snare of deceit.—R. B.

No XII.

TO MISS KENNEDY OF DALGARROCK.

[Miss Margaret Kennedy, the young lady to whom this letter and the enclosed song ("Young Peggy") were addressed, was the heroine of a melancholy story of betrayed love and cruel desertion : although now only seventeen years of age, the fatal intrigue with Captain M'Dowall of Logan had commenced ; but, of course, nothing was suspected by any one at this time. Miss Kennedy's case furnished the theme for the affecting song, "Ye Banks and Braes o' Bonnie Doon."]

Madam,

Permit me to present you with the enclosed song, as a small though grateful tribute for the honour of your acquaintance. I have, in these verses, attempted some faint sketches of your portrait in the unembellished manner of descriptive TRUTH. Flattery I leave to your LOVERS, whose exaggerating fancies may make them imagine you still nearer perfection than you really are.

Poets, Madam, of all mankind, feel most forcibly the powers of BEAUTY ;

as, if they are really POETS of Nature's making, their feelings must be finer, and their taste more delicate, than most of the world. In the cheerful bloom of SPRING, or the pensive mildness of AUTUMN, the grandeur of SUMMER, or the hoary majesty of WINTER, the poet feels a charm unknown to the rest of his species. Even the sight of a fine flower, or the company of a fine woman (by far the finest part of God's works below), have sensations for the poetic heart that the HERD of men are strangers to. On this last account, Madam, I am, as in many other things, indebted to Mr. H.'s kindness in introducing me to you. Your lovers may view you with a wish, I look on you with pleasure : their hearts, in your presence, may glow with desire, mine rises with admiration.

That the arrows of misfortune, however they should, as incident to humanity, glance a slight wound, may never reach your *heart*,—that the snares of villany may never beset you on the road of life,—that INNOCENCE may hand you by the path of HONOUR to the dwelling of PEACE,—is the sincere wish of him who has the honour to be, &c.—R. B.

[The song enclosed, " Young Peggy," will be found in page 35.]

No. XIII.
TO MR. JOHN RICHMOND,
EDINBURGH.

[John Richmond was an early friend of Burns' when clerk to the poet's patron and landlord, Mr. Gavin Hamilton, a Writer in Mauchline. Richmond was his companion in many a merry adventure at Mauchline, and afterwards received him in his lodging on his first arrival in Edinburgh.]

MY DEAR SIR,   MOSSGIEL, *February 17th*, 1786.

I have not time at present to upbraid you for your silence and neglect ; I shall only say I received yours with great pleasure. I have enclosed you a piece of rhyming ware for your perusal. I have been very busy with the Muses since I saw you, and have composed, among several others, " The Ordination," a poem on Mr. M'Kinlay's being called to Kilmarnock ; " Scotch Drink,' a poem ; "The Cotter's Saturday Night ;" "An Address to the Devil," &c. I have likewise completed my poem on the " Dogs," but have not shown it to the world. My chief patron now is Mr. Aiken in Ayr, who is pleased to express great approbation of my works. Be so good as send me Fergusson, by Connel, and I will remit you the money. I have no news to acquaint you with about Mauchline ; they are just going on in the old way. I have some very important news with respect to myself, not the most agreeable—news that I am sure you cannot guess, but I shall give you the particulars another time. I am extremely happy with Smith ; he is the only friend I have now in Mauchline. I can scarcely forgive your long neglect of me, and I beg you will let me hear from you regularly by Connel. If you would act your part as a friend, I am sure neither good nor bad fortune should strange or alter me. Excuse haste, as I got yours but yesterday.

I am, my dear Sir,
Yours,—R. B.

No. XIV.

TO MR. ROBERT MUIR,

KILMARNOCK.

[This is the last of the Poet's letters to which he has written his name Burness. Before this he had sometimes signed it as it now appears; and as his poems were about to go to the press, he decided upon abiding by BURNS.]

DEAR SIR, MOSSGIEL, *20th March,* 1786.

I am heartily sorry I had not the pleasure of seeing you as you returned through Mauchline; but as I was engaged, I could not be in town before the evening.

I here inclose you my "Scotch Drink," and "may the —— follow with a blessing for your edification." I hope, sometime before we hear the gowk, to have the pleasure of seeing you at Kilmarnock, when I intend we shall have a gill between us in a mutchkin-stoup; which will be a great comfort and consolation to,

Dear Sir, your humble Servant,
ROBERT BURNESS.

No. XV.

TO MR. DAVID BRICE.

[Burns had issued proposals for publishing his poems. In a letter written in April 1786, and supposed to be addressed to Mr. Ballantine of Ayr, he refers to the intended publication, and adds concerning his unhappy affair with Jean Armour— "Old Mr. Armour prevailed with him (Mr. Aiken) to mutilate that unlucky paper* yesterday. Would you believe it?—though I had not a hope, nor even a wish, to make her mine after her conduct, yet when he told me, the names were all out of the paper, my heart died within me, and he cut my veins with the news." To David Brice, a shoemaker in Glasgow, Burns speaks more fully.]

DEAR BRICE, MOSSGIEL, *June 12th,* 1786.

I received your message by G. Paterson, and as I am not very throng at present, I just write to let you know that there is such a worthless, rhyming reprobate, as your humble servant, still in the land of the living, though I can scarcely say, in the place of hope. I have no news to tell you that will give me any pleasure to mention, or you to hear.

Poor ill-advised, ungrateful Armour came home on Friday last. You have heard all the particulars of that affair, and a black affair it is. What she thinks of her conduct now, I don't know; one thing I do know—she has made me completely miserable. Never man loved, or rather adored, a woman more than I did her: and, to confess a truth between you and

---

* This was of course the informal marriage contract he had signed with Jean.

me, I do still love her to distraction after all, though I won't tell her so if I were to see her, which I don't want to do. My poor dear unfortunate Jean! how happy have I been in thy arms! It is not the losing her that makes me so unhappy, but for her sake I feel most severely : I foresee she is in the road to, I am afraid, eternal ruin.

May Almighty God forgive her ingratitude and perjury to me, as I from my very soul forgive her; and may His grace be with her and bless her in all her future life! I can have no nearer idea of the place of eternal punishment than what I have felt in my own breast on her account. I have tried often to forget her ; I have run into all kinds of dissipation and riots, mason-meetings, drinking matches, and other mischief, to drive her out of my head, but all in vain. And now for a grand cure: the ship is on her way home that is to take me out to Jamaica ; and then, farewell dear old Scotland ! and farewell dear ungrateful Jean ! for never, never will I see you more.

You will have heard that I am going to commence poet in print ; and to-morrow my works go to the press. I expect it will be a volume of about two hundred pages—it is just the last foolish action I intend to do ; and then turn a wise man as fast as possible.

Believe me to be, dear Brice,
Your Friend and Well-wisher,
R. B.

No. XVI.

TO JOHN RICHMOND,

ÆDINBURGH.

MOSSGIEL, *9th July,* 1786.

*   *   *   *   *   *

I have waited on Armour since her return home ; not from the least view of reconciliation, but merely to ask for her health, and, to you I will confess it, from a foolish hankering fondness, very ill-placed indeed. The mother forbade me the house, nor did Jean show that penitence that might have been expected. However, the priest, I am informed, will give me a certificate as a single man, if I comply with the rules of the Church, which for that very reason I intend to do.

I am going to put on sackcloth and ashes this day. I am indulged so far as to appear in my own seat.

Peccavi, pater ; miserere me.

My book will be ready in a fortnight. If you have any subscribers return them by Connell (the carrier). The Lord stand with the righteous. Amen, Amen !

R. B,

No. XVII.

TO MR. DAVID BRICE,

SHOEMAKER, GLASGOW.

MOSSGIEL, *17th July,* 1786.

I HAVE been so throng printing my Poems, that I could scarcely find as much time as to write to you. Poor Armour is come back again to Mauchline, and I went to call for her, and her mother forbade me the house ; nor did she herself express much sorrow for what she has done. I have already appeared publicly in church, and was indulged in the liberty of standing in my own seat. I do this to get a certificate as a bachelor, which Mr. Auld has promised me. I am now fixed to go for the West Indies in October. Jean and her friends insisted much that she should stand along with me in the kirk, but the minister would not allow it, which bred a great trouble, I assure you, and I am blamed as the cause of it, though I am sure I am innocent ; but I am very much pleased, for all that, not to have had her company. I have no news to tell you that I remember. I am really happy to hear of your welfare, and that you are so well in Glasgow. I must certainly see you before I leave the country. I shall expect to hear from you soon, and am,

Dear Brice, yours,

R. B.

No. XVIII.

TO MR. JOHN RICHMOND.

MY DEAR RICHMOND, OLD ROME FOREST, *30th July,* 1786.*

My hour is now come—you and I will never meet in Britain more. I have orders, within three weeks at farthest, to repair aboard the " Nancy," Captain Smith, from Clyde to Jamaica, and to call at Antigua. This, except to our friend Smith, whom God long preserve, is a secret about Mauchline. Would you believe it ? Armour has got a warrant to throw me in jail till I find security for an enormous sum. This they keep an entire secret, but I got it by a channel they little dream of ; and I am wandering from one friend's house to another, and, like a true son of the Gospel, "have nowhere to lay my head." I know you will pour an execration on her head, but spare the poor, ill-advised girl, for my sake ; though may all the furies that rend the injured, enraged lover's bosom, await her mother until her latest hour ! I write in a moment of rage, reflecting on my miserable situation—exiled, abandoned, forlorn. I can write no more. Let me hear from you by the return of coach. I will write you ere I go.

I am, dear Sir,

Yours, here and hereafter,

R. B.

* The Poet, when he wrote this letter, was skulking from Carrick to Kyle, and from Kyle to Carrick : " Some ill-advised persons," he said, " had uncoupled the merciless pack of the law at his heels." This was done, however, merely to get him to quit the country.

No. XIX.

TO MONS. JAMES SMITH,

MAUCHLINE.

My dear Sir,   *Monday morning*, Mossgiel [*August, 1786*].

I went to Dr. Douglas yesterday, fully resolved to take the opportunity of Captain Smith ; but I found the Doctor with a Mr. and Mrs. White, both Jamaicans, and they deranged my plans altogether. They assure him that to send me from Savannah-la-Mar to Port Antonio will cost my master, Charles Douglas, upwards of fifty pounds ; besides running the risk of throwing myself into a pleuritic fever in consequence of hard travelling in the sun. On these accounts, he refuses sending me with Smith, but a vessel sails from Greenock the first of September, right for the place of my destination. The Captain of her is an intimate friend of Mr. Gavin Hamilton's, and as good a fellow as heart could wish : with him I am destined to go. Where I shall shelter I know not, but I hope to weather the storm. Perish the drop of blood of mine that fears them ! I know their worst, and am prepared to meet it :—

> " I'll laugh, an' sing, an' shake my leg,
>   As lang's I dow."

On Thursday morning, if you can muster as much self-denial as to be out of bed about seven o'clock, I shall see you as I ride through to Cumnock. After all, Heaven bless the sex ! I feel there is still happiness for me among them :—

> " O woman, lovely woman ! Heaven designed you
> To temper man !—we had been brutes without you ! "

R. B.

No. XX.

TO MR. JOHN KENNEDY.

[It was towards the end of July, 1786, that " Poems, chiefly in the Scottish Dialect, by Robert Burns," was published, and the following letter was written in the course of the next month.]

My dear Sir,   Kilmarnock, *August, 1786.*

Your truly facetious epistle of the 3d inst. gave me much entertainment. I was sorry I had not the pleasure of seeing you as I passed your way, but we shall bring up all our lee way on Wednesday, the 16th current, when I hope to have it in my power to call on ycu and take a kind, very probably a last adieu, before I go for Jamaica; and I expect orders to repair to Greenock every day. I have at last made my public appearance, and am solemnly inaugurated into the numerous class. Could I have got a carrier, you should have had a score of vouchers for my Authorship ; but now you have them let them speak for themselves.

Farewell, dear Friend ! may guid luck hit you
And 'mang her favourites admit you !
If e'er Detraction shore to smit you,
       May nane believe him !
And ony de'il that thinks to get you,
      Good Lord deceive him.

R. B.

No. XXI.

TO MR. ROBERT MUIR,

KILMARNOCK.

MY FRIEND, MY BROTHER,   MOSSGIEL, *Friday noon [Sept. ?].*

*   *   *   *   *   *   *

You will have heard that poor Armour has repaid me double. A very fine boy and a girl have awakened a thought and feelings that thrill, some with tender pressure and some with foreboding anguish, through my soul.

*   *   *   *   *   *   *

I believe all hopes of staying at home will be abortive, but more of this when, in the latter part of next week, you shall be troubled with a visit from,

My dear Sir,
Your most devoted,
R. B.

No. XXII.

TO MR. BURNES,

MONTROSE.

MY DEAR SIR,   MOSSGIEL, *Sept. 26th,* 1786.

I this moment receive yours—receive it with the honest hospitable warmth of a friend's welcome. Whatever comes from you wakens always up the better blood about my heart, which your kind little recollections of my paternal friends carries as far as it will go. 'Tis there that man is blest ! 'Tis there, my friend, man feels a consciousness of something within him above the trodden clod ! The grateful reverence to the hoary (earthly) author of his being—the burning glow when he clasps the woman of his soul to his bosom—the tender yearnings of heart for the little angels to whom he has given existence—these nature has poured in milky streams about the human heart ; and the man who never rouses them to action, by the inspiring influences of their proper objects, loses by far the most pleasurable part of his existence.

My departure is uncertain, but I do not think it will be till after harvest. I will be on very short allowance of time indeed, if I do not comply with your friendly invitation.

*   *   *   *   *   *   *

R. B.

No. XXIII.

TO MR. ROBERT AIKEN.

[To the suffering of remorse and humiliation which befell Burns through Jean Armour, was added, about this time, the bitter grief of learning Highland Mary's death.]

SIR,   AYRSHIRE [*Oct.*], 1786.

I was with Wilson, my printer, t'other day, and settled all our by-gone matters between us. After I had paid him all demands, I made him the offer of the second edition, on the hazard of being paid out of the first and readiest, which he declines. By his account, the paper of a thousand copies would cost about twenty-seven pounds, and the printing about fifteen or sixteen : he offers to agree to this for the printing, if I will advance for the paper, but this you know is out of my power ; so farewell hopes of a second edition till I grow richer ! an epocha which, I think, will arrive at the payment of the British national debt.

There is scarcely anything hurts me so much in being disappointed of my second edition, as not having it in my power to show my gratitude to Mr. Ballantine, by publishing my poem of " The Brigs of Ayr." I would detest myself as a wretch, if I thought I were capable in a very long life of forgetting the honest, warm, and tender delicacy with which he enters into my interests. I am sometimes pleased with myself in my grateful sensations ; but I believe, on the whole, I have very little merit in it, as my gratitude is not a virtue, the consequence of reflection ; but sheerly the instinctive emotion of my heart, too inattentive to allow worldly maxims and views to settle into selfish habits.

I have been feeling all the various rotations and movements within, respecting the Excise. There are many things plead strongly against it ; the uncertainty of getting soon into business ; the consequences of my follies, which may perhaps make it impracticable for me to stay at home ; and besides I have for some time been pining under secret wretchedness, from causes which you pretty well know—the pang of disappointment, the sting of pride, with some wandering stabs of remorse, which never fail to settle on my vitals like vultures, when attention is not called away by the calls of society, or the vagaries of the Muse. Even in the hour of social mirth, my gaiety is the madness of an intoxicated criminal under the hands of the executioner. All these reasons urge me to go abroad, and to all these reasons I have only one answer—the feelings of a father. This, in the present mood I am in, overbalances everything that can be laid in the scale against it. . . . . . .

You may perhaps think it an extravagant fancy, but it is a sentiment which strikes home to my very soul : though sceptical in some points of our current belief, yet, I think, I have every evidence for the reality of a life beyond the stinted bourne of our present existence ; if so, then, how should I, in the presence of that tremendous Being, the Author of existence, how should I meet the reproaches of those who stand to me in the

dear relation of children, whom I deserted in the smiling innocency of helpless infancy ? O Thou great unknown Power !—Thou almighty God ! who hast lighted up reason in my breast, and blessed me with immortality !—I have frequently wandered from that order and regularity necessary for the perfection of Thy works, yet Thou hast never left me nor forsaken me ! . . . . . .

Since I wrote the foregoing sheet, I have seen something of the storm of mischief thickening over my folly-devoted head. Should you, my friends, my benefactors, be successful in your applications for me, perhaps it may not be in my power in that way to reap the fruit of your friendly efforts. What I have written in the preceding pages, is the settled tenor of my present resolution ; but should inimical circumstances forbid me closing with your kind offer, or enjoying it only threaten to entail farther misery—— . . . . . .

To tell the truth, I have little reason for complaint ; as the world, in general, has been kind to me fully up to my deserts. I was, for some time past, fast getting into the pining distrustful snarl of the misanthrope. I saw myself alone, unfit for the struggle of life, shrinking at every rising cloud in the chance-directed atmosphere of fortune, while, all defenceless, I looked about in vain for a cover. It never occurred to me, at least never with the force it deserved, that this world is a busy scene, and man, a creature destined for a progressive struggle ; and that, however I might possess a warm heart and inoffensive manners (which last, by the by, was rather more than I could well boast), still, more than these passive qualities, there was something to be done. When all my schoolfellows and youthful compeers (those misguided few excepted who joined, to use a Gentoo phrase, the "hallachores" of the human race) were striking off with eager hope and earnest intent, in some one or other of the many paths of busy life, I was " standing idle in the market-place," or only left the chace of the butterfly from flower to flower, to hunt fancy from whim to whim. . . . . . .

You see, Sir, that if to know one's errors were a probability of mending them, I stand a fair chance : but, according to the reverend Westminster divines, though conviction must precede conversion, it is very far from always implying it.—R. B.

No. XXIV.

TO MRS. DUNLOP,

OF DUNLOP.

[While suffering from the depression consequent upon a long and painful sickness, Mrs. Dunlop happened to meet with the "Cotter's Saturday Night," and was so stirred and delighted with it, that she at once despatched a messenger to Mossgiel, some fifteen miles off, with a letter expressing her admiration, and an order for half a dozen copies of the Kilmarnock edition of Burns' Poems.]

MADAM,   AYRSHIRE, 1786.

I am truly sorry I was not at home yesterday, when I was so much honoured with your order for my copies, and incomparably more by the

handsome compliments you are pleased to pay my poetic abilities. I am fully persuaded that there is not any class of mankind so feelingly alive to the titillations of applause as the sons of Parnassus : nor is it easy to conceive how the heart of the poor bard dances with rapture, when those, whose character in life gives them a right to be polite judges, honour him with their approbation. Had you been thoroughly acquainted with me, Madam, you could not have touched my darling heart-chord more sweetly than by noticing my attempts to celebrate your illustrious ancestor, the saviour of his country.

> " Great patriot hero ! ill-requited chief ! "*

The first book I met with in my early years, which I perused with pleasure, was "The Life of Hannibal ; " the next was "The History of Sir William Wallace :" for several of my earlier years I had few other authors ; and many a solitary hour have I stole out, after the laborious vocations of the day, to shed a tear over their glorious but unfortunate stories. In those boyish days I remember, in particular, being struck with that part of Wallace's story where these lines occur—

> " Syne to the Leglen wood, when it was late,
> To make a silent and a safe retreat."

I chose a fine summer Sunday, the only day my line of life allowed, and walked half a dozen of miles to pay my respects to the Leglen wood, with as much devout enthusiasm as ever pilgrim did to Loretto ; and, as I explored every den and dell where I could suppose my heroic countryman to have lodged, I recollect (for even then I was a rhymer) that my heart glowed with a wish to be able to make a song on him in some measure equal to his merits.—R. B.

No. XXV.

TO MRS. STEWART,

OF STAIR.

MADAM, 1786.

The hurry of my preparations for going abroad has hindered me from performing my promise so soon as I intended. I have here sent you a parcel of songs, &c. which never made their appearance, except to a friend or two at most. Perhaps some of them may be no great entertainment to you, but of that I am far from being an adequate judge. The song to the tune of "Ettrick Banks" [The Bonnie Lass of Ballochmyle] you will easily see the impropriety of exposing much, even in manuscript. I think, myself, it has some merit : both as a tolerable description of one of nature's sweetest scenes, a July evening ; and one of the finest pieces of nature's workmanship, the finest indeed we know anything of, an amiable, beautiful young woman ;† but I have no common friend to procure me that permission, without which I would not dare to spread the copy.

* Mrs. Dunlop, a daughter of Sir Thomas Wallace of Craigie, was descended from the brother of the hero.
† Miss Alexander.

I am quite aware, Madam, what task the world would assign me in this letter. The obscure bard, when any of the great condescend to take notice of him, should heap the altar with the incense of flattery. Their high ancestry, their own great and god-like qualities and actions, should be recounted with the most exaggerated description. This, Madam, is a task for which I am altogether unfit. Besides a certain disqualifying pride of heart, I know nothing of your connexions in life, and have no access to where your real character is to be found—the company of your compeers : and more, I am afraid that even the most refined adulation is by no means the road to your good opinion.

One feature of your character I shall ever with grateful pleasure remember ;—the reception I got when I had the honour of waiting on you at Stair.* I am little acquainted with politeness, but I know a good deal of benevolence of temper and goodness of heart. Surely did those in exalted stations know how happy they could make some classes of their inferiors by condescension and affability, they would never stand so high, measuring out with every look the height of their elevation, but condescend as sweetly as did Mrs. Stewart of Stair.—R. B.

No. XXVI.

TO DR. MACKENZIE,

MAUCHLINE ;

INCLOSING HIM VERSES ON DINING WITH LORD DAER.

[Of this meeting, which took place at Dugald Stewart's summer lodgings at Catrine, a few miles from Mossgiel, the Professor has left the following account :— " His manners were then, as they continued ever afterwards, simple, manly, and independent; strongly expressive of conscious genius and worth, but without anything that indicated forwardness, arrogance, and vanity. He took his share in conversation, but not more than belonged to him ; and listened with apparent attention and deference on subjects where his want of education deprived him of the means of information. If there had been a little more of gentleness and accommodation in his temper, he would, I think, have been still more interesting ; but he had been accustomed to give law in the circle of his ordinary acquaintance, and his dread of anything approaching to meanness and servility rendered his manner somewhat decided and hard. Nothing, perhaps, was more remarkable among his various attainments than the fluency, and precision, and originality of his language when he spoke in company, more particularly as he aimed at purity in his turn of expression, and avoided more successfully than most Scotchmen the peculiarities of Scottish phraseology."]

DEAR SIR, *Wednesday morning [Oct.]*.
I never spent an afternoon among great folks with half that pleasure as when, in company with you, I had the honour of paying my devoirs to that plain, honest, worthy man, the Professor [Dugald Stewart]. I

* Burns had accompanied a friend on a courting expedition to Mrs. Stewart's house, and the report of his genial humour and poetical powers having reached the parlour from the servants' room, Burns was invited to an interview with the lady of the house.

would be delighted to see him perform acts of kindness and friendship, though I were not the object ; he does it with such a grace.   I think his character, divided into ten parts, stands thus—four parts Socrates—four parts Nathaniel—and two parts Shakspeare's Brutus.

The foregoing verses (see page 111) were really extempore, but a little corrected since.   They may entertain you a little with the help of that partiality with which you are so good as to favour the performances of
Dear Sir,
Your very humble Servant,
R. B.

No. XXVII.

TO MISS ALEXANDER.

[Burns, walking one evening in the private grounds of Ballochmyle, met Miss Wilhelmina Alexander, the laird's sister, who, surprised to see a stranger there, started and hurried on.   It was as an apology for this intrusion that Burns composed the poem referred to in the following letter.   The lady's interpretation of its meaning was coloured by unfavourable reports of Burns' character, and neither letter nor poem was ever acknowledged.   Miss Alexander died in 1843, at the age of 88.]

MADAM,   MOSSGIEL, 18th November, 1786.
Poets are such outré beings, so much the children of wayward fancy and capricious whim, that I believe the world generally allows them a larger latitude in the laws of propriety, than the sober sons of judgment and prudence.   I mention this as an apology for the liberties that a nameless stranger has taken with you in the inclosed poem, which he begs leave to present you with.   Whether it has poetical merit any way worthy of the theme, I am not the proper judge ; but it is the best my abilities can produce ; and what to a good heart will, perhaps, be a superior grace, it is equally sincere as fervent.

The scenery was nearly taken from real life, though I dare say, Madam, you do not recollect it, as I believe you scarcely noticed the poetic *reveur* as he wandered by you.   I had roved out as chance directed, in the favourite haunts of my Muse, on the banks of the Ayr, to view nature in all the gaiety of the vernal year.   The evening sun was flaming over the distant western hills ; not a breath stirred the crimson opening blossom, or the verdant spreading leaf.   It was a golden moment for a poetic heart. I listened to the feathered warblers, pouring their harmony on every hand, with a congenial kindred regard, and frequently turned out of my path, lest I should disturb their little songs, or frighten them to another station.   Surely, said I to myself, he must be a wretch indeed, who, regardless of your harmonious endeavour to please him, can eye your elusive flights to discover your secret recesses, and to rob you of all the property nature gives you—your dearest comforts, your helpless nestlings.

Even the hoary hawthorn twig that shot across the way, what heart at such a time but must have been interested in its welfare, and wished it preserved from the rudely-browsing cattle, or the withering eastern blast? Such was the scene,—and such the hour, when in a corner of my prospect, I spied one of the fairest pieces of nature's workmanship that ever crowned a poetic landscape or met a poet's eye, those visionary bards excepted, who hold commerce with aërial beings! Had Calumny and Villany taken my walk, they had at that moment sworn eternal peace with such an object.

What an hour of inspiration for a poet! It would have raised plain dull historic prose into metaphor and measure.

The inclosed song was the work of my return home; and perhaps it but poorly answers what might have been expected from such a scene. . . . . . .

I have the honour to be, Madam,

Your most obedient and very humble Servant,

R. B.

No. XXVIII.

TO WILLIAM CHALMERS AND JOHN McADAM.

IN THE NAME OF THE NINE. Amen!

WE, Robert Burns, by virtue of a warrant from Nature, bearing date the twenty-fifth day of January, Anno Domini one thousand seven hundred and fifty-nine,* Poet Laureat, and Bard in Chief, in and over the districts and countries of Kyle, Cunningham, and Carrick, of old extent, To our trusty and well-beloved William Chalmers and John McAdam, student practitioners in the ancient and mysterious science of confounding right and wrong.

RIGHT TRUSTY :

Be it known unto you that whereas in the course of our care and watchings over the order and police of all and sundry the manufacturers, retainers, and vendors of poesy; bards, poets, poetasters, rhymers, jinglers, songsters, ballad-singers, &c. &c. &c. &c. male and female— We have discovered a certain nefarious, abominable, and wicked song or ballad, a copy whereof We have here inclosed ; Our Will therefore is, that Ye pitch upon and appoint the most execrable individual of that most execrable species, known by the appellation, phrase, and nickname of The Deil's Yell Nowte :† and after having caused him to kindle a fire at the Cross of Ayr, ye shall, at noontide of the day, put into the said wretch's merciless hands the said copy of the said nefarious and wicked

---

* His birthday.

† "The deil's yell nowte," according to Gilbert Burns, is here used as a scoffing epithet applied to sheriffs' officers, and other executors of the law.

song, to be consumed by fire in the presence of all beholders, in abhorrence of, and terrorem to, all such compositions and composers. And this in nowise leave ye undone, but have it executed in every point as this our mandate bears, before the twenty-fourth current, when in person we hope to applaud your faithfulness and zeal.

Given at Mauchline this twentieth day of November, Anno Domini one thousand seven hundred and eighty-six.

God save the Bard!

No. XXIX.

TO MR. ROBERT MUIR.

[The Edinburgh expedition was undertaken in consequence of the following letter, written by the blind poet, Thomas Blacklock, to the Rev. Mr. Lawrie, from whom it passed through Gavin Hamilton to Burns:—

" I ought to have acknowledged your favour long ago, not only as a testimony of your kind remembrance, but as it gave me an opportunity of sharing one of the finest, and perhaps one of the most genuine entertainments, of which the human mind is susceptible. A number of avocations retarded my progress in reading the poems ; at last, however, I have finished that pleasing perusal. Many instances have I seen of nature's force and beneficence, exerted under numerous and formidable disadvantages ; but none equal to that with which you have been kind enough to present me. There is a pathos and delicacy in his serious poems ; a vein of wit and humour in those of a more festive turn, which cannot be too much admired, nor too warmly approved ; and I think I shall never open the book without feeling my astonishment renewed and increased. It was my wish to have expressed my approbation in verse ; but whether from declining life, or a temporary depression of spirits, it is at present out of my power to accomplish that agreeable intention. Mr. Stewart, Professor of Morals in this University, had formerly read me three of the poems, and I had desired him to get my name inserted among the subscribers : but whether this was done or not I never could learn. I have little intercourse with Dr. Blair, but will take care to have the poems communicated to him by the intervention of some mutual friend. It has been told me by a gentleman, to whom I showed the performances, and who sought a copy with diligence and ardour, that the whole impression is already exhausted. It were therefore much to be wished, for the sake of the young man, that a second edition, more numerous than the former, could immediately be printed ; as it appears certain that its intrinsic merit, and the exertion of the author's friends, might give it a more universal circulation than anything of the kind which has been published within my memory."]

MY DEAR SIR, MOSSGIEL, 18*th November*, 1786.

Inclosed you have " Tam Samson," as I intend to print him. I am thinking for my Edinburgh expedition on Monday or Tuesday, come se'nnight, for pos. I will see you on Tuesday first.

I am ever,
Your much indebted,
R. B.

No. XXX.

TO GAVIN HAMILTON, ESQ.

MAUCHLINE.

[Burns reached Edinburgh on his first visit on the 28th November. Through Mr. Dalrymple, of Orangefield, near Ayr, Burns was introduced to that gentleman's brother-in-law, Lord Glencairn, to the Hon. Henry Erskine, and other influential people. Gavin Hamilton, a Writer in Mauchline, was one of Burns' chief patrons in Ayrshire.]

HONOURED SIR,   EDINBURGH, *December 7th,* 1786.

I have paid every attention to your commands, but can only say what perhaps you will have heard before this reach you, that Muirkirk-lands were bought by a John Gordon, W.S., but for whom I know not ; Mauchlands, Haugh Mill, &c., by a Frederick Fotheringham, supposed to be for Ballochmyle Laird, and Adam-hill and Shawood were bought for Oswald's folks. This is so imperfect an account, and will be so late ere it reach you, that were it not to discharge my conscience I would not trouble you with it ; but after all my diligence I could make it no sooner nor better.

For my own affairs, I am in a fair way of becoming as eminent as Thomas à Kempis or John Bunyan ; and you may expect henceforth to see my birthday inserted among the wonderful events, in the Poor Robin's and Aberdeen Almanacks, along with the Black Monday, and the battle of Bothwell Bridge. My Lord Glencairn and the Dean of Faculty, Mr. H. Erskine, have taken me under their wing ; and by all probability I shall soon be the tenth worthy, and the eighth wise man of the world. Through my Lord's influence it is inserted in the records of the Caledonian Hunt, that they universally, one and all, subscribe for the second edition. My subscription bills come out to-morrow, and you shall have some of them next post. I have met, in Mr. Dalrymple, of Orangefield, what Solomon emphatically calls " a friend that sticketh closer than a brother." The warmth with which he interests himself in my affairs is of the same enthusiastic kind which you, Mr. Aiken, and the few patrons that took notice of my earlier poetic days showed for the poor unlucky devil of a poet.

I always remember Mrs. Hamilton and Miss Kennedy in my poetic prayers, but you both in prose and verse.

> May cauld ne'er catch you but a hap,
> Nor hunger but in plenty's lap !
> Amen !

R. B.

No. XXXI.

TO JAMES DALRYMPLE, ESQ. OF ORANGEFIELD.

DEAR SIR,   [*December* 10, 1786?]

I suppose the devil is so elated with his success with you, that he is determined by a *coup de main* to complete his purposes on you all at once, in making you a poet. I broke open the letter you sent me—hummed over the rhymes—and as I saw they were extempore, said to myself they were very well ; but when I saw at the bottom a name that I shall ever value with grateful respect, " I gapit wide, but naething spak." I was nearly as much struck as the friends of Job, of affliction-bearing memory, when they sat down with him seven days and seven nights, and spake not a word. . . . . . .

I am naturally of a superstitious cast ; and as soon as my wonder-scared imagination regained its consciousness, and resumed its functions, I cast about what this mania of yours might portend. My foreboding ideas had the wide stretch of possibility ; and several events, great in their magnitude, and important in their consequences, occurred to my fancy. The downfall of the conclave, or the crushing of the cork rumps—a ducal coronet to Lord George Gordon, and the Protestant interest, or St. Peter's keys to——.

You want to know how I come on. I am just in *statu quo*, or, not to insult a gentleman with my Latin, in " auld use and wont." The noble Earl of Glencairn took me by the hand to-day, and interested himself in my concerns, with a goodness like that benevolent being whose image he so richly bears. He is a stronger proof of the immortality of the soul than any that philosophy ever produced. A mind like his can never die. Let the worshipful Squire H. L., or the Reverend Mass J. M., go into their primitive nothing. At best, they are but ill-digested lumps of chaos—only, one of them strongly tinged with bituminous particles and sulphureous effluvia. But my noble patron, eternal as the heroic swell of magnanimity, and the generous throb of benevolence, shall look on with princely eye at "the war of elements, the wreck of matter, and the crush of worlds."—R. B.

No. XXXII.

TO JOHN BALLANTINE, ESQ.,

BANKER, AYR.

MY HONOURED FRIEND,   EDINBURGH, *13th December*, 1786.

I would not write you till I could have it in my power to give you some account of myself and my matters, which by the by is often no easy task. I arrived here on Tuesday was se'nnight, and have suffered ever since I came to town with a miserable head-ache and stomach com-

plaint, but am now a good deal better. I have found a worthy warm friend in Mr. Dalrymple, of Orangefield, who introduced me to Lord Glencairn, a man whose worth and brotherly kindness to me I shall remember when time shall be no more. By his interest it is passed in the " Caledonian Hunt," and entered in their books, that they are to take each a copy of the second edition, for which they are to pay one guinea.— I have been introduced to a good many of the *noblesse*, but my avowed patrons and patronesses are, the Duchess of Gordon—the Countess of Glencairn, with my Lord, and Lady Betty*—the Dean of Faculty—Sir John Whiteford. I have likewise warm friends among the literati : Professors Stewart, Blair, and Mr. Mackenzie—the Man of Feeling. An unknown hand left ten guineas for the Ayrshire Bard with Mr. Sibbald, which I got. I since have discovered my generous unknown friend to be Patrick Miller, Esq., brother to the Justice Clerk ; and drank a glass of claret with him by invitation at his own house yesternight. I am nearly agreed with Creech to print my book, and I suppose I will begin on Monday. I will send a subscription bill or two, next post ; when I intend writing my first kind patron, Mr. Aiken. I saw his son to-day, and he is very well.

Dugald Stewart, and some of my learned friends, put me in the periodical paper called the Lounger,† a copy of which I here inclose you. I was, Sir, when I was first honoured with your notice, too obscure ; now I tremble lest I should be ruined by being dragged too suddenly into the glare of polite and learned observation.

I shall certainly, my ever-honoured patron, write you an account of my every step ; and better health and more spirits may enable me to make it something better than this stupid matter-of-fact epistle.

I have the honour to be,
Good Sir,
Your ever grateful humble Servant,
R. B.

---

* Lady Betty Cunningham, sister of Lord Glencairn.

† The paper here alluded to was written by Mr. Mackenzie, the celebrated author of " The Man of Feeling." It recognises in the poems " a genius of no ordinary rank," remarkable in itself without reference to the natural wonder excited by the fact that they were written by a man of such humble rank, without the advantages of a good education. "The power of genius," Mr. Mackenzie proceeds, " is not less admirable in tracing the manners, than in painting the passions or in drawing the scenery of nature. That intuitive glance with which a writer like Shakspeare discerns the characters of men, with which he catches the many changing hues of life, forms a sort of problem in the science of mind, of which it is easier to see the truth than to assign the cause. Though I am very far from meaning to compare our rustic bard to Shakspeare, yet whoever will read his lighter and more humorous poems, his Dialogue of the Dogs, his Dedication to G—— H——, Esq., his Epistle to a Young Friend, and to W—— S——, will perceive with what uncommon penetration and sagacity this heaven-taught ploughman, from his humble and unlettered station, has looked upon men and things." Mackenzie then referred to the misfortunes which, as he had heard most probably from Dugald Stewart, had befallen the bard, and expressed a hope that some means might be found to provide for him in his native land.

No. XXXIII.

TO MR. ROBERT MUIR.

My dear Friend,   Edinburgh, *December 20th,* 1786.

I have just time for the carrier, to tell you that I received your letter ; of which I shall say no more but what a lass of my acquaintance said of her bastard wean ; she said she " did na ken wha was the father exactly, but she suspected it was some o' thae bonny blackguard smugglers, for it was like them." So I only say your obliging epistle was like you. I inclose you a parcel of subscription bills. Your affair of sixty copies is also like you ; but it would not be like me to comply.

Your friend's notion of my life has put a crotchet in my head of sketching it in some future epistle to you. My compliments to Charles and Mr. Parker.—R. B.

No. XXXIV.

TO MR. WILLIAM CHALMERS,

WRITER, AYR.

My dear Friend,   Edinburgh, *December 27th,* 1786.

I confess I have sinned the sin for which there is hardly any forgiveness—ingratitude to friendship—in not writing you sooner ; but of all men living, I had intended to have sent you an entertaining letter ; and by all the plodding, stupid powers, that in nodding, conceited majesty, preside over the dull routine of business—a heavily solemn oath this !— I am, and have been, ever since I came to Edinburgh, as unfit to write a letter of humour, as to write a commentary on the Revelation of St. John the Divine, who was banished to the Isle of Patmos, by the cruel and bloody Domitian, son to Vespasian and brother to Titus, both emperors of Rome, and who was himself an emperor, and raised the second or third persecution, I forget which, against the Christians, and after throwing the said Apostle John, brother to the Apostle James, commonly called James the Greater, to distinguish him from another James, who was, on some account or other, known by the name of James the Less—after throwing him into a caldron of boiling oil, from which he was miraculously preserved, he banished the poor son of Zebedee to a desert island in the Archipelago, where he was gifted with the second sight, and saw as many wild beasts as I have seen since I came to Edinburgh ; which, a circumstance not very uncommon in story-telling, brings me back to where I set out.

To make you some amends for what, before you reach this paragraph, you will have suffered, I inclose you two poems I have carded and spun since I passed Glenbuck.

One blank in the Address to Edinburgh—" Fair B——," is heavenly Miss Burnet, daughter to Lord Monboddo, at whose house I have had the

honour to be more than once. There has not been anything nearly like her in all the combinations of beauty, grace, and goodness the great Creator has formed, since Milton's Eve on the first day of her existence.

My direction is—care of Andrew Bruce, merchant, Bridge-street.

R. E.

No. XXXV.

TO THE EARL OF EGLINTON.

MY LORD,   EDINBURGH, *January*, 1787.

As I have but slender pretensions to philosophy, I cannot rise to the exalted ideas of a citizen of the world, but have all those national prejudices, which I believe glow peculiarly strong in the breast of a Scotchman. There is scarcely anything to which I am so feelingly alive as the honour and welfare of my country : and as a poet, I have no higher enjoyment than singing her sons and daughters. Fate had cast my station in the veriest shades of life ; but never did a heart pant more ardently than mine to be distinguished ; though till very lately, I looked in vain on every side for a ray of light. It is easy then to guess how much I was gratified with the countenance and approbation of one of my country's most illustrious sons, when Mr. Wauchope called on me yesterday on the part of your lordship.* Your munificence, my lord, certainly deserves my very grateful acknowledgments ; but your patronage is a bounty peculiarly suited to my feelings. I am not master enough of the etiquette of life to know, whether there be not some impropriety in troubling your lordship with my thanks, but my heart whispered me to do it. From the emotions of my inmost soul I do it. Selfish ingratitude I hope I am incapable of ; and mercenary servility, I trust, I shall ever have so much honest pride as to detest.—R. B.

No. XXXVI.

TO JOHN BALLANTINE, ESQ.

MY HONOURED FRIEND,   EDINBURGH, *January 14th*, 1787.

It gives me a secret comfort to observe in myself that I am not yet so far gone as Willie Gaw's Skate, "past redemption ;"† for I have still this favourable symptom of grace, that when my conscience, as in the case of this letter, tells me I am leaving something undone that I ought to do, it teazes me eternally till I do it.

I am still "dark as was Chaos" in respect to futurity. My generous friend Mr. Patrick Miller, has been talking with me about the lease of some farm or other in an estate called Dalswinton, which he has lately bought near Dumfries. Some life-rented embittering recollections whisper me that I will be happier anywhere than in my old neighbourhood, but

---

* Mr. Wauchope brought him ten guineas as a subscription for two copies of his second edition.
† This is one of a great number of old saws that Burns, when a lad, had picked up from his mother, who had a vast collection of them.

B   Y

Mr. Miller is no judge of land ; and though I dare say he means to favour me, yet he may give me, in his opinion, an advantageous bargain that may ruin me.   I am to take a tour by Dumfries as I return, and have promised to meet Mr. Miller on his lands some time in May.

I went to a mason-lodge yesternight, where the most Worshipful Grand Master Chartres, and all the Grand Lodge of Scotland visited.   The meeting was numerous and elegant ; all the different lodges about town were present, in all their pomp.   The Grand Master, who presided with great solemnity and honor to himself as a gentleman and a mason, among other general toasts, gave " Caledonia, and Caledonia's Bard, Brother Burns," which rung through the whole assembly with multiplied honours and repeated acclamations.   As I had no idea such a thing would happen, I was downright thunderstruck, and, trembling in every nerve, made the best return in my power.   Just as I had finished, some of the grand officers said, so loud that I could hear, with a most comforting accent, "Very well indeed !" which set me something to rights again.

I have to-day corrected my 152d page.   My best good wishes to Mr. Aiken.

I am ever, dear Sir,
Your much indebted humble Servant,
R. B

No. XXXVII.

TO THE SAME.

January —, 1787.

WHILE here I sit, sad and solitary, by the side of a fire in a little country inn, and drying my wet clothes, in pops a poor fellow of a sodger, and tells me he is going to Ayr.   By heavens ! say I to myself, with a tide of good spirits which the magic of that sound, Auld Toon o' Ayr, conjured up, I will send my last song to Mr. Ballantine.   Here it is—

> Ye flowery banks o' bonnie Doon,
>   How can ye bloom sae fair ;
> How can ye chant, ye little birds,
>   And I sae fu' o' care ?

No. XXXVIII.

TO MRS. DUNLOP.

[This is an acknowledgment of some extracts which Mrs. Dunlop had sent to Burns from her correspondence with Dr. Moore, author of "Zeluco," &c.]

MADAM, EDINBURGH, *15th January*, 1787.

Yours of the 9th current, which I am this moment honoured with, is a deep reproach to me for ungrateful neglect. I will tell you the real truth, for I am miserably awkward at a fib—I wished to have written to Dr. Moore before I wrote to you ; but though every day since I received yours of December 30th, the idea, the wish to write to him has constantly pressed on my thoughts, yet I could not for my soul set about it. I know his fame and character, and I am one of "the sons of little men." To write him a mere matter-of-fact affair, like a merchant's order, would be disgracing the little character I have ; and to write the author of "The View of Society and Manners" a letter of sentiment—I declare every artery runs cold at the thought. I shall try, however, to write to him to-morrow or next day. His kind interposition in my behalf I have already experienced, as a gentleman waited on me the other day, on the part of Lord Eglinton, with ten guineas, by way of subscription for two copies of my next edition.

The word you object to in the mention I have made of my glorious countryman and your immortal ancestor, is indeed borrowed from Thomson ; but it does not strike me as an improper epithet. I distrusted my own judgment on your finding fault with it, and applied for the opinion of some of the literati here, who honour me with their critical strictures, and they all allow it to be proper. The song you ask I cannot recollect, and I have not a copy of it. I have not composed anything on the great Wallace, except what you have seen in print ; and the inclosed, which I will print in this edition.* You will see I have mentioned some others of the name. When I composed my "Vision" long ago, I had attempted a description of Kyle, of which the additional stanzas are a part, as it originally stood. My heart glows with a wish to be able to do justice to the merits of the "saviour of his country," which sooner or later I shall at least attempt.

You are afraid I shall grow intoxicated with my prosperity as a poet : alas ! Madam, I know myself and the world too well. I do not mean any airs of affected modesty ; I am willing to believe that my abilities deserve some notice ; but in a most enlightened, informed age and nation, when poetry is and has been the study of men of the first natural genius, aided with all the powers of polite learning, polite books, and polite company—to be dragged forth to the full glare of learned and polite observation, with all my imperfections of awkward rusticity and crude unpolished

---

* Stanzas in the "Vision," beginning "By stately tower or palace fair," and ending with the first Duan. Burns afterwards rejected several of the new stanzas before sending the book to press. Those omitted were chiefly panegyrics on country gentlefolk who had been kind to him.

ideas on my head—I assure you, Madam, I do not dissemble when I tell you I tremble for the consequences. The novelty of a poet in my obscure situat on, without any of those advantages which are reckoned necessary for that character, at least at this time of day, has raised a partial tide of public notice which has borne me to a height, where I am absolutely, feelingly certain my abilities are inadequate to support me ; and too surely do I see that time when the same tide will leave me, and recede, perhaps, as far below the mark of truth. I do not say this in the ridiculous affectation of self-abasement and modesty. I have studied myself, and know what ground I occupy ; and, however a friend or the world may differ from me in that particular, I stand for my own opinion, in silent resolve, with all the tenaciousness of property. I mention this to you once for all to disburthen my mind, and I do not wish to hear or say more about it. But,

"When proud fortune's ebbing tide recedes,"

you will bear me witness, that when my bubble of fame was at the highest, I stood unintoxicated, with the inebriating cup in my hand, looking forward with rueful resolve to the hastening time, when the blow of Calumny should dash it to the ground, with all the eagerness of vengeful triumph.

Your patronizing me and interesting yourself in my fame and character as a poet, I rejoice in ; it exalts me in my own idea ; and whether you can or cannot aid me in my subscription is a trifle. Has a paltry subscription-bill any charms to the heart of a bard, compared with the patronage of the descendant of the immortal Wallace?—R. B.

No. XXXIX.

TO DR. MOORE.

SIR,   EDINBURGH, *January* [16th?], 1787.

Mrs. Dunlop has been so kind as to send me extracts of letters she has had from you, where you do the rustic bard the honour of noticing him and his works. Those who have felt the anxieties and solicitudes of authorship, can only know what pleasure it gives to be noticed in such a manner, by judges of the first character. Your criticisms, Sir, I receive with reverence ; only I am sorry they mostly came too late : a peccant passage or two that I would certainly have altered, were gone to the press.

The hope to be admired for ages is, in by far the greater part of those even who are authors of repute, an unsubstantial dream. For my part, my first ambition was, and still my strongest wish is, to please my compeers, the rustic inmates of the hamlet, while ever-changing language and manners shall allow me to be relished and understood. I am very willing to admit that I have some poetical abilities ; and as few, if any, writers, either moral or poetical, are intimately acquainted with the classes of mankind among whom I have chiefly mingled, I may have seen men and manners in a different phasis from what is common, which may assist

originality of thought. Still I know very well the novelty of my character has by far the greatest share in the learned and polite notice I have lately had ; and in a language where Pope and Churchill have raised the laugh, and Shenstone and Gray drawn the tear ; where Thomson and Beattie have painted the landscape, and Lyttelton and Collins described the heart, I am not vain enough to hope for distinguished poetic fame.*—R. B.

No. XL.

TO THE REV. G. LAWRIE.

NEWMILLS, NEAR KILMARNOCK.

[Mr. Lawrie had written to Burns, urging him to visit Blacklock, the blind poet, and added a few kindly words of warning as to the temptations of the new life on which the Poet had entered.]

REVEREND AND DEAR SIR,   EDINBURGH, *February 5th,* 1787.

When I look at the date of your kind letter, my heart reproaches me severely with ingratitude in neglecting so long to answer it. I will not trouble you with any account by way of apology, of my hurried life and distracted attention : do me the justice to believe that my delay by no means proceeded from want of respect. I feel, and ever shall feel for you, the mingled sentiments of esteem for a friend and reverence for a father.

I thank you, Sir, with all my soul for your friendly hints, though I do not need them so much as my friends are apt to imagine. You are dazzled with newspaper accounts and distant reports ; but in reality, I have no great temptation to be intoxicated with the cup of prosperity. Novelty may attract the attention of mankind awhile ; to it I owe my present éclat ; but I see the time not far distant when the popular tide which has borne me to a height of which I am, perhaps, unworthy, shall recede with silent celerity, and leave me a barren waste of sand, to descend at my leisure to my former station. I do not say this in the affectation of modesty ; I see the consequence is unavoidable, and am prepared for it. I had been at a good deal of pains to form a just, impartial estimate of my intellectual powers before I came here ; I have not added, since I came to Edinburgh, anything to the account ; and I trust I shall take every atom of it back to my shades, the coverts of my unnoticed early years.

In Dr. Blacklock, whom I see very often, I have found what I would have expected in our friend, a clear head and an excellent heart.

---

* In his reply to this letter, dated Jan. 23rd, 1787, Dr. Moore says :—" If I may judge of the author's disposition from his works, with all the other good qualities of a poet, he has not the irritable temper ascribed to that race of men by one of their own number, whom you have the happiness to resemble in ease and curious felicity of expression. Indeed the poetical beauties, however original and brilliant, and lavishly scattered, are not all I admire in your works ; the love of your native country, that feeling sensibility to all the objects of humanity, and the independent spirit which breathes through the whole, give me a most favourable impression of the Poet, and have made me often regret that I did not see the poems, the certain effect of which would have been my seeing the author, last summer, when I was longer in Scotland than I have been for many years."

By far the most agreeable hours I spend in Edinburgh must be placed to the account of Miss Lawrie and her pianoforte. I cannot help repeating to you and Mrs. Lawrie a compliment that Mr. Mackenzie, the celebrated " Man of Feeling," paid to Miss Lawrie, the other night, at the concert. I had come in at the interlude, and sat down by him till I saw Miss Lawrie in a seat not very distant, and went up to pay my respects to her. On my return to Mr. Mackenzie, he asked me who she was ; I told him 'twas the daughter of a reverend friend of mine in the west country. He returned, there was something very striking, to his idea, in her appearance. On my desiring to know what it was, he was pleased to say " She has a great deal of the elegance of a well-bred lady about her, with all the sweet simplicity of a country girl."

My compliments to all the happy inmates of St. Margaret's.—R. B.

No. XLI.

TO DR. MOORE.

SIR, EDINBURGH, *February 15th,* 1787.

Pardon my seeming neglect in delaying so long to acknowledge the honour you have done me, in your kind notice of me, January 23rd. Not many months ago I knew no other employment than following the plough, nor could boast anything higher than a distant acquaintance with a country gentleman. Mere greatness never embarrasses me ; I have nothing to ask from the great, and I do not fear their judgment ; but genius, polished by learning, and at its proper point of elevation in the eye of the world, this of late I frequently meet with, and tremble at its approach. I scorn the affectation of seeming modesty to cover self-conceit. That I have some merit I do not deny ; but I see with frequent wringings of heart, that the novelty of my character, and the honest national prejudice of my countrymen, have borne me to a height altogether untenable to my abilities.

For the honour Miss Williams has done me, please, Sir, return her in my name my most grateful thanks. I have more than once thought of paying her in kind, but have hitherto quitted the idea in hopeless despondency. I had never before heard of her ; but the other day I got her Poems, which for several reasons, some belonging to the head, and others the offspring of the heart, give me a great deal of pleasure. I have little pretensions to critic lore ; there are, I think, two characteristic features in her poetry—the unfettered wild flight of native genius, and the querulous, sombre tenderness of "time-settled sorrow."

I only know what pleases me, often without being able to tell why.*

R. B.

* Dr. Moore, writing on 28th February, says:—" You are a very great favourite in my family ; and this is a higher compliment than perhaps you are aware of. It includes almost all the professions, and of course is a proof that your writings are adapted to various tastes and situations. My youngest son who is at Winchester School, writes to me that he is translating some stanzas of your ' Hallowe'en ' into Latin verse, for the benefit of his comrades."

No. XLII.

TO JOHN BALLANTINE, Esq.

[The picture from which Beugo engraved the portrait to which the Poet alludes, was painted by Alexander Nasmyth—the work in each case being done gratuitously. The engraving has a more melancholy air than the picture, and is of a swarthier hue : this change was made by the engraver, who caused the Poet to sit to him, and finished the copper from his face, in preference to working from the picture.]

My honoured Friend,   Edinburgh, *February 24th,* 1787.

I will soon be with you now, in guid black prent ;—in a week or ten days at farthest. I am obliged, against my own wish, to print subscribers' names ; so if any of my Ayr friends have subscription bills, they must be sent into Creech directly. I am getting my phiz done by an eminent engraver, and if it can be ready in time, I will appear in my book, looking like all other *fools* to my title-page.—R. B.

No. XLIII.

TO THE EARL OF GLENCAIRN.

My Lord,   Edinburgh, 1787.

I wanted to purchase a profile of your lordship, which I was told was to be got in town ; but I am truly sorry to see that a blundering painter has spoiled a "human face divine." The inclosed stanzas I intended to have written below a picture or profile of your lordship, could I have been so happy as to procure one with anything of a likeness.

As I will soon return to my shades, I wanted to have something like a material object for my gratitude ; I wanted to have it in my power to say to a friend, there is my noble patron, my generous benefactor. Allow me, my lord, to publish these verses. I conjure your lordship, by the honest throe of gratitude, by the generous wish of benevolence, by all the powers and feelings which compose the magnanimous mind, do not deny me this petition. I owe much to your lordship ; and, what has not in some other instances always been the case with me, the weight of the obligation is a pleasing load. I trust I have a heart as independent as your lordship's, than which I can say nothing more ; and I would not be beholden to favours that would crucify my feelings. Your dignified character in life, and manner of supporting that character, are flattering to my pride ; and I would be jealous of the purity of my grateful attachment, where I was under the patronage of one of the much favoured sons of fortune.

Almost every poet has celebrated his patrons, particularly when they were names dear to fame, and illustrious in their country ; allow me, then, my lord, if you think the verses have intrinsic merit, to tell the world how much I have the honour to be,

Your lordship's highly indebted,

And ever grateful humble Servant,

R. B.

No. XLIV.

TO THE EARL OF BUCHAN.

[The Earl of Buchan had advised Burns to seek inspiration for his muse in a pilgrimage to the chief battle-fields of Scotland, in the hope, it was suspected, that Ancrum Moor and his own family might be duly celebrated.]

MY LORD,

The honour your lordship has done me, by your notice and advice in yours of the 1st instant, I shall ever gratefully remember :—

> " Praise from thy lips 'tis mine with joy to boast,
> They best can give it who deserve it most."

Your lordship touches the darling chord of my heart, when you advise me to fire my muse at Scottish story and Scottish scenes. I wish for nothing more than to make a leisurely pilgrimage through my native country ; to sit and muse on those once hard-contended fields, where Caledonia, rejoicing, saw her bloody lion borne through broken ranks to victory and fame ; and, catching the inspiration, to pour the deathless names in song. But, my lord, in the midst of these enthusiastic reveries, a long-visaged, dry, moral-looking phantom strides across my imagination, and pronounces these emphatic words :—

" I, Wisdom, dwell with Prudence. Friend, I do not come to open the ill-closed wounds of your follies and misfortunes, merely to give you pain : I wish through these wounds to imprint a lasting lesson on your heart. I will not mention how many of my salutary advices you have despised : I have given you line upon line and precept upon precept ; and while I was chalking out to you the straight way to wealth and character, with audacious effrontery you have zigzagged across the path, contemning me to my face : you know the consequences. It is not yet three months since home was so hot for you that you were on the wing for the western shore of the Atlantic, not to make a fortune, but to hide your misfortune.

" Now that your dear-loved Scotia puts it in your power to return to the situation of your forefathers, will you follow these will-o'-wisp meteors of fancy and whim till they bring you once more to the brink of ruin ? I grant that the utmost ground you can occupy is but half a step from the veriest poverty ; but still it is half a step from it. If all that I can urge be ineffectual, let her who seldom calls to you in vain, let the call of Pride prevail with you. You know how you feel at the iron gripe of ruthless oppression : you know how you bear the galling sneer of contumelious greatness. I hold you out the conveniences, the comforts of life, independence, and character, on the one hand ; I tender you civility, dependence, and wretchedness, on the other. I will not insult your understanding by bidding you make a choice."

This, my lord, is unanswerable. I must return to my humble station, and woo my rustic muse in my wonted way at the plough-tail. Still, my lord, while the drops of life warm my heart, gratitude to that dear-loved country in which I boast my birth, and gratitude to those her distinguished

sons who have honoured me so much with their patronage and approbation, shall, while stealing through my humble shades, ever distend my bosom, and at times, as now, draw forth the swelling tear.—R. B.

No. XLV.

TO MR. JAMES CANDLISH.*

EDINBURGH, *March 21st,* 1787.

MY EVER DEAR OLD ACQUAINTANCE,

I was equally surprised and pleased at your letter, though I dare say you will think by my delaying so long to write to you that I am so drowned in the intoxication of good fortune as to be indifferent to old, and once dear connexions. The truth is, I was determined to write a good letter, full of argument, amplification, erudition, and, as Bayes says, *all that.* I thought of it, and thought of it, and, by my soul, I could not; and, lest you should mistake the cause of my silence, I just sit down to tell you so. Don't give yourself credit, though, that the strength of your logic scares me : the truth is, I never mean to meet you on that ground at all. You have shown me one thing which was to be demonstrated : that strong pride of reasoning, with a little affectation of singularity, may mislead the best of hearts. I likewise, since you and I were first acquainted, in the pride of despising old women's stories, ventured in "the daring path Spinosa trod;" but experience of the weakness, not the strength of human powers, made me glad to grasp at revealed religion.

I am still, in the Apostle Paul's phrase, "The old man with his deeds," as when we were sporting about the "Lady Thorn." I shall be four weeks here yet at least ; and so I shall expect to hear from you ; welcome sense, welcome nonsense.

I am, with the warmest sincerity,

R. B.

No. XLVI.

TO ———.

[One of the first things Burns did on his arrival in Edinburgh was, according to Allan Cunningham, to seek out the lowly grave of Fergusson, when kneeling down he kissed the sod. In February, 1787, he wrote to the Managers of the Kirk and Kirkyard Funds of Canongate, offering to "lay a simple stone over his (Fergusson's) revered ashes, to remain an unalienable property to his deathless fame,"—an offer which was cordially accepted.]

MY DEAR SIR,   EDINBURGH, *March,* 1787.

You may think, and too justly, that I am a selfish, ungrateful fellow, having received so many repeated instances of kindness from you, and yet never putting pen to paper to say thank you : but if you knew what a devil of a life my conscience has led me on that account, your good heart

* Father of the Rev. Dr. Candlish, of Edinburgh.

would think yourself too much avenged. By the by there is nothing in the whole frame of man which seems to be so unaccountable as that thing called conscience. Had the troublesome yelping cur powers efficient to prevent a mischief, he might be of use ; but at the beginning of the business, his feeble efforts are to the workings of passion as the infant frosts of an autumnal morning to the unclouded fervour of the rising sun : and no sooner are the tumultuous doings of the wicked deed over, than, amidst the bitter native consequences of folly, in the very vortex of our horrors, up starts conscience, and harrows us with the feelings of the damned.

The inscription on the stone is as follows :—

"HERE LIES ROBERT FERGUSSON, POET,

"Born, September 5th, 1751—Died, 16th September, 1774.

"No sculptur'd marble here, nor pompous lay,
' No storied urn nor animated bust ;'
This simple stone directs pale Scotia's way
To pour her sorrows o'er her poet's dust."

On the other side of the stone is as follows :—

"By special grant of the Managers to Robert Burns, who erected this stone, this burial place is to remain for ever sacred to the memory of Robert Fergusson."

No. XLVII.

TO MRS. DUNLOP.

MADAM,　　　　　　　　　　　　　EDINBURGH, *March 22d*, 1787.

I read your letter with watery eyes. A little, very little while ago, I had scarce a friend but the stubborn pride of my own bosom ; now I am distinguished, patronized, befriended by you. Your friendly advices—I will not give them the cold name of criticisms—I receive with reverence. I have made some small alterations in what I before had printed. I have the advice of some very judicious friends among the literati here, but with them I sometimes find it necessary to claim the privilege of thinking for myself. The noble Earl of Glencairn, to whom I owe more than to any man, does me the honour of giving me his strictures : his hints, with respect to impropriety or indelicacy, I follow implicitly.

You kindly interest yourself in my future views and prospects ; there I can give you no light. It is all

"Dark as was Chaos ere the infant sun
Was roll'd together, or had tried his beams
Athwart the gloom profound."

The appellation of a Scottish bard, is by far my highest pride ; to continue to deserve it is my most exalted ambition. Scottish scenes and Scottish story are the themes I could wish to sing. I have no dearer aim than to have it in my power, unplagued with the routine of business, for which heaven knows I am unfit enough, to make leisurely pilgrimages

through Caledonia ; to sit on the fields of her battles ; to wander on the romantic banks of her rivers ; and to muse by the stately towers or venerable ruins, once the honoured abodes of her heroes.

But these are all Utopian thoughts : I have dallied long enough with life ; 'tis time to be in earnest. I have a fond, an aged mother to care for : and some other bosom ties perhaps equally tender. Where the individual only suffers by the consequences of his own thoughtlessness, indolence, or folly, he may be excusable ; nay, shining abilities, and some of the nobler virtues, may half sanctify a heedless character ; but where God and nature have entrusted the welfare of others to his care ; where the trust is sacred, and the ties are dear, that man must be far gone in selfishness, or strangely lost to reflection, whom these connexions will not rouse to exertion.

I guess that I shall clear between two and three hundred pounds by my authorship ;* with that sum I intend, so far as I may be said to have any intention, to return to my old acquaintance, the plough, and, if I can meet with a lease by which I can live, to commence farmer. I do not intend to give up poetry ; being bred to labour, secures me independence, and the muses are my chief, sometimes have been my only enjoyment. If my practice second my resolution, I shall have principally at heart the serious business of life ; but while following my plough, or building up my shocks, I shall cast a leisure glance to that dear, that only feature of my character, which gave me the notice of my country, and the patronage of a Wallace.

Thus, honoured Madam, I have given you the bard, his situation, and his views, native as they are in his own bosom.—R. B.

No. XLVIII.

TO THE SAME.

Madam,   Edinburgh, 15th April, 1787.

There is an affectation of gratitude which I dislike. The periods of Johnson and the pauses of Sterne may hide a selfish heart. For my part, Madam, I trust I have too much pride for servility, and too little prudence for selfishness. I have this moment broken open your letter, but

> " Rude am I in speech,
> And therefore little can I grace my cause
> In speaking for myself—"

so I shall not trouble you with any fine speeches and hunted figures. I shall just lay my hand on my heart and say, I hope I shall ever have the truest, the warmest, sense of your goodness.

I come abroad, in print, for certain on Wednesday. Your orders I shall punctually attend to ; only by the way, I must tell you that I was paid before for Dr. Moore's and Miss Williams' copies, through the

---

* For the new edition of the Poems, which appeared on 21st April, 1787, there were 1,500 sub-scribers, engaging for 2,800 copies. Burns cleared about £500 by the whole.

medium of Commissioner Cochrane in this place, but that we can settle when I have the honour of waiting on you.

Dr. Smith* was just gone to London the morning before I received your letter to him.—R. B.

No. XLIX.

TO DR. MOORE.

EDINBURGH, 23*d April*, 1787.

I RECEIVED the books, and sent the one you mentioned to Mrs. Dunlop. I am ill skilled in beating the coverts of imagination for metaphors of gratitude. I thank you, Sir, for the honour you have done me ; and to my latest hour will warmly remember it. To be highly pleased with your book is what I have in common with the world ; but to regard these volumes as a mark of the author's friendly esteem, is a still more supreme gratification.

I leave Edinburgh in the course of ten days or a fortnight, and, after a few pilgrimages over some of the classic ground of Caledonia, Cowden Knowes, Banks of Yarrow, Tweed, &c. I shall return to my rural shades, in all likelihood never more to quit them. I have formed many intimacies and friendships here, but I am afraid they are all of too tender a construction to bear carriage a hundred and fifty miles. To the rich, the great, the fashionable, the polite, I have no equivalent to offer ; and I am afraid my meteor appearance will by no means entitle me to a settled correspondence with any of you, who are the permanent lights of genius and literature.

My most respectful compliments to Miss Williams. If once this tangent flight of mine were over, and I were returned to my wonted leisurely motion in my old circle, I may probably endeavour to return her poetic compliment in kind.—R. B.

No. L.

TO MRS. DUNLOP.

EDINBURGH, 30*th April*, 1787.

————YOUR criticisms, Madam, I understand very well, and could have wished to have pleased you better. You are right in your guess that I am not very amenable to counsel. Poets, much my superiors, have so flattered those who possessed the adventitious qualities of wealth and power, that I am determined to flatter no created being, either in prose or verse.

I set as little by princes, lords, clergy, critics, &c. as all these respective gentry do by my bardship. I know what I may expect from the world, by and by—illiberal abuse, and perhaps contemptuous neglect.

* Adam Smith, author of " Wealth of Nations."

I am happy, Madam, that some of my own favourite pieces are distinguished by your particular approbation. For my " Dream," which has unfortunately incurred your loyal displeasure, I hope in four weeks, or less, to have the honour of appearing, at Dunlop, in its defence in person.

R. B.

No. LI.

TO THE REV. DR. HUGH BLAIR.

LAWN MARKET, EDINBURGH, *3rd May,* 1787.

REVEREND AND MUCH RESPECTED SIR,

I leave Edinburgh to-morrow morning, but could not go without troubling you with half a line, sincerely to thank you for the kindness, patronage, and friendship you have shown me. I often felt the embarrassment of my singular situation; drawn forth from the veriest shades of life to the glare of remark; and honoured by the notice of those illustrious names of my country whose works, while they are applauded to the end of time, will ever instruct and mend the heart. However the meteor-like novelty of my appearance in the world might attract notice, and honour me with the acquaintance of the permanent lights of genius and literature, those who are truly benefactors of the immortal nature of man, I knew very well that my utmost merit was far unequal to the task of preserving that character when once the novelty was over ; I have made up my mind that abuse, or almost even neglect, will not surprise me in my quarters.

I have sent you a proof impression of Beugo's work* for me, done on Indian paper, as a trifling but sincere testimony with what heart-warm gratitude I am, &c.†—R. B.

* The portrait of the Poet after Nasmyth.

† A few sentences of Blair's reply may be quoted, partly as testimony to Burns' behaviour in the capital, and partly as an example of the pretentious patronage of common-place men which he had to endure :—" Your situation, as you say, was indeed very singular ; and in being brought out, all at once, from the shades of deepest privacy to so great a share of public notice and observation, you had to stand a severe trial. I am happy that you have stood it so well : and, as far I have known or heard, though in the midst of many temptations, without reproach to your character and behaviour. You are now, I presume, to retire to a more private walk of life ; and I trust will conduct yourself there with industry, prudence, and honour. You have laid the foundation for just public esteem. In the midst of those employments which your situation will render proper, you will not I hope neglect to promote that esteem, by cultivating your genius, and attending to such productions of it as may raise your character still higher. At the same time, be not in too great a haste to come forward. Take time and leisure to improve and mature your talents. For on any second production you give the world, your fate, as a poet, will very much depend. There is no doubt a gloss of novelty, which time wears off. As you very properly hint yourself, you are not to be surprised, if in your rural retreat you do not find yourself surrounded with that glare of notice and applause which here shone upon you. No man can be a good poet without being somewhat of a philosopher. He must lay his account, that any one, who exposes himself to public observation, will occasionally meet with the attacks of illiberal censure, which it is always best to overlook and despise. He will be inclined sometimes to court retreat, and to disappear from public view. He will not affect to shine always; that he may at proper seasons come forth with more advantage and energy. He will not think himself neglected if he be not always praised."

No. LII.

TO MR. W. NICOL,

MASTER OF THE HIGH SCHOOL, EDINBURGH.

KIND, HONEST-HEARTED WILLIE,   CARLISLE, *June 1st,* 1787.
    I'm sitten down here, after seven and forty miles ridin', e'en as for-jesket and forniaw'd as a forfoughten cock, to gie you some notion o' my land lowperlike stravaguin sin the sorrowfu' hour that I sheuk hands and parted with auld Reekie.
    My auld, ga'd gleyde o' a meere has huchyall'd up hill and down brae, in Scotland and England, as teugh and birnie as a vera devil wi' me.* It's true, she's as poor's a sang-maker and as hard's a kirk, and tipper-taipers when she taks the gate, first like a lady's gentlewoman in a minuwae, or a hen on a het girdle ; but she's a yauld, poutherie Girran for a' that, and has a stomack like Willie Stalker's meere that wad hae digeested tumbler-wheels, for she'll whip me aff her five stimparts o' the best aits at a down-sittin and ne'er fash her thumb.   When ance her ringbanes and spavies, her crucks and cramps, are fairly soupl'd, she beets to, beets to, and ay the hindmost hour the tightest.   I could wager her price to a thretty pennies, that for twa or three wooks ridin at fifty mile a day, the deil-sticket a five gallopers acqueesh Clyde and Whithorn could cast saut on her tail.
    I hae dander'd owre a' the kintra frae Dumbar to Selcraig, and hae for-gather'd wi' mony a guid fallow, and monie a weelfar'd hizzie.   I met wi' twa dink quines in particlar, ane o' them a sonsie, fine, fodgel lass, baith braw and bonnie ; the tither was a clean-shankit, straught, tight, weel-far'd winch, as blythe's a lintwhite on a flowerie thorn, and as sweet and modest's a new blawn plumrose in a hazle shaw.   They were baith bred to mainers by the beuk, and onie ane o' them had as muckle smeddum and rumblgumtion as the half o' some presbytries that you and I baith ken.   They play'd me sik a deevil o' a shavie that I daur say if my harigals were turn'd out, ye wad see twa nicks i'the heart o' me like the mark o' a kail-whittle in a castock.
    I was gaun to write you a lang pystle, but, Gude forgie me, I gat myself sae noutouriously bitchify'd the day after kail-time, that I can hardly stoiter but and ben.
    My best respecks to the guidwife and a' our common friens, especiall Mr. and Mrs. Cruikshank, and the honest guidman o' Jock's Lodge.
    I'll be in Dumfries the morn gif the beast be to the fore, and the branks bide hale.

Gude be wi' you, Willie ! Amen !

R. B.

---

* This mare was the Poet's favourite, Jenny Geddes.

No. LIII.

TO MR. JAMES SMITH,

LINLITHGOW.

MY EVER DEAR SIR,   MAUCHLINE, *June 11th,* 1787.

I date this from Mauchline, where I arrived on Friday even last. If anything had been wanting to disgust me completely at Armour's family, their mean, servile compliance would have done it.

Give me a spirit like my favourite hero, Milton's Satan :—

> " Hail, horrors ! hail,
> Infernal world ! and thou profoundest Hell,
> Receive thy new possessor ! he who brings
> A mind not to be changed by *place* or *time* !"

I cannot settle to my mind. Farming, the only thing of which I know anything, and heaven above knows but little do I understand of that, I cannot, dare not risk on farms as they are. If I do not fix, I will go for Jamaica. Should I stay in an unsettled state at home, I would only dissipate my little fortune, and ruin what I intend shall compensate my little ones for the stigma I have brought on their names.—R. B.

No. LIV.

TO WILLIAM NICOL, ESQ.

MY DEAR FRIEND,   MAUCHLINE, *June 18th,* 1787.

I am now arrived safe in my native country, after a very agreeable jaunt, and have the pleasure to find all my friends well. I breakfasted with your gray-headed, reverend friend, Mr. Smith ; and was highly pleased both with the cordial welcome he gave me, and his most excellent appearance and sterling good sense.

I have been with Mr. Miller at Dalswinton, and am to meet him again in August. From my view of the lands, and his reception of my bard-ship, my hopes in that business are rather mended ; but still they are but slender.

I am quite charmed with Dumfries folks—Mr. Burnside, the clergy-man, in particular, is a man whom I shall ever gratefully remember ; and his wife, Gude forgie me ! I had almost broke the tenth command-ment on her account. Simplicity, elegance, good sense, sweetness of disposition, good humour, kind hospitality, are the constituents of her manner and heart : in short—but if I say one word more about her, I shall be directly in love with her.

I never, my friend, thought mankind very capable of anything generous ; but the stateliness of the patricians in Edinburgh, and the servility of my plebeian brethren (who perhaps formerly eyed me askance) since I re-turned home, have nearly put me out of conceit altogether with my species. I have bought a pocket Milton, which I carry perpetually about with me, in order to study the sentiments—the dauntless magnanimity,

the intrepid, unyielding independence, the desperate daring, and noble defiance of hardship, in that great personage, SATAN. 'Tis true, I have just now a little cash ; but I am afraid the star that hitherto has shed its malignant, purpose-blasting rays full in my zenith, that noxious planet so baneful in its influences to the rhyming tribe, I much dread it is not yet beneath my horizon. Misfortune dodges the path of human life ; the poetic mind finds itself miserably deranged in, and unfit for the walks of business ; add to all, that thoughtless follies and hare-brained whims, like so many *ignes fatui*, eternally diverging from the right line of sober discretion, sparkle with step-bewitching blaze in the idly-gazing eyes of the poor heedless Bard, till, pop, " he falls like Lucifer, never to hope again." God grant this may be an unreal picture with respect to me ! but should it not, I have very little dependence on mankind. I will close my letter with this tribute my heart bids me pay you—the many ties of acquaintance and friendship which I have, or think I have in life, I have felt along the lines, and, damn them, they are almost all of them of such frail contexture, that I am sure they would not stand the breath of the least adverse breeze of fortune ; but from you, my ever dear Sir, I look with confidence for the Apostolic love that shall wait on me " through good report and bad report "—the love which Solomon emphatically says " is strong as death." My compliments to Mrs. Nicol, and all the circle of our common friends.

P.S. I shall be in Edinburgh about the latter end of July.—R. B.

No. LV.

TO ROBERT AINSLIE, ESQ.

[Burns was now on his first tour in the Highlands. His unsettled state, dissatisfaction with his present circumstances, and anxiety for the future, gave a somewhat morose, distempered turn to his thoughts, except when care was drowned in wild jollity.]

MY DEAR SIR, ARRACHAR, *June 28th,* 1787.

I write this on my tour through a country where savage streams tumble over savage mountains, thinly overspread with savage flocks, which staringly support as savage inhabitants. My last stage was Inverary —to-morrow night's stage Dumbarton. I ought sooner to have answered your kind letter, but you know I am a man of many sins.—R. B.

No. LVI.

TO MR. JAMES SMITH,

LINLITHGOW.

MY DEAR FRIEND, *June 30th,* 1787.

On our return, at a Highland gentleman's hospitable mansion, we fell in with a merry party, and danced till the ladies left us, at three in the morning. Our dancing was none of the French or English insipid formal

movements ; the ladies sung Scotch songs like angels, at intervals ; then we flew at " Bab at the Bowster," " Tullochgorum," " Loch Erroch Side,"* &c. like midges sporting in the mottie sun, or craws prognosticating a storm in a hairst day. When the dear lasses left us, we ranged round the bowl till the good-fellow hour of six ; except a few minutes that we went out to pay our devotions to the glorious lamp of day peering over the towering top of Benlomond. We all kneeled ; our worthy landlord's son held the bowl; each man a full glass in his hand ; and I, as priest, repeated some rhyming nonsense, like Thomas-a-Rhymer's prophecies I suppose. After a small refreshment of the gifts of Somnus, we proceeded to spend the day on Lochlomond, and reached Dumbarton in the evening. We dined at another good fellow's house, and consequently, pushed the bottle ; when we went out to mount our horses, we found ourselves " No vera fou but gaylie yet." My two friends and I rode soberly down the Loch side, till by came a Highlandman at the gallop, on a tolerably good horse, but which had never known the ornaments of iron or leather. We scorned to be out-galloped by a Highlandman, so off we started, whip and spur. My companions, though seemingly gaily mounted, fell sadly astern ; but my old mare, Jenny Geddes, one of the Rosinante family, strained past the Highlandman in spite of all his efforts with the hair halter : just as I was passing him, Donald wheeled his horse, as if to cross before me to mar my progress, when down came his horse, and threw his rider's breekless a—e in a clipt edge ; and down came Jenny Geddes over all, and my bardship between her and the Highlandman's horse. Jenny Geddes trode over me with such cautious reverence, that matters were not so bad as might well have been expected ; so I came off with a few cuts and bruises, and a thorough resolution to be a pattern of sobriety for the future.

I have yet fixed on nothing with respect to the serious business of life. I am, just as usual, a rhyming, mason-making, raking, aimless, idle fellow. However, I shall somewhere have a farm soon. I was going to say, a wife too ; but that must never be my blessed lot. I am but a younger son of the house of Parnassus, and, like other younger sons of great families, I may intrigue, if I choose to run all risks, but must not marry.

I am afraid I have almost ruined one source, the principal one indeed, of my former happiness ; that eternal propensity I always had to fall in love. My heart no more glows with feverish rapture. I have no paradisiacal evening interviews, stolen from the restless cares and prying inhabitants of this weary world. I have only * * * *. This last is one of your distant acquaintances, has a fine figure, and elegant manners ; and in the train of some great folks whom you know, has seen the politest quarters of Europe. I do like her a good deal ; but what piques me is her conduct at the commencement of our acquaintance. I frequently visited her when I was in ——, and after passing regularly the intermediate degrees between the distant formal bow and the familiar grasp round the waist, I ventured, in my careless way, to talk of friendship in rather ambiguous terms ; and after her return to ——, I wrote to her in the same style. Miss, construing my words

* Scotch reels.

farther I suppose than even I intended, flew off in a tangent of female dignity and reserve, like a mounting lark in an April morning ; and wrote me an answer which measured me out very completely what an immense way I had to travel before I could reach the climate of her favour.   But I am an old hawk at the sport, and wrote her such a cool, deliberate, prudent reply, as brought my bird from her aerial towerings, pop, down at my foot, like Corporal Trim's hat.

As for the rest of my acts, and my wars, and all my wise sayings, and why my mare was called Jenny Geddes, they shall be recorded in a few weeks hence at Linlithgow, in the chronicles of your memory, by R. B.

No. LVII.

TO MR. JOHN RICHMOND.

My dear Richmond,   Mossgiel, *July 7th,* 1787.

I am all impatience to hear of your fate since the old confounder of right and wrong has turned you out of place, by his journey to answer his indictment at the bar of the other world.   He will find the practice of the court so different from the practice in which he has for so many years been thoroughly hackneyed, that his friends, if he had any connexions truly of that kind, which I rather doubt, may well tremble for his sake. His chicane, his left-handed wisdom, which stood so firmly by him, to such good purpose, here, like other accomplices in robbery and plunder, will, now the piratical business is blown, in all probability turn king's evidence, and then the devil's bagpiper will touch him off " Bundle and go !"

If he has left you any legacy, I beg your pardon for all this ; if not, I know you will swear to every word I said about him.

I have lately been rambling over by Dumbarton and Inverary, and running a drunken race on the side of Loch Lomond with a wild High-landman ; his horse, which had never known the ornaments of iron or leather, zigzagged across before my old spavin'd hunter, whose name is Jenny Geddes, and down came the Highlandman, horse and all, and down came Jenny and my bardship ; so I have got such a skinful of bruises and wounds, that I shall be at least four weeks before I dare venture on my journey to Edinburgh.

Not one new thing under the sun has happened in Mauchline since you left it.   I hope this will find you as comfortably situated as formerly, or, if heaven pleases, more so ; but, at all events, I trust you will let me know of course how matters stand with you, well or ill.   'Tis but poor consola-tion to tell the world when matters go wrong ; but you know very well your connexion and mine stands on a different footing.

I am ever, my dear Friend, yours,

R. B.

No. LVIII.
TO DR. MOORE.*

SIR,   MAUCHLINE, *August 2d,* 1787.

For some months past I have been rambling over the country, but I am now confined with some lingering complaints, originating, as I take it, in the stomach. To divert my spirits a little in this miserable fog of ennui, I have taken a whim to give you a history of myself. My name has made some little noise in this country; you have done me the honour to interest yourself very warmly in my behalf; and I think a faithful account of what character of a man I am, and how I came by that character, may perhaps amuse you in an idle moment. I will give you an honest narrative, though I know it will be often at my own expense; for I assure you, Sir, I have, like Solomon, whose character, excepting in the trifling affair of wisdom, I sometimes think I resemble,—I have, I say, like him turned my eyes to behold madness and folly, and like him, too, frequently shaken hands with their intoxicating friendship. After you have perused these pages, should you think them trifling and impertinent, I beg leave to tell you, that the poor author wrote them under some twitching qualms of conscience, arising from a suspicion that he was doing what he ought not to do; a predicament he has more than once been in before.

I have not the most distant pretensions to assume that character which the pye-coated guardians of escutcheons call a gentleman. When at Edinburgh last winter, I got acquainted in the Herald's office; and, looking through that granary of honours, I there found almost every name in the kingdom; but for me,

> " My ancient but ignoble blood
> Has crept thro' scoundrels ever since the flood."

Gules, purpure, argent, &c. quite disowned me.

My father was of the north of Scotland, the son of a farmer, and was thrown by early misfortunes on the world at large; where, after many years' wanderings and sojournings, he picked up a pretty large quantity of observation and experience, to which I am indebted for most of my little pretensions to wisdom. I have met with few who understood men, their manners and their ways, equal to him; but stubborn, ungainly integrity, and headlong, ungovernable irascibility, are disqualifying circumstances; consequently, I was born a very poor man's son. For the first six or seven years of my life, my father was gardener to a worthy gentleman of small estate in the neighbourhood of Ayr. Had he continued in that station, I must have marched off to be one of the little underlings about a farmhouse; but it was his dearest wish and prayer to have it in his power to keep his children under his own eye, till they could discern between good and evil; so with the assistance of his generous master, my father ventured on a small farm on his estate. At those years, I was by no means a favourite with anybody. I was a good deal noted for a retentive memory, a stubborn sturdy something in my disposition, and an

* The original copy of this letter transmitted to Dr. Moore is now in the British Museum. It differs very much from the printed version.

Z 2

enthusiastic idiot* piety. I say idiot piety, because I was then but a child. Though it cost the schoolmaster some thrashings, I made an excellent English scholar ; and by the time I was ten or eleven years of age, I was a critic in substantives, verbs, and particles. In my infant and boyish days, too, I owe much to an old woman who resided in the family, remarkable for her ignorance, credulity, and superstition. She had, I suppose, the largest collection in the country of tales and songs concerning devils, ghosts, fairies, brownies, witches, warlocks, spunkies, kelpies, elf-candles, dead-lights, wraiths, apparitions, cantraips, giants, enchanted towers, dragons and other trumpery. This cultivated the latent seeds of poetry ; but had so strong an effect on my imagination, that to this hour, in my nocturnal rambles, I sometimes keep a sharp look-out in suspicious places ; and though nobody can be more sceptical than I am in such matters, yet it often takes an effort of philosophy to shake off these idle terrors. The earliest composition that I recollect taking pleasure in, was "The Vision of Mirza," and a hymn of Addison's beginning, "How are thy servants blest, O Lord!" I particularly remember one half-stanza which was music to my boyish ear —

> " For though in dreadful whirls we hung
> High on the broken wave—"

I met with these pieces in Mason's English Collection, one of my school-books. The first two books I ever read in private, and which gave me more pleasure than any two books I ever read since, were "The Life of Hannibal," and "The History of Sir William Wallace." Hannibal gave my young ideas such a turn, that I used to strut in raptures up and down after the recruiting drum and bag-pipe, and wish myself tall enough to be a soldier ; while the story of Wallace poured a Scottish prejudice into my veins, which will boil along there till the flood-gates of life shut in eternal rest.

Polemical divinity about this time was putting the country half mad, and I, ambitious of shining in conversation parties on Sundays, between sermons, at funerals, &c. used a few years afterwards to puzzle Calvinism with so much heat and indiscretion, that I raised a hue and cry of heresy against me, which has not ceased to this hour.

My vicinity to Ayr was of some advantage to me. My social disposition, when not checked by some modifications of spited pride, was like our catechism definition of infinitude, without bounds or limits. I formed several connexions with other younkers, who possessed superior advantages ; the youngling actors who were busy in the rehearsal of parts, in which they were shortly to appear on the stage of life, where, alas ! I was destined to drudge behind the scenes. It is not commonly at this green age, that our young gentry have a just sense of the immense distance between them and their ragged play-fellows. It takes a few dashes into the world, to give the young great man that proper, decent, unnoticing disregard for the poor, insignificant, stupid devils, the mechanics and peasantry around him, who were, perhaps, born in the

* Idiot for idiotic.

same village. My young superiors never insulted the clouterly appearance of my plough-boy carcase, the two extremes of which were often exposed to all the inclemencies of all the seasons. They would give me stray volumes of books; among them, even then, I could pick up some observations, and one, whose heart, I am sure, not even the "Munny Begum" scenes have tainted, helped me to a little French. Parting with these my young friends and benefactors, as they occasionally went off for the East or West Indies, was often to me a sore affliction; but I was soon called to more serious evils. My father's generous master died; the farm proved a ruinous bargain; and to clench the misfortune, we fell into the hands of a factor, who sat for the picture I have drawn of one in my tale of "Twa Dogs." My father was advanced in life when he married; I was the eldest of seven children, and he, worn out by early hardships, was unfit for labour. My father's spirit was soon irritated, but not easily broken. There was a freedom in his lease in two years more, and to weather these two years, we retrenched our expenses. We lived very poorly: I was a dexterous ploughman for my age; and the next eldest to me was a brother (Gilbert), who could drive the plough very well, and help me to thrash the corn. A novel-writer might, perhaps, have viewed these scenes with some satisfaction, but so did not I; my indignation yet boils at the recollection of the scoundrel factor's insolent threatening letters, which used to set us all in tears.

This kind of life—the cheerless gloom of a hermit, with the unceasing moil of a galley slave, brought me to my sixteenth year; a little before which period I first committed the sin of rhyme. You know our country custom of coupling a man and woman together as partners in the labours of harvest. In my fifteenth autumn, my partner was a bewitching creature, a year younger than myself. My scarcity of English denies me the power of doing her justice in that language, but you know the Scottish idiom: she was a "bonnie, sweet, sonsie lass." In short, she, altogether unwittingly to herself, initiated me in that delicious passion, which, in spite of acid disappointment, gin-horse prudence, and bookworm philosophy, I hold to be the first of human joys, our dearest blessing here below! How she caught the contagion I cannot tell; you medical people talk much of infection from breathing the same air, the touch, &c.; but I never expressly said I loved her. Indeed I did not know myself why I liked so much to loiter behind with her, when returning in the evening from our labours; why the tones of her voice made my heart-strings thrill like an Æolian harp; and particularly why my pulse beat such a furious ratan, when I looked and fingered over her little hand to pick out the cruel nettle-stings and thistles. Among her other love-inspiring qualities, she sung sweetly; and it was her favourite reel to which I attempted giving an embodied vehicle in rhyme. I was not so presumptuous as to imagine that I could make verses like printed ones, composed by men who had Greek and Latin; but my girl sung a song which was said to be composed by a small country laird's son, on one of his father's maids, with whom he was in love; and I saw no reason why I might not rhyme as well as he; for, excepting that he could smear

sheep, and cast peats, his father living in the moorlands, he had no more scholar-craft than myself.

Thus with me began love and poetry; which at times have been my only, and till within the last twelve months, have been my highest enjoyment. My father struggled on till he reached the freedom in his lease, when he entered on a larger farm, about ten miles farther in the country. The nature of the bargain he made was such as to throw a little ready money into his hands at the commencement of his lease, otherwise the affair would have been impracticable. For four years we lived comfortably here, but a difference commencing between him and his landlord as to terms, after three years' tossing and whirling in the vortex of litigation, my father was just saved from the horrors of a jail, by a consumption, which, after two years' promises, kindly stepped in, and carried him away, to where the wicked cease from troubling, and where the weary are at rest !

It is during the time that we lived on this farm, that my little story is most eventful. I was, at the beginning of this period, perhaps the most ungainly, awkward boy in the parish—no *solitaire* was less acquainted with the ways of the world. What I knew of ancient story was gathered from Salmon's and Guthrie's Geographical Grammars; and the ideas I had formed of modern manners, of literature, and criticism, I got from the Spectator. These, with Pope's Works, some Plays of Shakspeare, Tull and Dickson on Agriculture, The Pantheon, Locke's Essay on the Human Understanding, Stackhouse's History of the Bible, Justice's British Gardener's Directory, Boyle's Lectures, Allan Ramsay's Works, Taylor's Scripture Doctrine of Original Sin, A Select Collection of English Songs, and Hervey's Meditations, had formed the whole of my reading. The collection of songs was my *vade mecum*. I pored over them, driving my cart, or walking to labour, song by song, verse by verse ; carefully noting the true, tender, or sublime, from affectation and fustian. I am convinced I owe to this practice much of my critic-craft, such as it is.

In my seventeenth year, to give my manners a brush, I went to a country dancing-school. My father had an unaccountable antipathy against these meetings, and my going was, what to this moment I repent, in opposition to his wishes. My father, as I said before, was subject to strong passions ; from that instance of disobedience in me, he took a sort of dislike to me, which, I believe, was one cause of the dissipation which marked my succeeding years. I say dissipation, comparatively with the strictness, and sobriety, and regularity of Presbyterian country life ; for though the will-o'-wisp meteors of thoughtless whim were almost the sole lights of my path, yet early ingrained piety and virtue kept me for several years afterwards within the line of innocence. The great misfortune of my life was to want an aim. I had felt early some stirrings of ambition, but they were the blind gropings of Homer's Cyclops round the walls of his cave. I saw my father's situation entailed on me perpetual labour. The only two openings by which I could enter the temple of fortune were the gate of niggardly economy, or the path of

little chicaning bargain-making. The first is so contracted an aperture I never could squeeze myself into it: the last I always hated—there was contamination in the very entrance! Thus abandoned of aim or view in life, with a strong appetite for sociability, as well from native hilarity as from a pride of observation and remark; a constitutional melancholy or hypochondriasm that made me fly solitude; add to these incentives to social life, my reputation for bookish knowledge, a certain wild logical talent, and a strength of thought, something like the rudiments of good sense; and it will not seem surprising that I was generally a welcome guest where I visited, or any great wonder that always, where two or three met together, there was I among them. But far beyond all other impulses of my heart, was *un penchant à l'adorable moitié du genre humain*. My heart was completely tinder, and was eternally lighted up by some goddess or other; and, as in every other warfare in this world, my fortune was various; sometimes I was received with favour, and sometimes I was mortified with a repulse. At the plough, scythe, or reap-hook, I feared no competitor, and thus I set absolute want at defiance; and as I never cared farther for my labours than while I was in actual exercise, I spent the evenings in the way after my own heart. A country lad seldom carries on a love adventure without an assisting confidant. I possessed a curiosity, zeal, and intrepid dexterity that recommended me as a proper second on these occasions; and I dare say, I felt as much pleasure in being in the secret of half the loves of the parish of Tarbolton, as ever did statesman in knowing the intrigues of half the courts of Europe. The very goose-feather in my hand seems to know instinctively the well-worn path of my imagination, the favourite theme of my song; and is with difficulty restrained from giving you a couple of paragraphs on the love-adventures of my compeers, the humble inmates of the farm-house and cottage: but the grave sons of science, ambition, or avarice baptize these things by the name of follies. To the sons and daughters of labour and poverty they are matters of the most serious nature: to them the ardent hope, the stolen interview, the tender farewell, are the greatest and most delicious parts of their enjoyment.

Another circumstance in my life which made some alteration in my mind and manners, was, that I spent my nineteenth summer* on a smuggling coast, a good distance from home, at a noted school, to learn mensuration, surveying, dialling, &c. in which I made a pretty good progress. But I made a greater progress in the knowledge of mankind. The contraband trade was at that time very successful, and it sometimes happened to me to fall in with those who carried it on. Scenes of swaggering riot and roaring dissipation were, till this time, new to me; but I was no enemy to social life. Here, though I learnt to fill my glass, and to mix without fear in a drunken squabble, yet I went on with a high hand with my geometry, till the sun entered Virgo, a month which is always a carnival in my bosom, when a charming fillette, who lived next door to the school, overset my trigonometry, and set me off

* Seventeenth Summer in the M.S., Dr. Currie has written above it in pencil, " Nineteenth or twentieth."

at a tangent from the spheres of my studies. I, however, struggled on
with my sines and co-sines for a few days more; but stepping into the garden
one charming noon to take the sun's altitude, there I met my angel—

" Like Proserpine gathering flowers,
Herself a fairer flower——."

It was in vain to think of doing any more good at school. The remaining week I staid I did nothing but craze the faculties of my soul
about her, or steal out to meet her; and the two last nights of my stay
in the country, had sleep been a mortal sin, the image of this modest
and innocent girl had kept me guiltless.

I returned home very considerably improved. My reading was enlarged with the very important addition of Thomson's and Shenstone's
Works : I had seen human nature in a new phasis; and I engaged
several of my schoolfellows to keep up a literary correspondence with
me. This improved me in composition. I had met with a collection
of letters by the wits of Queen Anne's reign, and I pored over them
most devoutly. I kept copies of any of my own letters that pleased
me, and a comparison between them and the composition of most of
my correspondents flattered my vanity. I carried this whim so far,
that though I had not three-farthings' worth of business in the world,
yet almost every post brought me as many letters as if I had been a
broad plodding son of the day-book and ledger.

My life flowed on much in the same course till my twenty-third year.
Vive l'amour, et vive la bagatelle, were my sole principles of action.
The addition of two more authors to my library gave me great pleasure;
Sterne and Mackenzie—"Tristram Shandy" and the "Man of Feeling"—
were my bosom favourites. Poesy was still a darling walk for my mind,
but it was only indulged in according to the humour of the hour. I had
usually half a dozen or more pieces on hand; I took up one or other,
as it suited the momentary tone of the mind, and dismissed the work as
it bordered on fatigue. My passions, when once lighted up, raged like
so many devils, till they got vent in rhyme; and then the conning over
my verses, like a spell, soothed all into quiet! None of the rhymes of
those days are in print, except, "Winter, a dirge," the eldest of my printed
pieces; "The Death of poor Maillie," "John Barleycorn," and Songs
first, second, and third. Song second was the ebullition of that passion
which ended the forementioned school-business.

My twenty-third year was to me an important æra. Partly through
whim, and partly that I wished to set about doing something in life,
I joined a flax-dresser in a neighbouring town (Irvine), to learn his trade.
This was an unlucky affair. My * * * and to finish the whole,
as we were giving a welcome carousal to the new year, the shop took
fire and burned to ashes, and I was left, like a true poet, not worth
a sixpence.

I was obliged to give up this scheme; the clouds of misfortune were
gathering thick round my father's head; and, what was worst of all, he
was visibly far gone in a consumption; and to crown my distresses, a
belle fille, whom I adored, and who had pledged her soul to meet me

in the field of matrimony, jilted me, with ·peculiar circumstances of mortification. The finishing evil that brought up the rear of this infernal file, was my constitutional melancholy being increased to such a degree, that for three months I was in a state of mind scarcely to be envied by the hopeless wretches who have got their mittimus—depart from me, ye cursed !

From this adventure I learned something of a town life ; but the principal thing which gave my mind a turn, was a friendship I formed with a young fellow, a very noble character, but a hapless son of misfortune. He was the son of a simple mechanic ; but a great man in the neighbourhood taking him under his patronage, gave him a genteel education, with a view of bettering his situation in life. The patron dying just as he was ready to launch out into the world, the poor fellow in despair went to sea ; where, after a variety of good and ill-fortune, a little before I was acquainted with him he had been set on shore by an American privateer, on the wild coast of Connaught, stripped of every thing. I cannot quit this poor fellow's story without adding, that he is at this time master of a large West-Indiaman belonging to the Thames.

His mind was fraught with independence, magnanimity, and every manly virtue. I loved and admired him to a degree of enthusiasm, and of course strove to imitate him. In some measure I succeeded ; I had pride before, but he taught it to flow in proper channels. His knowledge of the world was vastly superior to mine, and I was all attention to learn. He was the only man I ever saw who was a greater fool than myself where woman was the presiding star ; but he spoke of illicit love with the levity of a sailor, which hitherto I had regarded with horror. Here his friendship did me a mischief, and the consequence was, that soon after I resumed the plough, I wrote the "Poet's Welcome."* My reading only increased while in this town by two stray volumes of Pamela, and one of Ferdinand Count Fathom, which gave me some idea of novels. Rhyme, except some religious pieces that are in print, I had given up ; but meeting with Fergusson's Scottish Poems, I strung anew my wildly-sounding lyre with emulating vigour. When my father died, his all went among the hell-hounds that growl in the kennel of justice ; but we made a shift to collect a little money in the family amongst us, with which, to keep us together, my brother and I took a neighbouring farm. My brother wanted my hair-brained imagination, as well as my social and amorous madness ; but in good sense, and every sober qualification, he was far my superior.

I entered on this farm with a full resolution, "come, go to, I will be wise !" I read farming books, I calculated crops ; I attended markets ; and in short, in spite of the devil, and the world, and the flesh, I believe I should have been a wise man ; but the first year, from unfortunately buying bad seed, the second from a late harvest, we lost half our crops. This overset all my wisdom, and I returned, "like the dog to his vomit, and the sow that was washed, to her wallowing in the mire."

* " Rob the Rhymer's Welcome to his Bastard Child."

I now began to be known in the neighbourhood as a maker of rhymes. The first of my poetic offspring that saw the light, was a burlesque lamentation on a quarrel between two reverend Calvinists, both of them *dramatis personæ* in my " Holy Fair." I had a notion myself that the piece had some merit ; but, to prevent the worst, I gave a copy of it to a friend, who was very fond of such things, and told him that I could not guess who was the author of it, but that I thought it pretty clever. With a certain description of the clergy, as well as laity, it met with a roar of applause. " Holy Willie's Prayer" next made its appearance, and alarmed the kirk-session so much, that they held several meetings to look over their spiritual artillery, if haply any of it might be pointed against profane rhymers. Unluckily for me, my wanderings led me on another side, within point-blank shot of their heaviest metal. This is the unfortunate story that gave rise to my printed poem, " The Lament." This was a most melancholy affair, which I cannot yet bear to reflect on, and had very nearly given me one or two of the principal qualifications for a place among those who have lost the chart, and mistaken the reckoning of rationality. I gave up my part of the farm to my brother ; in truth it was only nominally mine ; and made what little preparation was in my power for Jamaica. But before leaving my native country for ever, I resolved to publish my poems. I weighed my productions as impartially as was in my power ; I thought they had merit ; and it was a delicious idea that I should be called a clever fellow, even though it should never reach my ears—a poor negro-driver—or perhaps a victim to that inhospitable clime, and gone to the world of spirits ! I can truly say, that *pauvre inconnu* as I then was, I had pretty nearly as high an idea of myself and of my works as I have at this moment, when the public has decided in their favour. It ever was my opinion that the mistakes and blunders, both in a rational and religious point of view, of which we see thousands daily guilty, are owing to their ignorance of themselves. To know myself had been all along my constant study. I weighed myself alone ; I balanced myself with others ; I watched every means of information, to see how much ground I occupied as a man and as a poet ; I studied assiduously Nature's design in my formation—where the lights and shades in my character were intended. I was pretty confident my poems would meet with some applause ; but at the worst, the roar of the Atlantic would deafen the voice of censure, and the novelty of West Indian scenes make me forget neglect. I threw off six hundred copies, of which I had got subscriptions for about three hundred and fifty. My vanity was highly gratified by the reception I met with from the public ; and besides I pocketed, all expenses deducted, nearly twenty pounds. This sum came very seasonably, as I was thinking of indenting myself, for want of money to procure my passage. As soon as I was master of nine guineas, the price of wafting me to the torrid zone, I took a steerage passage in the first ship that was to sail from the Clyde, for

" Hungry ruin had me in the wind."

I had been for some days skulking from covert to covert, under all the terrors of a jail ; as some ill-advised people had uncoupled the merciless pack of the law at my heels. I had taken the last farewell of my few friends ; my chest was on the road to Greenock ; I had composed the last song I should ever measure in Caledonia—" The gloomy night is gathering fast," when a letter from Dr. Blacklock to a friend of mine, overthrew all my schemes, by opening new prospects to my poetic ambition. The doctor belonged to a set of critics for whose applause I had not dared to hope. His opinion, that I would meet with encouragement in Edinburgh for a second edition, fired me so much, that away I posted for that city, without a single acquaintance, or a single letter of introduction. The baneful star that had so long shed its blasting influence in my zenith, for once made a revolution to the nadir ; and a kind Providence placed me under the patronage of one of the noblest of men, the Earl of Glencairn. *Oublie moi, grand Dieu, si jamais je l'oublie !*

I need relate no farther. At Edinburgh I was in a new world ; I mingled among many classes of men, but all of them new to me, and I was all attention to " catch " the characters and " the manners living as they rise." Whether I have profited, time will show.

*   *   *   *   *

My most respectful compliments to Miss Williams. Her very elegant and friendly letter I cannot answer at present, as my presence is requisite in Edinburgh, and I set out to-morrow.—R. B.

No. LIX.

TO MR. ROBERT MUIR.

MY DEAR SIR, STIRLING, *26th August,* 1787.

I intended to have written you from Edinburgh, and now write you from Stirling to make an excuse. Here am I, on my way to Inverness, with a truly original, but very worthy man, a Mr. Nicol, one of the masters of the High-school in Edinburgh. I left Auld Reekie yesterday morning, and have passed, besides by-excursions, Linlithgow, Borrowstouness, Falkirk, and here am I undoubtedly. This morning I knelt at the tomb of Sir John the Graham, the gallant friend of the immortal Wallace ; and two hours ago I said a fervent prayer for Old Caledonia over the hole in a blue whinstone, where Robert de Bruce fixed his royal standard on the banks of Bannockburn ; and just now, from Stirling Castle, I have seen by the setting sun the glorious prospect of the windings of Forth through the rich carse of Stirling, and skirting the equally rich carse of Falkirk. The crops are very strong, but so very late that there is no harvest, except a ridge or two perhaps in ten miles, all the way I have travelled from Edinburgh.

I left Andrew Bruce and family all well. I will be at least three weeks in making my tour, as I shall return by the coast, and have many people to call for.

My best compliments to Charles, our dear kinsman and fellow-saint ; and Messrs. W. and H. Parkers. I hope Hughoc is going on and prospering with God and Miss M'Causlin.

If I could think on anything sprightly, I should let you hear every other post ; but a dull, matter-of-fact business like this scrawl, the less and seldomer one writes, the better.

Among other matters-of-fact I shall add this, that I am and ever shall be,

My dear Sir,

Your obliged

R. B.

No. LX.

TO GAVIN HAMILTON, ESQ.

[Mr. Tait, of Harvieston, was a connexion of Gavin Hamilton : Mrs. Tait, who was then dead, Mrs. Hamilton (Gavin's stepmother) who presided over the household at Harvieston, and Mrs. Chalmers, were sisters.]

MY DEAR SIR, STIRLING, *28th August,* 1787.

Here am I on my way to Inverness. I have rambled over the rich, fertile carses of Falkirk and Stirling, and am delighted with their appearance : richly waving crops of wheat, barley, &c. but no harvest at all yet, except, in one or two places, an old wife's ridge. Yesterday morning I rode from this town up the meandering Devon's banks, to pay my respects to some Ayrshire folks at Harvieston. After breakfast, we made a party to go and see the famous Caudron-linn, a remarkable cascade in the Devon, about five miles above Harvieston ; and after spending one of the most pleasant days I ever had in my life, I returned to Stirling in the evening. They are a family, Sir : though I had not had any prior tie, though they had not been the brother and sisters of a certain generous friend of mine, I would never forget them. I am told you have not seen them these several years, so you can have very little idea of what these young folks now are. Your brother is as tall as you are, but slender rather than otherwise ; and I have the satisfaction to inform you that he is getting the better of those consumptive symptoms which I suppose you know were threatening him. His make, and particularly his manner, resemble you, but he will still have a finer face. (I put in the word *still*, to please Mrs. Hamilton.) Good sense, modesty, and at the same time a just idea of that respect that man owes to man, and has a right in his turn to exact, are striking features in his character ; and, what with me is the Alpha and the Omega, he has a heart that might adorn the breast of a poet ! Grace has a good figure, and the look of health and cheerfulness, but nothing else remarkable in her person. I scarcely ever saw so striking a likeness as is between her and your little Beenie ; the mouth and chin particularly. She is reserved at first ; but as we grew better acquainted, I was delighted with the native frankness of her manner, and the sterling sense of her observation. Of Charlotte* I

* Daughter of Mrs. Hamilton.

cannot speak in common terms of admiration : she is not only beautiful, but lovely. Her form is elegant ; her features not regular, but they have the smile of sweetness and the settled complacency of good nature in the highest degree ; and her complexion, now that she has happily recovered her wonted health, is equal to Miss Burnet's. After the exercise of our riding to the Falls, Charlotte was exactly Dr. Donne's mistress :—

> ————————" Her pure and eloquent blood
> Spoke in her cheeks, and so distinctly wrought,
> That one would almost say her body thought."

Her eyes are fascinating ; at once expressive of good sense, tenderness, and a noble mind.

I do not give you all this account, my good Sir, to flatter you. I mean it to reproach you. Such relations the first peer in the realm might own with pride ; then why do you not keep up more correspondence with these so amiable young folks? I had a thousand questions to answer about you. I had to describe the little ones with the minuteness of anatomy. They were highly delighted when I told them that John was so good a boy, and so fine a scholar, and that Willie was going on still very pretty ; but I have it in commission to tell her from them that beauty is a poor silly bauble without she be good. Miss Chalmers I had left in Edinburgh, but I had the pleasure of meeting with Mrs. Chalmers, only Lady Mackenzie* being rather a little alarmingly ill of a sore throat somewhat marred our enjoyment.

I shall not be in Ayrshire for four weeks. My most respectful compliments to Mrs. Hamilton, Miss Kennedy, and Doctor Mackenzie. I shall probably write him from some stage or other.

I am ever, Sir,

Yours most gratefully,

R. B.

No. LXI.

TO MR. WALKER,

BLAIR OF ATHOLE.

[Mr. Josiah Walker, afterwards Professor, had met Burns at Edinburgh, and was then engaged at Blair Athole as a tutor. He introduced Burns to the Athole family, and it was in commemoration of his very kind reception that the Poet wrote the piece accompanying this letter, " The Humble Petition of Bruar-water." Mrs. Graham and Miss Çathcart, mentioned below, were sisters of the Duchess.]

MY DEAR SIR, INVERNESS, *5th September,* 1787.

I have just time to write the foregoing, and to tell you that it was (at least most part of it) the effusion of an half-hour I spent at Bruar. I do not mean it was extempore, for I have endeavoured to brush it up as well as Mr. Nicol's chat and the jogging of the chaise would allow. It eases my heart a good deal, as rhyme is the coin with which a poet pays his debts of honour or gratitude. What I owe to the noble family of

* One of Mrs. Chalmers' married daughters, wife of Sir Hector Mackenzie.

Athole, of the first kind, I shall ever proudly boast ; what I owe of the last, so help me God in my hour of need ! I shall never forget.

The "little angel-band !" I declare I prayed for them very sincerely to-day at the Fall of Fyers. I shall never forget the fine family-piece I saw at Blair ; the amiable, the truly noble Duchess, with her smiling little seraph in her lap, at the head of the table : the lovely "olive plants ;" as the Hebrew bard finely says, round the happy mother: the beautiful Mrs. G—— ; the lovely, sweet Miss C——, &c. I wish I had the powers of Guido to do them justice ! My Lord Duke's kind hospitality—markedly kind indeed. Mr. Graham of Fintry's charms of conversation—Sir W. Murray's friendship. In short, the recollections of all that polite, agreeable company raises an honest glow in my bosom – R. B.

No. LXII.

TO MR. GILBERT BURNS.

My dear Brother,   Edinburgh, *17th September, 1787.*

I arrived here safe yesterday evening, after a tour of twenty-two days, and travelling near six hundred miles, windings included. My farthest stretch was about ten miles beyond Inverness. I went through the heart of the Highlands by Crieff, Taymouth, the famous seat of Lord Bredalbane, down the Tay, among cascades and Druidical circles of stones, to Dunkeld, a seat of the Duke of Athole ; thence across Tay, and up one of his tributary streams to Blair of Athole, another of the Duke's seats, where I had the honour of spending nearly two days with his Grace and family ; thence many miles through a wild country among cliffs gray with eternal snows and gloomy savage glens, till I crossed Spey and went down the stream through Strathspey—so famous in Scottish music— Badenoch, &c. till I reached Grant Castle, where I spent half a day with Sir James Grant and family ; and then crossed the country for Fort George, but called by the way at Cawdor, the ancient seat of Macbeth ; there I saw the identical bed, in which tradition says King Duncan was murdered : lastly, from Fort George to Inverness.

I returned by the coast, through Nairn, Forres, and so on, to Aberdeen, thence to Stonehive, where James Burness, from Montrose, met me by appointment. I spent two days among our relations, and found our aunts, Jean and Isabel, still alive, and hale old women. John Cairn,[*] though born the same year with our father, walks as vigorously as I can : they have had several letters from his son in New York. William Brand is likewise a stout old fellow; but further particulars I delay till I see you, which will be in two or three weeks. The rest of my stages are not worth rehearsing : warm as I was from Ossian's country, where I had seen his very grave, what cared I for fishing-towns or fertile carses? I slept at the famous Brodie of Brodie's one night, and dined at Gordon Castle next day, with the Duke, Duchess, and family. I am thinking to

* Husband of Elizabeth Burns, another aunt. Mr. Brand was Isabel's husband.

cause my old mare to meet me, by means of John Ronald, at Glasgow ;
but you shall hear farther from me before I leave Edinburgh.   My duty
and many compliments from the north to my mother ; and my brotherly
compliments to the rest.   I have been trying for a berth for William,*
but am not likely to be successful.   Farewell.—R. B.

No. LXIII.

TO MISS MARGARET CHALMERS.

September 26th, 1787.

I SEND Charlotte† the first number of the songs ; I would not wait
for the second number ; I hate delays in little marks of friendship, as I
hate dissimulation in the language of the heart.   I am determined to pay
Charlotte a poetic compliment, if I could hit on some glorious old Scotch
air, in number second.‡   You will see a small attempt on a shred of paper
in the book ; but, though Dr. Blacklock commended it very highly, I am
not just satisfied with it myself.   I intend to make it a description of some
kind : the whining cant of love, except in real passion, and by a masterly
hand, is to me as insufferable as the preaching cant of old Father Smeaton,
Whig-minister at Kilmaurs.   Darts, flames, Cupids, loves, graces, and all
that farrago, are just a Mauchline . . . . a senseless rabble.

I got an excellent poetic epistle yesternight from the old, venerable
author of "Tullochgorum," "John of Badenyon," &c.§   I suppose you
know he is a clergyman.   It is by far the finest poetic compliment I ever
got.   I will send you a copy of it.

I go on Thursday or Friday to Dumfries, to wait on Mr. Miller about
his farms.   Do tell that to Lady Mackenzie, that she may give me credit
for a little wisdom.   " I Wisdom dwell with Prudence."   What a blessed
fire-side !   How happy should I be to pass a winter evening under their
venerable roof ! and smoke a pipe of tobacco, or drink water-gruel with
them !   What solemn, lengthened, laughter-quashing gravity of phiz !
What sage remarks on the good-for-nothing sons and daughters of
indiscretion and folly !   And what frugal lessons, as we straitened the
fire-side circle, on the uses of the poker and tongs !

Miss N.[immo] is very well, and begs to be remembered in the old way to
you.   I used all my eloquence, all the persuasive flourishes of the hand,
and heart-melting modulation of periods in my power, to urge her out to
Harvieston, but all in vain.   My rhetoric seems quite to have lost its effect
on the lovely half of mankind.   I have seen the day—but that is a "tale
of other years."   In my conscience I believe that my heart has been so
oft on fire that it is absolutely vitrified.   I look on the sex with something
like the admiration with which I regard the starry sky in a frosty December
night.   I admire the beauty of the Creator's workmanship ; I am charmed
with the wild but graceful eccentricity of their motions, and—wish them
good night.   I mean this with respect to a certain passion *dont j'ai eu*

* Burns' younger brother.   † Charlotte Hamilton.   ‡ Of the Scots Musical Museum.
§ Rev. John Skinner, father of Bishop Skinner.   The letter was in the shape of a poetical
address to the "Country Ploughman."

l'honneur d'être un miserable esclave : as for friendship, you and Charlotte have given me pleasure, permanent pleasure, "which the world cannot give nor take away," I hope ; and which will outlast the heavens and the earth.—R. B.

No. LXIV.

TO THE SAME.

Without date.

I HAVE been at Dumfries, and at one visit more shall be decided about a farm in that country. I am rather hopeless in it; but as my brother is an excellent farmer, and is, besides, an exceedingly prudent, sober man (qualities which are only a younger brother's fortune in our family), I am determined, if my Dumfries business fail me, to return into partnership with him, and at our leisure take another farm in the neighbourhood.

I assure you I look for high compliments from you and Charlotte on this very sage instance of my unfathomable, incomprehensible wisdom. Talking of Charlotte, I must tell her that I have, to the best of my power, paid her a poetic compliment, now completed. The air is admirable : true old Highland. It was the tune of a Gaelic song, which an Inverness lady sung me when I was there ; and I was so charmed with it that I begged her to write me a set of it from her singing ; for it had never been set before. I am fixed that it shall go in Johnson's next number ; so Charlotte and you need not spend your precious time in contradicting me. I won't say the poetry is first-rate ; though I am convinced it is very well ; and, what is not always the case with compliments to ladies, it is not only sincere, but just.

[Here follows the song of "The Banks of the Devon," given in page 215.]

R. B.

No. LXV.

TO JAMES HOY, ESQ.,

GORDON CASTLE.

[Hoy was librarian at Gordon Castle—a character of the Dominie Sampson kind. "It was," says Mr. Robert Carruthers, "the business of Hoy, during the day, to store his mind with all such knowledge as the publications of the time supplied ; and then over a bottle of claret, after dinner, impart to his Grace of Gordon, all that he reckoned valuable or important." Burns was delighted with his blunt, straightforward manner, and the librarian strove, it is said, to repay it by giving the postboy a crown to contrive, no matter how, to stop the bard's departure from Fochabers. The fierce impetuosity of Nicol prevented this.]

SIR, EDINBURGH, *20th October,* 1787.

I will defend my conduct in giving you this trouble, on the best of Christian principles—"Whatsoever ye would that men should do unto you, do ye even so unto them." I shall certainly, among my legacies, leave my latest curse to that unlucky predicament which hurried—tore me

away from Castle Gordon. May that obstinate son of Latin prose [Nicol] be curst to Scotch mile periods, and damned to seven league paragraphs ; while Declension and Conjugation, Gender, Number, and Time, under the ragged banners of Dissonance and Disarrangement, eternally rank against him in hostile array.

Allow me, Sir, to strengthen the small claim I have to your acquaintance, by the following request. An engraver, James Johnson, in Edinburgh, has, not from mercenary views, but from an honest Scotch enthusiasm, set about collecting all our native songs and setting them to music ; particularly those that have never been set before. Clarke, the well-known musician, presides over the musical arrangement, and Drs. Beattie and Blacklock, Mr. Tytler of Woodhouselee, and your humble servant to the utmost of his small power, assist in collecting the old poetry, or sometimes for a fine air make a stanza, when it has no words. The brats, too tedious to mention, claim a parental pang from my bardship. I suppose it will appear in Johnson's second number—the first was published before my acquaintance with him. My request is—" Cauld Kail in Aberdeen," is one intended for this number, and I beg a copy of his Grace of Gordon's words to it, which you were so kind as to repeat to me. You may be sure we won't prefix the author's name, except you like, though I look on it as no small merit to this work that the names of many of the authors of our old Scotch songs, names almost forgotten, will be inserted. I do not well know where to write to you—I rather write at you ; but if you will be so obliging, immediately on receipt of this, as to write me a few lines, I shall perhaps pay you in kind, though not in quality. Johnson's terms are :— each number a handsome pocket volume, to consist at least of a hundred Scotch songs, with basses for the harpsichord, &c. The price to subscribers, 5s. ; to non-subscribers, 6s. He will have three numbers, I conjecture.

My direction for two or three weeks will be at Mr. William Cruikshank's, St. James's-square, New-town, Edinburgh.

I am, Sir,

Yours to command,

R. B.

No. LXVI.

TO REV. JOHN SKINNER.

REVEREND AND VENERABLE SIR,   EDINBURGH, *October 25th,* 1787.

Accept, in plain dull prose, my most sincere thanks for the best poetical compliment I ever received. I assure you, Sir, as a poet, you have conjured up an airy demon of vanity in my fancy, which the best abilities in your other capacity would be ill able to lay. I regret, and while I live I shall regret, that when I was in the north, I had not the pleasure of paying a younger brother's dutiful respect to the author of the best Scotch song ever Scotland saw—" Tullochgorum's my delight ! " The world may think slightingly of the craft of song-making, if they

B   A A

please, but, as Job says—" O that mine adversary had written a book ! "
—let them try.   There is a certain something in the old Scotch songs, a
wild happiness of thought and expression, which peculiarly marks them,
not only from English songs, but also from the modern efforts of song-
wrights, in our native manner and language.   The only remains of this
enchantment, these spells of the imagination, rests with you.   Our true
brother, Ross of Lochlee, was likewise " owre cannie "—a " wild warlock ; "
but now he sings among the " sons of the morning."

I have often wished, and will certainly endeavour, to form a kind of
common acquaintance among all the genuine sons of Caledonian song.
The world, busy in low prosaic pursuits, may overlook most of us ; but
" reverence thyself." The world is not our *peers*, so we challenge the jury.
We can lash that world, and find ourselves a very great source of amusement and happiness independent of that world.

There is a work going on in Edinburgh, just now, which claims your
best assistance.   An engraver in this town has set about collecting and
publishing all the Scotch songs, with the music, that can be found.   Songs
in the English language, if by Scotchmen, are admitted, but the music
must all be Scotch.   Drs. Beattie and Blacklock are lending a hand, and
the first musician in town presides over that department.   I have been
absolutely crazed about it, collecting old stanzas, and every information
remaining respecting their origin, authors, &c. &c.   This last is but a very
fragment business ; but at the end of his second number—the first is
already published—a small account will be given of the authors, particularly to preserve those of latter times.   Your three songs, " Tullochgorum,"
" John of Badenyon," and " Ewie wi' the crookit Horn," go in this second
number.   I was determined, before I got your letter, to write you, begging
that you would let me know where the editions of these pieces may be
found, as you would wish them to continue in future times ; and if you
would be so kind to this undertaking as send any songs, of your own or
others, that you would think proper to publish, your name will be inserted
among the other authors,—" Nill ye, will ye."   One half of Scotland
already give your songs to other authors.   Paper is done.   I beg to hear
from you ; the sooner the better, as I leave Edinburgh in a fortnight or
three weeks.

I am, with the warmest sincerity, Sir,

Your obliged humble servant,
R. B.

No. LXVII.

TO JAMES HOY, ESQ.,

GORDON CASTLE.

DEAR SIR,   EDINBURGH, *6th November,* 1787.

I would have wrote you immediately on receipt of your kind letter,
but a mixed impulse of gratitude and esteem whispered to me that I ought
to send you something by way of return.   When a poet owes anything,

particularly when he is indebted for good offices, the payment that usually recurs to him— the only coin indeed in which he is probably conversant— is rhyme. Johnson sends the books by the fly, as directed, and begs me to enclose his most grateful thanks : my return I intended should have been one or two poetic bagatelles which the world have not seen, or, perhaps, for obvious reasons, cannot see. These I shall send you before I leave Edinburgh. They may make you laugh a little, which, on the whole, is no bad way of spending one's precious hours and still more precious breath : at any rate, they will be, though a small, yet a very sincere mark of my respectful esteem for a gentleman whose farther acquaintance I should look upon as a peculiar obligation.

The Duke's song, independent totally of his dukeship, charms me. There is I know not what of wild happiness of thought and expression peculiarly beautiful in the old Scottish song style, of which his Grace, old venerable Skinner, the author of " Tullochgorum," &c. and the late Ross at Lochlee, of true Scottish poetic memory, are the only modern instances that I recollect, since Ramsay, with his contemporaries, and poor Bob Fergusson, went to the world of deathless existence and truly immortal song. The mob of mankind, that many-headed beast, would laugh at so serious a speech about an old song ; but, as Job says, " O that mine adversary had written a book !" Those who think that composing a Scotch song is a trifling business—let them try.

I wish my Lord Duke would pay a proper attention to the Christian admonition—" Hide not your candle under a bushel," but " Let your light shine before men." I could name half a dozen dukes that I guess are a devilish deal worse employed ; nay, I question if there are half a dozen better : perhaps there are not half that scanty number whom Heaven has favoured with the tuneful, happy, and, I will say, glorious gift.

I am, dear Sir,
Your obliged humble Servant,
R. B.

No. LXVIII.

TO ROBERT AINSLIE, ESQ.,

EDINBURGH.

EDINBURGH, *Sunday Morning, November 23d,* 1787.

I BEG, my dear Sir, you would not make any appointment to take us to Mr. Ainslie's to-night. On looking over my engagements, constitution, present state of my health, some little vexatious soul concerns, &c., I find I can't sup abroad to-night. I shall be in to-day till one o'clock, if you have a leisure hour.

You will think it romantic when I tell you, that I find the idea of your friendship almost necessary to my existence. You assume a proper length of face in my bitter hours of blue-devilism, and you laugh fully up to my highest wishes at my good things. I don't know upon the

whole, if you are one of the first fellows in God's world, but you are so to me. I tell you this just now in the conviction that some inequalities in my temper and manner may perhaps sometimes make you suspect that I am not so warmly as I ought to be your friend.—R. B.

No. LXIX.

TO MISS MABANE [AFTERWARDS MRS. COL. WRIGHT].

Saturday noon, No. 2, St. James's Square, New Town, Edinburgh.

HERE have I sat, my dear Madam, in the stony altitude of perplexed study for fifteen vexatious minutes, my head askew, bending over the intended card ; my fixed eye insensible to the very light of day poured around ; my pendulous goose-feather, loaded with ink, hanging over the future letter, all for the important purpose of writing a complimentary card to accompany your trinket.

Compliment is such a miserable Greenland expression, lies at such a chilly polar distance from the torrid zone of my constitution, that I cannot, for the very soul of me, use it to any person for whom I have the twentieth part of the esteem every one must have for you who knows you.

As I leave town in three or four days, I can give myself the pleasure of calling on you only for a minute. Tuesday evening, some time about seven or after, I shall wait on you for your farewell commands.

The hinge of your box I put into the hands of the proper connoisseur. The broken glass, likewise, went under review ; but deliberative wisdom thought it would too much endanger the whole fabric.

I am, dear Madam,
With all sincerity of enthusiasm,
Your very obedient Servant,
R. B.

No. LXX.

TO MISS CHALMERS.

Edinburgh, *November* 21, 1787.

I HAVE one vexatious fault to the kindly-welcome, well-filled sheet which I owe to your and Charlotte's goodness—it contains too much sense, sentiment, and good spelling. It is impossible that even you two, whom I declare to my God I will give credit for any degree of excellence the sex are capable of attaining, it is impossible you can go on to correspond at that rate ; so, like those who, Shenstone says, retire because they have made a good speech, I shall, after a few letters, hear no more of you. I insist that you shall write whatever comes first : what you see, what you read, what you hear, what you admire, what you dislike, trifles, bagatelles, nonsense ; or to fill up a corner, e'en put down a laugh at full length. Now none of your polite hints about flattery : I leave that to your lovers, if you have or shall have any ; though, thank heaven, I have found at

last two girls who can be luxuriantly happy in their own minds and with one another, without that commonly necessary appendage to female bliss—a lover.

Charlotte and you are just two favourite resting-places for my soul in her wanderings through the weary, thorny wilderness of this world. God knows I am ill-fitted for the struggle : I glory in being a Poet, and I want to be thought a wise man—I would fondly be generous, and I wish to be rich. After all, I am afraid I am a lost subject. " Some folk hae a hantle o' fauts, an' I'm but a ne'er-do-weel."

Afternoon.—To close the melancholy reflections at the end of last sheet, I shall just add a piece of devotion commonly known in Carrick by the title of the " Wabster's grace : "

> " Some say we're thieves, and e'en sae are we,
> Some say we lie, and e'en sae do we !
> Gude forgie us, and I hope sae will he !
> ——Up and to your looms, lads."

R. B.

No. LXXI.

TO SIR JOHN WHITEFOORD.

SIR,   [EDINBURGH, *December,* 1787.]

Mr. Mackenzie, in Mauchline, my very warm and worthy friend, has informed me how much you are pleased to interest yourself in my fate as a man, and (what to me is incomparably dearer) my fame as a poet. I have, Sir, in one or two instances, been patronized by those of your character in life, when I was introduced to their notice by * * * * friends to them, and honoured acquaintances to me ; but you are the first gentleman in the country whose benevolence and goodness of heart has interested himself for me, unsolicited and unknown. I am not master enough of the etiquette of these matters to know, nor did I stay to inquire, whether formal duty bade, or cold propriety disallowed, my thanking you in this manner, as I am convinced, from the light in which you kindly view me, that you will do me the justice to believe this letter is not the manœuvre of the needy, sharping author, fastening on those in upper life, who honour him with a little notice of his or his works. Indeed, the situation of poets is generally such, to a proverb, as may, in some measure, palliate that prostitution of heart and talents they have at times been guilty of. I do not think prodigality is, by any means, a necessary concomitant of a poetic turn, but I believe a careless, indolent attention to economy is almost inseparable from it ; then there must be in the heart of every bard of Nature's making, a certain modest sensibility, mixed with a kind of pride, that will ever keep him out of the way of those windfalls of fortune which frequently light on hardy impudence and foot-licking servility. It is not easy to imagine a more helpless state than his whose poetic fancy unfits him for the world, and whose character as a scholar gives him some pretensions to the *politesse* of life—yet is as poor as I am.

For my part, I thank Heaven my star has been kinder ; learning never elevated my ideas above the peasant's shed, and I have an independent fortune at the plough-tail.

I was surprised to hear that any one who pretended in the least to the manners of the gentleman, should be so foolish, or worse, as to stoop to traduce the morals of such a one as I am, and so inhumanly cruel, too, as to meddle with that late most unfortunate, unhappy part of my story. With a tear of gratitude, I thank you, Sir, for the warmth with which you interposed in behalf of my conduct.   I am, I acknowledge, too frequently the sport of whim, caprice, and passion, but reverence to God, and integrity to my fellow-creatures, I hope I shall ever preserve.   I have no return, Sir, to make you for your goodness but one—a return which I am persuaded will not be unacceptable—the honest, warm wishes of a grateful heart for your happiness, and every one of that lovely flock, who stand to you in a filial relation.   If ever calumny aim the poisoned shaft at them, may friendship be by to ward the blow !—R. B.

No. LXXII.

TO GAVIN HAMILTON.

MY DEAR SIR,   [EDINBURGH, *December*, 1787.]

It is indeed with the highest pleasure that I congratulate you on the return of days of ease and nights of pleasure, after the horrid hours of misery in which I saw you suffering existence when last in Ayrshire ; I seldom pray for anybody, " I'm baith dead-sweer and wretched ill o't ;" but most fervently do I beseech the Power that directs the world, that you may live long and be happy, but live no longer than you are happy.   It is needless for me to advise you to have a reverend care of your health.   I know you will make it a point never at one time to drink more than a pint of wine (I mean an English pint), and that you will never be witness to more than one bowl of punch at a time, and that cold drams you will never more taste ; and, above all things, I am convinced, that after drinking perhaps boiling punch, you will never mount your horse and gallop home in a chill late hour.   Above all things, as I understand you are in habits of intimacy with that Boanerges of gospel powers, Father Auld, be earnest with him that he will wrestle in prayer for you, that you may see· the vanity of vanities in trusting to, or even practising the casual moral works of charity, humanity, generosity, and forgiveness of things, which you practised so flagrantly that it was evident you delighted in them, neglecting, or perhaps profanely despising, the wholesome doctrine of faith without works, the only author of salvation.   A hymn of thanksgiving would, in my opinion, be highly becoming from you at present, and in my zeal for your well-being, I earnestly press on you to be diligent in chaunting over the two enclosed pieces of sacred poesy.   My best compliments to Mrs. Hamilton and Miss Kennedy.

Yours, &c.

R. B.

No. LXXIII.

TO MISS CHALMERS.

MY DEAR MADAM,   EDINBURGH, *December,* 1787.

I just now have read yours. The poetic compliments I pay cannot be misunderstood. They are neither of them so particular as to point you out to the world at large ; and the circle of your acquaintances will allow all I have said. Besides, I have complimented you chiefly, almost solely, on your mental charms. Shall I be plain with you ? I will ; so look to it. Personal attractions, Madam, you have much above par ; wit, understanding, and worth, you possess in the first class. This is a cursed flat way of telling you these truths, but let me hear no more of your sheepish timidity. I know the world a little. I know what they will say of my poems ; by second sight I suppose, for I am seldom out in my conjectures ; and you may believe me, my dear Madam, I would not run any risk of hurting you by any ill-judged compliment. I wish to show the world the odds between a poet's friends and those of simple prosemen. More for your information, both the pieces go in. One of them, "Where braving angry winter's storms," is already set—the tune is " Neil Gow's Lamentation for *Abercairny;* " the other is to be set to an old Highland air in Daniel Dow's collection of ancient Scots music ; the name is " *Ha a Chaillich air mo Dheith.*" My treacherous memory has forgot every circumstance about *Las Incas,* only I think you mentioned them as being in Creech's possession. I shall ask him about it. I am afraid the song of " Somebody" will come too late—as I shall, for certain, leave town in a week for Ayrshire, and from that to Dumfries, but there my hopes are slender. I leave my direction in town, so anything, wherever I am, will reach me.

I saw yours to ———— ; it is not too severe, nor did he take it amiss. On the contrary, like a whipped spaniel, he talks of being with you in the Christmas days. Mr. ———— has given him the invitation, and he is determined to accept of it. O selfishness ! he owns, in his sober moments, that from his own volatility of inclination, the circumstances in which he is situated, and his knowledge of his father's disposition, the whole affair is chimerical—yet he *will* gratify an idle *penchant* at the enormous, cruel expense of perhaps ruining the peace of the very woman for whom he professes the generous passion of love ! He is a gentleman in his mind and manners—*tant pis !* He is a volatile school-boy—the heir of a man's fortune who well knows the value of two times two !

Perdition seize them and their fortunes, before they should make the amiable, the lovely ————, the derided object of their purse-proud contempt !

I am doubly happy to hear of Mrs. ————'s recovery, because I really thought all was over with her. There are days of pleasure yet awaiting her :

> " As I came in by Glenap,
> I met with an aged woman ;
> She bade me cheer up my heart,
> For the best o' my days was comin'."

This day will decide my affairs with Creech. Things are, like myself, not what they ought to be ; yet better than what they appear to be.

> " Heaven's Sovereign saves all beings, but Himself,
> That hideous sight—a naked human heart."

Farewell ! remember me to Charlotte.   R. B.

No. LXXIV.

TO MRS. M'LEHOSE.

[The correspondence with Clarinda records one of the most interesting, although by no means creditable episodes of Burns's romantic life. The circumstances under which the letters were exchanged are explained in the Biographical Preface. It was at the house of Miss Nimmo, an elderly lady, known both to Burns and his friend, Miss Chalmers, that they first met at tea, according to Mr. Robert Chambers's reckoning, about the 4th of December ; and the following letter, the first of a remarkable series, is an acceptance of Mrs. M'Lehose's invitation to tea, on Saturday the 8th. Mrs. M'Lehose preserved all Burns's letters, which she esteemed, in her own words, " precious memorials of an acquaintance, the recollection of which would influence me were I to live till fourscore." (Letter to Mr. Syme, 1796.) After his death she offered to select some passages for publication in the collected edition of his writings for the benefit of his widow and children. The person to whom she lent the letters for the transcription of the extracts she had chosen, copied them all, and published them in violation of his own engagement and against Mrs. M'Lehose's wish. Parts were given in Cromek's *Reliques.*]

MADAM,   THURSDAY EVENING [*December* 6, 1787].
  I had set no small store by my tea-drinking to-night, and have not often been so disappointed. Saturday evening I shall embrace the opportunity with the greatest pleasure. I leave town this day se'ennight, and probably for a couple of twelvemonths ; but must ever regret that I so lately got an acquaintance I shall ever highly esteem, and in whose welfare I shall ever be warmly interested.
  Our worthy common friend, in her usual pleasant way, rallied me a good deal on my new acquaintance, and in the humour of her ideas I wrote some lines, which I enclose you, as I think they have a good deal of poetic merit ; and Miss [Nimmo] tells me you are not only a critic, but a poetess. Fiction, you know, is the native region of poetry ; and I hope you will pardon my vanity in sending you the bagatelle as a tolerable off-hand *jeu d'esprit*. I have several poetic trifles, which I shall gladly leave with Miss [Nimmo] or you, if they were worth house-room ; as there are scarcely two people on earth by whom it would mortify me more to be forgotten, though at the distance of ninescore miles.
  I am, Madam, with the highest respect,
                    Your very humble Servant,
                                        *   *   *   *

No. LXXV.

TO MRS. M'LEHOSE.

[An accident through a drunken coachman prevented Burns from keeping his engagement.]

Saturday Even [*Dec.* 8].

I CAN say with truth, Madam, that I never met with a person in my life whom I more anxiously wished to meet again than yourself. To-night I was to have had that very great pleasure—I was intoxicated with the idea ; but an unlucky fall from a coach has so bruised one of my knees, that I can't stir my leg off the cushion. So, if I don't see you again, I shall not rest in my grave for chagrin. I was vexed to the soul I had not seen you sooner. I determined to cultivate your friendship with the enthusiasm of religion ; but thus has Fortune ever served me. I cannot bear the idea of leaving Edinburgh without seeing you. I know not how to account for it—I am strangely taken with some people, nor am I often mistaken. You are a stranger to me ; but I am an odd being. Some yet unnamed feelings—things, not principles, but better than whims—carry me farther than boasted reason ever did a philosopher.

Farewell ! every happiness be yours.

ROBERT BURNS.

No. LXXVi.

TO MRS. M'LEHOSE.

[Mrs. M'Lehose, in condoling with him on his accident, said, "Were I your sister I would call and see you," and enclosed some verses she had written after reading the little poem he had sent her, modestly disclaiming the idea of their being poetry.]

I STRETCH a point, indeed, my dearest Madam, when I answer your card on the rack of my present agony. Your friendship, Madam ! By heavens, I was never proud before ! Your lines, I maintain it, are poetry, and good poetry ; mine were indeed partly fiction, and partly a friendship which, had I been so blest as to have met with you *in time*, might have led me—God of love only knows where. Time is too short for ceremonies.

I swear solemnly (in all the tenor of my former oath) to remember you in all the pride and warmth of friendship until—I cease to be !

To-morrow, and every day, till I see you, you shall hear from me.

Farewell ! May you enjoy a better night's repose than I am likely to have.

No. LXXVII.

TO MRS. M'LEHOSE.

[In her rejoinder Mrs. M'Lehose reminded her correspondent that, though practically a widow, she was still a wife, and asked him playfully whether he could, Jacob-like, wait seven years for a wife at the risk of being even then disappointed.]

YOUR last, my dear Madam, had the effect on me that Job's situation had on his friends, when "they sat down seven days and seven nights astonied, and spake not a word." "Pay my addresses to a married woman!" I started as if I had seen the ghost of him I had injured: I recollected my expressions; some of them indeed were, in the law phrase, "habit and repute," which is being half guilty. I cannot positively say, Madam, whether my heart might not have gone astray a little; but I can declare, upon the honour of a poet, that the vagrant has wandered unknown to me. I have a pretty handsome troop of follies of my own; and, like some other people's retinue, they are but undisciplined black-guards: but the luckless rascals have something of honour in them: they would not do a dishonest thing.

To meet with an unfortunate woman, amiable and young, deserted and widowed by those who were bound by every tie of duty, nature, and gratitude to protect, comfort, and cherish her; add to all, when she is perhaps one of the first of lovely forms and noble minds, the mind, too, that hits one's taste as the joys of heaven do a saint—should a vague infant idea, the natural child of imagination, thoughtlessly peep over the fence—were you, my friend, to sit in judgment, and the poor, airy straggler brought before you, trembling, self-condemned, with artless eyes, brimful of contrition, looking wistfully on its judge, you could not, my dear Madam, condemn the hapless wretch to death "without benefit of clergy?"

I won't tell you what reply my heart made to your raillery of " seven years :" but I will give you what a brother of my trade says on the same allusion :—

> " The Patriarch to gain a wife,
>   Chaste, beautiful, and young,
> Served fourteen years a painful life,
>   And never thought it long.
>
> " Oh, were you to reward such cares,
>   And life so long would stay,
> Not fourteen but four hundred years
>   Would seem as but one day."

I have written you this scrawl because I have nothing else to do, and you may sit down and find fault with it, if you have no better way of con-suming your time; but finding fault with the vagaries of a poet's fancy is much such another business as Xerxes chastising the waves of the Hellespont.

My limb now allows me to sit in some peace: to walk I have yet no prospect of, as I can't mark it to the ground.

I have just now looked over what I have written, and it is such a chaos of nonsense that I daresay you will throw it into the fire, and call me an idle, stupid fellow ; but whatever you think of my brains, believe me to be, with the most sacred respect and heartfelt esteem,

My dear Madam, your humble Servant,

ROBERT BURNS.

No. LXXVIII.

TO MISS CHALMERS.

[It is worth while to break the continuity of the Clarinda correspondence, by interspersing other letters written by Burns at the same time, in order to illustrate his state of mind at that period, and to enable readers to judge of the artificial character of the passionate addresses to that lady.]

EDINBURGH, *Dec.* 12, 1787.

I AM here under the care of a surgeon, with a bruised limb extended on a cushion ; and the tints of my mind vying with the livid horror preceding a midnight thunderstorm. A drunken coachman was the cause of the first, and incomparably the lightest evil ; misfortune, bodily constitution, hell, and myself, have formed a "quadruple alliance" to guarantee the other. I got my fall on Saturday, and am getting slowly better.

I have taken tooth and nail to the Bible, and am got through the five books of Moses, and half-way in Joshua. It is really a glorious book. I sent for my bookbinder to-day, and ordered him to get me an octavo Bible in sheets, the best paper and print in town, and bind it with all the elegance of his craft.

I would give my best song to my worst enemy—I mean the merit of making it—to have you and Charlotte by me. You are angelic creatures, and would pour oil and wine into my wounded spirit.

I enclose you a proof copy of the *Banks of the Devon*, which present with my best wishes to Charlotte. The *Ochil-hills** you shall probably have next week for yourself. None of your fine speeches !—R. B.

No. LXXIX.

TO CHARLES HAY, ESQ.

ADVOCATE.

[Enclosing verses on the death of the Lord President, Robert Dundas of Arniston, who died December 13, 1787.]

SIR,

The enclosed poem was written in consequence of your suggestion last time I had the pleasure of seeing you. It cost me an hour or two of next morning's sleep, but did not please me ; so it lay by, an ill-digested

* The song in honour of Miss Chalmers, beginning, "Where braving angry winter's storms." (*Page* 198.)

effort, till the other day that I gave it a critic brush. These kind of subjects are much hackneyed ; and, besides, the wailings of the rhyming tribe over the ashes of the great are cursedly suspicious, and out of all character for sincerity. These ideas damped my muse's fire ; however, I have done the best I could, and, at all events, it gives me an opportunity of declaring that I have the honour to be, Sir,

Your obliged humble Servant,

R. B.

No. LXXX.

TO MISS CHALMERS.

EDINBURGH, 19th Dec. 1787.

I BEGIN this letter in answer to yours of the 17th current, which is not yet cold since I read it. The atmosphere of my soul is vastly clearer than when I wrote you last. For the first time, yesterday I crossed the room on crutches. It would do your heart good to see my bardship, not on poetic, but on my oaken stilts ; throwing my best leg with an air, and with as much hilarity in my gait and countenance, as a May frog leaping across the newly-harrowed ridge, enjoying the fragrance of the refreshed earth after the long-expected shower !

I can't say I am altogether at my ease when I see anywhere in my path that meagre, squalid, famine-faced spectre Poverty ; attended as he always is by iron-fisted Oppression, and leering Contempt ; but I have sturdily withstood his buffetings many a hard-laboured day already, and still my motto is—I DARE ! My worst enemy is *moi-même.* I lie so miserably open to the inroads and incursions of a mischievous, light-armed, well-mounted banditti, under the banners of imagination, whim, caprice, and passion, and the heavy-armed veteran regulars of wisdom, prudence, and forethought move so very, very slow, that I am almost in a state of perpetual warfare, and alas ! frequent defeat. There are just two creatures I would envy—a horse in his wild state traversing the forests of Asia, or an oyster on some of the desert shores of Europe. The one has not a wish without enjoyment, the other has neither wish nor fear.

R. B.

No. LXXXI.

TO CLARINDA.

[In the rest of the letters between Mrs. M'Lehose and Burns, she signs herself Clarinda, and he Sylvander.]

Friday Evening [*December* 21].

I BEG your pardon, my dear " Clarinda," for the fragment scrawl I sent you yesterday. I really do not know what I wrote. A gentleman for whose character, abilities, and critical knowledge I have the highest

veneration, called in just as I had begun the second sentence, and I would not make the porter wait. I read to my much-respected friend several of my own bagatelles, and, among others, your lines, which I had copied out. He began some criticisms on them as on the other pieces, when I informed him they were the work of a young lady in this town, which, I assure you, made him stare. My learned friend seriously protested that he did not believe any young woman in Edinburgh was capable of such lines ; and if you know anything of Professor Gregory, you will neither doubt of his abilities nor his sincerity. I do love you, if possible, still better for having so fine a taste and turn for poesy. I have again gone wrong in my usual unguarded way, but you may erase the word, and put esteem, respect, or any other tame Dutch expression you please in its place. I believe there is no holding converse, or carrying on correspondence, with an amiable woman, much less a *gloriously amiable fine woman*, without some mixture of that delicious passion whose most devoted slave I have more than once had the honour of being. But why be hurt or offended on that account? Can no honest man have a prepossession for a fine woman, but he must run his head against an intrigue? Take a little of the tender witchcraft of love, and add to it the generous, the honourable sentiments of manly friendship, and I know but *one* more delightful morsel, which few, few in any rank ever taste. Such a composition is like adding cream to strawberries : it not only gives the fruit a more elegant richness, but has a peculiar deliciousness of its own.

I enclose you a few lines I composed on a late melancholy occasion.* I will not give above five or six copies of it at all, and I would be hurt if any friend should give any copies without my consent.

You cannot imagine, Clarinda (I like the idea of Arcadian names in a commerce of this kind), how much store I have set by the hopes of your future friendship. I do not know if you have a just idea of my character, but I wish you to see me as I am. I am, as most people of my trade are, a strange Will-o'-wisp being ; the victim, too frequently, of much imprudence and many follies. My great constituent elements are *pride* and *passion*. The first I have endeavoured to humanise into integrity and honour ; the last makes me a devotee to the warmest degree of enthusiasm in love, religion, or friendship—either of them, or all together, as I happen to be inspired. 'Tis true I never saw you but once ; but how much acquaintance did I form with you in that once! Do not think I flatter you, or have a design upon you, Clarinda : I have too much pride for the one, and too little cold contrivance for the other ; but of all God's creatures I ever could approach in the beaten way of my acquaintance, you struck me with the deepest, the strongest, the most permanent impression. I say the most permanent, because I know myself well, and how far I can promise either in my prepossessions or powers. Why are you unhappy? And why are so many of our fellow-creatures, unworthy to belong to the same species with you, blest with all they can wish? You have a hand all benevolent to give : why were you denied the pleasure?

---

* Probably the verses on the Death of the Lord President.

You have a heart formed—gloriously formed—for all the most refined luxuries of love : why was that heart ever wrung ? Oh Clarinda ! shall we not meet in a state, some yet unknown state of being, where the lavish hand of plenty shall minister to the highest wish of benevolence, and where the chill north wind of prudence shall never blow over the flowery fields of enjoyment ? If we do not, man was made in vain ! I deserve most of the unhappy hours that have lingered over my head ; they were the wages of my labour : but what unprovoked demon, malignant as hell, stole upon the confidence of unmistrusting busy fate, and dashed *your* cup of life with undeserved sorrow ?

Let me know how long your stay will be out of town ; I shall count the hours till you inform me of your return. Cursed *etiquette* forbids your seeing me just now ; and so soon as I can walk I must bid Edinburgh adieu. Lord ! why was I born to see misery which I cannot relieve, and to meet with friends whom I cannot enjoy ? I look back with the pang of unavailing avarice on my loss in not knowing you sooner : all last winter, these three months past, what luxury of intercourse have I not lost ! Perhaps, though, 'twas better for my peace. You see I am either above or incapable of dissimulation. I believe it is want of that particular genius. I despise design, because I want either coolness or wisdom to be capable of it. I am interrupted. Adieu, my dear Clarinda !

SYLVANDER.

No. LXXXII.

TO CLARINDA.

MY DEAR CLARINDA,

Your last verses have so delighted me, that I have copied them in among some of my own most valued pieces, which I keep sacred for my own use. Do let me have a few now and then.

Did you, Madam, know what I feel when you talk of your sorrows !

Good God ! that one who has so much worth in the sight of heaven, and is so amiable to her fellow-creatures, should be so unhappy ! I can't venture out for cold. My limb is vastly better ; but I have not any use of it without my crutches. Monday, for the first time, I dine at a neighbour's, next door. As soon as I can go so far, *even in a coach*, my first visit shall be to you. Write me when you leave town, and immediately when you return ; and I earnestly pray your stay may be short. You can't imagine how miserable you made me when you hinted to me not to write. Farewell.

SYLVANDER.

No. LXXXIII.

TO MR. RICHARD BROWN

IRVINE.

[Richard Brown is the "very noble character, but hapless son of misfortune," to whom Burns refers in his memoir as having had a great influence on his youth.]

MY DEAR SIR,   EDINBURGH, *30th Dec.* 1787.

I have met with few things in life which have given me more pleasure than Fortune's kindness to you since those days in which we met in the vale of misery ; as I can honestly say, that I never knew a man who more truly deserved it, or to whom my heart more truly wished it.   I have been much indebted since that time to your story and sentiments for steeling my mind against evils, of which I have had a pretty decent share. My Will-o'-wisp fate you know : do you recollect a Sunday we spent together in Eglinton Woods?   You told me, on my repeating some verses to you, that you wondered I could resist the temptation of sending verses of such merit to a magazine.   It was from this remark I derived that idea of my own pieces which encouraged me to endeavour at the character of a poet.   I am happy to hear that you will be two or three months at home.   As soon as a bruised limb will permit me, I shall return to Ayrshire, and we shall meet ; "and faith I hope we'll not sit dumb, nor yet cast out !"

I have much to tell you "of men, their manners, and their ways ;" perhaps a little of the other sex.   Apropos, I beg to be remembered to Mrs. Brown.   There, I doubt not, my dear friend, but you have found substantial happiness.   I expect to find you something of an altered, but not a different man : the wild, bold, generous young fellow composed into the steady affectionate husband, and the fond careful parent.   For me, I am just the same Will-o'-wisp being I used to be.   About the first and fourth quarters of the moon, I generally set in for the trade wind of wisdom ; but about the full and change, I am the luckless victim of mad tornadoes, which blow me into chaos.   All-mighty love still reigns and revels in my bosom ; and I am at this moment ready to hang myself for a young Edinburgh widow, who has wit and wisdom more murderously fatal than the assassinating stiletto of the Sicilian bandit, or the poisoned arrow of the savage African.   My Highland dirk, that used to hang beside my crutches, I have gravely removed into a neighbouring closet, the key of which I cannot command, in case of spring-tide paroxysms.   You may guess of her wit by the following verses which she sent me the other day. . . .

My best compliments to our friend Allan.   Adieu !

R. B.

No. LXXXIV.

TO CLARINDA.

[Mrs. M'Lehose, as is evident from the allusions in Burns's letters, repeatedly sent him verses of her own composition. The lines referred to in the following letter will give a fair idea of her poetical gifts.

" Talk not of Love—it gives me pain,
     For Love has been my foe :
He bound me in an iron chain,
     And plunged me deep in woe.

" But Friendship's pure and lasting joys
     My heart was form'd to prove—
The worthy object be of those,
     But never talk of Love !

" The hand of Friendship I accept —
     May Honour be our guard !
Virtue our intercourse direct,
     Her smiles our dear reward."]

[*After New Year's day,* 1788.]

YOU are right, my dear Clarinda : a friendly correspondence goes for nothing, except one write their undisguised sentiments. Yours please me for their intrinsic merit, as well as because they are *yours*, which, I assure you, is to me a high recommendation. Your religious sentiments, Madam, I revere. If you have, on some suspicious evidence, from some lying oracle, learned that I despise or ridicule so sacredly important a matter as real religion, you have, my Clarinda, much misconstrued your friend ;—" I am not mad, most noble Festus !" Have you ever met a perfect character? Do we not sometimes rather exchange faults than get rid of them ? For instance, I am perhaps tired with and shocked at a life too much the prey of giddy inconsistencies and thoughtless follies ; by degrees I grow sober, prudent, and statedly pious—I say statedly, because the most unaffected devotion is not at all inconsistent with my first character—I join the world in congratulating myself on the happy change. But let me pry more narrowly into this affair. Have I, at bottom, anything of a secret pride in these endowments and emendations ? Have I nothing of a Presbyterian sourness, a hypocritical severity, when I survey my less regular neighbours ? In a word, have I missed all those nameless and numberless modifications of indistinct selfishness, which are so near our own eyes, we can scarcely bring them within the sphere of our vision, and which the known spotless cambric of our character hides from the ordinary observer ?

My definition of worth is short : truth and humanity respecting our fellow-creatures ; reverence and humility in the presence of that Being, my Creator and Preserver, and who, I have every reason to believe, will one day be my Judge. The first part of my definition is the creature of unbiassed instinct ; the last is the child of after reflection. Where I found these two essentials, I would gently note, and slightly mention,

any attendant flaws—flaws, the marks, the consequences of human nature.

I can easily enter into the sublime pleasures that your strong imagination and keen sensibility must derive from religion, particularly if a little in the shade of misfortune ; but I own I cannot, without a marked grudge, see Heaven totally engross so amiable, so charming a woman, as my friend Clarinda ; and should be very well pleased at *a circumstance* that would put it in the power of somebody (happy somebody !) to divide her attention, with all the delicacy and tenderness of an earthly attachment.

You will not easily persuade me that you have not a grammatical knowledge of the English language. So far from being inaccurate, you are elegant beyond any woman of my acquaintance, except one, whom I wish you knew.

Your last verses to me have so delighted me, that I have got an excellent old Scots air that suits the measure, and you shall see them in print in the *Scots Musical Museum*, a work publishing by a friend of mine in this town. I want four stanzas ; you gave me but three, and one of them alluded to an expression in my former letter ; so I have taken your two first verses, with a slight alteration in the second, and have added a third ; but you must help me to a fourth. Here they are : the latter half of the first stanza would have been worthy of Sappho ; I am in raptures with it.

> " Talk not of Love, it gives me pain,
>   For Love has been my foe :
> He bound me with an iron chain,
>   And sunk me deep in woe.
>
> " But Friendship's pure and lasting joys
>   My heart was form'd to prove :
> There, welcome, win and wear the prize,
>   But never talk of love."
>
> Your friendship much can make me blest,
>   O why that bliss destroy ?
>   [only]
> Why urge the odious one request,
>   [will]
>   You know I must deny ?

The alteration in the second stanza is no improvement, but there was a slight inaccuracy in your rhyme. The third I only offer to your choice, and have left two words for your determination. The air is " The Banks of Spey," and is most beautiful.

To-morrow evening I intend taking a chair, and paying a visit at Park Place to a much-valued old friend. If I could be sure of finding you at home (and I will send one of the chairmen to call), I would spend from five to six o'clock with you, as I go past. I cannot do more at this time, as I have something on my hand that hurries me much. I propose giving you the first call, my old friend the second, and Miss ——, as I return home. Do not break any engagement for me, as I will spend another evening with you at any rate before I leave town.

Do not tell me that you are pleased when your friends inform you of your faults. I am ignorant what they are ; but I am sure they must

be such evanescent trifles, compared with your personal and mental accomplishments, that I would despise the ungenerous narrow soul who would notice any shadow of imperfections you may seem to have any other way than in the most delicate agreeable raillery. Coarse minds are not aware how much they injure the keenly-feeling tie of bosom-friendship, when, in their foolish officiousness, they mention what nobody cares for recollecting. People of nice sensibility and generous minds have a certain intrinsic dignity, that fires at being trifled with, or lowered, or even too nearly approached.

You need make no apology for long letters : I am even with you. Many happy new-years to you, charming Clarinda ! I can't dissemble, were it to shun perdition. He who sees you as I have done, and does not love you, deserves to be damned for his stupidity ! He who loves you, and would injure you, deserves to be doubly damned for his villany ! Adieu.

SYLVANDER.

P.S.—What would you think of this for a fourth stanza ?

> Your thought, if love must harbour there,
>   Conceal it in that thought,
> Nor cause me from my bosom tear
>   The very friend I sought.

No. LXXXV.

TO CLARINDA.

[Reference is here made to the second interview between Burns and Mrs. M'Lehose ; along with the letter he sent his autobiography.]

SOME days, some nights, nay, some *hours*, like the "ten righteous persons in Sodom," save the rest of the vapid, tiresome, miserable months and years of life. One of these hours my dear Clarinda blest me with yesternight.

> "————— ———One well-spent hour,
> In such a tender circumstance for friends,
> Is better than an age of common time !"—THOMSON.

My favourite feature in Milton's Satan is his manly fortitude in supporting what cannot be remedied—in short, the wild broken fragments of a noble exalted mind in ruins. I meant no more by saying he was a favourite hero of mine.

I mentioned to you my letter to Dr. Moore, giving an account of my life : it is truth, every word of it, and will give you a just idea of the man whom you have honoured with your friendship. I am afraid you will hardly be able to make sense of so torn a piece. Your verses I shall muse on, deliciously, as I gaze on your image in my mind's eye, in my heart's core : they will be in time enough for a week to come. I am truly happy

your headache is better. Oh, how can pain or evil be so daringly unfeeling, cruelly savage as to wound so noble a mind, so lovely a form !

My little fellow is all my namesake. Write me soon. My every, strongest good wishes attend you, Clarinda !

SYLVANDER.

I know not what I have written, I am pestered with people around me.

No. LXXXVI.

TO CLARINDA.

[A tender rebuke from Clarinda about his want of religion drew from him this reply.]

Tuesday Night [*Jan.* 8?].

I AM delighted, charming Clarinda, with your honest enthusiasm for religion. Those of either sex, but particularly the female, who are luke-warm in that most important of all things, " O my soul, come not thou into their secrets ! " I feel myself deeply interested in your good opinion, and will lay before you the outlines of my belief. He who is our Author and Preserver, and will one day be our Judge, must be (not for His sake in the way of duty, but from the native impulse of our hearts) the object of our reverential awe and grateful adoration : He is almighty and all-bounteous, we are weak and dependent ; hence prayer and every other sort of devotion.——" He is not willing that any should perish, but that all should come to everlasting life ;" consequently it must be in every one's power to embrace His offer of " everlasting life ;" otherwise He could not, in justice, condemn those who did not. A mind pervaded, actuated, and governed by purity, truth, and charity, though it does not *merit* heaven, yet is an absolutely necessary prerequisite, without which heaven can neither be obtained nor enjoyed ; and, by Divine promise, such a mind shall never fail of attaining " everlasting life :" hence the impure, the deceiving, and the uncharitable extrude themselves from eternal bliss, by their unfitness for enjoying it. The Supreme Being has put the immediate administration of all this, for wise and good ends known to Himself, into the hands of Jesus Christ—a great personage, whose relation to Him we cannot comprehend, but whose relation to us is [that of] a guide and Saviour; and who, except for our own obstinacy and misconduct, will bring us all, through various ways, and by various means, to bliss at last.

These are my tenets, my lovely friend ; and which, I think, cannot be well disputed. My creed is pretty nearly expressed in the last clause of Jamie Deans's grace, an honest weaver in Ayrshire : " Lord, grant that we may lead a gude life ! for a gude life maks a gude end ; at least it helps weel."

I am flattered by the entertainment you tell me you have found in my packet. You see me as I have been, you know me as I am, and may guess at what I am likely to be. I too may say, " Talk not of love," &c.

B B 2

for indeed he has "plunged me deep in woe!" Not that I ever saw a woman who pleased unexceptionably, as my Clarinda elegantly says, "in the companion, the friend, and the mistress." *One* indeed I could except —*one*, before passion threw its mists over my discernment, I knew *the* first of women! Her name is indelibly written in my heart's core—but I dare not look in on it—a degree of agony would be the consequence. Oh, thou perfidious, cruel, mischief-making demon, who presidest over that frantic passion—thou mayst, thou dost poison my peace, but thou shalt not taint my honour—I would not, for a single moment, give an asylum to the most distant imagination, that would shadow the faintest outline of a selfish gratification, at the expense of her whose happiness is twisted with the threads of my existence.—— May she be as happy as she deserves! And if my tenderest, faithfulest friendship can add to her bliss, I shall at least have one solid mine of enjoyment in my bosom. *Don't guess at these ravings!*

I watched at our front window to-day, but was disappointed.* It has been a day of disappointments. I am just risen from a two hours' bout after supper, with silly or sordid souls, who could relish nothing in common with me but the port.——*One*——'Tis now "witching time of night;" and whatever is out of joint in the foregoing scrawl, impute it to enchantments and spells; for I can't look over it, but will seal it up directly, as I don't care for to-morrow's criticisms on it.

You are by this time fast asleep, Clarinda; may good angels attend and guard you as constantly and faithfully as my good wishes do!

> " Beauty, which, whether waking or asleep,
>   Shot forth peculiar graces."

John Milton, I wish thy soul better rest than I expect on my pillow to-night. Oh for a little of the cart-horse part of human nature! Good-night, my dearest Clarinda!

SYLVANDER.

No. LXXXVII.

TO CLARINDA.

[Clarinda writes to say she cannot imagine who is the fair one he alludes to in his last epistle. She first thought of his Jean, though uncertain whether she has his " tenderest, faithfulest friendship." She cannot understand that bonnie lassie— refusing him after such proofs of love; and admires him for his continued fondness towards her. She promises again to give him a nod at his window.]

Thursday Noon [*Jan.* 10?].

I AM certain I saw you, Clarinda; but you don't look to the proper storey for a poet's lodging,

> " Where Speculation roosted near the sky."

I could almost have thrown myself over for very vexation. Why didn't you look higher? It has spoilt my peace for this day. To be so near my

---

* Mrs. M'Lehose had promised to pass through his Square about two in the afternoon, and give him a nod if he were at the window of his room and she could discover it.

charming Clarinda ; to miss her look while it was searching for me ! I
am sure the soul is capable of disease, for mine has convulsed itself into
an inflammatory fever. I am sorry for your little boy : do let me know
to-morrow how he is.

You have converted me, Clarinda (I shall love that name while I live :
there is heavenly music in it !). Booth and Amelia I know well. Your
sentiments on that subject, as they are on every subject, are just and noble.
" To be feelingly alive to kindness and to unkindness " is a charming
female character.

What I said in my last letter, the powers of fuddling sociality only know
for me. By yours, I understand my good star has been partly in my
horizon when I got wild in my reveries. Had that evil planet, which has
almost all my life shed its baleful rays on my devoted head, been as usual
in its zenith, I had certainly blabbed something that would have pointed
out to you the dear object of my tenderest friendship, and, in spite of me,
something more. Had that fatal information escaped me, and it was
merely chance or kind stars that it did not, I had been undone. You
would never have written me, except, perhaps, *once* more. Oh, I could
curse circumstances ! and the coarse tie of human laws which keeps fast
what common sense would loose, and which bars that happiness itself
cannot give—happiness which otherwise love and honour would warrant !
But hold—I shall make no more " hairbreadth 'scapes."

My friendship, Clarinda, is a life-rent business. My likings are both
strong and eternal. I told you I had but one male friend : I have but two
female. I should have a third, but she is surrounded by the blandishments
of flattery and courtship. Her I register in my heart's core by Peggy
Chalmers : Miss Nimmo can tell you how divine she is. She is worthy
of a place in the same bosom with my Clarinda. That is the highest
compliment I can pay her. Farewell, Clarinda ! Remember

SYLVANDER.

No. LXXXVIII.

TO CLARINDA.

Saturday Morning.

YOUR thoughts on religion, Clarinda, shall be welcome. You may
perhaps distrust me when I say 'tis also my favourite topic ; but mine is
the religion of the bosom. I hate the very idea of a controversial divinity ;
as I firmly believe, that every honest, upright man, of whatever sect, will
be accepted of the Deity. If your verses, as you seem to hint, contain
censure, except you want an occasion to break with me, don't send them.
I have a little infirmity in my disposition, that where I fondly love, or
highly esteem, I cannot bear reproach.

" Reverence thyself " is a sacred maxim, and I wish to cherish it. I
think I told you Lord Bolingbroke's saying to Swift—" Adieu, dear Swift,
with all thy faults I love thee entirely ; make an effort to love me with all
mine." A glorious sentiment, and without which there can be no friend-

ship. I do highly, very highly esteem you indeed, Clarinda—you merit
it all. Perhaps, too, I scorn dissimulation. I could fondly love you :
judge, then, what a maddening sting your reproach would be. " Oh, I
have sins to *Heaven*, but none to *you !* " With what pleasure would I
meet you to-day, but I cannot walk to meet the Fly. I hope to be able
to see you on *foot*, about the middle of next week.

I am interrupted—perhaps you are not sorry for it, you will tell me—but
I won't anticipate blame. Oh Clarinda ! did you know how dear to me is
your look of kindness, your smile of approbation, you would not, either in
prose or verse, risk a censorious remark.

> " Curst be the verse, how well soe'er it flow,
> That tends to make one worthy man my foe ! "

SYLVANDER.

No. LXXXIX.

TO CLARINDA.

YOU talk of weeping, Clarinda : some involuntary drops wet your lines
as I read them. Offend me, my dearest angel ! You cannot offend me—
you never offended me. If you had ever given me the least shadow of
offence, so pardon me, my God, as I forgive Clarinda. I have read yours
again ; it has blotted my paper. Though I find your letter has agitated
me into a violent headache, I shall take a chair and be with you about
eight. A friend is to be with us at tea, on my account, which hinders me
from coming sooner. Forgive, my dearest Clarinda, my unguarded expressions. For Heaven's sake, forgive me, or I shall never be able to
bear my own mind.

Your unhappy
SYLVANDER.

No. XC.

TO CLARINDA.

[After a third interview Clarinda owns her high appreciation of Burns's
character : " Our last interview has raised you very high in mine [esteem].   I have
met with few, indeed, of your sex who *understood delicacy in such circumstances.*"
Still she fears she may be the victim of her sensibility.]

Monday Even, ıı *o'clock.*

WHY have I not heard from you, Clarinda ? To-day I expected it ; and
before supper, when a letter to me was announced, my heart danced with
rapture : but behold, 'twas some fool, who had taken it into his head to
turn poet, and made me an offering of the firstfruits of his nonsense. " It
is not poetry, but prose run mad." Did I ever repeat to you an epigram I
made on a Mr. Elphinstone, who has given a translation of Martial, a

famous Latin poet ?   The poetry of Elphinstone can only equal his prose-notes.   I was sitting in a merchant's shop of my acquaintance, waiting somebody ; he put Elphinstone into my hand, and asked my opinion of it ; I begged leave to write it on a blank leaf, which I did—

TO MR. ELPHINSTONE, ETC.

Oh thou, whom poesy abhors !
Whom prose has turnèd out of doors !
Heard'st thou yon groan ?—proceed no further !
'Twas laurell'd Martial calling murther !

I am determined to see you, if at all possible, on Saturday evening. Next week I must sing—

The night is my departing night,
   The morn's the day I maun awa' ;
There's neither friend nor foe o' mine
   But wishes that I were awa' !

What I hae done for lack o' wit,
   I never, never can reca' ;
I hope ye're a' my friends as yet—
   Gude night, and joy be wi' you a' !

If I could see you sooner, I would be so much the happier ; but I would not purchase the dearest gratification on earth, if it must be at your expense in worldly censure, far less inward peace.

I shall certainly be ashamed of thus scrawling whole sheets of inco-herence.   The only *unity* (a sad word with poets and critics !) in my ideas is CLARINDA.   There my heart " reigns and revels ! "

" What art thou, Love ? whence are those charms,
   That thus thou bear'st an universal rule ?
For thee the soldier quits his arms,
   The king turns slave, the wise man fool.
In vain we chase thee from the field,
   And with cool thoughts resist thy yoke :
Next tide of blood, alas, we yield,
   And all those high resolves are broke ! "

I like to have quotations for every occasion.   They give one's ideas so pat, and save one the trouble of finding expression adequate to one's feelings.   I think it is one of the greatest pleasures attending a poetic genius, that we can give our woes, cares, joys, loves, &c. an embodied form in verse, which to me is ever immediate ease.   Goldsmith says finely of his Muse—

" Thou source of all my bliss and all my woe,
Thou found'st me poor at first, and keep'st me so."

My limb has been so well to-day, that I have gone up and down stairs often without my staff.   To-morrow I hope to walk once again on my own legs to dinner.   It is only next street.   Adieu!

SYLVANDER.

No. XCI.

TO CLARINDA.

Tuesday Evening [*Jan.* 15?].

THAT you have faults, my Clarinda, I never doubted ; but I knew not where they existed, and Saturday night made me more in the dark than ever. Oh Clarinda ! why will you wound my soul by hinting that last night must have lessened my opinion of you ? True, I was "behind the scenes" with you ; but what did I see ? A bosom glowing with honour and benevolence ; a mind ennobled by genius, informed and refined by education and reflection, and exalted by native religion, genuine as in the climes of heaven ; a heart formed for all the glorious meltings of friendship, love, and pity. These I saw : I saw the noblest immortal soul creation ever showed me.

I looked long, my dear Clarinda, for your letter ; and am vexed that you are complaining. I have not caught you so far wrong as in your idea, that the commerce you have with *one* friend hurts you if you cannot tell every tittle of it to *another.* Why have so injurious a suspicion of a good God, Clarinda, as to think that Friendship and Love, on the sacred inviolate principles of Truth, Honour, and Religion, can be anything else than an object of His divine approbation ?

I have mentioned in some of my former scrawls, Saturday evening next. Do allow me to wait on you that evening. Oh, my angel ! how soon must we part ! and when can we meet again ? I look forward on the horrid interval with tearful eyes. What have I lost by not knowing you sooner ! I fear, I fear my acquaintance with you is too short, to make that *lasting* impression on your heart I could wish.

SYLVANDER.

No. XCII.

TO CLARINDA.

Sunday Night [*Jan.* 20?].

THE impertinence of fools has joined with a return of an old indisposition to make me good for nothing to-day. The paper has lain before me all this evening to write to my dear Clarinda ; but

" Fools rush'd on fools, as waves succeed to waves."

I cursed them in my soul : they sacrilegiously disturb my meditations on her who holds my heart. What a creature is man ! A little alarm last night and to-day that I am mortal, has made such a revolution in my spirits ! there is no philosophy, no divinity, comes half so home to the mind. I have no idea of courage that braves Heaven. 'Tis the wild ravings of an imaginary hero in Bedlam. I can no more, Clarinda ; I can scarce hold up my head ; but I am happy you don't know it, you would be so uneasy.

SYLVANDER.

I am, my lovely friend, much better this morning, on the whole ; but I have a horrid languor on my spirits—

> " Sick of the world and all its joy,
> My soul in pining sadness mourns :
> Dark scenes of woe my mind employ,
> The past and present in their turns.'

Have you ever met with a saying of the great and likewise good Mr. Locke, author of the famous *Essay on the Human Understanding ?* He wrote a letter to a friend, directing it " Not to be delivered till after my decease." It ended thus—" I know you loved me when living, and will preserve my memory now I am dead. All the use to be made of it is—that this life affords no solid satisfaction, but in the consciousness of having done well, and the hopes of another life. Adieu ! I leave my best wishes with you. —J. LOCKE."

Clarinda, may I reckon on your friendship for life ? I think I may. Thou Almighty Preserver of men ! Thy friendship, which hitherto I have too much neglected, to secure it shall all the future days and nights of my life be my steady care ! The idea of my Clarinda follows :—

> " Hide it, my heart, within that close disguise,
> Where, mix'd with God's, her loved idea lies."

But I fear inconstancy, the consequent imperfection of human weakness. Shall I meet with a friendship that defies years of absence, and the chances and changes of fortune ? Perhaps " such things are." *One* honest man I have great hopes from, that way ; but who, except a romance writer, would think on a *love* that could promise for life, in spite of distance, absence, chance, and change ; and that, too, with slender hopes of fruition ? For my own part, I can say to myself in both requisitions, " Thou art the man ;" I dare, in cool resolve, I dare declare myself that friend and that lover. If womankind is capable of such things, Clarinda is. I trust that she is ; and feel I shall be miserable if she is not. There is not one virtue which gives worth, or one sentiment which does honour to the sex, that she does not possess superior to any woman I ever saw : her exalted mind, aided a little perhaps by her situation, is, I think, capable of that nobly-romantic love-enthusiasm.

May I see you on Wednesday evening, my dear angel ? The next Wednesday again will, I conjecture, be a hated day to us both. I tremble for censorious remarks for your sake ; but in extraordinary cases, may not usual and useful precautions be a little dispensed with ? Three evenings, three swift-winged evenings, with pinions of down, are all the past—I dare not calculate the future. I shall call at Miss Nimmo's to-morrow evening ; 'twill be a farewell call.

I have written out my last sheet of paper, so I am reduced to my last half-sheet. What a strange, mysterious faculty is that thing called imagination ! We have no ideas almost at all of another world ; but I have often amused myself with visionary schemes of what happiness might be enjoyed by small alterations—alterations that we can fully enter to [*sic*], in

this present state of existence. For instance, suppose you and I just as we are at present, the same reasoning powers, sentiments, and even desires ; the same fond curiosity for knowledge and remarking observation in our minds—and imagine our bodies free from pain, and the necessary supplies for the wants of nature at all times and easily within our reach ; imagine further that we were set free from the laws of gravitation which bind us to this globe, and could at pleasure fly, without inconvenience, through all the yet unconjectured bounds of creation—what a life of bliss should we lead in our mutual pursuit of virtue and knowledge, and our mutual enjoyment of friendship and love !

I see you laughing at my fairy fancies, and calling me a voluptuous Mahometan ; but I am certain I should be a happy creature, beyond anything we call bliss here below ; nay, it would be a paradise congenial to you too. Don't you see us hand in hand, or rather my arm about your lovely waist, making our remarks on Sirius, the nearest of the fixed stars ; or surveying a comet flaming innoxious by us, as we just now would mark the passing pomp of a travelling monarch ; or in a shady bower of Mercury or Venus, dedicating the hour to love and mutual converse, relying honour, and revelling endearment—while the most exalted strains of poesy and harmony would be the ready, spontaneous language of our souls ? Devotion is the favourite employment of your heart, so is it of mine ; what incentives then to, and powers for reverence, gratitude, faith, and hope, in all the fervours of adoration and praise to that Being whose unsearchable wisdom, power, and goodness, so pervaded, so inspired every sense and feeling ! By this time, I daresay, you will be blessing the neglect of the maid that leaves me destitute of paper.

SYLVANDER.

No. XCIII.

TO MISS CHALMERS.

Now for that wayward unfortunate thing, myself. I have broke measures with Creech, and last week I wrote him a frosty, keen letter. He replied in terms of chastisement, and promised me upon his honour that I should have the account on Monday ; but this is Tuesday, and yet I have not heard a word from him. God have mercy on me ! a poor damned, incautious, duped, unfortunate fool ! The sport, the miserable victim of rebellious pride, hypochondriac imagination, agonizing sensibility, and bedlam passions.

" I wish that I were dead, but I'm no' like to die !" I had lately " a hairbreadth 'scape in th' imminent deadly breach" of love, too. Thank my stars, I got off heart-whole, " waur fleyed (worse frightened) than hurt."—Interruption.

I have this moment got a hint..... I fear I am something like—undone—but I hope for the best. Come, stubborn pride, and unshrinking resolution ; accompany me through this, to me, miserable world ! You must

not desert me. Your friendship I think I can count on, though I should date my letters from a marching regiment. Early in life, and all my life, I reckoned on a recruiting drum as my forlorn-hope. Seriously, though, life presents me with but a melancholy path : but—my limb will soon be sound, and I shall struggle on.—R. B.

No. XCIV.

TO MRS. DUNLOP.

EDINBURGH, *January* 21, 1788.

AFTER six weeks' confinement, I am beginning to walk across the room. They have been six horrible weeks ; anguish and low spirits made me unfit to read, write, or think.

I have a hundred times wished that one could resign life as an officer resigns a commission ; for I would not take in any poor ignorant wretch, by selling out. Lately I was a sixpenny private, and, God knows, a miserable soldier enough ; now I march to the campaign, a starving cadet —a little more conspicuously wretched.

I am ashamed of all this ; for though I do want bravery for the warfare of life, I could wish, like some other soldiers, to have as much fortitude or cunning as to dissemble or conceal my cowardice.

As soon as I can bear the journey, which will be, I suppose, about the middle of next week, I leave Edinburgh ; and soon after I shall pay my grateful duty at Dunlop House.—R. B.

No. XCV.

TO ROBERT GRAHAM, ESQ.

OF FINTRY.

[It had long been a favourite project with Burns to get a place in the Excise. Through the influence of the friends appealed to in the following letters, his name was placed on the list of candidates to be appointed as vacancies occurred.]

SIR,

When I had the honour of being introduced to you at Athole House, I did not so soon think of asking a favour of you. When Lear, in Shakspeare, asked old Kent why he wished to be in his service, he answers : ' Because you have that in your face which I would fain call master.' For some such reason, Sir, do I now solicit your patronage. You know, I dare say, of an application I lately made to your Board to be admitted an officer of Excise. I have, according to form, been examined by a supervisor, and to-day I gave in his certificate, with a request for an order for instructions. In this affair, if I succeed, I am afraid I shall but too much need a patronising friend. Propriety of conduct as a man, and fidelity

and attention as an officer, I dare engage for ; but with anything like business, except manual labour, I am totally unacquainted.

I had intended to have closed my late appearance on the stage of life in the character of a country farmer ; but after discharging some filial and fraternal claims, I find I could only fight for existence in that miserable manner which I have lived to see throw a venerable parent into the jaws of a jail ; whence death, the poor man's last and often best friend, rescued him.

I know, Sir, that to need your goodness is to have a claim on it ; may I, therefore, beg your patronage to forward me in this affair, till I be appointed to a division—where, by the help of rigid economy, I will try to support that independence so dear to my soul, but which has been too often so distant from my situation ?—R. B.

No. XCVI.

TO THE EARL OF GLENCAIRN.

[This appeal was not successful in obtaining Lord Glencairn's patronage in the matter.]

My Lord,
I know your lordship will disapprove of my ideas in a request I am going to make to you ; but I have weighed, long and seriously weighed, my situation, my hopes, and turn of mind, and am fully fixed to my scheme if I can possibly effectuate it. I wish to get into the Excise : I am told that your lordship's interest will easily procure me the grant from the commissioners ; and your lordship's patronage and goodness, which have already rescued me from obscurity, wretchedness, and exile, embolden me to ask that interest. You have likewise put it in my power to save the little tie of home that sheltered an aged mother, two brothers, and three sisters, from destruction. There, my lord, you have bound me over to the highest gratitude.

My brother's farm is but a wretched lease, but I think he will probably weather out the remaining seven years of it ; and after the assistance which I have given, and will give him, to keep the family together, I think, by my guess, I shall have rather better than two hundred pounds ; and instead of seeking, what is almost impossible at present to find, a farm that I can certainly live by, with so small a stock, I shall lodge this sum in a banking-house, a sacred deposit, excepting only the calls of uncommon distress or necessitous old age.

These, my lord, are my views : I have resolved from the maturest deliberation ; and now I am fixed, I shall leave no stone unturned to carry my resolve into execution. Your lordship's patronage is the strength of my hopes ; nor have I yet applied to anybody else. Indeed my heart sinks within me at the idea of applying to any other of the great who have honoured me with their countenance. I am ill-qualified to dog the heels

of greatness with the impertinence of solicitation, and tremble nearly as much at the thought of the cold promise as the cold denial ; but to your lordship I have not only the honour, the comfort, but the pleasure of being

Your lordship's much and deeply indebted humble Servant,

R. B.

No. XCVII.

TO CLARINDA.

[The next letter to Clarinda was written on the day following their fourth meeting.]

Thursday Morning [*January* 24?].

" UNLAVISH Wisdom never works in vain."

I have been tasking my reason, Clarinda, why a woman, who, for native genius, poignant wit, strength of mind, generous sincerity of soul, and the sweetest female tenderness, is without a peer, and whose personal charms have few, very, very few parallels among her sex ; why, or how she should fall to the blessed lot of a poor hairum-scairum poet whom Fortune had kept for her particular use, to wreak her temper on whenever she was in ill-humour. One time I conjectured, that as Fortune is the most capricious jade ever known, she may have taken, not a fit of remorse, but a paroxysm of whim, to raise the poor devil out of the mire, where he had so often and so conveniently served her as a stepping-stone, and given him the most glorious boon she ever had in her gift, merely for the maggot's sake, to see how his fool head and his fool heart will bear it. At other times I was vain enough to think that Nature, who has a great deal to say with Fortune, had given the coquettish goddess some such hint as, " Here is a paragon of female excellence, whose equal, in all my former compositions, I never was lucky enough to hit on, and despair of ever doing so again ; you have cast her rather in the shades of life ; there is a certain poet of my making ; among your frolics it would not be amiss to attach him to this masterpiece of my hand, to give her that immortality among mankind, which no woman of any age ever more deserved, and which few rhymesters of this age are better able to confer."

Evening, 9 *o'clock.*

I am here, absolutely so unfit to finish my letter—pretty hearty after a bowl, which has been constantly plied since dinner till this moment. I have been with Mr. Schetki, the musician, and he has set the song finely. I have no distinct ideas of anything, but that I have drunk your health twice to-night, and that you are all my soul holds dear in this world.

SYLVANDER.

No. XCVIII.

TO CLARINDA.

[Mrs. M'Lehose's letter after the last interview shows she was well aware of the delicate, not to say dangerous footing of her acquaintance with the Poet : "I am neither well nor happy to-day : my heart reproaches me for last night. If you wish Clarinda to regain her peace, determine against everything but what the strictest delicacy warrants. . . . Do not be displeased when I tell you I wish our parting was over. At a distance, we shall retain the same heartfelt affection and interestedness in each other's concerns ; but absence will mellow and restrain those violent heart agitations which, if continued much longer, would unhinge my very soul, and render me unfit for the duties of life."]

[Friday, February 1 ?]

CLARINDA, my life, you have wounded my soul. Can I think of your being unhappy, even though it be not described in your pathetic elegance of language, without being miserable ? Clarinda, can I bear to be told from you that " you will not see me to-morrow night—that you wish the hour of parting were come ?" Do not let us impose on ourselves by sounds. * * * * * Why, my love, talk to me in such strong terms ; every word of which cuts me to the very soul? You know, a hint, the slightest signification of your wish, is to me a sacred command.

Be reconciled, my angel, to your God, yourself, and me ; and I pledge you Sylvander's honour—an oath I daresay you will trust without reserve—that you shall never more have reason to complain of his conduct. Now, my love, do not wound our next meeting with any averted looks. * * * I have marked the line of conduct—a line, I know, exactly to your taste— and which I will inviolably keep ; but do not you show the least inclination to make boundaries. Seeming distrust, where you know you may confide, is a cruel sin against sensibility.

" Delicacy, you know, it was which won me to you at once : take care that you do not loosen the dearest, most sacred tie that unites us." Clarinda, I would not have stung *your* soul—I would not have bruised *your* spirit, as that harsh, crucifying " Take care," did *mine ;* no, not to have gained heaven ! Let me again appeal to your dear self, if Sylvander, even when he seemingly half transgressed the laws of decorum, if he did not show more chastised, trembling, faltering delicacy, than the many of the world do in keeping these laws ?

O Love and Sensibility, ye have conspired against my peace ! I love to madness, and I feel to torture ! Clarinda, how can I forgive myself that I have ever touched a single chord in your bosom with pain ! Would I do it willingly ? Would any consideration, any gratification make me do so ? Oh, did you love like me, you would not, you could not, deny or put off a meeting with the man who adores you ; who would die a thousand deaths before he would injure you ; and who must soon bid you a long farewell !

I had proposed bringing my bosom friend, Mr. Ainslie, to-morrow evening, at his strong request, to see you ; as he has only time to stay

with us about ten minutes, for an engagement. But I shall hear from you ; this afternoon, for mercy's sake !—for, till I hear from you, I am wretched. Oh, Clarinda, the tie that binds me to thee is intwisted, incorporated with my dearest threads of life !

SYLVANDER.

No. XCIX.

TO CLARINDA.

I WAS on the way, my love, to meet you (I never do things by halves) when I got your card. Mr. Ainslie goes out of town to-morrow morning to see a brother of his, who is newly arrived from France. I am determined that he and I shall call on you together. So look you, lest I should never see to-morrow, we will call on you to-night. Mary* and you may put off tea till about seven, at which time, in the Galloway phrase, " an the beast be to the fore, and the branks bide hale," expect the humblest of your humble servants, and his dearest friend. We only propose staying half an hour—" for ought we ken." I could suffer the lash of misery eleven months in the year, were the twelfth to be composed of hours like yesternight. You are the soul of my enjoyment—all else is of the stuff of stocks and stones.

SYLVANDER.

No. C.

TO CLARINDA.

Sunday Noon.

I HAVE almost given up the Excise idea. I have been just now to wait on a great person, Miss ——'s friend ——. Why will great people not only deafen us with the din of their equipage, and dazzle us with their fastidious pomp, but they must also be so very dictatorily wise ? I have been questioned like a child about my matters, and blamed and schooled for my inscription on the Stirling window. Come, Clarinda !—" Come, curse me Jacob ; come, defy me Israel ! "

Sunday Night.

I have been with Miss Nimmo. She is indeed " a good soul," as my Clarinda finely says. She has reconciled me, in a good measure, to the world with her friendly prattle.

Schetki has sent me the song, set to a fine air of his composing. I have called the song 'Clarinda :' I have carried it about in my pocket, and hummed it over all day.

Monday Morning.

If my prayers have any weight in heaven, this morning looks in on you and finds you in the arms of peace, except where it is charmingly

---

* One of Mrs. M'Lehose's friends.

interrupted by the ardours of devotion. I find so much serenity of mind, so much positive pleasure, so much fearless daring toward the world, when I warm in devotion, or feel the glorious sensation—a consciousness of Almighty friendship—that I am sure I shall soon be an honest enthusiast.

> " How are thy servants blest, O Lord !
> How sure is their defence !
> Eternal wisdom is their guide,
> Their help Omnipotence ! "

I am, my dear Madam, yours,
SYLVANDER.

No. CI.

TO CLARINDA.

[In her next and several subsequent letters, Clarinda still dwells on Burns's want of religious faith. "Sylvander," she says, "I believe nothing were a more impracticable task than to make you feel a little of genuine Gospel humility. Believe me, I wish not to see you deprived of that noble fire of an exalted mind which you eminently possess. Yet a sense of your faults—a feeling sense of them—were devoutly to be wished." Another interview preceded the following letter from Sylvander.]

Sunday Morning.

I HAVE just been before the throne of my God, Clarinda ; according to my association of ideas, my sentiments of love and friendship, I next devote myself to you. Yesternight I was happy—happiness that the world cannot give. I kindle at the recollection ; but it is a flame where innocence looks smiling on, and honour stands by, a sacred guard. Your heart, your fondest wishes, your dearest thoughts, these are yours to bestow : your person is unapproachable by the laws of your country ; and he loves not as I do who would make you miserable.

You are an angel, Clarinda ; you are surely no mortal that " the earth owns." To kiss your hand, to live on your smile, is to me far more exquisite bliss than the dearest favours that the fairest of the sex, yourself excepted, can bestow.

Sunday Evening.

You are the constant companion of my thoughts. How wretched is the condition of one who is haunted with conscious guilt, and trembling under the idea of dreaded vengeance ! and what a placid calm, what a charming secret enjoyment it gives, to bosom the kind feelings of friendship and the formal throes of love ! Out upon the tempest of anger, the acrimonious gall of fretful impatience, the sullen frost of louring resentment, or the corroding poison of withered envy ! They eat up the immortal part of man. If they spent their fury only on the unfortunate objects of them, it would be something in their favour ; but these miserable passions, like traitor Iscariot, betray their lord and master.

Thou Almighty Author of peace, and goodness, and love! do Thou give me the social heart that kindly tastes of every man's cup! Is it a draught of joy?—warm and open my heart to share it with cordial, un-envying rejoicing. Is it the bitter potion of sorrow?—melt my heart with sincerely sympathetic wo. Above all, do Thou give me the manly mind that resolutely exemplifies, in life and manners, those sentiments which I would wish to be thought to possess. The friend of my soul; there, may I never deviate from the firmest fidelity and most active kindness! Clarinda, the dear object of my fondest love; there, may the most sacred inviolate honour, the most faithful kindling constancy, ever watch and animate my every thought and imagination!

Did you ever meet with the following lines spoken of religion—your darling topic?—

> "'*Tis this*, my friend, that streaks our morning bright;
> '*Tis this* that gilds the horrors of our night;
> When wealth forsakes us, and when friends are few,
> When friends are faithless, or when foes pursue;
> 'Tis this that wards the blow, or stills the smart,
> Disarms affliction, or repels its dart;
> Within the breast bids purest rapture rise,
> Bids smiling Conscience spread her cloudless skies."

I met with these verses very early in life, and was so delighted with them, that I have them by me, copied at school.

Good-night and sound rest, my dearest Clarinda!

SYLVANDER.

No. CII.

TO CLARINDA.

[Clarinda's letters grew more passionate as the correspondence draws to a close. "Never," she writes, "were there two hearts formed so exactly alike as ours. At all events, Sylvander, the storms of life will quickly pass, and 'one unbounded spring encircle all.' Love, there, is not a crime. I charge you to meet me there. Oh God! I must lay down my pen." Mr. Robert Chambers says he has heard Clarinda, at seventy-five, express the same hope to meet in another sphere the one heart that she had ever found herself able entirely to sympathise with, but which had been divided from her on earth by such pitiless obstacles.]

Thursday Night.

I CANNOT be easy, my Clarinda, while any sentiment respecting me in your bosom gives me pain. If there is no man on earth to whom your heart and affections are justly due, it may savour of imprudence, but never of criminality, to bestow that heart and those affections where you please. The God of love meant and made those delicious attachments to be bestowed on somebody; and even all the imprudence lies in bestowing them on an unworthy object. If this reasoning is conclusive, as it certainly is, I must be allowed to "talk of love."

It is, perhaps, rather wrong to speak highly to a friend of his letter: it is apt to lay one under a little restraint in their future letters, and restraint

is the death of a friendly epistle ; but there is one passage in your last charming letter, Thomson or Shenstone never exceeded it, nor often came up to it. I shall certainly steal it, and set it in some future poetic production, and get immortal fame by it. 'Tis when you bid the scenes of nature remind me of Clarinda. Can I forget you, Clarinda ? I would detest myself as a tasteless, unfeeling, insipid, infamous blockhead. I have loved women of ordinary merit, whom I could have loved for ever. You are the first, the only unexceptionable individual of the beauteous sex that I ever met with ; and never woman more entirely possessed my soul. I know myself, and how far I can depend on passion's swell. It has been my peculiar study.

I thank you for going to Miers. Urge him, for necessity calls, to have it done by the middle of next week : Wednesday the latest day. I want it for a breast-pin, to wear next my heart. I propose to keep sacred set times, to wander in the woods and wilds for meditation on you. Then, and only then, your lovely image shall be produced to the day, with a reverence akin to devotion.

* * * * * * *

To-morrow night shall not be the last. Good-night ! I am perfectly stupid, as I supped late yesternight.

SYLVANDER.

No. CIII.

TO CLARINDA.

Saturday Morning.

THERE is no time, my Clarinda, when the conscious thrilling chords of love and friendship give such delight, as in the pensive hours of what our favourite Thomson calls " philosophic melancholy." The sportive insects, who bask in the sunshine of prosperity, or the worms, that luxuriant crawl amid their ample wealth of earth ; they need no Clarinda—they would despise Sylvander, if they dared. The family of Misfortune, a numerous group of brothers and sisters ! they need a resting-place to their souls. Unnoticed, often condemned by the world—in some degree, perhaps, condemned by themselves—they feel the full enjoyment of ardent love, delicate, tender endearments, mutual esteem, and mutual reliance.

In this light I have often admired religion. In proportion as we are wrung with grief, or distracted with anxiety, the ideas of a compassionate Deity, an Almighty Protector, are doubly dear.

> " 'Tis this, my friend, that streaks our morning bright ;
> 'Tis this that gilds the horrors of our night."

I have been this morning taking a peep through, as Young finely says, " the dark postern of time long elapsed ; " and you will easily guess 'twas a rueful prospect. What a tissue of thoughtlessness, weakness, and folly ! My life reminded me of a ruined temple : what strength, what proportion in some parts !—what unsightly gaps, what prostrate ruins in others ! I

kneeled down before the Father of Mercies, and said, " Father, I have
sinned against Heaven, and in Thy sight, and am no more worthy to be
called Thy son !" I rose, eased and strengthened. I despise the superstition of a fanatic, but I love the religion of a man. "The future," said
I to myself, " is still before me : there let me

> ' On reason build resolve—
> That column of true majesty in man ! '

I have difficulties many to encounter," said I ; " but they are not absolutely insuperable : and where is firmness of mind shewn, but in exertion ?
Mere declamation is bombast rant. Besides, wherever I am, or in whatever situation I may be,

> ————' 'Tis nought to me,
> Since God is ever present, ever felt,
> In the void waste as in the city full ;
> And where He vital breathes, there must be joy.' "

Saturday Night, Half after Ten.

What luxury of bliss I was enjoying this time yesternight ! My ever
dearest Clarinda, you have stolen away my soul : but you have refined,
you have exalted it ; you have given it a stronger sense of virtue, and a
stronger relish for piety. Clarinda, first of your sex ! if ever I am the
veriest wretch on earth to forget you—if ever your lovely image is effaced
from my soul,

> " May I be lost, no eye to weep my end,
> And find no earth that's base enough to bury me !"

What trifling silliness is the childish fondness of the every-day children
of the world ! 'Tis the unmeaning toying of the younglings of the fields
and forests ; but, where sentiment and fancy unite their sweets, where
taste and delicacy refine, where wit adds the flavour, and good sense gives
strength and spirit to all. what a delicious draught is the hour of tender
endearment !

No. CIV.

TO CLARINDA.

*   *   * I AM a discontented ghost, a perturbed spirit.
Clarinda, if ever you forget Sylvander, may you be happy, but he will be
miserable.

Oh, what a fool I am in love ! what an extravagant prodigal of affection !
Why are your sex called the tender sex, when I never have met with one
who can repay me in passion ? They are either not so rich in love as I
am, or they are niggards where I am lavish.

O Thou, whose I am, and whose are all my ways ! Thou see'st me
here, the hapless wreck of tides and tempest in my own bosom : do Thou
direct to Thyself that ardent love, for which I have so often sought a return
in vain from my fellow-creatures ! If Thy goodness has yet such a gift in

store for me as an equal return of affection from her who, Thou knowest, is dearer to me than life, do Thou bless and hallow our band of love and friendship ; watch over us, in all our outgoings and incomings for good ; and may the tie that unites our hearts be strong and indissoluble as the thread of man's immortal life !

I am just going to take your blackbird, the sweetest, I am sure, that ever sung, and prune its wings a little.

SYLVANDER.

No. CV.

TO CLARINDA.

Tuesday Morning.

I CANNOT go out to-day, my dearest love, without sending you half a line by way of a sin offering ; but, believe me, 'twas the sin of ignorance. Could you think that I intended to hurt you by anything I said yester-night ? Nature has been too kind to you for your happiness, your delicacy, your sensibility. Oh why should such glorious qualifications be the fruitful source of wo ! You have " murdered sleep " to me last night. I went to bed impressed with an idea that you were unhappy ; and every start I closed my eyes, busy Fancy painted you in such scenes of romantic misery, that I would almost be persuaded you are not well this morning.

> ———" If I unwitting have offended,
> Impute it not."
> ———" But while we live
> But one short hour, perhaps, between us two
> Let there be peace."

If Mary has not gone by the time this reaches you, give her my best compliments. She is a charming girl, and highly worthy of the noblest love.

I send you a poem to read till I call on you this night, which will be about nine. I wish I could procure some potent spell, some fairy charm, that would protect from injury, or restore to rest, that bosom chord, " trembling alive all o'er," on which hangs your peace of mind. I thought, vainly I fear thought, that the devotion of love—love strong as even you can feel, love guarded, invulnerably guarded, by all the purity of virtue, and all the pride of honour—I thought such a love might make you happy. Shall I be mistaken ? I can no more, for hurry.

No. CVI.

TO CLARINDA.

Friday Morning. 7 o'clock.

YOUR fears for Mary are truly laughable. I suppose, my love, you and I showed her a scene which, perhaps, made her wish that she had a swain, and one who could love like me ; and 'tis a thousand pities that so good

a heart as hers should want an aim, an object. I am miserably stupid this morning. Yesterday I dined with a baronet, and sat pretty late over the bottle. And "who hath wo—who hath sorrow? they that tarry long at the wine; they that go to seek mixed wine." Forgive me, likewise, a quotation from my favourite author. Solomon's knowledge of the world is very great. He may be looked on as the *Spectator* or *Adventurer* of his day : and it is, indeed, surprising what a sameness has ever been in human nature. The broken, but strongly characterising hints, that the royal author gives us of the manners of the court of Jerusalem and country of Israel are, in their great outlines, the same pictures that London and England, Versailles and France, exhibit some three thousand years later. The loves in the "Song of Songs" are all in the spirit of Lady M. W. Montagu, or Madame Ninon de l'Enclos; though, for my part, I dislike both the ancient and modern voluptuaries; and will dare to affirm, that such an attachment as mine to Clarinda, and such evenings as she and I have spent, are what these greatly respectable and deeply experienced judges of life and love never dreamed of.

I shall be with you this evening between eight and nine, and shall keep as sober hours as you could wish.

> I am ever, my dear Madam, yours,
>
> SYLVANDER.

No. CVII.

TO CLARINDA

[The "Puritanic scrawl" is an allusion to some reproaches which had been addressed to Mrs. M'Lehose, on account of her intimacy with Burns.]

MY EVER DEAREST CLARINDA,

I make a numerous dinner-party wait me while I read yours and write this. Do not require that I should cease to love you, to adore you in my soul; 'tis to me impossible : your peace and happiness are to me dearer than my soul. Name the terms on which you wish to see me, to correspond with me, and you have them. I must love, pine, mourn, and adore in secret : this you must not deny me. You will ever be to me

> " Dear as the light that visits those sad eyes,
> Dear as the ruddy drops that warm my heart."

I have not patience to read the Puritanic scrawl. Damned sophistry! Ye heavens, thou God of nature, thou Redeemer of mankind! ye look down with approving eyes on a passion inspired by the purest flame, and guarded by truth, delicacy, and honour; but the half-inch soul of an unfeeling, cold-blooded, pitiful Presbyterian bigot cannot forgive anything above his dungeon-bosom and foggy head.

Farewell! I'll be with you to-morrow evening; and be at rest in your mind. I will be yours in the way you think most to your happiness. I dare not proceed. I love, and will love you; and will, with joyous

confidence, approach the throne of the Almighty Judge of men with your dear idea ; and will despise the scum of sentiment and the mist of sophistry.

SYLVANDER.

No. CVIII.

TO CLARINDA.

MADAM, *Wednesday, Midnight.*

After a wretched day, I am preparing for a sleepless night. I am going to address myself to the Almighty Witness of my actions—some time, perhaps very soon, my Almighty Judge. I am not going to be the advocate of Passion : be Thou my inspirer and testimony, O God, as I plead the cause of truth !

I have read over your friend's haughty, dictatorial letter : you are only answerable to your God in such a matter. Who gave any fellow-creature of yours (a fellow-creature incapable of being your judge, because not your peer) a right to catechise, scold, undervalue, abuse, and insult, wantonly and unhumanly to insult, you thus ? I don't wish, not even wish, to deceive you, Madam. The Searcher of hearts is my witness how dear you are to me ; but though it were possible you could be still dearer to me, I would not even kiss your hand at the expense of your conscience. Away with declamation ! let us appeal to the bar of common sense. It is not mouthing everything sacred ; it is not vague ranting assertions ; it is not assuming, haughtily and insultingly assuming, the dictatorial language of a Roman pontiff, that must dissolve a union like ours. Tell me, Madam, are you under the least shadow of an obligation to bestow your love, tenderness, caresses, affections, heart and soul, on Mr. M'Lehose—the man who has repeatedly, habitually, and barbarously broken through every tie of duty, nature, or gratitude to you ? The laws of your country, indeed, for the most useful reasons of policy and sound government, have made your person inviolate ; but are your heart and affections bound to one who gives not the least return of either to you ? You cannot do it ; it is not in the nature of things that you are bound to do it ; the common feelings of humanity forbid it. Have you, then, a heart and affections which are no man's right ? You have. It would be highly, ridiculously absurd to suppose the contrary. Tell me, then, in the name of common sense, can it be wrong, is such a supposition compatible with the plainest ideas of right and wrong, that it is improper to bestow the heart and these affections on another—while that bestowing is not in the smallest degree hurtful to your duty to God, to your children, to yourself, or to society at large ?

This is the great test ; the consequences : let us see them. In a widowed, forlorn, lonely situation, with a bosom glowing with love and tenderness, yet so delicately situated that you cannot indulge these nobler feelings except you meet with a man who has a soul capable . . . . .

No. CIX.

TO CLARINDA.

" I am distressed for thee, my brother Jonathan." I have suffered, Clarinda, from your letter. My soul was in arms at the sad perusal, I dreaded that I had acted wrong. If I have wronged you, God forgive me. But, Clarinda, be comforted. Let us raise the tone of our feelings a little higher and bolder. A fellow-creature who leaves us—who spurns us without just cause, though once our bosom friend—up with a little honest pride : let him go ! How shall I comfort you, who am the cause of the injury ? Can I wish that I had never seen you—that we had never met ? No, I never will. But, have I thrown you friendless ?—there is almost distraction in the thought. Father of mercies ! against Thee often have I sinned : through Thy grace I will endeavour to do so no more. She who, Thou knowest, is dearer to me than myself—pour Thou the balm of peace into her past wounds, and hedge her about with Thy peculiar care, all her future days and nights. Strengthen her tender, noble mind firmly to suffer and magnanimously to bear. Make me worthy of that friendship, that love she honours me with. May my attachment to her be pure as devotion, and lasting as immortal life ! O Almighty Goodness, hear me ! Be to her at all times, particularly in the hour of distress or trial, a friend and comforter, a guide and guard.

> " How are thy servants blest, O Lord,
>   How sure is their defence !
> Eternal wisdom is their guide,
>   Their help Omnipotence."

Forgive me, Clarinda, the injury I have done you. To-night I shall be with you, as indeed I shall be ill at ease till I see you.

SYLVANDER.

No. CX.

TO CLARINDA.

Two o'clock.

I just now received your first letter of yesterday, by the careless negligence of the penny-post. Clarinda, matters are grown very serious with us ; then seriously hear me, and hear me, Heaven—I met you, my dear . . . . ., by far the first of womankind, at least to me ; I esteemed, I loved you at first sight ; the longer I am acquainted with you, the more innate amiableness and worth I discover in you. You have suffered a loss, I confess, for my sake : but if the firmest, steadiest, warmest friendship—if every endeavour to be worthy of your friendship—if a love, strong as the ties of nature, and holy as the duties of religion—if all these can make anything like a compensation for the evil I have occasioned you, if they be worth your acceptance, or can in the least

add to your enjoyments—so help Sylvander, ye Powers above, in his hour of need, as he freely gives these all to Clarinda !

I esteem you, I love you as a friend ; I admire you, I love you as a woman beyond any one in all the circle of creation; I know I shall continue to esteem you, to love you, to pray for you—nay, to pray for myself for your sake.

Expect me at eight—and believe me to be ever, my dearest Madam,

Yours most entirely,

SYLVANDER.

No. CXI.

TO CLARINDA.

WHEN matters, my love, are desperate, we must put on a desperate face—

" On reason build resolve,
That column of true majesty in man"—

or, as the same author finely says in another place,

" Let thy soul spring up
And lay strong hold for help on Him that made thee "

I am yours, Clarinda, for life. Never be discouraged at all this. Look forward : in a few weeks I shall be somewhere or other, out of the possibility of seeing you ; till then, I shall write you often, but visit you seldom. Your fame, your welfare, your happiness, are dearer to me than any gratification whatever. Be comforted, my love ! the present moment is the worst ; the lenient hand of time is daily and hourly either lightening the burden, or making us insensible to the weight. None of these friends —I mean Mr.—— and the other gentleman—can hurt your worldly support ; and of their friendship, in a little time you will learn to be easy, and by and by to be happy without it. A decent means of livelihood in the world, an approving God, a peaceful conscience, and one firm trusty friend—can anybody that has these be said to be unhappy ? These are yours.

To-morrow evening I shall be with you about eight, probably for the last time till I return to Edinburgh. In the meantime, should any of these two unlucky friends question you respecting me, whether I am *the man*, I do not think they are entitled to any information. As to their jealousy and spying, I despise them. Adieu, my dearest Madam !

SYLVANDER.

No. CXII.

TO MR. JAMES CANDLISH.

MY DEAR FRIEND, [EDINBURGH, 1788.]

If once I were gone from this scene of hurry and dissipation, I promise myself the pleasure of that correspondence being renewed which has been so long broken. At present I have time for nothing. Dissipa-

tion and business engross every moment. I am engaged in assisting an honest Scotch enthusiast,* a friend of mine, who is an engraver, and has taken it into his head to publish a collection of all our songs set to music, of which the words and music are done by Scotsmen. This, you will easily guess, is an undertaking exactly to my taste. I have collected, begged, borrowed, and stolen, all the songs I could meet with. "Pompey's Ghost," words and music, I beg from you immediately, to go into his second number—the first is already published. I shall shew you the first number when I see you in Glasgow, which will be in a fortnight or less. Do be so kind as to send me the song in a day or two—you cannot imagine how much it will oblige me.

Direct to me at Mr. W. Cruikshank's, St. James's Square, New Town, Edinburgh.--R. B.

No. CXIII.

TO MRS. DUNLOP.

EDINBURGH, *February* 12, 1788.

SOME things in your late letters hurt me : not that *you say them*, but that *you mistake me*. Religion, my honoured Madam, has not only been all my life my chief dependence, but my dearest enjoyment. I have indeed been the luckless victim of wayward follies ; but, alas! I have ever been "more fool than knave." A mathematician without religion is a probable character ; an irreligious poet is a monster.—R. B.

No CXIV.

TO THE REV. JOHN SKINNER.

REVEREND AND DEAR SIR, EDINBURGH, 14*th February*, 1788.

I have been a cripple now near three months, though I am getting vastly better, and have been very much hurried besides or else I would have wrote you sooner. I must beg your pardon for the epistle you sent me appearing in the magazine. I had given a copy or two to some of my intimate friends, but did not know of the printing of it till the publication of the magazine. However, as it does great honour to us both, you will forgive it.

The second volume of the songs I mentioned to you in my last is published to-day. I send you a copy, which I beg you will accept as a mark of the veneration I have long had, and shall ever have, for your character, and of the claim I make to your continued acquaintance. Your songs appear in the third volume, with your name in the index ; as I assure you, Sir, I have heard your "Tullochgorum," particularly among our west-country folks, given to many different names, and most commonly to the immortal author of "The Minstrel," who indeed never wrote anything

* Mr. Johnson. publisher of the *Scots Musical Museum.*

superior to "Gie's a sang, Montgomery cried." Your brother has promised me your verses to the Marquis of Huntly's reel, which certainly deserve a place in the collection. My kind host, Mr. Cruikshank, of the High School here, and said to be one of the best Latins in this age, begs me to make you his grateful acknowledgments for the entertainment he has got in a Latin publication of yours, that I borrowed for him from your acquaintance, and much-respected friend in this place, the Reverend Dr. Webster. Mr. Cruikshank maintains that you write the best Latin since Buchanan. I leave Edinburgh to-morrow, but shall return in three weeks. Your song you mentioned in your last, to the tune of "Dumbarton Drums," and the other, which you say was done by a brother in trade of mine, a ploughman, I shall thank you for a copy of each.

I am ever, reverend Sir,
With the most respectful esteem and sincere veneration, yours,

R. B.

No. CXV.

TO MR. RICHARD BROWN.

MY DEAR FRIEND,   EDINBURGH, *February* 15, 1788.

I received yours with the greatest pleasure. I shall arrive at Glasgow on Monday evening; and beg, if possible, you will meet me on Tuesday. I shall wait you Tuesday all day. I shall be found at Davies's Black Bull Inn. I am hurried, as if hunted by fifty devils, else I should go to Greenock; but if you cannot possibly come, write me, if possible, to Glasgow, on Monday; or direct to me at Mossgiel by Mauchline; and name a day and place in Ayrshire, within a fortnight from this date, where I may meet you. I only stay a fortnight in Ayrshire, and return to Edinburgh.

I am ever, my dearest Friend, yours,

R. B.

No. CXVI.

TO MISS CHALMERS.

EDINBURGH, *Sunday* [*February* 17].

TO-MORROW, my dear Madam, I leave Edinburgh. I have altered all my plans of future life. A farm that I could live in, I could not find; and, indeed, after the necessary support my brother and the rest of the family required, I could not venture on farming in that style suitable to my feelings. You will condemn me for the next step I have taken: I have entered into the Excise. I stay in the west about three weeks, and then return to Edinburgh for six weeks' instructions; afterwards, for I get employ instantly, I go *où il plait à Dieu—et mon roi.* I have chosen this, my dear friend, after mature deliberation. The question is not at what

door of fortune's palace shall we enter in, but what doors does she open to us? I was not likely to get anything to do. I wanted *un bût*, which is a dangerous, an unhappy situation. I got this without any hanging on, or mortifying solicitation: it is immediate bread; and though poor in comparison of the last eighteen months of my existence, 'tis luxury in comparison of all my preceding life: besides, the commissioners are some of them my acquaintances, and all of them my firm friends.—R. B.

No. CXVII.

TO MRS. ROSE,

OF KILRAVOCK.

[This is an acknowledgment of two Highland airs which Mrs. Rose had sent him, with a very kind letter.]

MADAM, EDINBURGH, *February 17, 1788.*

You are much indebted to some indispensable business I have had on my hands, otherwise my gratitude threatened such a return for your obliging favour as would have tired your patience. It but poorly expresses my feelings to say, that I am sensible of your kindness. It may be said of hearts such as yours is, and such, I hope, mine is, much more justly than Addison applies it—

" Some souls by instinct to each other turn "

There was something in my reception at Kilravock so different from the cold, obsequious, dancing-school bow of politeness, that it almost got into my head that friendship had occupied her ground without the interme-diate march of acquaintance. I wish I could transcribe, or rather trans-fuse into language, the glow of my heart when I read your letter. My ready fancy, with colours more mellow than life itself, painted the beauti-ful wild scenery of Kilravock; the venerable grandeur of the castle; the spreading woods; the winding river, gladly leaving his unsightly, heathy source, and lingering with apparent delight as he passes the fairy walk at bottom of the garden; your late distressful anxieties; your present enjoy-ments; your dear little angel, the pride of your hopes; my aged friend, venerable in worth and years, whose loyalty and other virtues will strongly entitle her to the support of the Almighty Spirit here, and His peculiar favour in a happier state of existence. You cannot imagine, Madam, how much such feelings delight me: they are my dearest proofs of my own immortality. Should I never revisit the north, as probably I never will, nor again see your hospitable mansion, were I some twenty years' hence to see your little fellow's name making a proper figure in a newspaper paragraph, my heart would bound with pleasure.

I am assisting a friend in a collection of Scottish songs, set to their proper tunes; every air worth preserving is to be included: among others

I have given "Morag," and some few Highland airs which pleased me most, a dress which will be more generally known, though far, far inferior in real merit. As a small mark of my grateful esteem, I beg leave to present you with a copy of the work, as far as it is printed : the Man of Feeling, that first of men, has promised to transmit it by the first opportunity.

I beg to be remembered most respectfully to my venerable friend and to your little Highland chieftain.* When you see the "two fair spirits of the hill" at Kildrummie,* tell them that I have done myself the honour of setting myself down as one of their admirers for at least twenty years to come—consequently they must look upon me as an acquaintance for the same period ; but, as the Apostle Paul says, "this I ask of grace, not of debt."

I have the honour to be, Madam, &c.

R. B.

No. CXVIII.

TO CLARINDA.

[On the 18th of February, Burns left Edinburgh for Mossgiel, visiting Glasgow and Kilmarnock on his way. In a last fond interview, Sylvander and Clarinda had parted, but the correspondence was continued. Sylvander had disclosed to Clarinda his unhappy *liason* with Jean Armour and the prospect of a second pledge of illicit love. Clarinda in her replies speaks with kindness of Jean, but evidently looks forward on her own side to the prospect of a union with Burns, should her husband's death leave her free to marry again. "You know," she says, "I count all things (Heaven excepted) but loss, that I may win and keep you." How far Burns had any serious thoughts of marriage with Mrs. M'Lehose, should circumstances permit it, it is difficult to say ; but at any rate he reckoned himself released from all obligations towards Jean Armour, except those of common humanity.]

GLASGOW, *Monday Evening, Nine o'clock.*

THE attraction of love, I find, is in an inverse proportion to the attraction of the Newtonian philosophy. In the system of Sir Isaac, the nearer objects were to one another, the stronger was the attractive force. In my system, every milestone that marked my progress from Clarinda, awakened a keener pang of attachment to her. How do you feel, my love ? Is your heart ill at ease ? I fear it. God forbid that these persecutors should harass that peace, which is more precious to me than my own. Be assured I shall ever think on you, muse on you, and in my moments of devotion, pray for you. The hour that you are not in my thoughts, "be that hour darkness ; let the shadows of death cover it ; let it not be numbered in the hours of the day !"

> "When I forget the darling theme,
> Be my tongue mute ! my fancy paint no more !
> And, dead to joy, forget my heart to beat !"

---

* The references in these two sentences are to Mrs. Rose's mother and her son Hugh, and to young ladies of the neighbourhood.

I have just met with my old friend, the ship captain*—guess my pleasure : to meet you could alone have given me more.   My brother William, too, the young saddler, has come to Glasgow to meet me ; and here are we three spending the evening.

I arrived here too late to write by post ; but I'll wrap half-a-dozen sheets of blank paper together, and send it by the Fly, under the name of a parcel. You will hear from me next post-town.   I would write you a longer letter, but for the present circumstances of my friend.

Adieu, my Clarinda ! I am just going to propose your health by way of grace drink.

SYLVANDER.

No. CXIX.

TO CLARINDA.

KILMARNOCK, Friday [Feb. 22].

I WROTE you, my dear Madam, the moment I alighted in Glasgow. Since then I have not had opportunity ; for in Paisley, where I arrived next day, my worthy, wise friend Mr. Pattison did not allow me a moment's respite.   I was there ten hours ; during which time I was introduced to nine men worth six thousands ; five men worth ten thousands ; his brother, richly worth twenty thousands ; and a young weaver, who will have thirty thousands good when his father, who has no more children than the said weaver, and a Whig kirk, dies.   Mr. P. was bred a zealous Antiburgher ; but during his widowerhood he has found their strictness incompatible with certain compromises he is often obliged to make with those powers of darkness—the devil, the world, and the flesh. * * * His only daughter, who, " if the beast be to the fore, and the branks bide hale," will have seven thousand pounds when her old father steps into the dark factory-office of eternity with his well-thrummed web of life, has put him again and again in a commendable fit of indignation by requesting a harpsichord. " Oh these boarding-schools !" exclaims my prudent friend: " she was a good spinner and sewer till I was advised by her foes and mine to give her a year of Edinburgh !"

After two bottles more, my much-respected friend opened up to me a project—a legitimate child of Wisdom and Good Sense : 'twas no less than a long-thought-on and deeply-matured design, to marry a girl fully as elegant in her form as the famous priestess whom Saul consulted in his last hours, and who had been second maid of honour to his deceased wife.   This, you may be sure, I highly applauded ; so I hope for a pair of gloves by and by.   I spent the two bypast days at Dunlop House, with that worthy family to whom I was deeply indebted early in my poetic career ; and in about two hours I shall present your " twa wee sarkies " to the little fellow.   My dearest Clarinda, you are ever present with me ; and these hours, that drawl by among the fools and rascals of this world, are only supportable in the idea, that they are the forerunners of that happy hour that ushers me to " the mistress of my soul." Next week I shall visit

* Mr. Richard Brown.

Dumfries, and next again return to Edinburgh. My letters, in these hurrying dissipated hours, will be heavy trash ; but you know the writer. God bless you !

SYLVANDER.

No. CXX.

TO GAVIN HAMILTON, ESQ.

[This letter refers to a proposal that Robert should become guarantee for his brother for a considerable amount. That his reluctance to assume the obligation did not arise from selfish motives is shewn by his advance of 180*l.* to Gilbert soon afterwards, when he had realized the proceeds of his poems.]

MOSSGIEL, *Friday Morning.*

THE language of refusal is to me the most difficult language on earth, and you are the man in the world, excepting one of Right Honourable designation, to whom it gives me the greatest pain to hold such language. My brother has already got money, and shall want nothing in my power to enable him to fulfil his engagement with you ; but to be security on so large a scale, even for a brother, is what I dare not do, except I were in such circumstances of life as that the worst that might happen could not greatly injure me.

I never wrote a letter which gave me so much pain in my life, as I know the unhappy consequences : I shall incur the displeasure of a gentleman for whom I have the highest respect, and to whom I am deeply obliged.

I am ever, Sir,

Your obliged and very humble Servant,

ROBERT BURNS.

No. CXXI.

TO MR. RICHARD BROWN.

MY DEAR SIR,   MOSSGIEL, *24th February,* 1788.

I arrived here, at my brother's, only yesterday, after fighting my way through Paisley and Kilmarnock against those old powerful foes of mine—the devil, the world, and the flesh ; so terrible in the fields of dissipation. I have met with few incidents in my life which gave me so much pleasure as meeting you in Glasgow. There is a time of life beyond which we cannot form a tie worth the name of friendship. " Oh youth ! enchanting stage, profusely blest." Life is a fairy scene : almost all that deserves the name of enjoyment or pleasure is only a charming delusion ; and in comes repining age, in all the gravity of hoary wisdom, and wretchedly chases away the bewitching phantom. When I think of life, I resolve to keep a strict look-out in the course of economy, for the sake of worldly convenience and independence of mind ; to cultivate intimacy with a few of the companions of youth, that they may be the

.friends of age ; never to refuse my liquorish humour a handful of the sweetmeats of life, when they come not too dear ; and, for futurity—

> The present moment is our ain,
> The neist we never saw !

How like you my philosophy ? Give my best compliments to Mrs. B., and believe me to be,

My dear Sir, yours most truly,
R. B.

No. CXXII.

TO CLARINDA.

CUMNOCK [*Sunday*], 2*d March*, 1788.

I HOPE, and am certain, that my generous Clarinda will not think my silence, for now a long week, has been in any degree owing to my forget-fulness. I have been tossed about through the country ever since I wrote you ; and am here, returning from Dumfries-shire, at an inn, the post-office of the place, with just so long time as my horse eats his corn, to write you. I have been hurried with business and dissipation almost equal to the insidious decree of the Persian monarch's mandate, when he forbade asking petition of God or man for forty days. Had the venerable prophet been as throng [busy] as I, he had not broken the decree, at least not thrice a-day.

I am thinking my farming scheme will yet hold. A worthy, intelligent farmer, my father's friend and my own, has been with me on the spot : he thinks the bargain practicable. I am myself, on a more serious review of the lands, much better pleased with them. I wont mention this in writing to anybody but you and [Ainslie]. Don't accuse me of being fickle : I have the two plans of life before me, and I wish to adopt the one most likely to procure me independence. I shall be in Edinburgh next week. I long to see you: your image is omnipresent to me; nay, I am convinced I would soon idolatrize it most seriously—so much do absence and memory improve the medium through which one sees the much-loved object. To-night, at the sacred hour of eight, I expect to meet you—at the Throne of Grace. I hope, as I go home to-night, to find a letter from you at the post-office in Mauchline. I have just once seen that dear hand since I left Edinburgh—a letter indeed which much affected me. Tell me, first of womankind ! will my warmest attachment, my sincerest friendship, my correspondence—will they be any compensation for the sacrifices you make for my sake? If they will, they are yours. If I settle on the farm I propose, I am just a day and a half's ride from Edinburgh. We will meet—don't you say " perhaps too often ! "

Farewell, my fair, my charming poetess! May all good things ever attend you !

I am ever, my dearest Madam, yours,
SYLVANDER.

No. CXXIII.

TO MR. WILLIAM CRUIKSHANK.

MY DEAR SIR, MAUCHLINE, *3d March,* 1788.

Apologies for not writing are frequently like apologies for not singing—the apology better than the song. I have fought my way severely through the savage hospitality of this country, (the object of all hosts being) to send every guest drunk to bed if they can. * * *

I should return my thanks for your hospitality (I leave a blank for the epithet, as I know none can do it justice) to a poor wayfaring bard, who was spent and almost overpowered fighting with prosaic wickednesses in high places ; but I am afraid lest you should burn the letter whenever you come to the passage, so I pass over it in silence. I am just returned from visiting Mr. Miller's farm. The friend whom I told you I would take with me was highly pleased with the farm ; and as he is, without exception, the most intelligent farmer in the country, he has staggered me a good deal. I have the two plans of life before me : I shall balance them to the best of my judgment, and fix on the most eligible. I have written Mr. Miller, and shall wait on him when I come to town, which shall be the beginning or middle of next week : I would be in sooner, but my unlucky knee is rather worse, and I fear for some time will scarcely stand the fatigue of my Excise instructions. I only mention these ideas to you ; and, indeed, except Mr. Ainslie, whom I intend writing to to-morrow, I will not write at all to Edinburgh till I return to it. I would send my compliments to Mr. Nicol, but he would be hurt if he knew I wrote to anybody, and not to him ; so I shall only beg my best, kindest, kindest compliments to my worthy hostess and the sweet little Rosebud.

So soon as I am settled in the routine of life, either as an excise-officer or as a farmer, I propose myself great pleasure from a regular correspondence with the only man almost I ever saw who joined the most attentive prudence with the warmest generosity.

I am much interested for that best of men, Mr. Wood. I hope he is in better health and spirits than when I saw him last.

I am ever, my dearest Friend,

Your obliged, humble Servant,

R. B.

No. CXXIV.

TO MR. ROBERT AINSLIE.

MY DEAR FRIEND, MAUCHLINE, *3d March,* 1788.

I am just returned from Mr. Miller's farm. My old friend whom I took with me was highly pleased with the bargain, and advised me to accept of it. He is the most intelligent, sensible farmer in the county, and his advice has staggered me a good deal. I have the two plans before me : I shall endeavour to balance them to the best of my judgment, and

fix on the most eligible. On the whole, if I find Mr. Miller in the same favourable disposition as when I saw him last, I shall in all probability turn farmer.

I have been through sore tribulation, and under much buffeting of the Wicked One, since I came to this country. Jean I found banished like a martyr—forlorn, destitute, and friendless. I have reconciled her to her mother. . . . .

I shall be in Edinburgh the middle of next week. My farming ideas I shall keep quiet till I see. I got a letter from Clarinda yesterday, and she tells me she has got no letter of mine but one. Tell her that I wrote to her from Glasgow, from Kilmarnock, from Mauchline, and yesterday from Cumnock, as I returned from Dumfries. Indeed, she is the only person in Edinburgh I have written to till this day. How are your soul and body putting up?—a little like man and wife, I suppose.

Your faithful Friend,
R. B.

No. CXXV.

[TO —————?]

[The next letter is supposed by Allan Cunningham to be addressed to Mr. Robert Ainslie, under date Mauchline, July, 1787, but Mr. R. Chambers suspects there is an error here both as to date and superscription.]

MY DEAR SIR,   MAUCHLINE, *between 3d and 8th March,* 1788.

My life, since I saw you last, has been one continued hurry; that savage hospitality which knocks a man down with strong liquors is the devil. I have a sore warfare in this world—the devil, the world, and the flesh are three formidable foes. The first I generally try to fly from; the second, alas! generally flies from me; but the third is my plague, worse than the ten plagues of Egypt.

I have been looking over several farms in this country; one, in particular, in Nithsdale, pleased me so well, that if my offer to the proprietor is accepted, I shall commence farmer at Whitsunday. If farming do not appear eligible, I shall have recourse to my other shift;* but this to a friend.

I set out for Edinburgh on Monday morning: how long I stay there is uncertain, but you will know so soon as I can inform you myself. However, I determined poesy must be laid aside for some time; my mind has been vitiated with idleness, and it will take a good deal of effort to habituate it to the routine of business.

I am, my dear Sir,
Yours sincerely,
R. B.

* The Excise.

D D

No. CXXVI.

SYLVANDER TO CLARINDA.

[March 6th, 1788.]

I OWN myself guilty, Clarinda : I should have written you last week. But when you recollect, my dearest Madam, that yours of this night's post is only the third I have from you, and that this is the fifth or sixth I have sent to you, you will not reproach me, with a good grace, for unkindness. I have always some kind of idea not to sit down to write a letter, except I have time, and possession of my faculties, so as to do some justice to my letter ; which at present is rarely my situation. For instance, yesterday I dined at a friend's at some distance : the savage hospitality of this country spent me the most part of the night over the nauseous potion in the bowl. This day—sick—headache—low spirits—miserable—fasting, except for a draught of water or small beer. Now eight o'clock at night ; only able to crawl ten minutes' walk into Mauchline, to wait the post, in the pleasurable hope of hearing from the mistress of my soul.

But truce with all this ! When I sit down to write to you, all is happiness and peace. A hundred times a day do I figure you before your taper, your book or work laid aside as I get within the room. How happy have I been ! and how little of that scantling portion of time, called the life of man, is sacred to happiness, much less transport.

I could moralise to-night like a death's-head.

> "O what is life, that thoughtless wish of all !
> A drop of honey in a draught of gall."

Nothing astonishes me more, when a little sickness clogs the wheels of life, than the thoughtless career we run in the hour of health. "None saith, Where is God, my Maker, that giveth songs in the night : who teacheth us more knowledge than the beasts of the field, and more understanding than the fowls of the air ?"

Give me, my Maker, to remember Thee ! Give me to act up to the dignity of my nature ! Give me to feel "another's wo ;" and continue with me that dear loved friend that feels with mine !

The dignifying and dignified consciousness of an honest man, and the well-grounded trust in approving Heaven, are two most substantial foundations of happiness. . . . .

I could not have written a page to any mortal except yourself. I'll write you by Sunday's post. Adieu ! Good-night !

SYLVANDER.

No. CXXVII.

SYLVANDER TO CLARINDA.

MOSSGIEL, *7th March*, 1788.

CLARINDA, I have been so stung with your reproach for unkindness— a sin so unlike me, a sin I detest more than a breach of the whole Decalogue, fifth, sixth, seventh, and ninth articles excepted—that I believe

I shall not rest in my grave about it, if I die before I see you. You have often allowed me the head to judge and the heart to feel the influence of female excellence : was it not blasphemy then, against your own charms and against my feelings, to suppose that a short fortnight could abate my passion ?

You, my love, may have your cares and anxieties to disturb you ; but they are the usual occurrences of life. Your future views are fixed, and your mind in a settled routine. Could not you, my ever dearest Madam, make a little allowance for a man, after long absence, paying a short visit to a country full of friends, relations, and early intimates ? Cannot you guess, my Clarinda, what thoughts, what cares, what anxious forebodings, hopes, and fears, must crowd the breast of the man of keen sensibility, when no less is on the *tapis* than his aim, his employment, his very existence through future life ?

To be overtopped in anything else, I can bear ; but in the tests of generous love, I defy all mankind ! not even to the tender, the fond, the loving Clarinda ; she whose strength of attachment, whose melting soul, may vie with Eloise and Sappho ; not even she can overpay the affection she owes me !

Now that, not my apology, but my defence is made, I feel my soul respire more easily. I know you will go along with me in my justification : would to Heaven you could in my adoption, too ! I mean an adoption beneath the stars—an adoption where I might revel in the immediate beams of

> " She the bright sun of all her sex."

I would not have you, my dear Madam, so much hurt at Miss Nimmo's coldness. 'Tis placing yourself below her, an honour she by no means deserves. We ought, when we wish to be economists in happiness—we ought, in the first place, to fix the standard of our own character ; and when, on full examination, we know where we stand, and how much ground we occupy, let us contend for it as property ; and those who seem to doubt or deny us what is justly ours, let us either pity their prejudices or despise their judgment. I know, my dear, you will say this is self-conceit ; but I call it self-knowledge : the one is the overweening opinion of a fool, who fancies himself to be what he wishes himself to be thought ; the other is the honest justice that a man of sense, who has thoroughly examined the subject, owes to himself. Without this standard, this column in our own mind, we are perpetually at the mercy of the petulance, the mistakes, the prejudices, nay, the very weakness and wickedness of our fellow-creatures.

I urge this, my dear, both to confirm myself in the doctrine which, I assure you, I sometimes need, and because I know that this causes you often much disquiet. To return to Miss Nimmo. She is most certainly a worthy soul ; and equalled by very, very few in goodness of heart. But can she boast more goodness of heart than Clarinda ? Not even prejudice will dare to say so. For penetration and discernment, Clarinda sees far beyond her. To wit, Miss Nimmo dare make no pretence ; to Clarinda's

wit, scarce any of her sex dare make pretence. Personal charms, it would be ridiculous to run the parallel : and for conduct in life, Miss Nimmo was never called out, either much to do, or to suffer. Clarinda has been both ; and has performed her part, where Miss Nimmo would have sunk at the bare idea.

Away, then, with these disquietudes ! Let us pray with the honest weaver of Kilbarchan, " Lord, send us a gude conceit o' oursel' ! " or in the words of the auld sang,

> " Who does me disdain, I can scorn them again,
> And I'll never mind any such foes."

There is an error in the commerce of intimacy. . . . . Happy is our lot, indeed, when we meet with an honest merchant, who is qualified to deal with us on our own terms ; but that is a rarity : with almost everybody we must pocket our pearls, less or more, and learn, in the old Scots phrase, " To gie sic like as we get." For this reason we should try to erect a kind of bank or storehouse in our own mind ; or, as the Psalmist says, " We should commune with our own hearts and be still." . . . .

I wrote you yesternight, which will reach you long before this can. I may write Mr. Ainslie before I see him, but I am not sure.

Farewell ! and remember

SYLVANDER.

No. CXXVIII.

TO MR. RICHARD BROWN.

[Jean Armour having been put to the door by her father, Burns felt bound to provide her an asylum. She bore twins (daughters), who died in a few days. Of the first pair of twins, born in September, 1786, the girl died fourteen months after—the boy was taken charge of by his grandmother at Mossgiel.]

MAUCHLINE, 7th March, 1788.

I HAVE been out of the country, my dear friend, and have not had an opportunity of writing till now, when I am afraid you will be gone out of the country too. I have been looking at farms, and after all, perhaps I may settle in the character of a farmer. I have got so vicious a bent to idleness, and have ever been so little a man of business, that it will take no ordinary effort to bring my mind properly into the routine ; but you will say a " great effort is worthy of you." I say so myself, and butter up my vanity with all the stimulating compliments I can think of. Men of grave geometrical minds, the sons of " which was to be demonstrated," may cry up reason as much as they please ; but I have always found an honest passion, or native instinct, the truest auxiliary in the warfare of this world. Reason almost always comes to me like an unlucky wife to a poor devil of a husband—just in sufficient time to add her reproaches to his other grievances.

[After explaining his relations with Jean Armour, Burns says :—]

I am gratified with your kind inquiries after her ; as, after all, I may say with Othello—

————" Excellent wretch !
Perdition catch my soul, but i do love thee !"

I go for Edinburgh on Monday. Yours,

R. B.

No. CXXIX.

TO MR. ROBERT MUIR.

DEAR SIR,   MOSSGIEL, *7th March,* 1788.

I have partly changed my ideas, my dear friend, since I saw you. I took old Glenconner with me to Mr. Miller's farm ; and he was so pleased with it, that I have wrote an offer to Mr. Miller, which if he accepts, I shall sit down a plain farmer—the happiest of lives when a man can live by it. In this case I shall not stay in Edinburgh above a week. I set out on Monday, and would have come by Kilmarnock, but there are several small sums owing me for my first edition about Galston and Newmills, and I shall set off so early as to despatch my business and reach Glasgow by night. When I return, I shall devote a forenoon or two to make some kind of acknowledgment for all the kindness I owe your friendship. Now that I hope to settle with some credit and comfort at home, there was not any friendship or friendly correspondence that promised me more pleasure than yours ; I hope I will not be disappointed. I trust the spring will renew your shattered frame, and make your friends happy. You and I have often agreed that life is no great blessing, on the whole. The close of life, indeed, to a reasoning age, is

" Dark as was Chaos, ere the infant sun
Was rolled together, or had tried his beams
Athwart the gloom profound."

But an honest man has nothing to fear. If we lie down in the grave, the whole man a piece of broken machinery, to moulder with the clods of the valley, be it so ; at least there is an end of pain, care, woes, and wants : if that part of us called mind does survive the apparent destruction of the man—away with old-wife prejudices and tales ! Every age and every nation has had a different set of stories ; and as the many are always weak, of consequence they have often, perhaps always, been deceived. A man conscious of having acted an honest part among his fellow-creatures—even granting that he may have been the sport at times of passions and instincts—he goes to a great unknown Being, who could have no other end in giving him existence but to make him happy ; who gave him those passions and instincts, and well knows their force.

These, my worthy friend, are my ideas ; and I know they are not far different from yours. It becomes a man of sense to think for himself, particularly in a case where all men are equally interested, and where, indeed, all men are equally in the dark.

Adieu, my dear Sir. God send us a cheerful meeting !—R. B.

No. CXXX.

TO MRS. DUNLOP.

MADAM, Mossgiel, *7th March,* 1788.

The last paragraph in yours of the 30th February affected me most, so I shall begin my answer where you ended your letter. That I am often a sinner, with any little wit I have, I do confess : but I have taxed my recollection to no purpose to find out when it was employed against you. I hate an ungenerous sarcasm a great deal worse than I do the devil—at least as Milton describes him ; and though I may be rascally enough to be sometimes guilty of it myself, I cannot endure it in others. You, my honoured friend, who cannot appear in any light but you are sure of being respectable—you can afford to pass by an occasion to display your wit, because you may depend for fame on your sense ; or, if you choose to be silent, you know you can rely on the gratitude of many and the esteem of all ; but God help us who are wits or witlings by profession : if we stand not for fame there, we sink unsupported !

I am highly flattered by the news you tell me of Coila.* I may say to the fair painter who does me so much honour, as Dr. Beattie says to Ross, the poet of his muse Scota, from which, by the by, I took the idea of Coila ('tis a poem of Beattie's in the Scottish dialect, which perhaps you have never seen) :—

> " Ye shake your head, but o' my fegs,
> Ye've set auld Scota on her legs :
> Lang had she lien wi' beffs and flegs,
>   Bumbaz'd and dizzie,
> Her fiddle wanted strings and pegs,
>   Wae's me, poor hizzie."

R. B.

No. CXXXI.

TO MISS CHALMERS.

[Burns left Mauchline on the 10th of March to return to Edinburgh, and decided to lease a farm from Mr. Miller.]

EDINBURGH, *March* 14, 1788.

I KNOW, my ever dear friend, that you will be pleased with the news when I tell you I have at last taken a lease of a farm. Yesternight I completed a bargain with Mr. Miller of Dalswinton for the farm of Ellisland, on the banks of the Nith, between five and six miles above Dumfries. I began at Whitsunday to build a house, drive lime, &c. ; and Heaven be my help ! for it will take a strong effort to bring my mind into the routine of business. I have discharged all the army of my former pursuits, fancies, and pleasures—a motley host !—and have literally and strictly

* A daughter of Mrs. Dunlop was painting a sketch of Coila.

retained only the ideas of a few friends, which I have incorporated into a lifeguard. I trust in Dr. Johnson's observation, "Where much is attempted, something is done." Firmness, both in sufferance and exertion, is a character I would wish to be thought to possess ; and have always despised the whining yelp of complaint, and the cowardly, feeble resolve.

Poor Miss K[ennedy, sister of Mrs. Gavin Hamilton] is ailing a good deal this winter, and begged me to remember her to you the first time I wrote to you. Surely woman, amiable woman, is often made in vain. Too delicately formed for the rougher pursuits of ambition ; too noble for the dirt of avarice ; and even too gentle for the rage of pleasure ; formed indeed for, and highly susceptible of, enjoyment and rapture ; but that enjoyment, alas ! almost wholly at the mercy of the caprice, malevolence, stupidity, or wickedness of an animal at all times comparatively unfeeling, and often brutal.—R. B.

No. CXXXII.

SYLVANDER TO CLARINDA.

Monday Noon [17th March].

I WILL meet you to-morrow, Clarinda, as you appoint. My Excise affair is just concluded, and I have got my order for instructions : so far good. Wednesday night I am engaged to sup among some of the principals of the Excise, so can only make a call for you that evening ; but next day, I stay to dine with one of the Commissioners, so cannot go till Friday morning.

Your hopes, your fears, your cares, my love, are mine ; so don't mind them. I will take you in my hand through the dreary wilds of this world, and scare away the ravening bird or beast that would annoy you. I saw Mary in town to-day, and asked her if she had seen you. I shall certainly bespeak Mr. Ainslie, as you desire.

Excuse me, my dearest angel, this hurried scrawl and miserable paper : circumstances make both. Farewell till to-morrow.

SYLVANDER.

No. CXXXIII.

SYLVANDER TO CLARINDA.

Tuesday Morning [18th March].

I AM just hurrying away to wait on the Great Man, Clarinda ; but I have more respect to my own peace and happiness than to set out without waiting on you ; for my imagination, like a child's favourite bird, will fondly flutter along with this scrawl, till it perch on your bosom. I thank you for all the happiness you bestowed on me yesterday. The walk—

delightful; the evening—rapture. Do not be uneasy to-day, Clarinda; forgive me. I am in rather better spirits to-day, though I had but an indifferent night. Care, anxiety, sat on my spirits; and all the cheerfulness of this morning is the fruit of some serious, important ideas that lie, in their realities, beyond "the dark and the narrow house," as Ossian, prince of poets, says. The Father of Mercies be with you, Clarinda! and every good thing attend you!

SYLVANDER.

No. CXXXIV.

SYLVANDER TO CLARINDA.

Wednesday Morning [19th March].

CLARINDA, will that envious night-cap hinder you from appearing at the window as I pass? "Who is she that looketh forth as the morning; fair as the sun, clear as the moon, terrible as an army with banners?"

Do not accuse me of fond folly for this line; you know I am a cool lover. I mean by these presents greeting, to let you to wit, that archrascal Creech has not done my business yesternight, which has put off my leaving town till Monday morning. To-morrow at eleven I meet with him for the last time; just the hour I should have met far more agreeable company.

You will tell me this evening whether you cannot make our hour of meeting to-morrow one o'clock. I have just now written Creech such a letter, that the very goose-feather in my hand shrunk back from the line, and seemed to say, "I exceedingly fear and quake!" I am forming ideal schemes of vengeance. . . . . . Adieu, and think on

SYLVANDER.

No. CXXXV.

SYLVANDER TO CLARINDA.

Friday, Nine o'clock, Night [21st March].

I AM just now come in, and have read your letter. The first thing I did was to thank the divine Disposer of events, that He has had such happiness in store for me as the connexion I have with you. Life, my Clarinda, is a weary, barren path; and wo be to him or her that ventures on it alone! For me, I have my dearest partner of my soul: Clarinda and I will make out our pilgrimage together. Wherever I am, I shall constantly let her know how I go on, what I observe in the world around me, and what adventures I meet with. Will it please you, my love, to get every week, or at least every fortnight, a packet, two or three sheets, full of remarks, nonsense, news, rhymes, and old songs? Will you open, with satisfaction and delight, a letter from a man who loves you, who has loved you, and who will love you to death, through death, and for ever?

Oh, Clarinda! what do I owe to Heaven for blessing me with such a piece of exalted excellence as you! I call over your idea, as a miser counts over his treasure. Tell me, were you studious to please me last night? I am sure you did it to transport. How rich am I who have such a treasure as you! You know me; you know how to make me happy; and you do it most effectually. God bless you with

"Long life, long youth, long pleasure, and a friend!"

To-morrow night, according to your own direction, I shall watch the window: 'tis the star that guides me to paradise. The great relish to all is, that Honour, that Innocence, that Religion, are the witnesses and guarantees of our happiness. "The Lord God knoweth," and perhaps "Israel he shall know," my love and your merit. Adieu, Clarinda! I am going to remember you in my prayers.

SYLVANDER.

No. CXXXVI.

TO MR. RICHARD BROWN.

GLASGOW, 26th March, 1788.

I AM monstrously to blame, my dear Sir, in not writing to you, and sending you the Directory. I have been getting my tack extended, as I have taken a farm, and I have been racking shop accounts with Mr. Creech; both of which, together with watching, fatigue, and a load of care almost too heavy for my shoulders, have in some degree actually fevered me. I really forgot the Directory yesterday, which vexed me; but I was convulsed with rage a great part of the day.—R. B.

No. CXXXVII.

TO MR. ROBERT CLEGHORN.

[Burns's care and anxiety at this time were due not merely to business arrangements, but to the news he had just received of the birth and speedy death of his offspring by Jean Armour.]

MAUCHLINE, 31st March, 1788.

YESTERDAY, my dear Sir, as I was riding through a track of melancholy, joyless muirs, between Galloway and Ayrshire, it being Sunday, I turned my thoughts to psalms, and hymns, and spiritual songs; and your favourite air, "Captain O'Kean," coming at length into my head, I tried these words to it. You will see that the first part of the tune must be repeated.

> The small birds rejoice in the green leaves returning,
> The murmuring streamlet winds clear through the vale;
> The hawthorn trees blow in the dew of the morning,
> And wild scattered cowslips bedeck the green dale:
> But what can give pleasure, or what can seem fair,
> While the lingering moments are numbered by care,
> No flowers gaily springing, nor birds sweetly singing,
> Can soothe the sad bosom of joyless despair.

I am tolerably pleased with these verses ; but as I have only a sketch of the tune, I leave it with you to try if they suit the measure of the music.

I am so harassed with care and anxiety about this farming project of mine, that my muse has degenerated into the veriest prose-wench that ever picked cinders or followed a tinker. When I am fairly got into the routine of business, I shall trouble you with a longer epistle ; perhaps with some queries respecting farming : at present, the world sits such a load on my mind, that it has effaced almost every trace of the poet in me.

My very best compliments and good wishes to Mrs. Cleghorn.—R. B.

No. CXXXVIII.

TO MR. WILLIAM DUNBAR,

EDINBURGH.

Mauchline, 7th April, 1788.

I HAVE not delayed so long respecting you, my much respected friend, because I thought no farther of my promise. I have long since given up that kind of formal correspondence, where one sits down irksomely to write a letter, because we think we are in duty bound so to do.

I have been roving over the country, as the farm I have taken is forty miles from this place, hiring servants and preparing matters ; but most of all, I am earnestly busy to bring about a revolution in my own mind. As, till within these eighteen months, I never was the wealthy master of ten guineas, my knowledge of business is to learn ; add to this, my late scenes of idleness and dissipation have enervated my mind to an alarming degree. Skill in the sober science of life is my most serious and hourly study. I have dropt all conversation and all reading (prose reading) but what tends in some way or other to my serious aim. Except one worthy young fellow, I have not one single correspondent in Edinburgh. You have indeed kindly made me an offer of that kind. The world of wits, and *gens comme il faut* which I lately left, and with whom I never again will intimately mix—from that port, Sir, I expect your Gazette : what *les beaux esprits* are saying, what they are doing, and what they are singing. Any sober intelligence from my sequestered walks of life ; any droll original ; any passing remark, important forsooth, because it is mine ; any little poetic effort, however embryoth ; these, my dear Sir, are all you have to expect from me. When I talk of poetic efforts, I must have it always understood that I appeal from your wit and taste to your friendship and good-nature. The first would be my favourite tribunal, where I defied censure ; but the last, where I declined justice

I have scarcely made a single distich since I saw you. When I meet with an old Scots air that has any facetious idea in its name, I have a peculiar pleasure in following out that idea for a verse or two.

I trust that this will find you in better health than I did last time I called for you. A few lines from you, directed to me at Mauchline, were

it but to let me know how you are, will set my mind a good deal [at rest].
Now, never shun the idea of writing me, because perhaps you may be
out of humour or spirits. I could give you a hundred good consequences
attending a dull letter ; one, for example, and the remaining ninety-nine
some other time—it will always serve to keep in countenance, my much
respected Sir,

Your obliged Friend and humble Servant,
R. B.

No. CXXXIX.

TO MISS CHALMERS.

MAUCHLINE, 7th April, 1788.

I AM indebted to you and Miss Nimmo for letting me know Miss
Kennedy. Strange, how apt we are to indulge prejudices in our judg-
ments of one another ! Even I, who pique myself on my skill in marking
characters—because I am too proud of my character as a man to be
dazzled in my judgment for glaring wealth, and too proud of my situation
as a poor man to be biassed against squalid poverty—I was unacquainted
with Miss K.'s very uncommon worth.

I am going on a good deal progressive in *mon grand but*—the sober
science of life. I have lately made some sacrifices, for which, were I
vivâ voce with you to paint the situation and recount the circumstances,
you would applaud me.—R. B.

No. CXL.

TO MR. JAMES SMITH,

AVON PRINTFIELD, LINLITHGOW.

[Burns's allusion in the preceding letter to the "sacrifices" he had made is supposed to refer to his resolution to recognise Jean Armour as his wife, and make
her, in the familiar country phrase, an honest woman. In the following letter we
have the first distinct formal announcement of his new relations with Jean.]

MAUCHLINE, April 28, 1788.

BEWARE of your Strasburgh, my good Sir ! Look on this as the
opening of a correspondence, like the opening of a twenty-four gun
battery !

There is no understanding a man properly without knowing something
of his previous ideas—that is to say, if the man has any ideas ; for I know
many who, in the animal muster, pass for men, that are the scanty
masters of only one idea on any given subject, and by far the greatest
part of your acquaintances and mine can barely boast of ideas, 1·25—1·5
—1·75 (or some such fractional matter) ; so, to let you a little into the
secrets of my pericranium, there is, you must know, a certain clean-
limbed, handsome, bewitching young hussey of your acquaintance, to
whom I have lately and privately given a matrimonial title to my corpus.

> " Bode a robe and wear it,
> Bode a poke and bear it,"

says the wise old Scots adage ! I hate to presage ill-luck ; and as my girl has been doubly kinder to me than even the best of women usually are to their partners of our sex, in similar circumstances, I reckon on twelve times a brace of children against I celebrate my twelfth wedding-day. . . . .

"Light's heartsome," quo' the wife when she was stealing sheep. You see what a lamp I have hung up to lighten your paths, when you are idle enough to explore the combinations and relations of my ideas. 'Tis now as plain as a pikestaff why a twenty-four gun battery was a metaphor I could readily employ.

Now for business. I intend to present Mrs. Burns with a printed shawl, an article of which I daresay you have variety : 'tis my first present to her since I have irrevocably called her mine ; and I have a kind of whimsical wish to get the first said present from an old and much-valued friend of hers and mine—a trusty Trojan, whose friendship I count myself possessed of as a life-rent lease.

Look on this letter as a "beginning of sorrows ;" I will write you till your eyes ache reading nonsense.

Mrs. Burns ('tis only her private designation) begs her best compliments to you.—R. B.

No. CXLI.

TO MRS. DUNLOP.

MADAM, *MAUCHLINE, 28th April,* 1788.

Your powers of reprehension must be great indeed, as I assure you they made my heart ache with penitential pangs, even though I was really not guilty. As I commence farmer at Whitsunday, you will easily guess I must be pretty busy ; but that is not all. As I got the offer of the Excise business without solicitation, and as it costs me only six months'* attendance for instructions to entitle me to a commission—which commission lies by me, and at any future period, on my simple petition, can be resumed—I thought five-and-thirty pounds a-year was no bad *dernier ressort* for a poor poet, if Fortune in her jade tricks should kick him down from the little eminence to which she has lately helped him up.

For this reason, I am at present attending these instructions, to have them completed before Whitsunday. Still, Madam, I prepared with the sincerest pleasure to meet you at the Mount, and came to my brother's on Saturday night, to set out on Sunday ; but for some nights preceding I had slept in an apartment where the force of the winds and rains was only mitigated by being sifted through numberless apertures in the windows, walls, &c. In consequence I was on Sunday, Monday, and part of Tuesday, unable to stir out of bed, with all the miserable effects of a violent cold.

* Mistake for weeks.

You see, Madam, the truth of the French maxim, *le vrai n'est pas toujours le vraisemblable.* Your last was so full of expostulation, and was something so like the language of an offended friend, that I began to tremble for a correspondence which I had with grateful pleasure set down as one of the greatest enjoyments of my future life.

Your books have delighted me ; Virgil, Dryden, and Tasso, were all equally strangers to me ; but of this more at large in my next.

R. B.

No. CXLII.

TO PROFESSOR STEWART.

SIR,
MAUCHLINE, 3d *May*, 1788.

I enclose you one or two more of my bagatelles. If the fervent wishes of honest gratitude have any influence with that great unknown Being who frames the chain of causes and events, prosperity and happiness will attend your visit to the continent, and return you safe to your native shore.

Wherever I am, allow me, Sir, to claim it as my privilege to acquaint you with my progress in my trade of rhymes ; as I am sure I could say it with truth, that, next to my little fame, and the having it in my power to make life more comfortable to those whom nature has made dear to me, I shall ever regard your countenance, your patronage, your friendly good offices, as the most valued consequence of my late success in life.

R. B.

No. CXLIII.

TO MRS. DUNLOP.

MADAM,
MAUCHLINE, 4th *May*, 1788.

Dryden's Virgil has delighted me. I do not know whether the critics will agree with me, but the Georgics are to me by far the best of Virgil. It is indeed a species of writing entirely new to me, and has filled my head with a thousand fancies of emulation : but, alas ! when I read the Georgics, and then survey my own powers, 'tis like the idea of a Shetland pony, drawn up by the side of a thorough-bred hunter, to start for the plate. I own I am disappointed in the Æneid. Faultless correctness may please, and does highly please, the lettered critic ; but to that awful character I have not the most distant pretensions. I do not know whether I do not hazard my pretensions to be a critic of any kind, when I say that I think Virgil, in many instances, a servile copier of Homer. If I had the Odyssey by me, I could parallel many passages where Virgil has evidently copied, but by no means improved, Homer. Nor can I think there is anything of this owing to the translators ; for, from everything I have seen of Dryden, I think him, in genius and fluency of language, Pope's master. I have not perused Tasso enough to form an

opinion—in some future letter you shall have my ideas of him ; though I am conscious my criticisms must be very inaccurate and imperfect, as there I have ever felt and lamented my want of learning most.—R. B.

No. CXLIV.
TO MR. SAMUEL BROWN.

DEAR UNCLE,   MOSSGIEL, *4th May*, 1788.
    This I hope will find you and your conjugal yokefellow in your good old way. I am impatient to know if the Ailsa fowling be commenced for this season yet, as I want three or four stones of feathers, and I hope you will bespeak them for me. It would be a vain attempt for me to enumerate the various transactions I have been engaged in since I saw you last, but this know, I engaged in a *smuggling trade*, and God knows if ever any poor man experienced better returns—two for one ; but as freight and delivery have turned out so dear, I am thinking of taking out a licence and beginning in fair trade. I have taken a farm on the borders of the Nith, and, in imitation of the old patriarchs, get men-servants and maid-servants, and flocks and herds, and beget sons and daughters.
                                        Your obedient Nephew,
                                                    R. B.

No. CXLV.
TO MR. ROBERT AINSLIE.

MY DEAR FRIEND,   MAUCHLINE, *May* 26, 1788.
    I am two kind letters in your debt ; but I have been from home, and horridly busy, buying and preparing for my farming business, over and above the plague of my Excise instructions, which this week will finish.
    As I flatter my wishes that I foresee many future years' correspondence between us, 'tis foolish to talk of excusing dull epistles : a dull letter may be a very kind one. I have the pleasure to tell you that I have been extremely fortunate in all my buyings and bargainings hitherto—Mrs. Burns [Jean Armour] not excepted ; which title I now avow to the world. I am truly pleased with this last affair ; it has indeed added to my anxieties for futurity, but it has given a stability to my mind and resolutions unknown before ; and the poor girl has the most sacred enthusiasm of attachment to me, and has not a wish but to gratify my every idea of her deportment. I am interrupted. Farewell, my dear Sir.—R. B.

No. CXLVI.
TO MRS. DUNLOP.

MADAM,   *27th May*, 1788.
    I have been torturing my philosophy to no purpose, to account for that kind partiality of yours, which has followed me, in my return to the

shade of life, with assiduous benevolence. Often did I regret, in the fleeting hours of my late will-o'-wisp appearance, that "here I had no continuing city ; " and, but for the consolation of a few solid guineas, could almost lament the time that a momentary acquaintance with wealth and splendour put me so much out of conceit with the sworn companions of my road through life—insignificance and poverty.

There are few circumstances relating to the unequal distribution, of the good things of this life that give me more vexation (I mean in what I see around me) than the importance the opulent bestow on their trifling family affairs, compared with the very same things on the contracted scale of a cottage. Last afternoon I had the honour to spend an hour or two at a good woman's fireside, where the planks that compose the floor were decorated with a splendid carpet, and the gay table sparkled with silver and china. 'Tis now about term-day, and there has been a revolution among those creatures, who, though in appearance partakers, and equally noble partakers, of the same nature with Madam, are from time to time—their nerves, their sinews, their health, strength, wisdom, experience, genius, time, nay a good part of their very thoughts—sold for months and years, not only to the necessities, the conveniences, but the caprices of the important few. We talked of the insignificant creatures ; nay, notwithstanding their general stupidity and rascality, did some of the poor devils the honour to commend them. But light be the turf upon his breast who taught " Reverence thyself." We looked down on the unpolished wretches, their impertinent wives and clouterly brats, as the lordly bull does on the little dirty ant-hill, whose puny inhabitants he crushes in the carelessness of his ramble, or tosses in the air in the wantonness of his pride.—R. B.

No. CXLVII.

TO MRS. DUNLOP,

AT MR. DUNLOP'S, HADDINGTON.

[Burns was now fairly established at Ellisland, getting the farm in order, and superintending the erection of a new house. He was alone, vexed with present cares and anxieties for the future, and miserably lodged. In building his farm-house, Burns had, according to Allan Cunningham, to perform the part of superintendent of the works—to dig the foundations, collect the stones, seek the sand, cart the lime, and see that all was performed according to the specifications.]

ELLISLAND, 13*th* [14*th* ?] *June*, 1788.

" WHERE'ER I roam, whatever realms I see,
My heart, untravell'd, fondly turns to thee :
Still to my friend it turns with ceaseless pain,
And drags, at each remove, a lengthen'd chain."

GOLDSMITH.

This is the second day, my honoured friend, that I have been on my farm. A solitary inmate of an old, smoky spence ; far from every object I love, or by whom I am beloved ; nor any acquaintance older than yesterday, except Jenny Geddes, the old mare I ride on ; while uncouth

cares and novel plans hourly insult my awkward ignorance and bashful inexperience. There is a foggy atmosphere native to my soul in the hour of care, consequently the dreary objects seem larger than the life. Extreme sensibility, irritated and prejudiced on the gloomy side by a series of misfortunes and disappointments, at that period of my existence when the soul is laying in her cargo of ideas for the voyage of life, is, I believe, the principal cause of this unhappy frame of mind.

> " The valiant, in himself, what can he suffer?
> Or what need he regard his *single* woes? &c."

Your surmise, Madam, is just ; I am indeed a husband. . . . .

To jealousy or infidelity I am an equal stranger. My preservative from the first is the most thorough consciousness of her sentiments of honour, and her attachment to me : my antidote against the last is my long and deep-rooted affection for her.

In housewife matters, of aptness to learn and activity to execute she is eminently mistress ; and during my absence in Nithsdale, she is regularly and constantly apprentice to my mother and sisters in their dairy and other rural business.

The Muses must not be offended when I tell them the concerns of my wife and family will, in my mind, always take the *pas;* but I assure them their ladyships will ever come next in place.

You are right that a bachelor state would have insured me more friends ; but, from a cause you will easily guess, conscious peace in the enjoyment of my own mind, and unmistrusting confidence in approaching my God, would seldom have been of the number.

I found a once much-loved and still much-loved female, literally and truly cast out to the mercy of the naked elements ; but I enabled her to *purchase* a shelter—there is no sporting with a fellow-creature's happiness or misery.

The most placid good-nature and sweetness of disposition ; a warm heart, gratefully devoted with all its powers to love me ; vigorous health and sprightly cheerfulness, set off to the best advantage by a more than commonly handsome figure ; these, I think, in a woman, may make a good wife, though she should never have read a page but the Scriptures of the Old and New Testament, nor have danced in a brighter assembly than a penny pay wedding.—R. B.

No. CXLVIII.

TO MR. ROBERT AINSLIE.

ELLISLAND, *June* 14 [15?], 1788.

THIS is now the third day, my dearest Sir, that I have sojourned in these regions ; and during these three days you have occupied more of my thoughts than in three weeks preceding : in Ayrshire I have several variations of friendship's compass, here it points invariable to the pole. My farm gives me a good many uncouth cares and anxieties, but I hate

the language of complaint. Job, or some one of his friends, says well—
" Why should a living man complain ? "

I have lately been much mortified with contemplating an unlucky imperfection in the very framing and construction of my soul ; namely, a
blundering inaccuracy of her olfactory organs in hitting the scent of craft
or design in my fellow-creatures. I do not mean any compliment to my
ingenuousness, or to hint that the defect is in consequence of the unsuspicious simplicity of conscious truth and honour : I take it to be, in some
way or other, an imperfection in the mental sight ; or, metaphor apart,
some modification of dulness. In two or three instances lately I have
been most shamefully out.

I have all along hitherto, in the warfare of life, been bred to arms among
the light-horse—the picket-guards of fancy—a kind of hussars and Highlanders of the brain ; but I am firmly resolved to sell out of these giddy
battalions, who have no ideas of a battle but fighting the foe, or of a siege
but storming the town. Cost what it will, I am determined to buy in
among the grave squadrons of heavy-armed thought, or the artillery corps
of plodding contrivance.

What books are you reading, or what is the subject of your thoughts,
besides the great studies of your profession ? You said something about
religion in your last. I don't exactly remember what it was, as the letter
is in Ayrshire : but I thought it not only prettily said, but nobly thought.
You will make a noble fellow if once you were married. I make no reser-
vation of your being well married : you have so much sense and knowledge
of human nature, that, though you may not realize perhaps the ideas of
romance, yet you will never be ill married.

Were it not for the terrors of my ticklish situation respecting provision
for a family of children, I am decidedly of opinion that the step I have
taken is vastly for my happiness. As it is, I look to the Excise scheme
as a certainty of maintenance. A maintenance !—luxury, to what either
Mrs. Burns or I was born to. Adieu !—R. B.

No. CXLIX.

EXTRACT FROM COMMONPLACE BOOK.

ELLISLAND, *Sunday, 14th* [*15th ?*] *June,* 1788.*

THIS is now the third day that I have been in this country. " Lord !
what is man ? " What a bustling little bundle of passions, appetites, ideas,
and fancies ! And what a capricious kind of existence he has here ! . . .
There is indeed an elsewhere, where, as Thomson says, *virtue sole
survives.*

> ————" Tell us, ye dead ;
> Will none of you in pity disclose the secret,
> What 'tis you are, and we must shortly be ?
> ————A little time
> Will make us wise as you are, and as close."

* Mr. R. Chambers suggests that the 14th of June, 1788, having been a Saturday, it may be
surmised that Burns wrote several dates at this time a day too early.

B   E E

I am such a coward in life, so tired of the service, that I would almost at any time, with Milton's Adam, "gladly lay me in my mother's lap, and be at peace."

But a wife and children bind me to struggle with the stream, till some sudden squall shall overset the silly vessel; or, in the listless return of years, its own craziness reduce it to a wreck. Farewell now to those giddy follies, those varnished vices, which, though half sanctified by the bewitching levity of wit and humour, are at best but thriftless idling with the precious current of existence; nay, often poisoning the whole, that, like the plains of Jericho, *the water is naught and the ground barren*, and nothing short of a supernaturally-gifted Elisha can ever after heal the evils.

Wedlock—the circumstance that buckles me hardest to care—if virtue and religion were to be anything with me but names, was what in a few seasons I must have resolved on : in my present situation it was absolutely necessary. Humanity. generosity, honest pride of character, justice to my own happiness for after life, so far as it could depend (which it surely will a great deal) on internal peace ; all these joined their warmest suffrages, their most powerful solicitations, with a rooted attachment, to urge the step I have taken. Nor have I any reason on her part to repent it. I can fancy how, but have never seen where, I could have made a better choice. Come, then, let me act up to my favourite motto, that glorious passage in Young—

> " On reason build resolve.
> That column of true majesty in man ! "

No CL.

TO MR. ROBERT AINSLIE.

MY DEAR SIR, ELLISLAND, 30th *June*. 1788.

I just now received your brief epistle ; and, to take vengeance on your laziness, I have, you see, taken a long sheet of writing-paper, and have begun at the top of the page, intending to scribble on to the very last corner.

I am vexed at that affair of the * * * , but dare not enlarge on the subject until you send me your direction, as I suppose that will be altered on your late master and friend's death [Mr. Samuel Mitchelson, W.S.] I am concerned for the old fellow's exit only as I fear it may be to your disadvantage in any respect ; for an old man's dying, except he have been a very benevolent character, or in some particular situation of life that the welfare of the poor or the helpless depended on him, I think it an event of the most trifling moment to the world. Man is naturally a kind, benevolent animal, but he is dropped into such a needy situation here in this vexatious world, and has such a whoreson, hungry, growling, multiplying pack of necessities, appetites, passions, and desires about him, ready to devour him for want of other food, that in fact he must lay aside his cares for others that he may look properly to himself.

I desired the carrier to pay you; but as I mentioned only fifteen shillings to him, I will rather enclose you a guinea-note. I have it not, indeed, to spare here, as I am only a sojourner in a strange land in this place; but in a day or two I return to Mauchline, and there I have the bank-notes through the house like salt-permits.

There is a great degree of folly in talking unnecessarily of one's private affairs. I have just now been interrupted by one of my new neighbours, who has made himself absolutely contemptible in my eyes by his silly garrulous pruriency. I know it has been a fault of my own too; but from this moment I abjure it as I would the service of hell! Your poets, spendthrifts, and other fools of that kidney, pretend, forsooth, to crack their jokes on prudence; but 'tis a squalid vagabond glorying in his rags. Still, imprudence respecting money matters is much more pardonable than imprudence respecting character. I have no objection to prefer prodigality to avarice in some few instances; but I appeal to your observation if you have not met, and often met, with the same disingenuousness, the same hollow-hearted insincerity and disintegrative depravity of principle, in the hackneyed victims of profusion as in the unfeeling children of parsimony. I have every possible reverence for the much-talked-of world beyond the grave, and I wish that which piety believes and virtue deserves may be all matter of fact. But in things belonging to and terminating in this present scene of existence man has serious and interesting business on hand. Whether a man shall shake hands with welcome in the distinguished elevation of respect, or shrink from contempt in the abject corner of insignificance; whether he shall wanton under the tropic of plenty—at least enjoy himself in the comfortable latitudes of easy convenience—or starve in the arctic circle of dreary poverty; whether he shall rise in a manly consciousness of a self-approving mind, or sink beneath a galling load of regret and remorse—these are alternatives of the last moment.

You see how I preach. You used occasionally to sermonize too; I wish you would in charity favour me with a sheet full in your own way. I admire the close of a letter Lord Bolingbroke writes to Dean Swift:— "Adieu, dear Swift! with all thy faults I love thee entirely; make an effort to love me with all mine!" Humble servant, and all that trumpery, is now such a prostituted business, that honest friendship, in her sincere way, must have recourse to her primitive, simple, Farewell!—R. B.

No. CLI.

TO MR. PETER HILL.

[Mr. Peter Hill, Creech's chief assistant, who had now set up in business for himself.]

MAUCHLINE, *18th July,* 1788.

YOU injured me, my dear Sir, in your construction of the cause of my silence. From Ellisland in Nithsdale to Mauchline in Kyle is forty and

five miles. *There* a house a-building, and farm enclosures and improvements to tend ; *here* a new—not indeed so much a *new* as a *young* wife : good God, Sir, could my dearest brother expect a regular correspondence from me ! . . . I am certain that my liberal-minded and much-respected friend would have acquitted me, though I had obeyed to the very letter that famous statute among the irrevocable decrees of the Medes and Persians, not to ask petition, for forty days, of either God or man, save thee, O Queen, only !

I am highly obliged to you, my dearest Sir, for your kind, your elegant, compliments on my becoming one of that most respectable, that truly venerable, corps, they who are, without a metaphor, the fathers of posterity. . . .

Your book came safe, and I am going to trouble you with further commissions. I call it troubling you—because I want only *books :* the cheapest way the best ; so you may have to hunt for them in the evening auctions. I want Smollett's works, for the sake of his incomparable humour. I have already " Roderick Random " and " Humphrey Clinker ;" " Peregrine Pickle,"" Launcelot Greaves," and "Ferdinand Count Fathom," I still want ; but, as I said, the veriest ordinary copies will serve me. I am nice only in the appearance of my poets. I forget the price of " Cowper's Poems," but I believe I must have them. I saw the other day proposals for a publication entitled " Banks's New and Complete Christian's Family Bible," printed for C. Cooke, Paternoster Row, London. He promises at least to give in the work, I think it is, three hundred and odd engravings, to which he has put the names of the first artists in London. You will know the character of the performance, as some numbers of it are published ; and if it is really what it pretends to be, set me down as a subscriber, and send me the published numbers.

Let me hear from you your first leisure minute, and trust me you shall in future have no reason to complain of my silence. The dazzling perplexity of novelty will dissipate, and leave me to pursue my course in the quiet path of methodical routine.—R. B.

No. CLII.

TO MR. GEORGE LOCKHART,

MERCHANT, GLASGOW.

MY DEAR SIR,   MAUCHLINE, 18*th July*, 1788.

I am just going for Nithsdale, else I would certainly have transcribed some of my rhyming things for you. The Miss Baillies I have seen in Edinburgh. " Fair and lovely are thy works, Lord God Almighty ! Who would not praise Thee for these Thy gifts in Thy goodness to the sons of men ? " It needed not your fine taste to admire them. I declare, one day I had the honour of dining at Mr. Baillie's, I was almost in the

predicament of the children of Israel, when they could not look on Moses' face for the glory that shone in it when he descended from Mount Sinai.

I did once write a poetic address from the Falls of Bruar to his Grace of Athole when I was in the Highlands. When you return to Scotland let me know, and I will send such of my pieces as please myself best. I return to Mauchline in about ten days.

My compliments to Mr. Purden.

I am in truth, but at present in haste, yours,
R. B.

No. CLIII.

TO MRS. DUNLOP.

HONOURED MADAM,   MAUCHLINE, *August* 2, 1788.

Your kind letter welcomed me yesternight to Ayrshire. I am indeed seriously angry with you at the quantum of your luckpenny ; but vexed and hurt as I was, I could not help laughing very heartily at the noble lord's apology for the missed napkin.

I would write to you from Nithsdale, and give you my direction there, but I have scarce an opportunity of calling at a post-office once in a fortnight. I am six miles from Dumfries, am scarcely ever in it myself, and as yet have little acquaintance in the neighbourhood. Besides, I am now very busy on my farm, building a dwelling-house ; as at present I am almost an evangelical man in Nithsdale, for I have scarce "where to lay my head."

There are some passages in your last that brought tears in my eyes. "The heart knoweth its own sorrows, and a stranger intermeddleth not therewith." The repository of these "sorrows of the heart" is a kind of *sanctum sanctorum;* and 'tis only a chosen friend, and that, too, at particular sacred times, who dares enter into them :

> " Heaven oft tears the bosom-chords
> That nature finest strung."

You will excuse this quotation for the sake of the author. Instead of entering on this subject farther, I shall transcribe you a few lines I wrote in a hermitage belonging to a gentleman in my Nithsdale neighbourhood. They are almost the only favours the Muses have conferred on me in that country. . . .

[Here follow the verses composed in the Friars' Carse Hermitage, given in page 82.]

Since I am in the way of transcribing, the following were the production of yesterday, as I jogged through the wild hills of New Cumnock. I intend inserting them, or something like them, in an epistle I am going to write to the gentleman on whose friendship my Excise hopes depend—Mr. Graham of Fintry, one of the worthiest and most accomplished gentlemen not only of this country, but, I will dare to say it, of this age. The

following are just the first crude thoughts " unhousel'd, unanointed, unaneal'd : "—

> Pity the tuneful Muses' helpless train ;
> Weak, timid landsmen on life's stormy main :
> The world were blest, did bliss on them depend ;
> Ah, that " the friendly e'er should want a friend !"
> The little fate bestows they share as soon ;
> Unlike sage, proverb'd wisdom's hard-wrung boon.
> Let Prudence number o'er each sturdy son
> Who life and wisdom at one race begun,
> Who feel by reason and who give by rule ;
> Instinct's a brute and sentiment a fool !
> Who make poor *will do* wait upon *I should* ;
> We own they're prudent, but who owns they're good ?
>
> Ye wise ones, hence ! ye hurt the social eye ;
> God's image rudely etched on base alloy !
> But come   *   *   *   *

Here the Muse left me. I am astonished at what you tell me of Anthony's writing me. I never received it. Poor fellow ! you vex me much by telling me that he is unfortunate. I shall be in Ayrshire ten days from this date. I have just room for an old Roman " Farewell."

R. B.

No. CLIV.

TO MRS. DUNLOP.

MAUCHLINE, August [July ?] 10, 1788.

MY MUCH HONOURED FRIEND,
      Yours of the 24th June is before me. I found it, as well as another valued friend—my wife—waiting to welcome me to Ayrshire : I met both with the sincerest pleasure.

When I write you, Madam, I do not set down to answer every paragraph of yours, by echoing every sentiment, like the faithful Commons of Great Britain in Parliament assembled answering a speech from the best of kings. I express myself in the fulness of my heart, and may perhaps be guilty of neglecting some of your kind inquiries ; but not from your very odd reason, that I do not read your letters. All your epistles for several months have cost me nothing except a swelling throb of gratitude or a deep-felt sentiment of veneration.

Mrs. Burns, Madam, is the identical woman * * *. When she first found herself " as women wish to be who love their lords," as I loved her nearly to distraction, we took steps for a private marriage. Her parents got the hint ; and not only forbade me her company and their house, but, on my rumoured West Indian voyage, got a warrant to put me in jail till I should find security in my about-to-be paternal relation. You know my lucky reverse of fortune. On my *éclatant* return to Mauchline I was made very welcome to visit my girl. The usual consequences began to betray her ; and as I was at that time laid up a cripple in Edinburgh, she was turned, literally turned, out of doors, and I wrote to a friend to shelter her till my return, when our marriage was declared. Her

happiness or misery was in my hands, and who could trifle with such a deposit? . . .

I can easily fancy a more agreeable companion for my journey of life ; but, upon my honour, I have never seen the individual instance. . . .

Circumstanced as I am, I could never have got a female partner for life who could have entered into my favourite studies, relished my favourite authors, &c. without probably entailing on me, at the same time, expensive living, fantastic caprice, perhaps apish affectation, with all the other blessed boarding-school acquirements, which (*pardonnez moi, madame*) are sometimes to be found among females of the upper ranks, but almost universally pervade the misses of the would-be gentry. . . .

I like your way in your churchyard lucubrations. Thoughts that are the spontaneous result of accidental situations, either respecting health, place, or company, have often a strength, and always an originality, that would in vain be looked for in fancied circumstances and studied paragraphs. For me, I have often thought of keeping a letter in progression by me, to send you when the sheet was written out. Now I talk of sheets, I must tell you my reason for writing to you on paper of this kind is my pruriency of writing to you at large. A page of post is on such a dissocial, narrow-minded scale, that I cannot abide it ; and double letters, at least in my miscellaneous reverie manner, are a monstrous tax in a close correspondence.—R. B.

No. CLV.

TO MRS. DUNLOP.

ELLISLAND, 16*th August*, 1788.

I AM in a fine disposition, my honoured friend, to send you an elegiac epistle, and want only genius to make it quite Shenstonian :—

> " Why droops my heart, with fancied woes forlorn?
> Why sinks my soul beneath each wintry sky? "

My increasing cares in this as yet strange country—gloomy conjectures in the dark vista of futurity—consciousness of my own inability for the struggle of the world—my broadened mark to misfortune in a wife and children—I could indulge these reflections till my humour should ferment into the most acid chagrin, that would corrode the very thread of life.

To counterwork these baneful feelings I have sat down to write to you ; as I declare upon my soul I always find that the most sovereign balm for my wounded spirit.

I was yesterday at Mr. Miller's [of Dalswinton] to dinner, for the first time. My reception was quite to my mind ; from the lady of the house quite flattering. She sometimes hits on a couplet or two *impromptu*. She repeated one or two, to the admiration of all present. My suffrage as a professional man was expected : I for once went agonizing over the belly of my conscience. Pardon me, ye, my adored household gods,

independence of spirit and integrity of soul ! In the course of conversation " Johnson's Musical Museum," a collection of Scottish songs with the music, was talked of. We got a song on the harpsichord, beginning—

> " Raving winds around her blowing."

The air was much admired : the lady of the house asked me whose were the words. " Mine, Madam ; they are indeed my very best verses : " she took not the smallest notice of them ! The old Scottish proverb says well, " King's caff is better than ither folks' corn." I was going to make a New Testament quotation about " casting pearls," but that would be too virulent, for the lady is actually a woman of sense and taste. . . .

After all that has been said on the other side of the question, man is by no means a happy creature. I do not speak of the selected few, favoured by partial Heaven, whose souls are tuned to gladness amid riches, and honours, and prudence, and wisdom. I speak of the neglected many, whose nerves, whose sinews, whose days, are sold to the minions of fortune.

If I thought you had never seen it, I would transcribe for you a stanza of an old Scottish ballad, called " The Life and Age of Man," beginning thus :—

> " 'Twas in the sixteen hundredth year
> Of God and fifty-three
> Frae Christ was born, that bought us dear,
> As writings testifie."

I had an old grand-uncle, with whom my mother lived a while in her girlish years : the good old man, for such he was, was long blind ere he died, during which time his highest enjoyment was to sit down and cry, while my mother would sing the simple old song of " The Life and Age of Man."

It is this way of thinking, it is these melancholy truths, that make religion so precious to the poor miserable children of men. If it is a mere phantom, existing only in the heated imagination of enthusiasm,

> " What truth on earth so precious as the lie ? "

My idle reasonings sometimes make me a little sceptical, but the necessities of my heart always give the cold philosophizings the lie. Who looks for the heart weaned from earth ; the soul affianced to her God ; the correspondence fixed with heaven ; the pious supplication and devout thanksgiving, constant as the vicissitudes of even and morn ; who thinks to meet with these in the court, the palace, in the glare of public life ? No : to find them in their precious importance and divine efficacy, we must search among the obscure recesses of disappointment, affliction, poverty, and distress.

I am sure, dear Madam, you are now more than pleased with the length of my letters. I return to Ayrshire middle of next week : and it quickens my pace to think that there will be a letter from you waiting me there. I must be here again very soon for my harvest.—R. B.

No. CLVI.

TO MR. BEUGO,

ENGRAVER, EDINBURGH.

MY DEAR SIR, ELLISLAND, *9th Sept.* 1788.

There is not in Edinburgh above the number of the Graces whose letters would have given me so much pleasure as yours of the 3d instant, which only reached me yesternight.

I am here on my farm, busy with my harvest; but for all that most pleasurable part of life called social communication, I am here at the very elbow of existence. The only things that are to be found in this country, in any degree of perfection, are stupidity and canting. Prose they only know in graces, prayers, &c. and the value of these they estimate, as they do their plaiding webs, by the ell. As for the Muses, they have as much an idea of a rhinoceros as of a poet. For my old capricious but good-natured hussy of a Muse—

> " By banks of Nith I sat and wept
> When Coila I thought on :
> In midst thereof I hung my harp
> The willow trees upon."

I am generally about half my time in Ayrshire with my "darling Jean ;" and then I, at lucid intervals, throw my horny fist across my becobwebbed lyre, much in the same manner as an old wife throws her hand across the spokes of her spinning-wheel.

I will send you the "Fortunate Shepherdess" as soon as I return to Ayrshire, for there I keep it with other precious treasure. I shall send it by a careful hand, as I would not for anything it should be mislaid or lost. I do not wish to serve you from any benevolence, or other grave Christian virtue ; 'tis purely a selfish gratification of my own feelings whenever I think of you.

You do not tell me if you are going to be married. Depend upon it, if you do not make some foolish choice, it will be a very great improvement on the dish of life. I can speak from experience, though, God knows, my choice was as random as blind-man's buff. . . . .

If your better functions would give you leisure to write me, I should be extremely happy ; that is to say, if you neither keep nor look for a regular correspondence. I hate the idea of being obliged to write a letter. I sometimes write a friend twice a week, at other times once a quarter.

I am exceedingly pleased with your fancy in making the author you mention place a map of Iceland instead of his portrait before his works ; 'twas a glorious idea.*

Could you conveniently do one thing ?—whenever you finish any head, I should like to have a proof-copy of it. I might tell you a long story about

---

* It has been suggested that the work in question was a collection of articles in a very frigid style by Creech.

your fine genius ; but as what everybody knows cannot have escaped you, I shall not say one syllable about it.

If you see Mr. Nasmyth, remember me to him most respectfully, as he both loves and deserves respect ; though, if he would pay less respect to the mere carcass of greatness, I should think him much nearer perfection.

R. B.

No. CLVII.

TO MISS CHALMERS,

EDINBURGH.

ELLISLAND, NEAR DUMFRIES, *Sept.* 16, 1788.

WHERE are you? and how are you? and is Lady Mackenzie recovering her health ?—for I have had but one solitary letter from you.   I will not think you have forgot me, Madam ; and for my part—

> " When thee, Jerusalem, I forget,
>   Skill part from my right hand ! "

" My heart is not of that rock, nor my soul careless as that sea."   I do not make my progress among mankind as a bowl does among its fellows—rolling through the crowd without bearing away any mark or impression, except where they hit in hostile collision.

I am here, driven in with my harvest-folks by bad weather ; and as you and your sister once did me the honour of interesting yourselves much *à l'égard de moi,* I sit down to beg the continuation of your goodness.   I can truly say that, all the exterior of life apart, I never saw two whose esteem flattered the nobler feelings of my soul—I will not say more, but so much, as Lady Mackenzie and Miss Chalmers.   When I think of you—hearts the best, minds the noblest, of human kind—unfortunate even in the shades of life—when I think I have met with you, and have lived more of real life with you in eight days than I can do with almost anybody I meet with in eight years—when I think on the improbability of meeting you in this world again—I could sit down and cry like a child !   If ever you honoured me with a place in your esteem, I trust I can now plead more desert.   I am secure against that crushing grip of iron poverty, which, alas ! is less or more fatal to the native worth and purity of, I fear, the noblest souls ; and a late important step in my life has kindly taken me out of the way of those ungrateful iniquities, which, however overlooked in fashionable licence or varnished in fashionable phrase, are indeed but lighter and deeper shades of villany.

Shortly after my last return to Ayrshire I married " my Jean."   This was not in consequence of the attachment of romance, perhaps ; but I had a long and much-loved fellow-creature's happiness or misery in my determination, and I durst not trifle with so important a deposit.   Nor have I any cause to repent it.   If I have not got polite tattle, modish manners, and fashionable dress, I am not sickened and disgusted with the multiform

From "Ossian's "Oithonia", mid.

curse of boarding-school affectation ; and I have got the handsomest figure, the sweetest temper, the soundest constitution, and the kindest heart in the county. Mrs. Burns believes, as firmly as her creed, that I am *le plus bel esprit et le plus honnête homme* in the universe, although she scarcely ever in her life, except the Scriptures of the Old and New Testament and the Psalms of David in metre, spent five minutes together on either prose or verse. I must except also from this last a certain late publication of Scots poems, which she has perused very devoutly, and all the ballads in the country, as she has ("Oh, the partial lover !" you will cry) the finest "wood-note wild" I ever heard. I am the more particular in this lady's character, as I know she will henceforth have the honour of a share in your best wishes. She is still at Mauchline, as I am building my house ; for this hovel that I shelter in, while occasionally here, is pervious to every blast that blows and every shower that falls ; and I am only preserved from being chilled to death by being suffocated with smoke. I do not find my farm that pennyworth I was taught to expect ; but I believe in time it may be a saving bargain. You will be pleased to hear that I have laid aside idle *éclat*, and bind every day after my reapers.

To save me from that horrid situation of at any time going down, in a losing bargain of a farm, to misery, I have taken my Excise instructions, and have my commission in my pocket for any emergency of fortune. If I could set all before your view, whatever disrespect you, in common with the world, have for this business, I know you would approve of my idea.

I will make no apology, dear Madam, for this egotistic detail ; I know you and your sister will be interested in every circumstance of it. What signify the silly, idle gewgaws of wealth, or the ideal trumpery of greatness ! When fellow-partakers of the same nature fear the same God, have the same benevolence of heart, the same nobleness of soul, the same detestation at everything dishonest, and the same scorn at everything unworthy—if they are not in the dependence of absolute beggary, in the name of common sense, are they not equals ? And if the bias, the instinctive bias, of their soul run the same way, why may they not be friends ?

When I may have an opportunity of sending this Heaven only knows. Shenstone says : "When one is confined idle within doors by bad weather, the best antidote against *ennui* is to read the letters of or write to one's friends :" in that case, then, if the weather continues thus, I may scrawl you half a quire.

I very lately—namely, since harvest began—wrote a poem, not in imitation, but in the manner, of Pope's "Moral Epistles." It is only a short essay, just to try the strength of my Muse's pinion in that way. I will send you a copy of it when once I have heard from you. I have likewise been laying the foundation of some pretty large poetic works : how the superstructure will come on I leave to that great maker and marrer of projects—time. Johnson's collection of Scots songs is going on in the third volume ; and, of consequence, finds me a consumpt for a great deal of idle metre. One of the most tolerable things I have done in that way is two stanzas I made to an air a musical gentleman of

my acquaintance [Captain Riddell of Glenriddell] composed for the anniversary of his wedding-day, which happens on the 7th of November. Take it as follows :—

[Here comes "The day returns, my bosom burns."]

I shall give over this letter for shame. If I should be seized with a scribbling fit before this goes away, I shall make it another letter; and then you may allow your patience a week's respite between the two. I have not room for more than the old, kind, hearty Farewell !

To make some amends, *mes chères mesdames,* for dragging you on to this second sheet, and to relieve a little the tiresomeness of my unstudied and uncorrectible prose, I shall transcribe you some of my late poetic bagatelles ; though I have, these eight or ten months, done very little that way. One day, in a hermitage on the banks of the Nith, belonging to a gentleman in my neighbourhood, who is so good as give me a key at pleasure, I wrote as follows, [" Friars' Carse Hermitage,"] supposing myself the sequestered, venerable inhabitant of the lonely mansion. . . .

R. B.

No. CLVIII.

TO MRS. DUNLOP,

OF DUNLOP.

MAUCHLINE, 27th Sept. 1788.

I HAVE received twins, dear Madam, more than once, but scarcely ever with more pleasure than when I received yours of the 12th instant. To make myself understood : I had wrote to Mr. Graham, enclosing my poem addressed to him, and the same post which favoured me with yours brought me an answer from him. It was dated the very day he had received mine ; and I am quite at a loss to say whether it was most polite or kind.

Your criticisms, my honoured benefactress, are truly the work of a friend. They are not the blasting depredations of a canker-toothed, caterpillar critic ; nor are they the fair statement of cold impartiality, balancing with unfeeling exactitude the *pro* and *con* of an author's merits : they are the judicious observations of animated friendship, selecting the beauties of the piece. I am just arrived from Nithsdale, and will be here a fortnight. I was on horseback this morning by three o'clock ; for between my wife and my farm is just forty-six miles. As I jogged on in the dark, I was taken with a poetic fit as follows :—

[Here is transcribed Mrs. Fergusson of Craigdarroch's lamentation for the death of her son—an uncommonly promising youth of eighteen or nineteen years of age.*]

---

* " The Mother's Lament" served a double purpose, having been first written in reference to young Fergusson, and then applied to the death of Alexander Gordon Stewart, only son of Mrs. Stewart of Afton, Burns's early patroness.]

No. CLIX.

TO MR. PETER HILL.

MAUCHLINE, *1st October*, 1788.

I HAVE been here in this country about three days, and all that time my chief reading has been the " Address to Lochlomond " [by the Rev. Dr. Cririe] you were so obliging as to send to me. Were I empannelled one of the author's jury, to determinate his criminality respecting the sin of poesy, my verdict should be " Guilty ! A poet of Nature's making ! " It is an excellent method for improvement, and what I believe every poet does, to place some favourite classic author, in his own walks of study and composition, before him as a model. Though your author had not mentioned the name, I could have, at half a glance, guessed his model to be Thomson. Will my brother poet forgive me if I venture to hint that his imitation of that immortal bard is in two or three places rather more servile than such a genius as his required ?—*e. g.*

" To soothe the maddening passions all to peace."
Address.

" To soothe the throbbing passions into peace."
THOMSON.

I think the " Address " is in simplicity, harmony, and elegance of versification, fully equal to the " Seasons." Like Thomson, too, he has looked into nature for himself : you meet with no copied description. One particular criticism I made at first reading : in no one instance has he said too much. He never flags in his progress, but, like a true poet of Nature's making, kindles in his course. His beginning is simple and modest, as if distrustful of the strength of his pinion ; only I do not altogether like—

————" Truth,
The soul of every song that's nobly great."

Fiction is the soul of many a song that is nobly great. Perhaps I am wrong : this may be but a prose criticism. Is not the phrase in line 7, page 6, " Great lake," too much vulgarized by every-day language for so sublime a poem ?

" Great mass of waters, theme for nobler song,"

is perhaps no emendation. His enumeration of a comparison with other lakes is at once harmonious and poetic. Every reader's ideas must sweep the

" Winding margin of a hundred miles."

The perspective that follows, mountains blue—the imprisoned billows beating in vain—the wooded isles—the digression on the yew-tree—" Ben Lomond's lofty, cloud-enveloped head," &c. are beautiful. A thunderstorm is a subject which has been often tried, yet our poet in his grand picture has interjected a circumstance, so far as I know, entirely original :—

————" The gloom
Deep seam'd with frequent streaks of moving fire."

In his preface to the storm, "the glens how dark between," is noble Highland landscape ! The "rain ploughing the red mould," too, is beautifully fancied. " Ben Lomond's lofty, pathless top," is a good expression ; and the surrounding view from it is truly great : the

> —————— " silver mist,
> Beneath the beaming sun,"

is well described ; and here he has contrived to enliven his poem with a little of that passion which bids fair, I think, to usurp the modern Muses altogether. I know not how far this episode is a beauty upon the whole, but the swain's wish to carry "some faint idea of the vision bright," to entertain her "partial listening ear," is a pretty thought. But in my opinion the most beautiful passages in the whole poem are the fowls crowding, in wintry frosts, to Loch Lomond's "hospitable flood," their wheeling round, their lighting, mixing, diving, &c. and the glorious description of the sportsman. This last is equal to anything in the "Seasons." The idea of "the floating tribes distant seen, far glistering to the moon," provoking his eye as he is obliged to leave them, is a noble ray of poetic genius. "The howling winds," the "hideous roar" of "the white cascades," are all in the same style.

I forget that while I am thus holding forth with the heedless warmth of an enthusiast, I am perhaps tiring you with nonsense. I must, however, mention that the last verse of the sixteenth page is one of the most elegant compliments I have ever seen. I must likewise notice that beautiful paragraph beginning "The gleaming lake," &c. I dare not go into the particular beauties of the last two paragraphs, but they are admirably fine, and truly Ossianic.

I must beg your pardon for this lengthened scrawl ; I had no idea of it when I began. I should like to know who the author is : but whoever he be, please present him with my grateful thanks for the entertainment he has afforded me.

A friend of mine desired me to commission for him two books—" Letters on the Religion Essential to Man," a book you sent me before ; and " The World Unmasked, or the Philosopher the Greatest Cheat." Send me them by the first opportunity. The Bible you sent me is truly elegant ; I only wish it had been in two volumes.—R. B.

No. CLX.

TO THE EDITOR OF THE "STAR."

[The following protest was called forth as much by the " dour" Calvinism as by the violent Whiggism of a thanksgiving sermon preached by the Rev. Mr. Kirkpatrick of Dunscore, in accordance with an order of the General Assembly, in memory " of that glorious event, the Revolution."]

SIR, *November* 8, 1788.

Notwithstanding the opprobrious epithets with which some of our philosophers and gloomy sectarians have branded our nature—the

principle of universal selfishness, the proneness to all evil, they have given us — still, the detestation in which inhumanity to the distressed or insolence to the fallen are held by all mankind shows that they are not natives of the human heart. Even the unhappy partner of our kind who is undone—the bitter consequence of his follies or his crimes—who but sympathises with the miseries of this ruined profligate brother? We forget the injuries, and feel for the man.

I went, last Wednesday, to my parish church, most cordially to join in grateful acknowledgment to the Author of all good for the consequent blessings of the glorious Revolution. To that auspicious event we owe no less than our liberties, civil and religious ; to it we are likewise indebted for the present royal family, the ruling features of whose administration have ever been mildness to the subject and tenderness of his rights.

Bred and educated in Revolution principles, the principles of reason and common sense, it could not be any silly political prejudice which made my heart revolt at the harsh, abusive manner in which the reverend gentleman mentioned the House of Stuart, and which, I am afraid, was too much the language of the day. We may rejoice sufficiently in our deliverance from past evils without cruelly raking up the ashes of those whose misfortune it was, perhaps as much as their crime, to be the authors of those evils ; and we may bless God for all His goodness to us as a nation, without at the same time cursing a few ruined, powerless exiles, who only harboured ideas and made attempts that most of us would have done had we been in their situation.

" The bloody and tyrannical House of Stuart" may be said with propriety and justice, when compared with the present royal family and the sentiments of our days ; but is there no allowance to be made for the manners of the times? Were the royal contemporaries of the Stuarts more attentive to their subjects' rights? Might not the epithets of "bloody and tyrannical" be, with at least equal justice, applied to the House of Tudor, of York, or any other of their predecessors.

The simple state of the case, Sir, seems to be this :—At that period the science of government, the knowledge of the true relation between king and subject, was, like other sciences and other knowledge, just in its infancy, emerging from dark ages of ignorance and barbarity.

The Stuarts only contended for prerogatives which they knew their predecessors enjoyed, and which they saw their contemporaries enjoying : but these prerogatives were inimical to the happiness of a nation and the rights of subjects.

In this contest between prince and people—the consequence of that light of science which had lately dawned over Europe—the monarch of France, for example, was victorious over the struggling liberties of his people : with us, luckily, the monarch failed, and his unwarrantable pretensions fell a sacrifice to our rights and happiness. Whether it was owing to the wisdom of leading individuals, or to the justling of parties, I cannot pretend to determine ; but, likewise, happily for us, the kingly power was shifted into another branch of the family, who, as they owed

the throne solely to the call of a free people, could claim nothing inconsistent with the covenanted terms which placed them there.

The Stuarts have been condemned and laughed at for the folly and impracticability of their attempts in 1715 and 1745. That they failed, I bless God, but cannot join in the ridicule against them. Who does not know that the abilities or defects of leaders and commanders are often hidden until put to the touchstone of exigency, and that there is a caprice of fortune, an omnipotence in particular accidents and conjunctures of circumstances, which exalt us as heroes or brand us as madmen, just as they are for or against us?

Man, Mr. Publisher, is a strange, weak, inconsistent being : who would believe, Sir, that in this our Augustan age of liberality and refinement, while we seem so justly sensible and jealous of our rights and liberties, and animated with such indignation against the very memory of those who would have subverted them, that a certain people under our national protection should complain, not against our monarch and a few favourite advisers, but against our whole legislative body, for similar oppression, and almost in the very same terms, as our forefathers did of the House of Stuart? I will not, I cannot, enter into the merits of the case ; but I dare say the American Congress in 1776 will be allowed to be as able and as enlightened as the English Convention was in 1688, and that their posterity will celebrate the centenary of their deliverance from us as duly and sincerely as we do ours from the oppressive measures of the wrong-headed House of Stuart.

To conclude, Sir : let every man who has a tear for the many miseries incident to humanity feel for a family illustrious as any in Europe, and unfortunate beyond historic precedent ; and let every Briton (and particularly every Scotsman) who ever looked with reverential pity on the dotage of a parent cast a veil over the fatal mistakes of the kings of his forefathers.—R. B.

No. CLXI.

TO MRS. DUNLOP,

AT MOREHAM MAINS.

MADAM,   MAUCHLINE, 13*th November*, 1788.

I had the very great pleasure of dining at Dunlop yesterday. Men are said to flatter women because they are weak : if it be so, poets must be weaker still ; for Misses R. and K. and Miss G. M'K. with their flattering attentions and artful compliments absolutely turned my head. I own that they did not lard me over as many a poet does his patron ; but they so intoxicated me with their sly insinuations and delicate inuendoes of compliment, that if it had not been for a lucky recollection how much additional weight and lustre your good opinion and friendship must give me in that circle, I had certainly looked upon myself as a person of no small consequence. I dare not say one word how much I

was charmed with the Major's friendly, welcome, elegant manner, and acute remark, lest I should be thought to balance my orientalisms of applause over against the finest quey* in Ayrshire, which he made me a present of to help and adorn my farm-stock. As it was on Hallow-day, I am determined annually, as that day returns, to decorate her horns with an ode of gratitude to the family of Dunlop.

So soon as I know of your arrival at Dunlop, I will take the first conveniency to dedicate a day, or perhaps two, to you and friendship, under the guarantee of the Major's hospitality. There will soon be three-score and ten miles of permanent distance between us; and now that your friendship and friendly correspondence is entwisted with the heart-strings of my enjoyment of life, I must indulge myself in a happy day of "the feast of reason and the flow of soul."—R. B.

No. CLXII.

TO DR. BLACKLOCK.

REVEREND AND DEAR SIR,   MAUCHLINE, *November* 15, 1788.

As I hear nothing of your motions, but that you are or were out of town, I do not know where this may find you, or whether it will find you at all. I wrote you a long letter, dated from the land of matrimony, in June; but either it had not found you, or, what I dread more, it found you or Mrs. Blacklock in too precarious a state of health and spirits to take notice of an idle packet.

I have done many little things for Johnson since I had the pleasure of seeing you; and I have finished one piece in the way of Pope's "Moral Epistles:" but from your silence I have everything to fear; so I have only sent you two melancholy things, which I tremble lest they should too well suit the tone of your present feelings.

In a fortnight I move, bag and baggage, to Nithsdale: till then, my direction is at this place; after that period it will be at Ellisland, near Dumfries. It would extremely oblige me were it but half a line, to let me know how you are, and where you are. Can I be indifferent to the fate of a man to whom I owe so much—a man whom I not only esteem, but venerate?

My warmest good wishes and most respectful compliments to Mrs. Blacklock and Miss Johnson, if she is with you.

I cannot conclude without telling you that I am more and more pleased with the step I took respecting "my Jean." Two things, from my happy experience, I set down as apophthegms in life—A wife's head is immaterial compared with her heart; and, "Virtue's (for wisdom, what poet pretends to it?) ways are ways of pleasantness, and all her paths are peace." Adieu!

                                              R. B.

* A young heifer.

No. CLXIII.

TO MR. JAMES JOHNSON,

ENGRAVER.

MY DEAR SIR,   MAUCHLINE, *November* 15, 1788.
I have sent you two more songs. If you have got any tunes, or anything to correct, please send them by return of the carrier.

I can easily see, my dear friend, that you will very probably have four volumes. Perhaps you may not find your account lucratively in this business ; but you are a patriot for the music of your country, and I am certain posterity will look on themselves as highly indebted to your public spirit. Be not in a hurry ; let us go on correctly, and your name shall be immortal.

I am preparing a flaming preface for your third volume. I see every day new musical publications advertised ; but what are they ? Gaudy, painted butterflies of a day, and then vanish for ever : but your work will outlive the momentary neglects of idle fashion, and defy the teeth of time.

Have you never a fair goddess that leads you a wild-goose chase of amorous devotion ? Let me know a few of her qualities, such as whether she be rather black or fair, plump or thin, short or tall, &c., and choose your air, and I shall task my muse to celebrate her.— R. B.

No. CLXIV.

TO MRS. DUNLOP.

MY DEAR HONOURED FRIEND,   ELLISLAND, 17*th December*, 1788.
Yours dated Edinburgh, which I have just read, makes me very unhappy. " Almost blind and wholly deaf " are melancholy news of human nature ; but when told of a much-loved and honoured friend, they carry misery in the sound. Goodness on your part and gratitude on mine began a tie which has gradually entwisted itself among the dearest chords of my bosom, and I tremble at the omens of your late and present ailing habit and shattered health. You miscalculate matters widely when you forbid my waiting on you, lest it should hurt my worldly concerns. My small scale of farming is exceedingly more simple and easy than what you have lately seen at Moreham Mains. But, be that as it may, the heart of the man and the fancy of the poet are the two grand considera- tions for which I live : if miry ridges and dirty dunghills are to engross the best part of the functions of my soul immortal, I had better been a rook or a magpie at once, and then I should not have been plagued with any ideas superior to breaking of clods and picking up grubs ; not to mention barn-door cocks or mallards—creatures with which I could almost exchange lives at any time. If you continue so deaf, I am afraid a visit will be no great pleasure to either of us ; but if I hear you are got so well

again as to be able to relish conversation, look you to it, Madam, for I will make my threatening good. I am to be at the New Year Day fair of Ayr, and by all that is sacred in the world, friend, I will come and see you.

Your meeting, which you so well describe, with your old schoolfellow and friend was truly interesting. Out upon the ways of the world! they spoil these "social offsprings of the heart." Two veterans of the "men of the world" would have met with little more heart-workings than two old hacks worn out on the road. Apropos, is not the Scotch phrase, "auld lang syne," exceedingly expressive? There is an old song and tune which has often thrilled through my soul. You know I am an enthusiast in old Scotch songs. I shall give you the verses on the other sheet, as I suppose Mr. Ker will save you the postage.—R. B.

No. CLXV.

TO MISS DAVIES.

MADAM,

December, 1788.

I understand my very worthy neighbour, Mr. Riddel, has informed you that I have made you the subject of some verses. There is something so provoking in the idea of being the burthen of a ballad, that I do not think Job or Moses, though such patterns of patience and meekness, could have resisted the curiosity to know what that ballad was : so my worthy friend has done me a mischief, which I dare say he never intended, and reduced me to the unfortunate alternative of leaving your curiosity un-gratified, or else disgusting you with foolish verses, the unfinished produc-tion of a random moment, and never meant to have met your ear. I have heard or read somewhere of a gentleman who had some genius, much eccentricity, and very considerable dexterity with his pencil. In the accidental group of life into which one is thrown, wherever this gentleman met with a character in more than ordinary degree congenial to his heart, he used to steal a sketch of the face, merely, he said, as a *nota bene*, to point out the agreeable recollection to his memory. What this gentle-man's pencil was to him, my muse is to me ; and the verses I do myself the honour to send you are a memento exactly of the same kind that he indulged in.

It may be more owing to the fastidiousness of my caprice than the delicacy of my taste, but I am so often tired, disgusted, and hurt with the insipidity, affectation, and pride of mankind, that when I meet with a person "after my own heart," I positively feel what an orthodox Protestant would call a species of idolatry, which acts on my fancy like inspiration ; and I can no more desist rhyming on the impulse, than an Æolian harp can refuse its tones to the streaming air. A distich or two would be the consequence, though the object which hit my fancy were grey-bearded age ; but where my theme is youth and beauty, a young lady whose personal charms, wit, and sentiment are equally striking and unaffected—by

F F 2

heavens ! though I had lived threescore years a married man, and three-score years before I was a married man, my imagination would hallow the very idea ; and I am truly sorry that the enclosed stanzas have done such poor justice to such a subject.—R. B.

No. CLXVI.

TO MR. JOHN TENNANT.

December 22, 1788.

I YESTERDAY tried my cask of whisky for the first time, and I assure you it does you great credit. It will bear five waters, strong, or six, ordinary, toddy. The whisky of this country is a most rascally liquor ; and, by consequence, only drunk by the most rascally part of the inhabitants. I am persuaded, if you once get a footing here, you might do a great deal of business in the way of consumpt ; and should you commence distiller again, this is the native barley country. I am ignorant if, in your present way of dealing, you would think it worth your while to extend your business so far as this country side. I write you this on the account of an accident, which I must take the merit of having partly designed to. A neighbour of mine, a John Currie, miller in Carse-mill—a man who is, in a word, a " very " good man, even for a £500 bargain—he and his wife were in my house the time I broke open the cask. They keep a country public-house, and sell a great deal of foreign spirits, but all along thought that whisky would have degraded their house. They were perfectly astonished at my whisky, both for its taste and strength ; and, by their desire, I write you to know if you could supply them with liquor of an equal quality, and what price. Please write me by first post, and direct to me at Ellisland, near Dumfries. If you could take a jaunt this way yourself, I have a spare spoon, knife, and fork, very much at your service. My compliments to Mrs. Tennant and all the good folks in Glenconner and Barquharry.—R. B.

No. CLXVII.

TO MR. WILLIAM CRUIKSHANK.

ELLISLAND, [*December*] 1788.

I HAVE not room, my dear friend, to answer all the particulars of your last kind letter. I shall be in Edinburgh on some business very soon ; and as I shall be two days, or perhaps three, in town, we shall discuss matters *vivâ voce*. My knee, I believe, will never be entirely well ; and an unlucky fall this winter has made it still worse. I well remember the circumstance you allude to respecting Creech's opinion of Mr. Nicol ; but as the first gentleman owes me still about fifty pounds, I dare not meddle in the affair.

It gave me a very heavy heart to read such accounts of the consequence of your quarrel with that puritanic, rotten-hearted, hell-commissioned

scoundrel, A——. If, notwithstanding your unprecedented industry in public and your irreproachable conduct in private life, he still has you so much in his power, what ruin may he not bring on some others I could name?

Many and happy returns of seasons to you, with your dearest and worthiest friend, and the lovely little pledge of your happy union. May the great Author of life, and of every enjoyment that can render life delightful, make her that comfortable blessing to you both which you so ardently wish for, and which, allow me to say, you so well deserve! Glance over the foregoing verses, and let me have your blots. Adieu!—R. B.

No. CLXVIII.

TO MRS. DUNLOP.

ELLISLAND, *New-year-day Morning,* 1789.

THIS, dear Madam, is a morning of wishes, and would to God that I came under the Apostle James's description!—" the prayer of a righteous man availeth much." In that case, Madam, you should welcome in a year full of blessings: everything that obstructs or disturbs tranquillity and self-enjoyment should be removed, and every pleasure that frail humanity can taste should be yours. I own myself so little a Presbyterian, that I approve set times and seasons of more than ordinary acts of devotion, for breaking in on that habituated routine of life and thought which is so apt to reduce our existence to a kind of instinct, or even sometimes, and with some minds, to a state very little superior to mere machinery.

This day—the first Sunday of May—a breezy, blue-skied noon some time about the beginning, and a hoary morning and calm sunny day about the end, of autumn—these, time out of mind, have been with me a kind of holiday.

I believe I owe this to that glorious paper in the Spectator, "The Vision of Mirza," a piece that struck my young fancy before I was capable of fixing an idea to a word of three syllables : " On the 5th day of the moon, which, according to the custom of my forefathers, I always *keep holy,* after having washed myself and offered up my morning devotions, I ascended the high hill of Bagdad, in order to pass the rest of the day in meditation and prayer."

We know nothing, or next to nothing, of the substance or structure of our souls, so cannot account for those seeming caprices in them that one should be particularly pleased with this thing, or struck with that, which on minds of a different cast makes no extraordinary impression. I have some favourite flowers in spring, among which are the mountain-daisy, the harebell, the foxglove, the wild-brier rose, the budding birch, and the hoary hawthorn, that I view and hang over with particular delight. I never hear the loud, solitary whistle of the curlew in a summer noon, or the wild mixing cadence of a troop of grey plovers in an autumnal morning, without feeling an elevation of soul like the enthusiasm of devotion or poetry. Tell me, my dear friend, to what can this be owing?

Are we a piece of machinery, which, like the Æolian harp, passive takes the impression of the passing accident ? Or do these workings argue something within us above the trodden clod ? I own myself partial to such proofs of those awful and important realities—a God that made all things—man's immaterial and immortal nature—and a world of weal or wo beyond death and the grave !—R. B.

No. CLXIX.

TO DR. MOORE.

SIR, ELLISLAND, *4th January,* 1789.

As often as I think of writing to you, which has been three or four times every week these six months, it gives me something so like the idea of an ordinary-sized statue offering at a conversation with the Rhodian Colossus, that my mind misgives me, and the affair always miscarries somewhere between purpose and resolve. I have at last got some business with you, and business letters are written by the style-book. I say my business is with you, Sir ; for you never had any with me, except the business that benevolence has in the mansion of poverty.

The character and employment of a poet were formerly my pleasure, but are now my pride. I know that a very great deal of my late *éclat* was owing to the singularity of my situation and the honest prejudice of Scotsmen ; but still, as I said in the preface to my first edition, I do look upon myself as having some pretensions from Nature to the poetic character. I have not a doubt but the knack, the aptitude to learn the Muses' trade, is a gift bestowed by Him " who forms the secret bias of the soul ;" but I as firmly believe that *excellence* in the profession is the fruit of industry, labour, attention, and pains—at least I am resolved to try my doctrine by the test of experience. Another appearance from the press I put off to a very distant day—a day that may never arrive ; but poesy I am determined to prosecute with all my vigour. Nature has given very few, if any, of the profession the talents of shining in every species of composition. I shall try (for until trial it is impossible to know) whether she has qualified me to shine in any one. The worst of it is, by the time one has finished a piece, it has been so often viewed and reviewed before the mental eye, that one loses in a good measure the powers of critical discrimination. Here the best criterion I know is a friend, not only of abilities to judge, but with good-nature enough, like a prudent teacher with a young learner, to praise perhaps a little more than is exactly just, lest the thin-skinned animal fall into that most deplorable of all poetic diseases—heart-breaking despondency of himself. Dare I, Sir, already immensely indebted to your goodness, ask the additional obligation of your being that friend to me ? I enclose you an essay of mine, in a walk of poesy to me entirely new ; I mean the Epistle addressed to R. G., Esq. or Robert Graham of Fintry, Esq., a gentleman of uncommon worth, to whom I lie under very great obligations. The story of the poem, like most of my poems, is connected with my own story ; and to give you the

one I must give you something of the other. I cannot boast of Mr. Creech's ingenuous fair-dealing to me. He kept me hanging about Edinburgh from the 7th August, 1787, until the 13th April, 1788, before he would condescend to give me a statement of affairs ; nor had I got it even then, but for an angry letter I wrote him, which irritated his pride. "I could" not "a tale," but a detail, "unfold ;" but what am I that should speak against the Lord's anointed Bailie of Edinburgh.

I believe I shall in whole, £100 copyright included, clear about £400 some little odds ; and even part of this depends upon what the gentleman has yet to settle with me. I give you this information, because you did me the honour to interest yourself much in my welfare. I give you this information, but I give it to yourself only ; for I am still much in the gentleman's mercy. Perhaps I injure the man in the idea I am sometimes tempted to have of him : God forbid I should ! A little time will try, for in a month I shall go to town to wind up the business, if possible.

To give the rest of my story in brief : I have married "my Jean," and taken a farm. With the first step I have every day more and more reason to be satisfied ; with the last it is rather the reverse. I have a younger brother, who supports my aged mother ; another still younger brother, and three sisters, in a farm. On my last return from Edinburgh it cost me about £180 to save them from ruin. Not that I have lost so much : I only interposed between my brother and his impending fate by the loan of so much. I give myself no airs on this, for it was mere selfishness on my part : I was conscious that the wrong scale of the balance was pretty heavily charged, and I thought that throwing a little filial piety and fraternal affection into the scale in my favour might help to smooth matters at the *grand reckoning*. There is still one thing would make my circumstances quite easy ; I have an Excise-officer's commission, and I live in the midst of a country division. My request to Mr. Graham, who is one of the commissioners of Excise, was, if in his power, to procure me that division. If I were very sanguine, I might hope that some of my great patrons might procure me a treasury-warrant for supervisor, surveyor-general, &c.

Thus, secure of a livelihood, "to thee, sweet Poetry, delightful maid," I would consecrate my future days.—R. B.

No. CLXX.

TO MR. ROBERT AINSLIE.

ELLISLAND, *January* 6, 1789.

MANY happy returns of the season to you, my dear Sir. May you be comparatively happy, up to your comparative worth, among the sons of men ; which wish would, I am sure, make you one of the most blest of the human race.

I do not know if passing a "writer to the Signet" be a trial of scientific merit or a mere business of friends and interest. However it be, let me quote you my two favourite passages, which, though I have repeated them

ten thousand times, still they rouse my manhood and steel my resolution like inspiration.

> ————On Reason build resolve,
> That column of true majesty in man.—*Young.*
> Hear, Alfred, hero of the state,
> Thy Genius Heaven's high will declare ;
> The triumph of the truly great,
> Is never, never to despair !
> Is never to despair !—*Masque of Alfred.*

I grant you enter the lists of life to struggle for bread, business, notice, and distinction, in common with hundreds. But who are they ? Men like yourself, and of that aggregate body your compeers, seven-tenths of them come short of your advantages, natural and accidental ; while two of those that remain, either neglect their parts, as flowers blooming in a desert, or misspend their strength, like a bull goring a bramble bush.

But to change the theme : I am still catering for Johnson's publication ; and among others I have brushed up the following old favourite song a little, with a view to your worship. I have only altered a word here and there ; but if you like the humour of it, we shall think of a stanza or two to add to it.—R. B.

No. CLXXI.

TO PROFESSOR DUGALD STEWART.

[Of the "Poet's Progress" Burns composed several detached pieces, but none have been preserved except a dozen satirical lines, supposed to refer to Creech. Dr. Gregory's "iron criticism" related to the "Wounded Hare."

SIR,   ELLISLAND, *20th Jan.* 1787.
The enclosed sealed packet I sent to Edinburgh a few days after I had the happiness of meeting you in Ayrshire, but you were gone for the Continent. I have now added a few more of my productions, those for which I am indebted to the Nithsdale Muses. The piece inscribed to R. G., Esq. is a copy of verses I sent Mr. Graham of Fintry, accompanying a request for his assistance in a matter, to me, of very great moment. To that gentleman I am already doubly indebted for deeds of kindness of serious import to my dearest interests, done in a manner grateful to the delicate feelings of sensibility. This poem is a species of composition new to me, but I do not intend it shall be my last essay of the kind, as you will see by the "Poet's Progress." These fragments, if my design succeed, are but a small part of the intended whole. I propose it shall be the work of my utmost exertions, ripened by years : of course I do not wish it much known. The fragment beginning "A little upright, pert, tart, &c." I have not shown to man living, till I now send it you. It forms the postulata, the axioms, the definition of a character, which, if it appear at all, shall be placed in a variety of lights. This particular part I send you merely as a sample of my hand at portrait-sketching ; but, lest idle conjecture should pretend to point out the original, please to let it be for your single, sole inspection.

Need I make any apology for this trouble, to a gentleman who has

treated me with such marked benevolence and peculiar kindness—who has entered into my interests with so much zeal, and on whose critical decisions I can so fully depend? A poet as I am by trade, these decisions are to me of the last consequence. My late transient acquaintance among some of the mere rank and file of greatness, I resign with ease ; but to the distinguished champions of genius and learning, I shall be ever ambitious of being known. The native genius and accurate discernment in Mr. Stewart's critical strictures, the justness (iron justice, for he has no bowels of compassion for a poor poetic sinner) of Dr. Gregory's remarks, and the delicacy of Professor Dalzel's taste, I shall ever revere.

I shall be in Edinburgh some time next month.

I have the honour to be, Sir,

Your highly obliged and very humble Servant,

R. B.

No. CLXXII.
TO BISHOP GEDDES.

[Bishop John Geddes was born at Enzie, Banffshire, in 1735. He was educated at the Scotch Roman Catholic College at Rome, ordained priest in 1759, had charge of a college in Madrid for several years, and was consecrated bishop in 1780. In 1781 he returned to Scotland, and resided chiefly at Edinburgh, but died in Aberdeen in 1799. He had met the poet at Lord Monboddo's. Bishop Geddes is often confounded with another Roman Catholic ecclesiastic and native of Enzie, Dr. Alexander Geddes, an eccentric but learned man, who published a translation of the Scriptures and various miscellaneous works, and who was author of the humorous Scotch song

"There was a wee bit wifiekie."

It does not appear that Burns ever met Dr. A. Geddes. The book to which he refers was a copy of the Edinburgh edition of his own poems, to which he had made manuscript additions. The volume is now in the possession of Mr. James Black, Detroit, America.]

VENERABLE FATHER,   ELLISLAND, *February 3d*, 1789.

As I am conscious that, wherever I am, you do me the honour to interest yourself in my welfare, it gives me pleasure to inform you, that I am here at last, stationary in the serious business of life, and have now not only the retired leisure, but the hearty inclination, to attend to those great and important questions—what I am? where I am? and for what I am destined.

In that first concern, the conduct of the man, there was ever but one side on which I was habitually blameable, and there I have secured myself in the way pointed out by Nature and Nature's God. I was sensible that to so helpless a creature as a poor poet a wife and family were incumbrances, which a species of prudence would bid him shun ; but when the alternative was, being at eternal warfare with myself, on account of habitual follies, to give them no worse name, which no general example, no licentious wit, no sophistical infidelity, would, to me, ever justify, I must have been a fool to have hesitated, and a madman to have made another choice. Besides, I had in "my Jean" a long and much-loved

fellow-creature's happiness or misery among my hands, and who could trifle with such a deposit?

In the affair of a livelihood, I think myself tolerably secure : I have good hopes of my farm ; but should they fail, I have an excise commission, which, on my simple petition, will at any time procure me bread.   There is a certain stigma affixed to the character of an excise officer, but I do not pretend to borrow honour from my profession ; and though the salary be comparatively small, it is luxury to anything that the first twenty-five years of my life taught me to expect.

Thus, with a rational aim and method in life, you may easily guess, my reverend and much-honoured friend, that my characteristical trade is not forgotten.   I am, if possible, more than ever an enthusiast to the Muses. I am determined to study man and nature, and in that view incessantly ; and to try if the ripening and corrections of years can enable me to produce something worth preserving.

You will see in your book, which I beg your pardon for detaining so long, that I have been tuning my lyre on the banks of Nith.   Some large poetic plans that are floating in my imagination, or partly put in execution, I shall impart to you when I have the pleasure of meeting with you ; which, if you are then in Edinburgh, I shall have about the beginning of March.

That acquaintance, worthy Sir, with which you were pleased to honour me, you must still allow me to challenge ; for with whatever unconcern I give up my transient connexion with the merely great, I cannot lose the patronizing notice of the learned and good without the bitterest regret.

R. B.

No. CLXXIII.
TO MR. JAMES BURNES.

MY DEAR SIR,

ELLISLAND, *9th February,* 1789.

Why I did not write to you long ago is what, even on the rack, I could not answer.   If you can in your mind form an idea of indolence, dissipation, hurry, cares, change of country, entering on untried scenes of life, all combined, you will save me the trouble of a blushing apology.   It could not be want of regard for a man for whom I had a high esteem before I knew him—an esteem which has much increased since I did know him ; and this caveat entered, I shall plead guilty to any other indictment with which you shall please to charge me.

After I parted from you, for many months my life was one continued scene of dissipation.   Here at last I am become stationary, and have taken a farm and—a wife.

The farm is beautifully situated on the Nith, a large river that runs by Dumfries, and falls into the Solway Frith.   I have gotten a lease of my farm as long as I pleased ; but how it may turn out is just a guess, and it is yet to improve and enclose, &c. ; however, I have good hopes of my bargain on the whole.

My wife is my Jean, with whose story you are partly acquainted.   I found I had a much-loved fellow-creature's happiness or misery among my hands, and I durst not trifle with so sacred a deposit.   Indeed I have

not any reason to repent the step I have taken, as I have attached myself to a very good wife, and have shaken myself loose of every bad failing.

I have found my book a very profitable business, and with the profits of it I have begun life pretty decently. Should Fortune not favour me in farming, as I have no great faith in her fickle ladyship, I have provided myself in another resource, which, however some folks may affect to despise it, is still a comfortable shift in the day of misfortune. In the heyday of my fame, a gentleman, whose name at least I daresay you know, as his estate lies somewhere near Dundee, Mr. Graham of Fintry, one of the Commissioners of Excise, offered me the commission of an excise officer. I thought it prudent to accept the offer ; and accordingly I took my instructions, and have my commission by me. Whether I may ever do duty, or be a penny the better for it, is what I do not know ; but I have the comfortable assurance that, come whatever ill fate will, I can, on my simple petition to the excise-board, get into employ.

We have lost poor uncle Robert this winter. He has long been very weak, and with a very little alteration on him, he expired 3d Jan.

His son William has been with me this winter, and goes in May to be an apprentice to a mason. His other son, the eldest, John, comes to me, I expect, in summer. They are both remarkably stout young fellows, and promise to do well. His only daughter, Fanny, has been with me ever since her father's death, and I purpose keeping her in my family till she be quite woman grown, and fit for better service. She is one of the cleverest girls, and has one of the most amiable dispositions, I have ever seen.

All friends in this country and Ayrshire are well. Remember me to all friends in the north. My wife joins me in compliments to Mrs. B. and family.

I am ever, my dear Cousin,

Yours sincerely,

R. B.

No. CLXXIV.

TO MRS. DUNLOP.

[The two following letters relate to some poems by Mr. Mylne, who had recently died, which had been sent to Burns for his judgment by the Rev. Mr. Carfrae, at the suggestion of Mrs. Dunlop.]

ELLISLAND, *4th March*, 1789.

HERE am I, my honoured friend, returned safe from the capital. To a man who has a home, however humble or remote—if that home is like mine, the scene of domestic comfort—the bustle of Edinburgh will soon be a business of sickening disgust.

"Vain pomp and glory of this world, I hate you !"

When I must skulk into a corner, lest the rattling equipage of some gaping blockhead should mangle me in the mire, I am tempted to exclaim, "What merits has he had, or what demerit have I had, in some state of pre-existence, that he is ushered into this state of being

with the sceptre of rule and the key of riches in his puny fist, and I am kicked into the world the sport of folly, or the victim of pride?" I have read somewhere of a monarch (in Spain I think it was), who was so out of humour with the Ptolemean system of astronomy, that he said, had he been of the Creator's council, he could have saved Him a great deal of labour and absurdity. I will not defend this blasphemous speech; but often, as I have glided with humble stealth through the pomp of Princes Street, it has suggested itself to me, as an improvement on the present human figure, that a man, in proportion to his own conceit of his consequence in the world, could have pushed out the longitude of his common size, as a snail pushes out his horns, or as we draw out a perspective. This trifling alteration, not to mention the prodigious saving it would be in the tear and wear of the neck and limb sinews of many of his Majesty's liege subjects, in the way of tossing the head and tiptoe strutting, would evidently turn out a vast advantage, in enabling us at once to adjust the ceremonials in making a bow, or making way to a great man, and that too within a second of the precise spherical angle of reverence, or an inch of the particular point of respectful distance, which the important creature itself requires; as a measuring-glance at its towering altitude would determine the affair like instinct.

You are right, Madam, in your idea of poor Mylne's poem, which he has addressed to me. The piece has a good deal of merit, but it has one great fault—it is, by far, too long. Besides, my success has encouraged such a shoal of ill-spawned monsters to crawl into public notice, under the title of Scottish poets, that the very term Scottish poetry borders on the burlesque. When I write to Mr. Carfrae, I shall advise him rather to try one of his deceased friend's English pieces. I am prodigiously hurried with my own matters, else I would have requested a perusal of all Mylne's poetic performances, and would have offered his friends my assistance in either selecting or correcting what would be proper for the press. What it is that occupies me so much, and perhaps a little oppresses my present spirits, shall fill up a paragraph in some future letter. In the mean time allow me to close this epistle with a few lines done by a friend of mine * * * * *. I give you them, that, as you have seen the original, you may guess whether one or two alterations I have ventured to make in them be any real improvement.

> " Like the fair plant that from our touch withdraws,
> Shrink, mildly fearful, even from applause ;
> Be all a mother's fondest hope can dream,
> And all you are, my charming * * * *, seem.
> Straight as the fox-glove, ere her bells disclose,
> Mild as the maiden-blushing hawthorn blows,
> Fair as the fairest of each lovely kind,
> Your form shall be the image of your mind ;
> Your manners shall so true your soul express,
> That all shall long to know the worth they guess ;
> Congenial hearts shall greet with kindred love,
> And even sick'ning envy must approve." *

R. B.

* These lines are supposed to have been written by Mrs. Dunlop herself.

No. CLXXV.

TO THE REV. P. CARFRAE.

REV. SIR,

1789.

I do not recollect that I have ever felt a severer pang of shame, than on looking at the date of your obliging letter which accompanied Mr. Mylne's poem.

I am much to blame : the honour Mr. Mylne has done me, greatly enhanced in its value by the endearing, though melancholy, circumstance of its being the last production of his muse, deserved a better return.

I have, as you hint, thought of sending a copy of the poem to some periodical publication ; but, on second thoughts, I am afraid that in the present case it would be an improper step. My success, perhaps as much accidental as merited, has brought an inundation of nonsense under the name of Scottish poetry. Subscription-bills for Scottish poems have so dunned, and daily do dun, the public, that the very name is in danger of contempt. For these reasons, if publishing any of Mr. Mylne's poems in a magazine, &c. be at all prudent, in my opinion it certainly should not be a Scottish poem. The profits of the labours of a man of genius are, I hope, as honourable as any profits whatever ; and Mr. Mylne's relations are most justly entitled to that honest harvest, which fate has denied himself to reap. But let the friends of Mr. Mylne's fame (among whom I crave the honour of ranking myself) always keep in eye his respectability as a man and as a poet, and take no measure that, before the world knows anything about him, would risk his name and character being classed with the fools of the times.

I have, Sir, some experience of publishing ; and the way in which I would proceed with Mr. Mylne's poems is this :—I will publish in two or three English and Scottish public papers any one of his English poems which should, by private judges, be thought the most excellent, and mention it, at the same time, as one of the productions of a Lothian farmer, of respectable character, lately deceased, whose poems his friends had it in idea to publish, soon, by subscription, for the sake of his numerous family ;—not in pity to that family, but in justice to what his friends think the poetic merits of the deceased ; and to secure, in the most effectual manner, to those tender connexions, whose right it is, the peeuniary reward of those merits.—R. B.

No. CLXXVI.

TO CLARINDA.

MADAM,

9th March, 1789

The letter you wrote me to Heron's carried its own answer in its bosom; you forbade me to write you, unless I was willing to plead guilty to a certain indictment that you were pleased to bring against me. As I am convinced of my own innocence, and though conscious of high imprudence and egregious folly, can lay my hand on my breast and attest

the rectitude of my heart, you will pardon me, Madam, if I do not carry my complaisance so far as humbly to acquiesce in the name of villain, merely out of compliment to your opinion, much as I esteem your judgment, and warmly as I regard your worth.

I have already told you, and I again aver it, that at the period of time alluded to I was not under the smallest moral tie to Mrs. Burns ; nor did I, nor could I, then know all the powerful circumstances that omnipotent necessity was busy laying in wait for me. When you call over the scenes that have passed between us, you will survey the conduct of an honest man, struggling successfully with temptations the most powerful that ever beset humanity, and preserving untainted honour in situations where the austerest virtue would have forgiven a fall ; situations that, I will dare to say, not a single individual of all his kind, even with half his sensibility and passion, could have encountered without ruin ; and I leave you to guess, Madam, how such a man is likely to digest an accusation of perfidious treachery.

Was I to blame, Madam, in being the distracted victim of charms which, I affirm it, no man ever approached with impunity ? Had I seen the least glimmering of hope that these charms could ever have been mine, or even had not iron necessity—but these are unavailing words.

I would have called on you when I was in town—indeed, I could not have resisted it—but that Mr. Ainslie told me that you were determined to avoid your windows while I was in town, lest even a glance of me should occur in the street.

When I have regained your good opinion, perhaps I may venture to solicit your friendship ; but, be that as it may, the first of her sex I ever knew shall always be the object of my warmest good wishes.—R. B.

No. CLXXVII.

TO DR. MOORE.

SIR, ELLISLAND, *23d March,* 1789.

The gentleman who will deliver you this is a Mr. Nielson, a worthy clergyman in my neighbourhood, and a very particular acquaintance of mine. As I have troubled him with this packet, I must turn him over to your goodness, to recompense him for it in a way in which he much needs your assistance, and where you can effectually serve him. Mr. Nielson is on his way for France, to wait on his Grace of Queensberry, on some little business of a good deal of importance to him, and he wishes for your instructions respecting the most eligible mode of travelling, &c. for him, when he has crossed the Channel. I should not have dared to take this liberty with you, but that I am told, by those who have the honour of your personal acquaintance, that to be a poor honest Scotchman is a letter of recommendation to you, and that to have it in your power to serve such a character gives you much pleasure.

The enclosed ode is a compliment to the memory of the late Mrs. Oswald, of Auchencruive. You, probably, knew her personally, an honour

of which I cannot boast ; but I spent my early years in her neighbourhood, and among her servants and tenants. I know that she was
detested with the most heartfelt cordiality. However, in the particular
part of her conduct which roused my poetic wrath, she was much less
blameable. In January last, on my road to Ayrshire, I had put up at
Bailie Whigham's, in Sanquhar, the only tolerable inn in the place.
The frost was keen, and the grim evening and howling wind were
ushering in a night of snow and drift. My horse and I were both
much fatigued with the labours of the day; and just as my friend the
Bailie and I were bidding defiance to the storm over a smoking bowl,
in wheels the funeral pageantry of the late great Mrs. Oswald, and poor
I am forced to brave all the horrors of the tempestuous night, and jade
my horse, my young favourite horse, whom I had just christened Pegasus,
twelve miles farther on, through the wildest moors and hills of Ayrshire,
to New Cumnock, the next inn. The powers of poesy and prose sink
under me, when I would describe what I felt. Suffice it to say, that when
a good fire at New Cumnock had so far recovered my frozen sinews, I sat
down and wrote the enclosed ode.

I was at Edinburgh lately, and settled finally with Mr. Creech ; and I
must own that at last he has been amicable and fair with me.—R. B.

No. CLXXVIII.

TO MR. HILL.

[The "library scheme" here referred to is now-a-days a common institution in
almost every village : but it is worth note that Burns appreciated the movement,
and interested himself actively in it, at its first beginnings.]

ELLISLAND, *2nd April,* 1789.

I WILL make no excuse, my dear Bibliopolus, (God forgive me for
murdering language !) that I have sat down to write you on this vile
paper.

It is economy, Sir ; it is that cardinal virtue, prudence ; so I beg you
will sit down, and either compose or borrow a panegyric. If you are going
to borrow, apply to * * * * to compose, or rather to compound, something
very clever on my remarkable frugality ; that I write to one of my most
esteemed friends on this wretched paper, which was originally intended
for the venal fist of some drunken exciseman, to take dirty notes in a
miserable vault of an ale-cellar.

O Frugality ! thou mother of ten thousand blessings !—thou cook of fat
beef and dainty greens !—thou manufacturer of warm Shetland hose and
comfortable surtouts !—thou old housewife, darning thy decayed stockings
with thy ancient spectacles on thy aged nose !—lead me, hand me in thy
clutching palsied fist, up those heights, and through those thickets, hitherto
inaccessible and impervious to my anxious, weary feet : not those Parnassian crags, bleak and barren, where the hungry worshippers of fame
are, breathless, clambering, hanging between heaven and hell, but those

glittering cliffs of Potosi, where the all-sufficient, all-powerful deity, Wealth, holds his immediate court of joys and pleasures ; where the sunny exposure of plenty and the hot walls of profusion produce those blissful fruits of luxury, exotics in this world and natives of paradise !   Thou withered sybil, my sage conductress, usher me into thy refulgent, adored presence !   The power, splendid and potent as he now is, was once the puling nursling of thy faithful care and tender arms !   Call me thy son, thy cousin, thy kinsman, or favourite, and adjure the god by the scenes of his infant years no longer to repulse me as a stranger or an alien, but to favour me with his peculiar countenance and protection !   He daily bestows his greatest kindness on the undeserving and the worthless : assure him, that I bring ample documents of meritorious demerits !   Pledge yourself for me, that for the glorious cause of Lucre I will do anything, be anything—but the horse-leech of private oppression, or the vulture of public robbery !

But to descend from heroics.

I want a Shakespeare ; I want likewise an English dictionary—Johnson's, I suppose, is best.   In these and all my prose commissions the cheapest is always the best for me.   There is a small debt of honour that I owe Mr. Robert Cleghorn, in Saughton Mills, my worthy friend, and your well-wisher.   Please give him, and urge him to take it, the first time you see him, ten shillings' worth of anything you have to sell, and place it to my account.

The library scheme that I mentioned to you is already begun, under the direction of Captain Riddel.   There is another in emulation of it going on at Closeburn, under the auspices of Mr. Monteith, of Closeburn, which will be on a greater scale than ours.   Capt. Riddel gave his infant society a great many of his old books, else I had written you on that subject ; but one of these days I shall trouble you with a commission for " The Monkland Friendly Society : " a copy of " The Spectator," "Mirror," and " Lounger," " Man of Feeling," " Man of the World," " Guthrie's Geographical Grammar," with some religious pieces, will likely be our first order.

When I grow richer, I will write to you on gilt post, to make amends for this sheet.   At present every guinea has a five guinea errand with,

My dear Sir,
Your faithful, poor, but honest Friend,
R. B.

No. CLXXIX.

TO MRS. DUNLOP.

ELLISLAND, *4th April*, 1789.

I NO sooner hit on any poetic plan or fancy, but I wish to send it to you : and if knowing and reading these give half the pleasure to you that communicating them to you gives to me, I am satisfied.

I have a poetic whim in my head, which I at present dedicate, or rather inscribe, to the Right Hon. Charles James Fox ; but how long that fancy

may hold, I cannot say. A few of the first lines I have just rough-sketched as follows :—

SKETCH.

How wisdom and folly meet, mix, and unite ;
How virtue and vice blend their black and their white ;
How genius, the illustrious father of fiction,
Confounds rule and law, reconciles contradiction—
I sing : if these mortals, the critics, should bustle,
I care not, not I ; let the critics go whistle.
 But now for a patron, whose name and whose glory
At once may illustrate and honour my story.

 Thou first of our orators, first of our wits,
Yet whose parts and acquirements seem mere lucky hits ;
With knowledge so vast, and with judgment so strong,
No man with the half of 'em e'er went far wrong ;
With passions so potent, and fancies so bright,
No man with the half of 'em e'er went quite right ;
A sorry, poor misbegot son of the Muses
For using thy name offers fifty excuses, &c.

(For the rest see page 107.)

On the 20th current I hope to have the honour of assuring you, in person, how sincerely I am.—R. B.

No. CLXXX.
TO MRS. McMURDO,
DRUMLANRIG.

MADAM,   ELLISLAND, *2d May*, 1789.

I have finished the piece* which had the happy fortune to be honoured with your approbation ; and never did little miss with more sparkling pleasure show her applauded sampler to partial mamma, than I now send my poem to you and Mr. McMurdo, if he is returned to Drumlanrig. You cannot easily imagine what thin-skinned animals, what sensitive plants, poor poets are. How do we shrink into the embittered corner of self-abasement, when neglected or condemned by those to whom we look up ! and how do we, in erect importance, add another cubit to our stature on being noticed and applauded by those whom we honour and respect ! My late visit to Drumlanrig has, I can tell you, Madam, given me a balloon waft up Parnassus, where on my fancied elevation I regard my poetic self with no small degree of complacency. Surely, with all their sins, the rhyming tribe are not ungrateful creatures. I recollect your goodness to your humble guest, I see Mr. McMurdo adding to the politeness of the gentleman the kindness of a friend, and my heart swells as it would burst, with warm emotions and ardent wishes ! It may be it is not gratitude ; it may be a mixed sensation. That strange, shifting, double animal man is so generally, at best,

---

* " Bonnie Jean ;" the heroine of which was the eldest daughter of Mrs. McMurdo, and sister to Phillis : their charms give lustre to some of the Poet's happiest lyrics.

but a negative, often a worthless, creature, that we cannot see real goodness and native worth without feeling the bosom glow with sympathetic approbation.

With every sentiment of grateful respect,

I have the honour to be, Madam,

Your obliged and grateful humble Servant,

R. B.

No. CLXXXI.

TO MR. CUNNINGHAM.

MY DEAR SIR, ELLISLAND, *4th May,* 1789.

Your *duty-free* favour of the 26th April I received two days ago. I will not say I received it with pleasure ; that is the cold compliment of ceremony : I perused it, Sir, with delicious satisfaction ;—in short, it is such a letter, that not you, nor your friend, but the legislature, by express proviso in their postage laws, should frank. A letter informed with the soul of friendship is such an honour to human nature, that they should order it free ingress and egress to and from their bags and mails, as an encouragement and mark of distinction to supereminent virtue.

I have just put the last hand to a little poem, which I think will be something to your taste. One morning lately, as I was out pretty early in the fields, sowing some grass seeds, I heard the burst of a shot from a neighbouring plantation, and presently a poor little wounded hare came crippling by me. You will guess my indignation at the inhuman fellow who could shoot a hare at this season, when all of them have young ones. Indeed there is something in that business of destroying for our sport individuals in the animal creation that do not injure us materially which I could never reconcile to my ideas of virtue.

Inhuman man ! curse on thy barb'rous art,
And blasted be thy murder-aiming eye !
May never pity sooth thee with a sigh,
Nor ever pleasure glad thy cruel heart !—&c. (*Page* 96.)

Let me know how you like my poem. I am doubtful whether it would not be an improvement to keep out the last stanza but one altogether.

Cruikshank is a glorious production of the Author of man. You, he, and the noble Colonel of the Crochallan Fencibles are to me

"Dear as the ruddy drops which warm my heart."

I have a good mind to make verses on you all to the tune of "Three guid fellows ayont the glen."—R. B.

No. CLXXXII.

TO RICHARD BROWN.

MY DEAR FRIEND, MAUCHLINE, *21st May,* 1789.

I was in the country by accident, and hearing of your safe arrival, I could not resist the temptation of wishing you joy on your return,

wishing you would write to me before you sail again, wishing you would always set me down as your bosom friend, wishing you long life and prosperity, and that every good thing may attend you, wishing Mrs. Brown and your little ones as free of the evils of this world as is consistent with humanity, wishing you and she were to make two at the ensuing lying-in with which Mrs. B. threatens very soon to favour me, wishing I had longer time to write to you at present, and, finally, wishing that if there is to be another state of existence, Mr. B., Mrs. B., our little ones, and both families, and you and I, in some snug retreat, may make a jovial party to all eternity !

My direction is at Ellisland, near Dumfries.

Yours,   R. B.

No. CLXXXIII.

TO MR. JAMES HAMILTON.

DEAR SIR, *Ellisland, 26th May,* 1789.

I would fain offer, my dear Sir, a word of sympathy with your misfortunes ; but it is a tender string, and I know not how to touch it. It is easy to flourish a set of high-flown sentiments on the subjects that would give great satisfaction to—a breast quite at ease ; but as one observes who was very seldom mistaken in the theory of life, " The heart knoweth its own sorrows, and a stranger intermeddleth not there-with."

Among some distressful emergencies that I have experienced in life, I ever laid this down as my foundation of comfort—*That he who has lived the life of an honest man has by no means lived in vain!*

With every wish for your welfare and future success,

I am, my dear Sir,
Sincerely yours,
R. B.

No. CLXXXIV.

TO WILLIAM CREECH, ESQ.

SIR, ELLISLAND. *30th May,* 1789.

I had intended to have troubled you with a long letter, but at present the delightful sensations of an omnipotent toothache so engross all my inner man, as to put it out of my power even to write nonsense. However, as in duty bound, I approach my bookseller with an offering in my hand—a few poetical clinches and a song:—to expect any other kind of offering from the rhyming tribe would be to know them much less than you do. I do not pretend that there is much merit in these *mor-ceaux;* but I have two reasons for sending them : *primo,* they are mostly ill-natured, so are in unison with my present feelings, while fifty troops of infernal spirits are driving post from ear to ear along my jaw-bones ; and

G G 2

secondly, they are so short, that you cannot leave off in the middle, and so hurt my pride in the idea that you found any work of mine too heavy to get through.

I have a request to beg of you, and I not only beg of you, but conjure you, by all your wishes and by all your hopes that the Muse will spare the satiric wink in the moment of your foibles ; that she will warble the song of rapture round your hymeneal couch ; and that she will shed on your turf the honest tear of elegiac gratitude ! Grant my request as speedily as possible : send me by the very first fly or coach for this place three copies of the last edition of my poems, which place to my account.

Now may the good things of prose, and the good things of verse, come among thy hands, until they be filled with the *good things of this life*, prayeth   R. B.

No. CLXXXV.

TO MR. JOHN McAULAY.

TOWN CLERK OF DUMBARTON.

DEAR SIR,   ELLISLAND, *4th June*, 1789.

Though I am not without my fears respecting my fate at that grand, universal inquest of right and wrong commonly called *The Last Day*, yet I trust there is one sin which that arch-vagabond Satan, who I understand is to be king's evidence, cannot throw in my teeth—I mean ingratitude. There is a certain pretty large quantum of kindness for which I remain, and from inability I fear must still remain, your debtor ; but though unable to repay the debt, I assure you, Sir, I shall ever warmly remember the obligation. It gives me the sincerest pleasure to hear by my old acquaintance, Mr. Kennedy, that you are, in immortal Allan's language, " Hale, and weel, and living ;" and that your charming family are well, and promising to be an amiable and respectable addition to the company of performers whom the Great Manager of the Drama of Man is bringing into action for the succeeding age.

With respect to my welfare, a subject in which you once warmly and effectively interested yourself, I am here in my old way, holding my plough, marking the growth of my corn, or the health of my dairy ; and at times sauntering by the delightful windings of the Nith, on the margin of which I have built my humble domicile ; praying for seasonable weather, or holding an intrigue with the Muses—the only gypsies with whom I have now any intercourse. As I am entered into the holy state of matrimony, I trust my face is turned completely Zionward ; and as it is a rule with all honest fellows to repeat no grievances, I hope that the little poetic licences of former days will of course fall under the oblivious influence of some good-natured statute of celestial prescription. In my family devotion, which, like a good presbyterian, I occasionally give to my household folks, I am extremely fond of the psalm, " Let not the errors of my youth," &c.

and that other, "Lo, children are God's heritage," &c. in which last Mrs. Burns, who, by the by, has a glorious "wood-note wild" at either old song or psalmody, joins me with the pathos of Handel's "Messiah."—R. B.

No. CLXXXVI.

TO MR. ROBERT AINSLIE.

MY DEAR FRIEND,　　　　ELLISLAND, *8th June,* 1789.

I am perfectly ashamed of myself when I look at the date of your last. It is not that I forget the friend of my heart and the companion of my peregrinations; but I have been condemned to drudgery beyond sufferance, though not, thank God, beyond redemption. I have had a collection of poems by a lady put into my hands to prepare them for the press; which horrid task, with sowing corn with my own hand, a parcel of masons, wrights, plasterers, &c. to attend to, roaming on business through Ayrshire—all this was against me, and the very first dreadful article was of itself too much for me.

13th.—I have not had a moment to spare from incessant toil since the 8th. Life, my dear Sir, is a serious matter. You know by experience that a man's individual self is a good deal, but, believe me, a wife and family of children, whenever you have the honour to be a husband and a father, will show you that your present and most anxious hours of solitude are spent on trifles. The welfare of those who are very dear to us, whose only support, hope, and stay we are—this, to a generous mind, is another sort of more important object of care than any concerns whatever which centre merely in the individual. On the other hand, let no young, unmarried, rakehelly dog among you make a song of his pretended liberty and freedom from care. If the relations we stand in to king, country, kindred, and friends, be anything but the visionary fancies of dreaming metaphysicians; if religion, virtue, magnanimity, generosity, humanity, and justice, be aught but empty sounds; then the man who may be said to live only for others, for the beloved, honourable female, whose tender, faithful embrace endears life, and for the helpless little innocents who are to be the men and women, the worshippers of his God, the subjects of his king, and the support, nay, the very vital existence, of his country, in the ensuing age;—compare such a man with any fellow whatever, who, whether he bustle and push in business among labourers, clerks, statesmen; or whether he roar and rant, and drink and sing, in taverns—a fellow over whose grave no one will breathe a single heigh-ho, except from the cobweb-tie of what is called good fellowship—who has no view nor aim but what terminates in himself: if there be any grovelling earthborn wretch of our species, a renegado to common sense, who would fain believe that the noble creature man is no better than a sort of fungus, generated out of nothing, nobody knows how, and soon dissipating in nothing, nobody knows where; such a stupid beast, such a crawling reptile, might balance the foregoing unexaggerated comparison, but no one else would have the patience.

Forgive me, my dear Sir, for this long silence. *To make you amends*, I shall send you soon, and, more encouraging still, without any postage, one or two rhymes of my later manufacture.—R. B.

No. CLXXXVII.

TO MR. [PETER STUART].

[Mr. Robert Chambers has discovered that this letter was addressed to Mr. Peter Stuart, editor of the *Star*, and afterwards connected with the *Morning Post* and *Chronicle*.]

MY DEAR SIR,   1789.
    The hurry of a farmer in this particular season and the indolence of a poet at all times and seasons will, I hope, plead my excuse for neglecting so long to answer your obliging letter of the 5th of August. . . .
    When I received your letter I was transcribing for * * * * my letter to the magistrates of the Canongate, Edinburgh, begging their permission to place a tombstone over poor Fergusson, and their edict in consequence of my petition; but now I shall send them to * * * *. Poor Fergusson! If there be a life beyond the grave, which I trust there is; and if there be a good God presiding over all nature, which I am sure there is; thou art now enjoying existence in a glorious world, where worth of the heart alone is distinction in the man; where riches, deprived of all their pleasure-purchasing powers, return to their native sordid matter; where titles and honours are the disregarded reveries of an idle dream; and where that heavy virtue, which is the negative consequence of steady dulness, and those thoughtless, though often destructive, follies which are the unavoidable aberrations of frail human nature, will be thrown into equal oblivion, as if they had never been! Adieu, my dear Sir! So soon as your present views and schemes are concentred in an aim, I shall be glad to hear from you, as your welfare and happiness is by no means a subject indifferent to   Yours,
                                                                                    R. B.

No. CLXXXVIII.

TO MISS WILLIAMS.

[Miss Helen Maria Williams, author of "Some Verses on the Slave Trade, and other Poems," was introduced to Burns by Dr. Moore.]

MADAM,   ELLISLAND, 1789.
    Of the many problems in the nature of that wonderful creature man, this is one of the most extraordinary, that he shall go on from day to day, from week to week, from month to month, or perhaps from year to year, suffering a hundred times more in an hour from the impotent consciousness of neglecting what he ought to do, than the very doing of it would cost him. I am deeply indebted to you, first for a most elegant

poetic compliment, then for a polite, obliging letter, and lastly, for your excellent poem on the Slave Trade ; and yet, wretch that I am ! though the debts were debts of honour, and the creditor a lady, I have put off and put off even the acknowledgment of the obligation, until you must indeed be the very angel I take you for, if you can forgive me.

Your poem I have read with the highest pleasure. I have a way whenever I read a book—I mean a book in our own trade, Madam, a poetic one—and when it is my own property, that I take a pencil and mark at the ends of verses, or note on margins and odd paper, little criticisms of approbation or disapprobation as I peruse along. I will make no apology for presenting you with a few unconnected thoughts that occurred to me in my repeated perusals of your poem. I want to show you that I have honesty enough to tell you what I take to be truths, even when they are not quite on the side of approbation ; and I do it in the firm faith that you have equal greatness of mind to hear them with pleasure.

I know very little of scientific criticism ; so all I can pretend to do in that intricate art is merely to note, as I read along, what passages strike me as being uncommonly beautiful, and where the expression seems to be perplexed or faulty.

The poem opens finely. There are none of these idle prefatory lines which one may skip over before one comes to the subject. Verses 9th and 10th in particular,

> "Where ocean's unseen bound
> Leaves a drear world of waters round,"

are truly beautiful. The simile of the hurricane is likewise fine ; and indeed, beautiful as the poem is, almost all the similes rise decidedly above it. From verse 31st to verse 50th is a pretty eulogy on Britain. Verse 36th, "That foul drama deep with wrong," is nobly expressive. Verse 46th, I am afraid, is rather unworthy of the rest : "to dare to feel" is an idea that I do not altogether like. The contrast of valour and mercy, from the 46th verse to the 50th, is admirable.

Either my apprehension is dull, or there is something a little confused in the apostrophe to Mr. Pitt. Verse 55th is the antecedent to verses 57th and 58th, but in verse 58th the connexion seems ungrammatical :—

> "Powers *   *   *   *   *
> With no gradations mark'd their flight,
> But rose at once to glory's height."

"Ris'n" should be the word instead of "rose." Try it in prose. Powers,—their flight marked by no gradations, but [the same powers] risen at once to the height of glory. Likewise, verse 53d, "For this" is evidently meant to lead on the sense of the verses 59th, 60th, 61st, and 62d ; but let us try how the thread of connexion runs :—

> "For this *   *   *   *
> The deeds of mercy, that embrace
> A distant sphere, an alien race,
> Shall virtue's lips record, and claim
> The fairest honours of thy name."

I beg pardon if I misapprehend the matter, but this appears to me the only imperfect passage in the poem. The comparison of the sunbeam is fine.

The compliment to the Duke of Richmond is, I hope, as just as it is certainly elegant. The thought,

> "Virtue * * * *
> Sends from her unsullied source
> The gems of thought their purest force,"

is exceeding beautiful. The idea, from verse 81st to the 85th, that the "blest decree" is like the beams of morning ushering in the glorious day of liberty, ought not to pass unnoticed or unapplauded. From verse 85th to verse 108th is an animated contrast between the unfeeling selfishness of the oppressor, on the one hand, and the misery of the captive, on the other. Verse 88th might perhaps be amended thus : "Nor ever *quit* her narrow maze." We are said to *pass* a bound, but we *quit* a maze. Verse 100th is exquisitely beautiful :—

> "They, whom wasted blessings tire."

Verse 110th is, I doubt, a clashing of metaphors ; "to load a span" is, I am afraid, an unwarrantable expression. In verse 114th, "Cast the universe in shade" is a fine idea. From the 115th verse to the 142d is a striking description of the wrongs of the poor African. Verse 120th, "The load of unremitted pain," is a remarkable, strong expression. The address to the advocates for abolishing the slave-trade, from verse 143d to verse 208th, is animated with the true life of genius. The picture of Oppression,—

> "While she links her impious chain,
> And calculates the price of pain ;
> Weighs agony in sordid scales,
> And marks if death or life prevails,"—

is nobly executed.

What a tender idea is in verse 180th ! Indeed, that whole description of home may vie with Thomson's description of home, somewhere in the beginning of his "Autumn." I do not remember to have seen a stronger expression of misery than is contained in these verses :—

> "Condemned, severe extreme, to live
> When all is fled that life can give."

The comparison of our distant joys to distant objects is equally original and striking.

The character and manners of the dealer in the infernal traffic is a well done, though a horrid, picture. I am not sure how far introducing the sailor was right ; for though the sailor's common characteristic is generosity, yet in this case he is certainly not only an unconcerned witness, but, in some degree, an efficient agent in the business. Verse 224th is a nervous . . . . expressive—"The heart convulsive anguish breaks." The description of the captive wretch when he arrives in the West Indies is carried on with equal spirit. The thought that the

oppressor's sorrow on seeing the slave pine is like the butcher's regret when his destined lamb dies a natural death is exceedingly fine.

I am got so much into the cant of criticism, that I begin to be afraid lest I have nothing except the cant of it ; and instead of elucidating my author, am only benighting myself. For this reason, I will not pretend to go through the whole poem. Some few remaining beautiful lines, however, I cannot pass over. Verse 280th is the strongest description of selfishness I ever saw. The comparison in verses 285th and 286th is new and fine ; and the line, "Your arms to penury you lend," is excellent.

In verse 317th, "like" should certainly be "as" or "so ;" for instance—

> "His sway the hardened bosom leads
> To cruelty's remorseless deeds ;
> As (*or* so) the blue lightning, when it springs
> With fury on its livid wings,
> Darts on the goal with rapid force,
> Nor heeds that ruin marks its course."

If you insert the word "like" where I have placed "as," you must alter "darts" to "darting," and "heeds" to "heeding," in order to make it grammar. A tempest is a favourite subject with the poets, but I do not remember anything even in Thomson's "Winter" superior to your verses from the 347th to the 351st. Indeed the last simile, beginning with "Fancy may dress," &c. and ending with the 350th verse, is, in my opinion, the most beautiful passage in the poem ; it would do honour to the greatest names that ever graced our profession.

I will not beg your pardon, Madam, for these strictures, as my conscience tells me, that for once in my life I have acted up to the duties of a Christian, in doing as I would be done by.—R. B.

No. CLXXXIX.

TO MRS. DUNLOP.

DEAR MADAM, . ELLISLAND, *21st June*, 1789.

Will you take the effusions, the miserable effusions, of low spirits, just as they flow from their bitter spring? I know not of any particular cause for this worst of all my foes besetting me ; but for some time my soul has been beclouded with a thickening atmosphere of evil imaginations and gloomy presages.

Monday Evening.

I have just heard Mr. Kirkpatrick preach a sermon. He is a man famous for his benevolence, and I revere him ; but from such ideas of my Creator, good Lord, deliver me! Religion, my honoured friend, is surely a simple business, as it equally concerns the ignorant and the learned, the poor and the rich. That there is an incomprehensible Great Being, to whom I owe my existence ; and that He must be intimately acquainted with the operations and progress of the internal machinery, and consequent outward deportment, of this creature which He has made ; these are, I

think, self-evident propositions. That there is a real and eternal distinction between virtue and vice, and, consequently, that I am an accountable creature; that from the seeming nature of the human mind, as well as from the evident imperfection, nay, positive injustice, in the administration of affairs, both in the natural and moral worlds, there must be a retributive scene of existence beyond the grave; must, I think, be allowed by every one who will give himself a moment's reflection. I will go farther, and affirm, that from the sublimity, excellence, and purity of His doctrine and precepts, unparalleled by all the aggregated wisdom and learning of many preceding ages, though, *to appearance*, He Himself was the obscurest and most illiterate of our species—therefore Jesus Christ was from God.

Whatever mitigates the woes, or increases the happiness, of others, this is my criterion of goodness; and whatever injures society at large, or any individual in it, this is my measure of iniquity.

What think you, Madam, of my creed? I trust that I have said nothing that will lessen me in the eye of one whose good opinion I value almost next to the approbation of my own mind.—R. B.

No. CXC.

TO LADY GLENCAIRN.

MY LADY,

The honour you have done your poor poet, in writing him so very obliging a letter, and the pleasure the enclosed beautiful verses have given him, came very seasonably to his aid amid the cheerless gloom and sinking despondency of diseased nerves and December weather. As to forgetting the family of Glencairn, Heaven is my witness with what sincerity I could use those old verses, which please me more in their rude simplicity than the most elegant lines I ever saw:—

" If thee, Jerusalem, I forget,
    Skill part from my right hand.

My tongue to my mouth's roof let cleave,
    If I do thee forget,
Jerusalem, and thee above
    My chief joy do not set."

When I am tempted to do anything improper, I dare not, because I look on myself as accountable to your ladyship and family. Now and then, when I have the honour to be called to the tables of the great, if I happen to meet with any mortification from the stately stupidity of self-sufficient squires or the luxurious insolence of upstart nabobs, I get above the creatures by calling to remembrance that I am patronised by the noble house of Glencairn; and at gala-times, such as New-year's day, a christening, or the Kirn-night, when my punch-bowl is brought from its dusty corner and filled up in honour of the occasion, I begin with, " The Countess of Glencairn ! " My good woman, with the enthusiasm of a grateful heart, next cries, " My Lord ! " and so the toast goes on until I end with " Lady Harriet's little angel ! " whose epithalamium I have pledged myself to write.

When I received your ladyship's letter, I was just in the act of transcribing for you some verses I have lately composed; and meant to have sent them my first leisure hour, and acquainted you with my late change of life. I mentioned to my lord my fears concerning my farm. Those fears were indeed too true: it is a bargain that would have ruined me but for the lucky circumstance of my having an excise commission.

People may talk as they please of the ignominy of the excise ; 50*l.* a year will support my wife and children, and keep me independent of the world ; and I would much rather have it said that my profession borrowed credit from me, than that I borrowed credit from my profession. Another advantage I have in this business is the knowledge it gives me of the various shades of human character, consequently assisting me vastly in my poetic pursuits. I had the most ardent enthusiasm for the Muses when nobody knew me but myself, and that ardour is by no means cooled now that my Lord Glencairn's goodness has introduced me to all the world. Not that I am in haste for the press. I have no idea of publishing, else I certainly had consulted my noble, generous patron ; but after acting the part of an honest man, and supporting my family, my whole wishes and views are directed to poetic pursuits. I am aware, that though I were to give performances to the world superior to my former works, still, if they were of the same kind with those, the comparative reception they would meet with would mortify me. I have turned my thoughts on the drama. I do not mean the stately buskin of the tragic Muse. . . . . .

Does not your ladyship think that an Edinburgh theatre would be more amused with affectation, folly, and whim of true Scottish growth, than manners which by far the greatest part of the audience can only know at second-hand?

> I have the honour to be,
> Your ladyship's ever devoted
> and grateful humble Servant,
> R. B.

No. CXCI.

TO MR. JOHN LOGAN

[OF KNOCKSHINNOCH, GLEN AFTON, AYRSHIRE].

DEAR SIR, ELLISLAND, *near Dumfries, 7th Aug.* 1789.

I intended to have written you long ere now, and, as I told you, I had gotten three stanzas and a half on my way in a poetic epistle to you ; but that old enemy of all *good works*, the devil, threw me into a prosaic mire, and for the soul of me I cannot get out of it. I dare not write you a long letter, as I am going to intrude on your time with a long ballad. I have, as you will shortly see, finished " The Kirk's Alarm ;" but now that it is done, and that I have laughed once or twice at the conceits in some of the stanzas, I am determined not to let it get into the public : so I send you this copy, the first that I have sent to Ayrshire, except some few of the stanzas, which I wrote off in embryo for Gavin Hamilton, under the

express provision and request that you will only read it to a few of us, and do not on any account give, or permit to be taken, any copy of the ballad. If I could be of any service to Dr. M'Gill, I would do it, though it should be at a much greater expense than irritating a few bigoted priests; but I am afraid serving him in his present *embarras* is a task too hard for me. I have enemies enow, God knows, though I do not wantonly add to the number. Still, as I think there is some merit in two or three of the thoughts, I send it to you as a small but sincere testimony how much, and with what respectful esteem,

I am, dear Sir,

Your obliged humble Servant,

R. B.

No. CXCII.

TO MRS. DUNLOP.

DEAR MADAM,   ELLISLAND, *6th Sept.* 1789.

I have mentioned in my last my appointment to the Excise and the birth of little Frank; who, by the by, I trust will be no discredit to the honourable name of Wallace, as he has a fine manly countenance, and a figure that might do credit to a little fellow two months older, and likewise an excellent good temper, though when he pleases he has a pipe only not quite so loud as the horn that his immortal namesake blew as a signal to take out the pin of Stirling bridge.

I had some time ago an epistle, part poetic, and part prosaic, from your poetess, Mrs. J. Little, a very ingenious but modest composition. I should have written her as she requested, but for the hurry of this new business. I have heard of her and her compositions in this country; and I am happy to add, always to the honour of her character. The fact is, I know not well how to write to her: I should sit down to a sheet of paper that I knew not how to stain. I am no dab at fine-drawn letter-writing; and, except when prompted by friendship or gratitude, or, which happens extremely rarely, inspired by the Muse (I know not her name) that presides over epistolary writing, I sit down, when necessitated to write, as I would sit down to beat hemp.

Some parts of your letter of the 20th August struck me with the most melancholy concern for the state of your mind at present.

Would I could write you a letter of comfort! I would sit down to it with as much pleasure as I would to write an epic poem of my own composition that should equal the "Iliad." Religion, my dear friend, is the true comfort! A strong persuasion in a future state of existence; a proposition so obviously probable, that, setting revelation aside, every nation and people, so far as investigation has reached, for at least near four thousand years, have in some mode or other firmly believed it. In vain would we reason and pretend to doubt. I have myself done so to a very daring pitch; but when I reflected, that I was opposing the most ardent wishes

and the most darling hopes of good men, and flying in the face of all human belief, in all ages, I was shocked at my own conduct.

I know not whether I have ever sent you the following lines, or if you have ever seen them ; but it is one of my favourite quotations, which I keep constantly by me in my progress through life, in the language of the book of Job,

> " Against the day of battle and of war"—

spoken of religion :

> " 'Tis *this*, my friend, that streaks our morning bright :
> 'Tis *this* that gilds the horror of our night :
> When wealth forsakes us, and when friends are few,
> When friends are faithless, or when foes pursue,
> 'Tis *this* that wards the blow, or stills the smart,
> Disarms affliction, or repels his dart ;
> Within the breast bids purest raptures rise,
> Bids smiling conscience spread her cloudless skies."

I have been busy with "Zeluco." The Doctor is so obliging as to request my opinion of it : and I have been revolving in my mind some kind of criticisms on novel-writing ; but it is a depth beyond my research. I shall however digest my thoughts on the subject as well as I can. "Zeluco" is a most sterling performance.

Farewell ! *A Dieu, le bon Dieu, je vous commende !*—R. B.

No. CXCIII.

TO CAPTAIN RIDDEL,

CARSE.

[The "important day" was that on which the contest with the famous Danish whistle was to take place at Captain Riddel's—the contest, who of the company could drink deepest and longest without losing the power of blowing the whistle.]

SIR,   ELLISLAND, *16th Oct.* 1789.

Big with the idea of this important day at Friars Carse, I have watched the elements and skies in the full persuasion that they would announce it to the astonished world by some phenomena of terrific portent. Yesternight until a very late hour did I wait with anxious horror for the appearance of some comet firing half the sky, or aerial armies of sanguinary Scandinavians, darting athwart the startled heavens, rapid as the ragged lightning, and horrid as those convulsions of nature that bury nations.

The elements, however, seem to take the matter very quietly : they did not even usher in this morning with triple suns and a shower of blood, symbolical of the three potent heroes and the mighty claret-shed of the day. For me, as Thomson in his "Winter" says of the storm, I shall "Hear astonished, and astonished sing"

> The whistle and the man : I sing
> The man that won the whistle, &c.

> Here are we met, three merry boys;
> Three merry boys I trow are we ;
> And mony a night we've merry been,
> And mony mae we hope to be.
>
> Wha first shall rise to gang awa,
> A cuckold coward loun is he :
> Wha *last* beside his chair shall fa',
> He is the king amang us three.

To leave the heights of Parnassus and come to the humble vale of prose—I have some misgivings that I take too much upon me, when I request you to get your guest, Sir Robert Lowrie, to frank the two enclosed covers for me ; the one of them to Sir William Cunningham of Robertland, Bart., at Kilmarnock ; the other to Mr. Allan Masterton, Writing-Master, Edinburgh. The first has a kindred claim on Sir Robert, as being a brother baronet, and likewise a keen Foxite ; the other is one of the worthiest men in the world, and a man of real genius ; so, allow me to say, he has a fraternal claim on you. I want them franked for to-morrow, as I cannot get them to the post to-night. I shall send a servant again for them in the evening. Wishing that your head may be crowned with laurels to-night, and free from aches to-morrow,

I have the honour to be, Sir,
Your deeply indebted humble Servant,
R. B.

No. CXCIV.

TO MR. ROBERT AINSLIE.

MY DEAR FRIEND,　　　　　ELLISLAND, *1st November*, 1789.

I had written you long ere now, could I have guessed where to find you ; for I am sure you have more good sense than to waste the precious days of vacation time in the dirt of business and Edinburgh. Wherever you are, God bless you, and lead you not into temptation, but deliver you from evil !

I do not know if I have informed you that I am now appointed to an excise division, in the middle of which my house and farm lie. In this I was extremely lucky. Without ever having been an expectant, as they call their journeymen excisemen, I was directly planted down to all intents and purposes an officer of excise, there to flourish and bring forth fruits—worthy of repentance.

I know not how the word exciseman, or, still more opprobrious, gauger, will sound in your ears. I too have seen the day, when my auditory nerves would have felt very delicately on this subject ; but a wife and children are things which have a wonderful power in blunting these kind of sensations. Fifty pounds a year for life, and a provision for widows and orphans, you will allow is no bad settlement for a *poet.* For the ignominy of the profession, I have the encouragement which I once heard a recruiting serjeant give to a numerous, if not a respectable, audience, in the streets of Kilmarnock : " Gentlemen, for your further and better encourage-

ment, I can assure you that our regiment is the most blackguard corps under the crown, and, consequently, with us an honest fellow has the surest chance for preferment."

You need not doubt that I find several very unpleasant and disagreeable circumstances in my business ; but I am tired with and disgusted at the language of complaint against the evils of life. Human existence in the most favourable situations does not abound with pleasures, and has its inconveniences and ills : capricious, foolish man mistakes these inconveniences and ills, as if they were the peculiar property of his particular situation; and hence that eternal fickleness, that love of change, which has ruined, and daily does ruin, many a fine fellow, as well as many a blockhead, and is, almost without exception, a constant source of disappointment and misery.

I long to hear from you how you go on—not so much in business, as in life. Are you pretty well satisfied with your own exertions, and tolerably at ease in your internal reflections? 'Tis much to be a great character as a lawyer, but beyond comparison more to be a great character as a man. That you may be both the one and the other is the earnest wish, and that you *will* be both is the firm persuasion, of,

My dear Sir, &c.

R. B.

No. CXCV.

TO MR. RICHARD BROWN.

Ellisland, *4th November,* 1789.

I HAVE been so hurried, my ever dear friend, that though I got both your letters, I have not been able to command an hour to answer them as I wished ; and even now you are to look on this as merely confessing debt, and craving days. Few things could have given me so much pleasure as the news that you were once more safe and sound on terra firma, and happy in that place where happiness is alone to be found, in the fireside circle. May the benevolent Director of all things peculiarly bless you in all those endearing connexions consequent on the tender and venerable names of husband and father! I have indeed been extremely lucky in getting an additional income of £50 a year, while, at the same time, the appointment will not cost me above £10 or £12 per annum of expenses more than I must have inevitably incurred. The worst circumstance is, that the excise division which I have got is so extensive, no less than ten parishes to ride over ; and it abounds besides with so much business, that I can scarcely steal a spare moment. However, labour endears rest, and both together are absolutely necessary for the proper enjoyment of human existence. I cannot meet you anywhere. No less than an order from the Board of Excise, at Edinburgh, is necessary before I can have so much time as to meet you in Ayrshire. But do you come and see me. We must have a social day, and perhaps lengthen it out with half the night, before you go again to sea. You are the earliest friend I now have on

earth, my brothers excepted; and is not that an endearing circumstance? When you and I first met, we were at the green period of human life. The twig would easily take a bent, but would as easily return to its former state. You and I not only took a mutual bent, but by the melancholy, though strong, influence of being both of the family of the unfortunate, we were entwined with one another in our growth towards advanced age; and blasted be the sacrilegious hand that shall attempt to undo the union! You and I must have one bumper to my favourite toast, " May the companions of our youth be the friends of our old age !" Come and see me one year ; I shall see you at Port Glasgow the next: and if we can contrive to have a gossiping between our two bedfellows, it will be so much additional pleasure. Mrs. Burns joins me in kind compliments to you and Mrs. Brown. Adieu !

I am ever, my dear Sir, yours,
R. B.

No. CXCVI.

TO R. GRAHAM, ESQ.

OF FINTRY.

SIR, *9th December,* 1789.

I have a good while had a wish to trouble you with a letter, and had certainly done it long ere now, but for a humiliating something that throws cold water on the resolution, as if one should say, " You have found Mr. Graham a very powerful and kind friend indeed, and that interest he is so kindly taking in your concerns, you ought by everything in your power to keep alive and cherish." Now, though since God has thought proper to make one powerful and another helpless, the connexion of obliger and obliged is all fair ; and though my being under your patronage is to me highly honourable, yet, Sir, allow me to flatter myself, that as a poet and an honest man you first interested yourself in my welfare, and principally as such still you permit me to approach you.

I have found the excise business go on a great deal smoother with me than I expected ; owing a good deal to the generous friendship of Mr. Mitchel, my collector, and the kind assistance of Mr. Findlater, my supervisor. I dare to be honest, and I fear no labour. Nor do I find my hurried life greatly inimical to my correspondence with the Muses. Their visits to me, indeed, and I believe to most of their acquaintance, like the visits of good angels, are short and far between ; but I meet them now and then as I jog through the hills of Nithsdale, just as I used to do on the banks of Ayr. I take the liberty to enclose you a few bagatelles, all of them the productions of my leisure thoughts in my excise rides.

If you know or have ever seen Captain Grose, the antiquarian, you will enter into any humour that is in the verses on him. Perhaps you have seen them before, as I sent them to a London newspaper. Though I dare say you have none of the solemn-league-and-covenant fire which

shone so conspicuous in Lord George Gordon and the Kilmarnock weavers, yet I think you must have heard of Dr. M'Gill, one of the clergymen of Ayr, and his heretical book. God help him, poor man ! Though he is one of the worthiest, as well as one of the ablest, of the whole priesthood of the Kirk of Scotland, in every sense of that ambiguous term, yet the poor Doctor and his numerous family are in imminent danger of being thrown out to the mercy of the winter winds. The enclosed ballad on that business is, I confess, too local ; but I laughed myself at some conceits in it, though I am convinced in my conscience that there are a good many heavy stanzas in it too.

The election ballad, as you will see, alludes to the present canvass in our string of boroughs. I do not believe there will be such a hard-run match in the whole general election.

I am too little a man to have any political attachments ; I am deeply indebted to, and have the warmest veneration for, individuals of both parties ; but a man who has it in his power to be the father of a country, and who * * * * * *, is a character that one cannot speak of with patience.*

Sir J. J. does what " what man can do," but yet I doubt his fate.

No. CXCVII.

TO MRS. DUNLOP.

ELLISLAND, 13*th December,* 1789.

MANY thanks, dear Madam, for your sheet-full of rhymes. Though at present I am below the veriest prose, yet from you everything pleases. I am groaning under the miseries of a diseased nervous system—a system, the state of which is most conducive to our happiness, or the most productive of our misery. For now near three weeks I have been so ill with a nervous headache, that I have been obliged for a time to give up my excise-books, being scarce able to lift my head, much less to ride once a week over ten muir parishes. What is man ?—To-day, in the luxuriance of health, exulting in the enjoyments of existence ; in a few days, perhaps in a few hours, loaded with conscious painful being, counting the tardy pace of the lingering moments by the repercussions of anguish, and refusing or denied a comforter. Day follows night, and night comes after day, only to curse him with life which gives him no pleasure ; and yet the awful, dark termination of that life is something at which he recoils.

> " Tell us, ye dead ; will none of you in pity
> Disclose the secret———— ————
> *What 'tis you are, and we must shortly be ?*
> ————————————'tis no matter :
> A little time will make us learned as you are."

Can it be possible, that when I resign this frail, feverish being, I shall still find myself in conscious existence ? When the last gasp of agony has

* This is evidently " Old Q.," the Duke of Queensberry.

H H

announced that I am no more to those that knew me, and the few who loved me ; when the cold, stiffened, unconscious, ghastly corse is resigned into the earth, to be the prey of unsightly reptiles, and to become in time a trodden clod, shall I be yet warm in life, seeing and seen, enjoying and enjoyed ? Ye venerable sages and holy flamens, is there probability in your conjectures, truth in your stories, of another world beyond death ; or are they all alike, baseless visions and fabricated fables ? If there is another life, it must be only for the just, the benevolent, the amiable, and the humane : what a flattering idea, then, is a world to come ! Would to God I as firmly believed it, as I ardently wish it ! There I shall meet an aged parent, now at rest from the many buffetings of an evil world, against which he so long and bravely struggled. There should I meet the friend, the disinterested friend, of my early life ; the man who rejoiced to see me, because he loved me and could serve me. Muir, thy weaknesses were the aberrations of human nature, but thy heart glowed with everything generous, manly, and noble ; and if ever emanation from the All-good Being animated a human form, it was thine ! There should I, with speechless agony of rapture, again recognise my lost, my ever dear Mary ! whose bosom was fraught with truth, honour, constancy, and love.

> " My Mary, dear departed shade
> 　　Where is thy place of heavenly rest?
> Seest thou thy lover lowly laid ?
> 　　Hear'st thou the groans that rend his breast ?"

Jesus Christ, thou amiablest of characters ! I trust Thou art no impostor, and that Thy revelation of blissful scenes of existence beyond death and the grave is not one of the many impositions which time after time have been palmed on credulous mankind. I trust that in Thee " shall all the families of the earth be blessed," by being yet connected together in a better world, where every tie that bound heart to heart in this state of existence shall be, far beyond our present conceptions, more endearing.

I am a good deal inclined to think with those who maintain, that what are called nervous affections are in fact diseases of the mind. I cannot reason, I cannot think ; and, but to you, I would not venture to write anything above an order to a cobbler. You have felt too much of the ills of life not to sympathise with a diseased wretch, who has impaired more than half of any faculties he possessed. Your goodness will excuse this distracted scrawl, which the writer dare scarcely read, and which he would throw into the fire, were he able to write anything better, or indeed anything at all.

Rumour told me something of a son of yours, who was returned from the East or West Indies. If you have gotten news from James or Anthony, it was cruel in you not to let me know ; as I promise you, on the sincerity of a man who is weary of one world, and anxious about another, that scarce anything could give me so much pleasure as to hear of any good thing befalling my honoured friend.

If you have a minute's leisure, take up your pen in pity to *le pauvre miserable.*—R. B.

No. CXCVIII.

TO SIR JOHN SINCLAIR.

SIR, 1790.

The following circumstance has, I believe, been omitted in the statistical account transmitted to you of the parish of Dunscore, in Nithsdale. I beg leave to send it to you, because it is new, and may be useful. How far it is deserving of a place in your patriotic publication, you are the best judge.

To store the minds of the lower classes with useful knowledge is certainly of very great importance, both to them as individuals, and to society at large. Giving them a turn for reading and reflection is giving them a source of innocent and laudable amusement, and, besides, raises them to a more dignified degree in the scale of rationality. Impressed with this idea, a gentlemen in this parish, Robert Riddel, Esq. of Glenriddel, set on foot a species of circulating library, on a plan so simple as to be practicable in any corner of the country ; and so useful, as to deserve the notice of every country gentleman who thinks the improvement of that part of his own species whom chance has thrown into the humble walks of the peasant and the artizan a matter worthy of his attention.

Mr. Riddel got a number of his own tenants and farming neighbours to form themselves into a society for the purpose of having a library among themselves. They entered into a legal engagement to abide by it for three years ; with a saving clause or two, in case of a removal to a distance, or death. Each member, at his entry, paid five shillings ; and at each of their meetings, which were held every fourth Saturday, sixpence more. With their entry-money, and the credit which they took on the faith of their future funds, they laid in a tolerable stock of books at the commencement. What authors they were to purchase was always decided by the majority. At every meeting all the books, under certain fines and forfeitures, by way of penalty, were to be produced ; and the members had their choice of the volumes in rotation. He whose name stood, for that night, first on the list, had his choice of what volume he pleased in the whole collection ; the second had his choice after the first ; the third after the second, and so on to the last. At next meeting, he who had been first on the list at the preceding meeting, was last at this ; he who had been second was first ; and so on, through the whole three years. At the expiration of the engagement the books were sold by auction, but only among the members themselves ; each man had his share of the common stock, in money or in books, as he chose to be a purchaser or not.

At the breaking up of this little society, which was formed under Mr. Riddel's patronage, what with benefactions of books from him, and what with their own purchases, they had collected together upwards of one hundred and fifty volumes. It will easily be guessed, that a good deal of trash would be bought. Among the books, however, of this little library

were Blair's Sermons, Robertson's History of Scotland, Hume's History of the Stewarts, "The Spectator," "Idler," "Adventurer," "Mirror," "Lounger," "Observer," "Man of Feeling," "Man of the World," "Chrysal," "Don Quixote," "Joseph Andrews," &c. A peasant who can read and enjoy such books is certainly a much superior being to his neighbour who, perhaps, stalks beside his team very little removed, except in shape, from the brutes he drives.

Wishing your patriotic exertions their so much merited success,

I am, Sir,

Your humble Servant,

A PEASANT.

No. CXCIX

TO LADY WINIFRED MAXWELL CONSTABLE.

[Lady Winifred was grand-daughter of the Earl of Nithsdale, the romantic story of whose escape from the Tower (where he was imprisoned for his share in the insurrection of 1715), through the heroism of his wife, is well known. She married William Haggerston Constable, of Everingham.]

ELLISLAND, *16th Dec.* 1789.

. . . . To court the notice or the tables of the great, except where I sometimes have had a little matter to ask of them, or more often the pleasanter task of witnessing my gratitude to them, is what I have never done, and I trust never shall do. But with your ladyship I have the honour to be connected by one of the strongest and most endearing ties in the whole moral world ; common sufferings in a cause where even to be unfortunate is glorious—the cause of heroic loyalty! Though my fathers had not illustrious honours and vast properties to hazard in the contest, though they left their humble cottages only to add so many units more to the unnoted crowd that followed their leaders, yet what they could they did, and what they had they lost : with unshaken firmness and unconcealed political attachments, they shook hands with ruin for what they esteemed the cause of their king and their country. This language and the enclosed verses [addressed to Mr. William Tytler] are for your ladyship's eyes alone. Poets are not very famous for their prudence ; but as I can do nothing for a cause which is now nearly no more, I do not wish to hurt myself.—R. B.

No. CC.

TO CHARLES SHARPE, ESQ.

OF HODDAM.

[Mr. Sharpe was a man of some accomplishments—a good violinist and a composer of original music. He also wrote verses for his own airs. The following letter was written by Burns under a fictitious signature, enclosing a ballad, in 1790 or 1791.]

IT is true, Sir, you are a gentleman of rank and fortune, and I am a poor devil ; you are a feather in the cap of society, and I am a very

hobnail in his shoes; yet I have the honour to belong to the same family with you, and on that score I now address you. You will perhaps suspect that I am going to claim affinity with the ancient and honourable house of Kirkpatrick. No, no, Sir: I cannot indeed be properly said to belong to any house, or even any province or kingdom; as my mother, who for many years was spouse to a marching regiment, gave me into this bad world, aboard the packet-boat, somewhere between Donaghadee and Portpatrick. By our common family I mean, Sir, the family of the Muses. I am a fiddler and a poet; and you, I am told, play an exquisite violin, and have a standard taste in the *belles lettres.* The other day, a brother catgut gave me a charming Scots air of your composition. If I was pleased with the tune, I was in raptures with the title you have given it; and taking up the idea, I have spun it into the three stanzas enclosed. Will you allow me, Sir, to present you them, as the dearest offering that a misbegotten son of poverty and rhyme has to give? I have a longing to take you by the hand and unburthen my heart by saying, "Sir, I honour you as a man who supports the dignity of human nature amid an age when frivolity and avarice have, between them, debased us below the brutes that perish!" But, alas, Sir! to me you are unapproachable. It is true, the Muses baptized me in Castalian streams, but the thoughtless gipsies forgot to give me a name. As the sex have served many a good fellow, the Nine have given me a great deal of pleasure, but, bewitching jades! they have beggared me. Would they but spare me a little of their cast-linen! Were it only in my power to say that I have a shirt on my back! But, the idle wenches! like Solomon's lilies, "they toil not, neither do they spin:" so I must e'en continue to tie my remnant of a cravat, like the hangman's rope, round my naked throat, and coax my galligaskins to keep together their many-coloured fragments. As to the affair of shoes, I have given that up. My pilgrimages in my ballad-trade, from town to town, and on your stony-hearted turnpikes too, are what not even the hide of Job's Behemoth could bear. The coat on my back is no more: I shall not speak evil of the dead. It would be equally unhandsome and ungrateful to find fault with my old surtout, which so kindly supplies and conceals the want of that coat. My hat indeed is a great favourite; and though I got it literally for an old song, I would not exchange it for the best beaver in Britain. I was, during several years, a kind of fac-totum servant to a country clergyman, where I pickt up a good many scraps of learning, particularly in some branches of the mathematics. Whenever I feel inclined to rest myself on my way, I take my seat under a hedge, laying my poetic wallet on the one side, and my fiddle-case on the other, and placing my hat between my legs, I can by means of its brim, or rather brims, go through the whole doctrine of the Conic Sections.

However, Sir, don't let me mislead you, as if I would interest your pity. Fortune has so much forsaken me, that she has taught me to live without her; and amid all my rags and poverty I am as independent, and much more happy, than a monarch of the world. According to the hackneyed metaphor, I value the several actors in the great drama of life simply as they act their parts. I can look on a worthless fellow of a duke with

unqualified contempt, and can regard an honest scavenger with sincere respect. As you, Sir, go through your *rôle* with such distinguished merit, permit me to make one in the chorus of universal applause, and assure you that, with the highest respect,

I have the honour to be, &c.

No. CCI.

TO MR. GILBERT BURNS.

DEAR BROTHER,   ELLISLAND, 11*th January*, 1790.

I mean to take advantage of the frank, though I have not in my present frame of mind much appetite for exertion in writing. My nerves are in a cursed state. I feel that horrid hypochondria pervading every atom of both body and soul. This farm has undone my enjoyment of myself. It is a ruinous affair on all hands. But let it go to hell! I'll fight it out and be off with it.

We have gotten a set of very decent players here just now. I have seen them an evening or two. David Campbell, in Ayr, wrote to me by the manager of the company, a Mr. Sutherland, who is a man of apparent worth. On New-year-day evening I gave him the following prologue, which he spouted to his audience with applause :—

> No song nor dance I bring from yon great city,
> That queens it o'er our taste—the more's the pity :
> Tho', by the by, abroad why will you roam?
> Good sense and taste are natives here at home.

I can no more.—If once I am clear of this curst farm, I should respire more at my ease.—R. B.

No. CCII.

TO MR. WILLIAM DUNBAR, W. S.

ELLISLAND, 14*th January*, 1790.

SINCE we are here creatures of a day, since a "few summer days, and a few winter nights, and the life of man is at an end," why, my dear, much-esteemed Sir, should you and I let negligent indolence—for I know it is nothing worse—step in between us, and bar the enjoyment of a mutual correspondence? We are not shapen out of the common, heavy, methodical clod, the elemental stuff of the plodding, selfish race, the sons of Arithmetic and Prudence ; our feelings and hearts are not benumbed and poisoned by the cursed influence of riches, which, whatever blessing there may be in other respects, are no friends to the nobler qualities of the heart ; in the name of random sensibility, then, let never the moon change on our silence any more. I have had a tract of bad health most part of this winter, else you had heard from me long ere now. Thank Heaven, I am now got so much better as to be able to partake a little in the enjoyments of life.

Our friend Cunningham will perhaps have told you of my going into the Excise. The truth is, I found it a very convenient business to have 50*l.* per annum, nor have I yet felt any of those mortifying circumstances in it that I was led to fear.

Feb. 2.

I HAVE not, for sheer hurry of business, been able to spare five minutes to finish my letter. Besides my farm business, I ride on my Excise matters at least 200 miles every week. I have not by any means given up the Muses. You will see in the third vol. of Johnson's " Scots Songs " that I have contributed my mite there.

But, my dear Sir, little ones that look up to you for parental protection are an important charge. I have already two fine, healthy, stout little fellows, and I wish to throw some light upon them. I have a thousand reveries and schemes about them and their future destiny—not that I am a Utopian projector in these things. I am resolved never to breed up a son of mine to any of the learned professions. I know the value of independence, and since I cannot give my sons an independent fortune, I shall give them an independent line of life. What a chaos of hurry, chance, and changes is this world, when one sits soberly down to reflect on it ! To a father, who himself knows the world, the thought that he shall have sons to usher into it must fill him with dread ; but if he have daughters, the prospect to a thoughtful man is apt to shock him.

I hope Mrs. Fordyce and the two young ladies are well. Do let me forget that they are nieces of yours, and let me say that I never saw a more interesting, sweeter pair of sisters in my life. I am the fool of my feelings and attachments. I often take up a volume of my Spenser [which Mr. Dunbar had presented to him] to realise you to my imagination, and think over those social scenes we have had together. God grant that there may be another world more congenial to honest fellows beyond this ; a world where these rubs and plagues of absence, distance, misfortunes, ill health, &c. shall no more damp hilarity and divide friendship.—R. B.

No. CCIII.

TO MRS. DUNLOP.

ELLISLAND, *25th January,* 1790.

IT has been owing to unremitting hurry of business that I have not written to you, Madam, long ere now. My health is greatly better, and I now begin once more to share in satisfaction and enjoyment with the rest of my fellow-creatures.

Many thanks, my much esteemed friend, for your kind letters : but why will you make me run the risk of being contemptible and mercenary in my own eyes ? When I pique myself on my independent spirit, I hope it is neither poetic licence, nor poetic rant ; and I am so flattered with the honour you have done me, in making me your compeer in friendship and

friendly correspondence, that I cannot without pain, and a degree of mortification, be reminded of the real inequality between our situations.

Most sincerely do I rejoice with you, dear Madam, in the good news of Anthony. Not only your anxiety about his fate, but my own esteem for such a noble, warm-hearted, manly young fellow in the little I had of his acquaintance, has interested me deeply in his fortunes.

Falconer, the unfortunate author of the "Shipwreck," which you so much admire, is no more. After witnessing the dreadful catastrophe he so feelingly describes in his poem, and after weathering many hard gales of fortune, he went to the bottom with the "Aurora" frigate!

I forget what part of Scotland had the honour of giving him birth; but he was the son of obscurity and misfortune. He was one of those daring adventurous spirits which Scotland, beyond any other country, is remarkable for producing. Little does the fond mother think, as she hangs delighted over the sweet little leech at her bosom, where the poor fellow may hereafter wander, and what may be his fate. I remember a stanza in an old Scottish ballad, which, notwithstanding its rude simplicity, speaks feelingly to the heart:—

> "Little did my mother think,
> That day she cradled me,
> What land I was to travel in,
> Or what death I should die!"

Old Scottish songs are, you know, a favourite study and pursuit of mine; and now I am on that subject, allow me to give you two stanzas of another old simple ballad, which I am sure will please you. The catastrophe of the piece is a poor ruined female, lamenting her fate. She concludes with this pathetic wish:—

> "O that my father had ne'er on me smil'd!
> O that my mother had ne'er to me sung!
> O that my cradle had never been rock'd;
> But that I had died when I was young!
>
> O that the grave it were my bed;
> My blankets were my winding sheet;
> The clocks and the worms my bedfellows a';
> And O sae sound as I should sleep!"

I do not remember, in all my reading, to have met with anything more truly the language of misery than the exclamation in the last line. Misery is like love; to speak its language truly, the author must have felt it.

I am every day expecting the doctor to give your little godson* the small-pox. They are *rife* in the country, and I tremble for his fate. By the way, I cannot help congratulating you on his looks and spirit. Every person who sees him, acknowledges him to be the finest, handsomest child he has ever seen. I am myself delighted with the manly swell of his little chest, and a certain miniature dignity in the carriage of his head, and the glance of his fine black eye, which promise the undaunted gallantry of an independent mind.

* His second son, Francis.

I thought to have sent you some rhymes, but time forbids. I promise you poetry until you are tired of it next time I have the honour of assuring you how truly I am, &c.—R. B.

No. CCIV.

TO MR. PETER HILL,

BOOKSELLER, EDINBURGH.

ELLISLAND, 2nd Feb. 1790.

NO! I will not say one word about apologies or excuses for not writing ; I am a poor, rascally gauger, condemned to gallop at least 200 miles every week to inspect dirty ponds and yeasty barrels, and where can I find time to write to, or importance to interest, anybody? The upbraidings of my conscience, nay, the upbraidings of my wife, have persecuted me on your account these two or three months past. I wish to God I was a great man, that my correspondence might throw light upon you, to let the world see what you really are; and then I would make your fortune, without putting my hand in my pocket for you, which, like all other great men, I suppose I would avoid as much as possible. What are you doing, and how are you doing? Have you lately seen any of my few friends? What has become of the Borough Reform, or how is the fate of my poor namesake Mademoiselle Burns decided? . . . O man! but for thee, and thy selfish appetites and dishonest artifices, that beauteous form, and that once innocent and still ingenuous mind, might have shone conspicuous and lovely in the faithful wife and the affectionate mother; and shall the unfortunate sacrifice to thy pleasures have no claim on thy humanity?

I saw lately in a Review some extracts from a new poem called "The Village Curate:" send it me. I want likewise a cheap copy of "The World." Mr. Armstrong, the young poet, who does me the honour to mention me so kindly in his works, please give him my best thanks for the copy of his book: I shall write him my first leisure hour. I like his poetry much, but I think his style in prose quite astonishing.—R. B.

No. CCV.

SYLVANDER TO CLARINDA.

[The Poet's marriage did not entirely break off his correspondence with Mrs. M'Lehose. She had written to him reproachfully, and the following is his reply.]

Feb. 1790 (?).

I HAVE indeed been ill, Madam, the whole winter. An incessant head-ache, depression of spirits, and all the truly miserable consequences of a deranged nervous system, have made dreadful havoc of my health and peace. Add to all this, a line of life into which I have lately entered

obliges me to ride, on the average, at least 200 miles every week. However, thank Heaven, I am now greatly better in my health. . . . .

I cannot, will not, enter into extenuatory circumstances; else I could show you how my precipitate, headlong, unthinking conduct leagued with a conjuncture of unlucky events to thrust me out of a possibility of keeping the path of rectitude to curse me, by an irreconcileable war between my duty and my nearest wishes, and to damn me with a choice only of different species of error and misconduct.

I dare not trust myself further with this subject. The following song is one of my latest productions, and I send it you as I would do anything else, because it pleases myself.

[Here follows " My Lovely Nancy," given in page 90.]

No. CCVI.

TO MR. W. NICOL.

MY DEAR SIR,   ELLISLAND, *Feb.* 9, 1790.

That d-mned mare of yours is dead. I would freely have given her price to have saved her; she has vexed me beyond description. Indebted as I was to your goodness beyond what I can ever repay, I eagerly grasped at your offer to have the mare with me. That I might at least show my readiness in wishing to be grateful, I took every care of her in my power. She was never crossed for riding above half a score of times by me or in my keeping. I drew her in the plough, one of three, for one poor week. I refused fifty five shillings for her, which was the highest bode I could squeeze for her. I fed her up and had her in fine order for Dumfries fair, when, four or five days before the fair, she was seized with an unaccountable disorder in the sinews, or somewhere in the bones of the neck; with a weakness or total want of power in her fillets; and, in short, the whole vertebræ of her spine seemed to be diseased and unhinged; and in eight and forty hours, in spite of the two best farriers in the country, she died—and be d-mned to her! The farriers said that she had been quite strained in the fillets beyond cure before you had bought her; and that the poor devil, though she might keep a little flesh, had been jaded and quite worn out with fatigue and oppression. While she was with me, she was under my own eye : and I assure you, my much valued friend, everything was done for her that could be done; and the accident has vexed me to the heart. In fact, I could not pluck up spirits to write to you on account of the unfortunate business.

There is little new in this country. Our theatrical company, of which you must have heard, leave us this week. Their merit and character are indeed very great, both on the stage and in private life; not a worthless creature among them; and their encouragement has been accordingly. Their usual run is from eighteen to twenty-five pounds a night : seldom less than the one, and the house will hold no more than the other. There have been repeated instances of sending away six, and eight, and ten

pounds a night for want of room. A new theatre is to be built by subscription : the first stone is to be laid on Friday first to come. Three
hundred guineas have been raised by thirty subscribers, and thirty more
might have been got if wanted. The manager, Mr. Sutherland, was introduced to me by a friend from Ayr ; and a worthier or cleverer fellow I
have rarely met with. Some of our clergy have slipped in by stealth now
and then ; but they have got up a farce of their own. You must have
heard how the Rev. Mr. Lawson of Kirkmahoe, seconded by the Rev. Mr.
Kirkpatrick of Dunscore, and the rest of that faction, have accused in
formal process the unfortunate and Rev. Mr. Heron of Kirkgunzeon, that
in ordaining Mr. Nielson to the cure of souls in Kirkbean he, the said
Heron, feloniously and treasonably bound the said Nielson to the confession of faith, *so far as it was agreeable to reason and the Word of God!*

Mrs. B. begs to be remembered most gratefully to you. Little Bobby
and Frank are charmingly well and healthy. I am jaded to death with
fatigue. For these two or three months, on an average, I have not ridden
less than two hundred miles per week. I have done little in the poetic
way : I have given Mr. Sutherland two prologues ; one of which was
delivered last week. I have likewise strung four or five barbarous stanzas,
to the tune of Chevy Chase, by way of Elegy on your poor unfortunate
mare, beginning (the name she got here was Peg Nicholson) :

> " Peg Nicholson was a good bay mare,
>   As ever trod on airn :
> But now she's floating down the Nith,
>   And past the mouth o' Cairn."—&c.   *(Page* 155.)

My best compliments to Mrs. Nicol, and little Neddy, and all the
family. I hope Ned is a good scholar, and will come out to gather nuts
and apples with me next harvest.—R. B.

No. CCVII.

TO MR. CUNNINGHAM.

ELLISLAND, 13*th February,* 1790.

I BEG your pardon, my dear and much valued friend, for writing to you
on this very unfashionable, unsightly sheet—

> " My poverty, but not my will, consents."

But to make amends, since of modish post I have none, except one poor
widowed half-sheet of gilt, which lies in my drawer among my plebeian
foolscap pages, like the widow of a man of fashion, whom that unpolite
scoundrel, Necessity, has driven from Burgundy and Pineapple to a dish
of Bohea, with the scandal-bearing helpmate of a village priest ; or a glass
of whisky-toddy, with a ruby-nosed yoke-fellow of a foot-padding exciseman ; I make a vow to enclose this sheet-full of epistolary fragments in
that my only scrap of gilt paper.

I am indeed your unworthy debtor for three friendly letters. I ought
to have written to you long ere now ; but it is a literal fact, I have scarcely

a spare moment.   It is not that I *will not* write to you ; Miss Burnet is
not more 'dear to her guardian angel, nor his Grace the Duke of Queensberry to the powers of darkness, than my friend Cunningham to me.   It is
not that I *cannot* write to you : should you doubt it, take the following
fragment, which was intended for you some time ago, and be convinced
that I can *antithesize* sentiment, and *circumvolute* periods, as well as any
coiner of phrase in the regions of philology :—

MY DEAR CUNNINGHAM,   *December,* 1789.
    Where are you?   And what are you doing?   Can you be that son
of levity who takes up a friendship as he takes up a fashion? or are you,
like some other of the worthiest fellows in the world, the victim of
indolence, laden with fetters of ever-increasing weight?

What strange beings we are!   Since we have a portion of conscious
existence equally capable of enjoying pleasure, happiness, and rapture, or
of suffering pain, wretchedness, and misery, it is surely worthy of an
inquiry, whether there be not such a thing as a science of life ; whether
method, economy, and fertility of expedients be not applicable to enjoyment ; and whether there be not a want of dexterity in pleasure, which
renders our little scantling of happiness still less, and a profuseness, an
intoxication in bliss, which leads to satiety, disgust, and self-abhorrence.
There is not a doubt but that health, talents, character, decent competency, respectable friends, are real substantial blessings ; and yet do we
not daily see those who enjoy many or all of these good things contrive,
notwithstanding, to be as unhappy as others to whose lot few of them have
fallen?   I believe one great source of this mistake or misconduct is owing
to a certain stimulus, with us called ambition, which goads us up the hill
of life, not as we ascend other eminences, for the laudable curiosity
of viewing an extended landscape, but rather for the dishonest pride of
looking down on others of our fellow-creatures, seemingly diminutive in
humbler stations, &c. &c.

Sunday, 14th February, 1790.
   GOD help me ! I am now obliged to join

            "Night to day, and Sunday to the week."

If there be any truth in the orthodox faith of these churches, I am d-mned
past redemption, and, what is worse, d-mned to all eternity.   I am deeply
read in Boston's " Fourfold State," Marshal on Sanctification, Guthrie's
" Trial of a Saving Interest," &c. ; but " there is no balm in Gilead, there is
no physician there," for me : so I shall e'en turn Arminian, and trust to
" sincere though imperfect obedience."

Tuesday, 16th.
   LUCKILY for me, I was prevented from the discussion of the knotty
point at which I had just made a full stop.   All my fears and care are of
this world : if there is another, an honest man has nothing to fear from it.
I hate a man that wishes to be a Deist ; but I fear every fair, unprejudiced

inquirer must in some degree be a Sceptic. It is not that there are any very staggering arguments against the immortality of man ; but, like electricity, phlogiston, &c., the subject is so involved in darkness, that we want data to go upon. One thing frightens me much : that we are to live for ever seems *too good news to be true.* That we are to enter into a new scene of existence, where, exempt from want and pain, we shall enjoy ourselves and our friends without satiety or separation—how much should I be indebted to any one who could fully assure me that this was certain !

My time is once more expired. I will write to Mr. Cleghorn soon. God bless him and all his concerns ! And may all the powers that preside over conviviality and friendship be present with all their kindest influence when the bearer of this, Mr. Syme, and you meet !—I wish I could also make one.

Finally, brethren, farewell ! Whatsoever things are lovely, whatsoever things are gentle, whatsoever things are charitable, whatsoever things are kind, think on these things, and think on

R. B.

No. CCVIII.

TO MR. HILL.

[The order for the works of the dramatists is supposed to indicate a design on Burns's part to try his own hand at dramatic composition.]

ELLISLAND, *2d March,* 1790.

. . . . IN addition to the books I commissioned in my last, I want very much " An Index to the Excise Laws, or an Abridgement of all the Statutes now in force relative to the Excise," by Jellinger Symons : I want three copies of this book ; if it is now to be had, cheap or dear, get it for me. An honest country neighbour of mine wants too a Family Bible, the larger the better, but second-handed, for he does not choose to give above ten shillings for the book. I want likewise for myself, as you can pick them up, second-handed or cheap, copies of Otway's Dramatic Works, Ben Jonson's, Dryden's, Congreve's, Wycherley's, Vanbrugh's, Cibber's, or any Dramatic Works of the more modern, Macklin, Garrick, Foote, Colman, or Sheridan. A good copy too of Molière, in French, I much want. Any other good dramatic authors in that language I want also; but comic authors chiefly, though I should wish to have Racine, Corneille, and Voltaire too. I am in no hurry for all or any of these, but if you accidentally meet with them very cheap, get them for me.

And now, to quit the dry walk of business, how do you do, my dear friend? and how is Mrs. Hill ? I trust, if now and then not so *elegantly* handsome, at least as amiable, and sings as divinely as ever. My good wife too has a charming " wood-note wild ;" now could we four————.

I am out of all patience with this vile world for one thing. Mankind are by nature benevolent creatures, except in a few scoundrelly instances.

I do not think that avarice of the good things we chance to have is born with us ; but we are placed here amid so much nakedness, and hunger, and poverty, and want, that we are under a cursed necessity of studying selfishness, in order that we may exist ! Still there are, in every age, a few souls, that all the wants and woes of life cannot debase to selfishness, or even to the necessary alloy of caution and prudence. If ever I am in danger of vanity, it is when I contemplate myself on this side of my disposition and character. God knows I am no saint; I have a whole host of follies and sins to answer for; but if I could, and I believe I do it as far as I can, I would wipe away all tears from all eyes. Adieu !

R. B.

No. CCIX.

TO MRS. DUNLOP.

ELLISLAND, 10*th April,* 1790.

I HAVE just now, my ever honoured friend, enjoyed a very high luxury, in reading a paper of the " Lounger." You know my national prejudices. I have often read and admired the " Spectator," " Adventurer," "Rambler," and " World ;" but still with a certain regret, that they were so thoroughly and entirely English. Alas ! have I often said to myself, what are all the boasted advantages which my country reaps from the union, that can counterbalance the annihilation of her independence, and even her very name ! I often repeat that couplet of my favourite poet, Goldsmith—

> " ———— States of native liberty possest,
> Tho' very poor, may yet be very blest."

Nothing can reconcile me to the common terms, " English ambassador, English court," &c. And I am out of all patience to see that equivocal character, Hastings, impeached by " the Commons of England." Tell me, my friend, is this weak prejudice ? I believe in my conscience such ideas as " my country ; her independence ; her honour ; the illustrious names that mark the history of my native land ;" &c.—I believe these, among your *men of the world*, men who in fact guide for the most part and govern our world, are looked on as so many modifications of wrongheadedness. They know the use of bawling out such terms, to rouse or lead the rabble ; but for their own private use, with almost all the *able statesmen* that ever existed, or now exist, when they talk of right and wrong, they only mean proper and improper ; and their measure of conduct is, not what they ought, but what they dare. For the truth of this I shall not ransack the history of nations, but appeal to one of the ablest judges of man that ever lived—the celebrated Earl of Chesterfield. In fact, a man who could thoroughly control his vices whenever they interfered with his interests, and who could completely put on the appearance of every virtue as often as it suited his purposes, is, on the Stanhopian plan, the *perfect man ;* a man to lead nations. But are great abilities,

complete without a flaw, and polished without a blemish, the standard of human excellence? This is certainly the staunch opinion of *men of the world;* but I call on honour, virtue, and worth, to give the Stygian doctrine a loud negative! However, this must be allowed, that, if you abstract from man the idea of an existence beyond the grave, *then* the true measure of human conduct is *proper* and *improper:* virtue and vice, as dispositions of the heart, are, in that case, of scarcely the same import and value to the world at large as harmony and discord in the modifications of sound; and a delicate sense of honour, like a nice ear for music, though it may sometimes give the possessor an ecstacy unknown to the coarser organs of the herd, yet, considering the harsh gratings and inharmonic jars in this ill-tuned state of being, it is odds but the individual world be as happy, and certainly would be as much respected by the true judges of society, as it would then stand, without either a good ear or a good heart.

You must know I have just met with the "Mirror" and "Lounger" for the first time, and I am quite in raptures with them: I should be glad to have your opinion of some of the papers. The one I have just read, "Lounger," No. 61, has cost me more honest tears than anything I have read a long time. Mackenzie has been called the Addison of the Scots, and, in my opinion, Addison would not be hurt at the comparison. If he has not Addison's exquisite humour, he as certainly outdoes him in the tender and the pathetic. His "Man of Feeling" (but I am not counsel learned in the laws of criticism) I estimate as the first performance in its kind I ever saw. From what book, moral or even pious, will the susceptible young mind receive impressions more congenial to humanity and kindness, generosity and benevolence—in short, more of all that ennobles the soul to herself, or endears her to others—than from the simple affecting tale of poor Harley?

Still, with all my admiration of Mackenzie's writings, I do not know if they are the fittest reading for a young man who is about to set out, as the phrase is, to make his way into life. Do not you think, Madam, that among the few favoured of Heaven in the structure of their minds (for such there certainly are) there may be a purity, a tenderness, a dignity, an elegance of soul, which are of no use, nay, in some degree, absolutely disqualifying, for the truly important business of making a man's way into life? If I am not much mistaken, my gallant young friend A——— is very much under these disqualifications: and for the young females of a family I could mention, well may they excite parental solicitude; for I, a common acquaintance, or, as my vanity will have it, an humble friend, have often trembled for a turn of mind which may render them eminently happy—or peculiarly miserable!

I have been manufacturing some verses lately; but as I have got the most hurried season of Excise business over, I hope to have more leisure to transcribe anything that may show how much I have the honour to be, Madam,

Yours, &c.

R. B.

No. CCX.

TO COLLECTOR MITCHELL.

[This letter refers to an Excise case, a farmer having reclaimed against a fine imposed by Collector Mitchell.]

SIR,　　　　　　　　　　　　　　　　　　ELLISLAND, 1790.

　　I shall not fail to wait on Captain Riddel to-night—I wish and pray that the Goddess of Justice herself would appear to-morrow among our hon. gentlemen, merely to give them a word in their ear that mercy to the thief is injustice to the honest man. For my part, I have galloped over my ten parishes these four days, until this moment that I am just alighted, or, rather, that my poor jackass-skeleton of a horse has let me down, for the miserable devil has been on his knees half a score of times within the last twenty miles, telling me in his own way, "Behold, am not I thy faithful jade of a horse, on which thou hast ridden these many years!"

　　In short, Sir, I have broke my horse's wind, and almost broke my own neck, besides some injuries in a part that shall be nameless, owing to a hardhearted stone for a saddle. I find that every offender has so many great men to espouse his cause, that I shall not be surprised if I am not committed to the stronghold of the law to-morrow for insolence to the dear friends of the gentlemen of the country.

　　　　　　　　　I have the honour to be, Sir,

　　　　　　　　　　　　　Your obliged and obedient humble

　　　　　　　　　　　　　　　　　　　　R. B.

No. CCXI.

TO DR. MOORE.

SIR,　　　　　　　DUMFRIES, EXCISE-OFFICE, 14*th July*, 1790.

　　Coming into town this morning to attend my duty in this office, it being collection-day, I met with a gentleman who tells me he is on his way to London ; so I take the opportunity of writing to you, as franking is at present under a temporary death. I shall have some snatches of leisure through the day, amid our horrid business and bustle, and I shall improve them as well as I can ; but let my letter be as stupid as * * * *, as miscellaneous as a newspaper, as short as a hungry grace-before-meat, or as long as a law-paper in the Douglas cause, as ill-spelt as country John's *billet-doux*, or as unsightly a scrawl as Betty Byre-Mucker's answer to it, I hope, considering circumstances, you will forgive it ; and as it will put you to no expense of postage, I shall have the less reflection about it.

　　I am sadly ungrateful in not returning you my thanks for your most valuable present, "Zeluco." In fact, you are in some degree blameable for my neglect. You were pleased to express a wish for my opinion of the

work, which so flattered me, that nothing less would serve my over-weening fancy than a formal criticism on the book. In fact, I have gravely planned a comparative view of you, Fielding, Richardson, and Smollett, in your different qualities and merits as novel-writers. This, I own, betrays my ridiculous vanity, and I may probably never bring the business to bear ; and I am fond of the spirit young Elihu shews in the book of Job—" And I said, I will also declare my opinion." I have quite disfigured my copy of the book with my annotations. I never take it up without at the same time taking my pencil, and marking with asterisms, parentheses, &c. wherever I meet with an original thought, a nervous remark on life and manners, a remarkable well-turned period, or a character sketched with uncommon precision.

Though I should hardly think of fairly writing out my "Comparative View," I shall certainly trouble you with my remarks, such as they are.

I have just received from my gentleman that horrid summons in the book of Revelation—" That time shall be no more ! "

The little collection of sonnets [by Mrs. Charlotte Smith] have some charming poetry in them. If *indeed* I am indebted to the fair author for the book, and not, as I rather suspect, to a celebrated author of the other sex, I should certainly have written to the lady, with my grateful acknow-ledgments, and my own ideas of the comparative excellence of her pieces. I would do this last, not from any vanity of thinking that my remarks could be of much consequence to Mrs. Smith, but merely from my own feelings as an author, doing as I would be done by.—R. B.

No. CCXII.

TO MR. MURDOCH,

TEACHER OF FRENCH, LONDON.

MY DEAR SIR,   ELLISLAND, *July 16th*, 1790.

I received a letter from you a long time ago, but unfortunately, as it was in the time of my peregrinations and journeyings through Scotland, I mislaid or lost it, and, by consequence, your direction along with it. Luckily my good star brought me acquainted with Mr. Kennedy, who I understand is an acquaintance of yours ; and by his means and mediation I hope to replace that link which my unfortunate negligence had so unluckily broke in the chain of our correspondence. I was the more vexed at the vile accident, as my brother William, a journeyman saddler, has been for some time in London ; and wished above all things for your direction, that he might have paid his respects to his father's friend.

His last address he sent me was, " Wm. Burns, at Mr. Barber's, saddler, No. 181, Strand." I writ him by Mr. Kennedy, but neglected to ask him for your address ; so, if you find a spare half-minute, please let my brother know by a card where and when he will find you, and the poor

fellow will joyfully wait on you, as one of the few surviving friends of the man whose name, and Christian name too, he has the honour to bear.

The next letter I write you shall be a long one ; I have much to tell you of " hair-breadth 'scapes in th' imminent deadly breach," with all the eventful history of a life,* the early years of which owed so much to your kind tutorage ; but this at an hour of leisure. My kindest compliments to Mrs. Murdoch and family.

I am ever, my dear Sir,
Your obliged Friend,
R. B.

No. CCXIII.

TO MR. McMURDO.

Sir,   ELLISLAND, *2d August,* 1790.
    Now that you are over with the sirens of Flattery, the harpies of Corruption, and the furies of Ambition, these infernal deities that on all sides, and in all parties, preside over the villanous business of Politics, permit a rustic muse of your acquaintance to do her best to sooth you with a song.†

You knew Henderson—I have not flattered his memory.

I have the honour to be, Sir,
Your obliged humble Servant,
R. B.

No. CCXIV.

TO MRS. DUNLOP.

DEAR MADAM,   *8th August,* 1790.
    After a long day's toil, plague, and care, I sit down to write to you. Ask me not why I have delayed it so long. It was owing to hurry, indolence, and fifty other things ; in short, to anything—but forgetfulness of *la plus aimable de son sexe.* By the by, you are indebted your best courtesy to me for this last compliment ; as I pay it from my sincere conviction of its truth—a quality rather rare in compliments of these grinning, bowing, scraping times.

Well, I hope writing to *you* will ease a little my troubled soul. Sorely has it been bruised to-day ! A *ci-devant* friend of mine, and an intimate acquaintance of yours, has given my feelings a wound that I perceive will gangrene dangerously ere it cure. He has wounded my pride !—R. B.

---

* This promised account of himself, as far as is known, was never written.
† A poem on the death of Captain Matthew Henderson, with whom Burns was acquainted when in Edinburgh. Henderson died Nov. 21, 1788.

No. CCXV.

TO MR. CUNNINGHAM.

ELLISLAND, *8th August,* 1788.

FORGIVE me, my once dear, and ever dear friend, my seeming negligence. You cannot sit down and fancy the busy life I lead.

I laid down my goose-feather to beat my brains for an apt simile, and
had some thoughts of a country grannum at a family christening ; a bride
on the market-day before her marriage; or a tavern-keeper at an election-
dinner ; but the resemblance that hits my fancy best is that blackguard
miscreant Satan, who roams about like a roaring lion, seeking, *searching*
whom he may devour. However, tossed about as I am, if I choose (and
who would not choose ?) to bind down with the crampets of Attention the
brazen foundation of Integrity, I may rear up the superstructure of Independence, and from its daring turrets bid defiance to the storms of fate.
And is not this a "consummation devoutly to be wished"?

> "Thy spirit, Independence, let me share;
> Lord of the lion-heart and eagle-eye !
> Thy steps I follow with my bosom bare,
> Nor heed the storm that howls along the sky !"

Are not these noble verses ? They are the introduction of Smollett's
Ode to Independence : if you have not seen the poem, I will send it to
you. How wretched is the man that hangs on by the favours of the
great ! To shrink from every dignity of man at the approach of a lordly
piece of self-consequence, who, amid all his tinsel glitter and stately
hauteur, is but a creature formed as thou art—and perhaps not so well
formed as thou art—came into the world a puling infant as thou didst,
and must go out of it as all men must, a naked corse.—R. B.

No. CCXVI.

TO DR. ANDERSON.

[Dr. James Anderson was editor of the "Bee," and through Dr. Blacklock had
asked Burns to become a contributor.]

SIR,   [1790.]

I am much indebted to my worthy friend Dr. Blacklock for introducing me to a gentleman of Dr. Anderson's celebrity; but when you do
me the honour to ask my assistance in your proposed publication, alas,
Sir ! you might as well expect to cheapen a little honesty at the sign of
an advocate's wig, or humility under the Geneva band. I am a miserable
hurried devil, worn to the marrow in the friction of holding the noses of
the poor publicans to the grindstone of the Excise ! and, like Milton's
Satan, for private reasons, am forced

> "To do what yet tho' damn'd I would abhor;"

—and except a couplet or two of honest execration * * * *—R. B.

No. CCXVII.

TO CRAUFORD TAIT, ESQ.

EDINBURGH.

DEAR SIR,   ELLISLAND, 15*th October,* 1790.

Allow me to introduce to your acquaintance the bearer, Mr. Wm. Duncan, a friend of mine, whom I have long known and long loved. His father, whose only son he is, has a decent little property in Ayrshire, and has bred the young man to the law, in which department he comes up an adventurer to your good town. I shall give you my friend's character in two words : as to his head, he has talents enough and more than enough, for common life ; as to his heart, when Nature had kneaded the kindly clay that composes it, she said, " I can no more."

You, my good Sir, were born under kinder stars ; but your fraternal sympathy, I well know, can enter into the feelings of the young man who goes into life with the laudable ambition to *do* something, and to *be* something among his fellow-creatures, but whom the consciousness of friendless obscurity presses to the earth and wounds to the soul !

Even the fairest of his virtues are against him. That independent spirit and that ingenuous modesty—qualities inseparable from a noble mind—are, with the million, circumstances not a little disqualifying. What pleasure is in the power of the fortunate and the happy, by their notice and patronage, to brighten the countenance and glad the heart of such depressed youth ! I am not so angry with mankind for their deaf economy of the purse ; the goods of this world cannot be divided without being lessened : but why be a niggard of that which bestows bliss on a fellow-creature, yet takes nothing from our own means of enjoyment ? We wrap ourselves up in the cloak of our own better fortune, and turn away our eyes, lest the wants and woes of our brother-mortals should disturb the selfish apathy of our souls !

I am the worst hand in the world at asking a favour. That indirect address, that insinuating implication, which, without any positive request, plainly expresses your wish, is a talent not to be acquired at a plough-tail. Tell me then, for you can, in what periphrasis of language, in what circumvolution of phrase, I shall envelope, yet not conceal, this plain story : "My dear Mr. Tait, my friend Mr. Duncan, whom I have the pleasure of introducing to you, is a young lad of your own profession, and a gentleman of much modesty and great worth. Perhaps it may be in your power to assist him in the, to him, important consideration of getting a place : but, at all events, your notice and acquaintance will be a very great acquisition to him ; and I dare pledge myself that he will never disgrace your favour."

You may possibly be surprised, Sir, at such a letter from me ; 'tis, I own, in the usual way of calculating these matters, more than our acquaintance entitles me to ; but my answer is short : Of all the men at your time of life whom I knew in Edinburgh, you are the most accessible on the side on which I have assailed you. You are very much altered indeed from

what you were when I knew you, if generosity point the path you will not tread, or humanity call to you in vain.

As to myself, a being to whose interest I believe you are still a well wisher, I am here, breathing at all times, thinking sometimes, and rhyming now and then. Every situation has its share of the cares and pains of life, and my situation I am persuaded has a full ordinary allowance of its pleasures and enjoyments.

My best compliments to your father and Miss Tait. If you have an opportunity, please remember me in the solemn league and covenant of friendship to Mrs. Lewis Hay. I am a wretch for not writing her ; but I am so hackneyed with self-accusation in that way, that my conscience lies in my bosom with scarce the sensibility of an oyster in its shell. Where is Lady McKenzie? wherever she is, God bless her ! I likewise beg leave to trouble you with compliments to Mr. Wm. Hamilton, Mrs. Hamilton and family, and Mrs. Chalmers, when you are in that country. Should you meet with Miss Nimmo, please remember me kindly to her.

R. B.

No. CCXVIII.

TO ———

[This letter was perhaps addressed to Gavin Hamilton.]

DEAR SIR, ELLISLAND, 1790.

Whether in the way of my trade I can be of any service to the Rev. Doctor is, I fear, very doubtful. Ajax's shield consisted, I think, of seven bull-hides and a plate of brass, which altogether set Hector's utmost force at defiance. Alas ! I am not a Hector, and the worthy Doctor's foes are as securely armed as Ajax was. Ignorance, superstition, bigotry, stupidity, malevolence, self-conceit, envy—all strongly bound in a massy frame of brazen impudence. Good God, Sir ! to such a shield, humour is the peck of a sparrow, and satire the pop-gun of a school-boy. Creation-disgracing *scélérats* such as they God only can mend, and the devil only can punish. In the comprehending way of Caligula, I wish they all had but one neck. I feel impotent as a child to the ardour of my wishes ! O for a withering curse to blast the germins of their wicked machinations. O for a poisonous tornado, winged from the torrid zone of Tartarus, to sweep the spreading crop of their villanous contrivances to the lowest hell !—R. B.

No. CCXIX.

TO MRS. DUNLOP.

ELLISLAND, *November,* 1790.

"As cold waters to a thirsty soul, so is good news from a far country." Fate has long owed me a letter of good news from you, in return for the many tidings of sorrow which I have received. In this instance I most

cordially obey the Apostle—" Rejoice with them that do rejoice." For me. *to sing* for joy, is no new thing ; but to *preach* for joy, as I have done in the commencement of this epistle, is a pitch of extravagant rapture to which I never rose before.

I read your letter—I literally jumped for joy : how could such a mercurial creature as a poet lumpishly keep his seat on the receipt of the best news from his best friend ? I seized my gilt-headed Wangee rod, an instrument indispensably necessary in my left hand, in the moment of inspiration and rapture ; and stride, stride—quick and quicker—out skipt I among the broomy banks of Nith to muse over my joy by retail. To keep within the bounds of prose was impossible. Mrs. Little's* is a more elegant, but not a more sincere, compliment to the sweet little fellow than I, extempore almost, poured out to him in the following verses :—

> " Sweet flow'ret, pledge o' meikle love,
>   And ward o' mony a prayer,
> What heart o' stane wad thou na move,
>   Sae helpless, sweet, an' fair ?
> November hirples o'er the lea
>   Chill on thy lovely form ;
> But gane, alas ! the shelt'ring tree
>   Should shield thee frae the storm. "

I am much flattered by your approbation of my "Tam o' Shanter," which you express in your former letter ; though, by the by, you load me in that said letter with accusations heavy and many ; to all which I plead, *not guilty !* Your book is, I hear, on the road to reach me. As to printing of poetry, when you prepare it for the press, you have only to spell it right, and place the capital letters properly : as to the punctuation, the printers do that themselves.—R. B.

No. CCXX.

TO MR. PETER HILL.

ELLISLAND, *17th January,* 1791.

TAKE these two guineas, and place them over against that d-mned account of yours, which has gagged my mouth these five or six months ! I can as little write good things as apologies to the man I owe money to. O the supreme curse of making three guineas do the business of five ! Not all the labours of Hercules, not all the Hebrews' three centuries of Egyptian bondage, were such an insuperable business, such an infernal task ! Poverty ! thou half-sister of death, thou cousin-german of hell ! where shall I find force of execration equal to the amplitude of thy demerits ? Oppressed by thee, the venerable ancient, grown hoary in the practice of every virtue, laden with years and wretchedness, implores a little, little aid to support his existence from a stony-hearted son of Mammon, whose sun of prosperity never knew a cloud ; and is by him denied and insulted. Oppressed by thee, the man of sentiment, whose

---

* The poetical milkmaid.

heart glows with independence and melts with sensibility, inly pines under the neglect, or writhes in bitterness of soul under the contumely, of arrogant, unfeeling wealth. Oppressed by thee, the son of genius, whose ill-starred ambition plants him at the tables of the fashionable and polite, must see in suffering silence his remark neglected and his person despised, while shallow greatness, in his idiot attempts at wit, shall meet with countenance and applause. Nor is it only the family of worth that have reason to complain of thee : the children of folly and vice, though in common with thee the offspring of evil, smart equally under thy rod. Owing to thee, the man of unfortunate disposition and neglected education is condemned as a fool for his dissipation ; despised and shunned as a needy wretch, when his follies, as usual, bring him to want ; and when his unprincipled necessities drive him to dishonest practices, he is abhorred as a miscreant, and perishes by the justice of his country. But far otherwise is the lot of the man of family and fortune. *His* early follies and extravagance are spirit and fire ; *his* consequent wants are the embarrassments of an honest fellow ; and when, to remedy the matter, he has gained a legal commission to plunder distant provinces, or massacre peaceful nations, he returns, perhaps, laden with the spoils of rapine and murder, lives wicked and respected, and dies a scoundrel and a lord. Nay, worst of all, alas ! for helpless woman. The needy prostitute, who has shivered at the corner of the street, waiting to earn the wages of casual prostitution, is left neglected and insulted, ridden down by the chariot-wheels of the coroneted RIP, hurrying on to the guilty assignation ; she who, without the same necessities to plead, riots nightly in the same guilty trade.

Well ! divines may say of it what they please, but execration is to the mind what phlebotomy is to the body : the vital sluices of both are wonderfully relieved by their respective evacuations.—R. B.

No. CCXXI.

TO A. F. TYTLER, ESQ.*

SIR,   ELLISLAND, *February* [*April?*], 1791.

Nothing less than the unfortunate accident I have met with could have prevented my grateful acknowledgments for your letter. His own favourite poem, and that an essay in the walk of the Muses entirely new to him, where consequently his hopes and fears were on the most anxious alarm for his success in the attempt,—to have that poem so much applauded by one of the first judges, was the most delicious vibration that ever thrilled along the heart-strings of a poor poet. However, Providence, to keep up the proper proportion of evil with the good, which it seems is necessary in this sublunary state, thought proper to check my exultation by a very serious misfortune. A day or two after I received your letter my horse came down with me and broke my right arm. As this is the first service my arm has done me since its disaster, I find myself unable to do more than just in general terms thank you for this additional instance of

* Lord Woodhouslee.

your patronage and friendship. As to the faults you detected in the piece, they are truly there : one of them, the hit at the lawyer and priest, I shall cut out ; as to the falling off in the catastrophe, for the reason you justly adduce, it cannot easily be remedied. Your approbation, Sir, has given me such additional spirits to persevere in this species of poetic composition, that I am already revolving two or three stories in my fancy. If I can bring these floating ideas to bear any kind of embodied form, it will give me an additional opportunity of assuring you how much I have the honour to be, &c. --R. B.

No. CCXXII.

TO MRS. DUNLOP.

ELLISLAND, *7th Feb.* [*April ?*], 1791.

WHEN I tell you, Madam, that by a fall, not from my horse, but with my horse,* I have been a cripple some time, and that this is the first day my arm and hand have been able to serve me in writing, you will allow that it is too good an apology for my seemingly ungrateful silence. I am now getting better, and am able to rhyme a little, which implies some tolerable ease ; as I cannot think that the most poetic genius is able to compose on the rack.

I do not remember if ever I mentioned to you my having an idea of composing an elegy on the late Miss Burnet of Monboddo. I had the honour of being pretty well acquainted with her, and have seldom felt so much at the loss of an acquaintance, as when I heard that so amiable and accomplished a piece of God's work was no more. I have as yet gone no farther than the following fragment, of which please let me have your opinion. You know that elegy is a subject so much exhausted, that any new idea on the business is not to be expected : 'tis well if we can place an old idea in a new light. How far I have succeeded as to this last you will judge from what follows.

[Here comes the Elegy.]

I have proceeded no further.

Your kind letter, with your kind *remembrance* of your godson, came safe. This last, Madam, is scarcely what my pride can bear. As to the little fellow, he is, partiality apart, the finest boy I have of a long time seen. He is now seventeen months old, has the small-pox and measles over, has cut several teeth, and never had a grain of doctor's drugs in his bowels.

I am truly happy to hear that the " little floweret " is blooming so fresh and fair, and that the " mother plant " is rather recovering her drooping head. Soon and well may her " cruel wounds " be healed ! I have written thus far with a good deal of difficulty. When I get a little abler you shall hear farther from,

Madam, yours,

R. B.

* He had a bad fall and broke his right arm.

No. CCXXIII.

TO THE REV. ARCH. ALISON.

[The Rev. Arch. Alison, a clergyman of the English Church, is best known as the author of "An Essay on Taste," and as the father of the late Sir Archibald Alison, the historian of Europe. Dugald Stewart has referred to this letter as proof that Burns, imperfectly educated as he was, had formed "a distinct conception of the general principles of the doctrine of association."]

SIR,   ELLISLAND, *near Dumfries*, 14*th Feb.* 1791.

You must by this time have set me down as one of the most ungrateful of men. You did me the honour to present me with a book which does honour to science and the intellectual powers of man, and I have not even so much as acknowledged the receipt of it. The fact is, you yourself are to blame for it. Flattered as I was by your telling me that you wished to have my opinion of the work, the old spiritual enemy of mankind, who knows well that vanity is one of the sins that most easily beset me, put it into my head to ponder over the performance with the look-out of a critic, and to draw up, forsooth ! a deep learned digest of strictures on a composition of which, in fact, until I read the book, I did not even know the first principles. I own, Sir, that at first glance several of your propositions startled me as paradoxical. That the martial clangor of a trumpet had something in it vastly more grand, heroic, and sublime, than the twingle-twangle of a jews-harp ; that the delicate flexure of a rose-twig, when the half-blown flower is heavy with the tears of the dawn, was infinitely more beautiful and elegant than the upright stub of a burdock, and that from something innate and independent of all associations of ideas ;—these I had set down as irrefragable, orthodox truths, until perusing your book shook my faith. In short, Sir, except Euclid's "Elements of Geometry," which I made a shift to unravel by my father's fireside, in the winter evenings of the first season I held the plough, I never read a book which gave me such a quantum of information, and added so much to my stock of ideas, as your "Essays on the Principles of Taste." One thing, Sir, you must forgive my mentioning as an uncommon merit in the work—I mean the language. To clothe abstract philosophy in elegance of style sounds something like a contradiction in terms ; but you have convinced me that they are quite compatible.

I enclose you some poetic bagatelles of my late composition. The one in print is my first essay in the way of telling a tale.

I am, Sir, &c.

R. B.

No. CCXXIV.

TO DR. MOORE.

ELLISLAND, 28*th January*, 1791.

I DO not know, Sir, whether you are a subscriber to Grose's "Antiquities of Scotland." If you are, the enclosed poem will not be altogether new to you. Captain Grose did me the favour to send me a dozen copies of the

proof sheet, of which this is one. Should you have read the piece before, still this will answer the principal end I have in view : it will give me another opportunity of thanking you for all your goodness to the rustic bard ; and also of showing you, that the abilities you have been pleased to commend and patronize are still employed in the way you wish.

The "Elegy on Captain Henderson" is a tribute to the memory of a man I loved much. Poets have in this the same advantage as Roman Catholics ; they can be of service to their friends after they have passed that bourne where all other kindness ceases to be of avail. Whether, after all, either the one or the other be of any real service to the dead is, I fear, very problematical ; but I am sure they are highly gratifying to the living : and as a very orthodox text, I forget where, in Scripture says, "Whatsoever is not of faith is sin," so say I, Whatsoever is not detrimental to society, and is of positive enjoyment, is of God, the Giver of all good things, and ought to be received and enjoyed by His creatures with thankful delight. As almost all my religious tenets originate from my heart, I am wonderfully pleased with the idea, that I can still keep up a tender intercourse with the dearly beloved friend, or still more dearly beloved mistress, who is gone to the world of spirits.

The ballad on Queen Mary was begun while I was busy with Percy's "Reliques of English Poetry." By the way, how much is every honest heart, which has a tincture of Caledonian prejudice, obliged to you for your glorious story of Buchanan and Targe ! 'Twas an unequivocal proof of your loyal gallantry of soul, giving Targe the victory. I should have been mortified to the ground if you had not.*

I have just read over, once more of many times, your "Zeluco." I marked with my pencil, as I went along, every passage that pleased me particularly above the rest ; and one or two, I think, which, with humble deference, I am disposed to think unequal to the merits of the book. I have sometimes thought to transcribe these marked passages, or at least so much of them as to point where they are, and send them to you. Original strokes that strongly depict the human heart is your and Fielding's province, beyond any other novelist I have ever perused. Richardson, indeed, might perhaps be excepted ; but, unhappily, his *dramatis personæ* are beings of another world ; and however they may captivate the unexperienced, romantic fancy of a boy or a girl, they will ever, in proportion as we have made human nature our study, dissatisfy our riper years.

As to my private concerns, I am going on, a mighty tax-gatherer before the Lord, and have lately had the interest to get myself ranked on the list of Excise as a supervisor. I am not yet employed as such, but in a few years I shall fall into the file of supervisorship by seniority. I have had an immense loss in the death of the Earl of Glencairn, the patron from whom all my fame and fortune took its rise. Independent of my grateful attachment to him, which was indeed so strong that it pervaded my very soul, and was entwined with the thread of my existence, so soon as the

---

* Targe, representing the Cavalier Highland spirit, overcomes Buchanan, representing the colder Lowland feeling in a quarrel about Queen Mary.

Prince's friends had got in (and every dog, you know, has his day, my getting forward in the Excise would have been an easier business than otherwise it will be. Though this was a consummation devoutly to be wished, yet, thank Heaven, I can live and rhyme as I am ; and as to my boys, poor little fellows ! if I cannot place them on as high an elevation in life as I could wish, I shall, if I am favoured so much of the Disposer of events as to see that period, fix them on as broad and independent a basis as possible. Among the many wise adages which have been treasured up by our Scottish ancestors, this is one of the best, *Better be the head o' the commonalty than the tail o' the gentry.*

But I am got on a subject which, however interesting to me, is of no manner of consequence to you ; so I shall give you a short poem on the other page, and close this with assuring you how sincerely I have the honour to be,

Yours, &c.

R. B.

Written on the blank leaf of a book, which I presented to a very young lady, whom I had formerly characterised under the denomination of *The Rose-bud.*

No. CCXXV.

TO MR. CUNNINGHAM.

ELLISLAND, *12th March,* 1791.

IF the foregoing piece* be worth your strictures, let me have them. For my own part, a thing that I have just composed always appears through a double portion of that partial medium in which an author will ever view his own works. I believe, in general, novelty has something in it that inebriates the fancy, and not unfrequently dissipates and fumes away like other intoxication, and leaves the poor patient, as usual, with an aching heart. A striking instance of this might be adduced in the revolution of many a hymeneal honeymoon. But lest I sink into stupid prose, and so sacrilegiously intrude on the office of my parish priest, I shall fill up the page in my own way, and give you another song of my late composition, which will appear perhaps in Johnson's work, as well as the former.

You must know a beautiful Jacobite air, "There'll never be peace till Jamie comes hame." When political combustion ceases to be the object of princes and patriots, it then, you know, becomes the lawful prey of historians and poets.

> " By yon castle wa' at the close of the day
> I heard a man sing, tho' his head it was gray ;
> And as he was singing, the tears fast down came—
> There'll never be peace till Jamie comes hame."

If you like the air, and if the stanzas hit your fancy, you cannot imagine, my dear friend, how much you would oblige me, if, by the charms of your

---

* By this Burns means the annexed verses, " By yon castle wa'."

delightful voice, you would give my honest effusion to "the memory of joys that are passed" to the few friends whom you indulge in that pleasure. But I have scribbled on till I hear the clock has intimated the near approach of

> "That hour, o' night's black arch the key-stane."

So good-night to you! Sound be your sleep, and delectable your dreams! *Apropos*, how do you like this thought in a ballad I have just now on the *tapis*?—

> "I look to the west when I gae to rest,
>   That happy my dreams and my slumbers may be :
> Far, far in the west is he I lo'e best,
>   The lad that is dear to my babie and me."

Good-night, once more, and God bless you! –R. B.

No. CCXXVI.

TO MR. ALEXANDER DALZEL,

FACTOR, FINDLAYSTON.

[The poem was on the recent death of Lord Glencairn, for whom Mr. Dalzel had acted as factor.]

MY DEAR SIR,   ELLISLAND, *19th March,* 1791.
        I have taken the liberty to frank this letter to you, as it encloses an idle poem of mine, which I send you ; and, God knows, you may perhaps pay dear enough for it if you read it through. Not that this is my own opinion ; but the author, by the time he has composed and corrected his work, has quite pored away all his powers of critical discrimination.

I can easily guess from my own heart what you have felt on a late most melancholy event. God knows what I have suffered at the loss of my best friend, my first and dearest patron and benefactor; the man to whom I owe all that I am and have! I am gone into mourning for him, and with more sincerity of grief than I fear some will, who by nature's ties ought to feel on the occasion.

I will be exceedingly obliged to you indeed, to let me know the news of the noble family—how the poor mother and the two sisters support their loss. I had a packet of poetic bagatelles ready to send to Lady Betty, when I saw the fatal tidings in the newspaper. I see by the same channel that the honoured remains of my noble patron are designed to be brought to the family burial-place. Dare I trouble you to let me know privately before the day of interment, that I may cross the country, and steal among the crowd, to pay a tear to the last sight of my ever-revered benefactor? It will oblige me beyond expression.—R. B.

No. CCXXVII.

TO MRS. GRAHAM,

OF FINTRY.

[To Mrs. Graham the Poet afterwards presented the new edition of his poems, with these characteristic words written on one of the blank leaves : "It is probable, Madam, that this page may be read, when the hand that now writes it shall be mouldering in the dust. May it then bear witness, that I present you these volumes as a tribute of gratitude, on my part ardent and sincere, as your and Mr. Graham's goodness to me has been generous and noble ! May every child of yours, in the hour of need, find such a friend as I shall teach every child of mine that their father found in you.—ROBERT BURNS."]

MADAM, ELLISLAND, 1791.

Whether it is that the story of our Mary Queen of Scots, has a peculiar effect on the feelings of a poet, or whether I have in the enclosed ballad succeeded beyond my usual poetic success, I know not ; but it has pleased me beyond any effort o₁ my muse for a good while past : on that account I enclose it particularly to you. It is true, the purity of my motives may be suspected. I am already deeply indebted to Mr. Graham's goodness ; and what, *in the usual ways of men*, is of infinitely greater importance, Mr. G. can do me service of the utmost importance in time to come. I was born a poor dog ; and however I may occasionally pick a better bone than I used to do, I know I must live and die poor : but I will indulge the flattering faith that my poetry will considerably outlive my poverty ; and without any fustian affectation of spirit, I can promise and affirm, that it must be no ordinary craving of the latter shall ever make me do anything injurious to the honest fame of the former. Whatever may be my failings, for failings are a part of human nature, may they ever be those of a generous heart and an independent mind ! It is no fault of mine that I was born to dependence ; nor is it Mr. Graham's chiefest praise that he can command influence : but it is his merit to bestow, not only with the kindness of a brother, but with the politeness of a gentleman ; and I trust it shall be mine, to receive with thankfulness and remember with undiminished gratitude.—R. B.

No. CCXXVIII.

TO THE REV. G. BAIRD.

[This is an answer to an application to revise the poems of Michael Bruce, and to add some verses of his own to an edition which was about to be published for the benefit of Bruce's mother, then 80 years of age, poor and helpless.]

REVEREND SIR, ELLISLAND, 1791.

Why did you, my dear Sir, write to me in such a hesitating style on the business of poor Bruce ? Don't I know, and have I not felt, the many

ills, the peculiar ills, that poetic flesh is heir to? You shall have your choice of all the unpublished poems I have; and had your letter had my direction, so as to have reached me sooner (it only came to my hand this moment), I should have directly put you out of suspense on the subject. I only ask, that some prefatory advertisement in the book, as well as the subscription bills, may bear, that the publication is solely for the benefit of Bruce's mother. I would not put it in the power of ignorance to surmise, or malice to insinuate, that I clubbed a share in the work from mercenary motives. Nor need you give me credit for any remarkable generosity in my part of the business. I have such a host of peccadilloes, failings, follies, and backslidings (anybody but myself might perhaps give some of them a worse appellation), that by way of some balance, however trifling, in the account, I am fain to do any good that occurs in my very limited power to a fellow-creature, just for the selfish purpose of clearing a little the vista of retrospection.—R. B.

No. CCXXIX.

TO MRS. DUNLOP.

ELLISLAND, 11*th April*, 1791.

I AM once more able, my honoured friend, to return you, with my own hand, thanks for the many instances of your friendship, and particularly for your kind anxiety in this last disaster that my evil genius had in store for me. However, life is chequered—joy and sorrow—for on Saturday morning last Mrs. Burns made me a present of a fine boy ; rather stouter but not so handsome as your godson was at his time of life. Indeed I look on your little namesake to be my *chef d'œuvre* in that species of manufacture, as I look on "Tam o' Shanter" to be my standard performance in the poetical line. 'Tis true, both the one and the other discover a spice of roguish waggery that might perhaps be as well spared ; but then they also show, in my opinion, a force of genius and a finishing polish that I despair of ever excelling. Mrs. Burns is getting stout again, and laid as lustily about her to-day at breakfast as a reaper from the corn-ridge. That is the peculiar privilege and blessing of our hale, sprightly damsels, that are bred among the *hay and heather*. We cannot hope for that highly polished mind, that charming delicacy of soul, which is found among the female world in the more elevated stations of life, and which is certainly by far the most bewitching charm in the famous cestus of Venus. It is indeed such an inestimable treasure, that, where it can be had in its native heavenly purity, unstained by some one or other of the many shades of affectation, and unalloyed by some one or other of the many species of caprice, I declare to Heaven I should think it cheaply purchased at the expense of every other earthly good ! But as this angelic creature is, I am afraid, extremely rare in any station and rank of life, and totally denied to such a humble one as mine, we meaner mortals must put up with the next rank of female excellence. As fine a figure and face we can produce as any rank of life whatever ; rustic, native grace ; unaffected

modesty and unsullied purity ; nature's mother-wit and the rudiments of
taste ; a simplicity of soul, unsuspicious of, because unacquainted with,
the crooked ways of a selfish, interested, disingenuous world ; and, the
dearest charm of all the rest, a yielding sweetness of disposition and a
generous warmth of heart, grateful for love on our part and ardently
glowing with a more than equal return ; these, with a healthy frame, a
sound, vigorous constitution, which your higher ranks can scarcely ever
hope to enjoy, are the charms of lovely woman in my humble walk
of life.

This is the greatest effort my broken arm has yet made. Do let me
hear, by first post, how *cher petit Monsieur* comes on with his small-pox.
May Almighty Goodness preserve and restore him !—R. B.

No. CCXXX.

TO —————

Dear Sir,   Ellisland, 1791.

I am exceedingly to blame in not writing you long ago ; but the
truth is, that I am the most indolent of all human beings ; and when I
matriculate in the herald's office, I intend that my supporters shall be two
sloths, my crest a slow-worm, and the motto, " Deil tak' the foremost."
So much by way of apology for not thanking you sooner for your kind
execution of my commission.—R. B.

No. CCXXXI.

TO —————

[This tremendous scolding is supposed to have been sent to a snarling critic who
had complained of the false grammar and uncouthness of Burns's poems.]

                                                            Ellisland, 1791.

Thou eunuch of language : thou Englishman, who never was south the
Tweed : thou servile echo of fashionable barbarisms : thou quack, vend-
ing the nostrums of empirical elocution : thou marriage-maker between
vowels and consonants, on the Gretna-green of caprice : thou cobbler,
botching the flimsy socks of bombast oratory : thou blacksmith, hammering the rivets of absurdity : thou butcher, embruing thy hands in the
bowels of orthography : thou arch-heretic in pronunciation : thou pitch-
pipe of affected emphasis : thou carpenter, mortising the awkward joints
of jarring sentences : thou squeaking dissonance of cadence : thou pimp of
gender : thou Lyon Herald to silly etymology : thou antipode of grammar : thou executioner of construction : thou brood of the speech-dis-
tracting builders of the Tower of Babel : thou lingual confusion worse
confounded : thou scape-gallows from the land of syntax : thou scavenger
of mode and tense : thou murderous accoucheur of infant learning : thou
ignis fatuus, misleading the steps of benighted ignorance : thou pickle-

herring in the puppet-show of nonsense : thou faithful recorder of barbarous idiom : thou persecutor of syllabication : thou baleful meteor,
foretelling and facilitating the rapid approach of Nox and Erebus.—R. B.

No. CCXXXII.

TO MR. CUNNINGHAM.

11th June, 1791.

LET me interest you, my dear Cunningham, in behalf of the gentleman
who waits on you with this. He is a Mr. Clarke, of Moffat, principal
schoolmaster there, and is at present suffering severely under the persecution of one or two powerful individuals of his employers. He is accused of harshness to boys that were placed under his care. God help
the teacher, if a man of sensibility and genius, and such is my friend
Clarke, when a booby father presents him with his booby son, and insists
on lighting up the rays of science in a fellow's head whose skull is impervious and inaccessible by any other way than a positive fracture with a
cudgel, a fellow whom, in fact, it savours of impiety to attempt making
a scholar of, as he has been marked a blockhead in the book of fate, at
the almighty fiat of his Creator.

The patrons of Moffat School are the ministers, magistrates, and town-
council of Edinburgh ; and as the business comes now before them, let me
beg my dearest friend to do everything in his power to serve the interests
of a man of genius and worth, and a man whom I particularly respect
and esteem. You know some good fellows among the magistracy and
council, but particularly you have much to say with a reverend gentleman,
to whom you have the honour of being very nearly related, and whom this
country and age have had the honour to produce. I need not name the
historian of Charles V. I tell him, through the medium of his nephew's
influence, that Mr. Clarke is a gentleman who will not disgrace even his
patronage. I know the merits of the cause thoroughly, and say it, that
my friend is falling a sacrifice to prejudiced ignorance.

God help the children of dependence ! Hated and persecuted by
their enemies, and too often, alas ! almost unexceptionably, received by
their friends with disrespect and reproach, under the thin disguise of cold
civility and humiliating advice. Oh, to be a sturdy savage, stalking in
the pride of his independence amid the solitary wilds of his deserts,
rather than, in civilized life, helplessly to tremble for a subsistence, precarious as the caprice of a fellow-creature ! Every man has his virtues, and
no man is without his failings ; and curse on that privileged plain-dealing
of friendship which in the hour of my calamity cannot reach forth the
helping hand, without at the same time pointing out those failings, and
apportioning them their share in procuring my present distress. My
friends, for such the world calls ye, and such ye think yourselves to be,
pass by my virtues if you please, but do, also, spare my follies : the first
will witness in my breast for themselves, and the last will give pain enough
to the ingenuous mind without you. And since deviating more or less

from the paths of propriety and rectitude must be incident to human nature, do thou, Fortune, put it in my power, always from myself, and of myself, to bear the consequences of those errors! I do not want to be independent that I may sin, but I want to be independent in my sinning.

To return in this rambling letter to the subject I set out with, let me recommend my friend, Mr. Clarke, to your acquaintance and good offices; his worth entitles him to the one, and his gratitude will merit the other. I long much to hear from you. Adieu!—R. B.

No. CCXXXIII.

TO THE EARL OF BUCHAN.

[Lord Buchan had projected a fête in honour of the poet Thomson, including the opening of a temple to his memory on Ednam Hill.]

My Lord,   Ellisland, 1791.

Language sinks under the ardour of my feelings when I would thank your lordship for the honour you have done me in inviting me to make one at the coronation of the bust of Thomson. In my first enthusiasm in reading the card you did me the honour to write me, I overlooked every obstacle, and determined to go; but I fear it will not be in my power. A week or two's absence, in the very middle of my harvest, is what I much doubt I dare not venture on. I once already made a pilgrimage *up* the whole course of the Tweed, and fondly would I take the same delightful journey *down* the windings of that delightful stream.

Your lordship hints at an ode for the occasion: but who would write after Collins? I read over his verses to the memory of Thomson, and despaired. I got indeed to the length of three or four stanzas, in the way of address to the shade of the bard, on crowning his bust. I shall trouble your lordship with the subjoined copy of them, which, I am afraid, will be but too convincing a proof how unequal I am to the task. However, it affords me an opportunity of approaching your lordship, and declaring how sincerely and gratefully I have the honour to be, &c.—R. B.

[Here follows the poem, for which see page 97.]

No. CCXXXIV.

TO MR. THOMAS SLOAN.

My dear Sloan,   Ellisland, *Sept.* 1, 1791.

Suspense is worse than disappointment; for that reason I hurry to tell you that I just now learn that Mr. Ballantine does not choose to interfere more in the business. I am truly sorry for it, but cannot help it.

You blame me for not writing you sooner, but you will please to recollect that you omitted one little necessary piece of information—your address.

However, you know equally well my hurried life, indolent temper, and strength of attachment. It must be a longer period than the longest

B   K K

life "in the world's hale and undegenerate days," that will make me forget so dear a friend as Mr. Sloan. I am prodigal enough at times, but I will not part with such a treasure as that.

I can easily enter into the *embarras* of your present situation. You know my favourite quotation from Young—

> ————"On Reason build RESOLVE,
> That column of true majesty in man."

And that other favourite one from Thomson's Alfred—

> "What proves the hero truly GREAT
> Is, never, never, to despair."

Or, shall I quote you an author of your acquaintance ?

> "————Whether DOING, SUFFERING, or FORBEARING,
> You may do miracles by—PERSEVERING."

I have nothing new to tell you. The few friends we have are going on in the old way. I sold my crop on this day se'ennight, and sold it very well : a guinea an acre, on an average, above value. But such a scene of drunkenness was hardly ever seen in this country. After the roup was over, about thirty people engaged in a battle, every man for his own hand, and fought it out for three hours. Nor was the scene much better in the house. No fighting, indeed, but folks lying drunk on the floor, and decanting, until both my dogs got so drunk by attending them, that they could not stand. You will easily guess how I enjoyed the scene ; as I was no farther over than you used to see me.

Mrs. B. and family have been in Ayrshire these many weeks.

Farewell ! and God bless you, my dear friend !—R. B.

No. CCXXXV.

TO LADY E. CUNNINGHAM.

MY LADY,

I would, as usual, have availed myself of the privilege your good-ness has allowed me, of sending you anything I compose in my poetical way ; but as I had resolved, so soon as the shock of my irreparable loss would allow me, to pay a tribute to my late benefactor, I determined to make that the first piece I should do myself the honour of sending you. Had the wing of my fancy been equal to the ardour of my heart, the enclosed had been much more worthy your perusal : as it is, I beg leave to lay it at your ladyship's feet. As all the world knows my obligations to the late Earl of Glencairn, I would wish to show as openly that my heart glows, and shall ever glow, with the most grateful sense and remem-brance of his lordship's goodness. The sables I did myself the honour to wear to his lordship's memory were not the " mockery of woe." Nor shall my gratitude perish with me ! If, among my children, I shall have a son that has a heart, he shall hand it down to his child as a family

honour, and a family debt, that my dearest existence I owe to the noble house of Glencairn !

I was about to say, my lady, that if you think the poem may venture to see the light, I would, in some way or other, give it to the world.—R. B.

No. CCXXXVI.

TO MR. AINSLIE.

MY DEAR AINSLIE, ELLISLAND, 1791.
Can you minister to a mind diseased ? Can you, amid the horrors of penitence, regret, remorse, headache, nausea, and all the rest of the d——d hounds of hell that beset a poor wretch who has been guilty of the sin of drunkenness—can you speak peace to a troubled soul ?

Miserable perdu that I am, I have tried everything that used to amuse me, but in vain : here must I sit, a monument of the vengeance laid up in store for the wicked, slowly counting every chick of the clock as it slowly, slowly, numbers over these lazy scoundrels of hours, who, d—n them ! are ranked up before me, every one at his neighbour's backside, and every one with a burthen of anguish on his back, to pour on my devoted head—and there is none to pity me. My wife scolds me, my business torments me, and my sins come staring me in the face, every one telling a more bitter tale than his fellow. When I tell you even * * * has lost its power to please, you will guess something of my hell within, and all around me. I began " Elibanks and Elibraes," but the stanzas fell un-enjoyed and unfinished from my listless tongue : at last I luckily thought of reading over an old letter of yours, that lay by me, in my bookcase, and I felt something, for the first time since I opened my eyes, of pleasur-able existence.——Well—I begin to breathe a little, since I began to write to you. How are you, and what are you doing? How goes Law ? *Apropos*, for connexion's sake do not address to me supervisor, for that is an honour I cannot pretend to : I am on the list, as we call it, for a supervisor, and will be called out by and by to act as one ; but at present I am a simple gauger, tho' t'other day I got an appointment to an Excise division of 25*l.* per annum better than the rest. My present income, down money, is 70*l.* per annum.

I have one or two good fellows here whom you would be glad to know.
R. B.

No. CCXXXVII.

TO MISS DAVIES.

IT is impossible, Madam, that the generous warmth and angelic purity of your youthful mind can have any idea of that moral disease under which I unhappily must rank as the chief of sinners : I mean a torpitude of the moral powers, that may be called a lethargy of conscience. In

vain Remorse rears her horrent crest, and rouses all her snakes : beneath the deadly-fixed eye and leaden hand of Indolence their wildest ire is charmed into the torpor of the bat, slumbering out the rigours of winter in the chink of a ruined wall. Nothing less, Madam, could have made me so long neglect your obliging commands. Indeed, I had one apology —the bagatelle was not worth presenting. Besides, so strongly am I interested in Miss Davies's fate and welfare in the serious business of life, amid its chances and changes, that to make her the subject of a silly ballad is downright mockery of these ardent feelings ; 'tis like an impertinent jest to a dying friend.

Gracious Heaven ! why this disparity between our wishes and our powers ? Why is the most generous wish to make others blest impotent and ineffectual, as the idle breeze that crosses the pathless desert ? In my walks of life I have met with a few people to whom how gladly would I have said : " Go, be happy ! I know that your hearts have been wounded by the scorn of the proud, whom accident has placed above you—or, worse still, in whose hands are, perhaps, placed many of the comforts of your life. But there ! ascend that rock, Independence, and look justly down on their littleness of soul. Make the worthless tremble under your indignation, and the foolish sink before your contempt ; and largely impart that happiness to others, which I am certain will give yourselves so much pleasure to bestow."

Why, dear Madam, must I wake from this delightful reverie, and find it all a dream ? Why, amid my generous enthusiasm, must I find myself poor and powerless, incapable of wiping one tear from the eye of pity, or of adding one comfort to the friend I love ? Out upon the world, say I, that its affairs are administered so ill ! They talk of reform : good Heaven ! what a reform would I make among the sons, and even the daughters, of men ! Down, immediately, should go fools from the high places where misbegotten chance has perked them up, and through life should they skulk, ever haunted by their native insignificance, as the body marches accompanied by its shadow. As for a much more formidable class, the knaves, I am at a loss what to do with them : had I a world, there should not be a knave in it.

But the hand that could give, I would liberally fill : and I would pour delight on the heart that could kindly forgive and generously love.

Still, the inequalities of life are among men comparatively tolerable ; but there is a delicacy, a tenderness, accompanying every view in which we can place lovely woman, that are grated and shocked at the rude, capricious distinctions of Fortune. Woman is the blood-royal of life : let there be slight degrees of precedency among them—but let them be all sacred. Whether this last sentiment be right or wrong, I am not accountable ; it is an original component feature of my mind.

R. B.

No. CCXXXVIII.

SYLVANDER TO CLARINDA.

[Burns had been to Edinburgh at the end of November and beginning of December, and had there seen Mrs. M'Lehose. She had resolved to go to her worthless but repentant husband in Jamaica, and sailed in February, 1792.]

I HAVE received both your last letters, Madam, and ought and would have answered the first long ago. But on what subject shall I write you? How can you expect a correspondent should write you when you declare that you mean to preserve his letters, with a view, sooner or later, to expose them in the pillory of derision and the rock of criticism? This is gagging me completely as to speaking the sentiments of my bosom ; else, Madam, I could perhaps too truly—

" Join grief with grief, and echo sighs to thine !"

I have perused your most beautiful but most pathetic poem ; do not ask me how often, or with what emotions. You know that " I dare to *sin*, but not to *lie*." Your verses wring the confession from my inmost soul, that —I will say it, expose it if you please—that I have more than once in my life been the victim of a damning conjuncture of circumstances ; and that to see you must be ever—

" Dear as the light that visits these sad eyes."

I have just, since I had yours, composed the following stanzas. Let me know your opinion of them.

[Here are transcribed the lines beginning, "Sweet Sensibility, how charming," &c.]

No. CCXXXIX.

TO CLARINDA.

[Enclosing the " Lament of Mary, Queen of Scots," Burns wrote as follows:—]

LEADHILLS, *Thursday Noon* [*Dec.* 11, 1791].

SUCH, my dearest Clarinda, were the words of the amiable but unfortunate Mary. Misfortune seems to take a peculiar pleasure in darting her arrows against " honest men and bonny lasses." Of this you are too, too just a proof ; but may your future be a bright exception to the remark. In the words of Hamlet—

" Adieu, adieu, adieu ! Remember me."

SYLVANDER.

No. CCXL.

TO CLARINDA.

DUMFRIES [15*th December* (?), 1791].

I HAVE some merit, my ever dearest of women, in attracting and securing the honest heart of Clarinda. In her I meet with the most

accomplished of all womankind, the first of all God's works, and yet I, even I, have the good fortune to appear amiable in her sight.

By the by, this is the sixth letter that I have written since I left you ; and if you were an ordinary being, as you are a creature very extra-ordinary—an instance of what God Almighty, in the plenitude of His power and the fulness of His goodness can make !—I would never forgive you for not answering my letters.

I have sent your hair, a part of the parcel you gave me, with a measure, to Mr. Brice, the jeweller, to get a ring done for me. I have likewise sent in the verses " On Sensibility," altered to—

> " Sensibility, how charming,
> Dearest Nancy, thou can tell," &c.

to the editor of " Scots Songs," of which you have three volumes, to set to a most beautiful air—out of compliment to the first of women, my ever-beloved, my ever-sacred Clarinda. I shall probably write you to-morrow. In the meantime, from a man who is literally drunk accept and forgive !—R. B.

No. CCXLI.

TO MRS. DUNLOP.

ELLISLAND, 17th December, 1791.

MANY thanks to you, Madam, for your good news respecting the little floweret and the mother-plant. I hope my poetic prayers have been heard, and will be answered up to the warmest sincerity of their fullest extent ; and then Mrs. Henri will find her little darling the representative of his late parent, in everything but his abridged existence.

I have just finished the following song, which to a lady the descendant of Wallace, and many heroes of his truly illustrious line, and herself the mother of several soldiers, needs neither preface nor apology :—

> "Scene—A Field of Battle. Time of the Day—Evening. The wounded and dying of the victorious army are supposed to join in the following

> SONG OF DEATH.
> Farewell, thou fair day, thou green earth, and ye skies
>   Now gay with the broad setting sun :
> Farewell, loves and friendships, ye dear, tender ties—
>   Our race of existence is run !"—&c.

The circumstance that gave rise to the foregoing verses was, looking over with a musical friend McDonald's collection of Highland airs, I was struck with one, an Isle of Skye tune, entitled " Oran an Aoig ; or, the Song of Death," to the measure of which I have adapted my stanzas. I have of late composed two or three other little pieces, which, ere yon full-orbed moon, whose broad impudent face now stares at old mother earth all night, shall have shrunk into a modest crescent, just peeping forth at dewy dawn, I shall find an hour to transcribe for you. *A Dieu je vous commende.*—R. B.

No. CCXLII.

TO MR. WILLIAM SMELLIE,

PRINTER.

[This letter introduces Mrs. Riddel to Smellie, the self-taught scholar and naturalist.]

DUMFRIES, *22d January,* 1792.

I SIT down, my dear Sir, to introduce a young lady to you, and a lady in the first ranks of fashion, too. What a task ! to you—who care no more for the herd of animals called young ladies, than you do for the herd of animals called young gentlemen. To you—who despise and detest the groupings and combinations of Fashion, as an idiot painter that seems industrious to place staring fools and unprincipled knaves in the foreground of his picture, while men of sense and honesty are too often thrown in the dimmest shades. Mrs. Riddel, who will take this letter to town with her, and send it to you, is a character that, even in your own way, as a naturalist and a philosopher, would be an acquisition to your acquaintance. The lady, too, is a votary to the Muses ; and as I think myself somewhat of a judge in my own trade, I assure you that her verses, always correct and often elegant, are much beyond the common run of the *lady poetesses* of the day. She is a great admirer of your book ; and, hearing me say that I was acquainted with you, she begged to be known to you, as she is just going to pay her first visit to our Caledonian capital. I told her that her best way was, to desire her near relation, and your intimate friend, Craigdarroch, to have you at his house while she was there ; and lest you might think of a lively West Indian girl of eighteen, as girls of eighteen too often deserve to be thought of, I should take care to remove that pre- judice. To be impartial, however, in appreciating the lady's merits, she has one unlucky failing ; a failing which you will easily discover, as she seems rather pleased with indulging in it, and a failing that you will pardon, as it is a sin which very much besets yourself :—where she dislikes, or despises, she is apt to make no more a secret of it than where she esteems and respects.

I will not present you with the unmeaning *compliments of the season*, but I will send you my warmest wishes and most ardent prayers, that Fortune may never throw your subsistence to the mercy of a knave, or set your character on the judgment of a fool ; but that, upright and erect, you may walk to an honest grave, where men of letters shall say, Here lies a man who did honour to science, and men of worth shall say, Here lies a man who did honour to human nature.—R. B.

No. CCXLIII.

TO MR. PETER HILL.

MY DEAR FRIEND,

DUMFRIES, *5th Feb.* 1792.

I send you by the bearer, Mr. Clarke, a particular friend of mine, six pounds and a shilling, which you will dispose of as follows ;—five

pounds ten shillings, per account, I owe Mr. R. Burn, architect, for erecting the stone over the grave of poor Fergusson. He was two years in erecting it after I had commissioned him for it, and I have been two years in paying him after he sent me his account ; so he and I are quits. He had the *hardiesse* to ask the interest on the sum ; but considering that the money was due by one poet for putting a tombstone over another, he may, with grateful surprise, thank Heaven that he ever saw a farthing of it.

With the remainder of the money pay yourself for the "Office of a Messenger" that I bought of you ; and send me by Mr. Clarke a note of its price. Send me likewise the fifth vol. of the "Observer" by Mr. Clarke ; and if any money remains, let it stand to account.

I sent you a maukin [hare] by last week's fly, which I hope you received.

R. B.

No. CCXLIV.

TO MR. W. NICOL.

[This is an ironical reply to a letter containing (according to Dr. Currie) good advice.]

20th February, 1792.

O THOU, wisest among the wise, meridian blaze of prudence, full moon of discretion, and chief of many counsellors ! How infinitely is thy puddle-headed, rattle-headed, wrong-headed, round-headed slave indebted to thy supereminent goodness, that from the luminous path of thy own right-lined rectitude thou lookest benignly down on an erring wretch, of whom the zigzag wanderings defy all the powers of calculation, from the simple copulation of units up to the hidden mysteries of fluxions ! May one feeble ray of that light of wisdom which darts from thy sensorium, straight as the arrow of heaven, and bright as the meteor of inspiration, may it be my portion, so that I may be less unworthy of the face and favour of that father of proverbs and master of maxims, that antipode of folly, and magnet among sages, the wise and witty Willie Nicol ! Amen ! Amen ! Yea, so be it !

For me, I am a beast, a reptile, and know nothing ! From the cave of my ignorance, amid the fogs of my dulness, and pestilential fumes of my political heresies, I look up to thee, as doth a toad through the iron-barred lucerne of a pestiferous dungeon to the cloudless glory of a summer sun ! Sorely sighing in bitterness of soul, I say, when shall my name be the quotation of the wise, and my countenance be the delight of the godly, like the illustrious lord of Laggan's many hills ? As for him, his works are perfect : never did the pen of calumny blur the fair page of his reputation, nor the bolt of hatred fly at his dwelling.

Thou mirror of purity, when shall the elfine lamp of my glimmerous understanding, purged from sensual appetites and gross desires, shine like the constellation of thy intellectual powers ? As for thee, thy thoughts are pure, and thy lips are holy. Never did the unhallowed breath of the powers of darkness, and the pleasures of darkness, pollute the sacred flame of thy sky-descended and heaven-bound desires : never did the vapours of

impurity stain the unclouded serene of thy cerulean imagination. O that like thine were the tenor of my life, like thine the tenor of my conversation! Then should no friend fear for my strength, no enemy rejoice in my weakness. Then should I lie down and rise up, and none to make me afraid. May thy pity and thy prayer be exercised for, O thou lamp of wisdom and mirror of morality! thy devoted slave.—R. B.

No. CCXLV.

TO FRANCIS GROSE, ESQ. F.S.A.

SIR,   DUMFRIES, 1792.

I believe among all our Scots *literati* you have not met with Professor Dugald Stewart, who fills the Moral Philosophy chair in the University of Edinburgh. To say that he is a man of the first parts, and, what is more, a man of the first worth, to a gentleman of your general acquaintance, and who so much enjoys the luxury of unencumbered freedom and undisturbed privacy, is not perhaps recommendation enough : but when I inform you that Mr. Stewart's principal characteristic is your favourite feature—*that* sterling independence of mind which, though every man's right, so few men have the courage to claim, and fewer still the magnanimity to support ; when I tell you, that unseduced by splendour, and undisgusted by wretchedness, he appreciates the merits of the various actors in the great drama of life merely as they perform their parts ;—in short, he is a man after your own heart, and I comply with his earnest request in letting you know that he wishes above all things to meet with you. His house, Catrine, is within less than a mile of Sorn Castle, which you proposed visiting ; or if you could transmit him the enclosed, he would, with the greatest pleasure, meet you anywhere in the neighbourhood. I write to Ayrshire to inform Mr. Stewart that I have acquitted myself of my promise. Should your time and spirits permit your meeting with Mr. Stewart, 'tis well ; if not, I hope you will forgive this liberty : and I have at least an opportunity of assuring you with what truth and respect,

I am, Sir,
Your great Admirer
And very humble Servant,
R. B.*

* Another letter to Capt. Grose, giving the legends of Alloway Kirk, will be found in the notes to the poem.

No. CCXLVI.

TO MRS. DUNLOP.

ANNAN WATER FOOT, *22d August*, 1792.

Do not blame me for it, Madam ; my own conscience, hackneyed and weather-beaten as it is in watching and reproving my vagaries, follies, indolence, &c. has continued to punish me sufficiently. . . . .

Do you think it possible, my dear and honoured friend, that I could be so lost to gratitude for many favours, to esteem for much worth, and to the honest, kind, pleasurable tie of, now, old acquaintance, and I hope and I am sure of progressive, increasing friendship, as for a single day not to think of you, to ask the Fates what they are doing and about to do with my much-loved friend and her wide-scattered connexions, and to beg of them to be as kind to you and yours as they possibly can?

Apropos (though how it is *apropos* I have not leisure to explain), do you know that I am almost in love with an acquaintance of yours?—Almost! said I?—I am in love; souse! over head and ears, deep as the most unfathomable abyss of the boundless ocean: but the word Love, owing to the *intermingledoms* of the good and the bad, the pure and the impure, in this world, being rather an equivocal term for expressing one's sentiments and sensations, I must do justice to the sacred purity of my attachment. Know, then, that the heart-struck awe; the distant, humble approach; the delight we should have in gazing upon and listening to a Messenger of Heaven, appearing in all the unspotted purity of his celestial home among the coarse, polluted, far inferior sons of men, to deliver to them tidings that make their hearts swim in joy, and their imaginations soar in transport—such, so delighting and so pure, were the emotions of my soul on meeting the other day with Miss Lesley Baillie, your neighbour, at M——. Mr. B. with his two daughters, accompanied by Mr. H. of G., passing through Dumfries a few days ago, on their way to England, did me the honour of calling on me; on which I took my horse (though God knows I could ill spare the time), and accompanied them fourteen or fifteen miles, and dined and spent the day with them. 'Twas about nine, I think, when I left them, and, riding home, I composed the following ballad, of which you will probably think you have a dear bargain, as it will cost you another groat of postage. You must know that there is an old ballad beginning with—

> " My bonnie Lizie Baillie,
> I'll rowe thee in my plaidie,"— &c.

So I parodied it as follows, which is literally the first copy, "unanointed, unanneal'd," as Hamlet says :—

> " O saw ye bonnie Lesley,
> As she gaed o'er the border?
> She's gane, like Alexander,
> To spread her conquests farther."

So much for ballads. I regret that you are gone to the east country, as I am to be in Ayrshire in about a fortnight. This world of ours, notwithstanding it has many good things in it, yet it has ever had this curse, that two or three people, who would be the happier the oftener they met together, are, almost without exception, always so placed as never to meet but once or twice a year; which, considering the few years of a man's life, is a very great " evil under the sun," which I do not recollect that Solomon has mentioned in his catalogue of the miseries of man. I hope and believe that there is a state of existence beyond the grave, where the worthy of

this life will renew their former intimacies, with this endearing addition, that "we meet to part no more!" . . . .

> "Tell us, ye dead;
> Will none of you in pity disclose the secret,
> What 'tis you are, and we must shortly be?"

A thousand times have I made this apostrophe to the departed sons of men, but not one of them has ever thought fit to answer the question. " O that some courteous ghost would blab it out!" but it cannot be ; you and I, my friend, must make the experiment by ourselves, and for ourselves. However, I am so convinced that an unshaken faith in the doctrines of religion is not only necessary, by making us better men, but also by making us happier men, that I should take every care that your little godson, and every little creature that shall call me father, shall be taught them.

So ends this heterogeneous letter, written at this wild place of the world, in the intervals of my labour of discharging a vessel of rum from Antigua.—R. B.

No. CCXLVII.

TO MR. CUNNINGHAM.

Dumfries, 10th September, 1792.

No! I will not attempt an apology. Amid all my hurry of business, grinding the faces of the publican and the sinner on the merciless wheels of the Excise : making ballads, and then drinking, and singing them ; and, over and above all, the correcting the press-work of two different publications; still, still I might have stolen five minutes to dedicate to one of the first of my friends and fellow-creatures. I might have done, as I do at present, snatched an hour near " witching time of night," and scrawled a page or two. I might have congratulated my friend on his marriage ; or I might have thanked the Caledonian archers for the honour they have done me (though, to do myself justice, I intended to have done both in rhyme ; else I had done both long ere now). Well, then, here is to your good health! for you must know I have set a nipperkin of toddy by me, just by way of spell, to keep away the meikle-horned Deil, or any of his subaltern imps who may be on their nightly rounds.

But what shall I write to you? "The voice said, Cry," and I said, " What shall I cry?" O thou spirit! whatever thou art, or wherever thou makest thyself visible!—be thou a bogle by the eerie side of an auld thorn, in the dreary glen through which the herd-callan maun bicker in his gloamin route frae the faulde !—Be thou a brownie, set, at dead of night, to thy task by the blazing ingle, or in the solitary barn, where the repercussions of thy iron flail half affright thyself, as thou performest the work of twenty of the sons of men, ere the cock-crowing summon thee to thy ample cog of substantial brose !—Be thou a kelpie, haunting the ford or ferry, in the starless night, mixing thy laughing yell with the howling of the storm and

the roaring of the flood, as thou viewest the perils and miseries of man on the foundering horse, or in the tumbling boat!—Or, lastly, be thou a ghost, paying thy nocturnal visits to the hoary ruins of decayed grandeur ; or performing thy mystic rites in the shadow of the time-worn church, while the moon looks, without a cloud, on the silent, ghastly dwellings of the dead around thee ; or, taking thy stand by the bedside of the villain or the murderer, portraying on his dreaming fancy pictures dreadful as the horrors of unveiled hell, and terrible as the wrath of incensed Deity !— Come, thou spirit, but not in these horrid forms ; come with the milder, gentle, easy inspirations which thou breathest round the wig of a prating advocate, or the *téte* of a tea-sipping gossip, while their tongues run at the light-horse gallop of clish-maclaver for ever and ever ; come and assist a poor devil who is quite jaded in the attempt to share half an idea among half a hundred words, to fill up four quarto pages, while he has not got one single sentence of recollection, information, or remark worth putting pen to paper for.

I feel, I feel the presence of supernatural assistance ! Circled in the embrace of my elbow-chair, my breast labours, like the bloated Sybil on her three-footed stool, and, like her too, labours with Nonsense.—Nonsense, auspicious name ! Tutor, friend, and finger-post in the mystic mazes of law, the cadaverous paths of physic, and particularly in the sightless soarings of school divinity ; who—leaving Common Sense confounded at his strength of pinion, Reason delirious with eyeing his giddy flight, and Truth creeping back into the bottom of her well, cursing the hour that ever she offered her scorned alliance to the wizard power of Theologic Vision—raves abroad on all the winds : " On earth Discord ! a gloomy heaven above, opening her jealous gates to the nineteen-thousandth part of the tithe of mankind ! and below, an inescapable and inexorable hell, expanding its leviathan jaws for the vast residue of mortals ! ! !" O doc- trine comfortable and healing to the weary, wounded soul of man ! Ye sons and daughters of affliction, ye *pauvres misérables*, to whom day brings no pleasure, and night yields no rest, be comforted ! " 'Tis but *one* to nineteen hundred thousand that your situation will mend in this world." So, alas ! the experience of the poor and needy too often affirms ; and 'tis nineteen hundred thousand to *one*, by the dogmas of * * * *, that you will be damned eternally in the world to come !

But, of all Nonsense, Religious Nonsense is the most nonsensical ; so enough, and more than enough of it. Only, by the by, will you, or can you, tell me, my dear Cunningham, why a sectarian turn of mind has always a tendency to narrow and illiberalize the heart ? They are orderly ; they may be just ; nay, I have known them merciful ; but still your children of sanctity move among their fellow-creatures with a nos- tril snuffing putrescence and a foot spurning filth,—in short, with a con- ceited dignity that your titled * * * * or any other of your Scottish lordlings of seven centuries' standing display, when they accidentally mix among the many-aproned sons of mechanical life. I remember, in my ploughboy days, I could not conceive it possible that a noble lord could be a fool, or a godly man could be a knave. How ignorant are plough-

boys! Nay, I have since discovered that a *godly woman* may be a
* * * * * !—But hold—Here's t' ye again—this rum is generous Antigua ;
so a very unfit menstruum for scandal.

Apropos, how do you like—I mean *really* like—the married life? Ah,
my friend, matrimony is quite a different thing from what your love-sick
youths and sighing girls take it to be! But marriage, we are told, is
appointed by God, and I shall never quarrel with any of His institutions.
I am a husband of older standing than you, and shall give you *my* ideas
of the conjugal state (*en passant*—you know I am no Latinist—is not *conjugal* derived from *jugum*, a yoke?). Well, then, the scale of good wife-
ship I divide into ten parts :—Goodnature, four ; Good Sense, two ; Wit,
one ; Personal Charms, viz. a sweet face, eloquent eyes, fine limbs, graceful carriage (I would add a fine waist too, but that is so soon spoilt, you
know), all these, one ; as for the other qualities belonging to, or attending
on, a wife, such as Fortune, Connexions, Education (I mean education
extraordinary), Family Blood, &c., divide the two remaining degrees among
them as you please ; only remember that all these minor properties must
be expressed by *fractions*, for there is not any one of them, in the afore-
said scale, entitled to the dignity of an *integer*.

As for the rest of my fancies and reveries—how I lately met with Miss
Lesley Baillie, the most beautiful, elegant woman in the world—how I
accompanied her and her father's family fifteen miles on their journey, out
of pure devotion, to admire the loveliness of the works of God in such an
unequalled display of them—how, in galloping home at night, I made a
ballad on her, of which these two stanzas make a part—

> Thou, bonie Lesley, art a queen,
>   Thy subjects we before thee ;
> Thou, bonie Lesley, art divine,
>   The hearts o' men adore thee.
>
> The very Deil he could na scathe
>   Whatever wad belang thee !
> He'd look into thy bonie face
>   And say, " I canna wrang thee."

—behold all these things are written in the chronicles of my imaginations,
and shall be read by thee, my dear friend, and by thy beloved spouse, my
other dear friend, at a more convenient season.

Now, to thee, and to thy before-designed *bosom*-companion, be given
the precious things brought forth by the sun, and the precious things
brought forth by the moon, and the benignest influences of the stars, and
the living streams which flow from the fountains of life, and by the tree of
life, for ever and ever ! Amen.—R. B.

No. CCXLVIII.

TO MR. G. THOMSON.

[In the autumn of 1792 Mr. G. Thomson of Edinburgh planned "A select Collection of original Scottish Airs ; to which are added Symphonies and Accompaniments by Pleyel and Kozeluck, with characteristic Verses by the most esteemed Scottish Poets;" and as Burns was the only poet of that period worthy of the name, he was instantly applied to, to furnish verses to some airs which were not already supplied with any, or at least with satisfactory, words.]

SIR,　　　　　　　　　　　　　　　　　DUMFRIES, *16th Sept.* 1792.

　　I have just this moment got your letter. As the request you make to me will positively add to my enjoyments in complying with it, I shall enter into your undertaking with all the small portion of abilities I have, strained to their utmost exertion by the impulse of enthusiasm. Only don't hurry me: "Deil tak' the hindmost" is by no means the *cri de guerre* of my muse. Will you, as I am inferior to none of you in enthusiastic attachment to the poetry and music of old Caledonia, and, since you request it, have cheerfully promised my mite of assistance—will you let me have a list of your airs, with the first line of the printed verses you intend for them, that I may have an opportunity of suggesting any alteration that may occur to me? You know 'tis in the way of my trade ; still leaving you, gentlemen, the undoubted right of publishers to approve or reject, at your pleasure, for your own publication. *Apropos,* if you are for English verses, there is, on my part, an end of the matter. Whether in the simplicity of the ballad, or the pathos of the song, I can only hope to please myself in being allowed at least a sprinkling of our native tongue. English verses, particularly the works of Scotsmen, that have merit, are certainly very eligible. "Tweedside"—"Ah, the poor shepherd's mournful fate!" —"Ah, Chloris! could I now but sit," &c., you cannot mend ; but such insipid stuff as "To Fanny fair could I impart," &c., usually set to "The Mill, Mill, O!" is a disgrace to the collections in which it has already appeared, and would doubly disgrace a collection that will have the very superior merit of yours. But more of this in the farther prosecution of the business, if I am called on for my strictures and amendments ;—I say amendments ; for I will not alter except where I myself, at least, think that I amend.

　　As to any remuneration, you may think my songs either above or below price ; for they shall absolutely be the one or the other. In the honest enthusiasm with which I embark in your undertaking, to talk of money, wages, fee, hire, &c. would be downright prostitution of soul! A proof of each of the songs that I compose or amend I shall receive as a favour. In the rustic phrase of the season, "Gude speed the wark!"

　　　　　　　　　　　　　　I am, Sir,
　　　　　　　　　　　　Your very humble Servant,
　　　　　　　　　　　　　　　　　　R. BURNS.

No. CCXLIX.

TO MRS. DUNLOP.

[Mrs. Henri, Mrs. Dunlop's widowed daughter, had gone to France to introduce her boy to his father's family, and found herself in the midst of the terrible convulsion of the great Revolution.]

DUMFRIES, *24th September*, 1792.

I HAVE this moment, my dear Madam, yours of the 23d. All your other kind reproaches, your news, &c., are out of my head when I read and think on Mrs. Henri's situation. Good God! a heart-wounded, helpless young woman in a strange, foreign land, and that land convulsed with every horror that can harrow the human feelings—sick—looking, longing for a comforter, but finding none—a mother's feelings, too ;—but it is too much : He who wounded (He only can), may He heal ! . . . .

I wish the farmer great joy of his new acquisition to his family. . . . . I cannot say that I give him joy of his life as a farmer. 'Tis, as a farmer paying a dear, unconscionable rent, a *cursed life !* As to a laird farming his own property ; sowing his own corn in hope, and reaping it, in spite of brittle weather, in gladness ; knowing that none can say unto him, 'What dost thou?' fattening his herds ; shearing his flocks ; rejoicing at Christmas ; and begetting sons and daughters, until he be the venerated, grey-haired leader of a little tribe—'tis a heavenly life ! but devil take the life of reaping the fruits that another must eat.

Well, your kind wishes will be gratified, as to seeing me when I make my Ayrshire visit. I cannot leave Mrs. B. until her nine months' race is run, which may perhaps be in three or four weeks. She, too, seems determined to make me the patriarchal leader of a band. However, if Heaven will be so obliging as to let me have them in the proportion of three boys to one girl, I shall be so much the more pleased. I hope, if I am spared with them, to show a set of boys that will do honour to my cares and name ; but I am not equal to the task of rearing girls.* Besides, I am too poor ; a girl should always have a fortune. *Apropos*, your little godson is thriving charmingly, but is a very devil. He, though two years younger, has completely mastered his brother. Robert is indeed the mildest, gentlest creature I ever saw. He has a most surprising memory, and is quite the pride of his schoolmaster.

You know how readily we get into prattle upon a subject dear to our heart : you can excuse it. God bless you and yours !—R. B.

No. CCL.

TO G. THOMSON.

Friday Night.

YOUR observation as to the aptitude of Dr. Percy's ballad, " O, Nancy, wilt thou go with me ?" to the air, " Nannie, O ! " is just. It is, besides, perhaps the most beautiful ballad in the English language. But

* The child proved to be a girl, born 21st November : she was named Elizabeth Riddel.

let me remark to you, that in the sentiment and style of our Scottish airs there is a pastoral simplicity, a something that one may call the Doric style and dialect of vocal music, to which a dash of our native tongue and manners is particularly, nay peculiarly, apposite. For this reason, and, upon my honour, for this reason alone, I am of opinion (but, as I told you before, my opinion is yours, freely yours, to approve or reject, as you please) that my ballad of " Nannie, O !" might perhaps do for one set of verses to the tune. Now don't let it enter into your head, that you are under any necessity of taking my verses. I have long ago made up my mind as to my own reputation in the business of authorship, and have nothing to be pleased or offended at in your adoption or rejection of my verses. Though you should reject one half of what I give you, I shall be pleased with your adopting the other half, and shall continue to serve you with the same assiduity.

In the printed copy of my " Nannie, O !" the name of the river is horribly prosaic. I will alter it :—

" Behind yon hills where Lugar flows." *

Girvan is the name of the river that suits the idea of the stanza best, but Lugar is the most agreeable modulation of syllables.

I will soon give you a great many more remarks on this business ; but I have just now an opportunity of conveying you this scrawl free of postage, an expense that it is ill able to pay : so, with my best compliments to honest Allan, Gude be wi' ye, &c.

Saturday Morning.

IN my very early years, when I was thinking of going to the West Indies, I took the following farewell of a dear girl. It is quite trifling, and has nothing of the merits of " Ewe-bughts ;" but it will fill up this page. You must know that all my earlier love-songs were the breathings of ardent passion ; and though it might have been easy in after-times to have given them a polish, yet that polish, to me, whose they were, and who perhaps alone cared for them, would have defaced the legend of my heart, which was so faithfully inscribed on them. Their uncouth simplicity was, as they say of wines, their race.

[Here are inserted the verses "Will ye go to the Indies, my Mary." *Page* 236.]

No. CCLI.
TO MRS. DUNLOP.
[Supposed to have been written on the death of Mrs. Henri, her daughter.]

[*October,* 1792.]

I HAD been from home, and did not receive your letter until my return the other day. What shall I say to comfort you, my much-valued, much-afflicted friend ! I can but grieve with you ; consolation I have none to offer, except that which religion holds out to the children of affliction.

* Although after the date of this letter, during the poet's life, two editions of his poems were published (1793 and 1794) the name of the river remained unaltered.

Children of affliction! — how just the expression! and like every other family, they have matters among them which they hear, see, and feel in a serious, all-important manner, of which the world has not, nor cares to have, any idea. The world looks indifferently on, makes the passing remark, and proceeds to the next novel occurrence.

Alas, Madam! who would wish for many years? What is it but to drag existence until our joys gradually expire, and leave us in a night of misery : like the gloom which blots out the stars one by one from the face of night, and leaves us, without a ray of comfort, in the howling waste!

I am interrupted, and must leave off. You shall soon hear from me again.—R. B.

No. CCLII.

TO MRS. DUNLOP.

DUMFRIES, *6th December,* 1792.

I SHALL be in Ayrshire, I think, next week ; and, if at all possible, I shall certainly, my much esteemed friend, have the pleasure of visiting at Dunlop House.

Alas, Madam! how seldom do we meet in this world, that we have reason to congratulate ourselves on accessions of happiness! I have not passed half the ordinary term of an old man's life, and yet I scarcely look over the obituary of a newspaper that I do not see some names that I have known, and which I, and other acquaintances, little thought to meet with there so soon. Every other instance of the mortality of our kind makes us cast an anxious look into the dreadful abyss of uncertainty, and shudder with apprehension for our own fate. But of how different an importance are the lives of different individuals! Nay, of what importance is one period of the same life, more than another! A few years ago I could have laid down in the dust, " careless of the voice of the morning ;" and now not a few, and these most helpless individuals, would, on losing me and my exertions, lose both their " staff and shield." By the way, these helpless ones have lately got an addition ; Mrs. B. having given me a fine girl since I wrote you. There is a charming passage in Thomson's " Edward and Eleanora :"—

> " The valiant, *in himself,* what can he suffer ?
> Or what need he regard his *single* woes ?"—&c.

As I am got in the way of quotations, I shall give you another from the same piece, peculiarly—alas ! too peculiarly—apposite, my dear Madam, your present frame of mind :—

> " Who so unworthy but may proudly deck him
> With his fair-weather virtue, that exults
> Glad o'er the summer main ? the tempest comes :
> The rough winds rage aloud ; when from the helm
> This virtue shrinks, and in a corner lies
> Lamenting.—Heavens ! if privileged from trial
> How cheap a thing were virtue !"

I do not remember to have heard you mention Thomson's dramas. I pick up favourite quotations, and store them in my mind as ready armour, offensive or defensive, amid the struggle of this turbulent existence. Of these is one, a very favourite one, from his " Alfred : "—

> " Attach thee firmly to the virtuous deeds
> And offices of life ; to life itself,
> With all its vain and transient joys, sit loose."

Probably I have quoted some of these to you formerly, as indeed, when I write from the heart, I am apt to be guilty of such repetitions. The compass of the heart, in the musical style of expression, is much more bounded than that of the imagination ; so the notes of the former are extremely apt to run into one another ; but in return for the paucity of its compass, its few notes are much more sweet. I must still give you another quotation, which I am almost sure I have given you before, but I cannot resist the temptation. The subject is religion : speaking of its import-ance to mankind, the author says,

> " 'Tis this, my friend, that streaks our morning bright."

I see you are in for double postage, so I shall e'en scribble out t'other sheet. We in this country here have many alarms of the reforming, or rather the republican, spirit of your part of the kingdom. Indeed, we are a good deal in commotion ourselves. For me, I am a placeman, you know ; a very humble one indeed, Heaven knows, but still so much as to gag me. What my private sentiments are, you will find out without an interpreter. . . . .

I have taken up the subject, and the other day, for a pretty actress's benefit-night, I wrote an address, which I will give on the other page, called " The Rights of Woman :"—

> " While Europe's eye is fixed on mighty things." *(Page* 111.)

I shall have the honour of receiving your criticisms in person at Dunlop.—R. B.

No. CCLIII.

TO G. THOMSON.

November 8th, 1792.

IF you mean, my dear Sir, that all the songs in your collection shall be poetry of the first merit, I am afraid you will find more difficulty in the undertaking than you are aware of. There is a peculiar rhythmus in many of our airs, and a necessity of adapting syllables to the emphasis, or what I would call the feature-notes of the tune, that cramp the poet, and lay him under almost insuperable difficulties. For instance, in the air, " My wife's a wanton wee thing," if a few lines smooth and pretty can be adapted to it, it is all you can expect. The following were made extempore to it ; and though, on farther study, I might give you some-

thing more profound, yet it might not suit the light-horse gallop of the air so well as this random clink :—

[" The Winsome Wee Thing." *Page* 180.]

No. CCLIV.

TO G. THOMSON.

MY DEAR SIR,   *14th November, 1792.*

I agree with you that the song, " Katharine Ogie," is very poor stuff, and unworthy, altogether unworthy, of so beautiful an air. I tried to mend it; but the awkward sound, Ogie, recurring so often in the rhyme, spoils every attempt at introducing sentiment into the piece. The foregoing song ["Highland Mary," page 226] pleases myself; I think it is in my happiest manner: you will see at first glance that it suits the air. The subject of the song is one of the most interesting passages of my youthful days; and I own that I should be much flattered to see the verses set to an air which would ensure celebrity. Perhaps, after all, 'tis the still glowing prejudice of my heart that throws a borrowed lustre over the merits of the composition.

I have partly taken your idea of " Auld Rob Morris." I have adopted the two first verses, and am going on with the song on a new plan, which promises pretty well. I take up one or another, just as the bee of the moment buzzes in my bonnet-lug; and do you, *sans cérémonie*, make what use you choose of the productions.—Adieu, &c.— R. B.

No. CCLV.

TO MISS FONTENELLE.

[Burns was very fond of the theatre, and had, as we have seen, some notion of trying his hand at dramatic writing. Miss Fontenelle was a youthful member of the company which at stated seasons visited Dumfries, playing such parts as " Little Pickle:" she was very sprightly and *petite* in figure.]

MADAM,

In such a bad world as ours, those who add to the scanty sum of our pleasures are positively our benefactors. To you, Madam, on our humble Dumfries boards, I have been more indebted for entertainment than ever I was in prouder theatres. Your charms as a woman would ensure applause to the most indifferent actress, and your theatrical talents would ensure admiration to the plainest figure. This, Madam, is not the unmeaning or insidious compliment of the frivolous or the interested : I pay it from the same honest impulse that the sublime in nature excites my admiration, or her beauties give me delight.

Will the foregoing lines [" The Rights of Woman : An Address"] be of any service to you in your approaching benefit-night ? If they will, I shall

be prouder of my muse than ever. They are nearly extempore : I know they have no great merit; but though they should add but little to the entertainment of the evening, they give me the happiness of an opportunity to declare how much I have the honour to be, &c.—R. B.

No. CCLVI.

TO A LADY,

IN FAVOUR OF A PLAYER'S BENEFIT.

MADAM, DUMFRIES.

You were so very good as to promise me to honour my friend with your presence on his benefit-night. That night is fixed for Friday first ; the play a most interesting one, " The Way to keep Him." I have the pleasure to know Mr. G. well. His merit as an actor is generally acknow-ledged. He has genius and worth which would do honour to patronage : he is a poor and modest man ; claims which from their very *silence* have the more forcible power on the generous heart. Alas, for pity ! that from the indolence of those who have the good things of this life in their gift, too often does brazen-fronted importunity snatch that boon, the rightful due of retiring, humble want ! Of all the qualities we assign to the Author and Director of Nature, by far the most enviable is to be able " to wipe away all tears from all eyes." O what insignificant, sordid wretches are they, however chance may have loaded them with wealth, who go to their graves, to their magnificent mausoleums, with hardly the consciousness of having made one poor honest heart happy !

But I crave your pardon, Madam ; I came to beg, not to preach.—R. B.

No. CCLVII.

TO MRS. RIDDEL.

I WILL wait on you, my ever valued friend, but whether in the morning I am not sure. Sunday closes a period of our curst revenue business, and may probably keep me employed with my pen until noon. Fine employ-ment for a poet's pen ! There is a species of human genius that I call *the gin-house class:* what enviable dogs they are ! Round and round and round they go. Mundell's ox, that drives his cotton-mill,* is their exact prototype—without an idea or wish beyond their circle—fat, sleek, stupid, patient, quiet, and contented ; while here I sit, altogether Novemberish, a d——d *mélange* of fretfulness and melancholy ; not enough of the one to rouse me to passion, nor of the other to repose me in torpor ; my soul flouncing and fluttering round his tenement like a wild-finch, caught among the horrors of winter, and newly thrust into a cage. Well, I am persuaded that it was of me the Hebrew sage prophesied when he fore-

* This was a primitive cotton-mill near Dumfries.

told : " And, behold, on whatsoever this man doth set his heart, it shall not prosper ! " If my resentment is awakened, it is sure to be where it dare not squeak ; and if— . . . Pray that wisdom and bliss be the frequent visitors of — R. B.

No. CCLVIII.

TO G. THOMSON.

[Mr. Thomson, criticizing the songs with the ear of a musician, excuses himself for pointing out what he deems defects—" the wren will oversee what has been overlooked by the eagle."]

DUMFRIES, 1st Dec. 1792.

YOUR alterations of my " Nannie, O ! " are perfectly right. So are those of " My wife's a winsome wee thing : " your alteration of the second stanza is a positive improvement. Now, my dear Sir, with the freedom which characterises our correspondence, I must not, cannot, alter " Bonie Lesley." You are right, the word " Alexander " makes the line a little uncouth ; but I think the thought is pretty. Of Alexander, beyond all other heroes, it may be said, in the sublime language of Scripture, that " he went forth conquering and to conquer."

> " For Nature made her what she is,
> And never made anither." (Such a person as she is.)

This is, in my opinion, more poetical than " Ne'er made sic anither." However, it is immaterial : make it either way. " Caledonie," I agree with you, is not so good a word as could be wished, though it is sanctioned in three or four instances by Allan Ramsay ; but I cannot help it. In short, that species of stanza is the most difficult that I have ever tried.

R. B.

No. CCLIX.

TO R. GRAHAM, ESQ.

FINTRY.

SIR,   *December, 1792.*

I have been surprised, confounded, and distracted by Mr. Mitchell, the collector, telling me that he has received an order from your Board to inquire into my political conduct, and blaming me as a person disaffected to Government.

Sir, you are a husband—and a father. You know what you would feel to see the much-loved wife of your bosom, and your helpless, prattling little ones turned adrift into the world, degraded and disgraced from a situation in which they had been respectable and respected, and left almost without the necessary support of a miserable existence. Alas, Sir ! must I think that such, soon, will be my lot ! and from the d-mned, dark insinuations of hellish, groundless envy too ! I believe, Sir, I may

aver it. and in the sight of Omniscience, that I would not tell a deliberate falsehood—no, not though even worse horrors, if worse can be, than those I have mentioned, hung over my head ; and I say, that the allegation, whatever villain has made it, is a lie ! To the British Constitution, on revolution principles, next after my God, I am most devoutly attached. You, Sir, have been much and generously my friend. Heaven knows how warmly I have felt the obligation, and how gratefully I have thanked you. Fortune, Sir, has made you powerful, and me impotent; has given you patronage, and me dependence. I would not for my single self call on your humanity ; were such my insular, unconnected situation, I would despise the tear that now swells in my eye—I could brave misfortune, I could face ruin ; for, at the worst, " Death's thousand doors stand open :" but, good God ! the tender concerns that I have mentioned, the claims and ties that I see at this moment, and feel around me, how they unnerve Courage, and wither Resolution ! To your patronage, as a man of genius, you have allowed me a claim ; and your esteem, as an honest man, I know is my due : to these, Sir, permit me to appeal ; by these may I adjure you to save me from that misery which threatens to overwhelm me, and which, with my latest breath I will say it, I have not deserved.—R. B.

No. CCLX.

TO MRS. DUNLOP.

DEAR MADAM, DUMFRIES, 31st December, 1792.
A hurry of business, thrown in heaps by my absence, has until now prevented my returning my grateful acknowledgments to the good family of Dunlop, and you in particular, for that hospitable kindness which rendered the four days I spent under that genial roof four of the pleasantest I ever enjoyed. Alas, my dearest friend ! how few and fleeting are those things we call pleasures ! On my road to Ayrshire, I spent a night with a friend whom I much valued, a man whose days promised to be many ; and on Saturday last we laid him in the dust !

Jan. 2, 1793.
I HAVE just received yours of the 30th, and feel much for your situation. However, I heartily rejoice in your prospect of recovery from that vile jaundice. As to myself, I am better, though not quite free of my complaint. You must not think, as you seem to insinuate, that in my way of life I want exercise. Of that I have enough ; but occasional hard drinking is the devil to me. Against this I have again and again bent my resolution, and have greatly succeeded. Taverns I have totally abandoned : it is the private parties in the family way, among the hard-drinking gentlemen of this country, that do me the mischief ; but even this I have more than half given over.
Mr. Corbet can be of little service to me at present ; at least I should be shy of applying. I cannot possibly be settled as a supervisor for several years. I must wait the rotation of the list, and there are twenty

names before mine. I might indeed get a job of officiating, where a settled supervisor was ill, or aged ; but that hauls me from my family, as I could not remove them on such an uncertainty. Besides, some envious, malicious devil has raised a little demur on my political principles, and I wish to let that matter settle before I offer myself too much in the eye of my supervisors. I have set, henceforth, a seal on my lips as to these unlucky politics ; but to you I must breathe my sentiments. In this, as in everything else, I shall show the undisguised emotions of my soul. War I deprecate ; misery and ruin to thousands are in the blast that announces the destructive demon.—R. B.

No. CCLXI.

TO MRS. DUNLOP.

5th January, 1793.

YOU see my hurried life, Madam ; I can only command starts of time : however, I am glad of one thing ; since I finished the other sheet, the political blast that threatened my welfare is overblown. I have corresponded with Commissioner Graham, for the Board had made me the subject of their animadversions ; and now I have the pleasure of informing you that all is set to rights in that quarter. Now, as to these informers, may the devil be let loose to —— But, hold ! I was praying most fervently in my last sheet, and I must not so soon fall a-swearing in this.

Alas ! how little do the wantonly or idly officious think what mischief they do by their malicious insinuations, indirect impertinence, or thoughtless blabbings. What a difference there is in intrinsic worth, candour, benevolence, generosity, kindness—in all the charities and all the virtues—between one class of human beings and another. For instance, the amiable circle I so lately mixed with in the hospitable hall of Dunlop—their generous hearts, their uncontaminated, dignified minds, their informed and polished understandings—what a contrast, when compared (if such comparing were not downright sacrilege) with the soul of the miscreant who can deliberately plot the destruction of an honest man that never offended him, and with a grin of satisfaction see the unfortunate being, his faithful wife, and prattling innocents, turned over to beggary and ruin !

Your cup, my dear Madam, arrived safe. I had two worthy fellows dining with me the other day, when I, with great formality, produced my whigmeeleerie cup, and told them that it had been a family-piece among the descendants of William Wallace. This roused such an enthusiasm, that they insisted on bumpering the punch round in it ; and, by and by, never did your great ancestor lay a *Suthron* more completely to rest, than for a time did your cup my two friends. *Apropos,* this is the season of wishing. May God bless you, my dear friend, and bless me, the humblest and sincerest of your friends, by granting you yet many returns of the season ! May all good things a tend you and yours, wherever they are scattered over the earth !—R. B.

No. CCLXII.

TO G. THOMSON.

26th January, 1793.

I APPROVE greatly, my dear Sir, of your plans. Dr. Beattie's essay will of itself be a treasure. On my part, I mean to draw up an appendix to the Doctor's essay, containing my stock of anecdotes, &c. of our Scots songs. All the late Mr. Tytler's anecdotes I have by me, taken down, in the course of my acquaintance with him, from his own mouth I am such an enthusiast, that in the course of my several peregrinations through Scotland I made a pilgrimage to the individual spot from which every song took its rise, " Lochaber" and the " Braes of Ballenden " excepted. So far as the locality, either from the title of the air or the tenor of the song, could be ascertained, I have paid my devotions at the particular shrine of every Scots muse.

I do not doubt but you might make a very valuable collection of Jacobite songs, but would it give no offence? In the meantime, do not you think that some of them, particularly " The Sow's Tail to Geordie," as an air, with other words, might be well worth a place in your collection of lively songs?

If it were possible to procure songs of merit, it would be proper to have one set of Scots words to every air, and that the set of words to which the notes ought to be set. There is a *naïveté*, a pastoral simplicity, in a slight intermixture of Scots words and phraseology, which is more in unison (at least to my taste, and, I will add, to every genuine Caledonian taste) with the simple pathos or rustic sprightliness of our native music, than any English verses whatever.

The very name of Peter Pindar is an acquisition to your work. His " Gregory" is beautiful. I have tried to give you a set of stanzas in Scots, on the same subject, which are at your service. Not that I intend to enter the lists with Peter; that would be presumption indeed. My song, though much inferior in poetic merit, has, I think, more of the ballad simplicity in it.—R. B.

No. CCLXIII.

TO CLARINDA.

[Poor Mrs. M'I ehose, finding her brutal husband's company quite unbearable, and her health breaking down, returned from Jamaica in August, 1792; but Burns did not know of it till some time afterwards.]

I SUPPOSE, my dear Madam, that by your neglecting to inform me of your arrival in Europe—a circumstance that could not be indifferent to me, as indeed no occurrence relating to you can—you meant to leave me to guess and gather that a correspondence I once had the honour and felicity to enjoy is to be no more. Alas! what heavy-laden sounds are

these—"No more!" The wretch who has never tasted pleasure has never known woe: what drives the soul to madness is the recollection of joys that are "no more!" But this is not language to the world: they do not understand it. But come, ye few—the children of feeling and sentiment!—ye whose trembling bosom-chords ache to unutterable anguish as recollection gushes on the heart!—ye who are capable of an attachment keen as the arrows of Death, and strong as the vigour of immortal being—come! and your ears shall drink a tale—But hush! I must not, cannot, tell it; agony is in the recollection, and frenzy in the recital!

But, Madam, to leave the paths that lead to madness, I congratulate your friends on your return; and I hope that the precious health, which Miss P. tells me is so much injured, is restored or restoring. . . . .

I present you a book: may I hope you will accept it? I daresay you will have brought your books with you. The fourth vol. of the "Scots Songs" is published. [*August,* 1792.] I will presume to send it you. Shall I hear from you? But first hear me. No cold language—no prudential documents: I despise advice and scorn control. If you are not to write such language, such sentiments, as you know I shall wish, shall delight to receive, I conjure you, by wounded pride, by ruined peace, by frantic disappointed passion, by all the many ills that constitute that sum of human woes, a broken heart!!! to me be silent for ever. . . . . R.B

No. CCLXIV.

TO MR. CUNNINGHAM.

3d March, 1793.

SINCE I wrote to you the last lugubrious sheet, I have not had time to write you farther. When I say that I had not time, that, as usual, means, that the three demons, indolence, business, and ennui, have so completely shared my hours among them, as not to leave me a five minutes' fragment to take up a pen in.

Thank Heaven, I feel my spirits buoying upwards with the renovating year. Now I shall in good earnest take up Thomson's songs. I dare say he thinks I have used him unkindly, and I must own with too much appearance of truth. *Apropos,* do you know the much-admired old Highland air called "The Sutor's Dochter?" It is a first-rate favourite of mine, and I have written what I reckon one of my best songs to it. I will send it to you as it was sung with great applause in some fashionable circles by Major Robertson, of Lude, who was here with his corps. . . . .

There is one commission that I must trouble you with. I lately lost a valuable seal, a present from a departed friend, which vexes me much.

I have gotten one of your Highland pebbles, which I fancy would make a very decent one; and I want to cut my armorial bearing on it; will you be so obliging as inquire what will be the expense of such a business? I do not know that my name is matriculated, as the heralds call it, at all; but I have invented arms for myself,—so you know I shall be chief of the

name ; and, by courtesy of Scotland, will likewise be entitled to supporters. These, however, I do not intend having on my seal. I am a bit of a herald, and shall give you, *secundum artem*, my arms. On a field azure a holly bush, seeded, proper, in base ; a shepherd's pipe and crook, saltierwise, also proper, in chief. On a wreath of the colours a woodlark perching on a sprig of bay-tree, proper, for crest. Two mottoes : round the top of the crest, " Wood-notes wild ; " at the bottom of the shield, in the usual place, " Better a wee bush than nae bield." By the shepherd's pipe and crook I do not mean the nonsense of painters of Arcadia, but a " Stock and Horn," and a " Club," such as you see at the head of Allan Ramsay, in Allan's quarto edition of the " Gentle Shepherd." By the by, do you know Allan ? He must be a man of very great genius.—Why is he not more known ? Has he no patrons ? or do " poverty's cold wind and crushing rain beat keen and heavy" on him ? I once, and but once, got a glance of that noble edition of the noblest pastoral in the world ; and dear as it was—I mean, dear as to my pocket—I would have bought it ; but I was told that it was printed and engraved for subscribers only. He is the *only* artist who has hit *genuine* pastoral *costume*. What, my dear Cunningham, is there in riches, that they narrow and harden the heart so ? I think, that were I as rich as the sun, I should be as generous as the day ; but as I have no reason to imagine my soul a nobler one than any other man's, I must conclude that wealth imparts a bird-lime quality to the possessor, at which the man, in his native poverty, would have revolted. What has led me to this is the idea of such merit as Mr. Allan possesses, and such riches as a nabob or government contractor possesses, and why they do not form a mutual league. Let wealth shelter and cherish unprotected merit, and the gratitude and celebrity of that merit will richly repay it.—R. B

No. CCLXV.

TO MISS BENSON,

AFTERWARDS MRS. BASIL MONTAGUE.

MADAM,   DUMFRIES, 21st *March*, 1793.

Among many things for which I envy those hale, long-lived old fellows before the Flood, is this in particular, that when they met with anybody after their own heart, they had a charming long prospect of many, many happy meetings with them in after-life.

Now, in this short, stormy, winter day of our fleeting existence, when you now and then, in the chapter of accidents, meet an individual whose acquaintance is a real acquisition, there are all the probabilities against you, that you shall never meet with that valued character more. On the other hand, brief as this miserable being is, it is none of the least of the miseries belonging to it, that if there is any miscreant whom you hate, or creature whom you despise, the ill run of the chances shall be so against you, that in the overtakings, turnings, and jostlings of life, pop, at some

unlucky corner, eternally comes the wretch upon you, and will not allow your indignation or contempt a moment's repose. As I am a sturdy believer in the powers of darkness, I take these to be the doings of that old author of mischief, the Devil. It is well known that he has some kind of shorthand way of taking down our thoughts, and I make no doubt that he is perfectly acquainted with my sentiments respecting Miss Benson : how much I admired her abilities and valued her worth, and how very fortunate I thought myself in her acquaintance. For this last reason, my dear Madam, I must entertain no hopes of the very great pleasure of meeting with you again.

Miss Hamilton tells me that she is sending a packet to you, and I beg leave to send you the enclosed sonnet; though, to tell you the real truth, the sonnet is a mere pretence, that I may have the opportunity of declaring with how much respectful esteem I have the honour to be, &c.—R. B.

No. CCLXVI.

TO PATRICK MILLER, ESQ.

OF DALSWINTON.

SIR,   DUMFRIES, *April*, 1793.

My poems having just come out in another edition, will you do me the honour to accept of a copy ? A mark of my gratitude to you, as a gentleman to whose goodness I have been much indebted ; of my respect for you, as a patriot who, in a venal, sliding age, stands forth the champion of the liberties of my country ; and of my veneration for you, as a man whose benevolence of heart does honour to human nature.

There *was* a time, Sir, when I was your dependent :* this language *then* would have been like the vile incense of flattery—I could not have used it. Now that connexion is at an end, do me the honour to accept of this *honest* tribute of respect from, Sir,

Your much-indebted humble Servant,
R. B.

No. CCLXVII.

TO G. THOMSON.

7th April, 1793.

THANK you, my dear Sir, for your packet. You cannot imagine how much this business of composing for your publication has added to my enjoyments. What with my early attachment to ballads, your book, &c. ballad-making is now as completely my hobby-horse as ever fortification was Uncle Toby's ; so I'll e'en canter it away till I come to the limit of my race, (God grant that I may take the right side of the winning-post !), and then, cheerfully looking back on the honest folks with whom I have

---

* This was when he held the farm of Ellisland as tenant to Mr. Miller.

been happy, I shall say, or sing, "Sae merry as we a' hae been," and raising my last looks to the whole human race, the last words of the voice of Coila shall be "Good night, and joy be wi' you a'!" So much for my last words: now for a few present remarks, as they have occurred at random on looking over your list.

The first lines of "The last time I came o'er the moor," and several other lines in it, are beautiful; but, in my opinion—pardon me, revered shade of Ramsay!—the song is unworthy of the divine air. I shall try to make or mend. "For ever, Fortune, wilt thou prove," is a charming song; but "Logan Burn and Logan Braes" are sweetly susceptible of rural imagery: I'll try that likewise, and, if I succeed, the other song may class among the English ones. I remember the two last lines of a verse in some of the old songs of "Logan Water," (for I know a good many different ones), which I think pretty :—

> "Now my dear lad maun face his faes,
> Far, far frae me and Logan braes."

"My Patie is a Lover gay" is unequal. "His mind is never muddy," is a muddy expression indeed.

> "Then I'll resign and marry Pate,
> And syne my cockernony!"

This is surely far unworthy of Ramsay, or your book. My song, "Rigs of Barley," to the same tune, does not altogether please me; but if I can mend it and thresh a few loose sentiments out of it, I will submit it to your consideration. "The Lass o' Patie's Mill" is one of Ramsay's best songs; but there is one loose sentiment in it which my much-valued friend Mr. Erskine will take into his critical consideration. In Sir J. Sinclair's statistical volumes are two claims—one, I think, from Aberdeenshire, and the other from Ayrshire—for the honour of this song. The following anecdote, which I had from the present Sir William Cunningham of Robertland, who had it of the late John, Earl of Loudon, I can, on such authorities, believe :—

Allan Ramsay was residing at Loudon Castle with the then Earl, father to Earl John; and one forenoon, riding or walking out together, his lordship and Allan passed a sweet, romantic spot on Irwine Water, still called "Patie's Mill," where a bonie lass was "tedding hay, bareheaded, on the green." My lord observed to Allan that it would be a fine theme for a song. Ramsay took the hint, and, lingering behind, he composed the first sketch of it, which he produced at dinner.

"One Day I heard Mary say" is a fine song; but, for consistency's sake, alter the name "Adonis." Were there ever such banns published as a purpose of marriage between Adonis and Mary? I agree with you that my song, "There's nought but Care on every Hand," is much superior to "Poortith cauld." The original song, "The Mill, Mill, O!" though excellent, is, on account of delicacy, inadmissible; still I like the title, and think a Scottish song would suit the notes best; and let your chosen song, which is very pretty, follow as an English set. "The Banks of the

Dee" is, you know, literally " Langolee," to slow time. The song is well enough, but has some false imagery in it ; for instance,

> " And sweetly the nightingale sung from the *tree*."

In the first place, the nightingale sings in a low bush, but never from a tree ; and in the second place, there never was a nightingale seen, or heard, on the banks of the Dee, or on the banks of any other river in Scotland. Exotic rural imagery is always comparatively flat. If I could hit on another stanza equal to " The small birds rejoice," &c., I do myself honestly avow that I think it a superior song. " John Anderson my Jo," the song to this tune in Johnson's " Museum," is my composition, and I think it not my worst : if it suits you, take it and welcome. Your collection of sentimental and pathetic songs is, in my opinion, very complete ; but not so your comic ones. Where are " Tullochgorum," " Lumps o' Puddin'," " Tibbie Fowler," and several others, which, in my humble judgment, are well worthy of preservation ? There is also one sentimental song of mine in the " Museum," which never was known out of the immediate neighbourhood until I got it taken down from a country girl's singing. It is called " Craigieburn Wood ; " and, in the opinion of Mr. Clarke, is one of the sweetest Scottish songs. He is quite an enthusiast about it ; and I would take his taste in Scottish music against the taste of most connoisseurs.

You are quite right in inserting the last five in your list, though they are certainly Irish. " Shepherds, I have lost my love ! " is to me a heavenly air. What would you think of a set of Scottish verses to it ? I have made one to it [" The Gowden Locks of Anna"] a good while ago, but in its original state it is not quite a lady's song. I enclose an altered, not amended, copy for you, if you choose to set the tune to it, and let the Irish verses follow.—R. B.

No. CCLXVIII.

TO JOHN FRANCIS ERSKINE, ESQ.

OF MAR.

[Mr. Erskine, afterwards Earl of Mar, had written to Mr. Riddel, offering to head a public subscription for Burns, under the impression that he had been dismissed from the Excise for his political opinions.]

SIR,   DUMFRIES, 13*th April*, 1793.

Degenerate as human nature is said to be ; and, in many instances, worthless and unprincipled it is ; still there are bright examples to the contrary—examples that even in the eyes of superior beings must shed a lustre on the name of Man.

Such an example have I now before me, when you, Sir, came forward to patronise and befriend a distant obscure stranger, merely because poverty had made him helpless, and his British hardihood of mind had

provoked the arbitrary wantonness of power. My much-esteemed friend,
Mr. Riddel of Glenriddel, has just read me a paragraph of a letter he had
from you. Accept, Sir, of the silent throb of gratitude ; for words would
but mock the emotions of my soul.

You have been misinformed as to my final dismission from the Excise ;
I am still in the service. Indeed, but for the exertions of a gentleman
who must be known to you, Mr. Graham of Fintry, a gentleman who has
ever been my warm and generous friend, I had, without so much as a
hearing, or the slightest previous intimation, been turned adrift, with my
helpless family, to all the horrors of want. Had I had any other resource, probably I might have saved them the trouble of a dismission ;
but the little money I gained by my publication is almost every guinea
embarked to save from ruin an only brother, who, though one of the
worthiest, is by no means one of the most fortunate, of men.

In my defence to their accusations I said, that whatever might be my
sentiments of republics, ancient or modern, as to Britain I abjured the
idea : that a constitution, which, in its original principles, experience
had proved to be every way fitted for our happiness in society, it would be
insanity to sacrifice to an untried visionary theory : that, in consideration of my being situated in a department, however humble, immediately
in the hands of people in power, I had forborne taking any active part,
either personally or as an author, in the present business of Reform :
but that, where I must declare my sentiments, I would say there existed
a system of corruption between the executive power and the representative part of the Legislature, which boded no good to our glorious constitution, and which every patriotic Briton must wish to see amended.
Some such sentiments as these I stated in a letter to my generous patron
Mr. Graham, which he laid before the Board at large ; where, it seems,
my last remark gave great offence ; and one of our supervisors general, a
Mr. Corbet, was instructed to inquire on the spot, and to document me—
" that my business was to act, *not to think ;* and that whatever might be
men or measures, it was for me to be *silent* and *obedient.*"

Mr. Corbet was likewise my steady friend ; so, between Mr. Graham
and him, I have been partly forgiven ; only I understand that all hopes of
my getting officially forward are blasted.

Now, Sir, to the business in which I would more immediately interest
you. The partiality of my countrymen has brought me forward as a
man of genius, and has given me a character to support. In the poet I
have avowed manly and independent sentiments, which I trust will be
found in the man. Reasons of no less weight than the support of a wife
and family have pointed out as the eligible, and, situated as I was, the only
eligible line of life for me, my present occupation. Still my honest fame
is my dearest concern ; and a thousand times have I trembled at the idea
of those *degrading* epithets that malice or misrepresentation may affix to
my name. I have often, in blasting anticipation, listened to some future
hackney scribbler, with the heavy malice of savage stupidity, exulting in
his hireling paragraphs : " Burns, notwithstanding the *fanfaronade* of independence to be found in his works, and after having been held forth to

public view and to public estimation as a man of some genius, yet, quite destitute of resources within himself to support his borrowed dignity, he dwindled into a paltry exciseman, and slunk out the rest of his insignificant existence in the meanest of pursuits, and among the vilest of mankind."

In your illustrious hands, Sir, permit me to lodge my disavowal and defiance of these slanderous falsehoods. Burns was a poor man from birth, and an exciseman by necessity; but—*I will* say it !—the sterling of his honest worth no poverty could debase, and his independent British mind oppression might bend, but could not subdue. Have not I, to me, a more precious stake in my country's welfare than the richest dukedom in it? I have a large family of children, and the prospect of many more. I have three sons, who, I see already, have brought into the world souls ill qualified to inhabit the bodies of slaves. Can I look tamely on, and see any machination to wrest from them the birthright of my boys—the little independent Britons, in whose veins runs my own blood? No! I will not ! should my heart's blood stream around my attempt to defend it!

Does any man tell me, that my full efforts can be of no service ; and that it does not belong to my humble station to meddle with the concern of a nation?

I can tell him, that it is on such individuals as I that a nation has to rest, both for the hand of support and the eye of intelligence. The uninformed mob may swell a nation's bulk ; and the titled, tinsel, courtly throng may be its feathered ornament ; but the number of those who are elevated enough in life to reason and to reflect, yet low enough to keep clear of the venal contagion of a court—these are a nation's strength.

I know not how to apologize for the impertinent length of this epistle ; but one small request I must ask of you farther.—When you have honoured this letter with a perusal, please to commit it to the flames. Burns, in whose behalf you have so generously interested yourself, I have here, in his native colours, drawn *as he is ;* but should any of the people in whose hands is the very bread he eats get the least knowledge of the picture, *it would ruin the poor* BARD *for ever!*

My poems having just come out in another edition, I beg leave to present you with a copy as a small mark of that high esteem and ardent gratitude with which I have the honour to be, Sir,

Your deeply indebted

And ever devoted humble Servant,

R. B.

No. CCLXIX.

TO THE EARL OF GLENCAIRN.

MY LORD, [*May,* 1794?].

When you cast your eye on the name at the bottom of this letter, and on the title-page of the book [a new edition of the poems] I do myself the honour to send your lordship, a more pleasurable feeling than my

vanity tells me that it must be a name not entirely unknown to you. The generous patronage of your late illustrious brother found me in the lowest obscurity : he introduced my rustic muse to the partiality of my country ; and to him I owe all. My sense of his goodness, and the anguish of my soul at losing my truly noble protector and friend, I have endeavoured to express in a poem to his memory, which I have now published. This edition is just from the press ; and in my gratitude to the dead, and my respect for the living (fame belies you, my lord, if you possess not the same dignity of man which was your noble brother's characteristic feature), I had destined a copy for the Earl of Glencairn. I learnt just now that you are in town :—allow me to present it you.

I know, my lord, such is the vile, venal contagion which pervades the world of letters, that professions of respect from an author, particularly from a poet, to a lord, are more than suspicious. I claim my by-past conduct, and my feelings at this moment, as exceptions to the too just conclusion. Exalted as are the honours of your lordship's name, and unnoted as is the obscurity of mine, with the uprightness of an honest man I come before your lordship, with an offering—however humble, 'tis all I have to give—of my grateful respect ; and to beg of you, my lord—'tis all I have to ask of you—that you will do me the honour to accept of it.

I have the honour to be,

R. B.

No. CCLXX.

TO G. THOMSON.

April, 1793.

. . . . GIVE me leave to criticise your taste in the only thing in which it is, in my opinion, reprehensible. You know I ought to know something of my own trade. Of pathos, sentiment, and point you are a complete judge ; but there is a quality more necessary than either in a song, and which is the very essence of a ballad ; I mean simplicity : now, if I mistake not, this last feature you are a little apt to sacrifice to the foregoing.

Ramsay, as every other poet, has not been always equally happy in his pieces : still I cannot approve of taking such liberties with an author as Mr. W. proposes doing with " The last time I came o'er the moor." Let a poet, if he chooses, take up the idea of another, and work it into a piece of his own ; but to mangle the works of the poor bard whose tuneful tongue is now mute for ever, in the dark and narrow house—by Heaven, 'twould be sacrilege ! I grant that Mr. W.'s version is an improvement ; but—I know Mr. W. well, and esteem him much—let him mend the song as the Highlander mended his gun : he gave it a new stock, a new lock, and a new barrel.

I do not, by this, object to leaving out improper stanzas, where that can be done without spoiling the whole. One stanza in " The Lass o' Patie's Mill" must be left out : the song will be nothing worse for it. I am not sure if we can take the same liberty with " Corn Rigs are bonie : "

perhaps it might want the last stanza, and be the better for it. "Cauld Kail in Aberdeen" you must leave with me yet a while. I have vowed to have a song to that air, on the lady whom I attempted to celebrate in the verses, "Poortith cauld and restless love." At any rate, my other song, "Green grow the Rashes," will never suit. That song is current in Scotland under the old title, and to the merry old tune of that name; which, of course, would mar the progress of your song to celebrity. Your book will be the standard of Scots songs for the future : let this idea ever keep your judgment on the alarm.

I send a song, on a celebrated toast in this country, to suit "Bonie Dundee." I send you also a ballad to the "Mill, Mill, O !"

"The last time I came o'er the moor" I would fain attempt to make a Scots song for, and let Ramsay's be the English set. You shall hear from me soon. When you go to London on this business, can you come by Dumfries ? I have still several MS. Scots airs by me which I have picked up, mostly from the singing of country lasses. They please me vastly ; but your learned lugs would perhaps be displeased with the very feature for which I like them. I call them simple ; you would pronounce them silly. Do you know a fine air, called "Jackie Hume's Lament "? I have a song of considerable merit to that air. I'll enclose you both the song and tune, as I had them ready to send to Johnson's "Museum." I send you likewise, to me, a beautiful little air, which I had taken down from *vivâ voce.*—Adieu !—R. B.

No. CCLXXI.

TO G. THOMSON.

April, 1793.

. . . . ONE hint let me give you. Whatever Mr. Pleyel does, let him not alter one iota of the original Scottish airs—I mean in the song department—but let our national music preserve its native features. They are, I own, frequently wild and irreducible to the more modern rules ; but on that very eccentricity, perhaps, depends a great part of their effect.

No. CCLXXII.

TO MR. ROBERT AINSLIE.

April 26, 1793.

I AM damnably out of humour, my dear Ainslie, and that is the reason why I take up the pen to *you:* 'tis the nearest way (*probatum est*) to recover my spirits again.

I received your last, and was much entertained with it ; but I will not at this time, nor at any other time, answer it. Answer a letter? I never could answer a letter in my life ! I have written many a letter in return for letters I have received ; but then they were original matter—spurt-away ! zig, here ; zag, there ; as if the devil that, my grannie (an old woman indeed) often told me, rode on will-o'-wisp, or, in her more classic phrase, Spunkie, were looking over my elbow.—Happy thought that

B

idea has engendered in my head : Spunkie, thou shalt henceforth be my symbol, signature, and tutelary genius ! Like thee, hap-step-and-lowp, here-awa-there-awa, higglety-pigglety, pell-mell, hither-and-yon, ram-stam, happy-go-lucky, up-tails-a'-by-the-light-o'-the-moon, has been, is, and shall be, my progress through the mosses and moors of this vile, bleak, barren wilderness of a life of ours.

Come, then, my guardian spirit ! like thee, may I skip away, amusing myself by and at my own light : and if any opaque-souled lubber of mankind complain that my elfine, lambent, glimmerous wanderings have misled his stupid steps over precipices, or into bogs ; let the thick-headed Blunderbuss recollect, that he is not Spunkie ; that

> Spunkie's wanderings could not copied be :
> Amid these perils none durst walk but he.

* * * * *

I have no doubt but scholarcraft may be caught, as a Scotsman catches the itch—by friction. How else can you account for it, that born block-heads, by mere dint of *handling* books, grow so wise that even they themselves are equally convinced of and surprised at their own parts ? I once carried this philosophy to that degree, that in a knot of country folks who had a library amongst them, and who, to the honour of their good sense, made me factotum in the business, one of our members,—a little, wise-looking, squat, upright, jabbering body of a tailor,—I advised him, instead of turning over the leaves, *to bind the book on his back.* Johnie took the hint ; and as our meetings were every fourth Saturday, and Pricklouse having a good Scots mile to walk in coming, and, of course, another in returning, Bodkin was sure to lay his hand on some heavy quarto, or ponderous folio, with and under which, wrapt up in his grey plaid, he grew wise, as he grew weary, all the way home. He carried this so far, that an old musty Hebrew concordance, which we had in a present from a neighbouring priest, by mere dint of applying it, as doctors do a blistering plaster, between his shoulders, Stitch, in a dozen pilgrim-ages, acquired as much rational theology as the said priest had done by forty years' perusal of the pages.

Tell me, and tell me truly, what you think of this theory.

Yours,
SPUNKIE.

No. CCLXXIII.

TO G. THOMSON.

[In a letter to Peter Hill about this time Burns also bewails the condition of the country : " O may the wrath and curse of all mankind haunt and harass these turbulent, unprincipled miscreants who have involved a people in this ruinous business ! "]

June, 1793.

WHEN I tell you, my dear Sir, that a friend of mine, in whom I am much interested, has fallen a sacrifice to these accursed times, you will easily allow that it might unhinge me for doing any good among ballads.

My own loss, as to pecuniary matters, is trifling : but the total ruin of a much-loved friend is a loss indeed. Pardon my seeming inattention to your last commands. . . . .

No. CCLXXIV.

TO G. THOMSON.

June 25th, 1793.

HAVE you ever, my dear Sir, felt your bosom ready to burst with indignation on reading of those mighty villains who divide kingdom against kingdom, desolate provinces, and lay nations waste, out of the wantonness of ambition, or often from still more ignoble passions? In a mood of this kind to-day I recollected the air of "Logan Water," and it occurred to me that its querulous melody probably had its origin from the plaintive indignation of some swelling, suffering heart, fired at the tyrannic strides of some public destroyer, and overwhelmed with private distress, the consequence of a country's ruin. If I have done anything at all like justice to my feelings, the following song, composed in three-quarters of an hour's meditation in my elbow-chair, ought to have some merit.

[Here follows " Logan Water."]

No. CCLXXV.

TO G. THOMSON.

[Mr. Thomson had sent Burns £5, as an instalment of remuneration for his songs.]

July, 1793.

I ASSURE you, my dear Sir, that you truly hurt me with your pecuniary parcel. It degrades me in my own eyes. However, to return it would savour of affectation ; but, as to any more traffic of that debtor and creditor kind, I swear, by that honour which crowns the upright statue of Robert Burns's integrity, on the least motion of it I will indignantly spurn the by-past transaction, and from that moment commence entire stranger to you! Burns's character for generosity of sentiment and independence of mind will, I trust, long outlive any of his wants, which the cold unfeeling ore can supply : at least, I will take care that such a character he shall deserve.

Thank you for my copy of your publication. Never did my eyes behold in any musical work such elegance and correctness. Your preface, too, is admirably written ; only your partiality to me has made you say too much : however, it will bind me down to double every effort in the future progress of the work. The following are a few remarks on the songs in the list you sent me. I never copy what I write to you ; so I may be often tautological, or perhaps contradictory.

" The Flowers o' the Forest " is charming as a poem, and should be,

and must be, set to the notes; but, though out of your rule, the three stanzas beginning,

" I hae seen the smiling o' fortune beguiling, '

are worthy of a place, were it but to immortalize the author of them, who is an old lady of my acquaintance, and at this moment living in Edinburgh. She is a Mrs. Cockburn; I forget of what place; but from Roxburghshire. What a charming apostrophe is —

" O fickle Fortune, why this cruel sporting?
Why, why torment us—poor sons of a day?"

The old ballad, " I wish I were where Helen lies," is silly, to contemptibility. My alteration of it, in Johnson's, is not much better. Mr. Pinkerton, in his, what he calls, ancient ballads (many of them notorious, though beautiful enough, forgeries) has the best set. It is full of his own interpolations—but no matter.

In my next I will suggest to your consideration a few songs which may have escaped your hurried notice. In the mean time allow me to congratulate you now, as a brother of the quill. You have committed your character and fame; which will now be tried, for ages to come, by the illustrious jury of the Sons and Daughters of Taste—all whom poesy can please, or music charm.

Being a bard of Nature, I have some pretensions to second sight; and I am warranted by the spirit to foretel, and affirm, that your great-grandchild will hold up your volumes, and say, with honest pride, " This so much admired selection was the work of my ancestor ! "—R. B.

No. CCLXXVI.

TO MISS HELEN CRAIK,

OF ARBIGLAND.

MADAM,

DUMFRIES, *August*, 1793.

I enclose you two of my late pieces, as some kind of return for the pleasure I have received in perusing a certain MS. volume of poems in the possession of Captain Riddel. To repay one with an *old song* is a proverb whose force you, Madam, I know, will not allow. What is said of illustrious descent is, I believe, equally true of a talent for poetry—none ever despised it who had pretensions to it. The fates and characters of the rhyming tribe often employ my thoughts when I am disposed to be melancholy. There is not, among all the martyrologies that ever were penned, so rueful a narrative as the lives of the poets. In the comparative view of wretches, the criterion is not what they are doomed to suffer, but how they are formed to bear. Take a being of our kind; give him a stronger imagination and a more delicate sensibility, which between them will ever engender a more ungovernable set of passions than are the usual lot of man; implant in him an irresistible impulse to some idle vagary, such as arranging wild flowers in fantastical nosegays, tracing the

grasshopper to his haunt by his chirping song, watching the frisks of the little minnows in the sunny pool, or hunting after the intrigues of butterflies —in short, send him adrift after some pursuit which shall eternally mislead him from the paths of lucre, and yet curse him with a keener relish than any man living for the pleasures that lucre can purchase ; lastly, fill up the measure of his woes by bestowing on him a spurning sense of his own dignity ; and you have created a wight nearly as miserable as a poet. To you, Madam, I need not recount the fairy pleasures the Muse bestows to counterbalance this catalogue of evils. Bewitching poetry is like bewitching woman ; she has in all ages been accused of misleading mankind from the councils of wisdom and the paths of prudence, involving them in difficulties, baiting them with poverty, branding them with infamy, and plunging them in the whirling vortex of ruin : yet, where is the man but must own that all our happiness on earth is not worthy the name ; that even the holy hermit's solitary prospect of paradisiacal bliss is but the glitter of a northern sun rising over a frozen region, compared with the many pleasures, the nameless raptures, that we owe to the lovely Queen of the heart of Man !—R. B.

No. CCLXXVII.

TO G. THOMSON.

August, 1793.

I HAVE tried my hand on " Robin Adair," and, you will probably think, with little success ; but it is such a cursed, cramp, out-of-the-way measure, that I despair of doing anything better to it.

[Here follow three stanzas of " Phillis the Fair." *Page* 184.]

So much for namby-pamby. I may, after all, try my hand on it in Scots verse. There I always find myself most at home.

I have just put the last hand to the song I meant for " Cauld Kail in Aberdeen." If it suits you to insert it, I shall be pleased, as the heroine is a favourite of mine : if not, I shall also be pleased ; because I wish, and will be glad, to see you act decidedly on the business. 'Tis a tribute as a man of taste, and as an editor, which you owe yourself.

No. CCLXXVIII.

TO G. THOMSON.

August, 1793.

THAT crinkum-crankum tune, " Robin Adair," has run so in my head, and I succeeded so ill in my last attempt, that I have ventured, in this morning's walk, one essay more.

[" Had I a Cave." *Page* 185.]

By the way, I have met with a musical Highlander, in Breadalbane's Fencibles, which are quartered here, who assures me that he well remembers his mother's singing Gaelic songs to both " Robin Adair" and

" Gramachree." They certainly have more of the Scotch than Irish taste in them.

This man comes from the vicinity of Inverness ; so it could not be any intercourse with Ireland that could bring them ;—except, what I shrewdly suspect to be the case, the wandering minstrels, harpers, and pipers, used to go frequently errant through the wilds both of Scotland and Ireland, and so some favourite airs might be common to both.   A case in point.— They have lately, in Ireland, published an Irish air, as they say, called " Caun du delish."   The fact is, in a publication of Corri's, a great while ago, you will find the same air called a Highland one, with a Gaelic song set to it.   Its name there, I think, is " Oran Gaoil," and a fine air it is. Do ask honest Allan, or the Rev. Gaelic Parson, about these matters.

No. CCLXXIX.

TO G. THOMSON.

August, 1793.

THAT tune, " Cauld Kail," is such a favourite of yours, that I once more roved out yesterday for a gloamin-shot at the Muses ; when the Muse that presides o'er the shores of Nith, or rather my old inspiring dearest nymph, Coila, whispered me the following.   I have two reasons for thinking that it was my early, sweet, simple inspirer that was by my elbow, " smooth gliding without step," and pouring the song on my glowing fancy.   In the first place, since I left Coila's native haunts, not a fragment of a poet has arisen to cheer her solitary musings, by catching inspiration from her ; so I more than suspect that she has followed me hither, or at least makes me occasional visits : secondly, the last stanza of this song I send you is the very words that Coila taught me many years ago, and which I set to an old Scots reel in Johnson's " Museum."

[" Come, let me take thee to my breast."]

If you think the above will suit your idea of your favourite air, I shall be highly pleased.   " The last time I came o'er the moor" I cannot meddle with as to mending it ; and the musical world have been so long accustomed to Ramsay's words, that a different song, though positively superior, would not be so well received.   I am not fond of choruses to songs, so I have not made one for the foregoing.

No. CCLXXX.

TO G. THOMSON

Sept. 1793.

YOU know that my pretensions to musical taste are merely a few of nature's instincts, untaught and untutored by art.   For this reason many musical compositions, particularly where much of the merit lies in coun- terpoint, however they may transport and ravish the ears of you connois- seurs, affect my simple lug no otherwise then merely as melodious din. On the other hand, by way of amends, I am delighted with many little melodies, which the learned musician despises as silly and insipid.   I do

not know whether the old air, " Hey, tuttie taitie," may rank among this number ; but well I know that, with Fraser's hautboy, it has often filled my eyes with tears. There is a tradition, which I have met with in many places of Scotland, that it was Robert Bruce's march at the battle of Bannockburn. This thought, in my solitary wanderings, warmed me to a pitch of enthusiasm on the theme of liberty and independence, which I threw into a kind of Scottish ode, fitted to the air, that one might suppose to be the gallant Royal Scot's address to his heroic followers on that eventful morning.

[" Scots, wha hae wi' Wallace bled."] *

So may God ever defend the cause of truth and liberty, as He did that day !—Amen.

P. S. I showed the air to Urbani, who was highly pleased with it, and begged me to make soft verses for it ; but I had no idea of giving myself any trouble on the subject, till the accidental recollection of that glorious struggle for freedom, associated with the glowing ideas of some other struggles of the same nature, not quite so ancient, roused my rhyming mania. Clarke's set of the tune, with his bass, you will find in the " Museum ; " though I am afraid that the air is not what will entitle it to a place in your elegant selection.

No. CCLXXXI.

TO G. THOMSON.

Sept. 1793.

I DARESAY, my dear Sir, that you will begin to think my correspondence is persecution. No matter, I can't help it ; a ballad is my hobby-horse, which, though otherwise a simple sort of harmless idiotical beast enough, has yet this blessed headstrong property, that when once it has fairly made off with a hapless wight, it gets so enamoured with the tinkle-gingle, tinkle-gingle of its own bells, that it is sure to run poor pilgarlick, the bedlam jockey, quite beyond any useful point or post in the common race of man.

The following song I have composed for " Oran Gaoil," the Highland air, that, you tell me in your last, you have resolved to give a place to in your book. I have this moment finished the song, so you have it glowing from the mint. If it suit you, well !—If not, 'tis also well !

[" Behold the Hour."]

No. CCLXXXII.

TO G. THOMSON.

September, 1793.

" LADDIE, lie near me," must lie by me for some time. I do not know the air ; and until I am complete master of a tune, in my own singing

---

* It is related that Burns composed this noble song under the influence of a storm of rain and lightning among the wilds of Glenken in Galloway.

(such as it is), I can never compose for it. My way is : I consider the poetic sentiment correspondent to my idea of the musical expression ; then choose my theme ; begin one stanza ; when that is composed, which is generally the most difficult part of the business, I walk out, sit down now and then, look out for objects in nature round me that are in unison or harmony with the cogitations of my fancy and workings of my bosom ; humming every now and then the air, with the verses I have framed. When I feel my muse beginning to jade, I retire to the solitary fireside of my study, and there commit my effusions to paper ; swinging, at intervals, on the hind-legs of my elbow-chair, by way of calling forth my own critical strictures, as my pen goes on. Seriously, this, at home, is almost invariably my way.

What cursed egotism !

" Blythe hae I been o'er the hill " is one of the finest songs I ever made in my life ; and, besides, is composed on a young lady, positively the most beautiful, lovely woman in the world. As I purpose giving you the names and designations of all my heroines, to appear in some future edition of your work, perhaps half a century hence, you must certainly include " The boniest lass in a' the warld " in your collection.

" Saw ye my Father ? " is one of my greatest favourites. The evening before last I wandered out, and began a tender song, in what I think is its native style. I must premise that the old way, and the way to give most effect, is to have no starting-note, as the fiddlers call it, but to burst at once into the pathos. Every country girl sings " Saw ye my Father ? " &c. . . . .

One song more and I have done —" Auld Lang Syne." The air is but mediocre ; but the following song, the old song of the olden times, and which has never been in print, nor even in manuscript, until I took it down from an old man's singing, is enough to recommend any air :—

[Here follows " Auld Lang Syne," of which Allan Cunningham attributes the second, third, and fourth verses to Burns.]

Now, I suppose, I have tired your patience fairly. You must, after all is over, have a number of ballads, properly so called. " Gil Morice," " Tranent Muir," " Macpherson's Farewell," " Battle of Sheriff-Muir," or, " We ran and they ran " (I know the author of this charming ballad, and his history), " Hardiknute," " Barbara Allan " (I can furnish a finer set of this tune than any that has yet appeared) ; and, besides, do you know that I really have the old tune to which " The Cherry and the Slae " was sung, and which is mentioned as a well-known air in " Scotland's Complaint," a book published before poor Mary's days. It was then called " The Banks o' Helicon," an old poem which Pinkerton has brought to light. You will see all this in Tytler's " History of Scottish Music." The tune, to a learned ear, may have no great merit ; but it is a great curiosity. I have a good many original things of this kind.

No. CCLXXXIII.

TO G. THOMSON.

September, 1793.

" WHO shall decide when doctors disagree?" My ode "Bannockburn" pleases me so much that I cannot alter it. . . . .

I have finished my song to "Saw ye my Father?" and in English, as you will see. That there is a syllable too much for the expression of the air, it is true; but allow me to say, that the mere dividing of a dotted crotchet into a crotchet and a quaver is not a great matter : however, in that I have no pretensions to cope in judgment with you. Of the poetry I speak with confidence ; but the music is a business where I hint my ideas with the utmost diffidence.

No. CCLXXXIV.

TO G. THOMSON.

. . . . YOUR Irish airs are pretty, but they are downright Irish. If they were like the "Banks of Banna," for instance, though really Irish, yet in the Scottish taste, you might adopt them. Since you are so fond of Irish music, what say you to twenty-five of them in an additional number? We could easily find this quantity of charming airs ; I will take care that you shall not want songs ; and I assure you that you would find it the most saleable of the whole. If you do not approve of "Roy's Wife," for the music's sake, we shall not insert it. "Deil tak the Wars" is a charming song ; so is "Saw ye my Peggy?" "There's nae Luck about the House" well deserves a place. I cannot say that "O'er the hills and far awa" strikes me as equal to your selection. "This is no my ain House" is a great favourite air of mine ; and if you will send me your set of it, I will task my muse to her highest effort. What is your opinion of "I hae laid a Herrin' in Sawt?" I like it much. Your Jacobite airs are pretty : and there are many others of the same kind, pretty ; but you have not room for them. You cannot, I think, insert "Fye, let's a' to the Bridal," to any other words than its own.

What pleases me as simple and *naïve*, disgusts you as ludicrous and low. For this reason "Fye, gie me my coggie, Sirs," "Fye, let's a' to the Bridal," with several others of that cast, are, to me, highly pleasing ; while "Saw thee my Father, or saw ye my Mother?" delights me with its descriptive simple pathos. Thus my song, "Ken ye what Meg o' the Mill has gotten?" pleases myself so much, that I cannot try my hand at another song to the air ; so I shall not attempt it. I know you will laugh at all this ; but "Ilka man wears his belt his ain gait."

No. CCLXXXV.

TO JOHN McMURDO, ESQ.

SIR, *Dumfries, December,* 1793.

It is said that we take the greatest liberties with our greatest friends, and I pay myself a very high compliment in the manner in which

I am going to apply the remark. I have owed you money longer than ever I owed it to any man. Here is Ker's account, and here are six guineas ; and now I don't owe a shilling to man—or woman either. But for these damned dirty, dog's-ear'd little pages [Scottish banknotes], I had done myself the honour to have waited on you long ago. Independent of the obligations your hospitality has laid me under, the consciousness of your superiority in the rank of man and gentleman of itself was fully as much as I could ever make head against ; but to owe you money too was more than I could face.

I think I once mentioned something of a collection of Scots songs I have for some years been making : I send you a perusal of what I have got together. I could not conveniently spare them above five or six days, and five or six glances of them will probably more than suffice you. A very few of them are my own. When you are tired of them, please leave them with Mr. Clint, of the King's Arms. There is not another copy of the collection in the world ; and I should be sorry that any unfortunate negligence should deprive me of what has cost me a good deal of pains.

R. B.

No. CCLXXXVI.

TO CAPTAIN [ROBERTSON OF LUDE ?].

SIR,   DUMFRIES, *5th December,* 1793.

    Heated as I was with wine yesternight, I was perhaps rather seemingly impertinent in my anxious wish to be honoured with your acquaintance. You will forgive it : it was the impulse of heart-felt respect. "He is the father of the Scottish country reform, and is a man who does honour to the business at the same time that the business does honour to him," said my worthy friend Glenriddel to somebody by me who was talking of your coming to this country with your corps. "Then," I said, "I have a woman's longing to take him by the hand, and say to him, ' Sir, I honour you as a man to whom the interests of humanity are dear, and as a patriot to whom the rights of your country are sacred.'"

In times like these, Sir, when our commoners are barely able by the glimmer of their own twilight understandings to scrawl a frank, and when lords are what gentlemen would be ashamed to be, to whom shall a sinking country call for help ? To the independent country gentleman ! To him who has too deep a stake in his country not to be in earnest for her welfare, and who in the honest pride of man can view with equal contempt the insolence of office and the allurements of corruption.

I mentioned to you a Scots ode or song I had lately composed, and which I think has some merit. Allow me to enclose it. When I fall in with you at the theatre, I shall be glad to have your opinion of it. Accept of it, Sir, as a very humble but most sincere tribute of respect from a man who, dear as he prizes poetic fame, yet holds dearer an independent mind.

I have the honour to be,
R. B.

No. CCLXXXVII.

TO THE EARL OF BUCHAN,

WITH A COPY OF BRUCE'S ADDRESS TO HIS TROOPS AT BANNOCKBURN.

MY LORD, DUMFRIES, *12th January*, 1794.

Will your lordship allow me to present you with the enclosed little composition of mine, as a small tribute of gratitude for the acquaintance with which you have been pleased to honour me. Independent of my enthusiasm as a Scotsman, I have rarely met with anything in history which interests my feelings as a man equal with the story of Bannockburn. On the one hand, a cruel but able usurper, leading on the finest army in Europe to extinguish the last spark of freedom among a greatly daring and greatly injured people ; on the other hand, the desperate relics of a gallant nation devoting themselves to rescue their bleeding country, or perish with her.

Liberty ! thou art a prize truly and indeed invaluable ; for never canst thou be too dearly bought !—R. B.

No. CCLXXXVIII.

TO MRS. RIDDEL.

[Burns's repugnance to officers of the army was probably due in some measure to his hostility to the political cause with which he identified them.]

DEAR MADAM,

I meant to have called on you yesternight, but as I edged up to your box-door, the first object which greeted my view was one of those lobster-coated puppies, sitting like another dragon, guarding the Hesperian fruit. On the conditions and capitulations you so obligingly offer, I shall certainly make my weather-beaten rustic phiz a part of your box-furniture on Tuesday ; when we may arrange the business of the visit.

Among the profusion of idle compliments which insidious craft, or unmeaning folly, incessantly offer at your shrine—a shrine, how far exalted above such adoration!—permit me, were it but for rarity's sake, to pay you the honest tribute of a warm heart and an independent mind ; and to assure you that I am, thou most amiable and most accomplished of thy sex, with the most respectful esteem and fervent regard, thine, &c.

R. B.

No. CCLXXXIX.

TO MR. SAMUEL CLARKE, JUN.

DUMFRIES.

[At a supper-table Burns proposed the toast, " May our success in the present war be equal to the justice of our cause," which was resented by an officer present as a reflection on the Government and the army. Next morning Burns wrote this note.]

DEAR SIR,   *Sunday Morning.*

    I was, I know, drunk last night, but I am sober this morning. From the expressions Capt. ———— made use of to me, had I had nobody's welfare to care for but my own, we should certainly have come, according to the manners of the world, to the necessity of murdering one another about the business. The words were such as generally, I believe, end in a brace of pistols ; but I am still pleased to think that I did not ruin the peace and welfare of a wife and a family of children in a drunken squabble. Farther, you know that the report of certain political opinions being mine has already once before brought me to the brink of destruction. I dread lest last night's business may be misrepresented in the same way. You, I beg, will take care to prevent it. I tax your wish for Mr. Burns's welfare with the task of waiting as soon as possible on every gentleman who was present, and state this to him, and, as you please, show him this letter. What, after all, was the obnoxious toast ? " May our success in the present war be equal to the justice of our cause "—a toast that the most outrageous frenzy of loyalty cannot object to. I request and beg that this morning you will wait on the parties present at the foolish dispute. I shall only add, that I am truly sorry that a man who stood so high in my estimation as Mr. —— should use me in the manner in which I conceive he has done.—R. B.

No. CCXC.

TO MRS. RIDDEL.

[Burns's intimacy with the Riddels was interrupted about this time in consequence of the Poet's rough behaviour to the lady after a bout of hard drinking at the dinner-table. The following letter of apology is supposed to be written from the Dead to the Living.]

MADAM,

    I daresay that this is the first epistle you ever received from this nether world. I write you from the regions of hell, amid the horrors of the damned. The time and manner of my leaving your earth I do not exactly know, as I took my departure in the heat of a fever of intoxication, contracted at your too hospitable mansion ; but, on my arrival here, I was fairly tried, and sentenced to endure the purgatorial tortures of this

infernal confine for the space of ninety-nine years, eleven months, and twenty-nine days, and all on account of the impropriety of my conduct yesternight under your roof. Here am I, laid on a bed of pitiless furze, with my aching head reclined on a pillow of ever-piercing thorn, while an infernal tormentor, wrinkled, and old, and cruel—his name I think is *Recollection*—with a whip of scorpions, forbids peace or rest to approach me, and keeps anguish eternally awake. Still, Madam, if I could in any measure be reinstated in the good opinion of the fair circle whom my conduct last night so much injured, I think it would be an alleviation to my torments. For this reason I trouble you with this letter. To the men of the company I will make no apology. Your husband, who insisted on my drinking more than I chose, has no right to blame me ; and the other gentlemen were partakers of my guilt. But to you, Madam, I have much to apologize. Your good opinion I valued as one of the greatest acquisitions I had made on earth, and I was truly a beast to forfeit it. There was a Miss I—— too, a woman of fine sense, gentle and unassuming manners—do make, on my part, a miserable d-mned wretch's best apology to her. A Mrs. G——, a charming woman, did me the honour to be prejudiced in my favour; this makes me hope that I have not outraged her beyond all forgiveness. To all the other ladies please present my humblest contrition for my conduct, and my petition for their gracious pardon. O all ye powers of decency and decorum ! whisper to them that my errors, though great, were involuntary—that an intoxicated man is the vilest of beasts—that it was not in my nature to be brutal to any one—that to be rude to a woman, when in my senses, was impossible with me—but—

* * * * * * *

Regret ! Remorse ! Shame ! ye three hellhounds that ever dog my steps and bay at my heels, spare me ! spare me !

Forgive the offences, and pity the perdition of, Madam,

Your humble Slave,

R. B.

No. CCXCI.

TO MRS. RIDDEL.

Madam,

I return your common-place book. I have perused it with much pleasure, and would have continued my criticisms ; but as it seems the critic has forfeited your esteem, his strictures must lose their value.

If it is true that " offences come only from the heart," before you I am guiltless. To admire, esteem, and prize you as the most accomplished of women and the first of friends—if these are crimes, I am the most offending thing alive.

In a face where I used to meet the kind complacency of friendly confidence, *now* to find cold neglect and contemptuous scorn, is a wrench that my heart can ill bear. It is, however, some kind of miserable good luck, that while *de-haut-en-bas* rigour may depress an unoffending wretch to the ground, it has a tendency to rouse a stubborn something in his

bosom, which, though it cannot heal the wounds of his soul, is at least an opiate to blunt their poignancy.

With the profoundest respect for your abilities; the most sincere esteem, and ardent regard, for your gentle heart and amiable manners; and the most fervent wish and prayer for your welfare, peace, and bliss, I have the honour to be, Madam,

Your most devoted humble Servant,
R. B.

No. CCXCII.

TO MRS. RIDDEL.

[In spite of Burns's rather abject pleadings the breach of friendship was not repaired. The lampoons on Mrs. Riddel, in which Burns vented his anger, cast a dark shadow on this part of his life.]

I HAVE this moment got the song from Syme, and I am sorry to see that he has spoilt it a good deal. It shall be a lesson to me how I lend him anything again.

I have sent you " Werter," truly happy to have any the smallest opportunity of obliging you.

'Tis true, Madam, I saw you once since I was at Woodlea; and that once froze the very life-blood of my heart. Your reception of me was such, that a wretch meeting the eye of his judge, about to pronounce sentence of death on him, could only have envied my feelings and situation. But I hate the theme, and never more shall write or speak on it.

One thing I shall proudly say, that I can pay Mrs. R. a higher tribute of esteem, and appreciate her amiable worth more truly, than any man whom I have seen approach her.—R. B.

No. CCXCIII.

TO MR. CUNNINGHAM.

["They," says Mr. Lockhart, "who have been told that Burns was ever a degraded being, who have permitted themselves to believe that his only consolations were those of 'the opiate guilt applies to grief,' will do well to pause over this noble letter and judge for themselves."]

25th February, 1794.

CANST thou minister to a mind diseased? Canst thou speak peace and rest to a soul tost on a sea of troubles, without one friendly star to guide her course, and dreading that the next surge may overwhelm her? Canst thou give to a frame, tremblingly alive as the tortures of suspense, the stability and hardihood of the rock that braves the blast? If thou canst not do the least of these, why wouldst thou disturb me in my miseries, with thy inquiries after me? . . . .

For these two months I have not been able to lift a pen. My constitution and frame were, *ab origine*, blasted with a deep incurable taint of

hypochondria, which poisons my existence. Of late a number of domestic vexations, and some pecuniary share in the ruin of these cursed times— losses which, though trifling, were yet what I could ill bear—have so irritated me, that my feelings at times could only be envied by a reprobate spirit listening to the sentence that dooms it to perdition.

Are you deep in the language of consolation? I have exhausted in reflection every topic of comfort. *A heart at ease* would have been charmed with my sentiments and reasonings; but as to myself, I was like Judas Iscariot preaching the Gospel : he might melt and mould the hearts of those around him, but his own kept its native incorrigibility.

Still there are two great pillars that bear us up, amid the wreck of misfortune and misery. The one is composed of the different modifications of a certain noble, stubborn something in man, known by the names of courage, fortitude, magnanimity. The other is made up of those feelings and sentiments which, however the sceptic may deny them or the enthusiast disfigure them, are yet, I am convinced, original and component parts of the human soul; those *senses of the mind*, if I may be allowed the expression, which connect us with, and link us to, those awful obscure realities—an all-powerful and equally beneficent God, and a world to come, beyond death and the grave. The first gives the nerve of combat, while a ray of hope beams on the field : the last pours the balm of comfort into the wound which time can never cure.

I do not remember, my dear Cunningham, that you and I ever talked on the subject of religion at all. I know some who laugh at it, as the trick of the crafty few, to lead the undiscerning many; or at most as an uncertain obscurity, which mankind can never know anything of, and with which they are fools if they give themselves much to do. Nor would I quarrel with a man for his irreligion, any more than I would for his want of musical ear. I would regret that he was shut out from what, to me and to others, were such superlative sources of enjoyment. It is in this point of view, and for this reason, that I will deeply imbue the mind of every child of mine with religion. If my son should happen to be a man of feeling, sentiment, and taste, I shall thus add largely to his enjoyments. Let me flatter myself that this sweet little fellow, who is just now running about my desk, will be a man of a melting, ardent, glowing heart, and an imagination delighted with the painter and rapt with the poet. Let me figure him wandering out in a sweet evening, to inhale the balmy gales, and enjoy the growing luxuriance of the spring; himself the while in the blooming youth of life. He looks abroad on all nature, and through nature up to nature's God. His soul, by swift delighting degrees, is rapt above this sublunary sphere, until he can be silent no longer, and bursts out into the glorious enthusiasm of Thomson—

> "These, as they change, Almighty Father, these
> Are but the varied God.—The rolling year
> Is full of Thee : "

and so on in all the spirit and ardour of that charming hymn. These are no ideal pleasures, they are real delights; and I ask, what of the delights among the sons of men are superior, not to say equal, to them? And they

have this precious, vast addition, that conscious virtue stamps them for her own, and lays hold on them to bring herself into the presence of a witnessing, judging, and approving God.—R. B.

No. CCXCIV.

TO MISS LAWRIE.

[When Capt. Riddel died, in April 1794, no reconciliation had taken place between him and Burns ; but the latter, recollecting only the kindness he had received at Carse, wrote a sonnet (the only verses he composed during the first half of 1794) on the death of his former friend, which was published in a local paper. The following letter was addressed to Mrs. Riddel's sister in order to procure the return of some manuscript pieces which had been lent to Capt. Riddel, but which, for various reasons, Burns was very anxious should be suppressed.]

MADAM, DUMFRIES, 1794.

Nothing short of a kind of absolute necessity could have made me trouble you with this letter. Except my ardent and just esteem for your sense, taste, and worth, every sentiment arising in my breast, as I put pen to paper to you, is painful. The scenes I have passed with the friend of my soul and his amiable connexions ! the wrench at my heart to think that he is gone, for ever gone from me, never more to meet in the wanderings of a weary world ! and the cutting reflection of all, that I had most unfortunately, though most undeservedly, lost the confidence of that soul of worth, ere it took its flight !

These, Madam, are sensations of no ordinary anguish. However, you also may be offended with some *imputed* improprieties of mine : sensibility you know I possess, and sincerity none will deny me.

To oppose those prejudices which have been raised against me is not the business of this letter. Indeed it is a warfare I know not how to wage. The powers of positive vice I can in some degree calculate, and against direct malevolence I can be on my guard ; but who can estimate the fatuity of giddy caprice, or ward off the unthinking mischief of precipitate folly?

I have a favour to request of you, Madam; and of your sister Mrs. Riddel, through your means. You know that, at the wish of my late friend, I made a collection of all my trifles in verse which I had ever written. They are many of them local, some of them puerile and silly, and all of them unfit for the public eye. As I have some little fame at stake—a fame that I trust may live when the hate of those who " watch for my halting," and the contumelious sneer of those whom accident has made my superiors, will, with themselves, be gone to the regions of oblivion—I am uneasy now for the fate of those manuscripts. Will Mrs. Riddel have the goodness to destroy them, or return them to me ? As a pledge of friendship they were bestowed ; and that circumstance indeed was all their merit. Most unhappily for me, that merit they no longer possess ; and I hope that Mrs. Riddel's goodness, which I well know, and ever will revere, will

not refuse this favour to a man whom she once held in some degree of estimation.

With the sincerest esteem, I have the honour to be, Madam, &c.

R. B.

No. CCXCV.

TO MRS. DUNLOP.

CASTLE DOUGLAS, *25th June*, 1794.

HERE in a solitary inn, in a solitary village, am I set by myself, to amuse my brooding fancy as I may. Solitary confinement, you know, is Howard's favourite idea of reclaiming sinners ; so let me consider by what fatality it happens that I have so long been exceeding sinful as to neglect the correspondence of the most valued friend I have on earth. To tell you that I have been in poor health will not be excuse enough, though it is true. I am afraid that I am about to suffer for the follies of my youth. My medical friends threaten me with a flying gout ; but I trust they are mistaken.

I am just going to trouble your critical patience with the first sketch of a stanza I have been framing as I passed along the road. The subject is Liberty : you know, my honoured friend, how dear the theme is to me. I design it an irregular ode for General Washington's birthday. After having mentioned the degeneracy of other kingdoms I come to Scotland thus :—

> " Thee, Caledonia, thy wild heaths among,
> Thee, famed for martial deed and sacred song,
>   To thee I turn with swimming eyes ;
> Where is that soul of freedom fled ?
> Immingled with the mighty dead,
>   Beneath the hallowed turf where Wallace lies !
> Hear it not, Wallace, in thy bed of death :
>   Ye babbling winds, in silence sweep ;
>   Disturb ye not the hero's sleep.

With the additions of—

> " Behold that eye which shot immortal hate,
>   Braved usurpation's boldest daring ;
> That arm which, nerved with thundering fate,
>   Crushed the despot's proudest bearing !
> One quenched in darkness like the sinking star,
>   And one the palsied arm of tottering, powerless age."

You will probably have another scrawl from me in a stage or two.

R. B.

No. CCXCVI.

TO MR. JAMES JOHNSON.

MY DEAR FRIEND,

DUMFRIES, 1794.

You should have heard from me long ago ; but, over and above some vexatious share in the pecuniary losses of these accursed times, I

B
N N

have all this winter been plagued with low spirits and blue devils, so that *I have almost hung my harp on the willow trees.*

I am just now busy correcting a new edition of my poems; and this, with my ordinary business, finds me in full employment.

I send you by my friend Mr. Wallace forty-one songs for your fifth volume ; if we cannot finish it any other way, what would you think of Scots words to some beautiful Irish airs ? In the mean time, at your leisure, give a copy of the " Museum " to my worthy friend Mr. Peter Hill, bookseller, to bind for me, interleaved with blank leaves, exactly as he did the Laird of Glenriddel's, that I may insert every anecdote I can learn, together with my own criticisms and remarks on the songs. A copy of this kind I shall leave with you, the editor, to publish at some after period, by way of making the " Museum " a book famous to the end of time, and you renowned for ever.—R. B.

No. CCXCVII.

TO CLARINDA.

BEFORE you ask me why I have not written you, first let me be informed by you, *how* I shall write you ? " In friendship," you say ; and I have many a time taken up my pen to try an epistle of " friendship" to you, but it will not do ; 'tis like Jove grasping a popgun after having wielded his thunder. When I take up the pen, recollection ruins me. Ah, my ever-dearest Clarinda ! Clarinda ! What a host of memory's tenderest offspring crowd on my fancy at that sound ! But I must not indulge that subject ; you have forbid it.

I am extremely happy to learn that your precious health is re-established, and that you are once more fit to enjoy that satisfaction in existence which health alone can give us. My old friend Ainslie has indeed been kind to you. Tell him, that I envy him the power of serving you. I had a letter from him a while ago, but it was so dry, so distant, so like a card to one of his clients, that I could scarce bear to read it, and have not yet answered it. He is a good, honest fellow, and *can* write a friendly letter, which would do equal honour to his head and his heart, as a whole sheaf of his letters which I have by me will witness ; and though Fame does not blow her trumpet at my approach *now* as she did *then*, when he first honoured me with his friendship, yet I am as proud as ever ; and when I am laid in my grave, I wish to be stretched at my full length, that I may occupy every inch of ground I have a right to.

You would laugh were you to see me where I am just now. Would to Heaven you were here to laugh with me, though I am afraid that crying would be our first employment ! Here am I set, a solitary hermit, in the solitary room of a solitary inn, with a solitary bottle of wine by me, as grave and as stupid as an owl, but, like that owl, still faithful to my old song ; in confirmation of which, my dear Mrs. Mac, here is your good health ! May the hand-waled benisons o' Heaven bless your bonnie face ; and the

wratch wha skellies at your welfare, may the auld tinkler deil get him, to clout his rotten heart! Amen.

You must know, my dearest Madam, that these now many years, whereever I am, in whatever company, when a married lady is called as a toast, I constantly give you; but as your name has never passed my lips, even to my most intimate friend, I give you by the name of Mrs. Mac. This is so well known among my acquaintances, that when any married lady is called for, the toast-master will say: "Oh, we need not ask him who it is: here's Mrs. Mac!" I have also, among my convivial friends, set on foot a round of toasts, which I call a round of Arcadian Shepherdesses—that is, a round of favourite ladies, under female names celebrated in ancient song; and then you are my Clarinda. So, my lovely Clarinda, I devote this glass of wine to a most ardent wish for your happiness.

> In vain would Prudence, with decorous sneer,
> Point out a censuring world, and bid me fear:
> Above that world on wings of love I rise;
> I know its worst, and can that worst despise.
>
> "Wronged, injured, shunned, unpitied, unredrest—
> The mocked quotation of the scorner's jest"—
> Let Prudence' direst bodements on me fall,
> Clarinda, rich reward! o erpays them all.

I have been rhyming a little of late, but I do not know if they are worth postage.

Tell me what you think of the following monody. [*See page* 117.]

The subject of the foregoing is a woman of fashion in this country,* with whom at one period I was well acquainted. By some scandalous conduct to me, and two or three other gentlemen here as well as me, she steered so far to the north of my good opinion, that I have made her the theme of several ill-natured things. . . . .

R. B.

No. CCXCVIII.

TO G. THOMSON.

July, 1794.

Is there no news yet of Pleyel? Or is your work to be at a dead stop until the allies set our modern Orpheus at liberty from the savage thraldom of democratic discords? Alas the day! And woe is me! That auspicious period, pregnant with the happiness of millions, ... seems by no means near.†

No. CCXCIX.

TO G. THOMSON.

30*th August*, 1794.

THE last evening, as I was straying out, and thinking of "O'er the Hills and Far Away," I spun the following stanza for it; but whether my

* Mrs. Riddel.

† The suppressed portion of the letter was an ironical tirade on the mishaps of Prussia in her war against France.

spinning will deserve to be laid up in store, like the precious thread of the silk-worm, or brushed to the devil, like the vile manufacture of the spider, I leave, my dear Sir, to your usual candid criticism. I was pleased with several lines in it, at first; but I own that now it appears rather a flimsy business.

This is just a hasty sketch, until I see whether it be worth a critique. We have many sailor songs; but, as far as I at present recollect, they are mostly the effusions of the jovial sailor, not the wailings of his love-lorn mistress. I must here make one sweet exception—" Sweet Annie frae the Sea-beach came." Now for the song :—

[" On the Seas and Far Away." Given in *page* 187.]

No. CCC.

TO G. THOMSON.

Sept. 1794.

I SHALL withdraw my " On the Seas and Far Away" altogether : it is unequal, and unworthy the work. Making a poem is like begetting a son : you cannot know whether you have a wise man or a fool, until you produce him to the world to try him.

No. CCCI.

TO G. THOMSON.

Sept. 1794.

. . . . To compare small things with great, my taste in music is like the mighty Frederick of Prussia's taste in painting : we are told that he frequently admired what the connoisseurs decried, and always, without any hypocrisy, confessed his admiration. I am sensible that my taste in music must be inelegant and vulgar, because people of undisputed and cultivated taste can find no merit in my favourite tunes. Still, because I am cheaply pleased, is that any reason why I should deny myself that pleasure ? Many of our strathspeys, ancient and modern, give me most exquisite enjoyment, where you and other judges would probably be showing disgust. For instance, I am just now making verses for " Rothe-murche's Rant," an air which puts me in raptures ; and, in fact, unless I be pleased with the tune, I never can make verses to it. . . . .

I have begun anew " Let me in this ae night." Do you think that we ought to retain the old chorus ? I think we must retain both the old chorus and the first stanza of the old song. I do not altogether like the third line of the first stanza, but cannot alter it to please myself. I am just three stanzas deep in it. Would you have the *dénouement* to be successful or otherwise ? Should she " let him in" or not ? . . . .

How do you like the following epigram, which I wrote the other day, on a lovely young girl's recovery from a fever ? Doctor Maxwell was the

physician who seemingly saved her from the grave ; and to him I address the following. (*See page* 161.)

TO DR. MAXWELL.

ON MISS JESSIE CRAIG'S RECOVERY.

Maxwell, if merit here you crave,
   That merit I deny ;
You save fair Jessie from the grave ?—
   An angel could not die.

God grant you patience with this stupid epistle

No. CCCII.

TO G. THOMSON.

MY DEAR FRIEND,   *19th October,* 1794.

By this morning's post I have your list, and, in general, I highly approve of it. I shall, at more leisure, give you a critique on the whole. Clarke goes to your town by to-day's fly, and I wish you would call on him and take his opinion in general : you know his taste is a standard. He will return here again in a week or two ; so please do not miss asking for him. One thing I hope he will do, persuade you to adopt my favourite, " Craigie-burn Wood," in your selection : it is as great a favourite of his as of mine. The lady on whom it was made is one of the finest women in Scotland ; and, in fact (*entre nous*), is in a manner to me what Sterne's Eliza was to him—a mistress, or friend, or what you will, in the guileless simplicity of Platonic love. (Now don't put any of your squinting constructions on this, or have any clishmaclaiver about it among our acquaintances.) I assure you that to my lovely friend you are indebted for many of your best songs of mine. Do you think that the sober, gin-horse routine of existence could inspire a man with life, and love, and joy— could fire him with enthusiasm, or melt him with pathos equal to the genius of your book ?—no ! no ! Whenever I want to be more than ordinary in song, to be in some degree equal to your diviner airs, do you imagine I fast and pray for the celestial emanation ? *Tout au contraire!* I have a glorious recipe ; the very one that for his own use was invented by the divinity of healing and poetry, when erst he piped to the flocks of Admetus. I put myself on a regimen of admiring a fine woman ; and in proportion to the adorability of her charms, in proportion you are delighted with my verses. The lightning of her eye is the godhead of Parnassus, and the witchery of her smile the divinity of Helicon ! . . . .

These English songs gravel me to death. I have not that command of the language that I have of my native tongue. I have been at " Duncan Gray," to dress it in English, but all I can do is deplorably stupid.

No. CCCIII.

TO G. THOMSON.

[" Chloris," otherwise Jean, was the eldest daughter of Mr. W. Lorimer, a farmer on the banks of the Nith—a very handsome girl.   She made an unfortunate love-match with a young gentleman from Cumberland named Whelpdale, who, being pursued for debts, abandoned his wife.   She returned to her parents, being then only about eighteen years of age, and did not see her husband again for twenty-three years.]

November, 1794.

ON my visit the other day to my fair Chloris (that is the poetic name of the lovely goddess of my inspiration), she suggested an idea which I, in my return from the visit, wrought into the following song [Chloris].

I like you for entering so candidly and so kindly into the story of " *ma chere Amie.*"   I assure you, I was never more in earnest in my life than in the account of that affair which I sent you in my last.   Conjugal love is a passion which I deeply feel, and highly venerate ; but, somehow, it does not make such a figure in poesy as that other species of the passion,

/" Where Love is liberty, and Nature law."

Musically speaking, the first is an instrument of which the gamut is scanty and confined, but the tones inexpressibly sweet ; while the last has powers equal to all the intellectual modulations of the human soul.   Still, I am a very poet in my enthusiasm of the passion.   The welfare and happiness of the beloved object is the first and inviolate sentiment that pervades my soul ; and whatever pleasure I might wish for, or whatever might be the raptures they would give me, yet, if they interfere with that first principle, it is having these pleasures at a dishonest price ; and justice forbids, and generosity disdains, the purchase !

Despairing of my own powers to give you variety enough in English songs, I have been turning over old collections, to pick out songs of which the measure is something similar to what I want ; and, with a little alter-ation, so as to suit the rhythm of the air exactly, to give you them for your work.   Where the songs have hitherto been but little noticed, nor have ever been set to music, I think the shift a fair one. . . . .

No. CCCIV.

TO G. THOMSON.

. . . . THERE is an air, "The Caledonian Hunt's Delight," to which I wrote a song that you will find in Johnson.   " Ye Banks and Braes o' bonnie Doon :" this air, I think, might find a place among your hundred, as Lear says of his knights.   Do you know the history of the air?   It is curious enough.   A good many years ago Mr. James Miller, writer in your good

town—a gentleman whom, possibly, you know—was in company with our friend Clarke; and talking of Scottish music, Miller expressed an ardent ambition to be able to compose a Scots air. Mr. Clarke, partly by way of joke, told him to keep to the black keys of the harpsichord, and preserve some kind of rhythm, and he would infallibly compose a Scots air. Certain it is that, in a few days, Mr. Miller produced the rudiments of an air, which Mr. Clarke, with some touches and corrections, fashioned into the tune in question. Ritson, you know, has the same story of the black keys; but this account which I have just given you Mr. Clarke informed me of several years ago. Now, to show you how difficult it is to trace the origin of our airs, I have heard it repeatedly asserted that this was an Irish air; nay, I met with an Irish gentleman who affirmed he had heard it in Ireland among the old women; while, on the other hand, a Countess informed me that the first person who introduced the air into this country was a baronet's lady of her acquaintance, who took down the notes from an itinerant piper in the Isle of Man. How difficult, then, to ascertain the truth respecting our poesy and music! I myself have lately seen a couple of ballads sung through the streets of Dumfries, with my name at the head of them as the author, though it was the first time I had ever seen them. . . . .

I am ashamed, my dear fellow, to make the request; 'tis dunning your generosity: but, in a moment when I had forgotten whether I was rich or poor, I promised Chloris a copy of your songs. It wrings my honest pride to write you this, but an ungracious request is doubly so by a tedious apology. To make you some amends, as soon as I have extracted the necessary information out of them, I will return you Ritson's volumes.

The lady is not a little proud that she is to make so distinguished a figure in your collection, and I am not a little proud that I have it in my power to please her so much. Lucky it is for your patience that my paper is done, for when I am in a scribbling humour, I know not when to give over.—R. B.

No. CCCV.

TO G. THOMSON.

19th November, 1794.

YOU see, my dear Sir, what a punctual correspondent I am; though indeed you may thank yourself for the tedium of my letters, as you have so flattered me on my horsemanship with my favourite hobby, and have praised the grace of his ambling so much, that I am scarcely ever off his back. For instance, this morning, though a keen blowing frost, in my walk before breakfast I finished my duet [" O Philly, happy be that Day"] which you were pleased to praise so much. . . . .

I remember your objections to the name Philly; but it is the common abbreviation of Phillis. Sally, the only other name that suits, has, to my ear, a vulgarity about it which unfits it for anything except burlesque. The legion of Scottish poetasters of the day, whom your brother editor

Mr. Ritson, ranks with me, as my coevals, have always mistaken vulgarity for simplicity; whereas simplicity is as much *eloignée* from vulgarity, on the one hand, as from affected point and puerile conceit on the other.

I agree with you, as to the air " Craigie-burn Wood," that a chorus would, in some degree, spoil the effect ; and shall certainly have none in my projected song to it. It is not, however, a case in point with " Rothe-murche ; " there, as in " Roy's Wife of Aldivalloch," a chorus goes, to my taste, well enough. As to the chorus going first, that is the case with " Roy's Wife " as well as " Rothemurche." In fact, in the first part of both tunes the rhythm is so peculiar and irregular, and on that irregu-larity depends so much of their beauty, that we must e'en take them with all their wildness, and humour the verse accordingly. Leaving out the starting-note in both tunes has, I think, an effect that no regularity could counterbalance the want of :—

Try	{ *O Roy's* Wife of Aldivalloch, { *O Lassie* wi' the lint-white locks,
and compare with	{ *Roy's* Wife of Aldivalloch, { *Lassie* wi' the lint-white locks.

Does not the tameness of the prefixed syllable strike you? In the last case, with the true furor of genius, you strike at once into the wild originality of the air ; whereas in the first insipid method it is like the grating screw of the pins before the fiddle is brought into tune. This is my taste ; if I am wrong, I beg pardon of the *cognoscenti.*

" The Caledonian Hunt " is so charming, that it would make any subject in a song go down ; but pathos is certainly its native tongue. Scottish Bacchanalians we certainly want, though the few we have are excellent. For instance " Todlin Hame " is, for wit and humour, an unparalleled composition ; and " Andrew and his cutty Gun " is the work of a master. By the way, are you not quite vexed to think that those men of genius, for such they certainly were, who composed our fine Scottish lyrics, should be unknown ? It has given me many a heart-ache.—R. B.

No. CCCVI.

TO G. THOMSON.

SINCE yesterday's penmanship I have framed a couple of English stanzas, by way of an English song to " Roy's Wife."

[The song " Canst thou leave me thus, my Katy," is given in *page* 221.]

Well ! I think this, to be done in two or three turns across my roor and with two or three pinches of Irish blackguard, is not so far amiss. You see I am determined to have my quantum of applause from some-body.

Tell my friend Allan (for I am sure that we only want the trifling circumstance of being known to one another, to be the best friends on earth) that I much suspect he has, in his plates, mistaken the figure of the

stock and horn. I have at last gotten one ; but it is a very rude instrument : it is composed of three parts ; the stock, which is the hinder thigh-bone of a sheep, such as you see in a mutton-ham ; the horn, which is a common Highland cow's horn, cut off at the smaller end, until the aperture be large enough to admit the stock, to be pushed up through the horn, until it be held by the thicker end of the thigh-bone ; and, lastly, an oaten reed exactly cut and notched, like that which you see every shepherd-boy have when the corn-stems are green and full-grown. The reed is not made fast in the bone, but is held by the lips, and plays loose in the smaller end of the stock ; while the stock, with the horn hanging on its larger end, is held by the hands in playing. The stock has six or seven ventiges on the upper side, and one back-ventige, like the common flute. This of mine was made by a man from the braes of Athole, and is exactly what the shepherds are wont to use in that country.

However, either it is not quite properly bored in the holes, or else we have not the art of blowing it rightly ; for we can make little of it. If Mr. Allan chooses, I will send him a sight of mine ; as I look on myself to be a kind of brother-brush with him. "Pride in poets is nae sin," and, I will say it, that I look on Mr. Allan and Mr. Burns to be the only genuine and real painters of Scottish costume in the world.—R. B.

No. CCCVII.

TO PETER MILLER, JUN., ESQ.

OF DALSWINTON.

[This is a reply to an offer by Mr. Perry (through Mr. Peter Miller) of an engagement on the *Morning Chronicle*, of which he was editor.]

DEAR SIR, DUMFRIES, *November*, 1794.

Your offer is indeed truly generous, and most sincerely do I thank you for it ; but in my present situation I find that I dare not accept it. You well know my political sentiments ; and were I an insular individual, unconnected with a wife and a family of children, with the most fervid enthusiasm I would have volunteered my services : I then could and would have despised all consequences that might have ensued.

My prospect in the Excise is something ; at least, it is, encumbered as I am with the welfare, the very existence, of near half a score of helpless individuals, what I dare not sport with.

In the mean time they are most welcome to my Ode ; only let them insert it as a thing they have met with by accident and unknown to me. Nay, if Mr. Perry, whose honour, after your character of him, I cannot doubt ; if he will give me an address and channel by which anything will come safe from those spies with which he may be certain that his correspondence is beset, I will now and then send him any bagatelle that I may write. In the present hurry of Europe nothing but news and politics will

be regarded ; but against the days of peace, which Heaven send soon, my little assistance may perhaps fill up an idle column of a newspaper. I have long had it in my head to try my hand in the way of little prose essays, which I propose sending into the world through the medium of some newspaper ; and should these be worth his while, to these Mr. Perry shall be welcome ; and all my reward shall be, his treating me with his paper—which, by the by, to anybody who has the least relish for wit, is a high treat indeed.

With the most grateful esteem, I am ever, dear Sir,

R. B.

No. CCCVIII.

TO G. THOMSON.

January, 1795.

I FEAR for my songs ; however a few may please, yet originality is a coy feature in composition, and in a multiplicity of efforts in the same style disappears altogether. For these three thousand years we poetic folks have been describing the spring, for instance ; and, as the spring continues the same, there must soon be a sameness in the imagery, &c. of these said rhyming folks.

A great critic (Aikin) on songs says that love and wine are the exclusive themes for song-writing. The following is on neither subject, and consequently is no song ; but will be allowed, I think, to be two or three pretty good prose thoughts inverted into rhyme :—

["Is there, for honest poverty." *Page* 227.]

No. CCCIX.

TO G. THOMSON.

MY DEAR THOMSON, ECCLEFECHAN, *7th February,* 1795.

You cannot have any idea of the predicament in which I write to you. In the course of my duty as supervisor (in which capacity I have acted of late) I came yesternight to this unfortunate, wicked little village. I have gone forward, but snows, of ten feet deep, have impeded my progress : I have tried to "gae back the gate I cam again," but the same obstacle has shut me up within insuperable bars. To add to my misfortune, since dinner a scraper has been torturing catgut, in sounds that would have insulted the dying agonies of a sow under the hands of a butcher, and thinks himself, on that very account, exceeding good company. In fact, I have been in a dilemma—either to get drunk, to forget these miseries ; or to hang myself, to get rid of them : like a prudent man (a character congenial to my every thought, word, and deed), I, of two evils, have chosen the least, and am very drunk, at your service !

No. CCCX.

TO MR. HERON,

OF HERON.

[Mr. Heron was at this time a candidate for the representation of the Stewartry of Kirkcudbright ; and there can be no question that Burns's poetical advocacy of his cause, however generous, was extremely imprudent in any Government official in that time of keen political excitement.   Mr. Heron carried the election.]

SIR,

DUMFRIES, 1794 *or* 1795.

I enclose you some copies of a couple of political ballads ; one of which, I believe, you have never seen.   Would to Heaven I could make you master of as many votes in the Stewartry ! but—

" Who does the utmost that he can,
Does well, acts nobly ; angels could no more."

In order to bring my humble efforts to bear with more effect on the foe I have privately printed a good many copies of both ballads, and have sent them among friends all about the country.

To pillory on Parnassus the rank reprobation of character, the utter dereliction of all principle, in a profligate junto, which has not only outraged virtue, but violated common decency, spurning even hypocrisy as paltry iniquity below their daring ;—to unmask their flagitiousness to the broadest day—to deliver such over to their merited fate—is surely not merely innocent, but laudable; is not only propriety, but virtue.   You have already, as your auxiliary, the sober detestation of mankind on the heads of your opponents ; and I swear by the lyre of Thalia to muster on your side all the votaries of honest laughter and fair, candid ridicule !

I am extremely obliged to you for your kind mention of my interests in a letter which Mr. Syme showed me.   At present my situation in life must be in a great measure stationary, at least for two or three years.   The statement is this : I am on the supervisors' list, and as we come on there by precedency, in two or three years I shall be at the head of that list, and be appointed *of course.   Then* friend might be of service to me in getting me into a place of the kin ,dom which I would like.   A supervisor's income varies from about a hundred and twenty to two hundred a year ; but the business is an incessant drudgery, and would be nearly a complete bar to every species of literary pursuit.   The moment I am appointed supervisor, in the common routine, I may be nominated on the collector's list ; and this is always a business purely of political patronage.   A collectorship varies much, from better than two hundred a year to near a thousand.   They also come forward by precedency on the list ; and have, besides a handsome income, a life of complete leisure.   A life of literary leisure, with a decent competency, is the summit of my wishes.   It would be the prudish affectation of silly pride in me to say that I do not need, or would not be indebted to, a political friend : at the same time, Sir, I by no means lay my affairs before you thus, to hook my dependant situation on

your benevolence. If, in my progress of life, an opening should occur where the good offices of a gentleman of your public character and political consequence might bring me forward, I shall petition your goodness with the same frankness as I now do myself the honour to subscribe myself,—R. B.

No. CCCXI.

TO G. THOMSON.

[Enclosing "How cruel are the Parents," and "Mark yonder Pomp."]

. . . . WELL! this is not amiss. You see how I answer your orders; your tailor could not be more punctual. I am just now in a high fit of poetizing, provided that the strait-jacket of criticism don't cure me. If you can in a post or two administer a little of the intoxicating potion of your applause, it will raise your humble servant's phrenzy to any height you want. I am at this moment "holding high converse" with the Muses, and have not a word to throw away on such a prosaic dog as you are.

No. CCCXII.

TO G. THOMSON.

May, 1795.

TEN thousand thanks for your elegant present ;* though I am ashamed of the value of it, being bestowed on a man who has not by any means merited such an instance of kindness. I have shown it to two or three judges of the first abilities here, and they all agree with me in classing it as a first-rate production. My phiz is sae kenspeckle, that the very joiner's apprentice whom Mrs. Burns employed to break up the parcel (I was out of town that day) knew it at once. My most grateful compliments to Allan, who has honoured my rustic muse so much with his masterly pencil. One strange coincidence is, that the little one who is making the felonious attempt on the cat's tail is the most striking likeness of an ill-deedie, d—n'd wee rumble-gairie urchin of mine, whom, from that propensity to witty wickedness and manfu' mischief which even at twa days auld I foresaw would form the striking features of his disposition, I named Willie Nicol; after a certain friend of mine, who is one of the masters of a grammar-school in a city which shall be nameless.

No. CCCXIII.

TO G. THOMSON.

IN " Whistle, and I'll come to ye, my Lad," the iteration of that line is tiresome to my ear. Here goes what I think is an improvement :—

---

* The picture alluded to was painted by David Allan from the "Cotter's Saturday Night:" it displays at once the talent and want of taste of the ingenious artist. The scene is a solemn one : but the serenity of the moment is disturbed by what some esteem as a beauty—namely, the attempt to cut the tip of the cat's tail by the little merry urchin seated on the floor.—*Allan Cunningham.*

" O whistle, and I'll come to ye, my lad ;
O whistle, and I'll come to ye, my lad ;
Tho' father, and mother, and a' should gae mad,
Thy Jeany will venture wi' ye, my lad."

In fact, a fair dame, at whose shrine I, the Priest of the Nine, offer up the incense of Parnassus ; a dame, whom the Graces have attired in witchcraft, and whom the Loves have armed with lightning ; a fair one, herself the heroine of the song, insists on the amendment, and dispute her commands if you dare !

No. CCCXIV.

TO MRS. RIDDEL.

DUMFRIES, 1793.

MR. BURNS'S compliments to Mrs. Riddel ; is much obliged to her for her polite attention in sending him the book. Owing to Mr. B. being at present acting as supervisor of Excise, a department that occupies his every hour of the day, he has not that time to spare which is necessary for any *belle-lettre* pursuit ; but, as he will, in a week or two, again return to his wonted leisure, he will then pay that attention to Mrs. R.'s beautiful song, "To thee, loved Nith," which it so well deserves. When "Anacharsis' Travels" come to hand, which Mrs. Riddel mentioned as her gift to the public library, Mr. B. will feel honoured by the indulgence of a perusal of them before presentation : it is a book he has never yet seen, and the regulations of the library allow too little leisure for deliberate reading.

Friday Evening.

P.S. Mr. Burns will be much obliged to Mrs. Riddel if she will favour him with a perusal of any of her poetical pieces which he may not have seen.

No. CCCXV.

TO MRS. DUNLOP.

MY DEAR FRIEND,   *15th December*, 1795.

As I am in a complete Decemberish humour, gloomy, sullen, stupid, as even the Deity of Dulness herself could wish, I shall not drawl out a heavy letter with a number of heavier apologies for my late silence. Only one I shall mention, because I know you will sympathize in it : these four months a sweet little girl, my youngest child, has been so ill, that every day a week or less threatened to terminate her existence. There had much need be many pleasures annexed to the states of husband and father, for, God knows, they have many peculiar cares. I cannot describe to you the anxious, sleepless hours these ties frequently give me. I see a train of helpless little folks ; me and my exertions all their stay : and on what a brittle thread does the life of man hang ! If I am nipt off at the command of fate ! even in all the vigour of manhood as I am—such

things happen every day—gracious God ! what would become of my little flock ! 'Tis here that I envy your people of fortune. A father on his death-bed, taking an everlasting leave of his children, has indeed woe enough ; but the man of competent fortune leaves his sons and daughters independency and friends, while I—but I shall run distracted if I think any longer on the subject !

To leave talking of the matter so gravely, I shall sing with the old Scots ballad—

> " O that I had ne'er been married !
> I would never had nae care :
> Now I've gotten wife and bairns,
> They cry crowdie ! evermair.
>
> Crowdie ! ance ; crowdie ! twice ;
> Crowdie ! three times in a day ;
> An ye, crowdie ! ony mair,
> Ye'll crowdie ! a' my meal away."

* * * * * *

December 24th.

We have had a brilliant theatre here this season ; only, as all other business does, it experiences a stagnation of trade from the epidemical complaint of the country, *want of cash.* I mentioned our theatre merely to lug in an occasional Address which I wrote for the benefit-night of one of the actresses, and which is as follows : —

[Here the Address is transcribed. *See page* 112.]

25th, Christmas Morning.

This, my much-loved friend, is a morning of wishes ; accept mine—so Heaven hear me as they are sincere !—that blessings may attend your steps, and affliction know you not ! In the charming words of my favourite author, " The Man of Feeling," " May the Great Spirit bear up the weight of thy grey hairs, and blunt the arrow that brings them rest ! "

Now that I talk of authors, how do you like Cowper ?* Is not the " Task " a glorious poem ? The religion of the " Task," bating a few scraps of Calvinistic divinity, is the religion of God and nature ; the religion that exalts, that ennobles man. Were not you to send me your " Zeluco " in return for mine ? Tell me how you like my marks and notes through the book. I would not give a farthing for a book, unless I were at liberty to blot it with my criticisms.

I have lately collected, for a friend's perusal, all my letters ; I mean those which I first sketched, in a rough draught, and afterwards wrote out fair. On looking over some old musty papers, which, from time to time, I had parcelled by, as trash that were scarce worth preserving, and which yet at the same time I did not care to destroy, I discovered many of these rude sketches, and have written, and am writing them out, in a

---

* Burns generally carried Cowper's " Task " in his pocket, and took it out when he found himself in a lonely road, or in a brewhouse where he had to wait sometimes to " gauge the browst." The copy which he used was one lent to him by Mrs. Dunlop, the margins of which he enriched with notes, critical and commendatory.

bound MS. for my friend's library. As I wrote always to you the rhapsody of the moment, I cannot find a single scroll to you except one, about the commencement of our acquaintance. If there were any possible conveyance, I would send you a perusal of my book.—R. B.

No. CCCXVI.

TO MRS. DUNLOP,

IN LONDON.

DUMFRIES, *20th December,* 1795.

I HAVE been prodigiously disappointed in this London journey of yours. In the first place, when your last to me reached Dumfries, I was in the country, and did not return until too late to answer your letter ; in the next place, I thought you would certainly take this route ; and now I know not what is become of you, or whether this may reach you at all. God grant that it may find you and yours in prospering health and good spirits ! Do let me hear from you the soonest possible.

As I hope to get a frank from my friend Captain Miller, I shall every leisure hour take up the pen, and gossip away whatever comes first, prose or poetry, sermon or song. In this last article I have abounded of late. I have often mentioned to you a superb publication of Scottish Songs, which is making its appearance in your great metropolis, and where I have the honour to preside over the Scottish verse, as no less a personage than Peter Pindar does over the English.

December 29*th.*

SINCE I began this letter, I have been appointed to act in the capacity of supervisor here ; and I assure you, what with the load of business, and what with that business being new to me, I could scarcely have commanded ten minutes to have spoken to you, had you been in town, much less to have written you an epistle. This appointment is only temporary, and during the illness of the present incumbent ; but I look forward to an early period when I shall be appointed in full form—a consummation devoutly to be wished ! My political sins seem to be forgiven me.

This is the season (New-year's-day is now my date) of wishing ; and mine are most fervently offered up for you. May life to you be a positive blessing while it lasts, for your own sake ; and that it may yet be greatly prolonged is my wish, for my own sake, and for the sake of the rest of your friends ! What a transient business is life ! Very lately I was a boy ; but t'other day I was a young man ; and I already begin to feel the rigid fibre and stiffening joints of old age coming fast o'er my frame. With all my follies of youth, and I fear a few vices of manhood, still I congratulate myself on having had in early days religion strongly impressed on my mind. I have nothing to say to any one as to which sect he belongs to, or what creed he believes : but I look on the man who is firmly persuaded of infinite Wisdom and Goodness superintending and directing every circumstance that can happen in his lot—I felicitate such

a man, as having a solid foundation for his mental enjoyment; a firm prop
and sure stay in the hour of difficulty, trouble, and distress; and a never-
failing anchor of hope, when he looks beyond the grave.

January 12th.

YOU will have seen our worthy and ingenious friend, the Doctor, long
ere this. I hope he is well, and beg to be remembered to him. I have
just been reading over again, I daresay for the hundred and fiftieth time,
his "View of Society and Manners;" and still I read it with delight.
His humour is perfectly original: it is neither the humour of Addison,
nor Swift, nor Sterne, nor of anybody but Dr. Moore. By the by, you
have deprived me of "Zeluco:" remember that, when you are disposed
to rake up the sins of my neglect from among the ashes of my laziness.

He has paid me a pretty compliment, by quoting me in his last
publication.—R. B.

No. CCCXVII.

TO THE HON. THE PROVOST, BAILIES, AND TOWN COUNCIL OF DUMFRIES.

[1795.]

GENTLEMEN,

The literary taste and liberal spirit of your good town has so ably
filled the various departments of your schools, as to make it a very great
object for a parent to have his children educated in them. Still, to me, a
stranger, with my large family and very stinted income, to give my young
ones that education I wish, at the high school fees which a stranger pays,
will bear hard upon me.

Some years ago your good town did me the honour of making me an
honorary Burgess. Will you allow me to request that this mark of distinction may extend so far as to put me on a footing of a real freeman of
the town in the schools?

That I may not appear altogether unworthy of this favour allow me to
state to you some little services I have lately done a branch of your
revenue—the two pennies exigible on foreign ale vended within your
limits. In this rather neglected article of your income, I am ready to
show that within these few weeks my exertions have secured for you of
those duties nearly the sum of Ten Pounds; and in this, too, I was the
only one of the gentlemen of the Excise (except Mr. Mitchell, whom *you*
pay for his trouble) who took the least concern in the business.

If you are so very kind as to grant my request, it will certainly be a
constant incentive to me to strain every nerve where I can officially serve
you, and will, if possible, increase that grateful respect with which I have
the honour to be,

Gentlemen,

Your devoted humble Servant,

R. B.*

* The original draft of this letter is in the British Museum. Cromek, who first published it
(omitting, however, the third paragraph) states that the poet's request was immediately complied
with.

No. CCCXVIII.

TO MRS. RIDDEL.

DUMFRIES, *20th January,* 1796.

I CANNOT express my gratitude to you for allowing me a longer perusal of "Anacharsis." In fact, I never met with a book that bewitched me so much ; and I, as a member of the library, must warmly feel the obligation you have laid us under. Indeed, to me the obligation is stronger than to any other individual of our society ; as " Anacharsis " is an indispensable desideratum to a son of the Muses.

The health you wished me in your morning's card is, I think, flown from me for ever. I have not been able to leave my bed to-day till about an hour ago. These wickedly unlucky advertisements I lent (I did wrong) to a friend, and I am ill able to go in quest of him.

R. B.

No. CCCXIX.

TO MRS. DUNLOP.

[There seems about this time to have been some coldness between Burns and Mrs. Dunlop, probably caused by her displeasure at his confirmed habits of conviviality.]

DUMFRIES, *31st January,* 1796.

THESE many months you have been two packets in my debt : what sin of ignorance I have committed against so highly valued a friend I am utterly at a loss to guess. Alas, Madam ! ill can I afford, at this time, to be deprived of any of the small remnant of my pleasures. I have lately drunk deep of the cup of affliction. The autumn robbed me of my only daughter and darling child, and that at a distance too, and so rapidly, as to put it out of my power to pay the last duties to her. I had scarcely begun to recover from that shock, when I became myself the victim of a most severe rheumatic fever, and long the die spun doubtful ; until, after many weeks of a sick bed, it seems to have turned up life, and I am beginning to crawl across my room, and once indeed have been before my own door in the street.

> " When pleasure fascinates the mental sight,
> Affliction purifies the visual ray,
> Religion hails the drear, the untried night,
> And shuts, for ever shuts, life's doubtful day."

R. B.

No. CCCXX.

TO MRS. RIDDEL,

[Who had desired him to go to the Birthday Assembly on that day to show his loyalty.]

DUMFRIES, *4th June,* 1796.

I AM in such miserable health as to be utterly incapable of showing my loyalty in any way. Racked as I am with rheumatisms, I meet every face with a greeting like that of Balak to Balaam : " Come, curse me Jacob ; and come, defy me Israel ! " So say I : Come, curse me that east wind ;

and come, defy me the north! Would you have me in such circumstances copy you out a love-song?

I may perhaps see you on Saturday, but I will not be at the ball. Why should I? "Man delights not me, nor woman either!" Can you supply me with the song, "Let us all be unhappy together?"—do if you can, and oblige *le pauvre misérable.*—R.B.

No. CCCXXI.

TO G. THOMSON.

April, 1796.

ALAS! my dear Thomson, I fear it will be some time ere I tune my lyre again! "By Babel streams I have sat and wept" almost ever since I wrote you last. I have only known existence by the pressure of the heavy hand of sickness; and have counted time by the repercussions of pain. Rheumatism, cold, and fever have formed to me a terrible combination. I close my eyes in misery, and open them without hope. I look on the vernal day, and say with poor Fergusson—

> " Say, wherefore has an ill-indulgent Heaven
> Light to the comfortless and wretched given?"

This will be delivered to you by a Mrs. Hyslop, landlady of the Globe Tavern here, which for these many years has been my howff,* and where our friend Clarke and I have had many a merry squeeze. I am highly delighted with Mr. Allan's etchings. "Woo'd and married an' a'" is admirable! The grouping is beyond all praise. The expression of the figures, conformable to the story in the ballad, is absolutely faultless perfection. I next admire "Turnimspike." What I like least is "Jenny said to Jocky." Besides the female being in her appearance quite a virago, if you take her stooping into the account, she is at least two inches taller than her lover.

Poor Cleghorn! I sincerely sympathize with him! Happy I am to think that he yet has a well-grounded hope of health and enjoyment in this world. As for me—but that is a damning subject!

No. CCCXXII.

TO G. THOMSON.

I HAVE no copies of the songs I have sent you, and I have taken a fancy to review them all, and possibly may send some of them; so, when you have complete leisure, I will thank you for either the originals or copies. I had rather be the author of five well-written songs than of ten otherwise. I have great hopes that the genial influence of the approaching summer will set me to rights, but as yet I cannot boast of returning health. I have now reason to believe that my complaint is a flying gout: a sad business!

---

* The "howff" of which Burns speaks was a small, comfortable tavern, situated in the mouth of the Globe close, and it held at that time the rank as third among the houses of public accommodation in Dumfries.

This should have been delivered to you a month ago. I am still **very** poorly, but should much like to hear from you.

No. CCCXXIII.
TO MR. JAMES JOHNSON,
EDINBURGH.

[About *May* 17, 1796.]

HOW are you, my dear friend, and how comes on your fifth volume? You may probably think that for some time past I have neglected you and your work; but, alas! the hand of pain, and sorrow, and care, has these many months lain heavy on me! Personal and domestic affliction have almost entirely banished that alacrity and life with which I used to woo the rural Muse of Scotia. In the meantime let us finish what we have so well begun. The gentleman, Mr. Lewars, a particular friend of mine, will bring out any proofs (if they are ready) or any message you may have. Farewell!—R.B.

[Turn over.

[About *June* 17.]

YOU should have had this when Mr. Lewars called on you, but his saddle-bags miscarried. I am extremely anxious for your work, as, indeed, I am for everything concerning you and your welfare. You are a good, worthy, honest fellow, and have a good right to live in this world —because you deserve it. Many a merry meeting this publication has given us, and possibly it may give us more, though, alas! I fear it. This protracting, slow, consuming illness which hangs over me will, I doubt much, my ever dear friend, arrest my sun before he has well reached his middle career, and will turn over the poet to far more important concerns than studying the brilliancy of wit or the pathos of sentiment! However, *hope* is the cordial of the human heart, and I endeavour to cherish it as well as I can.

Let me hear from you as soon as convenient. Your work is a great one; and now that it is near finished, I see, if we were to begin again, two or three things that might be mended; yet I will venture to prophesy, that to future ages your publication will be the text-book and standard of Scottish song and music.

I am ashamed to ask another favour of you, because you have been so very good already; but my wife has a very particular friend of hers, a young lady who sings well, to whom she wishes to present the "Scots Musical Museum." If you have a spare copy, will you be so obliging as to send it by the very first *fly*, as I am anxious to have it soon.

Yours ever,
R. B.

[In this humble and delicate manner did poor Burns ask for a copy of a work of which he was principally the founder, and to which he had contributed, gratuitously, not less than 184 original, altered, and collected songs! The Editor has seen

O O 2

180 transcribed by his own hand for the *Museum*. This letter was written on the 4th of July—the Poet died on the 21st.—*Cromek.* A fac-simile of this interesting letter is given in the latest edition of Johnson's *Museum*, 1839. The date "July 4," affirmed by Cromek, is conjectural and evidently wrong.]

No. CCCXXIV.

TO MR. CUNNINGHAM.

BROW, SEA-BATHING QUARTERS, *7th July*, 1796.

MY DEAR CUNNINGHAM,

I received yours here this moment, and am indeed highly flattered with the approbation of the literary circle you mention—a literary circle inferior to none in the two kingdoms. Alas! my friend, I fear the voice of the bard will soon be heard among you no more! For these eight or ten months I have been ailing, sometimes bed-fast and sometimes not; but these last three months I have been tortured with an excruciating rheumatism, which has reduced me to nearly the last stage. You actually would not know me if you saw me. Pale, emaciated, and so feeble as occasionally to need help from my chair—my spirits fled! fled!—but I can no more on the subject—only the medical folks tell me that my last and only chance is bathing, and country quarters, and riding. The deuce of the matter is this: when an exciseman is off duty, his salary is reduced to 35*l.* instead of 50*l.* What way, in the name of thrift, shall I maintain myself, and keep a horse in country quarters, with a wife and five children at home, on 35*l.*? I mention this, because I had intended to beg your utmost interest, and that of all the friends you can muster, to move our Commissioners of Excise to grant me the full salary;* I dare say you know them all personally. If they do not grant it me, I must lay my account with an exit truly *en poëte*—if I die not of disease, I must perish with hunger.

I have sent you one of the songs; the other my memory does not serve me with, and I have no copy here; but I shall be at home soon, when I will send it you. *Apropos* to being at home, Mrs. Burns threatens in a week or two to add one more to my paternal charge, which, if of the right gender, I intend shall be introduced to the world by the respectable designation of *Alexander Cunningham Burns*. My last was *James Glencairn*, so you can have no objection to the company of nobility. Farewell.—R. B.

No. CCCXXV.

TO MR. GILBERT BURNS.

10th July, 1796.

DEAR BROTHER,

It will be no very pleasing news to you to be told that I am dangerously ill, and not likely to get better. An inveterate rheumatism has reduced me to such a state of debility, and my appetite is so totally gone, that I can scarcely stand on my legs. I have been a week at sea-

---

* The Poet's humble request of the continuance of his full salary was not granted.

bathing, and I will continue there, or in a friend's house in the country, all the summer. God keep my wife and children! if I am taken from their head, they will be poor indeed. I have contracted one or two serious debts, partly from my illness these many months, partly from too much thoughtlessness as to expense when I came to town, that will cut in too much on the little I leave them in your hands. Remember me to my mother.

Yours,

R. B.

No. CCCXXVI.

TO G. THOMSON.

MY DEAR SIR,   BROW, *4th July.*

I received your songs: but my health is so precarious, nay, dangerously situated, that as a last effort I am here at sea-bathing quarters. Besides my inveterate rheumatism, my appetite is quite gone, and I am so emaciated as to be scarce able to support myself on my own legs! Alas! is this a time for me to woo the Muses? However, I am still anxiously willing to serve your work, and, if possible, shall try. I would not like to see another employed, unless you could lay your hand upon a poet whose productions would be equal to the rest. You will see my remarks and alterations on the margin of each song. My address is still Dumfries. Farewell, and God bless you!—R.B.

[The handwriting of this note is smaller and less steady than the other letters —like the writing of one who, in the interval, had become an old man.— *Robert Chambers.*]

No. CCCXXVII.

TO MRS. BURNS.

MY DEAREST LOVE,   BROW, *Thursday.*

I delayed writing until I could tell you what effect sea-bathing was likely to produce. It would be injustice to deny that it has eased my pains, and I think has strengthened me; but my appetite is still extremely bad. No flesh nor fish can I swallow: porridge and milk are the only things I can taste. I am very happy to hear, by Miss Jess Lewars, that you are all well. My very best and kindest compliments to her, and to all the children. I will see you on Sunday.

Your affectionate Husband,

R. B.

No. CCCXXVIII.

TO MRS. DUNLOP.

MADAM,   BROW, *Saturday, 12th July,* 1796.

I have written you so often, without receiving any answer, that I would not trouble you again, but for the circumstances in which I am. An illness which has long hung about me in all probability will speedily

send me beyond that *bourn whence no traveller returns.* Your friendship, with which for many years you honoured me, was a friendship dearest to my soul. Your conversation, and especially your correspondence, were at once highly entertaining and instructive. With what pleasure did I use to break up the seal! The remembrance yet adds one pulse more to my poor palpitating heart. Farewell ! ! !—R. B.

No. CCCXXIX.

TO MR. JAMES BURNES,

WRITER, MONTROSE.

MY DEAR COUSIN, DUMFRIES, *12th July.*

When you offered me money assistance, little did I think I should want it so soon. A rascal of a haberdasher, to whom I owe a considerable bill, taking it into his head that I am dying, has commenced a process against me, and will infallibly put my emaciated body into jail. Will you be so good as to accommodate me, and that by return of post, with ten pounds? O, James! did you know the pride of my heart, you would feel doubly for me. Alas! I am not used to beg. The worst of it is, my health was coming about finely; you know, and my physician assured me, that melancholy and low spirits are half my disease: guess, then, my horrors since this business began. If I had it settled, I would be, I think, quite well in a manner. How shall I use the language to you, O do not disappoint me! but strong necessity's curst command.

I have been thinking over and over my brother's affairs, and I fear I must cut him up; but on this I will correspond at another time, particularly as I shall [require] your advice.

Forgive me for once more mentioning by return of post;—save me from the horrors of a jail!

My compliments to my friend James, and to all the rest. I do not know what I have written. The subject is so horrible, I dare not look it over again. Farewell.*—R. B.

No. CCCXXX.

TO G. THOMSON.

BROW, ON THE SOLWAY FRITH, *12th July,* 1796.

AFTER all my boasted independence, curst necessity compels me to implore you for five pounds.† A cruel wretch of a haberdasher, to whom I owe an account, taking it into his head that I am dying, has commenced

---

* James Burnes sent his cousin ten pounds the moment he received his letter, and shortly afterwards (June 29) five pounds to the poet's widow, offering at the same time to bring up and educate her son Robert, if she was disposed to part with him. Such substantial kindness is worthy of special notice.

† The dying Poet wrote entreatingly for five pounds, and Thomson sent the exact sum which he requested, from inability to send more; or, as he avers, from a dread of giving offence to the sensitive mind of Burns.

ply put me into jail. Do, for God's sake, send me
turn of post. Forgive me this earnestness, but
made me half distracted. I do not ask all this
urning health, I hereby promise and engage to
s' worth of the neatest song-genius you have
emurche" this morning. The measure
infuse much genius into the lines ;
now'st." *Page* 197.) Forgive,

Dumfries,

THE BORD

[The notes which Burns l
one through the Border
characteristic that we
of the Border tour
then a writer'
horseback, l

LE
bu

indiscriminate complaisance—from his situation past and present, an admirer of everything that bears a splendid title, or that possesses a large estate.* Mrs. Brydone a most elegant woman in her person and manners ; the tones of her voice remarkably sweet—my reception extremely flattering—sleep at Coldstream.

Tuesday.—Breakfast at Kelso—charming situation of Kelso—fine bridge over the Tweed—enchanting views and prospects on both sides of the river, particularly the Scotch side ; introduced to Mr. Scott of the Royal Bank, an excellent, modest fellow—fine situation of it—ruins of Roxburgh Castle—a holly-bush growing where James II. of Scotland was accidentally killed by the bursting of a cannon. A small old religious ruin, and a fine old garden planted by the religious, rooted out and destroyed by an English Hottentot, a *maître d'hôtel* of the Duke's, a Mr. Cole. Climate and soil of Berwickshire, and even Roxburghshire, superior to Ayrshire—bad roads. Turnip and sheep husbandry, their great improvements—Mr. M'Dowal, at Caverton Mill, a friend of Mr. Ainslie's, with whom I dined to-day, sold his sheep, ewe and lamb together, at two guineas apiece—wash their sheep before shearing—seven or eight pounds of washen wool in a fleece—low markets, consequently low rents—fine lands not above sixteen shillings a Scotch acre—magnificence of farmers and farm-houses—come up Teviot and up Jed to Jedburgh to lie, and so wish myself a good night.

Wednesday.—Breakfast with Mr. —— in Jedburgh—a squabble between Mrs. ——, a crazed, talkative slattern, and a sister of hers, an old maid, respecting a relief minister—Miss gives Madam the lie ; and Madam, by way of revenge, upbraids her that she laid snares to entangle the said minister, then a widower, in the net of matrimony. Go about two miles out of Jedburgh to a roup of parks—meet a polite, soldier-like gentleman, a Captain Rutherford, who had been many years through the wilds of America, a prisoner among the Indians—charming, romantic situation of Jedburgh, with gardens, orchards, &c. intermingled among the houses —fine old ruins—a once magnificent cathedral, and strong castle. All the towns here have the appearance of old, rude grandeur, but the people extremely idle—Jed a fine romantic little river.

Dine with Capt. Rutherford—the Captain a polite fellow, fond of money in his farming way ; showed a particular respect to my bardship—his lady exactly a proper matrimonial second part for him. Miss Rutherford a beautiful girl, but too far gone woman to expose so much of a fine swelling bosom—her face very fine.

Return to Jedburgh—walk up Jed with some ladies to be shown Love-lane and Blackburn, two fairy scenes. Introduced to Mr. Potts, writer,

---

* Mr. Brydone had been travelling tutor to several men of rank, and was the author of "A Tour in Sicily and Malta." In after years Scott visited Brydone, and in Marmion speaks of him as a " reverend pilgrim,"

> " Well worth the whole Bernardine brood
>   That e'er wore sandal, frock, or hood."

a very clever fellow ; and Mr. Somerville, the clergyman of the place, a man, and a gentleman, but sadly addicted to punning. The walking party of ladies : Mrs. —— and Miss —— her sister, before mentioned.—N.B. These two appear still more comfortably ugly and stupid, and bore me most shockingly.—Two Miss ——, tolerably agreeable. Miss Hope, a tolerably pretty girl, fond of laughing and fun. Miss Lindsay, a good-humoured, amiable girl ; rather short *et embonpoint*, but handsome and extremely graceful—beautiful hazel eyes, full of spirit, and sparkling with delicious moisture—an engaging face—*un tout ensemble* that speaks her of the first order of female minds. Her sister, a bonie, strappan, rosy, sonsie lass. Shake myself loose, after several unsuccessful efforts, of Mrs. —— and Miss ——, and somehow or other get hold of Miss Lindsay's arm. My heart is thawed into melting pleasure after being so long frozen up in the Greenland Bay of indifference, amid the noise and nonsense of Edinburgh. Miss seems very well pleased with my bardship's distinguishing her, and after some slight qualms, which I could easily mark, she sets the titter round at defiance, and kindly allows me to keep my hold ; and when parted by the ceremony of my introduction to Mr. Somerville, she met me half, to resume my situation.——*Nota Bene.* The Poet within a point and a half of being d-mnably in love—I am afraid my bosom is still nearly as much tinder as ever.

The old, cross-grained, whiggish, ugly, slanderous Miss ——, with all the poisonous spleen of a disappointed, ancient maid, stops me very unseasonably to ease her bursting breast, by falling abusively foul on the Miss Lindsays, particularly on my Dulcinea ;—I hardly refrain from cursing her to her face for daring to mouth her calumnious slander on one of the finest pieces of the workmanship of Almighty Excellence ! Sup at Mr. ——'s ; vexed that the Miss Lindsays are not of the supper-party, as they only are wanting. Mrs. —— and Miss —— still improve infernally on my hands.

Set out next morning for Wauchope, the seat of my correspondent, Mrs. Scott—breakfast by the way with Dr. Elliot, an agreeable, good-hearted, climate-beaten old veteran, in the medical line ; now retired to a romantic but rather moorish place, on the banks of the Roole—he accompanies us almost to Wauchope—we traverse the country to the top of Bochester, the scene of an old encampment, and Woolee Hill.

Wauchope.—Mr. Scott exactly the figure and face commonly given to Sancho Panca—very shrewd in his farming matters, and not unfrequently stumbles on what may be called a strong thing rather than a good thing. Mrs. Scott all the sense, taste, intrepidity of face, and bold, critical decision, which usually distinguish female authors. Sup with Mr. Potts—agreeable party. Breakfast next morning with Mr. Somerville—the *bruit* of Miss Lindsay and my bardship, by means of the invention and malice of Miss ——. Mr. Somerville sends to Dr. Lindsay ; begging him and family to breakfast if convenient, but at all events to send Miss Lindsay ; accordingly Miss Lindsay only comes. I find Miss Lindsay would soon play the devil with me—I met with some little flattering attentions from her. Mrs. Somerville an excellent, motherly, agreeable woman, and a fine

family. Mr. Ainslie and Mrs. S. junrs., with Mr. ——, Miss Lindsay, and myself, go to see *Esther*, a very remarkable woman for reciting poetry of all kinds, and sometimes making Scotch doggrel herself : she can repeat by heart almost everything she has ever read, particularly Pope's Homer from end to end ; has studied Euclid by herself ; and, in short, is a woman of very extraordinary abilities. On conversing with her I find her fully equal to the character given of her. She is very much flattered that I send for her, and that she sees a poet who has "put out a book," as she says. She is, among other things, a great florist—and is rather past the meridian of once celebrated beauty.

I walk in *Esther's* garden with Miss Lindsay, and after some little chit-chat of the tender kind, I presented her with a proof print of my Nob, which she accepted with something more tender than gratitude. She told me many little stories which Miss —— had retailed concerning her and me, with prolonging pleasure—God bless her ! Was waited on by the magistrates, and presented with the freedom of the burgh.

Took farewell of Jedburgh, with some melancholy, disagreeable sensations.—Jed, pure be thy crystal streams, and hallowed thy sylvan banks ! Sweet Isabella Lindsay, may peace dwell in thy bosom, uninterrupted except by the tumultuous throbbings of rapturous love ! That love-kindling eye must beam on another, not on me ; that graceful form must bless another's arms, not mine !

Kelso.—Dine with the farmers' club—all gentlemen, talking of high matters—each of them keeps a hunter from thirty to fifty pounds' value, and attends the fox-huntings in the country. Go out with Mr. Ker, one of the club, and a friend of Mr. Ainslie's, to lie—Mr. Ker a most gentlemanly, clever, handsome fellow, a widower with some fine children—his manner astonishingly like my dear old friend Robert Muir, in Kilmarnock—everything in Mr. Ker's most elegant—he offers to accompany me in my English tour. Dine with Sir Alexander Don—a pretty clever fellow, but far from being a match for his divine lady. A very wet day. . . . . Sleep at Stodrig again ; and set out for Melrose—visit Dryburgh, a fine old ruined abbey —still bad weather—cross Leader, and come up Tweed to Melrose—dine there, and visit that far-famed glorious ruin—come to Selkirk, up Ettrick ; the whole country hereabout, both on Tweed and Ettrick, remarkably stony.

Monday.—Come to Inverleithing, a famous shaw, and in the vicinity of the palace of Traquair, where having dined, and drank some Galloway whey, I here remain till to-morrow. Saw Elibanks and Elibraes, on the other side of the Tweed.

Tuesday.—Drank tea yesternight at Pirn, with Mr. Horsburgh. Breakfasted to-day with Mr. Ballantyne of Hollowlee. Proposal for a four-horse team, to consist of Mr. Scott of Wauchope, Fittieland ; Logan of Logan, Fittiefurr ; Ballantine of Hollowlee, Forewynd ; Horsburgh of Horsburgh. Dine at a country inn, kept by a miller, in Earlston, the birth-place and residence of the celebrated Thomas à Rhymer—saw the ruins of his castle—come to Berrywell.

Wednesday.—Dine at Dunse with the farmers' club-company—impossible to do them justice. Rev. Mr. Smith a famous punster, and Mr. Meikle a celebrated mechanic, and inventor of the threshing-mills.

Thursday.—Breakfast at Berrywell, and walk into Dunse to see a famous knife made by a cutler there, and to be presented to an Italian prince. A pleasant ride with my friend Mr. Robert Ainslie and his sister to Mr. Thomson's, a man who has newly commenced farmer, and has married a Miss Patty Grieve, formerly a flame of Mr. Robert Ainslie's. Company—Miss Jacky Grieve, an amiable sister of Mrs. Thomson's, and Mr. Hood, an honest, worthy, facetious farmer in the neighbourhood.

Friday.—Ride to Berwick—an idle town, rudely picturesque. Meet Lord Errol in walking round the walls—his lordship's flattering notice of me. Dine with Mr. Clunzie, merchant—nothing particular in company or conversation. Come up a bold shore, and over a wild country, to Eyemouth—sup and sleep at Mr. Grieve's.

Saturday.—Spend the day at Mr. Grieve's—made a royal arch mason of St. Abb's Lodge. Mr. William Grieve, the oldest brother, a joyous, warm-hearted, jolly, clever fellow—takes a hearty glass, and sings a good song. Mr. Robert, his brother, and partner in trade, a good fellow, but says little. Take a sail after dinner. Fishing of all kinds pays tithes at Eyemouth.

Sunday.—A Mr. Robinson, brewer at Ednam, sets out with us to Dunbar. The Miss Grieves very good girls—my bardship's heart got a brush from Miss Betsey.

Mr. William Grieve's attachment to the family-circle so fond, that when he is out, which by the by is often the case, he cannot go to bed till he see if all his sisters are sleeping well——Pass the famous Abbey of Coldingham, and Pease-bridge. Call at Mr. Sheriff's, where Mr. A. and I dine. Mr. S. talkative and conceited. I talk of love to Nancy the whole evening, while her brother escorts home some companions like himself. Sir James Hall of Dunglass, having heard of my being in the neighbourhood, comes to Mr. Sheriff's to breakfast—takes me to see his fine scenery on the stream of Dunglass—Dunglass the most romantic, sweet place I ever saw—Sir James and his lady a pleasant happy couple. He points out a walk for which he has an uncommon respect, as it was made by an aunt of his, to whom he owes much.

Miss —— will accompany me to Dunbar, by way of making a parade of me as a sweetheart of hers, among her relations. She mounts an old cart-horse, as huge and as lean as a house ; a rusty old side-saddle, without girth or stirrup, but fastened on with an old pillion-girth ; herself as fine as hands could make her, in cream-coloured riding clothes, hat and feather, &c. I, ashamed of my situation, ride like the devil, and almost shake her to pieces on old Jolly—get rid of her by refusing to call at her uncle's with her.

Passed through the most glorious corn-country I ever saw, till I reach Dunbar, a neat little town.—Dine with Provost Fall, an eminent merchant and most respectable character, but undescribable, as he exhibits no marked traits. Mrs. Fall a genius in painting ; fully more clever in the fine arts and sciences than my friend Lady Wauchope, without her consummate assurance of her own abilities.—Call with Mr. Robinson (who, by the by, I find to be a worthy, much-respected man, very modest ; warm, social heart, which with less good sense than his would be perhaps, with the children of prim precision and pride, rather inimical to that respect which is man's due from man)—with him I call on Miss Clark, a maiden, in the Scotch phrase, "guid enough, but no brent new :" a clever woman, with tolerable pretensions to remark and wit ; while time had blown the blushing bud of bashful modesty into the flower of easy confidence. She wanted to see what sort of *raree show* an author was, and to let him know, that though Dunbar was but a little town, yet it was not destitute of people of parts.

Breakfast next morning at Skateraw, at Mr. Lee's, a farmer of great note. Mr. Lee an excellent, hospitable, social fellow, rather oldish ; warm-hearted and chatty—a most judicious, sensible farmer. Mr. Lee detains me till next morning. Company at dinner—my Rev. acquaintance Dr. Bowmaker, a reverend, rattling old fellow ; two sea-lieutenants ; a cousin of the landlord's, a fellow whose looks are of that kind which deceived me in a gentleman at Kelso, and has often deceived me—a goodly handsome figure and face, which incline one to give them credit for parts which they have not ; Mr. Clarke, a much cleverer fellow, but whose looks, a little cloudy, and his appearance, rather ungainly, with an every-day observer may prejudice the opinion against him ; Dr. Brown, a medical young gentleman from Dunbar, a fellow whose face and manners are open and engaging. Leave Skateraw for Dunse next day, along with Collector ——, a lad of slender abilities and bashfully diffident to an extreme.

Found Miss Ainslie, the amiable, the sensible, the good-humoured, the sweet Miss Ainslie, all alone at Berrywell. Heavenly powers, who know the weakness of human hearts, support mine ! What happiness must I see only to remind me that I cannot enjoy it !

Lammermuir hills, from East Lothian to Dunse, very wild. Dine with the farmers' club at Kelso. Sir John Hume and Mr. Lumsden there, but nothing worth remembrance when the following circumstance is considered—I walk into Dunse before dinner, and out to Berrywell in the evening with Miss Ainslie—how well-bred, how frank, how good she is ! Charming Rachael ! may thy bosom never be wrung by the evils of this life of sorrows, or by the villany of this world's sons !

Thursday.—Mr. Ker and I set out to dine at Mr. Hood's on our way to England.

I am taken extremely ill, with strong feverish symptoms, and take a servant of Mr. Hood's to watch me all night—embittering remorse scares my fancy at the gloomy forebodings of death. I am determined to live for the future in such a manner as not to be scared at the approach of death :

I am sure I could meet him with indifference, but for " the something beyond the grave." Mr. Hood agrees to accompany us to England if we will wait till Sunday.

Friday.—I go with Mr. Hood to see a roup of an unfortunate farmer's stock—rigid economy and decent industry, do you preserve me from being the principal *dramatis persona* in such a scene of horror !

Meet my good old friend Mr. Ainslie, who calls on Mr. Hood in the evening to take farewell of my bardship. This day I feel myself warm with sentiments of gratitude to the Great Preserver of men, who has kindly restored me to health and strength once more.

A pleasant walk with my young friend Douglas Ainslie, a sweet, modest, clever young fellow.

Sunday, 27th May.—Cross Tweed, and traverse the moors through a wild country till I reach Alnwick—Alnwick Castle a seat of the Duke of Northumberland, furnished in a most princely manner.—A Mr. Wilkin, agent of his Grace's, shows us the house and policies—Mr. Wilkin a discreet, sensible, ingenious man.

Monday.—Come, still through by-ways, to Warkworth, where we dine. Hermitage and old castle. Warkworth situated very picturesque, with Coquet Island, a small rocky spot, the seat of an old monastery, facing it a little in the sea ; and the small but romantic river Coquet running through it. Sleep at Morpeth, a pleasant enough little town, and on next day to Newcastle. Meet with a very agreeable, sensible fellow, a Mr. Chattox, who shows us a great many civilities, and who dines and sups with us.

Wednesday.—Left Newcastle early in the morning, and rode over a fine country to Hexham to breakfast—from Hexham to Wardrue, the celebrated Spa, where we slept.

Thursday.—Reach Longtown to dine, and part there with my good friends Messrs Hood and Ker—a hiring day in Longtown—I am uncommonly happy to see so many young folks enjoying life. I come to Carlisle. (Meet a strange enough romantic adventure by the way, in falling in with a girl and her married sister : the girl, after some overtures of gallantry on my side, sees me a little cut with the bottle, and offers to take me in for a Gretna-green affair. I not being such a gull as she imagines, make an appointment with her, by way of *vive la bagatelle*, to hold a conference on it when we reach town. I meet her in town and give her a brush of caressing and a bottle of cyder ; but finding herself *un peu trompé* in her man she sheers off.) Next day I meet my good friend Mr. Mitchell, and walk with him round the town and its environs, and through his printing-works, &c.—four or five hundred people employed, many of them women and children. Dine with Mr. Mitchell, and leave Carlisle. Come by the coast to Annan. Overtaken on the way by a curious old fish of a shoemaker, and miner from Cumberland mines.

[*Here the Manuscript abruptly terminates.*]

THE HIGHLAND TOUR.

[Nicol, Burns's companion on this Highland expedition, was then an under teacher in the High School of Edinburgh. He was a Dumfriesshire man, of humble birth, possessed considerable natural ability and scholarship, but was of a somewhat coarse, hot-tempered character.]

25th August, 1787.—I leave Edinburgh for a northern tour, in company with my good friend Mr. Nicol, whose originality of humour promises me much entertainment. Linlithgow—a fertile improved country—West Lothian. The more elegance and luxury among the farmers, I always observe, in equal proportion the rudeness and stupidity of the peasantry. This remark I have made all over the Lothians, Merse, Roxburgh, &c. For this, among other reasons, I think that a man of romantic taste, a "man of feeling,' will be better pleased with the poverty, but intelligent minds, of the peasantry in Ayrshire (peasantry they are all below the justice of peace) than the opulence of a club of Merse farmers, when at the same time he considers the vandalism of their plough-folks, &c. I carry this idea so far, that an uninclosed, half-improven country is to me actually more agreeable, and gives me more pleasure as a prospect, than a country cultivated like a garden.—Soil about Linlithgow light and thin. The town carries the appearance of rude, decayed grandeur— charmingly rural, retired situation. The old royal palace a tolerably fine, but melancholy, ruin—sweetly situated on a small elevation, by the brink of a loch. Shown the room where the beautiful, injured Mary Queen of Scots was born—a pretty good old Gothic church. The infamous stool of repentance standing, in the old Romish way, on a lofty situation.

What a poor, pimping business is a Presbyterian place of worship; dirty, narrow, and squalid ; stuck in a corner of old popish grandeur such as Linlithgow, and much more, Melrose ! Ceremony and show, if judiciously thrown in, absolutely necessary for the bulk of mankind, both in religious and civil matters.—Dine—go to my friend Smith's, at Avon, printfield—find nobody but Mrs. Miller, an agreeable, sensible, modest, good body ; as useful but not so ornamental as Fielding's Miss Western— not rigidly polite *à la Francais*, but easy, hospitable, and housewifely.

An old lady from Paisley, a Mrs. Lawson, whom I promise to call for in Paisley : like old lady W——, and still more like Mrs. C——, her conversation is pregnant with strong sense and just remark, but, like them, a certain air of self-importance and a *duresse* in the eye seem to indicate, as the Ayrshire wife observed of her cow, that "she had a mind o' her ain."

Pleasant view of Dumfermline and the rest of the fertile coast of Fife, as we go down to that dirty, ugly place, Burrowstones—see a horse-race and call on a friend of Mr. Nicol's, a Bailie Cowan, of whom I know too little to attempt his portrait—come through the rich carse of Falkirk to pass the night. Falkirk nothing remarkable except the tomb of Sir John the Graham, over which, in the succession of time, four stones have been placed. Camelon, the ancient metropolis of the Picts, now a small village in the neighbourhood of Falkirk. Cross the grand canal to Carron—come past Larbert, and admire a fine monument of cast-iron erected by Mr. Bruce, the African traveller, to his wife.

Pass Dunipace, a place laid out with fine taste—a charming amphitheatre, bounded by Denny village, and pleasant seats down the way to Dunipace. —The Carron running down the bosom of the whole makes it one of the most charming little prospects I have seen.

Dine at Auchinbowie—Mr. Monro an excellent, worthy old man—Miss Monro an amiable, sensible, sweet young woman, much resembling Mrs. Grierson. Come to Bannockburn—shown the old house where James III. finished so tragically his unfortunate life. The field of Bannockburn —the hole where glorious Bruce set his standard. Here no Scot can pass uninterested. I fancy to myself that I see my gallant, heroic countrymen coming o'er the hill and down upon the plunderers of their country, the murderers of their fathers, noble revenge and just hate glowing in every vein, striding more and more eagerly as they approach the oppressive, insulting, blood-thirsty foe ! I see them meet in gloriously-triumphant congratulation on the victorious field, exulting in their heroic royal leader and rescued liberty and independence !—Come to Stirling.

Monday.—Go to Harvieston. Go to see Caudron linn, and Rumbling brig, and Diel's mill. Return in the evening. Supper—Messrs. Doig, the schoolmaster ; Bell ; and Captain Forrester of the castle. Doig a queerish figure, and something of a pedant—Bell a joyous fellow, who sings a good song—Forrester a merry, swearing kind of man, with a dash of the sodger.

Tuesday Morning.—Breakfast with Captain Forrester—Ochel hills— Devon river—Forth and Tieth—Allan river—Strathallan, a fine country, but little improved—cross Earn to Crieff—dine, and go to Arbruchil—cold reception at Arbruchil—a most romantically pleasant ride up Earn, by Auchtertyre and Comrie, to Arbruchil—sup at Crieff.

Wednesday Morning.—Leave Crieff—Glen Amond—Amond river— Ossian's grave—Loch Fruoch—Glenquaich—landlord and landlady remarkable characters—Taymouth described in rhyme—meet the Hon. Charles Townshend.

Thursday.—Come down Tay to Dunkeld—Glenlyon House—Lyon river—Druids' temple—three circles of stones, the outermost sunk ; the second has thirteen stones remaining, the innermost has eight ; two

large detached ones, like a gate, to the south-east—say prayers in it—pass Taybridge—Aberfeldy—described in rhyme—Castle Menzies—Inver—Dr. Stewart—sup.

Friday.—Walk with Mrs. Stewart and Beard to Birnam top—fine prospect down Tay—Craigieburn hills—hermitage on the Branwater, with a picture of Ossian—breakfast with Dr. Stewart—Neil Gow plays—a short, stout-built, honest Highland figure, with his grayish hair shed on his honest social brow ; an interesting face, marking strong sense, kind openheartedness, mixed with unmistrusting simplicity—visit his house—Marget Gow.

Ride up Tummel river to Blair—Fascally a beautiful romantic nest—wild grandeur of the pass of Gilliecrankie—visit the gallant Lord Dundee's stone.

Blair—Sup with the Duchess—easy and happy from the manners of the family—confirmed in my good opinion of my friend Walker.

Saturday.—Visit the scenes round Blair—fine, but spoiled with bad taste—Tilt and Gairie rivers—Falls on the Tilt—heather seat—ride in company with Sir William Murray and Mr. Walker, to Loch Tummel—meanderings of the Rannach, which runs through quondam Struan Robertson's estate, from Loch Rannach to Loch Tummel. Dine at Blair : company—General Murray ; Captain Murray, an honest tar ; Sir William Murray, an honest, worthy man, but tormented with the hypochondria ; Mrs. Graham, *belle et aimable;* Miss Catchcart ; Mrs. Murray, a painter ; Mrs. King ; Duchess and fine family, the Marquis, Lords James, Edward, and Robert. Ladies Charlotte, Emilia, and children dance. Sup—Mr. Graham of Fintry.

Come up the Garrie—Falls of Bruar—Daldecairoch—Dalwhinnie—dine—snow on the hills seventeen feet deep—no corn from Loch Gairie to Dalwhinnie—cross the Spey, and come down the stream to Pitnin—Straths rich—*les environs* picturesque—Craigow hill—Ruthven of Badenoch—barracks—wild and magnificent—Rothemurche on the other side, and Glenmore—Grant of Rothemurche's poetry, told me by the Duke of Gordon—Strathspey, rich and romantic. Breakfast at Aviemore, a wild spot—dine at Sir James Grant's—Lady Grant a sweet, pleasant body—come through mist and darkness to Dulsie to lie.

Tuesday.—Findhorn river—rocky banks—come on to Castle Cawdor, where Macbeth murdered King Duncan—saw the bed in which King Duncan was stabbed—dine at Kilravock—Mrs. Rose, sen. a true chieftain's wife—Fort George—Inverness.

Wednesday.—Loch Ness—Braes of Ness—General's hut—Falls of Fyers—Urquhart Castle and Strath.

Thursday.—Come over Culloden Muir—reflections on the field of battle—breakfast at Kilravock—old Mrs. Rose, sterling sense, warm heart,

strong passions, and honest pride, all in an uncommon degree—Mrs. Rose,
jun. a little milder than the mother; this perhaps owing to her being
younger—Mr. Grant, minister at Calder, resembles Mr. Scott at Inverleithing—Mrs. Rose and Mrs. Grant accompany us to Kildrummie—two
young ladies : Miss Rose, who sung two Gaelic songs, beautiful and lovely ;
Miss Sophia Brodie, most agreeable and amiable ; both of them gentle,
mild, the sweetest creatures on earth, and happiness be with them !—
Dine at Nairn—fall in with a pleasant enough gentleman, Dr. Stewart,
who had been long abroad with his father in the Forty-five ; and Mr.
Falconer, a spare, irascible, warm-hearted Norland, and a Nonjuror—
Brodie-house to lie.

Friday.—Forres—famous stone at Forres—Mr. Brodie tells me that the
muir where Shakespeare lays Macbeth's witch-meeting is still haunted—
that the country folks won't pass it by night. . . . .
Venerable ruins of Elgin Abbey—a grander effect at first glance than
Melrose, but not near so beautiful—cross Spey to Fochabers—fine palace,
worthy of the generous proprietor. Dine—company, Duke and Duchess,
Ladies Charlotte and Magdeline, Col. Abercrombie and lady, Mr. Gordon
and Mr. ——, a clergyman, a venerable, aged figure : the Duke makes me
happier than ever great man did—noble, princely, yet mild, condescending,
and affable, gay and kind—the Duchess witty and sensible—God bless
them !
Come to Cullen to lie—hitherto the country is sadly poor and unim-
proven.
Come to Aberdeen—meet with Mr. Chalmers, printer, a facetious fellow
—Mr. Ross, a fine fellow, like Professor Tytler—Mr. Marshal, one of the
poetæ minores—Mr. Sheriffs, author of " Jamie and Bess," a little decrepid
body with some abilities—Bishop Skinner, a Nonjuror, son of the author
of " Tullochgorum," a man whose mild venerable manner is the most
marked of any in so young a man—Professor Gordon, a good-natured,
jolly-looking professor—Aberdeen, a lazy town—near Stonhive, the coast
a good deal romantic—meet my relations—Robert Burns, writer, in Stonhive, one of those who love fun, a gill, and a punning joke, and have not
a bad heart—his wife a sweet hospitable body, without any affectation of
what is called town-breeding.

Tuesday.—Breakfast with Mr. Burns—lie at Lawrence Kirk—album
library—Mrs. —— a jolly, frank, sensible, love-inspiring widow—Howe of
the Mearns, a rich, cultivated, but still unenclosed country.

Wednesday.—Cross North Esk river, and a rich country to Craigow.

*　　*　　*　　*　　*　　*

Go to Montrose, that finely-situated, handsome town—breakfast at
Muthie, and sail along that wild rocky coast, and see the famous caverns,
particularly the Gairiepot—land and dine at Arbroath—stately ruins of
Arbroath Abbey—come to Dundee, through a fertile country—Dundee a

low-lying but pleasant town—old steeple—Tayfrith—Broughty Castle, a finely situated ruin, jutting into the Tay.

Friday.—Breakfast with the Miss Scotts—Miss Bess Scott like Mrs. Greenfield ; my bardship almost in love with her—come through the rich harvests and fine hedge-rows of the carse of Gowrie, along the romantic margin of the Grampian hills, to Perth—fine, fruitful, hilly, woody country round Perth.

Saturday Morning.—Leave Perth—come up Strathearn to Endermay —fine, fruitful, cultivated strath—the scene of "Bessie Bell and Mary Gray," near Perth—fine scenery on the banks of the May—Mrs. Belcher, gawcie, frank, affable, fond of rural sports, hunting, &c.—lie at Kinross— reflections in a fit of the colic.

Sunday.—Pass through a cold, barren country to Queensferry—dine— cross the ferry, and on to Edinburgh.

NOTES.

NOTES.

Page 1. The tale of the 'Twa Dogs,' Gilbert Burns writes, was composed after the resolution of publishing was nearly taken. Robert had a dog which he called Luath, that was a great favourite. The dog had been killed by the wanton cruelty of some person the night before my father's death. Robert said to me, that he should like to confer such immortality as he could bestow on his old friend Luath, and that he had a great mind to introduce something into the book, under the title of Stanzas to the Memory of a Quadruped Friend ; but this plan was given up for the poem as it now stands. Cæsar was merely the creature of the poet's imagination, created for the purpose of holding chat with his favourite Luath.

Page 1, l 26. Luath, Cuchullin's dog in Ossian's Fingal. R. B.

Page 2, l 8. Var. In all editions up to 1794—

Till tired at last wi' many a farce,
They sat them down upon their a—.

Page 3, l 14. Burns alludes to the factor in the autobiographical sketch communicated to Dr. John Moore.
'My father's generous master died : the farm proved a ruinous bargain : and, to clench the misfortune, we fell into the hands of a factor who sat for the picture I have drawn of one in my tale of the "Twa Dogs" . . . my indignation yet boils at the recollection of the scoundrel factor's insolent threatening letters, which used to set us all in tears.'

Page 8, l 10. In the first edition the stanza closed as follows :—

Wae worth them for't!
While healths gae round to him, wha tight,
Gies famous sport

Page 9, l 2. Var. "Humble thanks" in edition of 1794.

Page 9, l 25. This was wrote before the Act anent the Scotch Distilleries, of Session, 1786 : for which Scotland and the author return their most grateful thanks. R. B.

Page 9, l 35. Var. 'Simple Poet's prayers' in edition of 1794.

Page 11, l 1. The allusion in the text is primarily to Hugh Montgomerie of Coilsfield, twelfth Earl of Eglintoune.

Page 11, l 2. James Boswell of Auchinleck, Johnson's biographer.

Page 11, l 17. George Dempster, Esq. of Dunnichen.

Page 11, l 18. Sir Adam Fergusson of Kilkerran, Bart.

Page 11, l 20. The Marquis of Graham, eldest son of the Duke of Montrose.

Page 11, l 22. The Right Hon. Henry Dundas, Treasurer of the Navy, and M.P. for the city of Edinburgh.

Page 11, l 24. Lord Frederick Campbell, second brother of the Duke of Argyle, and Ilay Campbell, Lord Advocate of Scotland.

Page 12, l 13. The Earl of Chatham, Pitt's father, was the second son of Robert Pitt of Boconnock, in the county of Cornwall.

Page 12, l 15. A worthy old hostess of the author's in Mauchline, where he sometimes studies politics over a glass of guid old Scotch drink. R. B. Nanse was surprised at her house and name being thus dragged before the public. She declared that Burns had never taken three half-mutchkins in her house in all his life.

Page 13, l 37. In edition of 1794 this stanza is altered as follows :—

"Scotland, my auld respected mither!
Tho' whiles ye moistify your leather,
Till when ye speak. ye aiblins blether ;
Yet deil mak matter!
Freedom and Whisky gang thegither,
Tak aff your whither.

This tasteless alteration (which we feel convinced was not made by the poet) was not adopted in any subsequent edition of the Poems.

Page 14, l 1. Holy Fair is a common phrase in the west of Scotland for a sacramental occasion. R. B.

Page 15, l 39. Var.

Bet B—r there, an' twa-three whores.

Racer Jess was a half-witted daughter of Poosie Nansie. She was a great pedestrian, and died at Mauchline in 1813.

Page 15, l 43. Var. An' there, a batch o' wabster brawls.

Page 16, l 2. Var. An' ithers on their claes.

Page 16, l 22. Var.

Wi' tidings o' salvation.

The change in the text was made at the suggestion of Dr. Blair.

Page 16, l 25. Var. The vera sight o' Sawnie's face.

Page 16, l 26. Var. Tae hell wi' speed had sent him.

Page 16, l 41. Var.

Geordie begins his cauld harangues.

The Rev. George Smith, minister at Galston.

Page 16, l 42. Var. On practice and of morals.

Page 17, l 12. Var.

For sairy Willy water-fit.

The Rev. William Peebles, minister of Newton-upon-Ayr.

Page 17, l 17. A street so called, which faces the tent in Mauchline. R. B.

Page 17, *l* 19. The Rev. W. Miller, assistant preacher at Auchinleck, and afterwards minister of Kilmaurs, near Kilmarnock. He was of short stature.

Page 18, *l* 13. *Var.*

Black Jock is na spairin.

The Rev. John Russel, minister of the Chapel of Ease, Kilmarnock.

Page 18, *l* 17. Shakespeare's Hamlet. R. B.

Page 18, *l* 32. *Var.* How yill gaed round in jugs an' caups.

Page 18, *l* 37. *Var.* Then comes a gaucie, gash guidwife.

Page 19. The composition of 'Death and Doctor Hornbook' was suggested by the circumstances related in the Preface. It was composed rapidly. Burns met the apothecary at a meeting of the Tarbolton Masonic lodge, and the next afternoon he repeated the entire poem to Gilbert. With reference to its composition, Mr. Allan Cunningham supplies the following tradition, which is nonsense on the face of it.

'On his way home,'—from the Masonic meeting—'the Poet found a neighbour lying tipsy by the road-side ; the idea of Death flashed on his fancy, and seating himself on the parapet of a bridge, he composed the poem, fell asleep, and when awakened by the morning sun, he recollected it all, and wrote it down on reaching Mossgiel.'

The laughter occasioned by the publication of the satire drove, it is said, John Wilson, schoolmaster and apothecary, out of the county. He ultimately settled in Glasgow, became Session Clerk of the Gorbals, and died in 1839. 'Death and Doctor Hornbook' first appeared in the Edinburgh edition of the poems.

Page 19, *l* 29. In all the editions up to 1794 this line stood :

Great lies and nonsense baith to vend.

Page 19, *l* 37. Mr. Robert Wright, in his Life of Major-General James Wolfe, states that 'Hell' was the name given to the arched passage in Dublin which led into the area on the south side of Christ Church, and east of the law courts. A representation of the Devil, carved in oak, stood above the entrance.

Page 20, *l* 32. This rencounter happened in seed-time, 1785. R. B.

Page 21, *l* 9. An epidemical fever was then raging in that country. R. B.

Page 21, *l* 21. This gentleman, Dr. Hornbook, is, professionally, a brother of the Sovereign Order of the Ferula, but by intuition and inspiration is at once an apothecary, surgeon, and physician. R. B.

Page 21, *l* 25. Buchan's Domestic Medicine. R. B.

Page 22, *l* 31. The grave-digger. R. B.

Page 24. The occasion of this poem was the erection of a new bridge across the river at Ayr, to supersede the inconvenient structure built in the reign of Alexander III. Mr. Ballantine, Burns' patron, and chief magistrate of the town, was mainly instrumental in raising funds for the work ; and to him the poem is dedicated.

Page 25, *l* 15. A noted tavern at the Auld Brig end. R. B.

Page 25, *l* 20. *Var.*

The drowsy steeple clock had numbered two.

The two steeples. R. B. The 'Dungeon Clock' in this, and the 'Wallace Tow'r' in the following line.

Page 25, *l* 28. *Var.*

When, lo ! before our Bardie's wond'ring e'en
The Brigs of Ayr's twa sprites are seen.

Page 25, *l* 31. The Gos-hawk or Falcon R. B.

Page 26, *l* 11 & 12. This couplet—the most picturesque and memorable in the poem—does not occur in the MS. copy.

Page 26, *l* 15. A noted ford, just above the Auld Brig. R. B.

Page 26, *l* 30. *Var.*

Or haunted Garpal draws its feeble source.

The banks of Garpal water is one of the few places in the west of Scotland where those fancy-scaring beings known by the name of Ghaists still continue pertinaciously to inhabit. R. B.

Page 26, *l* 31. *Var.* Aroused by blust'ring winds an' spotted thowes.

Page 26, *l* 35. 'Glenbuck,' the source of the river Ayr. R. B.

Page 26, *l* 36. 'Ratton-Key,' a small landing-place above the large key. R. B.

Page 28, *l* 3. *Var.* To liken them to your auld warld bodies.

Page 28, *l* 4. *Var.* I must needs say comparisons are odious.

Page 28, *l* 14. *Var.* Plain kind stupidity stept kindly in to aid them.

Page 28, *l* 25. A well-known performer of Scottish music on the violin. R. B.

Page 28, *l* 49. A stream near Coilsfield.

Page 28, *l* 51. Mrs. Stewart of Stair.

Page 29, *l* 2. The seat of Professor Dugald Stewart.

Page 29. 'The Ordination' was composed on the Rev. Mr. Mackinlay being called to Kilmarnock. It was first printed in the second edition of the Poems.

Page 29, *l* 17. Alluding to a scoffing ballad which was made on the admission of the late reverend and worthy Mr. Lindsay to the Laigh Kirk. R. B.

Page 29, *l* 3, 2 *col. Var.*

> Formula and confession:
> An' lay your hands upon his head,
> An' seal his high commission,
> The holy flock to tent an' feed.

Page 30, *l* 15, 2 *col. Var.*

> Will clap him in the torture.

Page 30, *l* 21, 2 *col.* 'New Light' is a cant phrase in the west of Scotland for those religious opinions which Dr. Taylor of Norwich has so strenuously defended. R. B.

Page 30, *l* 28. With reference to this piece Burns wrote to a correspondent:—'Warm recollection of an absent friend presses so hard upon my heart, that I send him the prefixed bagatelle, pleased with the thought that it will greet the man of my bosom, and be a kind of distant language of friendship. . . . It was merely an extemporaneous production, on a wager with Mr. Hamilton that I would not produce a poem on the subject in a given time.' The Rev. Mr. Steven was afterwards minister of one of the Scotch churches in London—where, in 1790, William Burns, the Poet's brother, heard him preach—and he finally settled at Kilwinning in Ayrshire, where he died in 1824.

Page 31. Gilbert Burns says: 'It was, I think, in the winter of 1784, as we were going together with carts for coal to the family fire (and I could yet point out the particular spot), that the author first repeated to me the "Address to the Deil." The curious idea of such an address was suggested to him by turning over in his mind the many ludicrous accounts and representations we have from various quarters of this august personage.'

Page 32, *l* 13. This stanza was originally as follows :—

> Lang syne in Eden's happy scene,
> When strappin' Adam's days were green,
> And Eve was like my bonie Jean,
>   My dearest part,
> A dancin', sweet, young, handsome quean,
>   Wi' guileless heart.

Page 32, *l* 11, 2 *col. Vide* Milton, Book vi. R. B.

Page 32, *l* 29. This was one of Burns' earliest poems, the first indication of that peculiar moral humour of which the 'Twa Dogs' is the finest example. It was written before 1784, and Gilbert Burns informed Dr. Currie that 'the circumstances of the poor sheep were pretty much as he has described them : he had, partly by way of frolic, bought a ewe and two lambs from a neighbour, and she was tethered in a field adjoining the house at Lochlea. He and I were going out with our teams, and our two younger brothers to drive for us, at mid-day, when Hugh Wilson, a curious-looking, awkward lad, clad in plaiding, came to us with much anxiety in his face, with the information that the ewe had entangled herself in the tether, and was lying in the ditch. Robert was much tickled with Hughoc's appearance and postures on the occasion. Poor Mailie was set to rights, and when we returned from the plough in the evening he repeated to me her "Death and Dying Words' pretty much in the way they now stand.'

Page 32, *l* 34. A neibor herd callan. R. B. 'In a copy of this poem in the Poet's handwriting, possessed by Miss Grace Aiken, Ayr, a more descriptive note is here given. "Hughoc was an odd, glowran, gapin' callan, about three-fourths as wise as other folk."' *Chambers.*

Page 33, *l* 26, 2 *col.* This stanza was originally written :—

> She was nae get o' runted rams,
> Wi' woo' like goats, and legs like trams ;
> She was the flower o' Fairlie lambs,
>   A famous breed ;
> Now Robin, greetin', chows the hams
>   O' Mailie dead.

Page 34. Mr. James Smith was, when this epistle was written, a shopkeeper in Mauchline. He afterwards removed to Avon near Linlithgow, where he established a calico-printing manufactory. Being unsuccessful in his speculations, he emigrated to the West Indies, where he died.

Page 35, *l* 19, 2 *col.* George Dempster, Esq. of Dunnichen.

Page 36. Certain of Burns' friends—Mrs. Dunlop, and Mrs. Stewart of Stair— considered the 'Dream' to contain perilous stuff. These ladies, it is said, vainly solicited the Poet to omit it in the second edition of his poems. The 'Dream,' if not a high, is a very characteristic effort : there never was an easier hand-gallop of verse.

Page 36, *l* 14, 2 *col.* An allusion to the loss of the North American colonies.

Page 37, *l* 7. 'On the supplies for the Navy being voted, Spring 1786, Captain Macbride counselled some changes in that force, particularly the giving up of sixty-four gun-ships, which occasioned a good deal of discussion.' *Chambers.*

Page 37, *l* 35. Charles James Fox.

Page 37, *l* 6, 2 *col.* Frederick, Bishop of Osnaburg, afterwards Duke of York.

Page 37, *l* 15, 2 *col.* William, afterwards Duke of Clarence, and King William IV.

Page 37, *l* 17, 2 *col.* Alluding to the newspaper account of a certain royal sailor's amour. R. B.

Page 38. Duan, a term of Ossian's for the different divisions of a digressive poem. See his 'Cath-Loda,' vol. ii. of McPherson's translation. R. B.

Page 38, *l* 27, 2 *col.* This line supplies a curious instance of the fluctuations of Burns' mind and passion. It was originally written as it stands in the text, but in the bitter feeling induced by the destruction of the marriage lines he had given to Jean Armour he transferred

the compliment to the reigning favourite of the hour. In the first edition the line stood—

And such a leg! my Bess, I ween.

In the Edinburgh edition, the old affection being in the ascendant again, the line was restored to its original shape.

Page 39, *l* 19. This and the six following stanzas appeared for the first time in the second edition.

Page 39, *l* 26. The Wallaces. R. B.

Page 39, *l* 1, 2 *col.* William Wallace. R. B.

Page 39, *l* 2, 2 *col.* Adam Wallace of Richardton, cousin of the immortal preserver of Scottish independence. R. B.

Page 39, *l* 3, 2 *col.* Wallace, Laird of Craigie, who was second in command, under Douglas, Earl of Ormond, at the famous battle on the banks of the Sark, fought anno 1448. That glorious victory was principally owing to the judicious conduct and intrepid valour of the gallant Laird of Craigie, who died of his wounds after the action. R. B.

Page 39, *l* 7 · *col.* Coilus, King of the Picts, from whom the district of Kyle is said to take its name, lies buried, as tradition says, near the family seat of the Montgomeries of Coilsfield, where his burial-place is still shown. R.B.

Page 39, *l* 13, 2 *col.* Barskimming, the seat of the Lord Justice Clerk. R. B. (Sir Thomas Miller of Glenlee, afterwards President of the Court of Session.)

Page 39, *l* 19, 2 *col.* Catrine, the seat of the late Doctor, and present Professor, Stewart. R. B.

Page 39, *l* 25, 2 *col.* Colonel Fullarton. R.B.

Page 41, *l* 18, 2 *col.* In the Appendix to the second volume of Mr. Robert Chambers' 'Life and Works of Burns' are printed the following additional stanzas of the 'Vision,' taken from a MS. in the possession of Mr. Dick, bookseller, Ayr. After the 18th stanza of printed copies :—

With secret throes I mark'd that earth,
That cottage, witness of my birth ;
And near I saw, bold issuing forth,
In youthful pride,
A Lindsay, race of noble worth,
Famed far and wide.

Where, hid behind a spreading wood,
An ancient Pict-built mansion stood,
I spied, among an angel brood,
A female pair ;
Sweet shone their high maternal blood
And father's air.

An ancient tower to memory brought
How Dettingen's bold hero fought ;
Still, far from sinking into nought,
It owns a lord
Who 'far in western' climates fought
With trusty sword.

There, where a sceptred Pictish shade
Stalk'd round his ashes lowly laid,
I saw a martial race portray'd
In colours strong :
Bold, sodger-featured, undismay'd,
They stalked along.

Among the rest I well could spy
One gallant, graceful, martial boy ;
The sodger sparkled in his eye,
A diamond water ;
I blest that noble badge with joy
That owned me frater. *

After the 20th stanza :—

Near by arose a mansion fine,
The seat of many a Muse divine ;
Not rustic Muses such as mine,
With holly crowned,
But th' ancient, tuneful, laurelled nine
From classic ground.

I mourned the card that fortune dealt,
To see where bonie Whitefoords dwelt ;
But other prospects made me melt,-
That village near.
There nature, friendship, love, I felt,
Fond—mingling dear.

Hail nature's pang, more strong than death !
Warm friendship's glow, like kindling wrath !
Love, dearer than the parting breath
Of dying friend !
Not even with life's wild devious path
Your force shall end.

The power that gave the soft alarms
In blooming Whitefoords' rosy charms,
Still threats the tiny-feathered arms,
The barbèd dart,
While lovely Wilhelmina charms
The coldest heart.

After the 21st :—

Where Lugar leaves his moorland plaid,
Where lately Want was idly laid,
I marked busy, bustling Trade
In fervid flame,
Beneath a patroness's air
Of noble name.

While countless hills I could survey,
And countless flocks as well as they ;
But other scenes did charms display
That better please,
Where polished manners dwelt with Gray
In rural ease.

Where Cessnock flows with gurgling sound,
And Irwine marking out the bound,
Enamoured of the scenes around,
Slow runs his race,
A name I doubly honoured found
With knightly grace.

Brydone's brave ward I saw him stand,
Fame humbly offering her hand,
And near his kinsman's rustic band
With one accord
Lamenting their late blessed land
Must change its lord.

The owner of a pleasant spot,
Near sandy wilds I did him note :
A heart too warm, a pulse too hot,
At times o'erran,
But, large in every feature wrote,
Appeared the man.

Page 41, *l* 19. This poem was first printed in the second edition of Burns' works.

Page 42, *l* 17. When this worthy old sportsman went out last muir-fowl season, he supposed it was to be, in Ossian's phrase, 'the last of his fields,' and expressed an ardent desire to die and be buried in the muirs. On this hint the author composed his Elegy and Epitaph. R. B.

---

* Captain James Montgomery, Master of St. James's Lodge, Torbolton, to which the author has the honour to belong. R. B.

Page 42, *l* 33. A certain preacher, a great favourite with the million. *Vide* the 'Ordination,' stanza ii. R. B.

Page 42, *l* 34. Another preacher, an equal favourite with the few, who was at that time ailing. For him see also the 'Ordination,' stanza ix. R. B.

Page 43, *l* 25. This stanza does not appear in the Edinburgh edition.

Page 43, *l* 22, *col* 2. Killie is a phrase the country folk sometimes use for the name of a certain town in the west (Kilmarnock). R. B.

Page 48. The scene of the 'Jolly Beggars' was the Change house of Poosie Nansie's in Mauchline, a favourite haunt of all kinds of vagrants. It is said that Burns witnessed the circumstances which gave rise to the poem in company with his friend James Smith. Although the most dramatic of all Burns' performances, it was not a favourite with his mother and brother, and he never seems to have thought it worthy of publication. Mr. George Thomson had heard of its existence, and in 1793 wrote the Poet on the subject. Burns replied, ' I have forgot the cantata you allude to, as I kept no copy, and, indeed, did not know of its existence ; however, I remember that none of the songs pleased myself except the last, something about

' Courts for cowards were erected,
Churches built to please the priest.'

It was first published in Glasgow in 1801.

Page 48, *l* 34. The heights of Abraham, where Wolfe gloriously fell.

Page 48, *l* 36. ' El Morro, the castle which defends the entrance to the harbour of Santiago, or St. Jago, a small island near the southern shore of Cuba. It is situated on an eminence, the abutments being cut out of the limestone rock. *Logan's Notes of a Tour, &c. Edinburgh*, 1838. In 1762 this castle was stormed and taken by the British, after which the Havana was surrendered, with spoil to the value of three millions.' *Chambers*.

Page 48, *l* 41. Captain Curtis, who destroyed the Spanish floating batteries during the siege of Gibraltar.

Page 48, *l* 43. The defender of Gibraltar, George Augustus Elliot, created Lord Heathfield for his services.

Page 54. Gilbert Burns states that the ' Verses to the Mouse' were composed while the author was holding the plough. Mr. Chambers relates a pleasant circumstance in relation to the event, and the poem to which it gave rise. ' John Blane, who had acted as gaudsman to Burns, and who lived sixty years afterwards, had a distinct recollection of the turning up of the mouse. Like a thoughtless youth as he was, he ran after the creature to kill it, but was checked and recalled by his master, who he observed became thereafter thoughtful and abstracted. Burns, who treated his servants with the familiarity of

fellow-labourers, soon after read the poem to Blane.' The gaudsman's rush after the terrified creature may have suggested the lines :—

' I wad be laith to rin an' chase thee,
Wi' murd'ring pattle.'

Page 55. ' A Winter Night' was first printed in the second edition of the poems.

Page 57. Davie was David Sillar, a member of the Torbolton Club, and author of a volume of poems printed at Kilmarnock in 1789. Gilbert Burns states that the ' Epistle ' was among the earliest of his brother's poems. ' It was,' he adds, ' I think, in summer, 1784, when, in the interval of harder labour, he and I were weeding in the garden (kailyard) that he repeated to me the principal part of the epistle. I believe the first idea of Robert's becoming an author was started on this occasion. I was much pleased with the epistle, and said to him I was of opinion it would bear being printed, and that it would be well received by people of taste ; that I thought it at least equal, if not superior, to many of Allan Ramsay's epistles ; and that the merit of these, and much other Scottish poetry, seemed to consist in the knack of the expression ; but here there was a stream of interesting sentiment, and the Scotticism of the language scarcely seemed affected, but appeared to be the natural language of the poet ; that, besides, there was certainly some novelty in a poet pointing out the consolations that were in store for him when he should go a-begging. Robert seemed very well pleased with my criticism, and we talked of sending it to some magazine ; but as the plan afforded no opportunity of how it would take, the idea was dropped.'

Page 57, *l* 37. Ramsay. R. B.

Page 59. With reference to the poem Gilbert Burns writes, ' It is scarcely necessary to mention that the " Lament " was composed on that unfortunate passage of his matrimonial history which I have mentioned in my letter to Mrs. Dunlop, after the first distraction of his feelings had a little subsided.'

Page 61, *l* 9. Dr. Young. R. B.

Page 61. Gilbert Burns, in writing of the ' Cotter's Saturday Night,' says, ' Robert had frequently remarked to me, that he thought there was something peculiarly venerable in the phrase, " Let us worship God," used by a decent sober head of a family introducing family worship. To this sentiment of the author the world is indebted for the " Cotter's Saturday Night." The hint of the plan and title of the poem were taken from Fergusson's " Farmer's Ingle." When Robert had not some pleasure in view in which I was not thought fit to participate, we used frequently to walk together, when the weather was favourable, on the Sunday afternoons (those precious breathing times to the labouring part of the community), and enjoyed such Sundays as would make one regret to see their number abridged. It was in one of these walks that I first had the pleasure of hearing the

author repeat the "Cotter's Saturday Night." I do not recollect to have read or heard anything by which I was more highly electrified. The fifth and sixth stanzas, and the eighteenth, thrilled with a peculiar ecstasy through my soul.'

Page 62, *l* 8. *Var.* Does a' his weary kiaugh and care beguile. First Edinb. edition.

Page 65, *l* 7. Pope's 'Windsor Forest.' R. B.

Page 65, *l* 23. *Var.*
That stream'd thro' great unhappy Wallace' heart.
First and second edition.

Page 65. Gilbert Burns writes, 'Several of the poems were produced for the purpose of bringing forward some favourite sentiment of the author. He used to remark to me that he could not well conceive a more mortifying picture of human life than a man seeking work. In casting about in his mind how this sentiment might be brought forward, the elegy 'Man was made to Mourn' was composed.

Page 66, *l* 33. In Burns' memoranda the following passage is prefixed to the prayer : 'A prayer, when fainting fits, and other alarming symptoms of pleurisy, or some other dangerous disorder, which indeed still threatens me, first put nature on the alarm.'

Page 67, *l* 14. *Var.* Again by passion would be led astray.

Page 67, *l* 20. *Var.*
If one so black with crimes dare call on Thee.

Page 67, *l* 24. *Var.*
Those rapid headlong passions to confine.

Page 67, *l* 25. *Var.*
For all unfit my native powers be.

Page 67, *l* 28. 'The first time,' says Gilbert Burns, 'Robert heard the spinnet played upon was at the house of Dr. Laurie, then minister of the parish of Loudon, now in Glasgow, having given up the parish in favour of his son. Dr. Laurie has several daughters : one of them played ; the father and mother led down the dance ; the rest of the sisters, the brother, the Poet, and the other guests, mixed in it. It was a delightful family scene for our Poet, then lately introduced to the world. His mind was roused to a poetic enthusiasm, and the stanzas were left in the room where he slept.' Mr. Chambers states that the morning after the dance Burns did not make his appearance at the breakfast table at the usual hour. Dr. Laurie's son went to inquire for him, and met him on the stair. The young man asked Burns if he had slept well. 'Not well,' was the reply : 'the fact is, I have been praying half the night. If you go up to my room, you will find my prayer on the table.'

Page 68, *l* 21. In Burns' memoranda the poem appears with the following sentences prefixed : 'There was a certain period of my life that my spirit was broke by repeated losses and disasters, which threatened, and indeed effected, the utter ruin of my fortune. My body, too, was attacked by that most dreadful disorder, a hypochondria or confirmed melancholy. In this wretched state, the recollection of which makes me yet shudder, I hung my harp on the willow-trees, except in some lucid intervals, in one of which I composed the following.'

Page 70, *l* 13. This poem was addressed to Andrew Aitken, son of the poet's patron, Robert Aitken, to whom the 'Cotter's Saturday Night' was dedicated. Mr. Chambers states that Mr. Niven of Kilbride always alleged that the 'Epistle' was originally addressed to him.

Page 70, *l* 22, *col.* 2. After this line, in a copy of the poem in Burns' handwriting, the following stanza occurs :—

If ye hae made a step aside,
  Some hap mistake o'erta'en you,
Yet still keep up a decent pride,
  And ne'er o'er far demean you.
Time comes wi' kind oblivious shade,
  And daily darker sets it ;
And if nae mair mistakes are made,
  The world soon forgets it.

Page 71. Burns when meditating emigration to the West Indies was in gloomy mood enough, and in this ode, although in it he mocks at fortune, there are not wanting touches of bitterness, which are all the more effective from the prevalent lightness and gaiety by which they are surrounded.

Page 71, *l* 29. *Var.*
Our billie, Rob, has ta'en a jink.

Page 71, *l* 35. *Var.*
He's canter't to anither shore.

Page 71, *l* 38. *Var.*
An' pray kind Fortune to redress him.

Page 71, *l* 39. *Var.*
'Twill gar her poor, auld heart, I fear.

Page 71, *l* 20, *col.* 2. *Var.*
An' scarce a bellyfu' 'o drummock.

Page 71, *l* 37, *col.* 2. *Var.*
Then fare you weel, my rhymin billie !

Page 71, *l* 7. This poem did not appear in the first edition.

Page 72. In the 'Caledonian Mercury,' of date 20th December, 1786, in which the 'Haggis' was printed, apparently for the first time, the concluding stanza appears as follows :—

Ye Pow'rs wha gie us a' that's gude,
Still bless auld Caledonia's brood
Wi' great John Barleycorn's heart's blude,
  In stowps or laggies ;
An' on our board that king of food,
  A glorious Haggice.

Page 72. The dedication to Gavin Hamilton, the poet's friend and patron, did not, as might have been expected, open the volume published at Kilmarnock. It, however, finds its place in the body of the work.

Page 74, l 30. The 'lady' referred to in this line was, Mr. Chambers informs us, a village belle. He adds that her name was well known in Mauchline.

Page 75. This Address was written in Edinburgh in 1786.

Page 75, l 29. 'Fair Burnet' was the daughter of Lord Monboddo. Burns' admiration for her was intense.

Page 75. 'The Epistle to John Lapraik was produced,' says Gilbert Burns, 'exactly on the occasion described by the author. It was at one of these *rockings* at our house, when we had twelve or fifteen young people with their *rocks,* that Lapraik's song, beginning, "When I upon thy bosom lean," was sung, and we were informed who was the author. Upon this Robert wrote his first epistle to Lapraik ; and his second was in reply to his answer.'

Page 78. William Simpson was the schoolmaster of Ochiltree parish.

Page 80. The postscript to the foregoing 'Epistle' may be considered as a pendant to 'The Twa Herds,' which was making a noise in Ayrshire at the time.

Page 81. John Rankine lived at Adam-hill, in Ayrshire ; he was a man of much humour, and was one of Burns' earliest friends.

Page 81, l 4. A certain humorous dream of his was then making noise in the country-side. R. B. Of this dream the substance is thus related by Allan Cunningham. 'Lord K—— was in the habit of calling his familiar acquaintances "brutes" or "damned brutes." One day meeting Rankine, his lordship said, "Brute, are ye dumb? have ye no queer story to tell us?" "I have nae story," said Rankine, "but last night I had an odd dream." "Out with it, by all means," said the other. "A weel, ye see," said Rankine, "I dreamed that I was dead, and that for keeping other than good company on earth, I was damned. When I knocked at hell-door, wha should open it but the deil ; he was in a rough humour, and said, 'Wha may you be, and what's your name?' 'My name,' quoth I, 'is John Rankine, and my dwelling-place was Adam-hill.' 'Gi wa' wi',' quoth Satan, 'ye canna be here ; yer ane of Lord K——'s damned brutes : Hell's fou o' them already !' "' This sharp rebuke, it is said, polished for the future his lordship's speech. The trick alluded to in the same line was Rankine's making tipsy one of the 'unco gude.'

Page 81, l 29. A song he had promised the author.

Page 82. Friar's Carse was the estate of Captain Riddel, of Glenriddel, beautifully situated on the banks of the Nith, near Ellisland. The Hermitage was a decorated cottage, which the proprietor had erected.

Page 82, l 6. In a copy printed in the *Gentleman's Magazine* the following couplet occurs here :—

> Day—how rapid in its flight !
> Day—how few must see the night !

Page 82, l 10. *Var.*
> Beneath thy morning sun advance. *Gent's. Mag.*

Page 82, l 25. *Var.*
> When thy shades of ev'ning close. *Gent's. Mag.*

Page 82, l 33. *Var.*
>   genuine estimate
> Say the criterion of their fate
> The important query of their state,
> Is not, &c. *Gent's. Mag.*

Page 82, l 36. *Var.*
>   ebb or flow?
> Wert thou cottager or king,
> Peer or peasant ?—No such thing.
> Tell them, &c. *Gent's. Mag.*

Page 82, l 22, col 2. *Var.*
> Fame, a restless airy dream. *Gent's. Mag.*

Page 82, l 23, col 2. *Var.*
> Pleasures, insects on the wing ;
> Round peace, the tenderest flower of spring.
>   *Gent's. Mag.*

Page 82, l 26, col 2. *Var.*
> Make the butterflies their own. *Gent's. Mag.*

Page 82, l 31, col 2. *Var.*
> But thy utmost duty done. *Gent's. Mag.*

Page 82, l 42, col 2. *Var.*
> Quod the Bedesman on Nitheside. *Gent's. Mag.*

Page 83. The subject of this ode was the widow of Richard Oswald, Esq. of Auchincruive. She died December 6, 1788. Burns himself states the cause of its composition. 'In January last, on my road to Ayrshire, I had to put up at Bailie Whigham's, in Sanquhar, the only tolerable inn in the place. The frost was keen, and the grim evening and howling wind were ushering in a night of snow and drift. My horse and I were both much fatigued by the labours of the day ; and just as my friend the Bailie and I were bidding defiance to the storm, over a smoking bowl, in wheels the funereal pageantry of the late Mrs. Oswald, and poor I am forced to brave all the terrors of the tempestuous night, and jade my horse—my young favourite horse, whom I had just christened Pegasus—farther on through the wildest hills and moors of Ayrshire to the next inn. The powers of poetry and prose sink under me when I would describe what I felt. Suffice it to say, that when a good fire at New Cumnock had so far recovered my frozen sinews, I sat down and wrote the enclosed ode.' Being *dead,* the poor lady could hardly be held responsible for disturbing the Poet's potations with his friend the Bailie !

Page 83. In February, 1791, Burns wrote respecting this poem : 'The Elegy on Captain Henderson is a tribute to the memory of a man I loved much. . . . As almost all my religous tenets originate from my heart, I am

wonderfully pleased with the idea that I can still keep up a tender intercourse with the dearly beloved friend, or still more dearly beloved mistress, who is gone to the world of spirits.'

Page 84. Readers curious in the transmission of poetic ideas may amuse themselves by comparing this epitaph with Wordsworth's *Poet's Epitaph.*

Page 85. Writing to Mrs. Graham, of Fintry, Burns says, 'Whether it is that the story of our Mary, Queen of Scots, has a peculiar effect on the feelings of a poet, or whether I have in the enclosed ballad succeeded beyond my usual poetic success, I know not ; but it has pleased me beyond any effort of my muse for a good while past : on that account I enclose it particularly to you.'

Page 86. Robert Graham, Esq. of Fintry, was one of the Commissioners of Excise. Burns met him at the house of the Duke of Athole. The 'Epistle' was the poet's earliest attempt in the manner of Pope. It has its merits, of course ; but it lacks the fire, ease, and sweetness of his earlier Epistles to Lapraik, Smith, and others.

Page 88, l 10. 'By a fall, not from my horse, but with my horse, I have been a cripple some time.' Burns to Mrs. Dunlop, 7th February, 1791.

Page 88, l 11. Var.
The peopled fold thy kindly care have found ;
The horned bull tremendous spurns the ground ;
The lowly lion has enough and more,—
The forest trembles at his very roar.

Page 88, l 14. Var.
The puny wasp, victorious, guards his cell.

Page 88, l 21. Var.
Even silly women have defensive arts—
Their eyes, their tongues, and nameless other parts.

Page 88, l 29. Var.
No claws to dig, his dreaded sight to shun.

Page 88, l 31. Var.
No nerves olfactory, true to Mammon's fool ;
Or grunting grub, sagacious, evil's root ;
Or grunting sage, to grub all-evil's root.

Page 88, l 39. Alexander Munro, Professor of Anatomy in the University of Edinburgh.

Page 88, l 46. Var.
The hapless Poet flounces on through life.

Page 89, l 31. James, Earl of Glencairn. See succeeding poem.

Page 89. This nobleman, for whom the Poet had a deep respect, died at Falmouth, in his forty-second year. Burns wore mourning for the Earl, and designed to attend his funeral in Ayrshire. He enclosed the poem to Lady Elizabeth Cunningham, sister of the deceased nobleman.

Page 91. 'When my father,' writes Gilbert Burns, '*feued* his little property near Alloway Kirk, the wall of the churchyard had gone to ruin, and cattle had free liberty of pasture in it. My father, with two or three other neighbours, joined in an application to the town council of Ayr, who were superiors of the adjoining land, for liberty to rebuild it, and raised by subscription a sum for enclosing this ancient cemetery with a wall ; hence he came to consider it as his burial-place, and we learned that reverence for it people generally have for the burial-place of their ancestors. My brother was living at Ellisland, when Captain Grose, on his peregrinations through Scotland, stayed some time at Carse House, in the neighbourhood, with Captain Robert Riddel, of Glenriddel, a particular friend of my brother's. The Antiquarian and the Poet were "unco pack and thick thegither." Robert requested of Captain Grose, when he should come to Ayrshire, that he would make a drawing of Alloway Kirk, as it was the burial-place of his father, and where he himself had a sort of claim to lay down his bones when they should be no longer serviceable to him ; and added, by way of encouragement, that it was the scene of many a good story of witches and apparitions, of which he knew the Captain was very fond. The Captain agreed to the request, provided the Poet would furnish a witch story, to be printed along with it. "Tam o' Shanter" was produced on this occasion, and was first published in Grose's "Antiquities of Scotland."' The following letter, sent by Burns to Captain Grose, deals with the witch stories that clustered round Alloway Kirk.

'Among the many witch stories I have heard relating to Alloway Kirk, I distinctly remember only two or three.

'Upon a stormy night, amid whistling squalls of wind and bitter blasts of hail—in short, on such a night as the devil would choose to take the air in—a farmer, or a farmer's servant, was plodding and plashing homeward with his plough-irons on his shoulder, having been getting some repairs on them at a neighbouring smithy. His way lay by the Kirk of Alloway, and being rather on the anxious look-out in approaching a place so well known to be a favourite haunt of the devil, and the devil's friends and emissaries, he was struck aghast by discovering, through the horrors of the storm and stormy night, a light, which, on his nearer approach, plainly showed itself to proceed from the haunted edifice. Whether he had been fortified from above on his devout supplication, as is customary with people when they suspect the immediate presence of Satan, or whether, according to another custom, he had got courageously drunk at the smithy, I will not pretend to determine ; but so it was, that he ventured to go up to—nay, into—the very Kirk. As luck would have it, his temerity came off unpunished.

'The members of the infernal junto were all out on some midnight business or other, and he

saw nothing but a kind of kettle or caldron, depending from the roof, over the fire, simmering some heads of unchristened children, limbs of executed malefactors, &c. for the business of the night. It was in for a penny, in for a pound, with the honest ploughman ; so, without ceremony, he unhooked the caldron from off the fire, and pouring out its damnable ingredients, inverted it on his head, and carried it fairly home, where it remained long in the family, a living evidence of the truth of the story.

'Another story, which I can prove to be equally authentic, was as follows :—

'On a market-day, in the town of Ayr, a farmer from Carrick, and consequently whose way lay by the very gate of Alloway Kirk-yard, in order to cross the river Doon at the old bridge, which is about two or three hundred yards farther on than the said gate, had been detained by his business, till by the time he reached Alloway it was the wizard hour, between night and morning.

'Though he was terrified with a blaze streaming from the Kirk, yet as it is a well known fact, that to turn back on these occasions is running by far the greatest risk of mischief, he prudently advanced on his road. When he had reached the gate of the Kirk-yard, he was surprised and entertained, through the ribs and arches of an old Gothic window, which still faces the highway, to see a dance of witches merrily footing it round their old sooty blackguard master, who was keeping them all alive with the power of his bagpipe. The farmer, stopping his horse to observe them a little, could plainly descry the faces of many of his acquaintance and neighbourhood. How the gentleman was dressed, tradition does not say, but that the ladies were all in their smocks; and one of them happening unluckily to have a smock which was considerably too short to answer all the purposes of that piece of dress, our farmer was so tickled that he involuntarily burst out, with a loud laugh, "Weel looppen Maggy wi' the short sark!" and, recollecting himself, instantly spurred his horse to the top of his speed. I need not mention the universally known fact, that no diabolical power can pursue you beyond the middle of a running stream. Lucky it was for the poor farmer that the river Doon was so near, for notwithstanding the speed of his horse, which was a good one, against he reached the middle of the arch of the bridge, and consequently the middle of the stream, the pursuing, vengeful hags were so close at his heels, that one of them actually sprang to seize him : but it was too late ; nothing was on her side of the stream but the horse's tail, which immediately gave way at her infernal grip, as if blasted by a stroke of lightning ; but the farmer was beyond her reach. However, the unsightly, tailless condition of the vigorous steed was, to the last hours of the noble creature's life, an awful warning to the Carrick farmers not to stay too late in Ayr markets.'

This letter is interesting, as showing the actual body of tradition on which Burns had to work— the soil out of which the consummate poem grew like a flower. And it is worthy of notice also

how, out of the letter, some of the best things in the poem have come : 'such a night as the devil would choose to take the air in' being, for instance, the suggestion of the couplet—

> That night a child might understand
> The Deil had business on his hand.

It is pleasant to know that Burns thought well of 'Tam o' Shanter.'

To Mrs. Dunlop he wrote on the 11th April, 1791 :—'On Saturday morning last Mrs. Burns made me a present of a fine boy, rather stouter, but not so handsome as your godson was at his time of life. Indeed, I look on your little namesake to be my *chef-d'œuvre* in that species of manufacture, as I look on "Tam o' Shanter" to be my standard performance in the poetical line. 'Tis true, both the one and the other discover a spice of roguish waggery, that might, perhaps, be as well spared ; but then they also show, in my opinion, a force of genius, and a finishing polish, that I despair of ever excelling.'

Page 93, l 46. The following lines originally occurred here :—

> Three lawyers' tongues turned inside out,
> Wi' lies seamed, like a beggar's clout ;
> Three priests' hearts rotten, black as muck,
> Lay stinking, vile, in every neuk.

They were omitted at the suggestion of Lord Woodhouselee.

Page 95, l 8. It is a well-known fact, that witches, or any evil spirits, have no power to follow a poor wight any further than the middle of the next running stream. It may be proper likewise to mention to the benighted traveller that when he falls in with bogles, whatever danger may be in his going forward, there is much more hazard in turning back. R. B.

Page 95, l 26. 'Tam o' Shanter,' as already stated, appeared first in Captain Grose's 'Antiquities of Scotland.' To the poem the editor appended the following note : 'To my ingenious friend, Mr. Robert Burns, I have been seriously obligated ; for he was not only at the pains of making out what was most worthy of notice in Ayrshire, the county honoured by his birth, but he also wrote expressly for this work the pretty tale annexed to Alloway Church.' Grose's book appeared at the close of April, 1791, and he died in Dublin shortly after.

Page 95. For information respecting Captain Grose's intimacy with Burns see preceding note.

Page 95, l 27. Vide his 'Antiquities of Scotland.' R. B.

Page 96, l 8. Vide his 'Treatise on Ancient Armour and Weapons.' R. B.

Page 96, l 27. Var.

> Seek, mangled innocent, some wonted form !
> That wonted form, alas ! thy dying bed ;
> The sheltering rushes whistling o'er thy head,
> The cold earth with thy blood-stain'd bosom warm.

> Perhaps a mother's anguish adds its woe ;
> The playful pair crowd fondly by thy side ;
> Ah ! helpless nurslings, who will now provide
> That life a mother only can bestow ?

Page 96, l 34.   Var.

And curse the ruthless wretch, and mourn thy hapless
fate.

The changes in this poem were made on the suggestion of Dr. Gregory, to whom the Poet had sent a copy.

Page 97. This poem was addressed to the daughter of Mr. William Cruikshank, one of the masters of the High School of Edinburgh.

Page 98. Bruar Falls, in Athol, are exceedingly picturesque and beautiful, but their effect is much impaired by the want of trees and shrubs. R. B.

Page 98, l 19, col 2.   Var.

The bairdie, music's youngest child.

Page 99, l 11, col 2. Mr. Walker in his letter to Dr. Currie, describing the impression Burns made at Blair, says, 'The Duke's fine family attracted much of his admiration ; he drank their health as *honest men and bonie lasses,* an idea which was much applauded by the company, and with which he has very felicitously closed his poem.'

Page 99. The occasion of the satire was as follows. In 1786 Dr. Wm. McGill, one of the ministers of Ayr, published an essay on 'The Death of Jesus Christ,' which was denounced as heterodox by Dr. Wm. Peebles, of Newton-upon-Ayr, in a sermon preached by him November 5th, 1788. Dr. McGill published a defence, and the case came before the Ayr presbytery, and finally before the synod of Glasgow and Ayr. In August, 1789, Burns wrote to Mr. Logan : 'I have, as you will shortly see, finished the "Kirk's Alarm ;" but now that it is done, and that I have laughed once or twice at the conceits of some of the stanzas, I am determined not to let it get into the public : so I send you this copy, the first I have sent to Ayrshire, except some few of the stanzas, which I wrote off in embryo for Gavin Hamilton, under the express provision and request that you will only read it to a few of us, and do not on any account give, or permit to be taken, any copy of the ballad.' With reference to the ballad he wrote to Mr. Graham of Fintry : 'I laughed myself at some conceits in it, though I am convinced in my conscience that there are a good many heavy stanzas in it too.'

Page 99, l 13.   Var.

Brother Scots, brother Scots, wha believe in John
Knox.

Page 99, l 17.   Dr. McGill.

Page 99, l 18.   Var.

To strike wicked writers wi' terror.

Page 99, l 23.   John Ballantyne, Esq. Provost of Ayr.

Page 99, l 24.   Mr. Robert Aitken.

Page 99, l 25.   Rev. Dr. Wm. Dalrymple.

Page 99, l 29.   Rev. John Russel : see 'Holy Fair.'

Page 99, l 33.   Rev. James Mackinlay : see 'Ordination.'

Page 100, l 1.   Rev. Alexander Moodie : see 'The Twa Herds.'

Page 100, l 5.   Rev. Mr. Auld.

Page 100, l 6.   Mr. Gavin Hamilton.

Page 100, l 9.   Mr. Grant, Ochiltree.

Page 100, l 13.   Mr. Young, Cumnock.

Page 100, l 17. Rev. Dr Wm. Peebles. He had written a poem which contained a ridiculous line :—

And bound in Liberty's endearing chain.

Page 100, l 21.   Dr. Andrew Mitchell, Monkton.

Page 100, l 25.   Rev. Stephen Young, Barr.

Page 100, l 29.   Rev. George Smith, Galston : see 'Holy Fair.'

Page 100, l 33.   Rev. John Shepherd, Muirkirk.

Page 100, l 37.   Mr. William Fisher, the 'Holy Willie' of the famous satire.

Page 102, l 2.   Var.

The eye with pleasure and amazement fills.

Page 102. Miss Susan Dunlop, daughter of Mr. Dunlop, married a French gentleman named Henri. The young couple were living at Loudon Castle when M. Henri died, leaving his wife pregnant. The verses were written on the birth of a son and heir. Mrs. Dunlop communicated the intelligence to Burns, and received the following letter in return : '"As cold waters to a thirsty soul, so is good news from a far country !" Fate has long owed me a letter of good news from you, in return for the many tidings of sorrow which I have received. In this instance I most cordially obey the Apostle —"Rejoice with them that do rejoice." For me to *sing* for joy is no new thing ; but to *preach* for joy, as I have done in the commencement of this epistle, is a pitch of extravagant rapture to which I never rose before. I read your letter —I literally jumped for joy : how could such a mercurial creature as a poet lumpishly keep his seat on the receipt of the best news from his best friend ? I seized my gilt-headed Wangee rod, an instrument indispensably necessary, in my left hand, in the moment of inspiration and rapture ; and stride, stride—quick and quicker —out skipped I among the blooming banks of Nith, to muse over my joy by retail. To keep within the bounds of prose was impossible.' Mr. Chambers traces the future history of Mrs. Henri and her son : 'In a subsequent letter Burns deplores her (Mrs. Henri's) dangerous and distressing situation in France, exposed to the tumults of the Revolution ; and he has soon after occasion to condole with his venerable friend on the death of her daughter in a foreign

land. When this sad event took place, the orphan child fell under the immediate care of his paternal grandfather, who, however, was soon obliged to take refuge in Switzerland, leaving the infant behind him. Years passed, he and the Scotch friends of the child heard nothing of it, and concluded that it was lost. At length, when the elder Henri was enabled to return to his ancestral domains, he had the unspeakable satisfaction of finding that his grandson and heir was alive and well, having never been removed from the place. The child had been protected and reared with the greatest care by a worthy female named Mademoiselle Susette, formerly a domestic in the family. This excellent person had even contrived, through all the levelling violence of the intervening period, to preserve in her young charge the feeling appropriate to his rank. Though absolutely indebted to her industry for his bread, she had caused him always to be seated by himself at table and regularly waited on, so that the otherwise plebeian circumstances in which he lived did not greatly affect him. The subject of Burns's stanzas was, a very few years ago, proprietor of the family estates; and it is agreeable to add that Mademoiselle Susette then lived in his paternal mansion, in the enjoyment of that grateful respect to which her fidelity and discretion so eminently entitled her.'

Page 103. This epistle was prefixed to the edition of Sillar's poems, published in Kilmarnock in 1789.

Page 104. The 'Inventory' was addressed to Mr. Aitken of Ayr, surveyor of taxes for the district. It was first printed in the Liverpool edition of the poems.

Page 105. ' As the authentic prose history of the Whistle is curious,' writes Burns, ' I shall here give it :—In the train of Anne of Denmark, when she came to Scotland with our James the Sixth, there came over also a Danish gentleman of gigantic stature and great prowess, and a matchless champion of Bacchus. He had a little ebony whistle, which, at the commencement of the orgies he laid on the table ; and whoever was last able to blow it, everybody else being disabled by the potency of the bottle, was to carry off the whistle as a trophy of victory. The Dane produced credentials of his victories, without a single defeat, at the courts of Copenhagen, Stockholm, Moscow, Warsaw, and several of the petty courts in Germany ; and challenged the Scots' Bacchanalians to the alternative of trying his prowess, or else acknowledging their inferiority. After many overthrows on the part of the Scots, the Dane was encountered by Sir Robert Lawrie of Maxwelton, ancestor of the present worthy baronet of that name, who after three days' and three nights' hard contest, left the Scandinavian under the table,

And blew on the whistle his requiem shrill.

Sir Walter, son to Sir Robert before mentioned, afterwards lost the whistle to Walter Riddel of

Glenriddel, who had married a sister of Sir Walter's. On Friday, the 16th October, 1690, at Friar's Carse, the whistle was once more contended for, as related in the ballad, by the present Sir Robert Lawrie of Maxwelton ; Robert Riddel, Esq. of Glenriddel, lineal descendant and representative of Walter Riddel, who won the whistle, and in whose family it had continued ; and Alexander Ferguson, Esq. of Craigdarroch, likewise descended of the great Sir Robert; which last gentleman carried off the hard-won honours of the field. R. B.'

Oddly enough, on the 16th October, 1789, we have a letter from Burns addressed to Captain Riddel, referring to the Bacchanalian contest. ' Big with the idea of this important day at Friar's Carse, I have watched the elements and skies in the full persuasion that they would announce it to the astonished world by some phenomena of terrific portent. Yesternight, till a very late hour, did I wait with anxious horror for the appearance of some comet firing half the sky, or aërial armies of sanguinary Scandinavians darting athwart the startled heaven, rapid as the ragged lightning, and horrid as the convulsions of nature that bury nations.

'The elements, however, seem to take the matter very quietly : they did not even usher in the morning with triple suns and a shower of blood, symbolical of the three potent heroes and the mighty claret-shed of the day. For me, as Thomson in his *Winter* says of the storm, I shall " Hear astonished, and astonished sing"

The whistle and the man : I sing
The man that won the whistle.'

And he concludes by wishing that the captain's head 'may be crowned by laurels tonight, and free from aches to-morrow.' Burns in his note is supposed to have made a mistake of a year. He says the whistle was contended for on Friday, the 16th October, 1790 ; but in 1789 the 16th October fell on a *Friday,* and in 1790 it fell on a *Saturday.*

It is not quite clear what share the poet took in the fray. Allan Cunningham states that the whistle was contended for ' in the dining-room of Friar's Carse in Burns' presence, who drank bottle after bottle with the competitors, and seemed disposed to take up the conqueror.' On the other hand, Mr. Hunter of Cockrune, in the parish of Closeburn, reports that he has a perfect recollection of the whole affair. He states that ' Burns was present the whole evening. He was invited to join the party to see that the gentlemen drank fair, and to commemorate the day by writing a song. I recollect well that, when the dinner was over, Burns quitted the table, and went to a table in the same room, that was placed in a window that looked south-east ; and there he sat down for the night. I placed before him a bottle of rum, and another of brandy, which he did not finish, but left a good deal of each when he rose from the table after the gentlemen had gone to bed. . . . When the gentlemen were put to bed,

B

Burns walked home without any assistance, not being the worse of drink. When Burns was sitting at the table in the window, he had pen, ink, and paper, which I brought him at his own request. He now and then wrote on the paper, and while the gentlemen were sober, he turned round often, and chatted with them, but drank none of the claret which they were drinking. . . . I heard him read aloud several parts of the poem, much to the amusement of the three gentlemen.' It is just possible that Burns is after all correct enough in his dates. His letter to Captain Riddel on the 16th October, 1789, although clear enough as to the impending 'claret-shed,' hardly suggests that the writer expected to be present. The theory that the revel had been originally arranged for that date, and, unknown to Burns, suddenly postponed for a year, would explain the matter.

Page 105, *l* 5. See Ossian's Caric-thura. R.B.

Page 105, *l* 9. See Johnson's 'Tour to the Hebrides.' R. B.

Page 107. Concerning this 'sketch' Burns wrote to Mrs. Dunlop, April, 1789:—

'I have a poetic whim in my head, which I at present dedicate, or rather inscribe, to the Right Hon. C. J. Fox ; but how long that fancy may hold, I cannot say. A few of the first lines I have just rough-sketched as follows.'

The poet's M.S. of the "Sketch" is in the British Museum. Dr. Currie altered one passage as follows :—

"With knowledge so vast, and with judgment so strong,
No man with the half of 'em e'er went far wrong ;
With passions so potent, and fancies so bright,
No man with the half of 'em e'er went quite right."

Page 108. Burns had sent a letter to Dr. Blacklock, under charge of Robert Heron, detailing certain recent changes in his circumstances. The letter miscarried, and Blacklock addressed Burns in the following epistle :—

Edinburgh, 24th *August*, 1789.

'Dear Burns, thou brother of my heart,
Both for thy virtues and thy art ;
If art it may be called in thee,
Which Nature's bounty large and free
With pleasure on thy heart diffuses,
And warms thy soul with all the Muses :
Whether to laugh with easy grace
Thy numbers move the sage's face,
Or bid the softer passions rise,
And ruthless souls with grief surprise,
'Tis Nature's voice distinctly felt,
Thro' thee, her organ, thus to melt.
'Most anxiously I wish to know
With thee, of late, how matters go :
How keeps thy much-loved Jean her health ?
What promises thy farm of wealth ?
Whether the Muse persists to smile,
And all thy anxious cares beguile ?
Whether bright fancy keeps alive ?
And how thy darling infants thrive ?
'For me, with grief and sickness spent,
Since I my journey homeward bent,
Spirits depressed no more I mourn,
But vigour, life, and health return.
No more to gloomy thoughts a prey,
I sleep all night, and live all day ;
By turns my book, and friend enjoy,
And thus my circling hours employ ;
Happy while yet these hours remain,
If Burns could join the cheerful train,
With wonted zeal, sincere and fervent,
Salute once more his humble servant,
'THOS. BLACKLOCK.'

To this graceful effusion, breathing interest and good wishes, Burns responded, in a light mood at first, but which becomes overclouded with bitterness towards the close.

Page 109. In writing to his brother Gilbert, 11th January, 1790, Burns says :—

'We have got a set of very decent players here just now. I have seen them an evening or two. David Campbell, in Ayr, wrote to me by the manager of the company, a Mr. Sutherland, who is a man of apparent worth. On New Year's Day evening, I gave him the following prologue, which he spouted to his audience with applause.'

Page 109. Miss Burnet, daughter of Lord Monboddo, celebrated in the *Address to Edinburgh*. This elegy seems to have cost the poet considerable trouble. In a letter to Mr. Cunningham, January, 1791, he says :—'I have these several months been hammering at an elegy on the amiable and accomplished Miss Burnet. I have got, and can get, no farther than the following fragment.'

Page 110. This epistle is supposed to have been sent to Mr. Peter Stuart, of the *Star* newspaper. From the remonstrance which follows it would seem that the newspaper did not arrive with the punctuality which was desired.

Page 111. Basil William, Lord Daer, son of the Earl of Selkirk, died in 1794, in his thirty-second year. Burns met him at Professor Dugald Stewart's villa at Catrine.

Page 111. Miss Fontenelle was an actress at the Dumfries' Theatre. In sending her the address, Burns writes : 'Will the foregoing lines be of any service to you in your approaching benefit-night ? If they will, I shall be prouder of my muse than ever. They are nearly *extempore ;* I know they have no great merit ; but though they should add but little to the entertainment of the evening, they give me the happiness of an opportunity to declare how much I have the honour to be, &c.'

Page 112, *l* 2. *Var.*
The Rights of Woman claim some small attention.

Page 112, *l* 9. *Var.*
Our second Right—but idle here is caution.

Page 112, *l* 15. *Var.*
Got drunk, would swagger, swear, kick up a riot.

Page 112, *l* 20. An ironical allusion to the saturnalia of the Caledonian Hunt.

Page 112, *l* 24. *Var.*
Must fall before—'tis dear, dear admiration.

Page 112, *l* 26. *Var.*
And thence that life of life—immortal Love.

Page 113. Burns wrote Mr. Thomson, July, 1794 : 'I have presented a copy of your songs to the daughter of a much-honoured friend of mine, Mr. Graham of Fintry. I wrote, on the blank side of the title-page, the following address to the young lady.'

Page 113, *l* 35. *Var.*
In strains divine and sacred numbers join'd.

Page 113, *l* 43. *Var.*
As modest want the secret tale reveals.

Page 113, *l* 44. *Var.*
While virtue, conscious, all the strain endears.

Page 114. Gilbert Burns doubted whether the Poem on Pastoral Poetry was written by his brother. Few readers, we fancy, can have any doubt on the matter. Burns is, unquestionably, the author. The whole poem is full of lines which are 'like autographs,' and the four closing stanzas are in the Poet's best manner.

Page 114. With reference to these verses Burns, in 1795, wrote Mr. Thomson: 'Written on the blank leaf of a copy of the last edition of my poems, presented to the lady whom, in so many fictitious reveries of passion, but with the most ardent sentiments of real friendship, I have so often sung under the name of Chloris.' The lady was Miss Jean Lorimer, daughter of a farmer residing at some little distance from Dumfries. Chloris was the most unfortunate of all Burns' heroines While very young she eloped with a gentleman named Whelpdale, and was shortly after deserted by him. She died in 1831, having lived the greater portion of her life in penury.

Page 115. Mr. Tytler had published an 'Inquiry, Historical and Critical, into the Evidence against Mary Queen of Scots.'

Page 115, *l* 37. An artist, named Miers, was then practising in Edinburgh as a maker of silhouette portraits. Burns sat to him, and to Mr. Tytler he forwarded one of Miers' performances.

Page 116. This sketch is descriptive of the family of Mr. Dunlop, of Dunlop.

Page 116, *l* 11. Afterwards General Dunlop, of Dunlop.

Page 116, *l* 13. Miss Rachel Dunlop was making a sketch of Coila.

Page 116, *l* 14. Miss Keith Dunlop, the youngest daughter.

Page 116. Burns and Smellie were members of a club in Edinburgh called the Crochallan Fencibles.

Page 117, *l* 8. Mrs. Riddel, of Woodley Park, was the lady satirized in these verses. Dr. Currie, in printing them, substituted 'Eliza' for Maria.

Page 118. Miss Jessie Lewars attended Burns in his last illness.

Page 119. Mr. John Syme was one of the Poet's constant companions. He possessed great talent, and Dr. Currie wished him to undertake the editing of the Poet's life and writings.

Page 120, *l* 41. Mr. Mackenzie, surgeon, Mauchline, was believed to be the gentleman to whom these lines were addressed.

Page 122. In enclosing these verses to Mr. Creech, Burns writes: 'The enclosed I have just wrote, nearly extempore, in a solitary inn in Selkirk, after a miserable wet day's riding.'

Page 122, *l* 1. "Auld chuckie Reekie:" Edinburgh.

Page 123. In a MS. in the possession of the Publisher the two last stanzas are given.

Page 124. Ruisseaux: a play upon the Poet's own name.

Page 125. Mrs. Scott, of Wauchope, Roxburghshire, had sent a rhymed epistle to Burns, displaying considerable vigour of thought and neatness of expression.

Page 126, *l* 57. *Var.*
These five and fifty summers past.

Page 127, *l* 5. *Var.*
Frae Calvin's fountain-head they drank.

Page 127, *l* 20. *Var.*
Or nobly swing the Gospel club.

Page 127, *l* 29. *Var.*
While enemies wi' laughin' spite.

Page 127, *l* 33. *Var.*
But chiefly thee, apostle Auld.

Page 127, *l* 36. *Var.*
To gar them gree.

Page 127, *l* 3, *col.* 2. *Var.*
I trust in heaven to see them yet.

Page 127, *l* 11, *col.* 2. *Var.*
Auld Wodrow lang has wrought mischief.

Page 127, *l* 12, *col.* 2. *Var.*
We trusted death wad bring relief.

Page 128. The Rev. Mr. M'Math was, when Burns addressed him, assistant and successor to the Rev. Peter Wodrow, minister of Tarbolton. He is said to have been an excellent preacher.

Page 130. 'Holy Willie' was William Fisher, the leading elder in the Rev. Mr. Auld's session. He was afterwards found guilty of embezzling money from the church offerings, and died in a ditch, into which he had fallen when drunk.

Page 132, *l* 1. Written while Burns was on a visit to Sir William Murray, of Ochtertyre.

Page 132. Master Tootie was a dealer in cows, who lived in Mauchline. It was his practice to disguise the age of his cattle, by polishing away the markings on their horns.

Page 133. The newspaper contained some strictures on Burns' poetry.

Page 134. John Maxwell, Esq. of Terraughty and Munches. He died in 1814, aged 94.

Page 135, *l* 1. It is very doubtful whether Burns is the author of this piece published by Cromek.

Page 135. The 'Sketch' is a portion of a work, 'The Poet's Progress,' which Burns meditated, but of which hardly any portion seems to have ever been written. The immediate object of his satire is said to have been his publisher Creech.

Page 138, *l* 17. This ode was first printed in a London newspaper.

Page 138, *l* 34. *Var.*
Dim, cloudy, sunk beyond the western wave.

Page 140. Miss Ferrier, authoress of *Marriage* and *Destiny.*

Page 140. Burns' illegitimate daughter married Mr. John Bishop, overseer at Polkemmet, and died in 1817. She is said to have been strikingly like her father. A coarser version of this piece is extant, entitled 'A Welcome to a Bastart Wean.'

Page 141. In 1780 Mr. John Goldie, or Goudie, a tradesman in Kilmarnock, published a series of Essays touching the authority of the Scriptures. A second edition of the work appeared in 1785. Burns' epistle to him, although written when Ayrshire was convulsed with the *New Light* and *Auld Light* controversies, was not published till 1801. It appeared first in a Glasgow edition of the poems.

Page 141, *l* 16, *col* 2. Dr. Taylor of Norwich, the author of a work entitled 'The Scripture Doctrine of Original Sin proposed to Free and Candid Examination,' which was extensively read by the *New Light* party in Ayrshire at the time.

Page 141. Mr. James Tennant of Glenconner was an old friend of the Poet, and was consulted by him respecting the taking of the farm of Ellisland.

Page 142. 'The Esopus of this strange epistle,' says Mr. Allan Cunningham, 'was Williamson the actor, and the Maria to whom it was addressed was Mrs. Riddel.' While Williamson and his brother actors were performing at Whitehaven, Lord Lonsdale committed the whole to prison.

Page 144. A person named Glendining, who took away his own life, was the subject of this epigram. Mr. Cunningham adds the following particulars : 'My friend Dr. Copland Hutchison happened to be walking out that way'—to a place called the 'Old Chapel near Dumfries,' where Glendining had been interred. 'He saw Burns with his foot on the grave, his hat on his knee, and paper laid on his hat, on which he was writing. He then took the paper, thrust it with his finger into the red mould of the grave, and went away. This was the above epigram, and such was the Poet's mode of publishing it.'

Page 144, *l* 10. These lines form the conclusion of a letter written by Burns to Mr. John Kennedy, dated August, 1786, while his intention yet held of emigrating to Jamaica.

Page 144. 'The Farewell' was written in the autumn of 1786, when the idea of emigration was firmly fixed in the Poet's mind.

Page 147, *l* 37. These verses were inscribed by Burns on the back of a window-shutter of an inn or toll-house near the scene of the devastations.

Page 148. Major Logan, a retired military officer, fond of wit, violin-playing, and conviviality, who lived at Park, near Ayr.

Page 149. Gabriel Richardson was a brewer in Dumfries. The epitaph was written on a goblet, which is still preserved in the family.

Page 150, *l* 5. Written in reply to the minister of Gladsmuir, who had attacked Burns in verse relative to the imprudent lines inscribed on a window-pane in Stirling.

Page 150. Written from Ellisland to his friend Mr. Hugh Parker of Kilmarnock.

Page 150. These verses were originally headed, 'To the Right Honourable the Earl of Breadalbane, President of the Right Honourable and Honourable the Highland Society, which met on the 23d of May last, at the Shakspeare, Covent Garden, to concert ways and means to frustrate the designs of five hundred Highlanders, who, as the Society were informed by Mr. Mackenzie of Applecross, were so audacious as to attempt an escape from their lawful lords and masters, whose property they were, by emigrating from the lands of Mr. M'Donald of Glengarry'to the wilds of Canada in search of that fantastic thing—LIBERTY.'

Page 151, *l* 25. These verses form the conclusion of a letter written to Mr. John Kennedy from Mossgiel, of date 3d March, 1786.

Page 152. Lord President Dundas died on the 13th December, 1787, and Burns composed the elegy at the suggestion of Mr. Charles Hay, advocate, afterwards elevated to the bench under the designation of Lord Newton. On a copy of the elegy Burns afterwards wrote : "The foregoing poem has some tolerable lines in it, but the incurable wound of my pride will not suffer me to correct, or even to peruse it. I sent a copy of it, with my best prose letter, to the son of the great man, by the hands of one of the noblest men in God's world, Alexander Wood, surgeon. When, behold ! his solicitorship took no more notice of my poem or me than if I had been a strolling fiddler, who had made free with his lady's name over a silly new reel. Did the gentleman imagine that I looked for any dirty gratuity ?'

Page 153, *l* 5. Written at Castle Kenmure at the request of Mr. Gordon, whose dog had recently died.

Page 153, *l* 9. These lines were preserved by Miss Louisa Laurie, and appear to have been written on the same evening with the well-known 'Verses left in the room where he slept.'

Page 155, *l* 9. 'The Grace' was repeated at St. Mary's Isle at the request of the Earl of Selkirk.

Page 155, *l* 13. The mare, which was named after the insane female who attempted the life of George III., was the property of Burns' friend, Mr. William Nicol.

Page 155, *l* 29. These lines were written on a page of the Statistical Account of Scotland, vol. xiii., containing a description of the parish of Balmaghie. The minister, after quoting one of the simple, rude martyrs' epitaphs, adds—'The author of which no doubt supposed himself to have been writing poetry.' This captious remark called forth Burns's lines. The book, with the poet's comment, is preserved in the Mechanics' Institute, Dumfries. It is curious as the only expression of sympathy with the Covenanting cause which occurs in Burns.

Page 156. While Miss Lewars was attending Burns she became slightly indisposed. 'You must not die yet,' said the poet; and writing the four lines on a goblet he presented it, saying, 'This will be a companion for the "Toast."'

Page 156, *l* 9. On Miss Lewars recovering he said, 'There is a poetic reason for it,' and wrote these lines.

Page 156, *l* 13. 'The Toast' was written by Burns on a goblet, and presented to Miss Lewars.

Page 157, *l* 13. Mr. Chalmers was a writer in Ayr, and in love. He desired Burns to address the lady in his behalf.

Page 158. Burns arrived at Wanlockhead on a winter day, and was anxious to have the shoes of his mare *frosted.* The smith was busy, and could not attend. Burns then scribbled these verses to Mr. John Taylor, a person of some importance in the place. Through Taylor's influence the smith's services were secured; and for thirty years afterwards it is said Vulcan was in the habit of boasting 'that he had never been weel paid but ance, and that was by a poet, who paid him in money, paid him in drink, and paid him in verse.'

Page 158, *l* 9. The note on which Burns wrote these lines is of the Bank of Scotland, dated 1st March, 1780.

Page 158, *l* 19. The *Loyal Natives* was a club in Dumfries, 'more distinguished,' says Cromek, 'for drunken loyalty than for respectability and poetic talent.'

Page 158, *l* 26. These lines—with one exception, the only attempt of Burns in blank verse—occur in his common-place book, April 1783. It will be seen that the poet had not attained any considerable mastery over the most difficult of poetic measures.

Page 159, *l* 17. This epigram, it is said, silenced a gentleman who was talking mightily of dukes at the table of Maxwell of Terraughty.

Page 159, *l* 25. These lines occur in one of the letters to Clarinda.

Page 159, *l* 37. These verses were first printed by Cromek.

Page 160, *l* 5. These lines occur in one of the letters to Clarinda.

Page 160. Mr. Cobbett, who first printed these lines, says: 'It is our fortune to know a Mr. Kennedy, an aged gentleman, a native of Scotland, and the early friend and associate of Robert Burns. Both were born in Ayrshire, near the town of Ayr, so frequently celebrated in the poems of the bard. Burns, as is well known, was a poor peasant's son; and in the "Cotter's Saturday Night" gives a noble picture of what we may presume to be the family circle of his father. Kennedy, whose boyhood was passed in the labours of a farm, subsequently became the agent to a mercantile house in a neighbouring town. Hence he is called, in an epitaph which his friend the Poet wrote on him, "The Chapman." These lines, omitted in all editions of Burns' works, were composed on Kennedy's recovery from a severe illness. On his way to kirk on a bright Sabbath morning, he was met by the Poet, who, having rallied him on the sombre expression of his countenance, fell back, and soon rejoined him, presenting him with the epitaph scrawled on a bit of paper with a pencil.'

Page 161, *l* 13. In some MS. copies these stanzas conclude 'The Epistle to John Lapraik, an Old Scottish Bard.'

Page 162, *l* 24. These verses, inscribed to Gavin Hamilton, were printed for the first time in Pickering's edition.

Page 163, *l* 17. These lines occur in a letter addressed by Burns to Mr. Robert Ainslie.

Page 163. Burns in early life sketched the outlines of a tragedy, and the 'Tragic Fragment' was 'an exclamation from a great character—great in occasional instances of generosity, and daring at times, in villanies. He is supposed to meet a child of misery and exclaims to himself.'

Page 164. The following fragments are extracted from Burns' commonplace book, but the authorship is doubtful.

Page 165, *l* 27. The Tailor's epistle is as follows. Burns' reply was first published at Glasgow in 1801.

EPISTLE FROM A TAILOR TO ROBERT BURNS.

What waefu' news is this I hear,
Frae greeting I can scarce forbear,
Folk tell me, ye'er gawn aff this year
   Out o'er the sea.
Aur lasses wham ye lo'e sae dear
   Will greet for thee.

Weel wad I like war ye to stay,
But, Robin, since ye will away,
I ha'e a word yet mair to say,
   And maybe twa;
May He protect us night and day
   That made us a'.

Whar thou art gaun, keep mind frae me.
Seek Him to bear thee companie,
And, Robin, whan ye come to die,
   Ye'll won aboon,
An' live at peace an' unity
   Ayont the moon.

Some tell me, Rab, ye dinna fear
To get a wean, an' curse an' swear;
I'm unco wae, my lad, to hear
　　O' sic a trade.
Cou'd I persuade ye to forbear
　　I wad be glad.

Fu' weel ye ken ye'll gang to hell,
Gin ye persist in doin' ill—
Waes me! ye're hurlin' down the hill
　　Withouten dread,
An' ye'll get leave to swear your fill
　　After ye re dead.

There, walth o' women ye'll get near,
But gettin' weans ye will forbear.
Ye'll never say, my bonie dear,
　　Come, gie's a kiss—
Nae kissing then—ye'll grin an' sneer,
　　An' ither hiss.

O Rab! lay by thy foolish tricks,
An' steer nae mair the female sex,
Or some day ye'll come through the pricks,
　　An' that ye'll see ;
Ye'll fin' hard living wi' Auld Nicks :
　　I'm wae for thee.

But what's this comes wi' sic a knell,
Amaist as loud as ony bell,
While it does mak' my conscience tell
　　Me what is true,
I'm but a ragged cowt mysel',
　　Owre sib to you!

We're owre like those wha think it fit,
To stuff their noddles fa' o' wit,
An' yet content in darkness sit,
　　Wha shun the light,
To let them see down to the pit,
　　That long dark night.

But farewell, Rab, I maun awa',
May He that made us keep us a',
For that wad be a dreadfu' fa',
　　And hurt us sair :
Lad, ye wad never mend ava' ;
　　Sae, Rab, tak' care.

Page 167.　This epitaph, and the following epigrams, appeared in the Kilmarnock, but were omitted in the first Edinburgh and subsequent editions.

Page 168, *l* 1.　These lines first appeared in the edition published at Glasgow in 1801.

Page 168, *l* 9.　These lines first appeared in the edition published at Glasgow in 1801.

Page 168, *l* 13.　On Burns' arrival at Inverary the castle and inn were filled with visitors to the Duke, and the innkeeper was too busy to pay attention to the Poet and his friend. The epigram, which was first published in the Glasgow edition, is supposed to have been written on one of the windows.

Page 169.　John Stewart, eighth Earl of Galloway, who died in 1796. Burns disliked this nobleman, and his dislike descended in a shower of brilliant epigrams.

Page 170, *l* 33.　Printed in Cromek's Reliques.

Page 171, *l* 1.　Printed in the Glasgow Collection, 1801.

Page 171, *l* 23.　Printed in Cromek's Reliques.

Page 172, *l* 5.　Printed in the Glasgow Collection, 1801.

Page 172.　Captain Grose was extremely corpulent. This epigram was printed in the *Scots Magazine*, June 1791.

Page 172.　Printed in the Glasgow Collection, 1801. In a letter to Clarinda, in 1787, Burns refers to this epigram. 'Did I ever repeat to you an epigram I made on a Mr. Elphinstone, who has given a translation of Martial, a famous Latin poet? The poetry of Elphinstone can only equal his prose-notes. I was sitting in a merchant's shop of my acquaintance, waiting for somebody : he put Elphinstone into my hand, and asked my opinion of it ; I begged leave to write it on a blank leaf, which I did.'

Page 173.　This epitaph was printed in the Kilmarnock edition. 'Jamie' was James Humphrey, a mason in Mauchline, who was wont to hold theological disputations with the Poet.

Page 173.　'Wee Johnny' was John Wilson, the printer of the Kilmarnock edition, in which edition Burns wickedly inserted the epitaph. Wilson printed, unconscious that he had any other interest in the matter than a commercial one.

Page 173, *l* 5.　This, and the two following epitaphs, were printed in the Kilmarnock edition.

Page 173.　In the Kilmarnock, Edinburgh, and several subsequent editions, the first line of the 'Bard's Epitaph' is printed :—

　　Is there a whim-inspir'd fool.

Page 174, *l* 19.　Printed in the Kilmarnock edition. In a copy in the Poet's handwriting the first line reads :—

　　O ye who sympathise with virtue's pains.

Page 174, *l* 26.　Goldsmith.　R. B.

Page 174, *l* 27.　Printed in the Glasgow edition, 1801.

Page 174, *l* 41.　Burns' friend. James Smith, of Mauchline. This epitaph was printed in the Glasgow Collection.

Page 176.　These lines were inscribed on a pane of glass in Mr. M'Murdo's house.

Page 177, *l* 2.　The Right Worshipful Master, Major-General James Montgomery. On the 24th of June (St. John's Day) the masonic club in Mauchline, of which Burns was a member, contemplated a procession. Burns sent the rhymed note to Dr. Mackenzie, with whom he had lately been discussing the origin of morals.

Page 177, *l* 16.　This tumbler came into the possession of Sir Walter Scott, and is still preserved at Abbotsford. 'Willie Stewart' was factor on the estate of Closeburn in Dumfriesshire. He died in 1812, aged 63.

Page 178.　This song was composed in honour of Miss Wilhelmina Alexander, sister of the Laird of Ballochmyle, whom Burns had met in one of his evening walks.

Page 178, *l* 15.　*Var.*

　　The lily hue and rose's dye
　　Bespoke the lass o' Ballochmyle.

Page 178, *l* 3, 2 *col. Var.*

　　And all her other charms are foil'd.

Page 178, *l* 5, 2 *col. Var.*

O if she were a country maid.

Page 178. Burns wrote to Mrs. Dunlop, December, 1791 :—
' I have just finished the following song, which, to a lady the descendant of Wallace, and many heroes of his truly illustrious line, and herself the mother of several soldiers, needs neither preface nor apology. The circumstance that gave rise to the following verses was, looking over with a musical friend M'Donald's collection of Highland airs, I was struck with one, an Isle of Skye tune, entitled *Oran an Aoig,* or *The Song of Death,* to the measure of which I have adapted my stanzas.'

Page 178, *l* 42. *Var.*

Now gay with the bright setting sun.

Page 179, *l* 13. *Var.*

Down by the burn, where birken buds.

Page 179, *l* 21. *Var.*

Altho' the night were ne'er sae wet.

Page 179, *l* 33. The two first lines of this song are taken from an old Scotch ballad, printed in Johnson's ' Museum.' Mr. Chambers states that the second stanza was designed as a description of Charlotte Hamilton.

Page 180, *l* 1. This song was written when Burns brought his wife home to Ellisland. The second line was originally—

I'll share wi' naebody.

Page 180, *l* 19. In Burns' MS. this line stood—

She is a winsome wee thing.

It was altered, as in the text, by Mr. Thomson.

Page 180. *Duncan Gray* was suggested by a somewhat licentious ditty published in Johnson's ' Museum ;' the first and part of the third line being retained. With reference to this song Burns wrote to Mr. Thomson, December, 1792 :—' The foregoing I submit to your better judgment: acquit them or condemn them as seemeth good in your sight. *Duncan Gray* is that kind of horse-gallop of an air which precludes sentiment. The ludicrous is its ruling feature.'

Page 181, *l* 13. *Var.*

How blest the wild-wood Indian's fate.—*MS.*

Page 181, 2 *col.* About this song Burns wrote to Mr. Thomson, January, 1793 :—
' The very name of Peter Pindar is an acquisition to your work. His " Gregory " is beautiful. I have tried to give you a set of stanzas in Scots on the same subject, which are at your service. Not that I intend to enter the lists with Peter ; that would be presumption indeed. My song, though much inferior in poetic merit, has, I think, more of the ballad simplicity in it.'
Dr. Wolcot's song (Peter Pindar) may be inserted here for purposes of comparison.

' Ah ope, Lord Gregory, thy door!
    A midnight wanderer sighs ;
Hard rush the rains, the tempest roar,
    And lightnings cleave the skies.

'Who comes with woe at this drear night,—
    A pilgrim of the gloom ?
If she whose love did once delight,
    My cot shall yield her room.

'Alas ! thou heard'st a pilgrim mourn,
    That once was prized by thee :
Think of the ring by yonder burn
    Thou gav'st to love and me.

' But should'st thou not poor Marion know,
    I 'll turn my feet and part ;
And think the storms that round me blow
    Far kinder than thy heart.'

Page 182, *l* 13. A song under this title appeared in Johnson's ' Museum ' in 1788, which is said to have been written by Burns. ' It is so rude and wretched a production,' says Mr. Chambers, ' that we cannot believe many words of it to have been supplied by so masterly a pen.'

Page 182. The heroine of this song was Miss Jessie Staig.

Page 183, *l* 16. *Var.*

As simmer to nature, so Willie to me. *Erskine.*

Page 183, *l* 19. *Var.*

Blow soft, ye breezes ; blow gently, ye billows.
                    Erskine.

Page 183, *l* 22. *Var.*

Flow still between us, thou dark-heaving main.
                    Erskine.

Page 183, *l* 24. *Var.*

While dying, I think that my Willie's my ain.
                    Erskine.

Page 183, *l* 31. This and the following line were taken from a song, to the same air, written by John Mayne, afterwards author of the *Siller Gun,* and published in the *Star* newspaper in 1789.

Page 183, *l* 13, 2 *col. Var.*

Ye mind na, 'mid your cruel joys,
    The widow's tears, the orphan's cries.

Page 184. In July, 1793, Burns wrote Mr. Thomson :—' I have just finished the following ballad, and, as I do think it in my best style, I send it to you. Mr. Clarke, who wrote down the air from Mrs. Burns' wood-note wild, is very fond of it, and has given it a celebrity by teaching it to some young ladies of the first fashion here. . . . The heroine of the foregoing is a Miss M'Murdo, daughter to Mr. M'Murdo of Drumlanrig, one of your subscribers. I have not painted her in the rank which she holds in life, but in the dress and character of a cottager.'

Page 184, *l* 21. In the original MS. Burns asks Mr. Thomson if this stanza is not original.

Page 184, *l* 1, 2 *col. Var.*

Thy handsome foot thou shalt not set
    In barn or byre to trouble thee. *MS. copy.*

Page 184, *l* 9, 2 *col.* In August, 1793, Burns wrote Mr. Thomson :—' I have tried my hand on *Robin Adair,* and you will probably think with little success ; but it is such a cursed, cramp, out-of-the-way measure, that I despair

of doing anything better to it. So much for namby-pamby. I may, after all, try my hand on it in Scots verse. There I always find myself most at home.' *Phillis the Fair* is said to have been Miss M'Murdo,—sister of the heroine of *There was a Lass,*—and with whom the musician Clarke (who gave lessons to the young ladies) was in love. *Phillis* afterwards became Mrs. Norman Lockhart of Carnwath.

Page 184, *l* 34, 2 *col.* A mountain west of Strathallan, 3009 feet high. R. B.

Page 185, *l* 17. Burns wrote Mr. Thomson in August, 1793 :—' That crinkum-crankum tune, *Robin Adair,* has run so in my head, and I succeeded so ill in my last attempt, that I have ventured, in this morning's walk, one essay more. You, my dear Sir, will remember an unfortunate part of our worthy friend Cunningham's story, which happened about three years ago. That struck my fancy, and I endeavoured to do the idea justice, as follows.' A lady with whom Cunningham was in love had jilted him on the appearance of a richer lover.

Page 185. In August, 1793, Burns wrote Mr. Thomson :—' Is *Whistle, and I'll come to you, my lad,* one of your airs? I admire it much ; and yesterday I set the following verses to it.' In some of the MSS. the first four lines run thus :—

> O whistle, and I'll come to thee, my jo
> O whistle, and I'll come to thee, my jo;
> Tho' father and mother and a' should say no,
> O whistle, and I'll come to thee, my jo.

In 1795 Burns wrote to Johnson :—' In *Whistle, and I'll come to ye, my lad,* the iteration of that line is tiresome to my ear. Here goes what I think is an improvement :—

> O whistle, and I'll come to ye, my lad ;
> O whistle, and I'll come to ye, my lad ;
> Tho' father and mother and a' should gae mad,
> Thy Jeanie will venture wi' ye, my lad.'

Page 186, *l* 33. In September, 1793, Burns wrote to Mr. Thomson :—' I have been turning over some volumes of songs, to find verses whose measures would suit the airs for which you have allotted me to find English songs. For *Muirland Willie* you have in Ramsay's *Tea-table* an excellent song, beginning, *Ah, why those tears in Willie's eyes?* As for *The Collier's Dochter,* take the following old bacchanal.'

Page 186, *l* 13, 2 *col.* In a letter to Clarinda (supposed to be written about February, 1790,) Burns writes :—' The following song is one of my latest productions, and I send it to you, as I should do anything else, because it pleases myself.' It has been conjectured that Mrs. M'Lehose was the heroine.

Page 186. In March, 1792, Burns wrote to Mr. Cunningham :—' *Apropos,* do you know the much-admired old Highland air called *The Sutor's Dochter?* It is a first-rate favourite of mine, and I have written what I reckon one of my best songs to it. I will send it to you as it was sung with great applause in some fashionable circles by Major Lobertson, of Lude, who was here with his corps.' Allan Cunningham states that *Wilt thou be my Dearie?* was said 'to have been composed in honour of Janet Miller of Dalswinton, mother of the present Earl of Mar, one of the most beautiful women of her time.'

Page 187. In May, 1794, Burns wrote to Mr. Thomson :—' Now, for six or seven months, I shall be quite in song, as you shall see by and by. I know you value a composition because it is made by one of the great ones as little as I do. However, I got an air, pretty enough, composed by Lady Elizabeth Heron, of Heron, which she calls *The Banks of Cree.* Cree is a beautiful romantic stream ; and as her ladyship is a particular friend of mine, I have written the following song to it.'

Page 187, *l* 26. Burns wrote Mr. Thomson in 1794 :—' The last evening, as I was straying out, and thinking of *O'er the Hills and far away,* I spun the following stanzas for it ; but whether my spinning will deserve to be laid up in store, like the precious thread of the silkworm, or brushed to the devil, like the vile manufacture of the spider, I leave, my dear Sir, to your usual candid criticism. I was pleased with several lines in it at first, but I own that now it appears rather a flimsy business.'

Page 187. In September, 1794, Burns wrote Mr. Thomson : ' I am flattered at your adopting *Ca' the Yowes to the Knowes,* as it was owing to me that ever it saw the light. About seven years ago I was acquainted with a worthy little fellow of a clergyman, a Mr. Clunie, who sang it charmingly ; and, at my request, Mr. Clarke took it down from his singing. When I gave it to Johnson, I added some stanzas to the song, and mended others, but still it will not do for you. In a solitary stroll which I took to-day I tried my hand on a few pastoral lines, following up the idea of the chorus, which I would preserve. Here it is, with all its crudities and imperfections on its head.' The copy published in Johnson's ' Museum' is much inferior to the text.

Page 188, *l* 21. In September, 1794, Burns wrote to Mr. Thomson :—' Do you know a blackguard Irish song, called *Onagh's Waterfall?* The air is charming, and I have often regretted the want of decent verses on it. It is too much, at least for my humble rustic muse, to expect that every effort of hers shall have merit ; still I think that it is better to have *mediocre* verses to a favourite air than none at all.'

Page 188, *l* 13, 2 *col.* In sending this song to Mr. Thomson, 19th October, 1794, Burns writes :— ' I met with some such words in a collection of songs somewhere, which I altered and enlarged : and to please you, and to suit your favourite air, I have taken a stride or two across my room, and have arranged it anew, as you will find on the other page.'

Page 188, *l* 31, *2 col.* The heroine of this song was Miss Lorimer, of Craigieburn. Dr. Currie prints the following variation :—

Now to the streaming fountain,
Or up the heathy mountain,
The hart, hind, and roe, freely, wildly-wanton, stray;
In twining hazel bowers
His lay the linnet pours;
The lav'rock to the sky
Ascends wi' sangs o' joy ;
While the sun and thou arise to bless the day.

When frae my Chloris parted,
Sad, cheerless, broken-hearted,
The night's gloomy shades, cloudy, dark, o'ercast my sky.
But when she charms my sight
In pride of beauty's light,
When through my very heart
Her beaming glories dart,
'Tis then, 'tis then, I wake to life and joy.

Page 189, *l* 19. In sending this song to Mr. Thomson, November, 1794, Burns says :—' This piece has at least the merit of being a regular pastoral : the vernal morn, the summer noon, the autumnal evening, and the winter night, are regularly rounded.'

Page 189, *l* 1, *2 col. Var.*

And should the howling wintry blast
Disturb my lassie's midnight rest.
I'll fauld thee to my faithfu' breast
And comfort thee, my dearie O.

Page 189, *l* 9, *2 col.* With reference to this song Burns wrote Mr. Thomson, 19th October, 1794 : —' I enclose you a musical curiosity, an East Indian air, which you would swear was a Scottish one. I know the authenticity of it, as the gentleman who brought it over is a particular acquaintance of mine. . . . Here follow the verses I intend for it.'

Page 189, *l* 25, *2 col.* Burns sent the first draft of this song to Mr. Thomson in April, 1793. It was then addressed to Maria (supposed to be Mrs. Riddel). When he sent the version in the text to Mr. Thomson in November, 1794, he had made some inconsiderable alterations, and substituted Eliza for Maria.

Page 190, *l* 13. Burns wrote to Mr. Thomson, November, 1794 :—' Scottish bacchanalians we certainly want, though the few we have are excellent. . . . *Apropos* to bacchanalian songs in Scottish, I composed one yesterday for an air I like much, *Lumps o' Pudding.*' Burns tells Mr. Thomson in a passage suppressed by Currie, that he intended this song as a picture of his own mind.

Page 190, *l* 29. Clarinda was the heroine of this song.

Var.

Now in her green mantle gay Nature arrays.

Page 190, *l* 31. *Var.*

And birds warble welcomes in ilka green shaw.

Page 190, *l* 33. *Var.*

The primrose and daisy our glens may adorn.

Page 190, *l* 35. *Var.*

They torture my bosom, sae sweetly they blaw.

Page 190, *l* 36. *Var.*

They mind me o' Nannie—and Nannie's awa.

Page 190, *l* 41. *Var.*

Come autumn sae pensive, in yellow array.

Page 191, *l* 1. The heroine of this song was Miss Lorimer, of Craigieburn.

Page 191, *l* 17. In February, 1795, Burns wrote to Mr. Thomson :—' Here is another trial at your favourite air. . . . I do not know whether it will do.'

Page 191, *l* 58. In May, 1795, Burns wrote to Mr. Thomson :—' The Irish air, *Humours of Glen,* is a great favourite of mine, and as, except the silly stuff in the *Poor Soldier,* there are not any decent verses for it, I have written for it as follows.'

Page 191, *l* 62. *Var.*

Far dearer to me are these humble broom bowers.

Page 191, *l* 63. *Var.*

Where blue-bells and gowans lurk lowly unseen.

Page 192, *l* 9. Miss Lorimer of Craigieburn was the heroine of this song.

Page 192, *l* 17. *Var.*

Jeanie, I'm thine wi' a passion sincerest.

Page 192, *l* 1, *2 col.* This song is altered from an old English one.

Page 193, *l* 25. The chorus of this song was originally written—

O this is no my ain body,
Kind though the body be, &c.

Page 193, *l* 27, *2 col.* With reference to this song Burns asked Mr. Thomson :—' How do you like the foregoing ? I have written it within this hour. So much for the *speed* of my Pegasus : but what say you to his *bottom ?*'

Page 194, *l* 33. In the original copy this line stood —

He up the Gateslack to my black cousin Bess.

And on 3d June, 1795, Mr. Thomson wrote, objecting to the introduction of the word Gateslack, and also to that of Dalgarnock in the verse which followed. On August 3d of the same year Burns replied :—' Gateslack, the word you object to, is the name of a particular place, a kind of passage up among the Lower Hills, on the confines of this county. Dalgarnock is also the name of a romantic spot near the Nith, where are still a ruined church and a burial-ground. However, let the first run "He up the lang loan," &c.'

Page 195, *l* 27. About May 17, 1796, Burns wrote to Mr. Thomson :—' I once mentioned to you an air which I have long admired, *Here's a health to them that's awa, hiney,* but I forget if you took any notice of it. I have just been trying to suit it with verses, and I beg leave to recommend the air to your attention once more. I have only begun it.' *Jessie,* the heroine of the song, was Miss Jessie Lewars, who acted as nurse during the Poet's illness.

Page 196, *l* 16. Burns composed this song while standing under the falls of Aberfeldy, near Moness, in Perthshire, September, 1787.

Page 197, *l* 11. This was the last song composed by Burns. It was written at Brow, on the Solway Frith, a few days before his death.

Page 197. William, fourth viscount of Strathallan, fell at the battle of Culloden, while serving on the side of the rebels. In original edition in Johnson's Museum the first stanza runs as follows:—

Thickest night, surround my dwelling!
Howling tempests, o'er me rave!
Turbid torrents, wintry swelling,
Roaring by my lonely cave.

Page 197, *l* 37. *Var.*

Farewell fleeting, fickle treasure,
Between Misfortune and Folly shar'd!
Farewell peace, and farewell pleasure!
Farewell flattering man's regard!

Ruin's wheel has driven o'er me,
Nor dare a hope my fate attend;
The wide world is all before me,
But a world without a friend!

Page 197, *l* 9, 2 *col.* 'I composed these verses on Miss Isabella M'Leod of Raasay, alluding to her feelings on the death of her sister, and the still more melancholy death of her sister's husband, the late Earl of Loudon, who shot himself out of sheer heart-break, at some mortifications he suffered, owing to the deranged state of his finances.'—B.

Page 197, *l* 25, 2 *col.* 'I composed these verses out of compliment to a Mrs. Maclachlan, whose husband is an officer in the East Indies.'—B.

Page 198, *l* 1. The heroine of this song was Miss Euphemia Murray, of Lintrose, who was an inmate of Ochtertyre House, when Burns was there on a visit.

Page 198, *l* 6, 2 *col.* The heroine of this song was Miss Margeret Chalmers.

Page 199, *l* 1. This song was written in celebration of Miss Jenny Cruikshank, daughter of Mr. Cruikshank, of the High School, Edinburgh.

Page 199. This song was composed by Burns when he was about seventeen years of age. The subject was a girl in his neighbourhood named Isabella Steven, or Stein. According to Allan Cunningham, 'Tibbie was the daughter of a pensioner of Kyle—a man with three acres of peat moss—an inheritance which she thought entitled her to treat a landless wooer with disdain.'

Page 199, *l* 26, 2 *col.* 'This song,' Burns writes in a note, 'I composed out of compliment to Mrs. Burns. N.B.—It was in the honeymoon.'

Page 200, *l* 1. This song was also composed out of compliment to Mrs. Burns. Corsincon is a hill at the head of Nithsdale, beyond which Mrs. Burns lived before the Poet brought her home to Ellisland.

Page 200, *l* 25. With regard to this song Burns writes:—'I composed it out of compliment to one of the happiest and worthiest married couples in the world, Robert Riddel, of Glenriddel, and his lady.'

Page 200, *l* 1, 2 *col.* 'Composed on the amiable and excellent family of Whitefoord leaving Ballochmyle, when Sir John's misfortunes obliged him to sell the estate.'—B.

Page 200, *l* 17, 2 *col.* Burns writes concerning this song:—'The air is Masterton's, the song mine. The occasion of it was this: Mr. William Nicol, of the High School of Edinburgh, during the autumn vacation, being at Moffat, honest Allan, who was at that time on a visit to Dalswinton, and I, went to pay Nicol a visit. We had such a joyous meeting, that Mr. Masterton and I agreed, each in our own way, that we should celebrate the business.'

Page 200, *l* 37, 2 *col.* In many editions this line is printed:—'Wha *last* beside his chair shall fa'.' In Johnson's 'Museum' it is given as in the text. It seems more in accordance with the splendid bacchanalian frenzy that *he* should be king who

Rushed into the field and foremost fighting fell.

Victory does not lie in stamina or endurance. For the moment intoxication is the primal good, and he is happiest who is first intoxicated.

Page 201, *l* 1. At Lochmaben Burns spent an evening at the manse with the Rev. Andrew Jeffrey. His daughter Jean, a blue-eyed blonde of seventeen, presided at the tea-table. Next morning at breakfast the poet presented the young lady with the song.

Page 201, *l* 33. This song appears in the 'Museum' with Burns' name attached. Mrs. Begg maintained that it was an old song which her brother brushed up and retouched.

Page 203, *l* 20. 'Charming lovely Davies' is the heroine of this song.

Page 203, *l* 17, 2 *col. Var.*
O weels me on my spinnin wheel.

Page 203, *l* 18, 2 *col. Var.*
O weels me on my rock and reel,

Page 203, *l* 24, 2 *col. Var.*
O weels me on my spinnin wheel

Page 203, *l* 29, 2 *col. Var.*
Alike to shield the birdie's nest.

Page 203, *l* 34, 2 *col. Var.*
And echoes con the doolfu' tale.

Page 204, *l* 4. *Var.*
Rejoice me at my spinnin wheel.

Page 204, *l* 7. *Var.*
O wha would change the humble state.

Page 204, *l* 9 and 10. *Var.*
Amang their flarin, idle toys,
Amang their cumbrous, dinsome joys.

Page 204, l 11, 2 col. In the original MS. the name of the heroine of this song was Rabina.

Page 205. It will be noticed that this song is not distinguished by botanical correctness. Into the *Posie* Burns has gathered the flowers of spring, summer, and autumn.

Page 206, l 1. This song appeared with Burns' name attached in Johnson's 'Museum.' The simple and finer version which follows was sent to Mr. Ballantine in 1787. 'While here I sit,' Burns writes, 'sad and solitary, by the side of a fire in a little country inn, and drying my wet clothes.'

Page 206, l 45. This song was addressed to Clarinda.

Page 206, l 47. Var.
Dire was the parting thou bidst me remember.

Page 207, l 1. Burns wrote to Mr. Thomson, September, 1793 :—' The following song I have composed for *Oran Gaoil*, the Highland air that you tell me in your last you have resolved to give a place to in your book. I have this moment finished the song ; so you have it glowing from the mint. If it suits you, well ! if not, 'tis also well !'

Page 207, l 47. According to Dr. Currie this song was composed in honour of Mrs. Stewart of Stair. Gilbert Burns thought the verses referred to Highland Mary. Afton is an Ayrshire stream, and flows into the Nith, near New Cumnock.

Page 208, l 13, 2 col. Clarinda is supposed to be the subject of this song.

Page 208, l 28, 2 col. The first four lines of this song are old.

Page 209, l 9. The foundation of this song was a short ditty, written, it is said, by one Lieutenant Hinches, as a farewell to his sweetheart.

Page 209, l 25. This song was composed in honour of Mrs. Oswald, of Auchincruive.

Page 209, l 35, 2 col. Var.
The tod was howling on the hill.

Page 210, l 1. Var.
The burn adown its hazelly path.

Page 210, l 3. Var.
To join you river on the strath.

Page 210, l 9. Var.
Now looking over firth and fauld
Her horn the pale-faced Cynthia rear'd,
When, lo, in form of minstrel auld
A stern and stalwart ghaist appear'd.

Page 210, l 1, 2 col. This song is supposed to connect itself with the attachment to Highland Mary and the idea of emigration to the West Indies.

Page 211, l 13. Written in celebration of the personal and mental attractions of Miss Chalmers.

Page 211, l 29. The chorus of the song is old.

Page 211, l 8, 2 col. Jean Armour is the *Jean* referred to.

Page 211, l 9, 2 col. This is one of Burns' earliest productions.

Page 211, l 25, 2 col. 'I composed this song out of compliment to Miss Ann Masterton, the daughter of my friend Allan Masterton, the author of the air, *Strathallan's Lament.*'—B.

Page 212, l 1. The first four lines of this song are old.

Page 212, l 12. Var.
The battle closes deep and bloody.

Page 212, l 17. The first stanza of this song is taken from a stall ditty, entitled *The Strong Walls of Derry.*

Page 212, l 33. Concerning this song Burns writes :—' This air is claimed by Neil Gow, who calls it *a lament for his brother.* The first half stanza of the song is old ; the rest is mine.'

Page 213, l 1. 'I composed this song,' Burns writes, 'pretty early in life, and sent it to a young girl, a very particular acquaintance of mine, who was at that time under a cloud.'

Page 213, l 1, 2 col. 'This song,' Burns writes, 'is altered from a poem by Sir Robert Ayton, private secretary to Mary and Anne, Queens of Scotland. . . . I think I have improved the simplicity of the sentiments by giving them a Scots dress.'

Page 213, l 33. 'This song,' says Burns, 'alludes to a part of my private history which it is of no consequence to the world to know.'

Page 214, l 1. Burns says : 'This tune is also known by the name of *Lass, an' I come near thee.* The words are mine.'

Page 214, l 25. These verses were inspired by Clarinda—the most beautiful and passionate strain to which that strange attachment gave birth.

Page 215, l 17. Allan Cunningham states that Burns considered this to be the finest love-song he had ever composed—an opinion in which few readers will concur.

Page 215, l 49. 'These verses,' says Burns, 'were composed on a charming girl, Miss Charlotte Hamilton, who is now married to James Mackittrick Adair, physician. She is sister to my worthy friend Gavin Hamilton, of Mauchline, and was born on the banks of the Ayr.'

Page 216, l 34. This song was written soon after Burns' visit to Gordon Castle in 1787. The variations are from a copy in the Poet's handwriting.

Page 216, l 37. Var.
There immix'd with foulest stains.

Page 216, l 38. Var.
From Tyranny's empurpled hands

Page 210, *l* 1, 2 *col.* Var.

I leave the tyrants and their slaves.

Page 216, *l* 4, 2 *col.* Var.

Torrid forests, ever gay.

Page 217. In September, 1793, Burns wrote to Mr. Thomson :—'*Blithe hae I been o'er the hill* is one of the finest songs ever I made in my life ; and, besides, is composed on a young lady, positively the most beautiful, lovely woman in the world.' The young lady was Miss Lesley Baillie.

Page 217, *l* 17. The first and second stanzas of this song are by Burns ; the third and fourth are old.

Page 217, *l* 33. In August, 1793, Burns wrote to Mr. Thomson :—'That tune, *Cauld Kail*, is such a favourite of yours, that I once more roved out yesterday for a gloamin-shot at the Muses ; when the Muse that presides o'er the banks of Nith, or rather my old inspiring dearest nymph, Coila, whispered me the following.'

Page 217, *l* 49. Burns wrote Mr. Thomson September, 1793 :—' I have finished my song to *Saw ye my Father ?* and in English, as you will see. That there is a syllable too much for the *expression* of the air is true ; but allow me to say that the mere dividing of a dotted crotchet into a crotchet and a quaver is not a great matter : however, in that I have no pretensions to cope in judgment with you. The old verses have merit, though unequal, and are popular. My advice is .to set the air to the old words, and let mine follow as English verses. Here they are.'

Page 218, *l* 13. On the 19th October, 1794, Burns wrote to Mr. Thomson :—' To descend to business ; if you like my idea of *When she cam ben, she bobbit*, the following stanzas of mine, altered a little from what they were formerly when set to another air, may perhaps do instead of worse stanzas.'

Page 218, *l* 25. In September, 1793, Burns wrote Mr. Thomson :—'*Fee him, Father*. I enclose you Fraser's set of this tune when he plays it slow ; in fact he makes it the language of despair. I shall here give you two stanzas in that style, merely to try if it will be any improvement. Were it possible in singing to give it half the pathos which Fraser gives it in playing, it would make an admirably pathetic song. I do not give these verses for any merit they have. I composed them at the time in which "Patie Allan's mither died—that was, about the back of midnight," and by the leeside of a bowl of punch which had overset every mortal in company except the hautbois and the Muse.'

Page 219, *l* 9. In November, 1794, Burns wrote Mr. Thomson :—'You may think meanly of this, but take a look at the bombast original, and you will be surprised that I have made so much of it.'

Page 220, *l* 21. This is partly composed on the plan of an old song known by the same name. R. B. The ballad appeared in the first Edinburgh edition.

Page 221, *l* 1. On the 19th November, 1794, Burns wrote to Mr. Thomson :—'Well ! I think this, to be done in two or three turns across my room, and with two or three pinches of Irish blackguard, is not so far amiss.'

Page 221, *l* 1, 2 *col.* This fragment appeared in the first Edinburgh edition.

Page 222, *l* 33. This song appeared in the Kilmarnock edition.

Page 222, *l* 29, 2 *col.* This song appeared in the Kilmarnock edition.

Page 223, *l* 1. The poet proposed, for the sake of euphony, to substitute *Lugar* for Stinchar, but in all his editions, from 1786 to 1794, 'Stinchar' is printed.

Page 223, *l* 33. This song was printed in the first Edinburgh edition.

Page 223, *l* 21, 2 *col.* Composed in August. This song appeared in the Kilmarnock edition.

Page 224, *l* 29. This song was printed in the first Edinburgh edition.

Page 224, *l* 49. Young's Night Thoughts. R. B.

Page 225, *l* 1. In the autobiographical sketch forwarded to Dr. Moore, Burns writes : —' I had taken the last farewell of my few friends ; my chest was on the road to Greenock ; and I had composed the last song I should ever measure in Caledonia—

The gloomy night is gathering fast;

when a letter from Dr. Blacklock to a friend of mine overthrew all my schemes, by opening new prospects to my poetic ambition.' The song was printed in the first Edinburgh edition.

Page 225. The 'Farewell' was printed in the Kilmarnock edition.

Page 225, *l* 21, 2 *col.* Mr. Chambers states that the grand master referred to in the text was Major-General James Montgomery ; elsewhere the grand master is said to have been Sir John Whiteford.

Page 225, *l* 33, 2 *col.* Menie is the common abbreviation of Marianne. R. B. This chorus is part of a song composed by a gentleman in Edinburgh, a particular friend of the author's. R. B. This song appeared in the first Edinburgh edition.

Page 226, *l* 29. Concerning this song Burns wrote Mr. Thomson on the 14th November. 1792 :—' The foregoing song pleases myself ; I think it is in my happiest manner : you will see at first glance that it suits the air. The subject of the song is one of the most interesting passages of my youthful days ; and I own that I should be

much flattered to see the verses set to an air which would insure celebrity. Perhaps, after all, 'tis the still glowing prejudice of my heart that throws a borrowed lustre over the merits of the composition.'

Page 226. Burns stated, both to Mrs. Dunlop and Mr. Thomson, that *Auld Lang Syne* was old. It is, however, generally believed that he was the entire, or almost the entire, author. In Pickering's edition the following variations are taken from a copy in the Poet's handwriting.

Page 226, *l* 26, 2 *col. Var.*
And never thought upon.

Page 226, *l* 27, 2 *col. Var.*
Let's hae a waught o' Malaga
For auld lang syne.

Page 226, *l* 29, 2 *col. Var.*
For auld lang syne, my jo.

Page 226, *l* 31, 2 *col. Var.*
Let's hae a waught o' Malaga.

Page 227. In September, 1793, Burns sent this song to Mr. Thomson. 'There is,' he wrote, 'a tradition, which I have met with in many places of Scotland, that it' (the old air *Hey tuttie taitie*) 'was Robert Bruce's march at the battle of Bannockburn. This thought in my yesternight's evening walk warmed me to a pitch of enthusiasm on the theme of Liberty and Independence, which I threw into a kind of Scottish ode, fitted to the air, that one might suppose to be the gallant royal Scot's address to his heroic followers on that eventful morning. So may God ever defend the cause of truth and liberty as He did that day. Amen.' Mr. Thomson wrote suggesting alterations, and Burns replied :—' "Who shall decide when doctors disagree?" My ode pleases me so much, that I cannot alter it. Your proposed alterations would, in my opinion, make it tame. I am exceedingly obliged to you for putting me on reconsidering it, as I think I have much improved it. . . . . I have scrutinised it over and over ; and to the world, some way or other, it shall go as it is.'

Page 227, *l* 21, 2 *col.* In January, 1795, Burns wrote Mr. Thomson :—' A great critic (Aikin) on songs says that love and wine are the exclusive themes for song-writing. The following is on neither subject, and consequently is no song; but will be allowed, I think, to be two or three pretty good prose thoughts converted into rhyme.'

Page 228, *l* 25. Of this song Burns says :—' The title of the song only is old ; the rest is mine.' In Johnson's 'Museum' he published an early version, with the burden, 'The gardener with his paidle.'

Page 230, *l* 21. Gilbert Burns did not consider his brother the author of this song.

Page 231, *l* 22. This song, which became immensely popular at the time, was published in the *Dumfries Journal*, 5th May, 1795.

Page 232, *l* 1. This was written in an envelope to Mr. Cardonnel, the antiquary, enclosing a letter to Captain Grose.

Page 232, *l* 2, 2 *col. Var.*
Sweet and harmless as a child.

Page 232, *l* 13, 2 *col.* This was one of Burns' earliest compositions.

Page 233, *l* 1. This song appears in Johnson's 'Museum' without Burns' name.

Page 233. M'Pherson was a Highland freebooter, of great personal strength and musical taste and accomplishment. While lying in prison under sentence of death, he composed his *Farewell*, words and air, the former of which began :—

' I've spent my time in rioting,
Debauch'd my health and strength ;
I squander'd fast as pillage came,
And fell to shame at length.
But dantonly and wantonly
And rantonly I'll gae :
I'll play a tune and dance it roun'
Beneath the gallows' tree.'

When brought to the gallows' foot at Banff, he played his *Farewell*, and then broke his violin across his knee. His sword is preserved at Duff House.

Page 233, *l* 6, 2 *col.* This ballad refers to the contest between Mr. Erskine and Mr. Dundas for the Deanship of the Faculty of Advocates. On the 12th January, 1796, Mr. Dundas was elected by a large majority.

Page 234, *l* 1, 2 *col.* Another version of this song is printed in Cromek's Reliques. The text is from a copy in the Poet's own handwriting.

Page 236. On 12th March, 1791, Burns wrote to Mr. Thomson :—' Lest I sink into stupid prose, and so sacrilegiously intrude on the office of my parish priest, I shall fill up the page in my own way, and give you another song of my late composition. . . . You must know a beautiful Jacobite air, *There'll never be peace till Jamie comes hame.* When political combustion ceases to be the object of princes and patriots, it then, you know, becomes the lawful prey of historians and poets.'

Page 236, *l* 17. In a copy of this song in the Poet's handwriting the first stanza and chorus are thus given : —

There was a Birkie born in Kyle,
But what na day o' what na style,
I doubt it's hardly worth the while
To be so nice with Davie.
Leeze me on thy curly pow,
Bonie Davie, daintie Davie :
Leeze me on thy curly pow,
Thou 'se ay my daintie Davie.

Page 236, *l* 26. Jan. 25th, 1759, the date of my bardship's vital existence. R. B.

Page 236, *l* 35. *Var.*
He'll gie his daddie's name a blaw.

Page 236, *l* 6, 2 *col. Var.*
Ye'll gar the lasses lie aspar.

Page 237, l 13. On 20th March, 1793, Burns wrote Mr. Thomson :—' This song is one of my juvenile works. I do not think it very remarkable, either for its merits or demerits.'

Page 237, l 13, 2 col. Var.
And ay I min't the witching smile.

Page 237, l 19, 2 col. Var.
Wha spied I but my ain dear lass.

Page 237, l 23, 2 col. Var.
Wi' fremit voice, quoth I, Sweet lass.

Page 237, l 32, 2 col. Var.
And lov'lier look'd than ever.

Page 237, l 40, 2 col. Var.
Syne wallow't like a lily.

Page 237, l 41, 2 col. Var.
And sank within my arms, and cried.

Page 238, l 3. Var.
Though wealth be sma', we're rich in love

Page 238, l 5. Var.
Quo' she, My grandsire left me gear.

Page 238, l 7. Var.
And come, my ain dear soger lad.

Page 238, l 17. Concerning this song Burns writes :—' The following song is a wild rhapsody, miserably deficient in versification ; but as the sentiments are the genuine feelings of my heart, for that reason I have a particular pleasure in conning it over.'

Page 239, l 1. Composed on the death of James Fergusson, Esq. Younger, of Craigdarroch.

Page 239. ' Bonie Lesley ' was Miss Lesley Baillie, daughter of Mr. Baillie of Ayrshire. Mr. Baillie, on his way to England with his two daughters, called on Burns at Dumfries. Burns mounted, accompanied them fifteen miles, and composed the song as he rode homewards.

Page 239, l 24, 2 col. Jean Armour is the ' Mauchline lady ' referred to.

Page 240. ' My Montgomerie's Peggy,' writes Burns, ' was my deity for six or eight months. . . . A vanity of showing my parts in courtship, particularly my abilities at a billet-doux, which I always piqued myself upon, made me lay siege to her.' Burns, after he had warmed into a passion for Peggy, found that she was pre-engaged, and confessed that it cost him some heartaches to get rid of the affair.

Page 240, l 29, 2 col. Dr. Currie inserted this in his first edition, but withdrew it on finding it was the composition of Helen Maria Williams. Burns had copied it ; his MS. is now in the British Museum.

Page 241, l 25. A song, in several stanzas, similar to this occurs in the *Jolly Beggars*.

Page 241, l 16, 2 col. This song was written on one of the anniversaries of Highland Mary's death.

Page 241, l 28, 2 col. Var.
Eternity can not efface.

Page 242, l 3. Var.
Time but the impression stronger makes.

Page 242, l 6. Var.
Where is thy place of heavenly rest?

Page 242, l 41. Burns chanted these verses on hearing some one express his joy at General Dumourier's defection from the service of the French Republic.

Page 243, l 19. Var.
The primroses blush in the dews of the morning.

Page 243, l 23. Var.
No birds sweetly singing, no flowers gaily springing.

Page 243, l 28. Var.
here the wild beasts find shelter, though I can find none.

Page 243, l 32. Var.
Alas ! can I make you no better return?

Page 245, l 43. Charles James Fox.

Page 246, l 3. Thomas Erskine. A somewhat different version of this piece is in *Scots Magazine* for January 1818.

Page 246, l 13. Burns writes :—' The chorus of this song is old ; the rest of it, such as it is, is mine.'

Page 248. The ' Five Carlins ' represent the five boroughs of Dumfries-shire and Kirkcudbright, which were at the time contested by Patrick Miller of Dalswinton in the Whig, and Sir James Johnstone of Westerhall in the Tory interest. Dumfries is ' Maggie by the banks o' Nith ;' Annan is ' blinkin Bess o' Annandale ;' Kirkcudbright ' whisky Jean ' of Galloway ; Sanquhar ' black Joan frae Creighton peel ;' and Lochmaben ' Marjorie o' the monie Lochs.'

Page 248, l 25, 2 col. Sir James Johnstone.

Page 248, l 33, 2 col. Captain Miller of Dalswinton.

Page 249, l 9. King George III.

Page 249, l 12. The Prince of Wales.

Page 249, l 25, 2 col. This song, founded on an old ballad, was printed in Johnson's ' Museum.'

Page 250, l 48. Var.
Sae kend in martial story.

Page 250, l 26, 2 col. Var.
I'll breathe this exclamation.

Page 251, l 1. Concerning this song Burns writes :—' The chorus I picked up from an old woman in Dunblane ; the rest of the song is mine.'

Page 251, l 25. Another version of this song will be found p. 191, l 1.

Page 252, l 11. Allan Cunningham mentions a report that Burns wrote these verses in humorous allusion to the condition in which Jean Armour found herself before marriage.

Page 252, l 31. This is founded on an old song.

Page 252, *l* 47. This is founded on an old song.

Page 253, *l* 25. This song was altered by Burns from a Jacobite ditty.

Page 254, *l* 17. Another version of this song will be found p. 181, l 24.

Page 257, *l* 33. It is doubted whether Burns was the author of this song.

Page 257, *l* 25, 2 *col.* Of this song Burns writes :—'These were originally English verses ; I gave them their Scots dress.'

Page 258, *l* 13. Part only of this song is by Burns.

Page 258, *l* 31. Part only of this song appears to have been written by Burns.

Page 258, *l* 13, 2 *col.* Of this song Burns writes :—'The chorus is old ; the rest of it is mine.'

Page 259, *l* 1, 2 *col.* The foundation of this song is old.

Page 260, *l* 1. This is founded on an old ballad.

Page 261, *l* 13. 'The last stanza of this song,' Burns writes, 'is mine. It was composed out of compliment to one of the worthiest fellows in the world, William Dunbar, Esq. W.S. Edinburgh, and colonel of the Crochallan Corps, a club of wits who took that title at the time of raising the Fencible regiments.'

Page 262, *l* 1, 2 *col.* The first four lines of this song are old.

Page 262, *l* 17. The second verse of this song is by Burns.

Page 262, *l* 33. Concerning this ballad Gilbert Burns says :—'When Mr. Cunninghame of Enterkin came to his estate, two mansion houses on it, Enterkin and Anbank, were both in a ruinous state. Wishing to introduce himself with some *eclat* to the county, he got temporary erections made on the banks of Ayr, tastefully decorated with shrubs and flowers, for a supper and ball, to which most of the respectable families in the county were invited. It was a novelty, and attracted much notice. A dissolution of Parliament was soon expected, and this festivity was thought to be an introduction to a canvass for representing the county. Several other candidates were spoken of, particularly Sir John Whitefoord, then residing at Cloncaird (commonly pronounced Glencaird), and Mr. Boswell, the well-known biographer of Dr. Johnson. The political views of the festive assemblage, which are alluded to in the ballad, if they ever existed, were, however, laid aside, as Mr. Cunninghame did not canvass the county.'

Page 265, *l* 9. Burns says the second and fourth stanzas of this song were written by him.

Page 266, *l* 1. This song is founded on an old ballad.

Page 268, *l* 25. The last two verses of this song are by Burns.

Page 269, *l* 37, 2 *col.* The ' Heron Ballads ' were written on the occasion of the Stewartry of Kirkcudbright being contested, in 1795, by Mr. Heron of Kerroughtree in the Whig, and Mr. Gordon of Balmaghie in the Tory, interest.

Page 270, *l* 14, 2 *col. Var.*
> For now what he wan in the Indies
> Has scoured up the laddie fu' clean.

Page 273, *l* 1. This song was produced at a festive meeting of the Kilmarnock Masonic Lodge, presided over by Mr. William Parker.

Page 275, *l* 7. Gilbert Burns was of opinion that his brother did not write this song.

Page 277, *l* 5, 2 *col.* Burns states concerning this song :—' I added the four last lines by way of giving a turn to the theme of the poem, such as it is.'

Page 278, *l* 1, 2 *col.* The text has been collated with a copy in the Poet's handwriting.

GLOSSARY

	Page	line	col.
Braw, *handsome*	1	13	
Brawly, *perfectly*	25	39	
Braxies, *morbid sheep*	79	38	2
Breastie, dim. of *breast*	54	20	
Breastit, *did spring up or forward*	54	9	
Brechan, *a horse-collar*	157	14	
Breckan, *fern*	191	27	
Bree, *juice, liquid*	8	15	
Breeks, *breeches*	9	20	
Brent, *straight*	93	22	
smooth, unwrinkled	201	20	
Brewin, *brewing*	29	33	2
Brief, *a writing*	166	1	
Brig, *bridge*	25	31	
Brither, *brother*	79	31	2
Brithers, *brothers*	11	28	
Brock, *a badger*	3	10	
Brogue, *a trick*	32	21	
Broo, *water*	27	28	
broth	163	10	
Brooses, *races at country weddings who shall first reach the bridegroom's house on returning from church*	53	15	2
Browst, *as much malt liquor as is brewed at a time*	255	15	2
Browster-wives, *ale-house wives*	126	23	
Brugh, *burgh*	25	12	
Brughs, *boroughs*	9	26	
Brulzie, *a broil*	80	42	2
Brunstane, *brimstone*	9	17	
Brunt, *burned*	45	6	2
Brust, *burst*	9	36	
Buckie, dim. of *buck*	111	10	
Buckskin, *an inhabitant of Virginia*	81	26	2
Buff, *to beat*	127	15	2
Bughtin-time, *the time of collecting the sheep in the pens to be milked*	179	10	
Buirdly, *strong, imposing-looking, well-knit*	3	3	
Buke, *book*	104	32	2
Bum, *to hum*	79	30	2
Bum-clock, *a beetle*	6	11	
Bumming, *making a noise like a bee*	31	33	
Bummle, *a blunderer*	71	32	
Bunker, *a chest*	93	25	
Burdies, *damsels*	94	12	
Bure, *bore, did bear*	53	32	
Burns, *streams*	43	3	
Burnie, dim. of *burn*	47	28	
Burnewin, i.e. *burn the wind, a blacksmith*	7	41	
Bur-thistle, *the spear-thistle*	125	21	
Busking, *dressing, decorating*	263	3	
Buskit, *dressed*	25	44	
Busks, *adorns*	114	21	
Buss, *a bush*	189	19	2
Bussle, *a bustle*	10	27	
But, *without*	189	56	2
But an' ben, *kitchen and parlour*	17	28	
By, *past*	32	34	
apart	54	12	2
By attour, *in the neighbourhood, outside*	254	33	2
Byke, *a multitude*	52	3	
a bee-hive	164	7	

	Page	line	col.
CA', *to drive*	32	35	2
a call	47	3	
Ca'd, *named*	1	26	
driven	91	25	
Ca's, *calls*	2	19	2
Ca't, *called*	53	12	2
Ca' throu', *to push forward*	268	25	2
Cadger, *a carrier*	48	12	2
Cadie, *a fellow*	12	10	
Caff, *chaff*	41	24	
Cairds, *tinkers*	35	17	
Calf-ward, *a small inclosure for calves*	22	33	
Callans, *boys*	80	7	
Caller, *fresh*	14	4	
Callet, *a trull*	48	32	
Cam, *came*	29	17	
Cankert, *cankered*	124	37	
Cankrie, *cankered*	148	40	
Canna, *cannot*	10	17	
Cannie, *carefully, softly*	12	2	
Cannilie, *dexterously*	17	24	
Cantie, *in high spirits*	4	7	
Cantin', *canting*	128	20	
Cantrip, *a charm, a spell*	93	33	
Cape-stane, *cope-stone*	33	27	
Cap'rin, *capering*	51	11	2
Careerin, *cheerfully*	47	31	2
Carl, *a carle*	148	36	
Carlie, dim. of *carle*	249	16	
Carlin, *an old woman*	11	6	
Cartes, *cards*	58	38	
Cartie, dim. of *cart*	159	4	2
Caudrons, *cauldrons*	30	15	
Cauf, *a calf*	255	21	2
Cauk and keel, *chalk and red clay*	95	38	
Cauld, *cold*	5	18	
Caulder, *colder*	156	20	
Caups, *wooden drinking vessels*	18	32	
Causey, *causeway*	27	23	
Cavie, *a hen-coop*	51	31	
Chamer, *chamber*	95	7	2
Change-house, *a tavern*	17	28	
Chap, *a fellow*	11	21	
Chapman, *a pedlar*	91	1	
Chaup, *a blow*	7	42	
Cheek for chow, *cheek by jowl*	10	33	
Cheep, *chirp*	29	23	2
Cheerfu', *cheerful*	58	23	
Chiels, *young fellows*	3	3	
Chimla, *chimney*	150	13	
Chimlie, *chimney*	45	26	
Chittering, *trembling with cold*	55	23	
Chows, *chews*	7	1	
Chuckie, dim. of *chuck*	108	27	
Christendie, *Christendom*	200	20	2
Chuffie, *fat-faced*	10	33	
Clachan, *a hamlet*	20	1	
Claise, *clothes*	32	12	
Claith, *cloth*	23	5	
Claith'd, *clothed*	214	5	2
Claithing, *clothing*	19	4	
Clamb, *clomb*	201	26	
Clankie, *a sharp stroke*	269	18	
Clap, *a clapper*	41	26	
Clark, *clerkly, pertaining to erudition*	124	8	

Page line col.

Gleib, *a glebe* 203 10
Glib-gabbet, *that speaks smoothly
  and readily* 11 19
Glinted, *glanced* 69 15
Glintin, *glancing* 14 6
Gloamin, *twilight* 6 10
Gloamin-shot, *a twilight interview* 255 41
Glowran, *staring* 52 3
Glowr'd, *looked earnestly, stared* . 14 10
Glunch, *a frown* 8 39
Goavan, *looking round with a
  strange inquiring gaze, star-
  ing stupidly* 111 10 2
Gotten, *got* 79 8
Gowan, *the daisy* 191 30
Gowany, *daisied* 114 16 2
Gowd, *gold* 81 25
Gowden, *golden* 114 12 2
Gowff'd, *knocked hither and thither* 222 26
Gowk, *a foolish person* . . . 26 19
Gowling, *howling* 73 26 2
Graff, *a grave* 167 1 2
Grained, *grinned* 22 37
Graip, *a pronged instrument for
  cleaning stables* . . . 46 8 2
Graith, *harness, field implements
  accoutrements* 15 19
Granes, *groans* 5 20
Grape, *to grope* 44 12 2
Graped, *groped* 171 21
Grapit, *groped* 45 25 2
Grat, *wept* 180 10 2
Gratefu', *grateful* 72 23 2
Graunie, *grandmother* . . . 31 25
Gree, *a prize* 79 35
  to agree 132 31 2
Gree't, *agreed* 21 6
Greet, *to weep* 11 6
Greetin, *weeping* 10 25
Griens, *covets, longs for* . . . 271 32
Grievin, *grieving* 43 24
Grippet, *gripped, caught hold of* . 45 14
Grissle, *gristle* 77 12 2
Grit, *great* 131 22
Grozet, *a gooseberry* . . . 74 13 2
Grumphie, *the sow* 46 32 2
Grun', *the ground* 131 34
Grunstane, *a grindstone* . . . 73 32
Gruntle, *the countenance* . . 8 39
  a grunting noise 46 20 2
Grunzie, *the mouth* . . . 207 22 2
Grushie, *thick, of thriving growth* 3 30
Grusome, *ill favoured* . . . 170 1
Grutten, *wept* 137 10 2
Gude, *the Supreme Being* . . 33 6 2
  good 50 6 2
Gudeen, *good even* 164 8 2
Gudeman, *goodman* . . . 20 43
Gudes, *goods, merchandise* . . 271 12 2
Guid, *good* 4 6
Guid-e'en, *good even* . . . 20 31
Guid-mornin, *good morning* . 36 10
Guidfather, *father-in-law* . 53 20
Guidwife, *the mistress of the house
  the landlady* 125 1
  . . . . 201 33 2
Gully, *a large knife* . . . 20 42

Page line col.

Gulravage, *riot* 128 3
Gumlie, *muddy, discoloured* . . 26 38
Gumption, *understanding* . . 141 12 2
Gusty, *tasteful* 7 36
Gutcher, *grandfather* . . . 254 25 2

HA', *hall* 95 7 2
Ha' Bible, *hall-Bible* 63 38
Ha' folk, *servants* 2 26
Haddin, *holding, inheritance* . . 270 11 2
Hae, *have* 4 10
  here (in the sense of *take*) . . 151 41 2
Haet, *the least thing.* Deil haet,
  an oath of negation . . . 5 34
  Damn'd haet, *nothing* . . . 21 34
Ha'f, *the half* 165 31
Haff, *the half* 140 22 2
Haffets, *the temples* . . . 63 40
Haffet locks, *locks at the temples* 257 18
Hafflins, *partly* 62 44
Hafflins-wise, *almost half* . . 17 26
Hag, *a scar, or gulf in mosses and
  moors* 43 7
Haggis, *a kind of pudding boiled
  in the stomach of a cow or
  sheep* 72 24 2
Hain, *to spare, to save* . . . 79 9
Hain'd, *spared* 54 16 2
Hairst, *harvest* 46 19
Haith, *a petty oath* . . . 4 21
Haivers, *idle talk* 125 14
Hal', *hall* 57 14 2
Hald, *an abiding-place* . . . 54 28 2
Hale, *whole, entire*; Hale breeks,
  breeches without holes . . . 9 20
  uninjured 95 17
Haly, *holy* 93 36
Hallan, *a particular partition
  wall in a cottage* 63 29
Hallions, *clowns, common fellows* 151 1 2
Hallowmas, *the 31st of October* . 165 8
Hame, *home* 23 23
Hamely, *homely* 53 29
Han', *hand* 9 15
Han' afore, *the foremost horse on
  the left hand in the plough* . 104 8
Han' ahin, *the hindmost horse on
  the left hand in the plough* . 104 10
Hand-breed, *a hand-breadth* . . 207 13 2
Hand-waled, *carefully chosen by
  hand* 148 29 2
Handless, *without hands, useless,
  awkward* 164 35 2
Hangit, *hanged* 251 6 2
Hansel, hansel throne, *a throne
  newly inherited* 234 27
  *a gift for a particular season,
  or the first money on any
  particular occasion* . . . 236 28
Han't, *handed* 204 39
Hap, *to wrap* 71 32
  Winter hap, *winter clothing* . 24 25
Hap, *hop* 150 28
Ha'pence, *half-pence* 15 29
Happer, *a hopper* 41 25
Happing, *hopping* 55 19

	Page	line	col.
Hap-step-an'-lowp, *hop, step, and jump, with a light airy step* .	14	23	
Harkit, *hearkened*	38	25	
Harn, *yarn*	94	27	
Har'sts, *harvests*	101	2	2
Hash, *a soft, useless fellow* . .	8	27	
Hash'd, *did smite, did disfigure* .	230	1	2
Haslock, *descriptive of the finest wool, being the lock that grows on the* hals *or throat* . . .	256	9	2
Has't, *has it*	22	22	
Hastit, *hasted*	54	11	
Haud, *to hold*	9	15	
would keep	96	9	
Hauds, *holds*	223	25	
Hauf, *the half*	161	7	2
Haughs, *low-lying lands, meadows*	6	29	
Hauns, *hands, as applied to work-men, persons*	103	29	
Haurl, *to drag*	83	19	
Haurls, *drags*	46	8	2
Haurlin, *peeling, dragging off* . .	47	19	
Hauver, *oatmeal*	262	17	
Havins, *good manners*	33	22	
Hav'rel, *half-witted*	44	14	2
Hawkie, *a cow, properly one with a white face*	31	23	2
Healsome, *wholesome*	63	27	
Heapet, *heaped*	41	25	
Heapit, *heaped*	54	11	2
Hearin', *hearing*	149	14	
Hearse, *hoarse*	9	31	
Hear't, *hear it*	76	13	
Heartie, dim. of *heart*	50	34	2
Hech, *an exclamation of wonder*	4	43	
Hecht, *foretold*	47	11	
offered	182	21	
Hechtin', *making to pant* . . .	177	4	2
Heckle, *a board, in which are fixed a number of sharp pins, used in dressing hemp, flax, &c.*	101	25	
Hee balou, *a term used by nurses when lulling children* . . .	255	1	2
Heels-o'er-gowdy, *head over heels*	121	13	2
Heeze, *to elevate, to hoist* . .	65	24	
Heft, *haft*	93	46	
Hein shinn'd, *in-shinned* . . .	207	12	2
Hellim, *the helm*	221	2	2
Hen-broo, *hen-broth*	276	2	2
Herriet, *harried*	151	2	2
Herrin, *herring*	23	34	
Herryment, *plundering, devasta-tion*	27	39	
Hersel, *herself*	23	21	
Het, *hot.* Gie him't het, *give him it hot*	12	9	
Heugh, *a coal pit*	31	15	
a steep	263	11	2
Heuk, *a reaping-hook*	248	16	
Hich, *high*	254	26	2
Hidin', *hiding*	71	21	2
Hie, *high*	200	30	2
Hilch, *to hobble*	58	41	2
Hilchin, *halting*	46	27	2
Hill-tap, *hill-top*	244	1	

	Page	line	col.
Hiltie skiltie, *helter skelter* . . .	103	11	2
Himsel, *himself*	2	17	
Hiney, *honey*	202	11	
Hing, *to hang*	29	21	2
Hingin', *hanging*	110	5	2
Hinging, *hanging*	239	2	2
Hirples, *walks with difficulty* . .	264	9	
Hirplin, *limping*	14	7	
Hissels, hissel, *so many cattle as one person can attend* . . .	80	32	
Histie, *dry, barren*	69	23	
Hitch, *a loop or knot*	32	31	
Hizzies, *young women*	3	3	
Hoast, *a cough*	9	9	
Hoble, *to hobble*	53	1	2
Hoddin, *the motion of a man on horseback*	15	20	
Hoggie, *a young sheep after it is smeared and before it is shorn*	269	25	
Hog-score, *a kind of distance-line drawn across the rink* . . .	42	21	2
Hog-shouther, *a kind of horse-play by justling with the shoulder*	79	26	2
Hol't, *holed, perforated* . . .	50	34	2
Hoodie-craw, *the hooded crow* . .	122	10	2
Hoodock, *miserly*	148	30	2
Hool, *the outer skin or case* . . .	47	10	2
Hoolie ! *stop !*	34	4	2
Hoord, *hoard*	31	31	2
Hoordet, *hoarded*	45	19	
Horn, *a spoon made of horn* . .	72	19	
a comb made of horn . . .	74	26	
Hornie, *Satan*	16	23	
Host, *a cough*	157	12	2
Hostin, *coughing*	35	5	
Hotch'd, *fidgetted*	94	40	
Houghmagandie, *fornication* . .	19	26	
Houlets, *owls*	84	31	
Housie, dim. of *house*	54	37	
Hov'd, *swelled*	23	20	
Howdie, *a midwife*	8	11	
Howe, *hollowly*	20	37	
a hollow or dell	33	21	2
Howe-backit, *sunk in the back* . .	53	3	
Howes, *hollows*	147	33	
Howkit, *digged*	2	4	
dug up	31	18	2
Howlet-faced, *faced like an owl* .	176	25	
Hoyse, *hoist*	30	16	2
Hoy't, *urged*	47	10	
Hoyte, *to amble crazily* . . .	53	1	2
Hughoc, *Hugh*	32	34	
Hunder, *a hundred*	94	8	
Hunkers, *hams*	51	33	
Huntit, *hunted*	230	22	2
Hurcheon, *a hedgehog*	83	20	
Hurchin, *an urchin*	51	28	2
Hurdies, *hips*	1	36	
Hurl, *to fall down ruinously to ride*	26	37	
	159	4	2
Hushion, *a cushion*	207	22	
Hyte, *mad*	149	10	
ICKER, *an ear of corn*	54	33	
Ier'oe, *a great-grandchild* . . .	73	40	2

	Page	line	col.
Ilk, *each*	38	5	
Ilka, *every*	1	32	
Ill-willie, *ill-natured*	71	38	2
Indentin, *indenturing*	4	20	
Ingine, *genius, ingenuity*	76	16	
ingle-cheek, *the fireside*	38	13	
Ingle-lowe, *the household fire*	38	3	2
In's, *in his*	25	46	
In't, *in it*	231	41	
I'se, *I shall or will*	78	37	
Isna, *is not*	121	1	2
Ither, *other*	2	1	
Itsel, *itself*	137	9	2
JAD, *a jade*	29	40	
Jads, *jades*	5	48	
Janwar, *January*	236	27	
Jauk, *to dally, to trifle*	62	31	
Jaukin, *trifling, dallying*	45	29	2
Jauner, *foolish talk*	254	30	2
Jauntie, *dim. of jaunt*	108	11	
Jaups, *splashes*	26	38	
Jaw, *to pour*	221	6	2
Jillet, *a jilt*	71	15	2
Jimp, *to jump*	58	41	2
slender	200	14	
Jimps, *a kind of easy stays*	246	11	2
Jimpy, *neatly*	211	31	2
Jink, *to dodge*	6	24	
Jinker, *that turns quickly*	53	3	2
Jinkers, *gay, sprightly girls*	149	8	
Jinkin, *dodging*	32	19	2
Jirkinet, *an outer jacket or jerkin worn by women*	246	11	2
Jirt, *a jerk*	78	1	
Jo, *sweetheart, a term expressing affection and some degree of familiarity*	164	4	2
Jobbin', *jobbing*	166	24	
Joctelegs, *clasp-knives*	45	6	
Joes, *lovers*	114	4	
Johnny Ged's Hole, *the grave-digger*	22	31	
Jokin, *joking*	75	35	2
Jorum, *the jug*	208	21	2
Jouk, *to duck*	35	33	2
to make obeisance	270	21	
Jow, *to swing and sound*	19	11	
Jumpit, *jumped*	43	9	
Jundie, *to justle*	79	26	2
KAES, *daws*	12	39	
Kail, *broth*	12	38	
Kail-blade, *the leaf of the colewort*	22	9	
Kail-runt, *the stem of the colewort*	21	46	
Kain, *farm produce paid as rent*	2	16	
Kebars, *rafters*	49	1	
Kebbuck, *a cheese*	18	39	
Kebbuck-heel, *the remaining portion of a cheese*	19	7	
Keckle, *to cackle, to laugh*	101	23	
Keekin'-glass, *a looking-glass*	176	27	
Keekit, *peeped*	236	22	
Keeks, *peeps*	2	22	
Keepit, *kept*	1	8	
Kelpies, *water-spirits*	25	38	

	Page	line	col.
Ken, *know*	4	21	
Kend, *known*	31	14	
Kenn'd, *known*	19	30	
Kennin, *a little bit*	42	3	2
Kent, *knew*	3	1	
Kep, *to catch anything when falling*	84	44	
Ket, *a fleece*	33	28	2
Kiaugh, *anxiety*	62	8	
Kickin', *kicking*	122	11	2
Kilbagie, *the name of a certain kind of whisky*	51	15	2
Killie, *Kilmarnock*	43	22	2
Kilt, *to tuck up*	11	42	
Kimmer, *a girl*	78	11	
Kin', *kind*	33	1	
King's-hood, *a part of the entrails of an ox*	21	24	
Kintra, *country*	124	4	2
Kintra cooser, *a country stallion*	111	13	
Kirn, *a churn*	31	20	2
Kirns, *harvest-homes*	3	42	
Kirsen, *to christen*	77	11	
Kissin', *kissing*	276	3	
Kist, *a shop counter*	78	14	
Kitchen, *anything that eats with bread to serve for soup or gravy*	163	11	
Kitchens, *seasons, makes palatable*	7	24	
Kittle, *to tickle*	17	44	
ticklish	27	45	
Kittlin, *a kitten*	47	20	
Kiutlin, *cuddling*	45	17	
Knaggie, *like knags, or points of rock*	53	3	
Knappin-hammers, *hammers for breaking stones*	76	12	2
Knowe, *a hillock*	2	8	
Knurl, *a churl*	182	19	
Knurlin, *a dwarf*	114	15	
Kye, *cows*	6	12	
Kyle, *a district of Ayrshire*	71	37	
Kytes, *bellies*	72	21	
Kythe, *discover*	44	3	2
LADDIE, *a lad*	49	8	
Lade, *a load*	90	22	
Laggen, *the angle between the side and bottom of a wooden dish*	37	40	2
Laigh, *low*	29	11	
Laik, *lack*	199	27	
Lair, *lore*	17	39	
Lairing, *wading and sinking in snow or mud*	55	17	
Laith, *loth*	54	23	
Laithfu', *bashful*	63	4	
Lallan, *lowland*	32	13	2
Lambie, *dim. of lamb*	14	20	
Lampit, *limpet*	10	30	
Lan', *land, estate*	2	32	
Lane, *alone*	42	24	
Lanely, *lonely*	31	26	
Lang, *long*	1	28	
Langer, *longer*	16	38	
Lap, *did leap*	1	30	
Laughin, *laughing*	21	27	

	Page	line	col.
Mirk, *dark*	181	9	2
Misca'd, *abused*	29	19	
Misguidin', *misguiding*	71	23	
Mishanter, *misfortune, disaste*, *calamity*	140	19	
Miska't, *abused*	128	25	
Mislear'd, *mischievous*	21	2	
Mist, *missed*	47	12	2
Misteuk, *mistook*	50	7	
Mither, *mother*	13	37	
Mixtie-maxtie, *confusedly mixed*	12	23	
Mizzl'd, *having different colours*	137	15	2
Moistify, *to make moist*	13	38	
Mony, *many*	3	12	
Mools, *the earth of graves*	101	3	2
Moop, *to nibble*	33	9	2
to keep company with	247	24	2
Moorlan', *moorland*	79	38	2
Moss, *a morass*	32	1	
Mou, *mouth*	45	16	2
Moudieworts, *moles*	2	4	
Mousie, dim. of *mouse*	54	31	2
Movin', *moving*	170	15	
Muckle, *great, big*	10	11	
much	27	43	
Musie, dim. of *muse*	78	40	
Muslin-kail, *broth composed simply of water, shelled barley, and greens*	35	27	2
Mutchkin, *an English pint*	10	26	
Mysel', *myself*	23	41	
NA', *not*	5	14	
no	42	21	
Nae, *no*	1	16	
Naebody, *nobody*	79	24	
Naething, *nothing*	20	34	
Naig, *a nag*	72	26	2
Naigies, dim. of *nags*	184	16	2
Nane, *none*	1	10	
Nappy, *ale*	3	33	
Natch, *grip, hold.* To natch, *to lay hold of violently*	165	31	
Near't, *near it*	76	17	
Neebors, *neighbours*	8	13	
Needna, *need not*	22	38	
Negleckit, *neglected*	111	6	
Neist, *next*	180	23	
Neuk, *nook, corner*	18	7	
New-ca'd, *newly driven*	77	18	
Nick, *to break, to sever suddenly*	21	12	
Nickan, *cutting*	125	40	
Nicket, *cut off*	96	3	2
caught, cut off	120	2	2
Nick-nackets, *curiosities*	96	7	
Nicks, *knocks, blows*	80	2	2
Auld crummie's nicks, *marks on the horn of a cow*	132	29	
Niest, *next*	5	44	
Nieve-fu', *a fist-full*	78	20	2
Nieves, *fists*	23	8	
Niffer, *exchange*	41	20	2
Niger, *a negro*	29	37	
Nits, *nuts*	44	16	
Nocht, *nothing*	90	7	
Norland, *Northland*	11	23	

	Page	line	col.
Notet, *noted*	104	35	2
Nowte, *cattle*	4	34	
O', *of*	1	1	
O'erlay, *an outside dress, an overall*	268	2	2
O'erword, *any term frequently repeated, a refrain*	153	11	2
Ony, *any*	6	6	
Orra, *supernumerary*	48	10	
O't, *of it*	3	24	
O'ts, *of it is*	165	26	
Ought, *aught, anything*	232	1	
Oughtlins, *anything in the least*	111	12	
Ourie, *shivering*	55	14	
Oursel, *ourselves*	19	38	
Out-cast, *a quarrel*	126	35	
Outler, *un-housed*	47	8	2
Owre, *over*	1	36	
too	4	11	
Owrehip, *a way of fetching a blow with the hammer over the arm*	8	3	
Owsen, *oxen*	179	11	
PACK, *pack an' thick, on friendly or intimate terms*	2	2	
Packs, *twelve stones*	32	38	2
Paidle, *to paddle*	104	26	2
Paidles, *wanders about without object or motive*	249	13	2
Paidl't, *paddled*	226	38	
Painch, *paunch, stomach*	2	33	
Paitricks, *partridges*	42	29	2
Pangs, *crams*	17	40	
Parishen, *the parish*	256	20	2
Parritch, *oatmeal boiled in water, stirabout*	7	23	
Parritch-pats, *porridge-pots*	96	11	
Pat, *put*	20	20	
a pot	45	30	2
Pattle, *a plough-staff*	54	24	
Paughty, *haughty*	37	10	2
Paukie, *cunning, sly*	34	1	
Pay't, *paid*	53	17	2
Pechan, *the stomach*	2	26	
Pechin, *panting*	157	16	
Peel, *a tower*	248	13	1
Peelin, *peeling*	30	6	2
Penny wheep, *small beer*	17	41	
Petticoatie, dim. of *petticoat*	254	3	
Pettle, *a plough-staff*	104	7	
Phraisin, *flattering*	78	41	
Pickle, *a small quantity*	46	37	2
Pit, *put*	2	33	
Pits, *puts*	45	11	2
Placads, *public proclamations*	222	11	
Plack, *an old Scotch coin, the third part of a Scotch penny, twelve of which make an English penny*	8	12	2
Pladie, dim. of *plaid*	210	27	
Plaiden, *plaiding*	248	19	
Plaister, *to plaister*	36	29	2
Platie, dim. of *plate*	6	1	
Pleugh, *plough*	5	27	
Pliskie, *a trick*	11	38	

	Page	line	col.
Pliver, *a plover*	51	29	
Plumpit, *plumped*	47	13	
Poeks, *wallets*	52	35	
Poind, *to seize for sequestration*	3	16	
Poind't, *poinded*	151	2	2
Poortith, *poverty*	3	22	
Posie, *a bouquet*	205	10	
Pou, *to pull*	44	16	
Pouchie, dim. of *pouch*	103	9	2
Pouk, *to pluck*	21	28	
Poupit, *the pulpit*	137	31	
Pouse, *a push*	165	18	2
Poussie, *a hare*	75	35	
Pou't, *pulled*	44	16	2
Pouts, *poults, chicks*	81	23	2
Pouther'd, *powdered*	157	2	2
Pouthery, *powdery*	57	6	
Pow, *the head, the skull*	78	4	
Pownie, *a pony, a small horse*	76	27	
Powther, *powder*	13	14	
Praise be blest, *an expression of thankfulness*	265	21	2
Prayin, *praying*	73	22	2
Pree, *to taste*	200	18	2
Preen, *a pin*	80	1	
Prent, *print*	34	2	2
Pridefu', *prideful*	45	5	2
Prie'd *tasted*	45	16	2
Prief, *proof*	34	5	
Priestie, dim. of *priest*	157	2	2
Priggin, *haggling*	28	9	
Primsie, *demure, precise*	45	2	2
Propone, *to propose*	41	26	
Proveses, *provosts*	27	20	
Pu', *to pull*	205	10	
Pu'd, *pulled*	206	17	
Puddin', *a pudding*	72	2	
Puddock-stools, *mushrooms*	122	21	
Pund, *pounds*	54	17	
Pursie, dim. of *purse*	50	31	
Pyet, *the magpie*	141	29	2
Pyke, *to pick*	51	14	
Pyles, *grains*	41	24	
QUAICK, *quack*	31	9	2
Quat, *quit*	36	7	2
quitted	96	4	
Quaukin, *quaking*	45	31	2
Quey, *a cow from one year to two years old*	47	8	2
Quo', *quoth*	165	5	
RAD, *afraid*	164	8	
Rade, *rode*	239	19	
Ragweed, *the plant ragwort*	31	14	2
Raibles, *rattles, nonsense*	17	20	
Rair, *to roar*	84	24	
Wad rair't, *would have roared*	53	35	2
Rairin, *roaring*	18	11	
Raise, *rose*	222	27	
Raize, *to madden, to inflame*	53	11	
Ramblin, *rambling*	5	5	
Ramfeezl'd, *fatigued*	77	30	
Ramgunshock, *rugged*	255	23	
Ram-stam, *forward*	36	9	
Randie, *quarrelsome*	48	8	

	Page	line	col.
Randy, *a term of opprobrium generally applied to a woman*	255	38	
Ranklin', *rankling*	151	4	
Ranting, *noisy, full of animal spirits*	1	24	
Rants, *jollifications*	7	26	
Rape, *a rope*	30	16	
Raploch, *coarse*	103	17	2
Rash, *a rush*	72	8	2
Rash-buss, *a bush of rushes*	31	5	2
Rattan, *a rat*	121	20	
Rattons, *rats*	38	17	
Raucle, *fearless*	12	25	
Raught, *reached*	46	1	2
Raw, *a row*	15	41	
Rax, *to stretch*	29	9	
Rax'd, *stretched out, extended*	111	6	
Raxin, *stretching*	128	22	
Ream, *cream*	4	3	
Rebute, *a rebut, a discomfiture*	262	13	2
Red, *counsel*	20	41	
Red-wud, *stark mad*	11	39	
Reekin, *smoking*	7	33	
Reekit, *smoked*	94	2	
smoky	32	26	
Reeks, *smokes*	4	3	
Reestit, *withered, singed*	32	26	
stood restive	54	7	
Reflec', *reflect*	137	17	
Reif randies, *sturdy beggars*	208	16	
Remead, *remedy*	12	6	
Remuve, *remove*	205	33	
Respeckit, *respected*	126	33	2
Restricked, *restricted*	70	26	
Rew, *to take pity*	204	13	2
Rickles, *stocks of grain*	126	2	
Rig, *a ridge*	54	16	2
Riggin, *rafters*	38	18	
Rigwooddie, *withered, sapless*	94	14	
Rin, *run*	11	45	
Rink, *the course of the stones, a term in curling*	42	19	2
Rinnin, *running*	46	26	2
Ripp, *a handful of unthrashed corn*	53	2	
Ripple, *weakness in the back and reins*	141	20	
Ripplin-kame, *a flax-comb*	255	33	
Ripps, *handfuls*	33	10	
Riskit, *made a noise like the tearing of roots*	53	35	2
Rive, *to burst*	72	23	
Rives, *tears to pieces*	4	32	
Rives't, *tears it*	81	18	
Roastin', *roasting*	141	24	2
Rock, *a distaff*	203	18	2
Rockin, *a social gathering, the women spinning on the rock or distaff*	75	33	2
Roon, *round*	80	15	
Roos'd, *praised*	233	6	
Roose, *to praise*	72	27	
Roosty, *rusty*	51	27	
Roun', *round*	62	11	
Roupet, *hoarse as with a cold*	9	31	
Routhie, *well filled, abundant*	204	24	
Rowes, *rolls*	26	32	

	Page	line	col.
Rowin, *rolling*	227	35	
Row't, *rolled*	71	23	
Rowte, *to low, to bellow*	29	12	
Rowth, *abundance*	9	21	
Rowtin, *lowing*	6	12	
Rozet, *rosin*	74	14	2
Ruefu', *rueful*	171	9	2
Rung, *a cudgel*	12	26	
Runkl'd, *wrinkled*	15	7	
Runts, *the stems of cabbage*	29	16	
Ryke, *reach*	51	1	
SABS, *sobs*	50	35	
Sae, *so*	3	21	
Saft, *soft*	19	22	
Sair, *sore*	2	43	
to serve	132	32	
Sairly, *sorely*	211	34	
Sair't, *served*	81	35	
Sang, *song*	1	27	
Sannock, *Alexander*	142	11	
Sark, *a shirt*	11	3	
Sarkit, *provided in shirts*	38	29	
Sauce, *scorn, insolence*	111	23	2
Saugh, *the willow*	53	24	2
Saugh woodies, *ropes made of willow withes*	108	5	2
Saul, *soul*	4	20	
Saunt, *saints*	7	27	
Saut, *salt*	33	24	
Saut backets, *salt buckets*	96	11	
Sautet, *salted*	37	36	2
Saw, *to sow*	46	39	
Sawin, *sowing*	20	32	
Sawmont, *a salmon*	42	23	2
Sax, *six*	21	17	
Saxpence, *sixpence*	142	12	
Say't, *say it*	236	7	
Scaith, *hurt*	239	29	
Scaur, *to scare*	21	20	
Scaur, *frightened*	31	18	
Scaud, *to scald*	31	6	
Scawl, *a scold*	32	7	2
Scho, *she*	236	14	2
Schoolin', *schooling, teaching*	170	27	
Scones, *barley cakes*	7	2	
Sconner, *to loathe*	35	18	2
loathing	72	4	2
Scraichin, *screaming*	75	34	
Scrapin', *scraping*	132	29	
Screed, *a tear, a rent*	14	36	
to repeat glibly	104	5	2
Scriechin, *screeching*	9	35	
Scrievin, *gliding easily*	7	11	
Scrimpit, *scanty*	34	14	
Scrimply, *scantly*	38	26	2
Scroggie, *covered with stunted shrubs*	269	32	
Sculdudd'ry, *a ludicrous term denoting fornication*	271	34	
See't, *see it*	45	36	
Seizin, *seizing*	10	28	
Sel, *self*	76	35	
Sell't, *sold*	54	15	
Sen', *send*	142	17	
Sen't, *send it*	81	29	

	Page	line	col.
Servan', *servant*	35	37	
Set, *lot*	16	7	
Sets, *becomes*	8	34	
sets off, starts	23	15	
Settlin, gat a fearfu' settlin, *was frightened into quietness*	47	22	
Shachl't, *deformed*	195	3	
Shaird, *a shred*	80	33	2
Sha'na, *shall not*	239	34	
Shangan, *a cleft stick*	29	18	
Shank, *the leg and foot*	53	15	
Shanks, *legs*	267	27	
Shanna, *shall not*	151	20	2
Sharin't, *sharing it*	240	20	
Shaul, *shallow*	127	32	
Shaver, *a wag*	37	4	2
Shavie, *a trick*	51	29	2
Shaw, *show*	34	6	2
Shaw'd, *showed*	93	32	
Shaws, *wooded dells*	47	21	
Sheep-shank, wha thinks himsel nae sheep-shank bane, *who thinks himself no unimportant personage*	78	21	
Sheers, *shears*	33	16	
scissors	62	25	
Sherra-moor, *Sheriff-muir*	46	19	
Sheugh, *a trench*	1	30	
Sheuk, *shook*	49	1	
Shiel, *a shieling, a hut*	204	3	
Shill, *shrill*	223	5	
Shillin's, *shillings*	255	22	2
Shog, *a shock*	32	25	
Shools, *shovels*	76	11	2
Shoon, *shoes*	34	9	
Shor'd, *threatened*	28	11	
offered	51	35	2
Shore, *to threaten*	132	21	2
Shouldna, *should not*	177	11	
Shouther, *shoulder*	13	13	
Shure, *did shear, did cut grain*	248	14	
Sic, *such*	3	4	
Sicker, *secure*	20	16	
Siclike, *suchlike*	2	38	
Sidelins, *sidelong*	78	39	
Sighin', *sighing*	128	20	
Siller, *money*	91	24	
of the colour of silver	205	23	
Simmer, *summer*	14	1	
Simmers, *summers*	5	18	
Sin', *since*	21	18	
Sindry, *sundry*	274	2	2
Sinfu', *sinful*	72	32	
Singet, *singed*	100	1	
Singin', *singing*	110	6	2
Sing't, *sing it*	57	25	2
Sinn, *the sun*	126	20	2
Sinny, *sunny*	204	30	
Sinsyne, *since*	183	27	
Skaith, *injury*	20	41	
Skaithing, *injuring*	81	19	
Skeigh, *high-mettled*	53	7	2
shy, proud, disdainful	180	2	2
Skellum, *a worthless fellow*	91	19	
Skelp, *a slap*	72	30	2
to run	157	15	2

	Page	line	col.
Widdle, *a struggle or bustle*	103	21	
Wiel, *a small whirlpool*	47	31	
Wifie, dim. of *wife*	62	6	
Wight, *strong, powerful*	104	9	
Wil' cat, *the wild cat*	127	7	
Willie-waught, *a hearty draught*	227	3	
Willow wicker, *the smaller species of willow*	121	17	
Willyart, *wild, strange, timid*	111	34	
Wimplin, *waving, meandering*	44	11	
Wimpl't, *wimpled*	47	20	
Win', *wind*	236	27	
Winkin, *winking*	30	13	
Winna, *will not*	11	10	
Winnock - bunker, *a seat in a window*	93	25	
Winnocks, *windows*	12	17	
Wins, *winds*	4	2	
Win't, *did wind*	45	28	2
Wintle, *a staggering motion*	47	22	
Wintles, *struggles*	170	8	
Winze, *an oath*	47	16	
Wiss, *wish*	71	25	
Witha', *withal*	212	27	
Withoutten, *without*	42	30	
Wonner, *a wonder, a contemptuous appellation*	2	29	
Wons, *dwells*	179	21	
Woo', *wool*	32	38	2
Woodie, *the gallows*	50	34	
a rope, more properly one made of withes or willows	83	18	
Wooer-babs, *garters knotted below the knee in a couple of loops*	44	5	2
Wordie, dim. of *word*	128	17	
Wordy, *worthy*	72	5	
Worl', *world*	4	30	

	Page	line	col.
Worset, *worsted*	46	8	
Wow, *an exclamation of pleasure or wonder*	95	37	
Wrang, *wrong*	36	25	
mistaken	76	6	2
Wranged, *wronged*	71	35	2
Wreeths, *wreaths*	55	9	
Wud, *mad*	8	14	
Wumble, *a wimble*	71	35	
Wyle, *to beguile, to decoy*	185	44	
Wyliecoat, *a flannel vest*	74	21	2
Wyling, *beguiling*	188	20	
Wyte, *to blame, to reproach*	8	20	
YARD, *a garden*	32	13	
Yaud, *a worn-out horse*	272	36	
Yell, *barren. As yell's the Bill, giving no more milk than the bull*	31	24	2
Yerd, *the churchyard*	236	10	
Yerket, *jerked, lashed*	34	21	
Yerl, *an earl*	272	24	
Ye'se, *you shall or will*	104	21	2
Yestreen, *yesternight*	21	35	
Yetts, *gates*	151	11	
Yeukin, *itching*	111	5	
Yeuks, *itches*	121	9	2
Yill, *ale*	18	30	
Yill-caup, *ale-stoup*	17	29	
Yird, *earth*	45	1	
Yirth, *the earth*	137	9	2
Yokin, *yoking, a bout, a set to*	75	57	2
Yont, *beyond*	31	33	
Yoursel, *yourselves*	19	5	
yourself	30	30	
Yowes, *ewes*	33	2	2
Yowie, dim. of *yowe*	33	5	2
Yule, *Christmas*	180	35	

INDEX TO FIRST LINES.

INDEX TO THE LETTERS.

THE END.

RICHARD CLAY AND SONS, LIMITED, LONDON AND BUNGAY.

NEW UNIFORM AND COMPLETE EDITIONS OF THE POETS.

Large Crown 8vo, cloth gilt, $1.75. Bound in morocco, extra, $4.00.

ALFRED, LORD TENNYSON, POET LAUREATE, COMPLETE WORKS. *With a New Portrait.*

"This single volume, convenient in size, printed on an excellent quality of paper, from clear type, in double columns, with a page that lies easily open in the hand, is, in our judgment, a model of what a low-priced book should be. . . . It is a pleasure to look upon a piece of book-making so thoroughly honest and so genuinely attractive at the same time, put upon the market at a price so low as to put it within reach of people of the most moderate means." — *Christian Union.*

"This latest edition of his works, which as a book is every way what a complete, compact edition should be, and which contains the only portrait we have ever seen which does his genius justice." — *N. Y. Mail and Express.*

COLERIDGE'S COMPLETE POETICAL WORKS.

Edited, with Introduction, by J. DYKES CAMPBELL.

MATTHEW ARNOLD'S POETICAL WORKS.

"Contains some of the wisest and most melodious verse that this age has produced." — *Athenæum.*

PERCY BYSSHE SHELLEY'S POETICAL WORKS.

Edited by PROFESSOR DOWDEN. With Portrait.

WILLIAM WORDSWORTH'S COMPLETE POETICAL WORKS.

With an Introduction by JOHN MORLEY, and Portrait.

"Mr. Morley has seldom written anything fresher or more vigorous than the essay on Wordsworth which he has prefixed to Macmillan's new and admirable one-volume edition of the poet — the only complete edition." — *Spectator.*

"The finest of all tributes to the memory of Wordsworth is a complete edition of his poetical works, printed in one volume, and sold at a few shillings. It runs to near a thousand pages, and is all that it need be in type and clearness of arrangement. It stands midway between the *éditions de luxe* and the cheap typographical renderings of other classics of the English school. In a good binding it would do perfectly well for the library of a millionaire; in serviceable cloth it would make almost a library in itself for the student of humble means. It has a good bibliography of all the poet's writings, a catalogue of biographies, an index of first lines and a complete list of the poems in the order of their production year by year. Above all, it has an introduction from the pen of Mr. John Morley." — *Daily News.*

SHAKESPEARE'S COMPLETE WORKS.

Edited by W. G. CLARK, M.A., and W. ALDIS WRIGHT, M.A. With Glossary. New Edition.

MORTE D'ARTHUR.

SIR THOMAS MALORY'S Book of King Arthur, and of his Noble Knights of the Round Table. The Edition of Caxton, revised for modern use. With an Introduction, Notes, and Glossary, by SIR EDWARD STRACHEY. New Edition.

ROBERT BURNS' COMPLETE WORKS.

The POEMS, SONGS, and LETTERS. Edited, with Glossarial Index, and Biographical Memoir, by ALEXANDER SMITH. New Edition.

SIR WALTER SCOTT'S POETICAL WORKS.

With Biographical and Critical Essay by FRANCIS TURNER PALGRAVE. New Edition.

OLIVER GOLDSMITH'S MISCELLANEOUS WORKS.

With Biographical Introduction by PROFESSOR MASSON. New Edition.

EDMUND SPENSER'S COMPLETE WORKS.

Edited with Glossary by R. MORRIS, and Memoir by J. W. HALES. New Edition.

ALEXANDER POPE'S POETICAL WORKS.

Edited, with Notes and Introductory Memoir, by PROFESSOR WARD. New Edition.

JOHN DRYDEN'S POETICAL WORKS.

Edited, with a Revised Text and Notes, by W. D. CHRISTIE, M.A., Trinity College, Cambridge. New Edition.

COWPER'S POETICAL WORKS.

Edited, with Notes and Biographical Introduction, by Rev. W. BENHAM, B.D. New Edition.

MILTON'S POETICAL WORKS.

With Introductions by PROFESSOR MASSON.

MACMILLAN & CO., PUBLISHERS, NEW YORK.